THE JUDEO-SPANISH BALLAD CHAPBOOKS OF YACOB ABRAHAM YONÁ

FOLK LITERATURE OF THE SEPHARDIC JEWS

I

THE JUDEO-SPANISH BALLAD CHAPBOOKS OF

Yacob Abraham Yoná

BY

SAMUEL G. ARMISTEAD JOSEPH H. SILVERMAN

UNIVERSITY OF CALIFORNIA PRESS
BERKELEY, LOS ANGELES, LONDON
1971

UNIVERSITY OF CALIFORNIA PRESS
BERKELEY AND LOS ANGELES, CALIFORNIA
UNIVERSITY OF CALIFORNIA PRESS, LTD.
LONDON, ENGLAND

ISBN: 0-520-01648-3
Library of Congress Catalog Card Number: 71-78565

PRINTED IN SPAIN

DEPÓSITO LEGAL: V. 5.216 - 1971

ARTES GRÁFICAS SOLER, S. A. - JÁVEA, 28 - VALENCIA (8) - 1971

For Pili and June

In memoriam

Ramón Menéndez Pidal　　*Antonio Rodríguez-Moñino*

PREFACE

In the spring of 1957 we began a research project aimed at recording and editing the rich fund of Judeo-Spanish folk literature, particularly lyriconarrative balladry, surviving in the Sephardic immigrant communities of the United States. Since that time we have carried on an intensive program of fieldwork among Eastern Mediterranean Sephardim now residing in Los Angeles, San Francisco, Seattle, and New York. To date, our fieldwork in the United States has yielded a total of more than 350 ballad texts, as well as a large number of traditional lyric songs, proverbs, folk remedies, and superstitions.

In 1959 our project was strengthened by the collaboration of our colleague, Dr. Israel J. Katz, who is editing the music of the ballads in our combined collection. To the texts already recorded by us in the United States, Dr. Katz added a magnificent collection of some 200 ballads, gleaned from oral tradition, during two years of fieldwork in Israel. He also acquired for us an important MS containing ten ballads copied in Hebrew letters by the lexicographer Salomon Israel Cherezli in Jerusalem during the early years of this century. This MS was published by us in *Studies in Honor of M. J. Benardete.* (See the bibliography at the end of the present study, under the abbreviation SICh.) Also, we have been very fortunate to acquire from other sources a number of important ballad MSS which have significantly amplified the geographic and thematic scope of our collection. In the Sephardic community of Los Angeles we discovered a precious old MS from the Island of Rhodes, containing ten ballad texts in Hebrew characters dating from as early as the eighteenth-century. These texts were published in our monograph, *Diez romances hispánicos en un manuscrito sefardí de la Isla de Rodas*. (See abbreviation DRH.) Professor Cynthia Crews of the University of Leeds very generously placed at our disposal her unedited MSS of 30 excellent ballad texts transcribed in Greece and Yugoslavia (1929-35). Dr. Shlomo Noble of the Yivo Institute for Jewish Research of New York gave us permission to photograph and edit a rich collection of ballads in manuscript form transcribed by the late Dr. William Milwitzky in various Balkan countries in 1899. Dr. S. Gaon of London provided us with an important collection of 22 *romances* printed (*ca.* 1939) in the Bosnian newspaper *Jevrejski Glas*. At the present time our total unedited holdings of ballads from the Eastern Mediterranean Sephardic communities comprise over 700 versions representing some 70 different text types.

In 1961 Professor Américo Castro was generous enough to place at our disposal a manuscript of 59 ballads collected by him in 1922 among the Sephardim of Morocco. In the summer of 1962, together with Dr. Katz, we traveled to Morocco for two months of fieldwork in all the major Spanish-speaking Sephardic communities: Tangier, Tetuán, Arcila, Larache, Alcazarquivir, Casablanca, and Melilla. During this time and during two subsequent field trips by Professor Armistead in 1963, we were able to record more than 550 traditional ballads, 25 dirges (*endechas*), 80 traditional wedding songs, and 75 folktales. At present, our complete ballad collection, counting both Eastern Mediterranean and Moroccan materials, comprises over 1,300 variant texts —representing some 160 different narrative themes— sung or recited by Spanish Jews from Turkey, Yugoslavia, Bulgaria, Rumania, Greece, the Island of Rhodes, Israel, and North Africa.

A requisite first step toward editing this mass of oral and manuscript material was the acquisition and mastery of the bibliography concerning the Judeo-Spanish traditional ballad. A major area of this field of investigation, hitherto almost completely neglected by Hispanic ballad scholars, concerns the popular ballad chapbooks printed in Hebrew characters (Ladino) in various Eastern Mediterranean Sephardic communities. The Ladino ballad booklets published by Yacob Abraham Yoná in Salonika and Sofia between 1891 and 1920 are without doubt the most representative and significant manifestations of this ephemeral genre, constituting in themselves a unique and precious corpus of traditional poetry that richly deserves detailed exploration. Apart from the chapbooks published by Yoná, we know of only three other booklets: Binyamin B. Yosef's *Sēfer rĕnānôθ* ([Jerusalem], 1908) and *Bukyeto de romansas* (Istanbul, 1926) and *'Endeğas de θišᶜāh bĕ-'Āb* ([Izmir], n.d.). We plan separate studies of these ballad booklets. The present edition and study of Yoná's chapbook ballads has been planned as the first in a series of monographic volumes devoted to the traditional balladry and other folk-literary forms of the Spanish-speaking Jews of the Eastern Mediterranean and North Africa.

In connection with the preparation of the present volume, we wish to express our gratitude to a number of friends and colleagues for their invaluable help and advice: to Rachael Castelete, Margaret I. Chaplin, Louis B. Dassa, Susan Kushner, Albert Matarasso, and Joseph Nehama for valuable unedited information concerning Yoná's life and times; to Arthur L.-F. Askins, Mair J. Benardete, Meir Benayahu, Henry V. Besso, Diego Catalán, Jonas C. Greenfield, Iacob M. Hassán, Israel J. Katz, Gonzalo Menéndez Pidal, Ramón Menéndez Pidal, Shlomo Noble, Federico Pérez Castro, Joanne B. Purcell, Israel S. Révah, and A. Rodríguez-Moñino for indispensable bibliographical indications and assistance; to Arnold J. Band, Herbert A. Davidson, Jonas C. Greenfield, and Iacob M. Hassán for their learned advice concerning various Hebrew and Aramaic problems; to Andreas Tietze for his erudite and unstinting help with Turkisms; to Anita Grillos Van Baelen for verifying translations of Neo-Hellenic texts; to Frede Jensen for his help with Scandinavian balladry; to Ann T. Hinckley, of the Interlibrary Loan Department at UCLA, for searching and obtaining many a rare ballad collection for us; to Joanne E. March and Jacqueline Thompson Elpers for their superb research assistance and expert, eminently patient editorial help; to Ralph R. Busick and James Kubeck of the University of California Press for making our text more readable; and finally to Wayland D. Hand for learned orientations concerning folkloric elements in our texts, as well as for unfailing and enthusiastic encouragement during every stage of our work. To the American Council of Learned Societies, the Del Amo Foundation, and the Ford Foundation Grant Committee on International and Comparative Studies (UCLA), we wish to express our sincere appreciation for their most generous support of our research. Thanks to the generosity of Mr. Harry Starr and the Lucius N. Littauer Foundation we have had sufficient funds to publish photographic reproductions of Yoná's extremely rare chapbooks. The Sephardic Hebrew Center of Los Angeles has been a source of advice and encouragement since the outset of this project and has also generously contributed toward the publication of the present volume.

S. G. A. and J. H. S.

Los Angeles, June 1967

CONTENTS

INTRODUCTION

In 1953, on referring to popular Judeo-Spanish ballad chapbooks printed in Hebrew characters, D. Ramón Menéndez Pidal —revered master of all who work in Spanish epic and ballad literature— made the following statement: "I do not believe that a bibliography [of these publications] or a transcription of them in Roman letters has ever been prepared: two endeavors much to be desired." [1] The present monograph attempts to fulfill Menéndez Pidal's wish by offering to him the bibliography, transcriptions, and commentary that his own monumental accomplishments have made possible.

Of all popular efforts to record in printed form the reliques of Judeo-Spanish balladry, Yacob Abraham Yoná's are without doubt the most extensive and worthy of study. It is no coincidence that, in Menéndez Pidal's brief discussion of Sephardic chapbooks, Yoná is the only editor of popular ballad booklets to be mentioned by name. In fact, the rarity and authenticity of his texts are favorably compared by D. Ramón to those of the splendid sixteenth-century "Cancionero de Amberes." [2]

Yacob Abraham Yoná

About Yoná himself there is scarcely any printed evidence. The late Rabbi Michael Molho, in his variegated anthology of Eastern Judeo-Spanish literature, observed only that "the minstrel Yacob Yoná published a great number of epigrams and poems in various pamphlets, which also contained many ballads, collected by the author from the

---

[1] *Romancero hispánico* (abbr. RoH), II, 330. Already at the turn of the century Menéndez Pidal was vitally interested in oral and manuscript versions of Sephardic ballads. At that time, however, he was unaware of the printed Ladino texts of similar materials. Note, however, his allusion to one of Y. A. Yoná's chapbooks in *El Romancero Español* (1910), pp. 87-88.

[2] RoH, II, 331.

lips of the people."[3] In his *Romancero sefaradí,* Moshe Attias characterized Yoná as "a Salonikan Jew of humble origin, a man endowed with a poetic soul, who was wont to publish small pamphlets of ballads which he would distribute himself among the community and in which he would even include poetry and prose of his own inspiration.... The pamphlets of Yacob Yoná and other similar ones were for the daily use of the people."[4]

In our efforts to reconstruct the outlines of Yoná's life, we have had the generous cooperation of his surviving relatives and contemporaries. Without their assistance, we could hardly have offered more than the sparse information already provided by Molho and Attias. One of Yoná's daughters, Mrs. Rachael Castelete, who now resides in London and is blind, dictated the following reminiscences to her daughter, Mrs. Susan Kushner:[5]

---

[3] LSO, p. 299.

[4] *Romancero sefaradí,* pp. 8 and 341 of the Hebrew and Spanish introductions.

[5] In 1959, Mrs. Castelete, following in her father's footsteps, published a small pamphlet—in Roman letters—containing a few traditional texts, as well as certain poems of her own invention, remarkably like the dialogs and debates of Medieval Spanish poetry. On the frontispiece she proudly declared: "Esta Gim[ri]ka es *el Tresoro de Rachael Castelete Ija de Jacov Yona.*" Mrs. Castelete's booklet includes an adaptation of one of the traditional texts published in her father's chapbooks—*La tormenta calmada + El idólatra* (no. 10 *infra*). We reprint it here, respecting the original orthography, punctuation, and verse arrangement:

El ombre religgiozo

Se pasea el pastor fiel,
Kon su ganado akea tadre,
Korre remolinos i truelos,
I los relamparos mui grandes.

Signor, Signor si piki
En mi ganado lo tope;
Si mi ganado lo kulpo,
Lo ke no es mio, eskapame.

Esto ke sintieron las naves,
Se avoltaron por otras partes;
Se davan los vapores,
De empegna en pegna
Por agua corria sangre.

FIG. 1.—Yacob Abraham Yoná (1847-1922).

"My father Yacob Yoná was born in Monastir [Yugoslavia], in 1847. When he was about 16 to 18 years of age, he went to Salonika with his two brothers. Yacob and his brother Leon settled in Salonika; the third brother was soon to leave for Western Europe. Yacob found work as a sweeper in a *stampería* [printing establishment], located near the Great Talmud Torah of Salonika, which belonged to *Han* [Mr.] Saadi Leví.[6] After Yacob had worked there for some time, Saadi Leví —not knowing how educated his employee was— asked him if he could read and write and handed him a newspaper. To Mr. Leví's amazement, my father was able to read and copy from the newspaper with great ease. Mr. Leví, who was an outstanding author of songs and *gimarás* ['pamphlets'], then put my father to work as a copyist in a room of his own. Yacob's new job was to copy all of Mr. Leví's work for publication. Some years passed and *Han* Saadi Leví asked Yacob if he would like to marry his niece, Dudún Matarasso, knowing full well that they loved each other. After they were married, my father looked for additional sources of income, and at the Talmud Torah he obtained a paying position as *hazán* ['cantor'], also blowing the *shofar* ['ram's horn'] on the High Holidays. Some time later he decided to leave *Han* Saadi Leví's printing shop to work on his own, simply because he was not earning enough to support a family. My father's work became more popular than Saadi's, whereupon the latter produced no further ballads

---

Yoraban los kapitanes,
Todos los ke en las mares;
Signora, la mi signora,
De esta fortuna eskapamos.
Si de esta fortuna me eskapas,
De oros vos enkoronare.

Un jidio ay entre eos,
Ke en ea no achetare.
Tenemos un Dio Bendicho,
Ke muchas maravias aze.

Me las aga en estas oras,
De prissa i ke no tadre.
Ansi aga kon los jazinos,
Ke stan grave en los spitales.

[6] Concerning this distinguished figure of Salonikan Jewry, see A. Pulido, *Españoles sin patria,* pp. 442-444.

or *gimarás,* but chose to concentrate on his newspaper, *La Época.*[7]

"My father composed approximately one *gimará* in six months, and when I became old enough to help him I would bind them for him at home. He did not earn enough money for us to live on, since the family consisted of three sons and three daughters —in all, eight mouths to feed. Father was regularly invited to all weddings, births, and other social functions and he would sing for all the people present, accompanied by a boys' choir he had founded. For these performances, the people would pay him, so that he might support his family.

"In the meantime, my brothers grew up, went to work, and helped to support my parents. My father died in 1922 at the age of 75. My mother died 10 years later, also in her seventy-fifth year."[8]

Mr. Albert Matarasso, who currently lives in New York City, sent us the following evocation written in Judeo-Spanish of Yoná's activities in Salonika: "I met Yacob Abraham Yoná early in the year 1900. I can still see him in my imagination walking along the streets of Salonika with a pencil behind his ear or between his fingers. And as he walked, he would be reading or checking a list of the Jewish families in Salonika. His occupation was what the Sephardic Jews called *combidador,* that is, an individual who went from house to house with a list of guests to invite the occupants to a wedding or a circumcision.[9] Yacob Yoná

[7] Concerning this newspaper, see M. D. Gaon, *A Bibliography of the Judeo-Spanish (Ladino) Press* (in Hebrew) (Tel Aviv, 1965), p. 19 (no. 20); also Pulido, *Españoles sin patria,* pp. 440, 442-444.

[8] Letter from Mrs. Susan Kushner, dated Nov. 24, 1966.

[9] In his monograph on *Usos y costumbres de los sefardíes de Salónica,* M. Molho discusses the occupation and the activities it entailed: "El papel [del *combidador*] era especialmente pintoresco. Como entonces todavía no se había establecido la costumbre de las invitaciones impresas, el *combidador* se hacía cargo de la doble lista de direcciones de parientes, amigos, y conocidos de las dos familias, y se iba con ella, para, durante todo el santo día, gritar de casa en casa anunciando la boda y haciendo las invitaciones. Al entrar en un patio tenía la obligación de llamar a la mujer interesada por su nombre y apellido, en muy alta e inteligible voz, anunciándole solemne y oficialmente la buena nueva y añadir que ella, su marido, sus hijos, sus amigos y conocidos estaban invitados a la boda que tendría lugar en tal o cual sitio. Terminaba indicando el nombre de la sinagoga a la que iría el novio el día mismo de la boda para la oración de la tarde. Fácil es adivinar el espectáculo al que esta curiosa forma de invitación, a la vez práctica y económica daba lugar. A los gritos del *combidador,* todas las comadres de la vecindad salían por puertas y ventanas, pidiendo detalles sobre las personas de los novios y sus familias. Dábase libre curso a

was outstanding in this activity. His sense of humor would often come into play, as he announced the invitation to one family or another. In fact, he would invite some families with a poetic invitation, in the form of a *compla,* as it was called in Salonika, made up on the spur of the moment. This was very pleasing to certain people. Women would throw him coins from their windows and many would wait on their terraces or at their doors and windows to hear the ballads of Yacob Yoná. And poor Yacob would have to shout answers from the street to the many questions they would put to him.

"The *combidador* or *combidadera,* in Salonika, was familiar with all the local gossip. And so, when he was given a list of guests, he was told to invite so-and-so, who was known by such-and-such a nickname, appropriate to his reputation, etc. The poor *combidador* had to seek out the houses of all the guests on the basis of the vaguest orientations: 'There's a stairway at the entrance, or an incline, and at the side of the house there's a vegetable stand, a liquor vendor (in Turkish, *meyhaneci*), a bakery, etc.' At times he would have to ask one guest where another lived, possibly a nephew or an in-law of the guest, and directions were then shouted from the window. In this way, with the sweat of his brow, Yacob Yoná earned his living and raised his family: his sons Samuel, Abraham, Daniel, and his daughters Mazaltov, Rachael, Miriam.

"Yacob Yoná wrote poems about many events in the life of Salonikan Jewry and sold his pamphlets during the evenings in the Jewish quarter of the city. Many Jews held him in great esteem and readily bought his pamphlets for the few pennies he charged. They read them avidly, as they were the favorite entertainment for many of them. Whenever our Yacob passed by some Jewish tavern he would be invited in to relax a while. And if he was offered a drink he would respond to the honor, without hesitation, in a poetic toast dedicated to the friend who had invited him.

"This is what I know and remember of the life of Yacob Yoná, who died in Salonika, old and tired, worn out by his difficult and

---

comentarios y críticas hasta el punto de que más de un ama de casa, al volver a su cocina, encontrábase con que se le había quemado la comida" (p. 19).

trying labors. Those of us who remember him and his times, say: 'A Jewish world that has gone forever.' "[10]

This, then, is the information we have been able to obtain concerning the life of Yacob Abraham Yoná. In truth, he appears as a humble and obscure figure, mentioned briefly and fleetingly in a few works devoted to Hispanic balladry or Sephardic literature and living now only in the fading memories of his surviving friends and relatives. His name does not even appear in Pulido's *Españoles sin patria,* whose

---

[10] The original Judeo-Spanish text of Mr. Matarasso's letter, dated Oct. 19, 1966, reads as follows: "Yo conocí a Yacob Abraham Yoná a los empesijos del año mil novecientos. Todavía lo veo en mi imaginación, caminando por las calles de Salónika con su lápiz sobre su oreja o entre sus dedos y en su otra mano tenía una hoja de papel, meldando o revisando una lista de nombres de familias judías de Salónika. Su oficio era lo que los Sephardim llaman *conbidador.* Esto era ir en las casas conbidar a envitados para bodas o fiestas de circumcisión. Yacob Yoná se distinguía en su oficio. Al conbidar una familia o otra, él tenía su senso de humor. Sin mucho pensar, como dizen, mientres estaba detenido sobre su pie, a algunas familias las envitaba en recitándoles una poesía corta, o como se llamaba en Salónika, una *compla.* Y esto a ciertos plasía. Y las mujeres le ronjaban por las ventanas unos centavos. Y muchas se aparaban por tarazas, ventanas y puertas por oir las baladas de Yacob Yoná. Y el pobre de Yacob tenía que gritar de la puerta de la calle repuestas a las preguntas que se le hacían.

"El conbidador o la conbidadera en Salónika sabían estorias de familias (*gossip*). Y así, cuando se les daba lista de envitados, se les decía de envitar a Fulanica de tal o a Fulano de tal que le pasó algo o que lo llaman *tal*—por mal nombre. Pobre de conbidador tenía que buscar también ónde moraban, cuando se le esplicaba: 'Fulano mora en la calle *tala* al lado y cerca de la casa de Sistrano. Se entra por una escalera o una abachada y al lado de esta casa hay uno que vende logumbres o licores (en turco, *meḥanağí*), un panadero, etc.' En veces el conbidador tenía que preguntar a otro envitado ónde mora Señor tal, que es su sobrino o cosfuegro y por la ventana le gritaban las informaciones. Así, Yacob Yoná ganó su pan a la sudor de su frente y engrandició su familia: sus hijos, Samuel, Abraham, Daniel; sus hijas, Mazaltov, Rachel, Miriam.

"Yacob Yoná escribía poesías sobre muchos evenimientos que se pasaban en la judería de Salónika y vendía sus brochuras y folletos, andando las noches por las calles de la judería. Y muchos judíos le tenían consideración y respecto, mercaban sus brochuras a la valor de aquellos tiempos—centavos. Las meldavan con buena gana; era el mijor pasatiempo de muchos. Y cuando nuestro Yacob pasaba por alguna taverna de judíos, lo llamaban que se sentara con ellos. Y si le trataban un beveraje, sin mucho pensar, les pagaba la honor: les recitaba una compla (*toast*) dedicada a el que le pagó por su beveraje.

"Esto conozco y me acodro de su vida del canez: Yacob Yoná el que murió en Salónika, viejo y arto de días, canso de mucho lavoro duro y penible. Los que bien nos recordamos de él y de su tiempo, decimos: 'un mundo judío que para siempre despareció'."

FIG. 2.—The tomb of Y. A. Yoná: The Jewish cemetery at Salonika was destroyed by Nazi occupation forces. The photograph was partially burned during the bombings of London.

pages on Salonika (pp. 437-448) are crowded with the names of distinguished Sephardim. And yet it is a truly moving experience to evoke, if only in part, the shadowy existence of this simple Judaic minstrel who wrote and sang his ballads to feed his family and keep body and soul together, [11] providing for the Sephardic community of Salonika over a great many years a favorite form of diversion at bargain prices. We know for sure that in 1920, only two years before his death, he was still writing and publishing his booklets of traditional and original verse. Thanks to his extraordinary tenacity and dedication, a treasure trove of Judeo-Spanish ballads has been rescued from oblivion and, in the process, Yoná himself has earned his own small measure of well-deserved immortality.

Toward a Bibliography of Y. A. Yoná

Yoná's booklets were ephemerae in the truest sense. Printed on cheap, fragile paper and priced at a few pennies, most copies were inevitably doomed to destruction, precisely because of their great popularity. [12] Just as is the case with many of the early Spanish ballad broadsides, [13] a number of Yoná's chapbooks have come down to us in but a single copy. Others can, in fact, boast two extant copies, but rare indeed is the booklet, such as *Gu'erta de romansos 'importantes* (GSA), of which four known copies have survived.

Twenty-five different publications by Yoná have thus far come to our attention. Many more, it seems quite certain, must have existed. Who can say how many may subsequently come to light? Prospects are, however, not particularly hopeful. The brutal extermination of

---

[11] Note Yoná's plea in the rhymed title page of his *Livriko de romansas 'importantes* (Sofia, 1908): "Vos rogo senyyores de tomar kada 'uno 'una gĕmārāh, syendo non kosta munğa pará 'i toda mi familyya vo lo rengrasyyará."

[12] An index of this popularity is the fact that some of Yoná's booklets bear the rather ingenuous admonition not to pass individual copies from hand to hand. Both *Ku'entos 'ermozos de pasatyempo* (Salonika, [1914]) and *Brośura por 'el fu'ego* (n.p., [1917]) carry on their title pages the warning: "'Es defendido de dar 'a meldar 'a 'otros."

[13] Cf. A. Rodríguez-Moñino's essential observations in *Pliegos de Morbecq,* pp. 9 ff., and *Construcción crítica y realidad histórica en la poesía española de los siglos XVI y XVII* (Madrid, 1965), p. 49.

Salonikan Jewry naturally brought with it the ruin of an entire cultural structure of which Yoná's publications were but one minute, though significant, material manifestation. Coupled then with the booklets' own ephemeral nature is the fact that the very community where they were printed and so avidly read has itself, for practical purposes, ceased to exist.

For many of Yoná's publications we have found specific locations in public or private libraries and, consequently, have been able to consult either photographic reproductions or, in some cases, the booklets themselves. In other instances, we have been able to obtain only indirect evidence: references or brief descriptions of chapbooks whose present whereabouts remains unknown. A number of these booklets, described by Molho in his *Sĕfārîm* and *Literatura sefardita de Oriente,* were available to him in Buenos Aires, but apparently not all of them formed part of the rich collection of Ladino literature which he so generously donated to the Instituto Arias Montano in Madrid. [14] The process of bibliographic attrition has thus continued down to the present and the very existence of some of Yoná's chapbooks remains perilous even today.

To date, we know of the following items published by Yoná. Where we have not actually seen a booklet, either in substance or in a photographic copy, we quote or, in the case of Ladino-Hebrew descriptions, we transliterate and translate the bibliographical reference given in our secondary source. Such references are placed in quotation marks. Chapbooks containing ballads edited in the present study are accorded a more detailed description elsewhere in this introduction:

(1) "*Cuentos hermosos de pasatiempo.* [Salónica, 1890. (En caracteres rashi.) Contiene cuatro romances.]" Reference: LSO, no. 62 (p. 409).
(2) *Sĕfer gĕdûlaθ Mōšeh,* n.p., 1891. See description no. I *infra.*
(3) *Kantiga por a̲l̲ [= 'el] fu'ego ...* , Salonika, 5651 (= 1891). 16 pp. Locations: Ben-Zvi Institute; private library of I. S.

[14] In a tantalizing footnote, Attias mentions that Molho had in his possession some sixteen of Yoná's chapbooks, published in Salonika between 1891 and 1921, and that he himself owns one published in Cairo in 1907. See *Romancero sefaradí,* p. 8, n. 12.

Révah. References: Molho, *Sĕfārîm,* no. 131 (he gives 8 instead of 16 pp.); Révah, no. I.

(4) *Komplas nu'evas por 'el pedrisko de Salonik,* Salonika, n.d. 16 pp. Location: Ben-Zvi Institute. Reference: Molho, *Sĕfārîm,* no. 130. He supplies the date 5659 (= 1899) in brackets and uses the form "Salóniko" in the title.

(5) "*Kantes mu'evos por los teretemblos* ... , Sofia, 1903 (= θRS"G). 16 pp. 8°." Reference: Molho, *Sĕfārîm,* no. 132.

(6) *Gu'erta de romansos 'importantes,* Salonika, before 1905. See description no. II *infra.*

(7) *Komplas nu'evas del felek 'i sala de pasatyempo,* Cairo, 5667 (= 1907). 32 pp. Location: Jewish National and University Library (Jerusalem): H88: 296.789.7. A handwritten note in Hebrew at the bottom of this copy's title page reads "printed in Jerusalem." References: Molho, *Sĕfārîm,* no. 133 (he lists 30 not 32 for the pagination); Yaari, no. 375.

(8) *Gu'erta de romansas antiguas de pasatyempo,* n.p., n.d. [before 1908?]. See description no. III *infra.*

(9) *Livriko de romansas 'importantes,* Sofia, 1908. See description no. IV *infra.*

(10) "*Kante mu'evo por mu'estro gran rabênû ḥ"r Yacăkōb Mē'îr nr"w.* ... Sofia, 1908. 16 pp. 8°. It also includes a dirge in Ladino on the demise of the Grand Rabbi Yacăkōb Ḥănanyāh Kobo, whose place R. Yacăkōb Mē'îr filled." We translate Molho's reference: *Sĕfārîm,* no. 135.

(11) *Romansos,* n.p., n.d. [before 1909]. See description no. V *infra.*

(12) *'El trezoro de Yacăkōb Yônāh* ... , Salonika, 5670 (= 1910). The *Trezoro* consists of five chapbooks of 16 pp. each. Subsequent volumes are numbered *Brośura segunda,* etc. *Brośuras* III, IV, and V simply bear the title *'El trezoro,* omitting the author's name. All are dated 5670. Location: Jewish National and University Library (Jerusalem): H88. *Brośuras* II and IV are in Révah's library. References: Gaon, no. 129; Révah, no. III; Yaari, no. 818.

(13) *Brošura de romansas 'importantes,* Salonika, 1913. See description no. VI *infra.*

(14) *Ku'entos 'ermozos de pasatyempo*, Salonika, [1914]. 16 pp. Location: Jewish National and University Library (Jerusalem).

(15) *'Un remorso por la Hagādāh de ḥag ha-Pesaḥ*, Salonika, 1915. See description no. VII *infra*.

(16) *Brośura por 'el fu'ego grande de Salóniko dezastrozo*, n.p., [1917]. 8 pp. Location: Jewish National and University Library (Jerusalem). References: Molho, *Sĕfārîm*, no. 136; Révah, no. IV.

(17) *Gu'erta de romansos 'inportantes*, [Salonika], 1920. See description no. VIII *infra*.

(18) "*Güerta de historia.*" Speaking of a text of *Gaiferos jugador* included in his Master's thesis, M. J. Benardete states: "Este romance tiene mucho que ver con el que publicó Jacob Yoná en su 'Güerta de Historia'; ninguna otra colección lo contiene" (p. 43). Cf. ballad no. 5, n. 16 *infra*.

(19) *Komplas mu'evas por ḥag ha-Pesaḥ*, Salonika, n.d. 14 pp. (?). Location: Ben-Zvi Institute. This copy includes odd pages from other publications of Yoná, which have been sewed together in disorderly fashion. Pp. 15-16 of GSA, comprising the final verses of *El chuflete* (GSA, no. 10) and most of the text of *El conde Alemán y la reina* (GSA, no. 11), have been sewed into this copy. Another copy, at the Instituto Arias Montano (Madrid), is listed as having neither place nor date of publication, in the *Catálogo de la Exposición Bibliográfica Sefardí Mundial* (no. 374).

(20) "*Romansas importantes (11) y complas y nuevas por* ... Salónica, sin año de impresión. (En caracteres rashi.)" Reference: LSO, no. 60 (p. 409).

(21) "*Sala de pasatyempo* ... , n.p., n.d., 24, [4] pp. 8°. Content: Songs in Ladino and miscellaneous subjects." We translate Molho's reference: *Sĕfārîm*, no. 134.

We have also seen photographs of the following broadsides, bearing no place or date of publication, now housed at the Ben-Zvi Institute (Jerusalem):

(22) *Kante mu'evo por mu'estro soverano Śultán ᶜAbdul Meḥmed Reśad sinkeno ǧok yyaśa.*

(23) *Suplemento de la libertad de Yaᶜăkōb Yônāh.*

(24) *Ku'entos 'ermozos de pasatyempo—Śarkís 'importantes.*

(25) *'El korasón: Kante por la fyesta briante de dí'a de alḥad del 17 de sîwān de 669* (=1909).

Yoná's Ballad Chapbooks

In the present volume we have edited the twenty-seven ballad text types that appear in eight of Yoná's chapbooks. Our edition of these texts takes into account the variant readings from all of the available chapbooks containing *romances*:

I. *Sēfer gĕdûlaθ Mōšeh,* n.p., 1891 (abbr. SGM).
II. *Gu'erta de romansos 'importantes,* Salonika, before 1905 (abbr. GSA).
III. *Gu'erta de romansas antiguas de pasatyempo,* n.p., before 1908? (abbr. GRA).
IV. *Livriko de romansas 'importantes,* Sofia, 1908 (abbr. LRI).
V. *Romansos,* n.p., before 1909 (abbr. RSA).
VI. *Brošura de romansas 'importantes,* Salonika, 1913 (abbr. BRI).
VII. *'Un remorso por la Hagādāh de ḥag ha-Pesaḥ,* Salonika, 1915 (abbr. RHP).
VIII. *Gu'erta de romansos 'inportantes,* [Salonika], 1920 (abbr. GRI).

At least three of Yoná's publications, which almost certainly contained ballads, have thus far eluded us. We have not been able to locate copies of Molho's *Cuentos hermosos de pasatiempo,* Salonika, 1890 (no. 1 *supra*) and *Romansas importantes y complas y nuevas,* Salonika, n.d. (no. 20 *supra*), nor the *Güerta de historia* as mentioned by Benardete (no. 18 *supra*). To judge by Molho's description, the *Sala de pasatyempo* (no. 21 *supra*) may also contain *romances.* We hope future investigations may bring copies of these publications to light.

Yoná as Collector and Editor

Certain aspects of the relationship of the various chapbook texts to one another elucidate Yoná's criteria as a collector and editor of ballads and point, not only to his initial acquisition of authentically traditional texts, but also to his continued reliance upon oral tradition for subsequent editorial modifications. Arbitrary omissions or changes in verse order are perhaps evident in his treatment of certain portions of *Roncesvalles + Las bodas en París* (no. 2B), *El villano vil* (no. 26B), and *El chuflete* (no. 27: GRI). However, unlike many an early Western European ballad editor, Yoná did not, in general, attempt to polish or otherwise tamper with the texts which he had selected from living tradition. His booklets offer us invaluable authentic versions whose characteristics are consistently corroborated by our own unedited field recordings, as well as by Judeo-Spanish variants published elsewhere. Rarely, if ever, do Yoná's texts strike a stylistically false note. His ballads reflect oral tradition with surprising and laudable exactitude. [15] Characterized by all the authentic irregularities, contaminations, and imperfections of traditional poetry, Yoná's ballads preserve for us precious evidence of the Salonikan *Romancero,* dating in many cases from a period before or at least contemporary with the very first erudite attempts to record Eastern Judeo-Spanish balladry.

In various instances, however, it does seem quite clear that Yoná referred back to oral tradition to emend or amplify ballads he had already published. His later printings of *Conde Alemán y la reina* (no. 7) and *El robo de Elena* (no. 11) clearly attest to his use of traditional variant readings for purposes of editorial revision, as also possibly do certain variations in *Roncesvalles + Las bodas en París* (no. 2) and *El falso hortelano* (no. 21).

---

[15] To what extent, on the other hand, Yoná's printed versions may have nourished subsequent oral tradition remains difficult to gauge, largely because of Yoná's own close adherence to that tradition and to the consequent identity of his texts with those already current among the folk. The influence of Yoná's widely and eagerly read booklets must, however, have been considerable. Attias is surely correct in assuming that "Estas publicaciones contribuyeron sin duda a refrescar la memoria de aquellos que se sentían atraídos por la romanza" (*Romancero sefaradí,* p. 341). The influence of printed sources upon the Judeo-Spanish *Romancero* has, in general, been quite considerable. Broadsides and even texts of a more erudite nature have certainly augmented the number of themes current in oral tradition. For now, see our remarks in "Sobre unos romances del Cid recogidos en Tetuán," pp. 395-396. For an instance of the influence of phonograph records on the Eastern Sephardic tradition, see our commentary to ballad no. 12 (*El conde Olinos*). On the fidelity of Yoná's texts to oral tradition, cf. also M. Molho, *Salonique: Ville-Mère en Israël* (Jerusalem—Tel Aviv, 1967), p. 100*a*.

The number of text types that appear but once in the eight chapbooks known to us attest to Yoná's efforts to renovate the content of his booklets in their successive reeditions. Several themes are, however, perpetuated as part of the "Yoná canon," being passed on with but minimal variations through a series of reprintings. Such, for example, is the case with our nos. 5 (*Gaiferos jugador*), 6 (*Melisenda sale de los baños*), 8 (*Robo de Dina*), 15 (*Amante abandonada*), 24 (*Bella en misa*), 26 (*Villano vil*), and 27 (*Chuflete*). The following table details the recurrences of each ballad type in the eight chapbooks we have edited.

TABLE I

	SGM (1891)	GSA (-1905)	GRA (-1908)	LRI (1908)	RSA (-1909)	BRI (1913)	RHP (1915)	GRI (1920)
1. *Almenas de Toro + Alcaide de Alhama*			2					
2. *Almerique de Narbona + Roncesvalles + Bodas en París*		1	7				1	
3. *Sueño de Doña Alda*			3					
4. *Conde Claros y el Emperador*		6	8	10		9	8	9
5. *Gaiferos jugador*		2		3				8
6. *Melisenda sale de los baños*				4		3	4	3
7. *Conde Alemán y la reina*		11			3			
8. *Robo de Dina*		5		12	2	11		11
9. *Paso del Mar Rojo*	p. 15			1				
10. *Tormenta calmada + Idólatra*		7	9	11	6	10		10
11. *Robo de Elena*		8		7		4	6	4
12. *Conde Olinos*			5					
13. *Esposa de Don García*			1					
14. *Mala suegra*		3						
15. *Amante abandonada*				8		5	5	5
16. *Adúltera (á-a)*				9		8		
17. *Celinos y la adúltera*		12						
18. *Rico Franco*					5			
19. *Triste amador*			4					
20. *Silvana*					1			
21. *Falso hortelano*			11	2		2	2	2
22. *Vos labraré un pendón*					4			
23. *Vuelta del hijo maldecido*			6					
24. *Bella en misa*		4		6		6		6
25. *Galana y su caballo*		9						
26. *Villano vil*			10			1	3	1
27. *Chuflete*		10		5		7	7	7

While most of Yoná's booklets—GSA, LRI, RSA, BRI, RHP, and GRI—seem to depend closely on one another in chronological succession, the *Gu'erta de romansas antiguas de pasatyempo* (GRA) sets itself apart from all the rest as a consistently distinctive and independent manifestation of Yoná's efforts as a ballad collector. GRA is distinguished not only by its preference for unique themes neglected in subsequent printings (i.e., our nos. 1, 3, 12, 13, 19, 23), but also by its absorption of variant versions which differ quite radically from those included in the other chapbooks (e.g., GRA's texts of *Conde Claros* and *La tormenta calmada* [our nos. 4 and 10]).

The importance of Yoná's activities as collector, editor, and publisher hinges upon his conservatism rather than upon any original, innovative creativity.[16] As a figure who seems to have purveyed his ballads not only in written but also in oral form, Yoná suggests some final, superannuated representative of medieval minstrelsy, just as his ballads themselves evoke the themes and protagonists of the Castilian epic: Urraca and the Cid, Roncevaux, Aude's tragic premonition, Gaiferos-Waltharius, Charlemagne. Yoná's techniques as an editor —faithfully reproducing traditional texts and later emending them in the light of other authentic variants—recall another, later stage in the history of Hispanic balladry: the sixteenth-century *Cancioneros,* whose compilers apparently followed almost identical editorial procedures.[17] At a moment when the cultural patterns of Sephardic Salonika were undergoing rapid and massive Westernization,[18] the figure of Yoná,

[16] Here we are not directly concerned with the many rhymes written by Yoná himself, which are abundantly represented in his publications.

[17] See, for example, Menéndez Pidal's observations in CSA, pp. v-vi, xlvii-xlviii; and "Poesía popular y Romancero," II, 12-15.

[18] In a recent letter (Dec. 17, 1966), the distinguished historian Joseph Nehama graphically evokes the intense cultural ferment of Salonikan life in the years around the turn of the century: "Notre troubadour appartient à une époque où Salonique sortait de son apathie, de sa somnolence presque deux fois séculaire. Depuis 1873, des écoles, où était distribué un enseignement moderne, en langue française et italienne, au grand scandale, à l'indignation des dirigeants qui voyaient dans les établissements scolaires des répreuves de Satan, des lieux de perdition, des pépinières de mécréants, ouvraient leurs portes, et dans l'intervalle de vingt-cinq ans, la population juive fit éruption dans la vie moderne, se livra à des activités diverses: le commerce prit un essor considérable avec son contact avec l'étranger; l'industrie prit un développement considérable; les banques se multiplièrent et favorisèrent le progrès général en prodigant le crédit. Parallèlement

genial street minstrel and self-appointed repository of the ancient folk poetry of his people, stands out as a remarkable and appealing archaism. And precisely therein lies the special quality of his contribution. Yoná's fine intuition for the style and values of traditional poetry has preserved for us a uniquely important cultural document: his superb selection of the very best of Salonikan balladry, captured at a crucial moment when, in competition with more modern lyrical forms, the Judeo-Spanish *Romancero* was verging upon a grave generic decline.[19] Scarcely two decades after Yoná's death this process was rushed to its inexorable end by the almost total annihilation of the great community of Salonika—the Jerusalem of Sephardic Jewry—which for almost half a millennium had cherished and preserved its ancient Hispanic ballad heritage.[20]

---

des quotidiens, des bihebdomadaires, des hebdomadaires foisonnèrent, des livres, par centaines, en espagnol local, furent traduits du français, de l'italien; les feuilles satiriques fourmillèrent. Déjà, à la fin du XIXe et aux premières années du XXe, l'Affaire Dreyfus avait profondément passionné tous les esprits à Salonique et toute la population juive, jusqu'à ses strates inférieures, s'était habituée à lire avec enthousiasme les journaux, ceux de France et ceux de la ville. Les esprits s'émancipèrent avec une rapidité vertigineuse. Nous eûmes une profusion d'écrivains, de publicistes, de poètes de premier rang, de tout acabit, des chansonniers. C'est vrai que l'ambiance politique a beaucoup aidé à cette soudaine éclosion: La Macédoine est devenue l'arène où se sont livré bataille des influences russes, autrichiennes et autres; l'effervescence jeune turque a triomphé du régime policier de Hamid II; les Balkans se sont ligués et ont expulsé le maître ottoman; les alliés ont ouvert à Salonique un front formidable; un incendie catastrophique a anéanti toute la zone résidentielle et commerciale de la ville; le régime hellénique s'est installé sur les territoires européens des Balkans; les turcs des nouvelles provinces helléniques ont été échangés contre les populations grecques d'Asie Mineure, etc. Nous avons eu un ébranlement gigantesque. Le milieu a changé du tout au tout. Cela a été une terre nouvelle, un ciel nouveau. Tout le passé a été aboli comme sous l'effet d'une baguette magique."

[19] Cf. the contemporary comments of Moisés Abravanel quoted by Menéndez Pidal in his "Catálogo del romancero judío-español" (abbr. MP): "La nueva generación de mujeres ... va desconociendo los hermosos y gustosos romances de España; es menester buscar las viejas. ... Me encuentro a veces con viejas mujeres, a las cuales les demando de cantar romances; ellas me responden que es moquería que les hago, pues ahora no cantan muchos, sino nuevas cantigas amorosas" (p. 1057).

[20] Today the Salonikan ballad tradition lives out its now tenuous and perilous existence in various diaspora communities, notably Israel and the United States.

Norms Followed in the Present Edition

Our transliteration has been carried out in accordance with the following table of equivalences:

'	*aleph.*	n	*nun.*
b	*beth.*	p	*pe.*
d	*daleth.*	r	*reš.*
đ	*daleth* with diacritic.	s	*samekh.*
f	*pe* with diacritic.	š	*šin.*
g	*gimel.*	ś	*sin.*
ğ	*gimel* with diacritic.	t	*teth.*
ḥ	*ḥeth.*	v	*beth* with diacritic.
k	*qoph.*	y	*yodh.*
l	*lamedh.*	z	*zayin.*
m	*mem.*	ž	*zayin* with diacritic.

We indicate with an apostrophe the *aleph* which in Ladino precedes *yodh* and *waw* in graphic-word-initial position. We also use the apostrophe for *aleph* before *he,* when the latter represents the morpheme *a* (verb or preposition) as an autonomous graphic word. Finally, the apostrophe represents the *aleph* used in Ladino as a sign of hiatus between any two vowels (with the usual exception of a = *aleph*).[21] We represent the final *he* of a graphic word by *a*. In any other position, *a* represents an *aleph* in the original. When *a* appears alone as a separate word in our transliteration it can be assumed to represent an *aleph* which is joined to the following word in the original (i.e., *ami* in the original will be written *a mi* in our transcriptions of ballad texts). Conversely, when *'a* appears at the beginning of a word—*'atan,* for instance—these two symbols, representing *aleph* + *he,* can be assumed to have constituted a separate graphic word in the original: i.e., *'a tan.* With a ligature (a͜l) we indicate a special digraph combining *aleph* and *lamedh.* We represent stressed *yodh* and *waw* by *e* or *i, o* or *u* respectively, following the pronunciation of Salonikan Judeo-Spanish.

---

[21] In Ladino the *aleph* of hiatus is not normally used between *aleph* (= *a*) and another vowel. However, some exceptions are found in the Yoná booklets: e.g., *sa'etas* (ballad no. 1.10); *ka'es* (no. 4A.17 f.); *A'ífto* (no. 9B.2); *tra'ída* (*passim*); *a'utor* (title page of BRI [no. VI *infra*], to avoid reading *'utor*).

In the case of unstressed *yodh* and *waw*, where the contrast between [*e*] and [*i*], [*o*] and [*u*] is apparently neutralized in the spoken language, we transliterate the *yodh* and the *waw* in accordance with modern Castilian or Turkish orthography (according to the origin of the word).[22] In the use of the written accent we follow the norms of standard Castilian.

In transcribing words written according to Hebrew usage we merely transliterate, making no attempt to reproduce Eastern Sephardic pronunciation.[23] We employ the following consonantal signs in addition to those used in transcribing Ladino:

ç	*çadhe.*	w	*waw.*
h	*he.*	θ	*thaw.*
ḳ	*kaph.*	ᶜ	*ayin.*

In transliterating Hebrew we do not indicate doubled consonants. We observe lenition only in the case of *pe*; that is to say, we ignore consonantal variations occasioned by the presence of *dagheš*. We transcribe all Hebrew words as if they carried complete vocalic pointing. We take as a model—with some slight modifications—the system of equivalences used by C. M. Crews in her excellent monograph on the *Meam Loez*:[24]

a	*pathaḥ.*	i	*ḥiriq.*
ā	*qamaç.*	î	*ḥiriq* + *yodh.*
â	*qamaç* + *yodh.*	ō	*ḥolam* without *waw.*
e	*seghol.*	ô	*ḥolam* + *waw.*
ē	*çere.*	u	*qubbuç.*
ê	*çere* + *yodh* and *seghol* + *yodh.*	û	*šuruq.*

The *šewa nac* and composite *šewaim* are represented as *ĕ, ă,* and *ŏ.* Sometimes the original makes use of vocalic pointing and consonantal

---

[22] For further discussion and a bibliography of Ladino transcription systems, see our DRH, pp. 21-24.

[23] Cf. C. M. Crews, "The Vulgar Pronunciation of Hebrew in the Judaeo-Spanish of Salonica," *The Journal of Jewish Studies,* XIII (1962), 83-95. We except from our system of transcription the names of the Hebrew letters, which we refer to by their conventional names.

[24] "Extracts from the *Meam Loez* (Genesis) with a Translation and a Glossary," *Proceedings of the Leeds Philosophical and Literary Society: Literary & Historical Section,* IX (1960), 13-106: p. 16.

diacritics for purely decorative purposes in the square letters of the titles. We make no attempt to indicate in our transliteration the capricious use of such symbols. In Hebrew texts we use a hyphen to separate the definite article, prepositions, and the conjunction *w* from following forms. Portions of the original printed in square Hebrew characters are transliterated in boldface.[24 bis] Rashi letters are represented by standard type.

In transliterating Ladino renderings of words or proper names of Turkish origin we underline any vowel which does not correspond to a written symbol in the original.

In our descriptions of the chapbooks, the symbol / indicates that a continuous text passes from one line to another in the original; two virgules (//) indicate the beginning of a separated line in the original. We follow modern norms of capitalization. In our bibliographic descriptions we preserve the punctuation and word division of the original (e.g., *ami, atomar,* etc.). In transcribing ballad texts punctuation and most graphic word boundaries (except for the prepositions *a* and *de* when joined to the definite articles) have been adjusted to modern norms.

All differences, both linguistic and orthographic, between the base text of each ballad (for which we usually use its earliest printing) and its successive reprintings, are normally recorded in the variants after each text. The following minor differences are not usually recorded: *al* vs. *a͜l, đ* vs. *d, š* vs. *ś, alos* or *alas* vs. *'a los* or *'a las* and other differences in graphic word boundaries when orthographic variations (e.g., *nun sofith*) are not involved. The presence of the word *'i* at the beginning of repeated lines in the variant texts is not normally noted.

[24 bis] Unfortunately, boldface type has not been available for certain "exotic" characters: š, ś, *θ*, ḥ.

Eight Ballad Chapbooks of Y. A. Yoná: Bibliographic Descriptions

I

SĒFER GĔDÛLAθ MŌŠEH

(n.p., 1891)

(abbr. SGM)

Sēfer gĕdûlaθ Mōšeh // — . — // 'En dita gĕmārā' kontyene la grandeza de Mōšeh rabênû / c"h de todo lo ke vido 'a los syelos, 'i lo ke / se aparesyyó 'el Santo Bendiğo 'Êl 'en Monte de / Sînay. // De más toparán la senyyorí'a detrás 'unos / romansos bastantes agrađavles tokante 'a / Mōšeh rabênû c"h, ke van atomar munğo plazer / tanto 'ombres komo mužeres. // Tra'iđa 'en la 'estamparí'a por mezo de 'el Se. Yacăkōb Yônāh hy"w. θaḥaθ memšeleθ 'Ădônênû ha-Meleḵ Śultán c*A*bdul Ḥamid Ḥan yr"h // Šĕnaθ **wĕ-Yacăkōb** 'îš θām **yôšēb** 'ôhālîm

15 pages (including the frontispiece). Size: approximately 181 × 134 mm. The margins of our copy are badly worn. Typographical frame of the frontispiece: 135 × 89 mm; of the text: 146 × 89 mm. Number of lines per page: 26-28. The date is indicated by means of a portion of Genesis 25:27: "and Jacob was a plain man, dwelling in tents." The sum of the numerical value of the letters that appear in boldface is equal to 651 (5651 = 1891). At the top of p. 2: **"Gĕdûlaθ Mōšeh."** The booklet has the following content:

Ḳĕ-θapûaḥ ba-căçê ha-yacar ḳēn dôdî bên ha-bānîm, 'este 'es Mōšeh rabênû c"h . . . (pp. 2-13).[25]

Romansos de Mōšeh rabênû // — . — // 'A Mōšeh Mōšeh 'en la sarsa mora . . . (14-15).[26]

---

[25] The Hebrew words at the beginning of the booklet are from the Song of Songs 2:3: "As the apple tree among the trees of the wood, so is my beloved among the sons."

[26] This narrative song, concerning Moses and the burning bush, which also appears in LRI (no. 1), is, metrically speaking, not a *romance*. For published

'En katorze de nîsān ... (15).

We use a copy found among papers of the late Professor William Milwitzky, which are now housed at the Yivo Institute for Jewish Research in New York. There is another copy at the Ben-Zvi Institute in Jerusalem. Description: "Algo más," no. I.

II

GU'ERTA DE ROMANSOS 'IMPORTANTES

(Salonika, before 1905)

(abbr. GSA)

Gu'erta // **de romansos** // **'importantes** // — // Dita gĕmārāh kontyene 'unos romansos 'ermozos, 'i / byen antikozos, 'i 'importantes, ke non se apa-/resyeron de antes, ke prevalen por kantarsen 'en / noğađas de vi'ola 'i noğađas de bu'eno de velar, / ke 'el kantađor se va namorar. // Si tambyén kontyene 'unos brindis para saluđar / 'en fyestas 'i zyafetes de bĕrîɵ mîlāh todos en / po'ezí'a. // — . — // Tra'íđa 'a la 'estamparí'a por mezo de // **Yaᶜăkōb 'Abrāhām** // **Yônāh s"t** // **Salóniko**

24 pages (including the frontispiece). Size: 200 × 136 mm. Typographical frame: 147 × 90 mm. Number of lines per page: 28. Molho (*Sĕfārîm,* no. 124), the *Catálogo de la Exposición Bibliográfica Sefardí Mundial* (no. 394) and H. V. Besso ("Bibliography of Judeo-Spanish Books," no. 78 [pp. 120-121]; or *Ladino Books,* no. 285 [= no. 78; p. 35]) attribute the date 1910 (= 5670) to this booklet. No such date appears anywhere in it. Hence we use the designation GSA (= "Gu'erta sin año"). Actually the collection must be considerably older than 1910. An apparent allusion to this *Gu'erta* in a lecture delivered by Menéndez Pidal in April of 1909 (*El Romancero Español,* pp. 87-88) in itself invalidates the 1910 attribution. William Milwitzky's papers include a complete transcription of this *Gu'erta,* whence Milwitzky extracted

---

versions, see Attias 78; Molho, *Usos,* pp. 254-255; Wiener 2. In Morocco there are two different *romances* on the same theme: Benoliel 367; Larrea, *Canciones,* nos. 83-84; MP 34, which are in *á-o* assonance; and Larrea 44; Larrea, *Canciones,* no. 87, which are in *ó.*

the version of *Gaiferos jugador* (no. 5 *infra*), which he published in 1905, without specifying its origin, in his article "El viajero filólogo y la antigua España" (*Cuba y América*, XIX). In 1899, Milwitzky had visited the principal Eastern Mediterranean Sephardic communities, where he collected a mass of linguistic, folkloric, and bibliographical materials. Very probably his transcription is based upon a copy of the *Gu'erta* acquired during this trip. In any event the publication of his article in *Cuba y América* gives us a firm *terminus* of 1905.

Romanso 1 // 'I akel konde 'i akel konde... (pp. 2-4).
Romanso 2 // Por los palasyyos de Karlo... (4-5).
Romanso 3 // Asentađa 'está la reyna... (5-7).
Romanso 4 // Tres damas van ala misa... (7-8).
Romanso 5 // Se pasean las 12 flores... (8-9).
Romanso 6 // Luz del dí'a 'i klaridad... (9-10).
Romanso 7 // Se pase'a pastor fi'el... (11-12).
Romanso 8 // **Dito romanso se kanta 'en 'el son de 'ôḥîlah** // 'Estava la reyna 'Izela... (12-13).
Romanso 9 // **Kantiga de novyya** // 'Estávanse [*sic*] la galana... (13-14).
Romanso 10 // Salir kere 'el mez de mağyyo... (14-15).
Romanso 11 // Pensativle 'está 'el bu'en rey... (15-17).
Romanso 12 // Ken kere tomar konsežo... (17-19).
Brindis // **'Importantes para fyestas** // Senyyores, todo modo de kîdûšîn... (19-22).
Brindis // **Para zyafetes de bĕrîɵ mîlāh** // Senyyores, nu'estro Dyyo 'es syempre 'Ēl mālē' raḥămîm... (22-23).
Dita kantiga se kanta 'en 'el son de Šābûᶜôɵ // sîmān **'ănî Yaᶜăkōb Yônāh** // 'En 'este tyempo 'espero de ser venturozo... (23-24).[27]

Actually there are two different printings of GSA: One is represented by an incomplete copy belonging to the Library of Congress described

---

[27] This composition is a veritable "ensalada," in which proverbs, popular sayings, and fragments of traditional songs alternate with prosaic verses composed by Yoná himself. The fourth strophe is of balladic interest:

> Yyo dudún ḥanum ami mužer la yyamarí'a,
> tener dovlet 'i asentarme kon 'elyya ala birerí'a,
> madre ke paryyó 'a Silvana ké 'onra le kedarí'a.

The last line is the conclusion of the incestuous ballad of *Silvana* (no. 20 *infra*).

by Besso ("Bibliography of Judeo-Spanish Books," no. 78; *Ladino Books,* no. 285). Pp. 3-4 and 5-6 are missing from this copy. A second printing, which incorporates a few very minor emendations, is represented by the copy belonging to the Instituto Arias Montano (Madrid) listed in the *Catálogo de la Exposición Bibliográfica Sefardí Mundial,* no. 394. This copy corrects the reading *klarirad* of the Library of Congress copy to *klaridad* in v. 1 of *Conde Claros y el Emperador* (GSA, no. 6, p. 9 = no. 4A *infra*). The Arias Montano copy adds the word *ver* to hemistich *b* of v. 5 of the same ballad; the word is lacking in the Library of Congress copy. Milwitzky's copy must have represented this earlier, uncorrected printing, since his transcription, like the Library of Congress copy, also lacks the word *ver* in hemistich *b* of v. 5 of *Conde Claros,* although Milwitzky emends *klarirad* to *klaridad.* The ballad of *Gaiferos jugador* (no. 5 *infra*) and portions of the texts of *Las bodas en París* (no. 2 *infra*) and *La mala suegra* (no. 14 *infra*), which are on pp. 3-6 of GSA, are missing in the lacunous Library of Congress copy. This first printing probably also differed from the later one (reflected in the Arias Montano copy) in the reading of the word for God in v. 7*b* of *Gaiferos jugador.* Here the Arias Montano copy reads " 'el Dyez," while Milwitzky's elsewhere scrupulously accurate MS copy reads "el Dio."

Menéndez Pidal's personal library includes an incomplete copy of the first printing (lacking the *portada,* pp. 1-4, and part of pp. 5-6) and a complete copy of the second printing. Cf. *El Romancero Español,* pp. 87-88; RoH, II, 330-331. Molho also mentions the booklet (*Sĕfārîm,* no. 124; LSO 409, no. 59). See also the description in "Algo más," no. II, which should be modified in the light of our observations in "Un romancerillo," p. 11, n. 8.

III

GU'ERTA DE ROMANSAS ANTIGUAS DE PASATYEMPO

(no place or date; before 1908?)

(abbr. GRA)

To the generosity of Don Ramón and Don Gonzalo Menéndez Pidal we owe the opportunity of consulting photographs of an apparently unique copy of this booklet. The title page of this copy is missing. However, the Menéndez Pidal library also houses a transliteration of GRA, including the lost title page, made by M. Manrique de Lara in Salonika in 1911 and generously placed at our disposal by Diego Catalán:

Güerta
de
romansas antiguas
de pasatiempo.

En dita guimará contiene tres artículos presentes.

I.—Once romansas, las más brillantes que puede ser por pasatiempo de los señores en todas las horas de alegria y de nochadas de velar.

II.—Una cantiga moral al ceder del alfabet(o) y se canta en todo modo de son que les plaze à los señores, si tambien en el son de *Xeborlimi mané.*

III.—Un cante del Felek que se canta en el son de las coplas de Xabuot.

Yo el autor
Jacob. Abraham Joná.

There are 14 pages in the Menéndez Pidal copy, which seems to be incomplete at the end as well. We do not have the dimensions. Number of lines per page: 26 or 28. The title, **"Gu'erta // de // romansas antiguas // de pasatyempo"**, appears at the top of p. 1. The booklet's date remains problematic. Manrique de Lara's dated transliteration places it before 1911. The *Sēfer rĕnānôθ* ([Jerusalem], 5668) apparently copies two ballads—*El conde Olinos* and *El falso hortelano* (nos. 12 and 21 *infra*) —from GRA. This would push the latter's publication back to some time before 1908.

Romansa 1 // Yyo me a̯levantí 'un lunes . . . (pp. 1-2).
Romansa 2 // Por los pa̯lasyyos de 'el re'e . . . (2-3).
Romansa 3 // 'En Paríž 'está Donyyalda . . . (4).

Romansa 4 // 'En akel verğel pekenyyo... (4-5).
Romansa 5 // 'En 'el verğel dela reyna... (5-6).
Romansa 6 // Dulse 'eraš la mi madre... (6-7).
Romansa 7 // Grandes bodas ayy 'en Fransyya... (7-8).
Romansa 8 // Luz del dí'a 'i klaridad... (8-9).
Romansa 9 // Se pase'a 'el pastor fi'el... (9-10).
Romansa 10 // 'En la sivdad de Manselyya [*sic*]... (10-11).
Romansa 11 // Aḥ! 'Índome por 'estas mares... (11-12).
Kantiga moral de la Ley kon la alma // — // 'Iža mí'a mi kerida... (12-14).
Komplas del felek // Se kantan 'en 'el son de las komplas de Šābûᶜôө. // Alavemos 'a 'el Dyyo kon avlas de alavasyón... (14).

References: *Catálogo de la Exposición Bibliográfica,* no. 835; RoH, II, 331; "Algo más," no. IV.

IV

LIVRIKO DE ROMANSAS 'IMPORTANTES

(Sofia, 1908)

(abbr. LRI)

Livriko // **de** // **romansas 'importantes** // — . — // Senyyores, // 'Esta dita brośura ke yyo vos prezento kontyene / 'unas kuantas romansas 'importantes. // — . — // 1 — Primero la kantiga de Mōšeh rabēnû ᶜ"h kuando sa-/limos los ğudyyós de A'ífto; // 2 — Doğe romansas 'una mežor de 'otra por kantarsen / 'en 'unas 'oras de alegrías; // — . — // Vos rogo senyyores de tomar kada 'uno 'una gĕmārāh, / syendo non kosta munğa pará 'i toda mi familyya vo lo / rengrasyyará, 'i 'el Dyyo demandas de vu'estro korasón / vos kumplirá. // — . — // **Šĕnaө wa-yikrĕbû yĕmê Yaᶜăkōb Yônāh lā-mûө wa-yikrā'**!!!

16 pages (including the frontispiece). We do not have the dimensions. Number of lines per page: 28-30. The Hebrew phrase which occupies the last line of the title page is adapted from Genesis 47:29: "And the time drew nigh that Israel must die and he called...." The editor has

substituted his own name for that of Israel (= the biblical Jacob). The fact that this phrase is preceded by the word *Šĕnaə* 'the year of' would seem to indicate that Yoná was using a versicle, as he had done on other occasions, to date the publication, but all efforts to relate the numerical values of the Hebrew letters to the date of the colophon have proved fruitless. Is it possible that Yoná was not dating the publication at all, but was simply giving voice to his emotional state at the time of the booklet's redaction? The colophon reads: "**Sofyya,** // 'Imprimerí'a de Raḥămîm Śimonov 'i Komp. // 1908."

Romansa 1. // — . — // **Kantiga por Mōšeh rabênû** **ᶜ"h de / ḥag ha-Pesaḥ.** // — . — // **'A** Mōšeh Mōšeh, 'en la sarza mora . . . (pp. 2-4).
Romansa 2. // — . — // **'Índome** por 'estas mares . . . (4-5).
Romansa 3. // — . — // Por los palasyyos de Karlo . . . (5-6).
Romansa 4. // — . — // 'Esta noǧe mis kavayeros . . . (6-7).
Romansa 5. // — . — // Salir kere 'el mez de mayyo . . . (7-8).
Romansa 6. // — . — // Tres damas van ala milsa . . . (8-9).
Romansa 7. // — . — // **Dita romansa se kanta 'en 'el son de 'ôḥîlāh la-'Ēl:** / 'Estava la reyna 'Izela . . . (9-10).
Romansa 8. // — . — // 'Un amor tan kerensyyoza . . . (11-12).
Romansa 9. // — . — // Yyo me alevantí 'i 'un lunes . . . (12).
Romansa 10. // — . — // Luz del dí'a 'i klaridad . . . (13-14).
Romansa 11. // — . — // Se pase'a pastor fi'el . . . (14-15).
Romansa 12. // — . — // Se pasean las 12 flores . . . (15-16).

We know of only two copies of LRI: One is in the private library of Professor Israel S. Révah, who very generously placed it at our disposal. Reference: Révah, "Para una bibliografía," p. 110 (no. II). Menéndez Pidal (RoH, II, 331) describes another copy in his personal library.

V

ROMANSOS

(n.p., before 1909)

(abbr. RSA)

Romansos // — . — // 'En dita gĕmārā' kontyene 'unos romansos tan 'ermozos / ke prevalen para kantar, tanto 'ombres komo // mužeres. //

'I 'unos refranes ke tomarán plazer los senyyores // 'en 'espanyyol 'i 'en turko muyy ğaveres, // 'i 'espero kon ayyuda del Dyyo 'i despu'és los / amigos ke de 'oyy 'i 'endelantre vos apareseré / munğas gemrikas, kon ke vos koste pokas parikas. // 'I todo volo trayygo kon bu'ena hăḳānāh, yyo 'el kom-//ponedor **Yăᶜakōb 'Abrāhām Yônāh hy"w** // — . — // **θm"'h Śultán ᶜ*A*bdul Ḥ*a*mid Ḥan yr"h** // Las ditas gĕmārôθ se topan 'en la 'Estamparí'a / de ᶜĒç ha-Ḥayîm por vendersen.

14 pages (including the frontispiece). We do not know the dimensions. Number of lines per page: 25-28. On the upper margin of the frontispiece, in cursive script, appears: "Mōšeh Šimĕᶜôn Pesaḥ st—." Although the booklet does not carry a date of publication, the reference to Abdu-l-Hamid provides a *terminus ad quem* of 1909, the year of the deposition of this monarch. The booklet has the following contents:

Romanso primo // — . — // Se paseava Silvana . . . (pp. 2-3).
Romanso segundo // Se pasean las doğe flores . . . (3-4).
Romanso tersyyo // Pensativle 'está 'el bu'en rey . . . (4-5).
Romanso kuarto // 'Era 'una mužer pompoza . . . (5).
Romanso kinto // Tres falkones van bolando . . . (6).
Proverbyyos 'espanyyoles // 'El Dyyo 'es tađri'ozo, non 'es 'olviđađozo. . . . (7-11).[28]
Proverbyyos turkos //Atylan taš, yyry dwnmys. . . . (11-13).[29]
Romanso sezeno // Se pase'a 'el pastor fi'el . . . (14).

---

[28] Cf. E. Saporta y Beja, *Refranero sefardí* (Madrid-Barcelona, 1957): "*El Dio es tadrozo, ma no es olvidozo.* (Dios es tardío, pero no olvidadizo.) No se debe perder confianza porque más o menos tarde llega el alivio a nuestros males" (p. 111). Concerning this proverb, see Liebrecht, *Zur Volkskunde,* p. 220 (no. 101). RSA contains a total of 100 Judeo-Spanish proverbs which we hope to publish on another occasion.

[29] Or, in Turkish orthography: *Atılan taş, geri dönmez* 'A thrown stone does not return.' The more usual form of the proverb is *Atilan ok* . . . 'A shot arrow.' The saying criticizes any irrevocable action. The pronunciation *yeri* (< *geri*) is typical of Judeo-Spanish Turkisms: cf. *yul* 'rose' (< T. *gül*); *yemes* 'reins' (< T. *gem* 'bit [of a horse]'). See NSR, p. 80. The Turkish proverb in its less usual form, with the "stone" reading, circulates in an exact Judeo-Spanish translation: "*Piedra que se arroja, atrás no torna.* . . . Quiere decir que los malos actos o las malas palabras van muy lejos, hacen daño y no se pueden enmendar después de haberlos cometido. Recomienda pensarlo bien antes, porque después es demasiado tarde para volver atrás" (Saporta, *Refranero,* p. 249). Cf. also "*Palavrada y piedrada no se atornan atrás*" (Saporta, p. 232). Peninsular paremiology knows an almost identical proverb: *La piedra y la palabra no se*

M. Molho apparently alludes to this booklet in the bibliography of LSO (p. 409: no. 61): "Romans(o)[a]s. Contiene unos romans(o)[a]s para cantar... y unos refranes en español y turco (sin año de impresión; en caracteres rashi)." Révah ("Para una bibliografía," p. 108) uses Molho's data. We do not know of any other references. We use photographs of a copy at the Ben-Zvi Institute (Jerusalem). Cf. the description in "Un romancerillo."

VI

BROŠURA DE ROMANSAS 'IMPORTANTES

(Salonika, 1913)

(abbr. BRI)

Brošura // **de** // **romansas 'importantes** // — . — // Senyyores, 'esta brośura kontyene los / artíkulos sigu'entes: // 1 — 'Unas romansas byen 'importantes. // 2 — Las bĕrāḳôɵ de **bĕrîɵ mîlāh** 'en fransés / 'i 'en 'espanyyol para toda la viđa del 'ombre / ke no penen los senyyores. // 3 — 'Una kantiga de 'el felek de lo ke 'egziste / agora. // — // Tra'íđa ala 'imprimerí'a mezo 'el a'utor // **Yaᶜăkōb 'Abrāhām Yônāh** // **Salóniko** 5673 // — . —

16 pages (in addition to the frontispiece). Size: 200 × 138 mm. Typographic frame of the frontispiece: 162 × 107 mm.; of the text: 147 × 105 mm. Number of lines per page: 28. The Hebrew date corresponds to 1913. The title is repeated on p. 1: **"Brošura** // **de** // **romansas 'importantes."**

Romansa 'una // — . — **'En** la sivdađ de Marselyya ... (pp. 1-2).
Romanso dos // — . — // ('Esta romansa aremira 'el pasaže de los mansevos ke / 'estuvyeron 'en la gera.) // — // **Aḥ**! 'Índome por 'estas mares ... (2-3).
Romansa tres // — . — // **'Esta** noğe mis kavalyeros ... (3-4).
Romansa kuatro // — . — // **'Estava** la reyna 'Izela ... (4-5).

---

recoge después de echada (Gonzalo de Correas, *Vocabulario de refranes y frases proverbiales* [Madrid, 1924], p. 394*a*). On pp. 11-13 of RSA appear 44 Turkish proverbs in alphabetical order.

Romansa sinko // — . — // **'Un** amor tan kerensyyoza . . . (5-6).
Romansa seš // — . — // **Tres** damas van 'a la milsa . . . (7).
Romansa syete // — // **S**alir kere 'el mez de mayyo . . . (7-8).
Romansa 'oğo // — // **Yyo** me alevantí 'i 'un lunes . . . (8-9).
Romansa mu'eve // — // **Luz** del dí'a 'i klariđađ . . . (9-10).
Romansa dyez // — . — // **Se** pase'a pastor fi'el . . . (11-12).
Romansa 'onze // — . — // Se pasean las doğe flores . . . (12).
Komplas mu'evas // **por** // **'el felek** / **de agora** // — . — // (Se kantan 'en 'el son delas komplas de (Šābûᵒôɵ) / 'O Dyyo? [*sic*] Mándales pas 'en todos los reynados . . . (13-15).
'En 'esta 'oža kontyene las bĕrāḳôɵ de **bĕrîɵ mîlāh** . . . (16).

We have at our disposal photographic reproductions of copies belonging to the Library of Congress (Washington, D.C.) and to the Ben-Zvi Institute (Jerusalem). Besso ("Bibliography of Judeo-Spanish Books . . . ," no. 26 [p. 121]; *Ladino Books,* no. 284) describes the Library of Congress copy. Other references: *Catálogo de la Exposición Bibliográfica,* no. 396 (= the Library of Congress copy); LSO 409 (no. 58); Molho, *Sĕfārîm,* no. 125; "Algo más," no. III. There is a copy in Menéndez Pidal's private library.

VII

'UN REMORSO POR LA HAGĀDĀH DE ḤAG HA-PESAḤ

(Salonika, 1915)

(abbr. RHP)

Môᵒădîm lĕ-śimḥāh Bonne Fête // **'Un remorso** // **por la** // **Hagādāh de** ḥag **ha-Pesaḥ** // — . — // ('En 'esta brošura kontyene 5 artíkulos) // ——— // 1 — 'Un remorso de 'unos kuantos verbos tokante // 'a la **Hagādāh.** // 2 — 'Una kantiga del felek que 'egziste agora. // 3 — **'Unas romansas 'importantes** / 4 — Las bĕrāḳôɵ de **bĕrîɵ mîlāh** 'en fransés 'i // 'en 'espanyyol, porke no pene 'el parido 'a / dezirlas // 5 — 'El nombre del a'utor **Yaᵒăkōb Yônāh** // **Salóniko** // **Šĕnaɵ Wĕ-'eɵ laḥăçênû Zeh ha-dĕḥak**

The words *Bonne Fête* are in Roman letters. The pamphlet consists of 16 unnumbered pages (not counting the frontispiece). We have assigned numbers to the pages of our photographic copy. We do not have the dimensions. There are some 33 lines per page. The date is appropriately indicated by a phrase from the Passover *Haggadah*: "And our oppression: this refers to the vexation" (*Haggadah*, "Wa-niçᶜak 'el [Adonay]"). The passage alludes to Deuteronomy 26:7: "We cried to the Lord, the God of our fathers, and the Lord heard our plea and saw our plight, our misery, and our oppression." The numerical value of the letters printed in boldface equals 675 (5675 = 1915). The title is repeated at the top of p. 1: "**'Un remorso de 'unos** // **kuantos verbos** // **'indikada** [*sic*] **ala Hagādāh de ḥag ha-Pesaḥ**".[30] The booklet has the following content:

Hā' laḥmā' ᶜanyā' // **'Este** 'el pan de la afri'isyyón... (pp. [1-5]).
Komplas de 'el felek // **ke 'egziste agora** // — . — // 'Ordení 'este kantar... ([6-7]).
Sîmān **Yaᶜăkōb Yônāh hy"w** // **Yyya** [*sic*] 'es 'ora de ser kon 'el Dyyo namorozo... ([7]).
Gu'erta // **de** // **romansas 'importantes** // — . — // **Romansa 'una** // Akel konde, 'i akel konde... ([8-9]).
Romans[a]**ḥ** [*sic*] **dos** // Aḥ! 'Índome por 'estas mares... ([9]).
Romansa tres // 'En la sivdad de Marselyya... ([10]).
Romansa kuatro // 'Esta noğe mis kavayeros... ([11]).
Romansa sinko // 'Un amor tan kerensyyoza... ([11-12]).
Romansa seś // **'Estava** la reyna 'Izela... ([12]).
Romansa syete // **Salir** kere 'el mez de mayyo... ([12-13]).
Romansa 'oğo // Luz del dí'a 'i klaridad... ([13]).
Proverbyyos 'importantes // — . — // **A** Kyen al Dÿyo yyama, nunka 'esklama... ([14-15]).[31]
'Estos 5 byervos dirá 'el parido // Achre tivhar outkarev yichkon hassérého. ... ([16]).[32]

[30] In *verbos*, the diacritic mark of the first *beth* follows the *yod*: *by'rbos.*
[31] Cf. "Quen a El yama, nunca se engania" (D. Elnecavé, "Folklore de los sefardíes de Turquía: Refranes y locuciones," *Sef*, XXV [1965], 189-212: no. 267); "Quen al Dio llama, nunca se engaña" (J. Subirá, "Romances y refranes sefardíes," *EMP*, V [Madrid, 1954], 319-333: p. 332). The *aleph* which precedes the proverb in RHP introduces a series of proverbs arranged in abecedarian fashion, according to the initial letter of the word immediately following *Kyen.*
[32] The Hebrew text, from Psalms 65:4, appears first in Roman transliteration and then in boldface Hebrew letters.

We use a photographic reproduction of the copy belonging to the Ben-Zvi Institute (Jerusalem). Molho apparently refers to this booklet: "*Un remanso* [*sic*] *por la Hagadá de Pesah* [Salónica (1900?). (En caracteres rashi.) Contiene ocho romances.]." [33]

VIII

GU'ERTA DE ROMANSOS 'INPORTANTES

([Salonika], 1920)

(abbr. GRI)

Gu'erta // **de** // **romansos 'inportantes** // — . — // **'En dita brośura kontyene los ditos artíkulos** / 1 — **'Onze romansos 'inportantes** / 2 — Las **bĕrāḳôɵ de bĕrîɵ mîlah** 'en fransés // 'i 'en **lĕšôn ha-kôd**eš // 3 — La kantiga alavađa de **Tĕberyāh** // 4 — 'El nombre del a'utor **Yaᶜăkōb Yônāh** // — . — // anyyo — **La-yĕ'ûdîm hāyĕɵāh 'ôrāh** wĕ-śi**m**ḥāh //: Presyyo 1 p"r.

Révah ("Para una bibliografía," no. V) includes the following information as part of the title page:

> emprimerí [*sic*] "EKLER", Mazi Ḥan.

This indication does not appear in the copy we used which, however, bears the same notice as does Révah's at the bottom of p. 1:

> Kompozada 'en la **'Imprimerí'a Novel** Kalye Salamín No" 2 (al porto).

Similar information appears at the bottom of p. 16:

'Imprimerí'a "Novel"
Kalye Salamín Número 2 ('Imobles del Porto)

16 pages (not including title page). We do not have dimensions. Number of lines per page: 24-26 or 32. The date is indicated by a verse from

---

[33] LSO, p. 409 (no. 56). *Sic* is ours.

Esther 8:16, also incorporated into the Habdālāh (a prayer recited at the conclusion of the Sabbath and festivals): "For the Jews there was light and joy." The editor has made what is undoubtedly an intentional "error" in the first word, substituting an *aleph* for a *he,* to achieve the necessary total for the date of his publication. The numerical value of the letters printed in boldface totals 680 (i.e., 5680 = 1920). See Révah, "Para una bibliografía," p. 111, n. 13. A variant general title is repeated at the top of p. 1: **"Gu'erta** // **de romansas 'importantes."**

Romansa 'una // 'En la sivdad de Marselyya... (pp. 1-2).
Romansa dos // 'Esta romansa admira 'el pasaže delos mansevos ke 'es-//tán sirvyendo al servisyyo militar // **Aḥ**! 'Índome por 'estas mares... (2-3).
Romansa tres // **'Esta** noğe mis kavalyeros... (3-4).
Romansa kuatro // **'Estava** la reyna 'Izela... (4-5).
Romansa sinko // **'Un** amor tan kerensyyoza... (5-6).
Romansa seś // **Tres** damas van ala milsa... (6-7).
Romansa syete // **Salir** kyere 'el mez de mayyo... (7-8).
Romansa 'oğo // **Por** los palasyyos de Karlo... (8-9).
Romansa mu'eve // **Luz** del dí'a 'i klaridad... (10-11).
Romansa dyez // **Se** pase'a pastor fi'el... (11-12).
Romansa 'onze // **Se** pase'a las doğe flores... (13).
Yāšār te yyamastes mos kondenastes... (13).[34]
Akí kontyene las bĕrāḳôɵ de bĕriɵ mîlāh 'en letras fransezas 'i lĕšôn ha-kōdeš // — . — // Achré tivhar outkarev yichkon hasséréha... (14).[35]
'Ordenar kero 'un kantar. Nombre de 'el Dyyo 'enmentar. ... (15-16).

We have used photographs of two complementary copies from the Jewish National and University Library: 51A726/H88 and 39A838/H88. Neither copy is complete: 51A726 lacks the title page, while 39A838 lacks one sheet (pp. 15-16). Other references: Attias, p. 261; LSO, p. 409 (no. 57); Révah, "Para una bibliografía," p. 111 (no. V); Yaari, *Rĕšîmaθ sifrê ladino,* no. 362.

[34] The *Y* of *Yāšār* is the initial letter of an acrostic which reads **Yᶜkb** (Yaᶜăkōb). The author's last name appears in the penultimate verse of the poem in the boldface letters of the words: **"Yyo navegaré** ..."
[35] See n. 32 above.

THE BALLADS

1

LAS ALMENAS DE TORO + EL ALCAIDE DE ALHAMA

(The Battlements of Toro + The Moorish Commander of Alhama)

Por los pa͜lasyyos de 'el re'e   se pase'a 'una donze'a.
Blanka 'es 'i kolorada,   'ermoza komo las 'estreas.
Visto la 'uvo 'el bu'en re'e,   namorarse 'uvo de 'elyya.
Demandó 'el rey 'a su ğente   kyén 'era 'esta donze'a:
Si 'era de a͜lta ğente,   fu'era la mi mužer primera.
Si 'era de baša ğente,   'era 'una de mis donzeas.
—Vu'estra 'ermana 'es, 'el bu'en re'e,   vu'estra 'ermana la pe-
[kenyya.
—Syendo ke 'es la mi 'ermana,   gran fu'ego le ayy 'en 'elyya.
Akí, akí, mis kavalyeros,   los ke del mi pan komyeraš,
toma͜lda 'a 'esta donze'a   'i arožа͜lde syen sa'etas.
Todo 'el 'ombre ke la 'enfita,   de dádivas ke yyo le dyera.
Todo 'el 'ombre ke no la 'enfita,   darle yyo su mayyor pena.
De a'i sa͜ltó 'el gran Sidi: —No agáš mal 'a 'esta donze'a.
—¿Ké atorgáš vos, 'el gran Siđi?   ¿Vu'estra namorađa fu'era?
—No 'es mi namorađa, 'el bu'en rey,   'es la mi mužer primera.
Ke me la đyyo 'el rey vu'estro pađre   muğo antes ke muryera.
Yya se parte 'el gran Siđi,   yya se parte 'i se fu'era.
—'El bu'en moro, 'el bu'en moro,   'el de la barva 'envelyyutađa,
vos mandó 'a yyamar 'el bu'en rey,   ke vos kyere 'una palavra.
—¿Ké palavra 'era 'ésta,   tan sekreta 'i tan notada?

—Kortarvos kyere la kavesa, 'eğarla 'en 'una mušama.
—Anda dezilde al bu'en rey ke yyo no le kulpo nađa.
De kuando fu'eron mis geras peđrí mi 'onra 'i mi fama.
Pedrí 'ižos 'i mužeres 'i 'una koza ke yyo amava.
Peđrí 'una 'iža donze'a ke no av'ía 'en Granada.
Peđrí mil 'i kinyentos molinos ke molían noğe 'i dí'a.
Los kinyentos molían 'oro 'i los kinyentos plata fina.
Los kinyentos molían polvo, para 'el rey se 'espartí'a.
Yya se parte 'el bu'en moro, yya se parte 'i se 'iva.

Source: GRA 2
3 + se torna.

Translation:

Through the halls of the King's palace there walks a young maiden. She is fair with rosy cheeks and is as beautiful as the stars. The moment the good King saw her he fell in love with her. He inquired of his vassals who this maid might be. (5) "If she were of noble lineage, she would be my first wife. If she were of low estate, she would be one of my maidens." "She is your sister, good King, the youngest of your sisters." "Since she is my sister, a great fire be upon her. Here, here, my knights, all you who eat of my bread, (10) take this maiden and hurl a hundred arrows at her. Every man who strikes her I shall reward with gifts. Every man who does not strike her I shall punish mightily." Then, the great Cid arose: "Do no harm to this maiden." "What concern of yours is this, great Cid? Might she be your beloved?" (15) "She is not my beloved, good King, she is my first wife. She was given to me by your father many years before he died. Now the great Cid departs, he departs and is gone. "Oh good Moor, good Moor, he of the flowing beard, the good King has sent for you, for he wishes a word with you." (20) "What word might that be, so secret and so important?" "He intends to cut off your head and put it in an oilcloth [sack]." "Go tell the good King that I do not blame him at all. Since the time when I waged war, I lost my honor and my fame. I lost my sons and my wives and something I loved most dearly. (25) I lost an unwed daughter without equal in Granada. I lost a thousand five hundred mills that worked night and day. Five hundred of them ground gold, five hundred fine silver. Five hundred ground powder to be strewn before the King." (29) Now the good Moor departs, he departs and is gone.

Motifs:

5 Cf. T415. *Brother-sister incest.* See n. 4 *infra.*
17 Q431. *Punishment: banishment (exile)* (?). See n. 14 *infra.*
21 Q421. *Punishment: beheading.*
26 Cf. D1263. *Magic mill.*

Yoná's text combines elements from three different narratives: *Las almenas de Toro* (vv. 1-17), *El alcaide de Alhama* (18-25), and the description of King Priam's mills from *El juicio de Paris* (26-28). The formulaic, migratory vv. 17 and 29 are a recurrent device for concluding ballads in the Eastern Sephardic tradition and cannot be connected exclusively to one specific narrative. [1]

Las almenas de Toro includes several remote and greatly distorted echoes of themes and characters known to medieval Castilian epic poetry. It is the only Eastern Sephardic ballad in which the Cid plays a significant rôle. The thirteenth-century epic *Cantar del cerco de Zamora,* apparently the ballad's ultimate source, told of the usurpations and subsequent assassination of Sancho II of Castile (1038?-1072). In a death-bed testament, Fernando I, *El Magno* (1016?-1065), had bequeathed the kingdoms of Castile, León, and Galicia to his sons, Sancho, Alfonso, and García respectively, and had given the towns of Zamora and Toro to his daughters, Urraca and Elvira. Sancho, in defiance of his father's will and of the curse which was to fall upon whoever dared disregard it, proceeded to dispossess his brothers of their lands, to seize the town of Toro from Doña Elvira, and to lay siege to

[1] For other occurrences, see *La esposa de Don García* (Attias 4.37 f.), *Celinos y la adúltera* (Attias 50.49 f.), *Conde Claros y el Emperador* (nos. 4A.16, 4B.18 *infra*; Attias 31.39 f.), *El triste amador* (no. 19 *infra*), *Silvana* (no. 20.12 *infra*). See also DRH, p. 36, n. 31.

Doña Urraca in Zamora, only to be assassinated by the traitor Vellido Dolfos, at Urraca's instigation.

The sixteenth-century ballad of *Las almenas de Toro* (*Primav.* 54), from which Yoná's Sephardic version derives, begins:

> En las almenas de Toro, allí estaba una doncella,
> vestida de paños negros, reluciente como estrella.

The situation referred to is evidently Sancho's seizure of Toro and the "doncella" is probably Elvira. In effect, Menéndez Pelayo has called *Las almenas* "el único romance relativo a la infanta Doña Elvira" (TRV, I, 309). However, the rôle of this princess in medieval epicry is tenuous indeed and it is open to question whether the Toro episode, mentioned only in a chronistic prosification, was really an authentic part of the now lost epic on the siege of Zamora. [2] Menéndez Pidal would see in *Las almenas de Toro* no direct, epic-based recollection of the taking of Toro, but rather a distorted, relocated reminiscence of a similar confrontation between Sancho and Urraca before the walls of Zamora. [3] To complicate matters, the besieging King in the sixteenth-century ballad is called Alonso, not Sancho, and his sudden infatuation (*Primav.* 54.3-5; Yoná, vv. 3-6) with the "maiden," who turns out to be his sister, may somehow echo the incestuous relationship which, according to contemporary historiographic testimony, existed between Alfonso VI of Castile and León (1040-1109) and his sister Doña Urraca —a relationship which was also known to medieval epicry. [4]

Although the epic reminiscences in the sixteenth-century *Almenas de Toro* may seem rather remote, modern traditional versions from three far-flung lateral areas of the Hispanic world (the Eastern Mediterranean, Morocco, and Portugal) offer two further epic parallels which, taken together with those mentioned above, argue strongly for the ballad's close relationship to epic tradition.

In the Eastern Sephardic versions, when the Cid speaks in the maiden's defense the King reacts by saying that she must be his (the

---

[2] See Armistead, "An Unnoticed Epic Reference to Doña Elvira," p. 146, n. 19.

[3] See RoH, I, 237-238.

[4] See E. Lévi-Provençal and R. Menéndez Pidal, "Alfonso VI y su hermana la infanta Urraca," *ALAn*, XIII (1948), 157-166.

Cid's) beloved. In the Moroccan texts, the girl is referred to as the "namorada del Sidi" or "Saide"; and a similar liaison is implied in the Portuguese versions ("Pois tu que lhe queres tanto, / por ventura tens com ella": Tavares-Martins). If, in fact, *Las almenas de Toro* is calked from a scene of the epic of the *Siege of Zamora,* as Menéndez Pidal suspects (RoH, I, 238 at n. 91), then the allusion to the beleaguered princess as the Cid's beloved may indeed constitute an ultimate survival of the tradition of Doña Urraca's love for the Cid, which is attested in a fourteenth-century, epic-based chronistic allusion and which reappears in the ballad of *Afuera, afuera, Rodrigo* (*Primav*. 37).[5]

The Cid's answer to the King's accusation, which appears only in versions from the modern oral tradition, is no less firmly rooted in medieval epic poetry. In the modern Portuguese texts, though he is not mentioned by name, the Cid justifies his interest in the girl by recalling that her dying father had designated him as her tutor or guardian:

Morreu lhe seu pae ha pouco, e eu ficava tutor d'ella.
(Tavares-Martins)
Morreu-le seu pai há pouco, fiquei por tutor dela.
(VRP 982)
Morreu seu pai há pouco, eu fiquei por titor dela.
(VRP 983)

One of the five known Moroccan texts offers an essentially identical allusion earlier in the dialog. On identifying the "doncella" as niece (not sister)[6] of the King, the Cid also mentions the dying father's request that he take charge of the Princess:

—Vuestra sobrina es, buen rey, vuestra sobrina es aquélla;
cuando murió su buen padre, a mí me encargó por ella,
que la diese buen marido o me casase con ella.
(Larrea 214.17-22)

In the Eastern Sephardic texts the deceased King's wishes also unite Princess and Cid, but the hero's rôle as guardian has been forgotten

[5] See Armistead, "'The Enamored Doña Urraca' in Chronicles and Balladry," *RPh*, XI (1957), 26-29.

[6] By contamination with the ballad of *Virgilios*. See Alvar, "Romances de Lope," p. 302.

and the Princess is referred to as his "first wife," having been given to him by the present King's father:

—No era mi namorada, sino mi mujer primera,
me la dio el rey vuestro padre mucho antes que muriera.
(Attias 2.29-32; Yoná 15-16)

The Cid's rôle as counselor and mediator between the dissident sons and daughters of Fernando I has its origin in the thirteenth-century *Cantar de la muerte del rey don Fernando,* [7] a brief epic poem which may have served as a prolog to the *Cerco de Zamora.* [8] The *Primera Crónica General* (*ca.* 1274), which summarized certain portions of the *Cantar de la muerte del rey don Fernando,* states that the King "mando llamar a Roy Diaz el Çid que era y, et comendol sus fijos et sus fijas

[7] Concerning this epic poem, see Menéndez Pidal, *La epopeya castellana,* pp. 55-57. For texts of the various chronistic versions, see Menéndez Pidal, *Reliquias,* pp. 240-256; Cintra, *Crónica de 1344,* III, 333-347; TRV, I, 282-291.

[8] Menéndez Pelayo sees the *Muerte del rey Fernando* and *Cerco de Zamora* as two different epic poems (TRV, I, 291). In *La epopeya castellana,* Menéndez Pidal maintains that "la solemne escena de la muerte del rey don Fernando" served as a prolog to the *Cerco de Zamora* (p. 55). In later traditional development, "la escena inicial del *Cerco de Zamora* pasó a ser escena final del dicho *Cantar de Don Fernando*" (p. 56, n. 1). In *Reliquias* Menéndez Pidal states: "Publicamos la escena de la muerte del rey Fernando omitiendo el resto del cantar de Fernando el Magno prosificado en la crónicas del s. XIV. ... La *Crónica de Veinte Reyes* ... nos da, bastante por extenso, la prosificación de un breve cantar de la *Partición de los reinos,* que es la parte final del cantar del *Rey Fernando Par de Emperador,* o sea de las Mocedades de Rodrigo, y es a la vez introducción al *Cantar del rey don Sancho*" (pp. 240 and lxv). On the other hand, D. Catalán claims that "'El Cantar del rey don Ferrando' y 'el Cantar del rey don Sancho' (o de Zamora), citados por la *Crónica de Veinte Reyes* eran parte de una sola gesta" ("El taller historiográfico alfonsí," p. 371, n. 1). Nevertheless, it must be understood that both the *Mocedades de Rodrigo* and the *Cantar del cerco de Zamora,* associated by Menéndez Pidal and Catalán with the *Cantar del rey Fernando,* constitute unified poems in their own right, as does the heroic narrative of the events surrounding King Fernando's death-bed partition of his realm. All three poems, however—and this is the crucial detail—were intimately and simultaneously present in the memories of minstrels and their audiences as common knowledge for anyone acquainted with the Castilian epic repertoire. In a sense, the entire Cidian cycle from the *Mocedades* through the end of the *Cantar de Mio Cid* could be taken to constitute one single "super-narrative" made up of semiautonomous segments. Quite apparently we cannot judge traditional, oral or semioral, cyclic epic poems as structurally "autonomous" works of art in the same sense as we would some literary work produced by an individual artist. While each segment possesses its own artistic structure, it is

que los conseiasse bien et touiesse con ellos do mester les fuesse."[9] In the *Crónica de Veinte Reyes* (*circa* 1300), which prosifies the lost epic poem *in extenso,* the dying King speaks to the Cid in identical terms:

> Bien seades venido, Çid, muy leal vasallo, ca nunca el rey tal conseiero ovo nin tan bueno commo vos sodes, ¿e donde tardastes tanto?; ruegovos pues que aquy sodes venido, que conseiedes sienpre bien a mis fijos ca sey que si vos quieren creer que sienpre seran bien consejados. ...[10]

The *Crónica de 1344,* which contains a variant version of the same prosification, describes at another point in the narrative a similar but more specific scene, in which the King enjoins his heirs to follow the Cid's counsel:

> Mando el rrey llamar sus fijos e encomendo a todos a Rrui Diaz el Çid, que le fiziesen sienpre bien e lo creyesen, ca el Çid los sirviera sienpre bien e muy lealmente e que sienpre se hallara muy bien de sus consejos. E ellos dixeron que lo farian muy de buena mente. ...[11]

Even more suggestive of the affinity between our ballad and epic tradition is the fact that the Cid appears specifically as the protector of Doña Urraca in this same *Cantar de la muerte del rey don Fernando*; for it is through the Cid's intercession that she is granted the town of Zamora as "alguna cosa en que biva e non finque ansi desanparada."[12] In this same rôle as counselor and conciliator of King

---

also inexorably linked to what follows outside the limits of its own poetic world. The boundaries between individual "cantares" in an epic cycle are quite naturally less clearly delineated than between "individual" works of art.

Concerning the possible existence of cyclic poems in the late epic tradition, see Menéndez Pidal, "Poesía popular y Romancero," I, 376-377. On the *Cantar del cerco de Zamora,* see C. Reig, *El cantar de Sancho II,* especially pp. 57 ff., and on the *Mocedades,* Armistead, "The Structure of the *Refundición de las Mocedades de Rodrigo.*"

[9] PCG 494*a*.34-37. Cf. Menéndez Pidal's commentary on the epic source, Vol. II, p. clxviii; also *España del Cid,* I, 141-142; Babbitt, *Crónica de Veinte Reyes,* p. 60; Catalán, "El taller historiográfico alfonsí," p. 372, n. 2.

[10] *Reliquias,* p. 247.5-8.

[11] *Reliquias,* p. 255.6-9. Cf. Cintra, *Crónica de 1344,* III, 346.5-8.

[12] *Reliquias,* p. 249.6-7 (*Crónica de Veinte Reyes*). Cf. also Menéndez Pidal, "Poesía popular y Romancero," II, 16.

Fernando's heirs and even as protector of Doña Urraca, the Cid dominates from the background the tumultuous events of the *Cantar del cerco de Zamora,* [13] wherein his supposed favoritism towards Urraca earns him banishment by order of King Sancho. The dramatic scene of his banishment parallels, as Menéndez Pidal has noted, the concluding verses of the sixteenth-century text of *Las almenas de Toro* (*Primav.* 54.14-17). [14]

The combined evidence of the modern and sixteenth-century versions of *Las almenas de Toro* reveals a number of points of contact with epic tradition: the confrontation of the besieging King and the embattled Princess; the possible incestuous relationship between Alfonso and Urraca; Urraca enamored of the Cid; the Cid as counselor to the Princess; and the Cid's banishment for alleged favoritism toward Urraca. Such an abundance of parallels seems to link *Las almenas de Toro* more closely to medieval epicry than previous critics have recognized. We conclude that whoever fashioned the ballad must have had a rather detailed, if somewhat incoherent, recollection of the more important interrelationships and motivations of the principal characters in some late, traditional version of the *Cantar del cerco de Zamora.*

A number of features of the Eastern Sephardic text merit comment: In Yoná and Attias, the battlements of Toro, which are preserved in

---

[13] In the prosified version of the *Cantar* embodied in the *Primera Crónica General,* King Sancho addresses the following words to the Cid: "Ruegouos que me conseiedes como faga en este fecho et que uos benga emiente de lo que mi padre vos dixo quando se querie finar que non seria mal aconsejado quien por vos se consejase et crer vos quisiese; et por eso vos dexo un condado en mi tierra et agora si de uos non me conseio, non lo atiendo de omne del mundo" (Reig, *El cantar de Sancho II,* pp. 224-225, ll. 32 ff.). The *Crónica particular del Cid* presents a more elaborate version of this passage: "Bien sabedes, mio Cid, que quando el Rey, mio padre, me vos encomendó, que me mandó sopena de la su maldicion que vos oviesse por consegero, e todo lo que oviesse de fazer fuesse con vuestro consejo, e yo assi lo fize fasta oy dia: e siempre me aconsejastes lo mejor: e yo por ende divos un Condado en el mio Reyno, e tengolo por bien compleado. E agora ruegovos que me aconsegedes lo mejor, en guisa que cobre los Reynos: ca si de vos non he consejo, non lo entiendo de haver de ome del mundo" (ed. Huber, pp. 46-47).

[14] RoH, I, 238. Cf. our article "Sobre unos romances del Cid," p. 391 at n. 16. Although Menéndez Pidal states that the Cid's banishment is lacking in the modern tradition, one wonders if the final formulistic verse of the Eastern versions ("Yya se parte 'el gran Siđi," etc.: Yoná, v. 17) may not constitute an

at least one Moroccan text, [15] become the more pedestrian "palasyyos de 'el re'e," thus destroying the heroic tension between the embattled Princess and her brother's besieging army, still implicit in the sixteenth-century text. The change may be due to the influence of the ballad of *Virgilios,* which sometimes begins: "Por los palasios del rey / se pasea una mužer." [16] In any event, the chances of survival for a toponym such as *Toro* would have been slim, in view of the Eastern tradition's consistent tendency to eliminate proper names. [17]

The Eastern and Moroccan Sephardic texts, as well as Lope de Vega's *comedia* on the same theme, replace the second verse of *Primavera* 54 ("vestida de paños negros, / reluciente como estrella") with a stock formulistic description of feminine beauty:

blanca es y corelada, hermosa como la strella.
(Attias 2.3-4)

blanca, rubia y colorada y hermosa com'una estreya.
(uned., Tetuán)

blanca, rubia y colorada: su cara, como una estrella.
(Alvar, "Rom. de Lope") [18]

---

ultimate, vague reflection of what is more specifically stated in the sixteenth-century text.

[15] "Por las almenas de Toro" (Larrea 214). Alvar's version reads: "Por las almenas de oro." Two unedited texts in our collection, from Tetuán and Alcazarquivir-Larache, read: "Por las alberjes del sielo" and "Por los jardines del rey." Larrea 215 begins "Por las anjibas del mundo," by contamination with some other ballad *incipit.* Cf. *El testamento del rey Felipe* (MP 126), which begins "Por las comarcas del mundo," and *Portocarrero* (MP 11), which begins "Por las andjibas del alba." Larrea 214 and 215 show evidence of further contamination with the latter ballad: i.e., 214.9-10, 215.7-8.

[16] As in two unedited versions from Salonika. For the influence of *Virgilios* on Moroccan versions of *Las almenas,* see Alvar, "Romances de Lope," p. 302. A king's palace as the scene of balladic action is, of course, much favored in the aristocratizing, chivalric atmosphere evoked by the Judeo-Spanish *romances.* See *Rico Franco* ("Hispanic Balladry," no. 4; no. 18 *infra*), *Gaiferos jugador* (Attias 26; no. 5 *infra*), *El rescate* (Attias 51). Cf. also the Castilian *Madre traidora* (*Romancero tradicional,* II, 280, no. 2*a*): "Por los palacios del rey / iba una dama corriendo. ..."

[17] See our "Dos romances fronterizos," p. 91, n. 7.

[18] Cf. Larrea 214.

Por las almenas de Toro se pasea una doncella,
pero dijera mejor que el mismo sol se pasea. . . .
Blanca es y colorada, que es de los amores reina.
(Lope: ASW 86)[19]

Identical or similar verses occur elsewhere in Sephardic tradition. In *Melisenda sale de los baños*: "blanca es y corelada / hermoza como la estrella"; [20] in *Virgilios*, the King's niece merits a similar description: "Blanca era y corelada / y hermosa como el chichek" (= Turkish *çiçek* 'flower'; *Attias* 7.5-6). In the Moroccan ballad, *Noche de amores*, the girl is "blanca, rubia y colorada / cuello gallardo" (MP 109, from Tangier). Both the archaic and the contemporary Peninsular traditions offer still other examples of this same formulaic pattern:

Blanca, rubia a maravilla, sobre todas agraciada.
(*Morica de Antequera*: *Primav.* 76)

---

[19] The same verse, probably borrowed from *Las almenas*, occurs at the beginning of *La Virgen romera*:

Por los senderos de un monte se pasea una romera
blanca, rubia y colorada, relumbra como una estrella.
(CVR, pp. 221, 219, 268; ASW 261, no. 61)

Por los campos de Ismael paseaba una romera
blanca, rubia y colorada, relumbra de media legua.
(RPM 358)

Por los campos de Troquillo vi venir una romera,
era blanca como un sol, relumbra como una estrella.
(RPM 360)

A Moroccan wedding song borrows the same description, combining verses from *Las almenas de Toro* and *El villano vil*:

Ven aquí, pastor amado, gozarás de esta donzella,
blanca, rubia y colorada, su cara como una estrella.
Digo yo ansí: yo al ganado me quiero ir.
(Larrea, *Canciones*, no. 28)

On the preference accorded a fair complexion in the early Castilian lyric, see Frenk Alatorre, *La lírica popular*, pp. 44-45; A. Sánchez Romeralo, *El villancico* (Madrid, 1969), pp. 56-59.

[20] LSO 91 (no. 24.3). The initial verses of this ballad, except for the verse quoted, seem to derive from *La Galiarda* (*Primav.* 139).

Blanca es y colorada, hermosa como una estrella.
(*Morica de Antequera*: Durán 114)

Ella es blanca y colorada, como la rosa y la leche.
("Vamonos Iuan al aldea": Joaquim, p. 82)

Blanca, rubia y encarnada, bonita que no era fea.
(*Serrana de la Vera*: RCan 2) [21]

Verse 4 of Yoná's version of *Las almenas,* "Demandó 'el rey 'a su ǧente / kyén 'era 'esta donze'a," which is lacking in the sixteenth-century text and in Lope, occurs in both the Eastern and Moroccan traditions. Although the context of the ballad calls for such a verse, one might imagine a possible reminiscence of *Virgilios.* [22] However, the occurrence of an essentially identical verse in the Peninsular *a lo divino* adaptation of *Las almenas* ("Jesús pregunta a San Juan / qui es aquella doncella" [Milá 61]), rules out the influence of *Virgilios* in the Yoná text and points to the verse's authenticity as a part of the narrative.

Verse 9 of the Eastern versions, which replaces *Primavera*'s "llámenme mis ballesteros; / tírenle sendas saetas," represents a recurrent formulaic pattern:

¡Aquí, aquí, mis caballeros, los que del mi pan comierais!
Tomalda a esta doncella y arrojalde cien saetas.
(Attias)

Compare:

Altos, altos, mis kavayeros, los ke del mi pan komíaš,
tomaréš a Dalgezina, en kadena la meteríaš.
(*Delgadina*: uned., Rhodes)

Criados, los mis criados, los que coméis del mi pan,
cogedme esta palomita, llevádmela al palomar.
(*Boda estorbada*: RPM 84) [23]

---

[21] The verse "blanca, rubia, colorada, / bella, sin ningún defeuto" appears in a *romance vulgar* published by Vicuña (no. 133). Certain versions of the Portuguese *Hortelão das flores* (Braga, I, 436, 439-440) also begin with similar verses.

[22] Cf. Alvar, "Romances de Lope," p. 302.

[23] The repeated invocation, *Aquí, aquí* ... , *Alto, alto* ... , is, of course, very frequent: "Aquí, aquí, los mis doscientos, / los que comedes mi pan"

Verses 18-25 of Yoná's text offer a version of one of the two known *romances fronterizos* current in the Eastern Sephardic tradition.[24] *El alcaide de Alhama,* in which the Moorish commander laments his personal losses after the Christian capture of the fortress town of Alhama, is based on historical fact. Alhama fell to the forces of Ferdinand and Isabel on February 28, 1482. Yoná's version of this rare ballad is more complete than the short text which we collected from oral tradition in California. The *romance* seems to be limited to the community of Salonika, where it may occur joined to *Las almenas de Toro* and followed by the description of Priam's mills (as in Yoná and Attias); combined only with the description of Priam's mills, as in an unedited text collected by Mrs. Crews; or as an autonomous ballad, as in the above-mentioned version published in our "Hispanic Balladry."

Hemistich *b* of v. 21 ("Kortarvos kyere la kavesa, / 'eğarla 'en 'una mušama") contributes little or nothing in its present form to the story. Why should the severed head be placed in oilcloth? The verse, which has undergone a series of transformations from the sixteenth century to the present, requires some clarification. Pérez de Hita's version read "y cortarte la cabeza / y ponerla en el Alhambra," but the toponym is

---

(*Bernardo del Carpio*: FN 67; *Primav.* 13); "Alto, alto, mis criados, / los que coméis del mi pan" (*Conde Dirlos*: RPM 48); "Alto, alto, meus creados, / vão lá selar o cavallo" (*Mala suegra*: Braga, I, 571); "Alto, alto, meus creados, / meus cavallos preparar" (*Difunta pleiteada*: Braga, I, 611); "Kavayeros, altos, altos, / los ke [en] mi komanda estava[n]" (*Infancia de Gaiferos*: uned., Tekirdağ [Turkey]). For other examples, see RPM 234, 362. References to eating bread as a sign of vassalage are legion in the *Romancero*: "Cuatrocientos soys, los míos, / los que coméis el mi pan" (*Bernardo del Carpio*: *Primav.* 13; RQDB-II 76); "Lleguéis vuestros caballeros / los que comen vuestro pan" (*Conde Dirlos*: *Primav.* 164); "Yo no soy vuestro criado, / nunca comí vuestro pan" (*Marqués de Mantua*: *Primav.* 165 [p. 353]); "Uno de los que allí dían / cas su padre comió pan" (*Infancia de Gaiferos*: RCan 8); "Criados, los mis criados, / los que estáis a mi mandar, // los que bebéis de mi vino, / los que coméis de mi pan" (*Valdovinos sorprendido en la caza*: RQDB-II 70); "¡Quién tuviera un pajecito / de esos que comen mi pan!" (*Conde Claros disfrazado de fraile*: RPC 9); "Adiós, criaos de mis padres, / que coméis su blanco pan" (*Mala suegra*: RPC 41); "Consigo [lleva] a los doce apóstoles / que en su mesa comen pan" (*Jesucristo va a decir misa*: RTR 36; RPM 447); other examples: *Primav.* 164 (p. 334), 173 (p. 384), 178 (p. 407), 195 (p. 459). For more on this formula, see PHP, p. 369; RoH, I, 243; Webber, *Formulistic Diction,* pp. 206, 208; Child, V, 292*b* (no. 65).

[24] See our article "Dos romances fronterizos," pp. 89 ff.

already barred from Joaquim's sixteenth-century, geographically Portuguese text: "Y cortaros la cabeça / y ponella en el alcaçoua." The rendition published in "Hispanic Balladry" and Mrs. Crews' unedited version read:

Kortarvos kiere la kavesa i metervos kiere a la almuxama. . . .
Kortarvos kiere la kavesa, metérvola al'almušama. . . .

Almušama, here replacing the toponym *Alhambra,* is apparently a Judeo-Spanish vestige of the Hispano-Arabism *almoxama,* which survives in Modern Castilian as *mojama* 'salt tunny fish'.[25] What is referred to is apparently the practice of curing the heads of executed prisoners in salt for better preservation before exposing them to public view.[26] The original idea of exemplary exposure is also carried over into the Moroccan versions, where the Commander's head is to be placed on a lance so as to inspire fear in others.[27] The readings of Yoná and Attias probably represent a further semantic development in which the Spanish Arabism has been associated with the Turkish and Pan-Balkanic form of the same word, *mušamá,* which is in current use in Eastern Judeo-Spanish with the meaning 'oilcloth.'[28]

The four verses which close Yoná's text, and occur also in Attias and in the unedited version collected by Mrs. Crews, apparently derive from a sixteenth-century version of *El juicio de Paris.* The contamination is all the more worthy of note since the verses in question survive in none of the modern Salonikan versions of the same ballad.[29] The sixteenth-century text, printed in the *Cancionero de romances sin año* (fol. 195r-v), reads:

---

[25] See DCELC, s.v.; R. Dozy and W. H. Engelmann, *Glossaire des mots espagnols et portugais dérivés de l'arabe,* 2d ed. (Leiden, 1869), pp. 178-179.

[26] The gate called Bab Segma at Fez is described as an "antique tour octogone où séchaient jadis les têtes des rebelles préalablement salées par les Israélites" (*Fès* [Syndicat d'Initiative et de Tourisme de Fès, Casablanca, n.d.], p. 14).

[27] The best text occurs as a contamination in the ballad of *Búcar sobre Valencia* (Alvar, *Textos dialectales,* II, 761):

le quitaré su cabesa y se la pondré en una lansa;
para ę sea el castigo y otros tema de mirálo.

Cf. Larrea 10.5-8; MP 9; our article on "Romances del Cid recogidos en Tetuán," p. 387; S139.2.2.1. *Heads of slain enemies impaled upon stakes.*

[28] See "Dos romances fronterizos," p. 90, n. 5.

[29] See Attias 5; Coello 11; MP 42. Cf. RoH, I, 348-349.

Por vna linda espessura   de arboleda muy florida
donde corren muchas fuẽtes   de agua clara muy luzida
vn río caudal la cerca   que nace dentro en Turquía
enlas tierras del soldán   & las del gran Can suría
mil & quinientos molinos   que dél muelen noche y día
quinientos muelen canela   y quinientos perla fina
y quinientos muelen trigo   para sustentar la vida
todos eran del gran rey [Príamo]   que alos reyes precedía. . . . [30]

This text embodies a favorite motif of European balladry: that of continuously operating mills as an indication of wealth [31] or, more specifically, of marvelous mills that grind an assortment of exquisite materials. The same commonplace exists elsewhere in Sephardic tradition, namely in Moroccan and Eastern versions of *La vuelta del marido* (*í* assonance):

[30] This ballad, which considerably antedates the mid-sixteenth-century *Cancionero,* was printed around 1525-1530 as part of the now lost folios of the *Libro de cincuenta romances.* See Rodríguez-Moñino, *Pliegos de Morbecq,* pp. 48-53, and, for the subsequent history of its printings, p. 53 in particular. For Menéndez Pelayo's comentary on the ballad: TRV, II, 366-367.

[31] Compare the following Child ballads:

'For I hae eighteen corn-mills,
Runs all in water clear,
And there's as much corn in each o' them
As they can grind in a year.'
(*Willie o Winsbury*: no. 100A.13, 100G.15)

Grant me my lyfe, my liege, my king,
And a bony gift I'll gie to thee;
Gude four-and-twenty ganging mills,
That gang throw a' the yeir to me.
(*Johnie Armstrong*: no. 169C.12)

It's I hae se'en weel gawn mills,
I wait they a' gang daily;
I'll gie them a' an amang ye a'
For the sparin o my Geordie.
(*Geordie*: no. 209B.16)

Cf. also Bartók and Lord, *Serbo-Croatian Folk Songs,* no. 27*a*.8. Mills as an indication of wealth also occur in the Spanish *Testamento del marinero,* where the devil offers the protagonist "cien molinos, / todos cien muelen de un agua" (RPM 294).

De tres molinos que tengo, le daré yo el más gentil.
El uno muele canela, el otro ajenjolí
y el otro harinita blanca que come el rey mi marí. [32]

Vos daré los tres mulinos, tres mulinos d'Amadí.
El uno muele canela y el otro zangifil,
el más chiquitico d'ellos muele harina d'Amadí. [33]

And in at least one Moroccan version of *Rosaflorida y Montesinos*:

Le daré los cien molinos que molen de noche y día;
los cientos molían clavos y los cientos canela fina,
y los cientos molen simiente para sostener la [vida]. [34]

Such mills and their exquisite produce have widely distributed parallels in European balladry:

---

[32] Unedited version from Tetuán, collected by S. G. A., from Aaron D. Essayag, at Melilla, March 3, 1963. Cf. also the similar verses which occur as a contamination in *Las bodas de París* from Alcazarquivir (MRuiz 78B).

[33] Attias 20.17-22. For other Sephardic variants, see SICh 6.11-13. Similar verses occur in Peninsular versions of the same ballad:

—De três moinhos que eu tenho todos três são p'ra ti:
Um de prata e canela, oitro de ouro e marfim,
oitro de bela farinha, esse queria-o eu p'ra mim!

(VRP 304)

—Le diera mis tres molinos, que ahí bajo están en el río:
El uno muele canela y el otro granos de trigo
y el otro granillos de oro que del mar habían venido.

(RQDB-I 50)

A distant French analog of the Hispanic ballad also contains the same *topos*. See Decombe, p. 221 (*Le prisonnier de Hollande*).

From some Catalan version of *La vuelta del marido* (*í*) the mills have been taken over, along with several other narrative features, by the ballad of *El maestro* (Milá 532.20-23; AFC 822; Capmany, no. 63; Subirá, p. 57):

Que ya 'n va á cercá l' aygua per donar als seus fills,
de las gotas qu' en queyan ya 'n molen tres molins,
lo un molt pebre y canella y l' altre un sucre fi,
l' altre farina blanca per vos y pera mi.

See also the contaminated variant of *La mala nova* published in the commentary to Capmany, no. 78.

[34] Larrea 38.27-32. We emend the editor's senseless reading "para sostener la lluvia."

J'ai trois moulins
Dessus la mer qui tournent.
L'un qui moud l'or
Et l'autre l'argenterie
Et le troisième
Les amours de ma mie. [35]

A casa del mio padre a i è mo du mulèin:
l'on fa farèina zala par fär al pulintèin,
l'äter farèina blanca par fär i zuccarèin. [36]

Ich hab' in meinem Vaterland
Wohl sieben Mühlen stehn. ...
Sie tun nichts mehr als mahlen
Muskat und rote Nägelein,
Muskat und gelbe Blümelein, ...
Und Zucker und Kaneel. [37]

I shall have a marvelous mill made for you,
Its first stone will cast forth white pearls,
Its second stone will cast forth small coins. [38]

"Yeg gyffwer hynne mynne møller ny,
de lyge paa wyllenne hedde:
oc de malle ecke annett mell
ænd ydelyg kanelle." [39]

---

[35] *Les trois tambours* (Rolland, I, 272). Cf. also Canteloube, III, 322; IV, 131; Tarbé, *Romancéro de Champagne,* II, 129. For further examples, see Nigra, pp. 419-420.

[36] *La bella Cecilia*: Bronzini, I, 468. See also Nigra 68 (*I mulini*).

[37] *Die sieben Mühlen*: Meier, *Balladen,* I, no. 16.2-4. For other variants, see DVM, nos. 42 (*Der betrügerische Freier* or *Stolz Heinrich*) and 84 (*Die neue Mühle*); important commentary and abundant Pan-European analogs: DVM, IV, 256-258.

[38] Leader, *Hungarian Classical Ballads,* p. 44. See also pp. 46, 47, 49-51 and n. 1, 53; Vargyas, *Researches,* pp. 69-70, 72-73; Aigner, p. 80; Járdányi, I, 99.

[39] *Skjön Anna* (DgF, V, no. 258A.17). Cf. Geijer-Afzelius, no. 5.18-19; Warrens 69; Prior, III, 303, vv. 22-23; Child, II, 65*b*; also *Herr Magnus och hafstrollet* (Geijer-Afzelius, no. 83:I.4; Warrens 26).

An analogous balladic *topos* is reflected in certain marvelous mills which are powered by a variety of unconventional liquids. A Greek Cypriot ballad—*Christ in Beggar's Guise*—collected by H. Lüdeke (*Im Paradies der Volksdichtung,* p. 129) provides an elaborate illustration:

—Fern auf der Höh' vor meiner Burg steht eine Wundermühle,
und hat der Müller Wasser nicht, mahlt sie von selbst mit Honig,
und hat der Imker Honig nicht, kann sie mit Milch auch mahlen,

An intriguing problem that invites speculation concerns the fusion or confusion of disparate ballad texts to make a new and inevitably traditional narrative. Obviously there is more involved than the mere blurring of balladic boundaries by the unsure memory of some singer. Yet one can scarcely do more than guess about the complicated processes of creation that are involved. Why were *Las almenas de Toro* and *El alcaide de Alhama,* for example, sung together as one ballad? Why was the description of Priam's mills appended to some versions and not to others? Is it possible that the legendary Cid could still evoke centuries later the memory of frontier clashes between Christians and Moors? Could his relationship with King Alfonso have merged with the tragic situation between the Commander of Alhama and the King of Granada? These questions, of course, are purely rhetorical, unanswerable. Nevertheless, just as the Cid was innocent yet sent into exile, so

---

und hat der Bauer keine Milch, kann sie mit Öl auch mahlen,
und gibt's kein Öl, so kann sie auch mit was es sonst gibt mahlen.

A less attractive congener of this motif occurs in the fragmentary Eastern Sephardic *Sierpe del río*: a mill which works with neither water nor wine, but uses only the blood of children (cf. S116.1. *Murder by grinding in mill,* and no. 16, n. 11 *infra*):

Aí más arriva avía un muelino.
No muele kon agua, ni muele kon vino,
muele kon la sangre de akeyos ižikos.

Ay más arriva avía 'n muelino.
Ni muelía agua, ni muelía vino,
sino muelía la sangre de los kristianikos.

We cite from two unedited Salonikan versions. Cf. Attias 29; Benardete 3; Díaz-Plaja 15. See also D1263. *Magic mill*; D1601.21. *Self-grinding mill. Grinds whatever owner wishes*; D1601.21.1. *Self-grinding salt-mill* (cf. Snorri Sturluson, *The Prose Edda,* trans. A. G. Brodeur [New York, 1960], pp. 162-169; A. Guichot, "El agua del mar en las supersticiones y creencias populares," *Boletín Folklórico Español* [Seville], I [1885], 4-5, 13-14: p. 4*b*; de Vries, *Heroic Song and Heroic Legend,* pp. 147, 149, 150).

Also worthy of mention here are marvelous fountains from which gold, silver, and pearls flow, as in the Castilian *Calumnia de la reina* (ART 200):

En la corte de Madrid hay una fuente muy clara;
cuatro caños tie la fuente, por todos los cuatro mana
por el uno mana oro, por el otro mana plata,
por el otro mana perlas, por el otro agua muy clara.

Cf. D925 ff. *Magic fountain*; D1467.1. *Magic fountain produces gold.*

the Commander had not been remiss in his duties yet was sentenced to death. Is it not possible that in some way the Cid and the Commander, both heroic and aggrieved figures, were drawn together in a poetic coalition through their misfortunes, centered in both ballads in the figure of a unique *doncella*?

The description of Priam's mills and its use in conjunction with *El alcaide de Alhama* is another matter and leads to conjecture about the intent of different balladic artists. In a version of the *Alcaide de Alhama* that we recorded the Commander epitomized all his losses—his honor, his reputation, his sons and wives, his wealth and power—in "una iža donzeya tan kerida i tan amada." It is as if the Commander were another Pleberio, negating the value of all his treasures because of the all-pervading emptiness of his life without Melibea.[40] Nothing else is remembered by the Commander but the loss of his daughter. The other members of his family, his position in society and the symbols of his opulence have been sacrificed by the balladeer who sought to achieve the heightened dramatic impact and tension characteristic of ballad gems like the fragmentary and impressionistic *El prisionero* and *El conde Arnaldos*. The singer of Yoná's version, on the other hand, was an artist of a different school. He felt the need of amplifying the dimensions of the Commander's tragedy. His technique was to be specific and to enumerate a detailed inventory of the Commander's great losses, which could not fail to impress the audience. It may well be that with this purpose in mind he borrowed the readily available description of Priam's wondrous mills to enhance through poetic licence the splendid estate of the Commander, thus making his losses seem even greater.

Whereas it is a truism, often observed by Menéndez Pidal, that the *Romancero* is characterized in its genesis and aesthetics by a propensity toward "fragmentism," it must also be remembered that there was another tendency, exemplified by texts like *Almenas de Toro* + *Alcaide*

[40] Cf. Fernando de Rojas, *La Celestina,* 2 vols., ed. J. Cejador y Frauca, ("Clásicos Castellanos," nos. 20 and 23, Madrid, 1951, 1949), II, 202-203: "¿Para quién edifiqué torres? ¿Para quién adquirí honrras? ¿Para quién planté árboles? ¿Para quién fabriqué nauíos? . . . ¡O fortuna variable, ministra e mayordoma de los temporales bienes! . . . ¿Por qué no destruyste mi patrimonio? ¿Por qué no quemaste mi morada? ¿Por qué no asolaste mis grandes heredamientos? Dexárasme aquella florida planta, en quien tú poder no tenías."

de Alhama + Priam's mills, toward completeness and specificity and for equally legitimate artistic purposes.

BIBLIOGRAPHY

Las almenas de Toro

Eastern J.-Sp.: Attias 2.1-34; PTJ 5 (= Attias).

Moroccan J.-Sp.: Alvar, "Romances de Lope," pp. 282-283, Var. B, vv. 1-20; Larrea 214-215; PTJ *5a* (= Alvar).

Portuguese: Martins, I, 236 (= Tavares); Tavares, *RL,* VIII, 73-74; VRP 982-983.

Castilian: The Central Peninsular tradition seems to have kept the ballad alive only *a lo divino*—, i.e., adapted to a religious theme: Cabal, *Las costumbres asturianas,* p. 48; García Sanz, "Las *Ramas,*" p. 582; Magaña, "Nuevas notas," p. 99; Milá 62; RQDB-I 4; RTR 30. Similar verses introduce some versions of *La Virgen romera*: ASW 261; RPM 356-360; Teresa León, p. 489; and n. 19 *supra.*

Spanish American: Vicuña 95 (*a lo divino*).

Archaic Texts: ASW 86-87; Durán 816; *Primavera* 54; Timoneda, *Rosa Española,* fol. xl*r-v.*

Studies: BNE 221; RoH, I, 237-238; TRV, I, 309-311.

El alcaide de Alhama

Eastern J.-Sp.: Armistead-Silverman, "Dos romances fronterizos," no. 1 (= "Hispanic Balladry"); Attias 2.35-58; "Hispanic Balladry," no. 1; PTJ 9-*9a* (= Attias, "Hispanic Balladry").

Moroccan J.-Sp.: Larrea 10; MP 9.

Archaic Texts: Durán 1062; Joaquim 8; Pérez de Hita, *Guerras Civiles,* I, 256-257; *Primavera* *84a* (= Pérez de Hita). Durán 1061 and *Primavera* 84 (= *Cancionero de 1550*) are a reworking in *í-a* assonance. See also our "Dos romances fronterizos," p. 90, n. 6; RVP, p. 66.

Studies: Alvar, *Granada y el Romancero,* pp. 23-29, 94-96; Cirot, "Deux notes sur les rapports entre romances et chroniques," pp. 250-252; RoH, I, 143-144, n. 121; TRV, II, 126.

Juicio de Paris

Eastern J.-Sp.: Attias 2.51-56.

Archaic Texts: CSA, fols. 195*r*-198*r*; Durán 469; Rodríguez-Moñino, *Pliegos de Morbecq,* pp. 48-53, 105, 166; *Silva de 1561,* fols. 144*r*-147*r*. Cf. also Rodríguez-Moñino, *Noticias bibliográficas sobre... El Cancionero general,* p. 125 (no. 241); Schaeffer, p. 419 (no. 56).

2

ALMERIQUE DE NARBONA + RONCESVALLES + LAS BODAS EN PARÍS

(Aymeri de Narbonne + The Battle of Roncevaux + The Wedding Feast in Paris)

2A

¡'I akel konde 'i akel konde,   ke 'en la mar se'a su fin!
Armó armas 'i galeras   'i para Fransyya kižo 'ir.
Las armó de todo punto   'i las 'eğó dyentro 'el sanğir.
'El sanğir komo 'era 'estrego   'i non las podi'a režir.
—¡Atrás, atrás, los fransezes,   non le deš vergu'ela así!
Si 'el gran duke lo save,   'a Fransyya non vos deša 'ir,
ni vos dan pan 'a komere,   ni kon las damas dormir.
'En la tornada ke atorna,   mataron setenta mil,
aparte de ğiketikos,   ke non ayy ku'enta ni fin.
Grandes bodas ayy 'en Fransyya   'i 'en la sala de París;
ke kazó la 'iža del rey   kon la 'iža de Amadí.

Source: GSA 1. Variants: RHP 1.
The second hemistich of each verse is repeated except in v. 33. There are no repetitions in RHP except in v. 1.

1*a* 'I *om. RHP.*
1*b* ke *om. RHP.*
2*b* + se torna *RHP.*
4*b* pu'edi'a *RHP.*
5*b* vergu'ensa *RHP.*
8*a* 'En la torna ke atorna *RHP.*

Bayylan damas 'i donzeas, kavayeros más de mí.
La ke agiava la tayyfa 'era 'una dama ǧentil.
Mirándola 'estava 'el bu'en konde 'i akel konde de Amadí.
—¿Ké miráš akí, 'el bu'en konde, konde, ké miráš akí?
'O miravaš ala tayyfa, 'o me miravaš a mí.
—Yyo non miro ala tayyfa, ni menos te miro a ti.
—Miro 'a 'este lindo pu'erpo, tan galano 'i tan ǧentil.
—Si vos agrađo, 'el konde, konsigo yevéšme a mí.
Mariđo 'en viaže tengo, lonǧe 'está para venir.
'Una 'esfu'egra vieža tengo, mala 'está para morir.
Dos 'ižikos ǧikos tengo, ke non se lo saven dezir.
La 'embružó 'en 'un mantel de 'oro, de afu'era dešó 'el ǧapín.
Por 'en međyyo del kamino, 'eskontró kon Amadí.
—¿Ké yeváš akí, 'el konde, 'i konde, ké yeváš akí?
—Yevo 'un pasežiko de 'oro, ke 'inda 'oyy me lo merkí.
—'Este pasežiko, konde, a mí me 'esfu'ele 'a servir,
'el dí'a para la meza 'i la noǧe para 'el dormir.
Non la konose 'en 'el garbe, ni menos 'en 'el vestir.
Konose 'el ǧapín de 'oro: —¡A'índa alyer se lo merkí!
'Esto ke sintyyó 'el konde, la dešó 'i se 'eǧó 'a fu'ir.
—Non vos fuyygáš, 'el bu'en konde, ni vos kižeraš fu'ir.
'Esto non 'es la vu'estra kulpa, sinon 'es yyo ke lo buškí.

12*b* kavalyeros más de mil *RHP*.
13*a* giava *RHP*.
14*a* bu'en *om*. *RHP*.
15*b* 'i konde *RHP*.
19*b* kon sigo *GSA* (*in repetition*) / *RHP*.
21*b* mu'erir *RHP*.
24*a* 'enmedyyo *RHP*.
24*b* 'enkontró *RHP*.
26*a*, 27*a* pasažiko *RHP*.
27*b* amí me lo 'es fi'el 'a servir *RHP*.
28*b* 'el *om*. *RHP*.
30*a* konose 'en 'el ǧapín *RHP*.
32 *om*. *RHP*.
33*b* sinon yyo ke lo kulpí *RHP*.

2B

Grandes bodas ayy 'en Fransyya,   'en la sala de París; (10)
ke kazó 'el 'ižo de 'el rey   kon la 'iža de Amadí.
Bayylan damas 'i donzeas,   kavayeros más de mil.
'El que gí'a la tayyfa   'es 'una dama ğentil.
Mirándola 'estava 'el konde   'i akel konde de Amadí.
—¿Ké miráš akí, 'el konde,   'i konde, ké miráš akí? (15)
'O miravaš ala tayyfa,   'o me miravaš a mí.
—Lyyo non miro ala tayyfa,   ni menos te miro a ti.
Miro 'a 'este lindo ku'erpo,   que 'es galano 'i tan ğentil.
—Si vos plazí'a, 'el bu'en konde,   konsigo yevéšme a mí.
Marido 'en viaže tengo   'i lonğe 'está para venir (20)
Dos 'ižikos ğikos tengo,   ke non se lo saven dezir. (22)
'Una 'esfu'egra vyeža tengo   'i mala 'está para morir. (21)
'Enbružóla 'en 'un mantel de 'oro   'i de afu'era dešó 'el ğapín. (23)
Ala salida dela pu'erta,   'enkontró kon Amadí.
—¿Ké yeváš akí, 'el bu'en konde,   'i konde, ké yeváš akí? (25)
—Yevo 'un pažežiko de 'oro,   ke a'índa alyer yyo lo merkí.
—'Este pažežiko, 'el konde,   ke a mí me 'esfu'ele 'a servir,
'el dí'a para la meza   'i la noğe para dormir. (28)
'Esto ke sintyyó 'el bu'en konde,   lo dešó 'i se 'eğó a fu'ir. (31)
—Non vos fuyygáš, 'el bu'en konde,   'i no vos kižeraš fu'ir. (32)
Ke no 'es la vu'estra kulpa,   sinon yyo ke lo buškí. (33)
¡Akel konde 'i akel konde   'i 'en la mar se'a su fin! (1)
Armó naves 'i galeas   'i para Fransyya kižo 'ir.
Las armó de todo punto   'i las 'eğó dyentro 'el sanğir.
El sanğir komo 'era 'estrego,   no las pu'edí'a režir.
—¡Atrás, atrás, los fransezes,   non le deš vergu'ensa así! (5)
Si 'el gran duke lo save,   'a Fransyya non mos deša 'ir,
ni vos dan pan 'a komere,   ni kon las damas dormir.
Ala tornada ke atornan,   mataron setenta mil,
aparte de ğiketikos,   ke non ayy ku'enta ni fin. (9)

Source: GRA 7.

2 *repeated.*

3*b* + setorna.

10*b* kon sigo.

Translations:

2A

Oh that Count, that Count, may he perish on the sea! He fitted out weapons and galleys and set out for France. He fitted them out completely and launched them upon the [river] San Gil. Since the river was narrow, he could not steer them well. (5) "Go back, go back, you Frenchmen, do not shame him so! If the Grand Duke learns of it, he'll not let you return to France. Nor will he give you bread to eat, nor let you sleep with ladies." In the counterattack, they killed seventy thousand, aside from foot soldiers, whose number is without end. (10) There are great wedding feasts in France, in the halls of Paris; for the daughter of the King has been married together with the daughter of Amadí. Ladies and maidens are dancing, and more than a thousand knights. She who was leading the dance was a graceful lady. The good Count was looking at her, that Count Amadí. (15) "What are you looking at, good Count? Count, what are you looking at here?" "Either you were looking at the dancing or you were looking at me." "I'm not looking at the dancing, and even less am I looking at you. I'm looking at your beautiful body, so graceful and fine." "If I please you, Count, take me with you. (20) My husband is on a journey; he is too far away to return. I have an old mother-in-law who is sick unto death. I have two small children who will not know how to tell him." He wrapped her in a golden mantle, but left her shoe outside. Along the way, he encountered Amadí: (25) "What are you carrying, Count? Count, what are you carrying here?" "I'm carrying a little golden page, that I bought only today." "This little page, Count, is wont to serve me, during the day at table and at night for bed." He does not recognize her in her gracefulness, and even less in her attire. (30) He recognizes the golden shoe: "Only yesterday I bought it!" When the Count heard this, he left her and started to flee. "Don't flee, good Count, do not think of fleeing. (33) This is no fault of yours, but mine, for I brought it on myself."

2B

There are great wedding feasts in France, in the halls of Paris; for the King's son has married the daughter of Amadí. Ladies and maidens are dancing, and more than a thousand knights. The one who leads the dancing is a graceful lady. (5) The Count was looking at her, that Count Amadí. "What are you looking at, Count? Count, what are you looking at here? Either you were looking at the dancing or you were looking at me." "I'm not looking at the dancing and even less am I looking at you. I'm looking at your beautiful body that is so graceful and fine." (10) "If it pleased you, good Count, take me with you. My husband is on a journey; he is too far away to return. I have two small children who will not know how to tell him. I have an old mother-in-law, who is sick unto death." He wrapped her in a golden mantle, but left her shoe outside. (15) On stepping through the door, he encountered Amadí: "What are you carrying, good Count? Count, what are you carrying here?" "I'm carrying a little golden page that I bought only yesterday." "This little page, Count, is wont to serve me, during the day at table and at night for bed." (20) When the good Count heard this, he left everything and started to flee. "Don't flee, good Count, do not think of fleeing, for it is not your fault, but mine, since I brought it on myself." Oh that Count, that Count, may he perish on the sea! He fitted out ships and galleys and set out for France. (25) He fitted them out completely and launched them upon the [river] San Gil. Since the river was narrow, he could not steer them well. "Go back, go back, you Frenchmen, do not shame him so! If the Grand Duke learns of it, he'll not let us return to France. Nor will he give you bread to eat, nor let you sleep with ladies." (30) In the counterattack, they killed seventy thousand, (31) aside from foot soldiers, whose number is without end.

Motifs:

14 Cf. N711.6. *Prince [Count] sees heroine at ball and is enamored.*
20 T230. *Faithlessness in marriage.*
22 Cf. K1500. *Deception connected with adultery.*
30 F823.1. *Golden shoes*; cf. H36.1. *Slipper test*; H36.1.1. *Recognition by shoes....*
33 J2301. *Gullible husbands.*

The narrative represented by Yoná's texts seems to be limited, in the Eastern tradition, to the community of Salonika. It is a composite of elements drawn from three independent sources: *Almerique de Nar-*

bona (2A, vv. 1-4), *Roncesvalles* (2A, vv. 5-9) and *Grandes bodas en Francia* (2A, vv. 10 ff.).

Version B (= GRA) is shorter than A, as represented by GSA, but embodies a number of minimal, though authentically traditional variants, some of which are preferable to GSA's readings: *vergu'ensa* (shared with RHP) instead of GSA's *vergu'ela* (2A.5), *atornan* (2B.30), *mil* (2B.3; shared with RHP) instead of GSA's senseless *mí* (2A.12), and *pažežiko* (2B.17) for GSA's *pasežiko* or RHP's *pasažíko* (2A.27). B's v. 2 is certainly better than A's v. 11. The reversed order of B's vv. 12-13 (= A. vv. 22 and 21) may also seem preferable, but A's sequence agrees with that of all versions we have seen from the Eastern tradition. B lacks vv. 29-30, which appear in almost all the Eastern versions published to date. B's placement of vv. 1-9 at the end of the narrative is altogether untraditional and might reflect nothing more than a typographic caprice.

The fragment of *Almerique de Narbona* (2A.1-4) is based upon *Primavera* 196, which derives in turn from the French epic tradition of Aymeri de Narbonne. The ballad, printed in the *Cancionero de 1550*, recreates certain incidents of the *chanson de geste* entitled *Mort Aymeri*:

> Del Soldán de Babilonia, de ése os quiero decir,
> que le dé Dios mala vida y a la postre peor fin.
> Armó naves y galeras, pasan de sesenta mil,
> para ir a combatir a Narbona la gentil.
> Allá van a echar áncoras, allá al puerto de Sant Gil,
> cativado han al conde, al conde Benalmenique. . . .
> (*Primav.* 196)

The Sephardic texts preserve the imprecation against the sea-going Sultan of Babylon (transformed into a nondescript Count) and a very brief, rather chaotic, description of his naval attack on Narbonne, quite naturally generalized to France. The sixteenth-century text's allusion to the port of Saint-Gilles explains the meaningless *sangí(r)* of the Sephardic versions. The final verse of *Primavera* 196, with its allusion to Roland, may help to explain the contamination of two essentially unrelated narratives at some earlier stage of Sephardic tradition. Though it is true that both *Almerique de Narbona* and *Roncesvalles* tell of Moorish onslaughts and both use *í* assonance, the partial identity of the last verse of *Almerique*: "Dios os lo eche en suerte / a ese Roldán paladín" and the fourth verse of *Domingo era de Ramos* (*Primav.* 183):

"¡Oh, cuán bien los esforzaba / ese Roldán paladín," undoubtedly contributed to the fusion of the two ballads.

Verses 5-9 of Yoná's text A offer a brief glimpse of the battle of Roncevaux, as it must have been narrated in some late Spanish redaction of the Roland epic. The Sephardic fragment is related to two known sixteenth-century ballads: *La fuga del Rey Marsín* ("Ya comienzan los franceses / con los moros pelear") and the briefer, monorhymed *Domingo era de Ramos,* but seems to derive directly from neither one. The Sephardic version contains several presumably authentic details which are absent from the extant sixteenth-century texts: that is, the reference to the "gran duke" or "konde," who is probably Charlemagne himself; the allusion to the benefits—sustenance and feminine companionship—which would be denied to the French warriors if they failed to return to battle; and the fragment's final verse (2A.9), which uses a well-known epic formula to stress the countless numbers of Moorish footsoldiers slaughtered by the French. [1] These details could well have been present in a now lost sixteenth-century ancestor text of the Sephardic version.

The fragments of *Almerique de Narbona* and *Roncesvalles* are known nowhere else in the modern Hispanic tradition. Thus, the Salonikan versions offer in this case two unique survivals of sixteenth-century material.

Las bodas en París (2A.10 ff.) is one of a number of Spanish ballads, known in fragmentary sixteenth-century versions, which can be substantially supplemented by evidence drawn from the present-day tradition. One of many Judeo-Spanish ballads on the adulteress theme, *Las bodas en París* tells of an intrigue between a dissatisfied wife and Count Amadí. The protagonists become infatuated during a dance and the lady allows herself to be "abducted." The fleeing lovers are found out

---

[1] For similar epic formulas, see our article "Para un gran romancero sefardí," no. II. See also *Cantar de Mio Cid,* vv. 1723, 1795, 2491, 2529. Cf. v. 418 and *Reliquias,* p. 159, v. 387. Analogous verses occur in various ballads: "Matan tantos de los griegos / que no los saben contar. // Más venían de otra parte / que no hay cuento ni par" (*Robo de Elena*: *Primav.* 109). "Miraba las torres espesas / que no las puede contar" (*Sobre Baza estaba el rey*: Barbieri 330; ASW 33); "árabes, rifeños, bárbaros, / no se podían contar" (*El Mostadí*: MP 16); "Os padres e a fidalguia / não tinham conta nem fim" (*Bernal Francés*: Fernandes Thomás, *Velhas canções,* pp. 17-18).

by the returning husband, who identifies his wife's golden slipper. One would expect a violent and bloody dénouement, for the *Romancero,* faithful to the Hispanic code of honor, usually takes a most restrictive view of such illicit activities. [2] Here, strangely enough, the husband blames neither wife nor lover, but explains the whole affair as the result of his own marital neglect: "Ken tiene mužer ermoza, / nunka ke la deše ansí" concludes one of our unedited Salonikan versions. In Moroccan variants the husband adopts an even more permissive and less credible attitude, saying that the Count is welcome to his wife's company for one night. Most Moroccan texts end: "Yevailde esta noche, el conde, / mañana traílde aquí" (Bénichou A; Larrea; Ortega). Bénichou B and Alvar are more complete and close on an ironic note, in which the Count takes advantage of the foolish husband's offer to acquire the errant wife's permanent companionship:

—Yevailde esta noche, el conde, mañana traílde aquí.
Ésa fue yevada, el conde, para siempre y nuncua aí.
(Bénichou B)

—Vaite esta noche, el conde, mañana tráimela aquí.
Ya se la yevó el conde esa noche y otrą mį[l].
(Alvar)

In Leite de Vasconcellos' lone, brutally direct Portuguese variant, matters go even worse for the poor husband. He tells the lover to take his wife for one night, but the Count claims her for an entire year ("from May to April") and when he finally does bring her back she is in a family way:

—Leva-a tu, por esta noite; amanhã trai-a m'aqui.
Levou-a no mês de Maio, trouxera-a no mês d'Abril.
Levara-a ele vazia, trouxera-a para parir.

We cannot be sure how the sixteenth-century texts ended, since all break off at a point corresponding to verse 20 of Yoná's text A. These early versions may have ended on a characteristically grim note of

---

[2] Cf. Menéndez Pidal's comments in FN 23; RoH, I, 331-332; also Bénichou, pp. 62, 65-66; M. R. Lida de Malkiel, *Davar,* 10, pp. 14-15; DRH, p. 79. For more on this, see no. 16, n. 33 *infra.*

marital vengeance, as Bénichou believes (pp. 65-66). However, the general agreement of the geographically separated modern versions bespeaks the antiquity of the ballad's cynical dénouement.

Most Eastern versions agree in incongruously applying the name *Amadí* to both lover and husband (cf. Yoná A, vv. 14 and 24). Attias' text and one of our own unedited versions call the husband *Almaví* or *Amadín,* while the lover is simply "el conde." That *Amadí* is properly the lover's and not the husband's name is borne out by evidence from other branches of the tradition. In Moroccan texts the lover is called "el conde de París" and in *Primavera* 157 he is "el buen conde don Martín," while the inadequate, permissive husband remains nameless in the Moroccan, Portuguese, and archaic versions.

The different branches of the tradition disagree as to the wife's motivation for going off with the Count. In all Eastern versions, it is because the husband is away traveling or at war:

Mariđo 'en viaže tengo, lonǧe 'está para venir...
(Yoná A, v. 20)

...el mi marido está en guerra, tarda inda de venir...
(Coello)

In Morocco, in place of the "absent husband," [3] we have the motif of the "aged husband," [4] as also in the sixteenth-century texts:

---

[3] For the husband's absence as an excuse for adultery, see *La adúltera* (*ó*) (MP 78; no. 16 *infra*), *Bernal Francés* (MP 83), and *La infanticida* (MP 84).

[4] In *La mujer del pastor,* the husband is "viejo, cano y rebelludo; / sus huesos traen [*read* trae en] dolor" (Larrea 102; MP 73). *La adúltera* (*í-a*) and *La condesa traidora* are likewise married to aged husbands (Larrea 117.21; Bénichou 41.9-10), as are *La bella malmaridada* (TRV, II, 387: "Que a este mi marido viejo / ya no le puedo sufrir"), the countess in *Celinos,* and the *Lavandera de San Juan* (DRH, pp. 73-74). There are abundant additional examples in the Catalan tradition: *Barba gris*: "Lo meu pare m'ha casada, / casada ab un barba gris. // Dia de las esposallas / no feya sino dormir" (Briz, V, 81; AFC 1098; Milá 426; Serra i Vilaró, p. 87); *Mensaje a los parientes*: "M'en ha casada ab un vell, / no'l puch veure ni m'agrada" (Milá 358; AFC 2300; Sarri 122; OCPC, I, 127-130; III, 166, 173-174, 285-286); *Casamiento desigual*: "M'han dada am un drotle / de quatre vint anys" (Milá 565); *Deseo no logrado* (Milá 439); *Casada amb un vell* (AFC 3310; Avenç, IV, 52-53; OCPC, II, 150; III, 236, 245); *La falguera* (AFC 2868; Avenç, III, 80-81); *La mal casada* (AFC 1100; Amades, I, 60-61); *Senyora Isabel* (AFC 2468; Avenç, II, 55); also AFC

el marido tengo y viejo, cansada estoy de servir.
(Alvar)

quel marido tengo viejo & no se curaua de mí.
(*Pliegos de Praga*)

In the Portuguese version, like those from the Eastern Mediterranean, it is again the husband's absence which seems to motivate his lady's infidelity:

—Tanho medo ao teu marido, que me mate já ali.
—O meu marido, ó conde, longes terras 'stá daqui.

The "absent husband," a ballad commonplace, could easily have entered the Eastern and Portuguese texts independently. Yet it is also possible that these variant versions from opposite extremities of the Hispanic world may derive from a common sixteenth-century text type, in which, unlike *Primavera* 157, the husband's distant travels moved the wife to seek other companionship.

The *Roncesvalles* fragment and *Las bodas en París* both use *í* assonance, but it is not unlikely that certain vague thematic similarities may also have helped to facilitate the combination of the two narratives. The initial cowardice of the French soldiers, the shirking of their military duties, may be compared to the husbands' disconcerting laxity in regard to his marital responsibilities as well as to the cowardly flight of the Count when the husband unexpectedly returns. In addition, there is the common ground of France in both ballads and a clear indication of the amorous proclivities of French knights. If an air of sensuality

1099; Milá 498; Serra i Vilaró, p. 72; Tomás i Parés, "L'Hereu Mill," pp. 935-936; in the French tradition: *La maumariée* (Davenson 64; Rolland, I, 79-86; II, 75, 77-90; Arbaud, I, 148-150; Barbeau, *Romancéro,* pp. 65-70), *La belle dans la vigne* (Rolland, I, 216-218), and other French instances: Canteloube, I, 230, 233, 278; II, 386, 416-417; III, 167, 258, 376; IV, 281, 302; Davenson 67; Puymaigre, *Pays Messin,* II, 26-34; Rolland, I, 101. The story of *Old Robin of Portingale* (Child 80), reminiscent of the Pan-Hispanic *Celinos*, provides a British example: "God let neuer soe old a man / marry soe yonge a wiffe." See also *The Marriage of Sir Gawain* (Child 31.46) and *Lord Ingram and Chiel Wyet* (Child 66c). For Greek songs on the same theme, see Chianis 16 and Pernot, *Anthologie,* pp. 197-198. Cf. J445.2. *Foolish marriage of old man and young girl*; T121. *Unequal marriage*; T237. *Old man married to young, unfaithful wife.*

pervades the *Bodas en París*, the threat of being deprived of feminine company goads the French warriors on to a victorious counterattack. Admittedly, these are tenuous connections. Still, they may help to explain, together with the *í* assonance, the union between two ballads of seemingly unrelated subject matter.

BIBLIOGRAPHY

Almerique de Narbona

Eastern J.-Sp.: See all texts listed for *Roncesvalles.*

Archaic Text: *Primavera* 196 (= *Cancionero de 1550*).

Studies: Bédier, *Les légendes épiques,* I, 416-417; EEB, p. 176; Entwistle, "Spanish Ballads in the French Epic Cycles," pp. 210-211; Riquer, *Cantares de gesta franceses,* pp. 179-186; RoH, I, 257-259; TRV, II, 300-302.

Roncesvalles

Eastern J.-Sp.: Attias 32; Benardete 9; Coello 8; Gil 25 (= Coello); Hemsi 14; Id., "Evocation," pp. 1056*a*, 1091 (= Hemsi 14); MP 20 (= *Coello*); PTJ 20 (= Attias); UYA 263 (= GSA).

Archaic Texts: *La fuga del rey Marsín* ("Ya comienzan los franceses"): ASW 67; Horrent, *Roncesvalles,* pp. 219-222; Menéndez Pidal, "Roncesvalles," pp. 170-172; *Pliegos góticos,* I, 131-132; II, 282*b*; Rodríguez-Moñino, *Cancionerillos góticos,* pp. 74-78. *Domingo era de Ramos*: ASW 127; CSA, fols. 229*v*-230*v*; Durán 394; *Pliegos de Praga,* I, 204-205; II, 161-164, 189-192; *Pliegos góticos,* II, 189-191; III, 193-196; Porębowicz, p. 16 (no. 84); *Primavera* 183; Rodríguez-Moñino, "Campo de Alanje," no. 40; Simón Díaz, III:2, 2975, 2980, 2981, 3026. See also Menéndez Pidal, "Poesía popular y romancero," II, 2-3; RVP, pp. 81-83.

Studies: Alonso, *Primavera temprana,* pp. 153-154, 156; EEB 173; Entwistle, "Spanish Ballads in the French Epic Cycles," pp. 207-208, 215; Horrent, *Chanson de Roland,* pp. 504-508; Id., *Roncesvalles,* pp. 93-94, 98-99, 217-222; Id., "Sur les *romances* carolingiens," pp. 163-167; Menéndez Pidal, *La Chanson de Roland y el neotradicionalismo,* pp. 154, 297, 381-382, 388, 400-402, 404, 406, 440; Id., *La Chanson de Roland et la tradition épique,* pp. 396, 415, 422, 436-438, 440, 442-443, 492; Id., Introduction to CSA, pp. xx-xxi, xxxvii; Id., "Roncesvalles," pp. 170-178; Id., "Sobre *Roncesvalles* y ... los romances carolingios," p. 397; Riquer, *Cantares de gesta franceses,* pp. 126-127; RoH, I, 76, 188, 192, 245-248, 264; II, 28; TRV, II, 261-264; Wilson-Sage 112.

Las bodas en París

Eastern J.-Sp.: Attias 32.24 ff.; Benardete 32; Coello 8.9 ff.; Gil 25 (= Coello); Hemsi 14.9 ff.; Hemsi, "Evocation," pp. 1056*a*, 1091 (= Hemsi 14); PTJ 95 (= Attias); UYA 263 (vv. 10 ff. = GSA).

Moroccan J.-Sp.: Alvar, *Textos dialectales,* II, 760, vv. 24 ff.; Bénichou 5; Gil 25 (= MP); Larrea 142-143; MP 95; MRuiz 78A-C; Ortega 214; PTJ 95*a* (= Alvar).

Portuguese: VRP 416.

Archaic Texts: Durán 290; *Pliegos de Praga,* II, 215-216; *Pliegos góticos,* II, 63-64, 285*b*; *Primavera* 157 (= *Cancionero de 1550*); Rodríguez-Moñino, *Espejo de enamorados,* pp. 65-69; Timoneda, *Rosa de Amores,* fol. lxvij*v*; Simón Díaz, III:1, 2825; III:2, 2957.

Studies: BNE 222-223; M. R. Lida de Malkiel, *Davar,* 10, p. 14; Menéndez Pidal, *El Romancero Español,* p. 124; Morley, "A New Jewish-Spanish *Romancero,*" p. 3, n. 7; RoH, II, 52, 69, 268, 331, 336, n. 65, 340, n. 74; TRV, II, 406-407.

3

EL SUEÑO DE DOÑA ALDA

(Lady Alda's Dream)

'En Paríž 'está Donyyalda 'i la 'espozika de Rovda͜le.
Trezyentas damas kon 'elyya, ke tođas son de a͜lto linaže.
Las syento 'eran de Burgo 'i las syento de Portugale;
las syento 'eran de Fransyya, la sivdad de gran korale.
No penséš ke 'están debaldes, ke tođas 'ofisyyo azen.
Las syento filavan perla 'i las syento tešen kardale;
las syento tanyen vigu'ela para Donyya͜lda folgare.
'I Donyyalda kon grande visyyo mal adormesida ka'e.
Tres días kon las tres noğes, no le 'uvo arefolgare.
A͜la fin de las tres noğes, se despertó kon pavor grande.
—Vení akí, mis donzeas, las ke 'en mi komande 'estareš.
'Esfu'enyyo sonyí, donzeas, 'en byen me lo asoltareš.
Si 'era mosa soltera, yyo la devo de kazare.
Si tal 'era kazada, ande su marido andare.
Me se kemavan kastí'os, me se kemavan sivdades.
Se les kemavan las barvas 'i la ko[r]ona reale.

Source: GRA 3
V. 2 is repeated.
3*b* + se torna *in parentheses.*
16*b* kodona.

Translation:

In Paris sits Doña Alda, the betrothed of Roland. Three hundred ladies are with her, all are of high degree. One hundred were from Burgo[s] and a hundred from Portugal; a hundred were from France, the city of great courage(?). (5) Do not think they are idle, for each has her chosen task. One hundred were embroidering pearls; and a hundred are weaving cloth (?); a hundred are playing instruments to entertain Doña Alda. And Doña Alda, [listening] with great pleasure, falls into an evil sleep. For three days and three nights she could not be awakened. (10) At the end of the three nights, she awoke in great terror: "Come here, my maidens, all who are at my command. I dreamt a dream, maidens; may you give it a happy meaning. If she [who can tell its meaning] were unmarried, I will see that she is married; if she were married, then she shall go to her husband. (15) [I dreamt that] my castles and my cities were burning; (16) their beards were on fire and the royal crown."

Motifs:

9 F564.3.2. *Person sleeps for three days and nights.*

15f. Cf. D1812.3.3. *Future revealed in dream*; D1812.3.3.5. *Prophetic dream allegorical*; D1812.5.1.2. *Bad dream as evil omen*; *D1812.3.3.9.1. *Dream of future reveals husband's death* (Bordman).

El sueño de Doña Alda, like the previous *Roncesvalles* fragment, is undoubtedly based upon one of the culminating scenes of a medieval Spanish reworking of the *Chanson de Roland,* namely, Aude's ominous dream presaging the announcement of the hero's death.

The ballad is quite rare in the Eastern Sephardic tradition. The text collected by Benardete is only a fragment. Like the unedited Salonikan version mentioned by Menéndez Pidal (MP 21), it is prefixed to the ballad of *Melisenda insomne* (MP 28) which, at a later stage in its narrative, incorporates other verses referring to Alda's dream (cf. Benardete 11.9-12). A text of *Alda* published by Menéndez Pidal in "El romancero y los sefardíes" is almost certainly synthetic and apparently combines readings from both branches of the Judeo-Spanish tradition. The two verses from Constantinople, appearing with music in RoH, agree with this synthetic version. Attias and Yoná thus offer the only two reasonably "complete" texts available from the East. In reality they represent a single version, since Attias differs from Yoná in only two minor details (*más* for *mal* in v. 8; *arrecodrare* instead of *arefolgare* in v. 9). Attias provides other variant readings in a footnote (p. 108, n. 6).

The Yoná-Attias version begins with a magnificent description of the courtly surroundings which serve as a background to Alda's dream. The impressive verses which specify different homelands for the three groups of maidens, lacking in *Primavera* 184, but present in Bénichou's Moroccan text, must go back to some other sixteenth-century variant. [1] Less felicitous are the verses concerning Alda's offer of rewards to whoever can interpret the dream. Such verses occur, with a rather exaggerated reinterpretation, in Morocco (cf. Bénichou), but not in the sixteenth-century version. Exclusive to our Eastern text are the formulistic "three days and three nights" of Alda's unnatural sleep, which recall verses from *El nacimiento de Montesinos*: "que tres días con sus noches / ha que no ha comido pan" (*Primav.* 175 [p. 392]) and *La novia abandonada*: "Siete días kon sus noches / i ni durmió ni komió pan" (unedited Sephardic version from Rhodes). [2]

---

[1] Cf. RoH, II, 336.

[2] The pattern is common to Pan-European balladry. Compare: "... tres dies i tres nits / ressonaren les campanes" (*Don Joan i Don Ramón*: Subirá, p. 43*b*); "Il y fut trois jours et trois nuits, / sans boire, manger, ni dormir. // Au bout de trois jours et trois nuits ..." (*Les anneaux de Marianson*: Davenson 2.22-23); "Ja krank, ja krank bis auf den Tod, / Drei Tag, drei Nacht sprach sie kein Wort" (*Der treue Knabe*: Erk-Böhme 93*a*.4; Meier, *Balladen*, II, no. 71; other instances: *Ulinger, Grausame Bruder*: Meier, *Balladen*, I, 112; II, 42-43); "Treĩs méres kaì treĩs núchtes tẽn ebastáxane" (*Tẽs hōriãs tò Kástro*: Dawkins, "Tragoúdia tõn Dōdekanḗsōn," no. 5.47); "Treĩs méres kánoun pólemo, treĩs méres kaì treĩs núchtes" (*Toũ Ziáka*: Petropoulos, I, 225, no. 73.6; other Greek instances: *Núfē koumpára* [no. 24 *infra*]; *Mavrianos and His Sister, Jannis and the Lamia,* and *The Sin* [Lüdeke-Megas, nos. 53, 117, 120]); "Spielte Dimo, spielte / drei Tag und drei Nächte" (*Die Vilen und der Spielmann*: Gesemann, *Zweiundsiebzig Lieder des bulgarischen Volkes,* p. 69). For other Balkan examples, see Abbott, *Songs,* pp. 30 f., 44 f.; Pernot, *Anthologie,* p. 121; Dozon, *Chansons populaires bulgares,* pp. 149, 169, 229, 230, 251, 284, 335; Strausz, *Bulgarische Volksdichtungen,* pp. 143, 150, 215; Camarda, *Grammatologia ... albanese,* pp. 124-125; Lambertz, *Die Volksepik der Albaner,* pp. 14, 20, 24, 67, 68, 121,

In spite of its promising beginnings, our Eastern text suffers a disappointing truncation. It closes abruptly by replacing the authentic account of Alda's vision (cf. Benardete 11.9-12, and the admirably complete Moroccan texts) with two verses from an omen-filled dream found in another Carolingian ballad, the previously mentioned *Nacimiento de Montesinos* (*Primav.* 175). Here Count Grimaltos describes an allegorical dream, not unlike Alda's in *Primavera* 184 and the Moroccan versions, where birds represent the protagonists. [3] The italicized material below doubtless corresponds to the last two verses of our Sephardic text:

133, 138, 145. Cf. also Bowra, *Heroic Poetry,* pp. 172, 285; DgF, I, no. 11A, v. 36.

[3] On ominous, usually allegorical dreams as a *topos* in Spanish Carolingian ballads and in medieval European epic and balladry, see Menéndez Pidal, RoH, I, 266; Id., "Roncesvalles," pp. 186-188; Id., *Leyenda de los Infantes de Lara,* p. 29, n. 1; Entwistle, "Spanish Ballads in the French Epic Cycles," pp. 209-210; Wimberly, *Folklore in the English and Scottish Ballads,* pp. 66, 80, 188-189, 241. Cf. also the following random examples: *Nibelungenlied,* vv. 921, 924, 1509; *Volsungasaga,* Chaps. 25, 34-35 (trans. M. Schlauch, pp. 120, 160-161); *Fair Margret and Sweet William* (Child 74); *Sir John Butler* (Child 165.16); *Lord Thomas Stuart* (Child 259.12); *Lord Livingston* (Child 262.20); *Marsk Stig dømmes fredløs* (DgF, III, no. 145B.2, M.3; Olrik, I, no. 26.2; Smith-Dampier, p. 155, v. 2); *Liden Engel* (DgF, V, no. 297A.4 etc.; Olrik, I, no. 33.4; Smith-Dampier, p. 196); Seemann, "Deutsch-litauische Volksliedbeziehungen," pp. 183-184 (nos. 74-75); Leader, *Hungarian Classical Ballads,* pp. 23, 33-34; Baud-Bovy, *Études sur la chanson cleftique,* p. 48 (vv. 4-7); Lambertz, *Die Volksepik der Albaner,* pp. 19, 34, 150-151. More specific correspondences in which the prophetic dream involves a hawk or eagle or represents the hero as a hawk are found in the *Volsungasaga,* chap. 25. Before Sigurd's death, Gudrun dreams of him as a hawk: "I dreamed that I saw a fair hawk on my hand, and his feathers were of a golden hue. ... There was nothing in the world I cared for more than that hawk, and I would rather have lost all my wealth than him" (trans. Schlauch, pp. 117-118). Analogous to Doña Alda's dream is one of a series of hideous, foreboding dreams seen by Kostbera: "Methought an eagle flew in here through the hall, and sprinkled me and all of us with blood, and that must betoken ill, for it seemed to me that that was the double of King Atli" (*Volsungasaga,* chap. 34, p. 160). Two famished hawks whose hearts, swollen with blood, are eaten by the heroine, appear in one of several prophetic dreams in the *Guđrúnarkviđa II* (trans. Hollander, *The Poetic Edda,* p. 276, v. 41). For yet another example, involving birds and eagles, see A. Prior, *Ancient Danish Ballads,* I, 196. Concerning such dreams, see also Bowra, *Heroic Poetry,* pp. 291-298; Wais, *Frühe Epik Westeuropas,* p. 138, n. 2; and K.-J. Steinmeyer, *Untersuchungen zur allegorischen Bedeutung der Träume im altfranzösischen Rolandslied* (Munich, 1963). In *Sir Aldingar,* the hero is seen as "a little hawk, flying

. . . un triste y mal sueño   alterado me hace estar.
Aunque en sueños no fiemos,   no sé a qué parte lo echar,
que parecía muy cierto   que vi una águila volar,
siete halcones tras ella   mal aquejándola van,
y ella por guardarse de ellos   retrújose a mi ciudad;
encima de una alta torre   allí se fuera a asentar;
por el pico echaba fuego,   por las alas alquitrán;
el fuego que de ella sale   la ciudad hace quemar;
a mí quemaba las barbas   y a vos quemaba el brial.
¡Cierto tal sueño como éste   no puede ser sino mal! [4]

---

out of the east" to strike down a "grimlie" griffin in a prophetic dream of happy import (Child 59A.19-21). Cf. *Infantes de Lara,* p. 295. Fundamental to the study of allegorical dreams is G. D. Kelchner, *Dreams in Old Norse Literature and Their Affinities in Folklore* (Cambridge, England, 1935).

The same motif is poignantly recreated by Lope de Vega in *El caballero de Olmedo* (ed. J. M. Blecua [Zaragoza: "Clásicos Ebro," 1947], Act II, vv. 870-871, 886-913):

De decirte me olvidaba
unos sueños que he tenido. . . .
Sobre una verde retama
veo ponerse un jilguero,
cuyas esmaltadas alas
con lo amarillo añadían
flores a las verdes ramas.
Y estando al aire trinando
de la pequeña garganta
con naturales pasajes
las quejas enamoradas,
sale un azor de un almendro,
adonde escondido estaba,
y como eran en los dos
tan desiguales las armas,
tiñó de sangre las flores,
plumas al aire derrama.
Al triste chillido, Tello,
débiles ecos del aura
respondieron, y, no lejos,
lamentando su desgracia,
su esposa, que en un jazmín
la tragedia viendo estaba.
Yo, midiendo con los sueños
estos avisos del alma,
apenas puedo alentarme;
que con saber que son falsas
todas estas cosas, tengo
tan perdida la esperanza,
que no me aliento a vivir.

[4] *Primavera* 175 (p. 388).

BIBLIOGRAPHY

Eastern J.-Sp.: Attias 28; Benardete 10; Menéndez Pidal, "El romancero y los sefardíes," p. xxii; RoH, I, 401.

Archaic J.-Sp. Incipit: "En sueño soñí, mis dueñas": ASW 438; Avenary 32 (pp. 383, 387); Kayserling, p. xi; RoH, II, 220.

Moroccan J.-Sp.: Alvar, *Textos dialectales,* II, 763-764; Bénichou 65; Cantera Burgos, *Los sefardíes,* pp. 12-13; Gil 51 (= MP); Larrea 24-25, 65.27-66; MP 21; MRuiz 34; PTJ 21-21*a* (= Alvar, MRuiz). Cf. FN 79-81 (final v.).

Archaic Texts: Durán 400; Horrent, *Roncesvalles,* pp. 224-226; *Primavera* 184 (= *Cancionero de 1550*); RVP, pp. 87-88.[5]

Studies: BNE 225; Entwistle, "Spanish Ballads in the French Epic Cycles," pp. 207, 215; FN 79-81; Horrent, *Chanson de Roland,* pp. 517-521; Id., *Roncesvalles,* pp. 100-101, 218; Id., "Sur les *romances* carolingiens," p. 167; Menéndez Pidal, *Chanson de Roland y el neotradicionalismo,* pp. 35, 39, 64, 166, 432; Id., *Chanson de Roland et la tradition épique,* pp. 35, 39-40, 67, 177, 485; PHP 351-352; Riquer, *Cantares de gesta franceses,* pp. 127-128; RoH, I, 245, 249-251, 266; II, 209-210, 254, 256, 331, 336, 340, 429; TRV, II, 264-267.

---

[5] The version published by Carré (no. 21) is simply a free, modern Galician translation of *Primavera* 184, which it follows verse by verse.

4

CONDE CLAROS Y EL EMPERADOR

(Count Claros and the Emperor)

4A

¡Luz del dí'a ['i luz del dí'a, luz del dí'a] 'i klaridad!
ke 'el dí'a me daš 'el sol 'i la noğe klaro lunar.
La manyyana las 'estreas kuando kere alvorear.
Se pasean tí'o 'i sovrino, ğuntos van a 'un barabar.
Ke kavayyos yevan de 'un presyyo 'i por ver kuál korí'a más.
Ke kore 'uno 'i kore 'otro, ğuntos van a 'un barabar,
avlando 'i platikando lo ke les 'importa más:

Source: GSA 6. Variants: LRI 10; BRI 9; RHP 8; GRI 9.
The second hemistich of each verse except vv. 1 and 19 is repeated and the word *'i* precedes each repetition. GSA / LRI / BRI / RHP / GRI.

1 Luz del dí'a 'i klarirad *GSA* (*in Library of Congress copy*; *printed as* klaridad *in the Instituto Arias Montano copy*), Luz del dí'a 'i klaridad *LRI / BRI / RHP / GRI. Bracketed material is supplied from Attias.*

1*a* Luz *in square letters BRI / GRI.*

2*a* mos daš *LRI / BRI / RHP / GRI,* sole *GRI.*

2*b* lunare *GRI.*

3*a* las manyyanikas *LRI / BRI / RHP / GRI.*

3*b* 'i kuando *BRI / RHP / GRI.*

4*a* se pase'a *LRI / BRI / RHP / GRI.*

4*b*, 6*b* a'un *GSA*, 'a 'un *LRI / BRI / RHP / GRI.*

5*a* kavalyyos *GRI.*

5*b* 'i por kual korí'a más *GSA, Library of Congress copy, but* 'i por ver.. *in the repetition. The verse is printed correctly in both cases in the Instituto Arias Montano copy and in LRI, BRI, GRI.*

7*a* Avlando van 'i pl. *LRI / BRI / RHP.*

—'Una mersed le rogo, tí'o,   kual me la avéš de atorgar:
ke me deš 'a Blankaninyya   por mužer 'i por 'igual.
—'Esta mersed, 'el mi sovrino,   non la pu'edo ağetar.
Kuando yyo la aví'a dado,   non la kižiteš tomar.
Ke dad[a] la tengo 'en Fransyya   por syen doblas 'i algo más.
Ke despozada la tengo 'en Fransyya   'i kon 'el konde Aligornar.
Gerero soš, 'el mi sovrino,   'i la pu'edéš muyy byen ganar.
—Dešme kamiza delgada,   sirma 'i perla 'en su koyyar.
Yya se 'esparte 'el kavayero,   yya se 'esparte 'i yya se va.
Por ka'es ke aví'a ğente,   kaminava de avagar.
Por las ka'es ke non aví'a ğente   senteas azí'a saltar.
¿Kén 'es 'este moro franko   ke la sivdad va derokar?

8*b* me *om. BRI* (me *included in repetition*) / *RHP. The* yod *is omitted from* me *in LRI* (*but the word is written properly in the repetition*).
10*b* non vola pu'edo *LRI* / *BRI,* no vola pu'edo *RHP,* non vola pu'edo atorgar *GRI.*
11*a* kuando vola aví'a dado *LRI* / *BRI* / *RHP* / *GRI.*
11*b* no la *RHP.*
12*a* dado *GSA* (*in both copies*), dada *LRI* / *BRI* / *RHP.*
12*b* doblas *LRI* (*in our copy, in the verse and its repetition,* daleth *is written in ink over whatever letter had been originally printed*), rublas *GRI.*
13*a* Ke *om. GRI.*
13*b* Aligornal *LRI* / *BRI* / *RHP in the repetition in GRI.*
14*b* muyy byen tomar *RHP.*
15*b* sirma perla *GRI* (*in repetition*).
16*a* 'I yya *GRI,* kavalyero *GRI.*
16*b* 'i yya *RHP* / *GRI.*
17*a,* 18*a* kalyes *BRI* / *RHP* / *GRI,* kayes *RHP,* no avían *RHP,* ğentes *RHP* / *GRI.*
18*b* sentelyyas *RHP.*
19*a* Kyen *RHP* / *GRI,* franko *om. GRI.*
19*b* ke *om. BRI,* aderokar *LRI,* 'a derokar *BRI* / *RHP.*

4B

¡Luz del dí'a ['i luz del dí'a,   luz del dí'a] 'i klaridad!
ke 'el dí'a le dyera 'el sol   'i la noğe 'el klaro lunar,
la manyyanika las 'estreas   'i kuando kere alvorear.

Source: GRA 8.
2*b* *repeated.*
3*b* + se torna.

Se pase'a tí'o 'i sovrino, ǧuntos van 'a 'un barabar.
Ke kavayyos yevan de 'un presyyo, por ver kual korí'a más. (5)
Ke kore 'uno 'i kore 'otro, ǧuntos van a 'un barabar,
avlando 'i platikando lo ke les 'importa más:
—'Una mersed le rogo, tí'o, kual me la avéš de atorgar:
ke me deš 'a Klaraninyya por mužer 'i por 'igual.
'Esta merseđ, 'el mi sovrino, no vola pu'edo aǧetar. (10)
Dezpozada la tengo 'en Fransyya kon 'el konde Aligornar. (13)
Gerero soš, 'el mi sovrino, sepášlas byen ganar. (14)
—Las armas tengo enpenyyadas por syen doblas 'i algo más. (X)
—Dalde syen doblas al konde para las armas kitar. (X)
'Otras tantas yyo le dyera para 'el kamino gastar. (X)
Daldeš kamiza de seda, sirma 'i perla 'en su koyyar. (15)
Daldeš ǧaketa de sirma, ke la lavró al bel lunar. (X)
Yya se 'esparte 'el kavalyero, yya se 'esparte 'i se va. (16)

10*b* vo la.
12*b* sepáš las.

Translations:

4A

Light of day, oh light of day, light of day and great clarity, which the sun gives me by day and at night the clear light of the moon and in the morning the stars, when dawn begins to break! Uncle and nephew ride along together, together they ride; (5) for they have horses of equal worth and want to see which might run faster. One rides and then the other, still they continue together apace, talking and discussing what concerns them most. "A favor I beg of you, uncle, which you must grant to me; that you give me Blancaniña for my wife and equal." (10) "This favor, my nephew, I cannot fulfil. When I offered her to you, you refused to accept her. Now I have betrothed her in France for one hundred doublings and more. I have betrothed her in France to Count Aligornar. You are a warrior, my nephew, and can surely win her back." (15) "Give me a fine shirt, with gold thread and pearls on the collar." Now the knight departs, he departs and already is gone.

Through the streets where there were people he rode slowly. Through the streets that were without people he made sparks fly. (19) Who is this foreign Moor who is going to destroy the city?

4B

Light of day, oh light of day, light of day and great clarity, which the sun gives him by day and at night the clear light of the moon, in the morning the stars, when dawn begins to break! Uncle and nephew ride along together, together they ride; (5) for they have horses of equal worth and want to see which might run faster. One rides and then the other, still they continue together apace, talking and discussing what concerns them most. "A favor I beg of you, uncle, which you must grant to me; that you give me Claraniña for my wife and equal." (10) "This favor, my nephew, I cannot fulfil. I have betrothed her in France to Count Aligornar. You are a warrior, my nephew, find a way to win her." "I have pawned my weapons for one hundred doublings and more." "Give the Count one hundred doublings to redeem his weapons. (15) I would give him another hundred to spend along the way. Give him a silken shirt, with gold thread and silver on the collar. Give him a jacket of golden thread, woven by the light of the beautiful moon." (18) Now the knight departs, now he departs and is gone.

This fragmentary, somewhat incoherent ballad is related to the sixteenth-century *romances* of *Conde Claros de Montalbán y el Emperador* ("A caza va el emperador . . ."; "A misa va el emperador . . .": *Primav*. 191-192). The Sephardic texts have suffered drastic contaminations and the story, what is left of it, has been radically reorganized.

The extraneous introductory verses (1-3) of Yoná's and Attias' texts offer a rather elaborate example of a device sometimes used in other Judeo-Spanish and Peninsular ballads—an invocatory reference to the time of day or the day on which the action is supposed to take place: "Noche buena y noche buena, / nochada de namorar . . ." (*Melisenda insomne*: Attias 33), "Noche buena, noche buena, / que es Pascua de Navidad . . ." (*Conde Claros fraile*: RPC 9),[1] "Mes de mayo, mes de mayo, / mes de la rica calor . . ." or "Días de mayo, días de mayo, /

[1] Cf. Menéndez Pidal, *et al.*, *Cómo vive un romance*, pp. 240-241.

días de las ricas calores..." (*El prisionero*),[2] "Mañanita, mañanita, / mañanita de San Juan..." (*Conde Olinos*),[3] "Mañanita, mañanita, / mañanita de San Simón..." (*Misa de amor*: RPE 90).

The first part of Yoná's and Attias' texts—the dialog between uncle and nephew—clearly corresponds to the initial verses of *Primavera* 191 and its reworked and expanded relative, *Primavera* 192:

191	192
A caza va el emperador	A misa va el emperador
a Sant Juan de Montiña;	a san Juan de la Montiña,
con él iba el conde Claros	con él iba el conde Claros
por le tener compañía.	por le tener compañía;
Contándole iba, contando	contándole iba contando
el gran menester que tenía: . . .	el menester que tenía: . . . (A-B 7, At 9 f.)
—Mis armas tengo empeñadas	—Mis armas tengo empeñadas
por mil marcos de oro y más,	por mil doblas de oro y más, (B 13, At 27 f.)
otros tantos debo en Francia	otras tantas debo en Francia
sobre mi buena verdad.	sobre mi buena verdad. . . .
—Llámenme mi camarero	Mandó llamar a su tesorero,
de mi cámara real;	su tesorero real: . . . (At 29 f.)
	—Da mil doblas de oro al conde
	para su verdad guardar,
dad mil marcos de oro al conde	y darle has otras mil
para sus armas quitar;	para sus armas quitar, (B 14, At 31 f.)
dad mil marcos de oro al conde	
para mantener verdad;	
dalde otros tantos al conde	
para vestir y calzar;	
dalde otros tantos al conde	
para las tablas jugar;	
dalde otros tantos al conde	
para torneos armar;	
dalde otros tantos al conde	dale también otras mil
para con damas folgar.	para con damas holgar.

[2] Unedited texts from San Ciprián de Sanabria (Zamora, Spain), collected July 6, 1963, by S. G. A.

[3] Unedited text, collected in Arroyo de la Luz (Cáceres, Spain), June 22, 1963, by S. G. A.

—Muchas mercedes, señor,	—Muchas gracias, el buen rey,
por esto y por mucho más.	por la buena voluntad,...
	más una merced os pido,
	ésta no me habéis de negar,
	(A-B 8, At 17 f.)
A la infanta Claraniña	que me caséis con la infanta
vos por mujer me la dad.	vuestra hija natural. ... (A-B 9,
	At 19 f.)
—Tarde acordastes, el conde,	—Ya no es tiempo, el conde Cla-
	[ros,
que mandada la tengo ya. ...	de aqueso vos hablar,
	que la tengo prometida
	al honrado don Beltrán, (A 13,
	B 11, At 23 f.)
	y por esto, el buen conde,
	a vos no la puedo dar:
	que vos sois niño y mochacho
	para tal mujer tomar.

The Sephardic text seems to agree more closely with *Primavera* 191, because of the latter's relative brevity in contrast with the expanded *Primavera* 192. The hunting expedition of 191 appears closer to the heroic comparison of horses in the Judeo-Spanish text than to the conversation on the way to Mass (192). Yoná's text B even preserves the name *Claraniña* as in 191. Nonetheless, the Sephardic texts contain two features which connect them to *Primavera* 192: " 'Una mersed le rogo...," etc. (A-B, v. 8) and the reference to Count Beltrán / Aligornar (A, v. 13, B, v. 11). Obviously the Judeo-Spanish version does not derive from either 191 or 192, but from some other early variant which combined the above-mentioned elements. [4] Such an impression is reinforced by the presence of the authentically epic passage, lacking in the early versions, in which the protagonists race each other to compare the strength of their horses. [5]

The Sephardic versions of *Conde Claros y el Emperador* have suffered a number of complex contaminations. Together with the knightly

[4] Compare the Moroccan versions (MP and Larrea), which combine abundant characteristics of 192 with the name *Claraniña* from 191. They must descend from a traditional text similar to the one which served as a basis for the reworking embodied in 192.

[5] There seems to be a distant analogy with the *Cantar de Mio Cid*, vv. 3507 ff. (section 150).

necessities of "doblas" to redeem his pawned weapons and for maintenance during the journey, the Emperor asks that Count Claros be given: "... kamiza de seda, / sirma 'i perla 'en su koyyar. // ... ğaketa de sirma, / ke la lavró al bel lunar" (B, vv. 16-17). These verses, describing the Count's rich apparel, recall the elaborate scene in which Count Claros arrays himself in regal style before going to visit the Princess in *Primavera* 192. [6] However, they seem to correspond even more closely to *Primavera* 190 (*Conde Claros y la infanta*: "Media noche era por filo . . ."):

—Levantá, mi camarero, dáme vestir y calzar.
Presto estaba el camarero para habérselo de dar:
diérale calzas de grana, borceguís de cordobán;
diérale jubón de seda aforrado en zarzahán;
diérale un manto rico que no se puede apreciar;
trescientas piedras preciosas al derredor del collar.
(*Primav.* 190.8-13)

The Sephardic ballad's connection with *Primavera* 190 is apparently confirmed by a verse which occurs in a hybrid text, *Gaiferos jugador* + *Conde Claros y el Emperador* + *La esposa de Don García,* collected by Mrs. Crews in Salonika (1935). The portion of this hybrid version corresponding to *Conde Claros y el Emperador* reads:

—Las armas tengo peñadas por sien doblas i algo más.
—Dešle sien doblas al konde para las armas kitare.
Presto demandó el vistido, presto demandó el kalsare.
Por kayes ke no ay ğente sinteyas aze saltare.
Por kayes k'avía ğente kaminava avagare.

The first two and the last two verses parallel B, vv. 13-14 and A, vv. 17-18 respectively. The third verse seems to derive from a version of *Conde Claros y la infanta* different from *Primavera* 190. Compare the second verse of the following fragment from a variant version absorbed by Luis Vélez de Guevara's drama, *Los hijos de la Barbuda*:

Conde Claros, con amores, non pudiera reposare,
apriesa pide el vestido, apriesa pide el calzare;
presto está su camarero para habérselo de dare.
(ASW 96)

---

[6] Cf. also ASW 73-75.

Yet the Moroccan versions of *Conde Claros y el Emperador,* much more unequivocally relatable to *Primavera* 192, also contain the above-mentioned features which we have traced to *Primavera* 190, as well as the reference to the Count's shirt being woven by moonlight (B, v. 17), although here the valet (*Primav.* 190.8) is replaced by a maiden:

Pronto demanda el vestido, pronto demanda el calzar;
ahí se aljadró una doncella que se lo solía dar.
Daile camisón de Holanda que el agua se beberá;
las cien damas lo tejieron a la sombra del lunar,
con el labre de la luna alrededor del collar.

(Larrea 30.42-51)

The evidence offered by texts from both Judeo-Spanish traditions seems to point to a most complex intertwining of elements from various ballads of *Conde Claros* at an early stage in the tradition.

One of the most striking features which set off the Eastern Sephardic versions of *Conde Claros y el Emperador* from both *Primavera* 191-192 and the latter's Moroccan derivatives is the different order of the dialog. In the archaic texts and in Morocco, Count Claros talks first of his material needs: he has pawned his arms and owes a thousand marks against his "buena verdad." Having been granted more than enough by the Emperor to redeem his pledges, he then boldly demands the hand of Claraniña (191 and Morocco) or "la infanta" (192), only to be rejected. In the Eastern versions, the Count first asks to marry Claraniña. The Emperor then explains that she has already been promised to Count Aligornar, but adds strangely enough—a possible reminiscence of the dénouement of *Primavera* 191—that she may still be won by force of arms: "Gerero soš, 'el mi sovrino, / 'i la pu'edéš muyy byen ganar" (A, v. 14). The pawned weapons are then mentioned by Count Claros as an excuse for not winning Claraniña. The Emperor forthwith orders that he be given the funds to redeem his arms and pay his traveling expenses. These features—the possibility of winning Claraniña by force of arms and the Emperor's co-operation—bespeak the intrusion of *Gaiferos jugador* (no. 5 *infra*) upon our narrative. In *Primavera* 173, Carlos "el emperante" reproaches Gaiferos for playing at dice instead of seeking to liberate Melisenda, his betrothed, who is being held captive by the Moors in Sansueña. Gaiferos flies into a rage but later explains his situation to Roland, giving as an excuse that he cannot rescue Melisenda because he has lent his weapons and horse to Montesinos for a tourney being held in the kingdom of Hungary. After some persuasion, Roland agrees to lend arms and a horse to Gaiferos. The episode of Gaiferos' excuse does not appear in contemporary Sephardic versions of *Gaiferos jugador,* which have themselves been severely and variously contaminated with *Conde Claros y el Emperador, La esposa de don García,* and *Juliana* (*Moriana*) *y Galván.* The episode must have migrated from some earlier Sephardic version to the ballad of *Conde Claros y el Emperador,* where it caused a profound alteration in the order and implications of the dialog and gave added conviction to the idea that Claraniña, like Melisenda, could be won or rescued by force of arms.

Yoná's and Attias' versions of *Conde Claros* give practically no hint as to how the narrative is to continue, once the hero, at the Emperor's behest, has been overwhelmed with money and apparel so that he may "win" Claraniña. The ballad's archaic forms are themselves at complete variance in regard to the outcome. After their initial parallelism, *Primavera* 191 and 192 begin to diverge: 191 tells the story of *Conde Claros en hábito de fraile,* a ballad with abundant modern Peninsular derivatives and far-ranging European counterparts,[7] while 192 tells a

[7] The **Moroccan** texts (Larrea 32-33; MP 24; MRuiz 36; PTJ 23*a* [= MRuiz]), like some **Castilian** (Kundert 87-88; RPC 12; RPM 58) and **Portuguese** versions (see below) combine *Conde Claros y la infanta* ("Media noche era por filo" *Primav.* 190, vv. 1-72) with *Conde Claros fraile* (*Primav.* 191, vv. 21 ff.). Cf. RoH, II, 397. The beginning of Larrea and MP is contaminated with *Guiomar* ("Ya se sale Guiomar / de los baños de bañar": *Primav.* 178). Cf. also *Aliarda* ("Ya se sale Aliarda / de los baños de bañar": *Primav.* 138, n. 4); Bénichou's remarks (p. 276); and RoH, II, 225, n. 47.

For versions of *Conde Claros fraile* from **Castilian** speaking areas, see ART 221; ASW 179-182; CPE, I, 32-33; II, 17-18; CVR 6-7; Espinosa, *Romancero canario,* pp. 47-48; Güéjar 1; Gutiérrez Macías 344-345; Kundert 87-88; Ledesma 181-182; Munthe 3; Pérez de Castro, "Nuevas variantes asturianas," 1; RCan 17; RPC 9-12; RPE 9-10; RPM 58-61; RTCN 30; RTO 14; RTR 4. The initial verses in *í-a* of the Salamancan, Extremeño, and Andalusian texts, with the Count's boast of his amorous conquest before the Court, recall the ballads of *Galiarda* I-II (*Primav.* 138-139), and also include verses from *La infanta deshonrada* (*í-a*: "Bien se pensaba la reina": *Primav.* 159); specifically "Ay, hija, si virgo estáis," etc. Cf. CPE, II, 17, vv. 7-8; Ledesma. The Asturian

very different tale, in which Count Claros sends the *infanta* to his own lands at Montalbán and the marriage of the lovers is arranged by the intercession of Roland and Oliver. Though the Moroccan versions seem to point to a dénouement based upon *Primavera* 192, the inarticulate

---

versions (ASW; Munthe), like certain Portuguese texts (*infra*), are preceded by *La apuesta ganada* (cf. Bénichou, p. 276).

For **Portugal** and **Brazil,** see VRP 52-91 and the bibliography listed on pp. 117-118; Michaëlis, "Estudos," pp. 199-201; S. Romero 7-9. Kundert's text of *Conde Claros fraile* (H3, pp. 86-87), in Galician-Portuguese, is from Hermisende in the Spanish province of Zamora. In some Portuguese versions, *Conde Claros y la infanta* combines with *Conde Claros fraile* (VRP 52-74), as in Castile and Morocco. In others, *La apuesta ganada* is followed by *Conde Claros fraile* (VRP 75-91, 987). Still others (Braga, I, 364-368; VRP 283) are contaminated with *El mal encanto* (*á-a*) (MP 108 *bis*; NSR, p. 71, no. 23); with *La adúltera* (*ó*); and with the *á-e* assonant version of *Galiarda* (*Primav.* 138, n. 4; Braga, I, 368; Delgado, *Subsídio,* II, 135-136); or with the theme of *La canción del huérfano* (Leite de Vasconcellos, "Romance popular de D. Carlos," pp. 189-191; VRP 986), concerning which see Catalán, "A caza de romances raros," pp. 466 ff., although the verses in question also occur in identical form in various other Portuguese ballads (cf. our review article, "Sobre unos romances del Cid recogidos en Tetuán," p. 393, n. 22).

For **Catalonia:** AFC 3263; Aguiló 317-328; Avenç, III, 34-37; Milá 258. Here *El mal encanto* (MP 108 bis) precedes *Conde Claros fraile.*

On the origin and geographic distribution of *Conde Claros fraile,* see RoH, I, 273; II, 397; VRP, I, 118. For the ballad's continental counterparts, see Child 65; Bronson 65 (*Lady Maisry*); DVM 67; Meier, *Balladen,* I, no. 29 (*König von Mailand*); and Aigner, pp. 215-218; Leader, pp. 179-223, 319, 321, 363; Vargyas, "Rapports," pp. 79-85; Id., *Researches,* pp. 105-110 (*The Dishonored Maiden*).

For the motif of the lover or husband who poses as a friar to confess his wife or beloved, compare Child 156 (*Queen Eleanor's Confession*); Nigra 97; Pitré, *Canti popolari siciliani,* II, 85-86; Bronzini, I, 43, 79, 114-115, 117-118, 127, 135, 164; II, 86, n. 36, 139-170, 178, n. 7 (*L'amante confessore*); RPM 329-330 (*La doncella que se confiesa con su galán*); Briz, II, 153-154, and AFC 2956 (*Lo confès fingit*); and the following motifs: J1141. *Confession obtained by a ruse*; J1545.2 . . . *A husband disguises as a priest to hear his wife's confession*; K1528. *Wife confesses to disguised husband.*

The **Portuguese, Brazilian, Catalan,** and **Argentine** traditions know versions of *Conde Claros y la infanta* in which the seduction of the Princess is followed by the imprisonment of Count Claros as in *Primavera* 190. Cf. Braga, I, 314-315; Leite de Vasconcellos, "Romance popular de D. Carlos," pp. 189-191; VRP 986; Boiteux, "Poranduba catarinense," pp. 20-21; Brandão, *Folklore de Alagoas* pp. 114-115; Pereira da Costa 313-314; S. Romero 7-8; Santos Neves, pp. 45 (no. 4), 51 (no. II); AFC 2973; Aguiló 305-314; Macabich 13-25; Moya, II, 23-24.

The **Eastern** and **Moroccan Sephardic** as well as the **Portuguese** traditions also know *Conde Claros y la infanta* as an independent ballad: e.g., Attias 30, PTJ 23*b* (= Attias); PTJ 23; and Braga, I, 306-309; VRP 50-51.

and almost totally formulistic endings of the Eastern texts can perhaps be linked to *Conde Claros en hábito de fraile* (*Primav.* 191, vv. 23 ff.). The final verse of Yoná's text B (= A, v. 16; Attias 31.39-40): "Yya se 'esparte 'el kavalyero, / yya se 'esparte 'i se va," though a recurrent formula (see no. 1, n. 1 *supra*), recalls *Primavera* 191, v. 44: "Ya se partía el conde, / ya se parte, ya se va."

The formulaic verses in which Count Claros travels slowly where he may be seen, but makes sparks fly from his horse's hoofs when he reaches deserted streets (A, vv. 17-18; Attias 31.41-44; LSO 77, vv. 14-15), occur in very similar form in many modern Peninsular versions of *Conde Claros fraile*:

Por donde le ve la gente   poquito a poquito va,
por donde no le ve nadie   corre como un gavilán.
(RPM 58)

Por onde no le ve gente   corre como un gavilán,
por onde le ve la gente   bien a poco a poco va.
(RPC 11) [8]

Such verses occur in at least one early ballad —*El desafío de Montesinos y Oliveros* ("En las salas de París": *Primav.* 177.29-30):

Por las calles que había gente,   íbase muy sosegado,
por do vía que no estaba,   va corriendo como un gamo. [9]

In the modern Peninsular and Eastern Sephardic traditions these verses lead a migratory existence. They occur in identical or similar form in *El Conde Dirlos* (RPM 48), *La mala suegra* (ASW 223; RPM 148) and *Galiarda enamorada en misa* (RPC 13; ART 218). [10] In the

---

[8] Cf. also RPM 59, 60, and RTO, pp. 44-45.

[9] Ultimately the same pattern is embodied in the following verses from *Cavalleros de Moclín*: "Por las calles de Alcalá, / corriendo va a media rienda; // y en saliendo de Alcalá, / corriendo va a rienda suelta" (Menéndez Pidal, *El Romancero Español,* p. 39).

[10] The examples from *Conde Dirlos* and *La mala suegra* are practically identical to those quoted from *Conde Claros fraile. Galiarda* reads:

Por donde les ve la gente   de amores se van tratando;
por donde no les ve nadie   de amores se van tomando.
(RPC 13)

Eastern tradition they are shared by *Conde Claros* and *La esposa de don García* (cf. no. 13, *infra*). One Moroccan text of *Conde Claros y el Emperador* offers a telescoped version of the same formula: "por la calle donde pasa / centellas hace saltar" (Larrea 30.56-57). In view of the formulistic and migratory nature of these verses, it is impossible to determine whether they formed part of some variant of *Conde Claros fraile* (*Primav*. 191), as the Peninsular texts seem to indicate, or if they belonged originally to a version of *Conde Claros y el Emperador*, like those current in the Moroccan tradition; or if, again, they are simply a borrowing from some other ballad, such as *La esposa de don García*.

BIBLIOGRAPHY

Eastern J.-Sp.: Attias 31; Hemsi, "Évocation," p. 1057*a* (= BRI); LSO 77, vv. 13-21; PTJ 22 (= Attias); UR 2 (= CBU 331-332; = GRI). LSO is preceded by verses from *La esposa de don García*. See also commentary above.

Moroccan J.-Sp.: Gil 31 (= MP); Larrea 27-31; MP 23; MRuiz 35; PTJ 22*a* (= MRuiz); Pulido 54 (= MP). Larrea 30 is preceded by *Isabel de Liar* (?) and followed by *La jactancia del Conde Vélez*. Larrea 31 and MRuiz are followed by the same ballad.

Archaic Texts: "A caza va el emperador": Durán 364; *Primavera* 191, vv. 1-18 (= *Cancionero de 1550*). "A misa va el emperador": *Pliegos góticos*, II, 293-297; *Pliegos de Praga*, I, 41-45; *Primavera* 192; Simón Díaz, III: 2, 2966; Wolf, "Ueber eine Sammlung," pp. 245-248. "Dormiendo está el Conde Claros":

Por donde la gente le vía el niño parece un santo,
por donde nadie le ve amores le van entrando.
(ART 218)

Analogous parallelistic formulas occur in versions of *La doncella guerrera* (RPM 266; FN 183) and *La mala suegra* (RPM 142):

Aquellas cuestas arriba corre como un gavilán,
aquellas cuestas abajo no hay ojos para mirar.

Por unas vegas alante no se tresvisa el andar,
por unas cuestas arriba parecía un gavilán.

For horses that strike sparks with their hoofs, see *Los estudiantes de Tolosa*: "De tan depressa qu'anava / las pedras van foguejant" (Milá 208.21); "Tant depressa que corria / les pedres van flamejant" (Sarri 126; AFC 2288; Aguiló, p. 261, vv. 85-86; Avenç, I, 13; Subirá, p. 31*b*); *La mala suegra*: "De tant que'l cavall corría / las pedras van fogueando" (Milá 243.17). Cf. also Canteloube, II, 196: "Qu'es aquel cabalhié / que fay flamba la ruyo?"

ASW 73-75; Durán 363; Castañeda-Huarte, II, 37-40; *Pliegos góticos,* III, 277-280; Simón Díaz, III: 2, 2986.

Studies (on the various ballads of *Conde Claros*): EEB, 104, 141, 183, 372; PHP 355-356, 362, 393; RoH, I, 64, 66, n. 9, 147, 273; II, 26, 28, 43-44, 47, 52, 84, 87-89, 100-101, 105-106, 187, 195-196, 200-201, 207, 211, 225, n. 47, 325, 331, 372, n. 16; RVP, pp. 107-114, 190, 259, n. 2, 270, n. 4, 274; TRV, II, 258-259, n. 2, 292-297, 402, 403. See also Menéndez Pidal, *La epopeya castellana,* pp. 147-148.

5

GAIFEROS JUGADOR

(Gaiferos the Gambler)

Por los palasyyos de Karlo   non pasan sinon ğugare.
Non ğugan plata ni 'oro,   sinon vías 'i sivdađes.
Ganó Karlo 'a Gayyfero   sus vías 'i sus sivdađes.
Ganó Gayyfero 'a Karlo   'i ala su mužer reale.
Más valí'a 'a peđrerla,   peđrerla ke non ganare:
—¡Sovrino, 'el mi sovrino,   'el mi sovrino karonale!
Yyo vos kre'í ğiketo,   'el Dyez te 'izo baragane.
'El te dyyo barvika rośa   'i 'en tu pu'erpo fu'ersa grande.
Lyyo vos di 'a Blankaninyya,   por mužer 'i por 'iguale.
Fu'iteś 'un 'ombre kovađo,   vola deśateś yevare,

Source: GSA 2. Variants: LRI 3; GRI 8.
Hemistich *b* of each verse, except v. 18, is repeated. GSA / LRI / GRI.
1*a* Por *in square letters GRI.*
1*b* ğugar *LRI.*
2*b* si non *GSA.*
3*a* Ganó Kayyro 'a Gafyero *LRI,* Ganó Kayyro 'a Gayyfero *GRI.*
4*a* Ganó Gayyfero 'a Kayyro *LRI.*
5*a* valyya *LRI.*
5*b* 'a pedrerla *GRI.*
6*b* 'i 'el mi *LRI / GRI.*
7*a* ğiketiko *GRI.*
7*b* 'el Dyyo *GRI. Milwitzky MS of GSA*: Dio.
9*a* Yyo *LRI / GRI.*
10*a* kovado *LRI / GRI.*
10*b* volo *GRI.*

'un dí'a 'estando 'en la milsa, 'en 'el verğel de vu'estro pađre,
kožendo rozas 'i flores, manyyana de Sanğiguare.
Maldisyyón vos 'eğo, 'el mi sovrino, si non la vaś 'a buśkare.
Por los kaminos ke vaś, non topéś vino ni pane,
ni menos dinero 'en bolsa para 'el kamino gastare.
Non deś sevađa 'a la mula, ni karne kruda al gavilane.
La mužer ke vos tuvyereś, non vos guadre kru'eldađe.
Los 'ižos ke vos paryere, non vos konoskan por padre.

11*a* 'estando *om. LRI / GRI.*

11*b* 'enel *in repetition GSA,* verğ 1 *GRI* (verğel *in repetition*).

14*b* non topéš ni vino ni pane *LRI / GRI* (non topéš vino ni pane *in repetition GRI*).

16*b* kruđa *in repetition GSA,* gavilano *GSA* (gavilane *in repetition*), gavilane *LRI,* gavilano *in both instances GRI.*

17*a* tuvyeraš *LRI / GRI.*

17*b* kru'eldad *GRI.*

Translation:

In the halls of Charlemagne's palace, they do nothing but gamble. They do not gamble for silver and gold, but for cities and towns. Charlemagne won from Gaiferos his cities and his towns. Gaiferos [then] beat Charlemagne and won his royal wife. (5) It would have been better to lose her, to lose her, not to win her. "Nephew, my nephew, blood nephew of mine! I raised you from childhood; God made you a valiant young man. He gave you a red beard and great strength in your body. I gave you Blancaniña for your wife and equal. (10) You were a coward, you let her be carried off one day from the chapel in your father's garden, while picking roses and flowers on the morning of Saint John. My curse be upon you, nephew, if you do not go in search of her: on the roads that you travel, may you find neither bread nor wine, (15) nor money in your purse to spend along the way. May you have no barley for your mule, nor raw meat for your hawk. May the wife that you take be unfaithful to you. (18) May the children that she bears you not recognize you as their father."

Motifs:

4 N2.6. *Wife as wager.*
10 R10.1. *Princess (maiden) abducted.*
13 Cf. H1219.3. *Quest assigned as punishment by father of abducted girl.*
14-18 M443. *Curse: privation*; M443.1. *Curse: lack of food, shelter, good company*; T230. *Faithlessness in marriage.*

The texts of *Gaiferos jugador* published to date (Attias; Díaz-Plaja) are both from Salonika, as are two unedited fragments in our collection. Menéndez Pidal reports versions from three additional localities: Jerusalem, Istib, and Istanbul (RoH, I, 289). The ballad seems to be unknown in Morocco.

The Eastern Judeo-Spanish *romance* is a rather distant and fragmentary congener of "Asentado está Gaiferos" (*Primav.* 173), which tells of the hero's single-handed expedition into the land of the Moors to rescue his wife, Melisenda, who is being held in captivity. The Judeo-Spanish texts comprise only the old ballad's initial scene, in which Charlemagne finds Gaiferos playing at dice [1] and reprimands him

[1] Gaiferos is playing *tablas,* a game probably not unlike backgammon. Concerning *tablas* and betting as a knightly activity and epic commonplace, see Menéndez Pidal, *Leyenda de los infantes de Lara,* p. 26, n. 2; Id., "Elena y María," *RFE,* I (1914), 52-96: p. 59 (vv. 130-141). In an episode of the prosified *Cantar del cerco de Zamora,* Alvar Fáñez begs King Sancho for a horse and weapons, explaining: "Yo iogue el cauallo et las armas que tenia" (PCG 501*a.* 19-20; Reig, *El cantar de Sancho II,* p. 230.20). In the second redaction of the *Cantar de los infantes de Lara* and in the ballad derived from it, Martín González is eulogized as a matchless player of *tablas*: "Tal jugador de tablas / non avia en toda España" (*Reliquias,* p. 207, v. 101); "Jugador era de tablas / el mejor de toda España" (*Primav.* 24). In a ballad of undoubted epic derivation concerning the childhood of Fernán González, recently discovered by Rodríguez-Moñino, instruction in the game of *tablas* forms part of the young hero's preparation for greatness:

Muéstrale a jugar las cañas y muéstrale a justador
también a jugar los dados y las tablas muy mejor.

See "Tres romances de la *Ensalada de Praga* (Siglo xvi)," p. 5. The text is reproduced, with important commentary, by Menéndez Pidal, *Romancero tradicional,* II, 283 ff.

for not continuing his efforts to rescue the captive Melisenda. Other branches of the Hispanic tradition, notably the archaic lateral areas of Portugal and Catalonia, preserve more comprehensive, though still radically abbreviated, versions of the sixteenth-century narrative. These Peninsular texts begin by representing Gaiferos engaged in a game of chance, but also go on to tell of Melisenda's rescue by the hero, as in *Primavera* 173. There seems to be little if any direct relationship

---

The ballad, "Caballero de lejas tierras," describes its protagonist as "muy gran jugador de tablas / y también del ajedrez" (*Vuelta del marido* [*é*]: *Primav.* 156). By contrast, gambling and *tablas* in particular are elsewhere scorned as unworthy of knighthood: for example, in *El desafío de Montesinos y Oliveros* (*Primav.* 177, p. 398) and in *El entierro de Fernand Arias* (FN 149; *Primav.* 50):

que ni morís por mesones,   ni por tableros jugando;
morís como caballero   en el campo peleando.

que no murió entre las damas,   ni menos tablas jugando:
mas murió sobre Zamora   vuestra honra resguardando.

The Spanish translation of Guido de Colonna's *Historia Destructionis Troiæ* alludes to "el juego de las tablas, el qual suele promouer los jugadores en arrebatada yra" (F. P. Norris, *La coronica troyana,* Ph.D. dissertation, UCLA, 1965, p. 133). For other references to *tablas,* see Prior, *Ancient Danish Ballads,* III, 143-144; *The Poetic Edda,* trans. Hollander, p. 127, n. 35.

Primavera 173, v. 3, presents Gaiferos in the act of throwing dice ("Los dados tiene en la mano / que los quiere arrojar"). A variant form of this verse, in which he actually throws the dice to the floor, has migrated to several ballads in the Moroccan Sephardic tradition: *Búcar sobre Valencia* (see our article "Sobre unos romances del Cid," p. 388), *La buena hija* (Larrea 180), and *El hijo vengador* (Larrea 182):

Los dados tiene en la mano,   al suelo los arronxara. . . .
(Arce 1.24)

Los dados tiene en la mano,   al suelo los arronxare. . . .
(Larrea 180.34-35)

Dados tenía en la mano   y al suelo los arrojase. . . .
(Larrea 182.17-18)

These verses are doubtless influenced by a variant form of a later stage of the narrative. In *Primavera* 173, Gaiferos, enraged by Charlemagne's reprimand, is about to throw the gaming board to the floor, but restrains himself out of respect for his partner Guarinos. In other traditional versions, his rage gets the better of him and he throws dice, cards, and board to the floor (cf. RoH, I, 288).

Concerning the game of chess as an epic and balladic commonplace, see Poncet y de Cárdenas, "El romance en Cuba," pp. 239-241; Chacón, "Romances tradicionales en Cuba," p. 108.

¶ Romãce de dõ gayferos y trata de como saco a su esposa q̃ estaua catiua en tierra de moros.

ASsentado esta gayferos
enel palacio real
assentado al tablero
para las tablas jugar
los dados tiene enla mano
que los queria arrojar
quando entrara por la sala
don carlos el emperante
desque ansi jugar lo vido
empeçole de mirare
hablando esta hablando
palabras de gran pesare
si tã bueno fuesseys gayferos
para las armas tomar
como soys para los dados
y para las tablas jugar
vuestra esposa tienen moros
yriades la a buscar
pesa me a mi por ello
porques mi hija carnal
de muchos fue demandada
y a nadie quiso tomar
pues cõ vos caso por amores
amores layan de sacar
si con otro fuera casada
nostuuiera en catiuidad
Gayferos que esto oyera
mouido de gran pesar
leuantosse del tablero
no queriendo mas jugar
a manos toma el tablero
para hauerlo de arrojar
sino por el que conel juega
quera hombre de linaje
jugaua conel guarinos
almirante dela mare
bozes da porel palacio
que al cielo quieren llegare
pregũtando va pregũtando
por su tio don roldane
hallaralo enel patin
que queria caualgare
conel estaua Oliueros
y el galan Durandarte
conel muchos caualleros
daquellos delos doze pares

FIG. 3.—Gayferos playing at *tablas* according to a broadside printed in Valencia, ca. 1540 (British Museum).

between the Sephardic ballad and its distant Portuguese and Catalan congeners, which, comparatively speaking, stay closer to the version printed in the sixteenth century.[2] The episode of Gaiferos' rescue of Melisenda is known in the Eastern Judeo-Spanish communities of Salonika and Jerusalem as a separate ballad, independent of *Gaiferos jugador,* but now joined to the *romance fronterizo* of *El moro de Antequera* (= *Primav.* 74).

The Sephardic *Gaiferos jugador,* in its present form, shows little similarity to the known sixteenth-century texts and probably goes back to a rather different archaic variant of the story. Numerous extraneous elements have also been added to the narrative. In the Judeo-Spanish ballad, Charlemagne has taken the part of Roland as Gaiferos' uncle. In *Primavera* 173, the Emperor appears as the hero's father-in-law, but the attribution of the traditional uncle-nephew relationship to Charlemagne and Gaiferos is also of respectable antiquity.[3] The sixteenth-

---

[2] All the same, they too derive from a slightly different archaic redaction. See RoH, I, 288.

[3] On nephews (sister's sons) in medieval epicry as a survival of matriarchal institutions, see especially F. B. Gummere, "The Sister's Son," *An English Miscellany Presented to Dr. Furnivall* ... (Oxford, 1901), pp. 133-149; W. A. Nitze, "The Sister's Son and the Conte del Graal," *MPh,* IX (1912), 291-322; W. O. Farnsworth, *Uncle and Nephew in the Old French Chansons de Geste,* New York, 1913; A. W. Aron, *Traces of Matriarchy in Germanic Hero-Lore,* in *University of Wisconsin Studies in Language and Literature,* no. 9 (Madison, 1920); C. H. Bell, *The Sister's Son in the Medieval German Epic, UCPMPh,* vol. 10 (Berkeley, 1922), pp. 67-182; also A. B. Franklin, "A Study of the Origins of the Legend of Bernardo del Carpio," *HR,* V (1937), 286-303: p. 301 at n. 23; R. Briffault, *The Mothers,* 3 vols. (New York, 1927), I, 414-415; F. B. Gummere, *The Oldest English Epic* (New York, 1910), p. 195, n. 1; Id., *The Popular Ballad,* pp. 121, 125, 182-184; Krappe, *The Science of Folklore,* p. 178, n. 14.

In the *Nota Emilianense,* the Twelve Peers are all said to be nephews of the Emperor (see D. Alonso, *Primavera temprana,* p. 99). The hero's fraternal nephews play an important rôle in later manifestations of the Cid epics. Cf. Armistead, "Para el texto de la *Refundición de las Mocedades de Rodrigo,*" p. 535. The same *topos* is probably reflected in the identification of Diego Ordóñez as "sobrino del conde don Garçia el Crespo de Grannon" in the prosified *Cantar del cerco de Zamora.* See Armistead, *A Lost Version of the ... Mocedades de Rodrigo ...* , p. 312, nn. 30-31. In a late variant of *El abad Don Juan de Montemayor,* the anti-hero García-Zulema is identified as nephew of the Abbot, thus emphasizing the odium of his traitorous actions. See Menéndez Pidal, *Historia y epopeya,* p. 163 at n. 2. Likewise, Ruy Velázquez's treachery against the Infantes de Lara is even more hateful since they are his nephews.

As in the *chansons de geste,* uncle-nephew relationships are frequently emphasized in the Carolingian and Pseudo-Carolingian *romances*: Dirlos and Don

century *Conde Dirlos,* like the Sephardic *Gaiferos jugador,* represents Gaiferos as "sobrino del emperante" (*Primav.* 164, p. 346).

The incongruous scene in which Charlemagne and Gaiferos play against each other in a game of chance and the Emperor loses his wife to Gaiferos has nothing to do with the original story. The Sephardic ballad has apparently been influenced by the *Wife, Daughter, Damsel as wager* motif (N2.6, N2.6.2, N2.6.3), which is known to several other Judeo-Spanish *romances*: that is, *Rico Franco* (no. 18 *infra*), *El jugador* (MP 112; MRuiz 86.14 ff.), and *La novia sorteada.*[4] There is also a distant similarity with another ballad which, like *Gaiferos,* concerns the rescue of a damsel held prisoner by the Moors. *Moriana y Galván* (*Primav.* 121) also begins by presenting the protagonists engaged in a game of *tablas*:

> Moriana en un castillo juega con el moro Galván;
> juegan los dos a las tablas por mayor placer tomar.
> Cada vez que el moro pierde bien perdía una cibdad;
> cuando Moriana pierde la mano le da a besar.

Perhaps the coincidence of both ballads' beginning with a gambling scene facilitated the migration of certain formulistic verses from *Moriana* to *Gaiferos jugador.* Yoná's vv. 11-12 agree with *Primavera* 121

Beltrán (*Primav.* 164), Valdovinos and the Marqués de Mantua (*Primav.* 165), Gaiferos and the uncle who helps him take revenge upon Galván (*Primav.* 171-172), Gaiferos and the Emperor (*Primav.* 164, p. 346), Gaiferos and Roland (*Primav.* 173), Grifos Lombardo and Don Golfo (*El conde preso*: RCan, pp. 15-16). See also the curious fragment published by M. Joaquim (no. 13: "Nora buena vengáis, tío, / hermano de la mi madre"). The same commonplace makes Count Claros Charlemagne's nephew in the Sephardic *Conde Claros y el Emperador* (no. 4 *supra*). "Tío y sobrino" are the protagonists of the problematic Eastern Judeo-Spanish *Sierpe del río* (Attias 29.21 ff.; Benardete 3) and the Moroccan *Rey envidioso de su sobrino* (MP 123).

[4] Attias 118; Besso, "Matrimonios sefardíes," p. 275; Hemsi 23; UR 4 (= CBU 333-334). Concerning the motif in *Rico Franco,* see "Hispanic Balladry," p. 238, n. 25.

For other examples of *The Damsel as Wager* motif in balladry, compare the Catalan *Bon caçador* (OCPC, III, 148-149, 153-155), the French *Retour du cavalier* (Tarbé, II, 123), the German *Schwabentöchterlein* (Meier, *Balladen,* II, no. 75), and the Scandinavian *Tærningspillet* (Dal, nos. 33 and 76; DgF, IV, no. 238; Olrik, I, no. 39; Prior, III, 143-149; Smith-Dampier, pp. 213-216), *Fæstemøens Hævn* (DgF, IV, no. 192), and *Den lille båtsmannen* (Arwidsson, II, no. 103; Geijer-Afzelius, no. 31; FSF, no. 51; Warrens, pp. 138-143) or *Taflkvæði* (Grundtvig-Sigurðsson, no. 38).

("Captiváronla los moros / la mañana de Sant Juan, // cogiendo rosas y flores / en la huerta de su padre."), [5] although the readings *mañanica* and *vergel* and the use of the name *Juliana* (*Ğuliana*) in Attias, in an unedited version collected by Mrs. Crews, and in others known to Menéndez Pidal (RoH, I, 289), suggest rather the influence of almost identical verses embodied in the *romance* of *Julianesa* ("¡Arriba, canes, arriba!": *Primav.* 124):

> Pues me la han tomado moros mañanica de Sant Juan,
> cogiendo rosas y flores en un vergel de su padre. [6]

In any case, the heroine who is abducted while picking flowers appears in several other ballads current in the modern Hispanic tradition. Under such circumstances, Blancaflor is carried off by the Moors in North African, Castilian, Portuguese, and Catalan versions of *Las hermanas reina y cautiva.* Sometimes it is even from her father's garden (VRP 634; RTR 13) as in *Julianesa*:

> que la cautivaron moros, día de Pascua Florida,
> cogiendo rosas y flores en las huertas de Almería.
> (Alvar, "Cinco romances," no. 1.53-56)

> que la cautivaron moros, días de Pascua Florida,
> cogiendo rosas y flores para la Virgen María.
> (*or* estando cogiendo flores en un jardín que tenía.)
> (RPM 205-206) [7]

---

[5] Attias' version places similar verses at the end of the ballad. Díaz-Plaja contains only the reference to the girl's capture on St. John's morn. Inexplicable, in this context, is the topic reference to *milsa* (= *misa* 'mass' or, by extension, 'chapel'), which occurs only in Yoná. On attendance at mass as a Pan-Hispanic ballad *topos,* see our study on "Christian Elements and De-Christianization in the Sephardic *Romancero,*" pp. 29, 32, 37.

[6] Actually *Moriana* and *Julianesa* are variants of one and the same narrative. Cf. RoH, I, 262. In Morocco, Julianesa is the principal character of a ballad which is essentially identical to *Moriana y Galván* (*Primav.* 121) and which continues with the Julianesa monolog (= *Primav.* 124), including the flashback concerning her abduction from her father's garden. Cf. Larrea 78-81, Ortega 230-231, FN 208-209, and Bénichou's important commentary, pp. 265-266. The same narrative components are similarly combined in the early Portuguese tradition, with an additional contamination (vv. 16 and 31-34) from the enigmatic historical ballad "A las armas, Moriscote." See Joaquim, no. 7 (cf. RoH, II, 55-57). Here the female protagonist is "Aliarda."

[7] Cf. Córdova y Oña, IV, 254; RTR 13.

que a cativaram os Mouros, dia de Páscoa florida,
andando a colher flores no jardim que meu pai tinha.
(VRP 634)

que'ls moros la cautivaron una mañanita fría,
cojiendo rosas y flores en un jardín que tenía.
(Milá 242.27-28)

Similar, and in some cases identical, verses to those of RPM 205 reappear in Castilian versions of the octosyllabic *Don Bueso y su hermana* (RPM 63, 196, 201, 202; RTR 11), in *La esposa de Don García* (RPM 16), and in a religious ballad recorded by Kundert (G8, pp. 89-90). Lope de Vega uses the same *topos,* probably borrowed from *Julianesa,* in a bi-lingual—Castilian and Galician—imitation of traditional ballad language: "Cautiváronla los moiros / mañanita de San Joan, // collendo rosas y frores // riberiñas de la mar." [8]

The Emperor's allusion to Gaiferos' upbringing and marriage (Yoná, vv. 7-9) also seems to be extraneous to the ballad's archaic form. The verses in question combine elements present in sixteenth-century variants of *La infancia de Gaiferos* ("Estábase la condesa": *Primav.* 171) and *Don García cercado en Urueña* ("Atal anda don García": *Primav.* 133):

Dios te dé barbas en rostro y te haga barragán.
(*Infancia*) [9]

Dios os dexe crecer, hijo, y llegar a barragán.
Dios os dé barba en el rostro & en el cuerpo fuerça grande.
(*Infancia*) [10]

Crióme el Rey de pequeño, hízome Dios barragane: ...
diérame a doña María por muger y por yguale.
(*Don García*) [11]

---

[8] RoH, II, 208. Cf. also Milá 115 (= a ballad entitled *Francisco*) which exemplifies the same *topos*; and *El palmero* (*Primav.* 195, pp. 459-460).

[9] *Primavera* 171 = CSA, fol. 103v. Cf. Castañeda-Huarte, II, 9; *Pliegos góticos,* II, 69; III, 273; *Pliegos de Praga,* I, 188.

[10] *Pliegos de Praga,* I, 201 (= variant to *Primav.* 171).

[11] Rodríguez-Moñino and Devoto, *Cancionero llamado Flor de enamorados,* fol. 49r-v; *Primavera* 133. Cf. also the Moroccan *Nacimiento de Montesinos* (MP 25; Bénichou 26; Larrea 34).

The curse with which Charlemagne threatens the hero if he fails to go in search of his captive wife also seems to belong exclusively to the Sephardic texts. Yoná and Attias are similar at this point, although the latter is less elaborate. In Díaz-Plaja, the curse is couched in rather different terms:

Maldición te echo, sobrino,   si no la vayas buscare:
desnudo vayas por los soles   y descalço por los muladares,
no topes árbol ni hoja   para tu cabayo lasare,
no topes pan ni vino   para tu alma abedivare,
la gente que te pregunten   no tengas piedade.

Verse 16 of Yoná's texts need not have been borrowed from *La mala suegra* (no. 14 *infra*), where a similar verse occurs in most Eastern Sephardic and in some Peninsular versions ("daré cebada a la mula / y carne cruda al gavilane" [Attias 38.21-22; cf. Yoná 14.10]; "cebada para la mula, / carne para el gavilán" [RPM 136]). An analogous reference to privations suffered jointly by the traveling or banished protagonist and his faithful horse occurs in at least one Azorian version of *Floresvento*: "Que não tenha pão, nem vinho, / nem comida o seu cavallo!" (Braga, I, 224). The verse involving mule and hawk, found in both *La mala suegra* and *Gaiferos,* is formulistic and occurs practically verbatim in the archaic *romancillo* of *La serranilla de la Zarzuela*:

Yo me yva, mi madre,   a Villa Reale,
errara yo el camino   en fuerte lugare.
Siete días anduve   que no comí pane,
cevada mi mula   carne el gavilán. [12]

Charlemagne's imprecations against Gaiferos have about them an authentic flavor of Carolingian balladry. Some of them might well have formed part of a now unknown archaic variant of *Gaiferos jugador*. The terms of the Emperor's curse are reminiscent of hardships which the hero, in *Primavera* 173, claims to have already undergone in a vain search for Melisenda:

Tres años anduve triste   por los montes y los valles,
comiendo la carne cruda,   bebiendo la roja sangre,

---

[12] R. Menéndez Pidal, "Serranilla de la Zarzuela," *StM,* II (1906-1907), p. 265; reprinted in *Poesía árabe y poesía europea,* p. 102.

trayendo los pies descalzos, las uñas corriendo sangre.
Nunca yo hallarla pude en cuanto pude buscar. [13]

The Emperor's curse also recalls the privations with which the retreating French are threatened in *Roncesvalles*: "ni vos da pan a comeres, / . . . // ni vos da moneda en bolsa / para puedervos rejir" (Attias 32.15, 17-18). Similar rigors attend the exile of Count Grimaltos, father of Montesinos, in *Primavera* 175 (p. 389):

Plazo le dan de tres días para el reino vaciar
y el destierro es de esta suerte: que gente no ha de llevar,
caballeros, ni criados no le hayan de acompañar,
ni lleve caballo o mula en que pueda cabalgar:
moneda de plata y oro deje y aun la de metal.

The final verses of Yoná's version, which evoke wifely infidelity and filial alienation as part of Gaiferos' misfortunes, agree with the Portuguese ballad on the banishment of *Floresvento*:

Vem-te cá, oh filho meu, que te quero amaldiçoar!
Que a mulher com quem casares nunca te seja leal.
(Braga, I, 225)

Vai-te embora, cruel vento, lá p'ràs ondinhas do mar,
Os rios onde tu passares, logo se hão-de turbar;
a fonte onde beberes, logo se há-de secar;
a mulher que tu tiveres, nunca t'há-de ser leal;
os filhos que tu tiveres, nunca os há-de lograr.
(VRP 36) [14]

---

[13] *Primavera* 173 (p. 377). On the formulistic nature of these verses, see RoH, I, 267; TRV, II, 256. Similar verses occur in *Moriana-Julianesa* (*Primav.* 121, 124), *La venganza de Montesinos* (*Primav.* 176), *De Mérida sale el palmero* (*Primav.* 195), *Airado va el escudero* (Barbieri, no. 325; MME, V, 142-143). Cf. also the *Refundición de las Mocedades de Rodrigo* (*Reliquias*, p. 282, vv. 888-890).

[14] For other versions of *Floresvento*, which derives from the *chanson de geste* of *Floovant*, see VRP 34-37 and the bibliography on p. 45; also Pérez Vidal, "*Floresvento* y *La esposa infiel*." The prohibition against supplying food to the banished person is present in the ballad's French source (cf. Menéndez Pidal, "Poesía tradicional en el Romancero hispano-portugués," p. 57). On the terms of Floresvento's exile and, by extension, of similar passages elsewhere in the *Romancero* as a possible reflection of Germanic legal practice, see Braga,

To summarize: In the course of its complex traditional life, the ballad of *Gaiferos jugador* has attracted to itself a number of extraneous elements: The *topos* of the wife as wager (N2.6), the abduction of Julianesa on St. John's morn, topic verses on the hero's education drawn from *La infancia de Gaiferos* and *Don García en Urueña,* to say nothing of noteworthy contaminations from *Conde Claros y el Emperador* and *La esposa de Don García,* which appear in unedited versions in our collection, as well as the formulistic terms of Charlemagne's curse, which may or may not be an original part of the ballad. In its multiple contaminations, *Gaiferos jugador* exemplifies a type of rhapsodic, pseudomorphic process, not uncommon in the Sephardic tradition, [15] through which essential elements of a ballad may be almost totally replaced by *topoi* and formulaic features drawn from other, sometimes quite unrelated sources. In *Gaiferos jugador,* the essential ingredients of the plot are still in evidence—the hero, playing a game of chance, is reproached for not rescuing his captive wife—but the individual components used to elaborate upon this basic situation are drawn mostly from extraneous sources. All that remains is a skeleton of the original narrative which has been almost completely reclothed in foreign materials.

BIBLIOGRAPHY

Eastern J.-Sp.: The Eastern tradition splits the archaic *Gaiferos* narrative into two separate ballads:

Gaiferos jugador

Attias 26; Benardete 50 (essentially identical to GSA); [16] Díaz-Plaja 11; Milwitzky, "El viajero filólogo," p. 325 (= GSA); PTJ 27-27*a* (= Attias, Díaz-Plaja). See also RoH, I, 289.

III, 404-405. The terms of the Cid's exile reflect the same usage. See *Cantar de Mio Cid,* III, vv. 21 ff., and II, 585-586 (s.v. *compra*), for historical and legal precedents.

[15] Cf. Alvar, "Patología y terapéutica rapsódicas," which concerns a Moroccan derivative of *La lavandera de San Juan.* For additional details, see DRH, p. 73, n. 67. For similar cases of successive contamination in the sixteenth-century tradition, see Menéndez Pidal, "Poesía popular y romancero," IX, 274-275.

[16] On p. 43 of his thesis, Benardete alludes to a relationship between this text and a certain "Güerta de Historia" published by Yoná. Is Benardete's text

Gaiferos y Melisenda

Attias 27; Coello 9; Gil 35 —first text only— (= Coello); Giménez Caballero, p. 371 (text G); MP 27 (= Coello); PTJ 26 (= Coello); SICh 3.1-5. Attias, Coello, and SICh are contaminated with *El moro de Antequera.* See "Dos romances fronterizos," no. 2 and pp. 92-93, n. 11; DRH 4.

Portuguese: Almeida Garrett, II, 261-276; Bellermann, pp. 30-55; Braga, I, 211-220; Hardung, II, 3-24; Pires de Lima-Lima Carneiro, *Romanceiro para o povo e para as escolas,* pp. 54-60; Chaves, "O ciclo dos descobrimentos," pp. 114-115; Id., "O Romanceiro e o teatro popular," pp. 371-372; Martins, I, 192-193; II, 39-40; Tavares, *RL,* VIII, 74; Id., *Ilustração Trasmontana,* II, 28; VRP 45-49. See also RoH, I, 287-288 and n. 76.

Catalan: AFC 3249; Aguiló 195-204; Macabich 111-127; Milá 247; RoH, I, 287-289.

Spanish American: On the ballads' possible currency in Peru during the colonial period, see E. Romero, *Perú,* p. 15; Simmons, nos. 1767-1768, 1798, 1811.

Archaic Texts:

"Asentado está Gaiferos"

ASW 134-135; Bibl. Nationale (Paris), Departement des Imprimés, Res. Y-G. 114-119 (entrés) 8.480; Castañeda-Huarte, II, 115-122; CSA, fols. 55*r*-65*v*; Durán 377; *Pliegos góticos,* III, 57-64; *Pliegos de Praga,* I, 5, 193-200; Porębowicz, p. 7; *Primavera* 173; Rodríguez-Moñino, *Pliegos de Morbecq,* pp. 41-44, 51, 103, 125-132; Id. "Tortajada," no. 3; Id., *Cancionero de 1511: Noticias bibliográficas,* p. 121 (no. 108); RVP, pp. 89-90; *Silva de 1561,* fols. 58*v*-68*v*; Simón Díaz, III:2, 2990, 7580; Thomas, *Romance de don Gayferos,* pp. 7-25; Wilson-Sage 46. See also the adaptation in *octavas* published by Foulché-Delbosc, "Les romancerillos de la Bibliothèque Ambrosienne," pp. 605-606 (no. 98: "Iugando está a las tablas don Gayferos"); cf. Simón Díaz, III:2, 3095; 7580; C. L. Penney, *Printed Books 1468-1700 in the Hispanic Society of America* (New York, 1965), p. 479.

"Caballero si a Francia ides"

ASW 76; Durán 319; Joaquim, no. 6 (pp. 157-158); Lucas Rodríguez, pp. 269-270; MME, V, no. 113; Id., VIII, no. 25; Ontañón de Lope, no. 10; *Primavera* 155; Rodríguez-Moñino, *Flor de romances, glosas,* etc., pp. 245-247; RoH, I, 287, 376-377; RVP, pp. 91, 92, 94, 270; Simón Díaz, III:2, 3095; Timoneda,

---

based on this publication, or on GSA itself, which figures in his bibliography (p. 2)?

Rosa de Amores, fol. 26*r-v*. Cf. also Barbieri 323 ("Si d'amor pena sentís"). For an *a lo divino* adaptation, see Menéndez Pidal, *El Romancero Español,* p. 90.

Continental analogs: Gaiferos' rescue of Melisenda is ultimately related to the Germanic epic of Walter of Aquitaine, exemplified by the Latin *Waltharius,* the Anglo-Saxon *Waldere, Thidrekssaga* (pp. 281-283), stanza 1756 of the *Nibelungenlied,* and other Germanic poetic remnants (cf. Strecker, *Ekkehards Waltharius,* pp. 100 ff.). The Franco-Catalan ballad of *Escrivette-Escriveta* and the Italian *Moro saracino* probably share a common intermediate source with *Gaiferos.* For **Catalan** texts: AFC 2222; Aguiló 183-192; Avenç, I, 40-46; Briz, III, 65-70; Capdevila 58-59; Capmany, no. 26; Milá 205; Sarri 116-117. **French:** Arbaud, II, 73-81; Canteloube, I, 111; II, 72; Davenson 5; Doncieux 8; Udry, pp. 99-104. **Italian:** Nigra 40. See also Peirone, "Un caso di trasumanza del ciclo carolingio." On *L'Escrivette,* see also DVM, V, 39-40. For a distant **Slavic** analog, see Schirmunski, p. 103 (no. 2). For an early, negative view of the traditional link between *Waltharius* and *Gaiferos,* see S. G. Morley, *Spanish Ballad Problems: The Native Historical Themes, UCPMPh,* 13 (Berkeley, 1925), 207-228: p. 224, n. 32.

Studies: Braga, III, 396-403; CSA, p. xii (fol. 55); EEB 78-79; Hanssen, "Sobre la poesía épica de los visigodos," pp. 300-306; Menéndez Pidal, *La epopeya castellana,* pp. 23-26; Id., "El estado latente en la vida tradicional," *Revista de Occidente,* I, no. 2 (1963), 129-152: pp. 146-151; Id., *Los godos y la epopeya española,* pp. 41-48; Id., "Poesía popular y romancero," VIII, 261; Id., *El Romancero Español,* pp. 22-23; Morley, "A New Jewish-Spanish *Romancero,*" p. 5; PHP 432-434; RoH, I, 169, 286-300; II, 419-420; RVP 89-91; TRV, II, 273-281, 383. Ch. V. Aubrun's unconvincing "Gaiferos, Calaínos, Almenique, et autres noms bizarres du Romancéro," *Miscelánea en Homenaje a Monseñor Higinio Anglés,* I (Barcelona, 1958-1961), 72-78, adds nothing to the understanding of the Gaiferos ballads' traditional development.

6

MELISENDA SALE DE LOS BAÑOS

(Melisenda Leaving the Baths)

'Esta noğe, mis kavayeros, dormir kon 'una senyyora.
'Un dí'a de los mis días non topí 'otra komo 'elyya.
Blanka 'es 'i korolada, 'ermoza komo la 'estre'a.
Ala baśada de 'un rí'o 'i ala suvida de 'un valye,
'eskontrí kon mi Lizelda, la 'iža del 'emperador,
ke vení'a de los banyyos 'i de los banyyos de lavarse,
de lavarse 'i 'entrensarse 'i de mudarse 'una delgada.
Diśo la kondesa al konde: —'I konde ¿por ké non kazateś?
—Kazaré si 'el Dyyo kere, kazaré si 'a 'El le plaze.

Sources: LRI 4. Variants: BRI 3; RHP 4; GRI 3.
Hemistich *b* of each verse is repeated except in the case of v. 14. LRI / BRI / RHP / GRI.

1*a* 'Esta *in square letters BRI / GRI,* kavalyeros *BRI / GRI.*
1*b* ¡'O! dormir *RHP,* dormir kero kon 'una senyyora *GRI.*
3*a* korelada *BRI,* kolorada *RHP / GRI.*
3*b* komo 'es la 'estre'a *RHP.*
4*a* 'A la abašada *BRI,* Ala abašada *RHP,* La abašada *GRI.*
5*a* 'Enkontrí *BRI / RHP / GRI,* mi 'Izela *GRI.*
6*a* venían *GRI.*
6*b* delos (*written as one word*) *GRI.*
7*b* demudarse (*written as one word*) *in repetition LRI.*
8*b* no *in repetition LRI.*
9*a* kyere *GRI.*
9*b* 'i kazaré *GRI,* 'i kazaré si 'a 'el Dyyo le plaze *in repetition GRI,* 'i kazaré si al Dyyo le plaze *RHP.*

10 Tomaré mužer ğiketa 'i ğika de la poka 'edade.
Ke se'a ğika de anyyos 'i de 'el 'entendimyento grande.
Ke se'a alta sin ğapines 'i 'ermoza sin afeytarse.
Los 'ižikos ke me paryere me asemežen 'a la madre.
14 Poko más, 'un poko manko, ke me asemežen al padre.

10*b* dela (*written as one word*) *in repetition GRI,* eđađ *BRI / RHP.*
13*b* ala *BRI / RHP / GRI.*
14*a* Poko más 'o poko manko *BRI / RHP / GRI.*
14*b* 'a 'el padre *GRI.*

Translation:

Tonight, my lords, I slept with a lady. Never in all my days did I find another like her. She is fair and rosy-cheeked, as beautiful as a star. Going down to the river, on the way out of the valley, (5) I met my Lizelda, the Emperor's daughter, who was returning from the baths, from bathing at the baths, from bathing and braiding her hair and changing into a fine chemise. Said the Countess to the Count, "Count, why don't you marry?" "I shall marry if God wills it; I shall marry if it please Him. (10) I shall take a young wife, a wife young in years but of great wisdom. She must be tall without raised slippers and beautiful without adornment. The children that she may bear me must resemble their mother, (14) and a little more or less must they resemble their father."

The ballad of *Melisenda leaving the baths,* a version of which was sung with mystical implications by Shabbethai Zevi, the false Messiah, in Smyrna in 1667, can be related to an otherwise unknown sixteenth-century Spanish *incipit,* recorded in the Prague Library's famous *Ensalada de muchos romances viejos y cantarcillos*: "Ya se sale Melisendra / de los baños de bañar" (*Pliegos de Praga,* I, 7). This verse is apparently echoed in Yoná's vv. 5-6.

The name *Melisendra, Melisenda, Melizelda,* or here, through popular etymology, *mi Lizelda,* is common to various Spanish ballad heroines. It derives from the Old French *Belissent* who, as in our *romance,* appears as Charlemagne's daughter in several *chansons de geste.*[1] The precise origin of the present ballad, in which the Princess is described as she is leaving the baths, has yet to be established.[2]

Today *Melisenda sale de los baños* seems to be known only in the Eastern Sephardic tradition. Most versions, Yoná's included, are disappointingly incomplete. Aside from minimal differences and the deformation of the initial verses, Uziel's text (UYA) is practically identical to that of Yoná. There is even closer identity (apart from the preferable readings "doncella" and "En día" in vv. 1b and 2a) between Molho's version (LSO) and that of BRI, although the former, unlike Yoná's text, attests in v. 6 to a contamination from the ballad of *Silvana* (no. 20 *infra*). Molho's reading "que venía de los baños, / y de los baños de agua fría" is paralleled in *Silvana,* where it is followed in some versions by a verse corresponding to 7 of Yoná's version of *Melisenda.* Attias' text of *Silvana* (no. 41.15-18) reads:

Déjame ir a los baños, a los baños d'agua fría,
a lavarme y a entrenzarme y a mudar una camisa.

The first three *é-a* assonant verses of Yoná-Uziel-Molho and of four unedited Salonikan texts in Menéndez Pidal's collection[3] are borrowed

---

1 See TRV, II, 279, 283-285; Menéndez Pidal, *El Romancero Español,* p. 31; RoH, I, 261. A "princesa Melisen" figures in the Catalan *Testament de n'Amelis* (Aguiló, p. 153). For occurrences of the French name, see Bédier, *Les légendes épiques,* II, 271, 273, 275, 283; Langlois, *Table de noms propres,* pp. 83-84 (s.v. *Belisant-Bellissent*). In Moroccan versions of *Melisenda insomne,* the protagonist is sometimes *Melisera,* sometimes *Belizera* (MP 28; Bénichou 2; Larrea 39-41). The Spanish forms in *M-* seem to be etymologically more correct. See E. G. Withycombe, *The Oxford Dictionary of English Christian Names,* 2d ed. (Oxford, 1963), s.v. *Millicent, Melicent* (Historically there was no daughter of Charlemagne by this name. See Einhard, *The Life of Charlemagne* [Ann Arbor, 1960], pp. 45-46, 75). For documentation of the name's Germanic etymon, *Amalasuintha,* and the development of such intermediate forms as *Malasintha,* see E. Förstemann, *Altdeutsches Namenbuch,* I: *Personennamen,* 2d ed. (Bonn, 1900), p. 95; W. Meyer-Lübke, *Romanische Namenstudien,* I: *Die altportugiesischen Personennamen germanischen Ursprungs* (Vienna, 1904), p. 11; M. Schönfeld, *Wörterbuch der Altgermanischen Personen- und Völkernamen* (Heidelberg, 1911), pp. 15-16, 159; J. M. Piel, "Sobre a formação dos nomes de mulher medievais hispano-visigodos," *EMP,* VI (Madrid, 1956), 111-150: pp. 130-131. Langlois (p. 450) records a single occurrence of the personal name *Milesent,* unconnected with Charlemagne, in the *chansons de geste.*

2 Cf. Menéndez Pidal, "Un viejo romance," p. 188; RoH, II, 225 at n. 47.

3 "Un viejo romance," p. 189, n. 2; RoH, II, 223, n. 41.

from some variant of *Galiarda y el alabancioso* or *Galiarda enamorada en misa.*[4] The archaic forms of this ballad (*Primav.* 139, etc.), as well as its modern Castilian counterpart (RPM 184; RPC 13-14), attest only to the origin of the first two verses of Yoná, while the Moroccan versions (Bénichou 34; Ortega 220) parallel Yoná's v. 1 and the formulistic, migratory v. 3.[5] Combined, the Moroccan and Peninsular forms of *Galiarda* integrate all the elements present in the initial contamination of the Eastern *Melisenda sale de los baños*:

Esta noche, caballeros, dormí con una doncella,
que en los días de mi vida, yo no vi cosa más bella.
(*Primav.*)

Anoche, los caballeros, dormí con una doncella.
De lo que ha que vine al mundo no he visto cama más bella.
(RPM)

Por los años de mi vida no pasé noche más bella,
que fue la noche pasada, dormí con una doncella.
(RPC)

Anoche, mis cabayeros, dormí con una donzeya,
blanca, rubia y colorada, su cara como una estreya.
(Bénichou)

Yoná's v. 4, which introduces the very brief portion of the ballad actually concerned with the protagonist, is formulistic. Compare the following line from *La muerte del Maestre de Santiago*: "A la pasada de un río, / pasándole por el vado" (*Primav.* 65). The Yoná-Uziel-Molho version of *Melisenda* agrees closely with the regrettably truncated, contaminated versions which can still be collected from the oral tradition of Salonikan immigrants in the United States. In all of these texts, as in Yoná, the ballad has been deprived of its principal charm and its most important feature—the rich accumulation of Oriental

[4] For archaic versions, see ASW 456; Bonilla, *Anales,* pp. 31-32; Durán 329; *Pliegos de Praga,* II, 117-118; *Primavera* 139; Timoneda, *Rosa de Amores,* fol. lxvj*r-v*.

Concerning the complex traditional life of the ballads of Galiarda, see Bénichou, pp. 274-276.

[5] Cf. the commentary to *Las almenas de Toro* (no. 1, supra).

metaphors used to describe *Melisenda*'s physical attractions. The poem's elaborate imagery can be sampled in the synthetic text published by Menéndez Pidal ("Un viejo romance," p. 186) and, more amply, in the two substantial versions collected by Attias.[6] In Yoná-Uziel-Molho, this metaphoric description has been replaced by a cryptic, unrelated ballad, *Dijo la condesa al conde,* for which we have been able to find no antecedent or counterpart elsewhere in Hispanic tradition. This *romance* is also sung in an autonomous, more extensive form among the Salonikan Sephardim (e.g., Attias 55).

BIBLIOGRAPHY

Melisenda sale de los baños

Eastern J.-Sp.: Attias 13-13a; Cantera Burgos, *Los sefardíes,* p. 12; LSO 91; Menéndez Pidal, "Un viejo romance," p. 186; PTJ 29 (= Attias); UYA 76 (= CBU 330). A curious text in *ó-e* from Damascus, published by Menéndez Pidal in "El romancero y los sefardíes," p. xxii, combines elements of our *Melisenda* ballad with verses from *La bella en misa* (no. 24 *infra*).

Archaic Text: Foulché-Delbosc, "Cancionerillos de Prague," p. 384*b*; *Pliegos de Praga,* I, 7*a*; Wolf, *Ueber eine Sammlung,* p. 201 (Stanza 9). See also **Studies.**

Studies: Bénichou, pp. 51-53; Lida de Malkiel, *Davar,* no. 10, p. 22; Id., *NRFH,* III (1949), 84-85; Menéndez Pidal, *El Romancero Español,* p. 87; Id., "Un viejo romance"; NSR, pp. 65-66; RoH, II, 222-226; TRV, II, 310, n. 1.

Dijo la condesa al conde

Eastern J.-Sp.: Attias 55; LSO 91, vv. 8-14; UYA 76 (= CBU 330, vv. 13-26).

---

[6] For more on these metaphors and their migratory nature, see DRH, pp. 26-27 and nn. 22-23; Alvar, "Patología y terapéutica rapsódicas" and "Interpretaciones judeo-españolas del árabe *ġabba.*"

7

EL CONDE ALEMÁN Y LA REINA

(Count Alemán and the Queen)

7A

Pensativle 'está 'el bu'en rey   'i 'unos penseryyos muyy grandes
  'i 'unos penseryyos muyy grandes,
ke non le a venido kartas,   kartas de la su sivdades,
  kartas de la sus sivdades.
'I 'el ke tra'í'a las kartas   syen 'i vente anyyos tení'a,
  syen 'i vente anyyos tení'a.
'I non vos toméš de maraví'a,   ke padre 'i madre tení'a,
  ke padre 'i madre tení'a.
'I 'atán alta va la luna,   kuando 'el sol salir kerí'a,
  kuando 'el sol salir kerí'a,
'i kuando 'el konde Alemare   kon la kondesa dormí'a,
  kon la kondesa 'olgava.
Non se lo save ningunos   kuantos 'en 'el korte aví'a,
  kuantos 'en 'el korte 'estavan,
si non 'era la su 'iža,   ke lo ví'a 'i lo 'enselava,
  ke lo ví'a 'i lo 'enkuvrí'a.
—Si algo viteš, la mi 'iža,   'enkuvrildo 'i 'enselaldo,
  'enkuvrildo 'i 'enselaldo.

Source: GSA 11.
2*b* *sic.*
5*a* 'a tan.
9*b* 'en kuvrildo.

Vos daré al konde Alemare,   kon sayyos de filo damasko,
kon sayyos de filo damasko.
—'I yyo malanyya los sus sayyos   'i 'atambyén ken los kerí'a
'i 'atambyén ken los kerí'a.
'En vida del rey mi padre,   yyo más mučo 'estru'í'a,
yyo más mučos 'estru'í'a.
—Ḥarán vos se aga, 'iža,   la leče ke yyo te dyera,
la leče ke yyo te dyera.
—Ḥarán vose aga, madre,   'el pan del mi padre komyeraś,
'el pan del mi padre komyeraš.
'En vida del rey mi padre,   tomateš mu'evo marido,
tomateš mu'evo amado.
Deša ke abaše 'el rey mi padre;   deša ke abaše de la misa,
deša ke abaše de la misa.
Yyo se lo vo 'a dezire;   yyo se lo vo 'a kontare,
yyo se lo vo 'a kontare.
'Estas palavras dizyendo,   'el bu'en rey ke yya arivare,
'i 'el bu'en rey ke yya vinyera.
Topa ala ninyya yyorando   lágrimas de tres 'en kuatro,
lágrimas de kuatro 'en sinko.
—¿De ké yyoráš, la mi 'iža,   lágrimas de tres 'en kuatro,
lágrimas de tres 'en kuatro?
—Yyo 'estando 'en la mi pu'erta   'i 'en mi bastidor lavrando,
'i 'en mi bastidor lavrando,
por a'í pasó 'el konde Alemare,   la travó por los trensados,
la travó por los trensados.
—Ansí rí'en, la mi 'iža,   ansí rí'en los mučačos,
ansí rí'en los mučačos.
—De detrás de 'estos re'íres   akontesen mučos danyyos,
akontesen mučos danyyos.
—Si vos plaze, la mi 'iža,   yyo lo mandaré 'a matare,
yyo lo mandaré 'a matare.
—Non lo matéš, 'el mi padre,   ni lo kižeraš matare,
ni lo kižeraš matare.

11*b* 'i 'a tambyén.

Ke 'el konde 'es ninyyo 'i muǧaǧo,   'el mundo kere gozare,
'el mundo kere gozare.
Desteraldo de 'estas tyeras,   ke de akí non koma pane.

7B

Pensativle 'está 'el bu'en rey,   'en 'unos penseryyos muyy grandes,
ke non le a veniđo kartas,   kartas de la su sivdađ.
'El ke tra'í'a las kartas   syen 'i vente anyyos tení'a.
Non vos toméš de maraví'a,   ke pađre 'i mađre tení'a.
'Atán alta va la luna,   kuando 'el sol salir kerí'a, (5)
kuando 'el konde Alemare   kon la kondesa dormí'a.
Non lo saví'a ningunos   kuantos 'en la korte aví'a,
si non 'era la su 'iža,   ke lo ví'a 'i lo 'enkuvrí'a.
—Si algo viteš, mi 'iža,   'enkuvrildo 'i 'enselaldo.
Vos dará 'el kondAlemare   kon sayyos de filo damasko. (10)
—Yyo malanyyo los sus sayyos   'i 'atambyén ken los kerí'a. (11)
'En viđa del rey mi pađre,   tomateš mu'evo amađo. (15)
—Ḥarán vose aga, 'iža,   la leǧe ke yyo te dyera. (13)
—Ḥarán vose aga, mađre,   'el pan del mi pađre komyeraš. (14)
Ša ke abaše 'el rey mi padre;   ša ke abaše de la milsa. (16)
Yyo se lo 'a [de] dezire,   yyo se lo a đe kontare. (17)
'Estas palavras dizyendo   'i 'el bu'en rey ke arivara. (18)
Tanto fu'e yyorando   lágrimas de tres 'a kuatro. (19)
—¿De ké yyoráš, la mi 'iža,   lágrimas de tres 'a kuatro? (20)
—Lyyo 'estando 'en mi pu'erta   'i 'en mi bastiđor lavrando,
kuando 'el konde Alemare   me travó por los vestiđos.
—Ansí rí'e, la mi 'iža,   ansí rí'e, la mi alma.
—De detrás de 'estos re'íres   akontesen munǧos males.
—Si vos plaze, la mi 'iža,   yyo lo mandaré 'a yyamare. (25)
—Non lo matéš, 'el mi padre,   ni lo kižeraš matare, (26)
ke 'el konde, ninyyo 'i muǧaǧo,   'el mundo kere gozare. (27)
Desteraldo de 'esta tyera,   ke de akí non koma pane. (28)

Source: RSA 3.
5*a* 'A tan.
11*b* 'A tam.

Translation:

7A

The good King is deep in thought, thinking grave thoughts, for no letters have come to him, no letters from his cities. He who carried the letters was a hundred and twenty years old. And do not be amazed, for his parents were still alive. (5) The moon rides so high, when the sun began to rise, when Count Alemán was sleeping with the Countess. Not a soul in all the Court knows of it, save her daughter, who saw it all and kept it silent. "If you saw anything, my daughter, conceal it and keep it silent. (10) I'll give you Count Alemán, with garments of damask thread." "Accursed be your garments and whoever might want them. In the lifetime of the King, my father, I have worn out many more." "May the milk that I gave you, daughter, do you no good." "May my father's bread, mother, do you no good. (15) In the lifetime of the King, my father, you took a new husband. Let the King, my father, come down; let him come down from the chapel. I'll tell him what has happened; I'll let him know." As she was saying these words, the good King arrived. He found the girl weeping, three and four tears at a time. (20) "Why are you crying, my daughter, three and four tears at a time?" "While I was sitting at my door, embroidering on a frame, Count Alemán passed by and seized me by my braids." "In that way, daughter, young men are playful." "After such jests many harmful things occur." (25) "If you like, my daughter, I shall have him killed." "Don't kill him, father, nor should you even want to kill him, for the Count is but a youth and wishes to enjoy the world. (28) Exile him from these lands, so that here he may eat no bread."

7B

The good King is deep in thought, in very grave thought, for no letters have come to him, no letters from his city. He who carried the letters was a hundred and twenty years old. Do not be amazed, for his parents were still alive. (5) The moon rides so high, when the sun began to rise, when Count Alemán was sleeping with the Countess. Not a soul in all the Court knows of it, save her daughter, who saw it all and kept it silent. "If you saw anything, my daughter, conceal it and keep it silent. (10) Count Alemán will give you garments of damask thread." "Accursed be your garments and whoever might want them. In the lifetime of the King, my father, you took a new lover." "May the milk that I gave you, daughter, do you no good." "May my father's bread, mother, do you no good. (15) Let the King, my father, come down; let him come down from the chapel. I'll tell him what has happened; I'll let him know." As she was saying these words, the good King arrived. She was weeping so bitterly, three and four tears at a time. "Why are you crying, my daughter, three and four tears at a time?" (20) "While I was sitting at my door, embroidering on a frame, Count Alemán seized me by my garments." "In that way he is playful, my daughter, in that way he is playful, my soul." "After such jests many evil things occur." "If you like, my daughter, I will have him summoned." (25) "Don't kill him, father, nor should you even want to kill him, for the Count, a mere youth, wishes to enjoy the world. (27) Exile him from this land, so that here he may eat no bread."

Motifs:

3 F571. *Extremely old person*; cf. L101.1. *Unpromising hero*: *aged man.*
6 T481. *Adultery.*
28 Q431.5.1. *Banishment for attempted seduction.*

El conde Alemán y la reina is atypical of the usually monorhymed Spanish ballads in that its proto-text seems to have been written in parallelistic couplets (*coplas pareadas*). The unique sixteenth-century version (*Primav.* 170), with its relatively long assonant series in *í-a, í-o,* and *á,* is already on the way toward developing a regularized *romance*-type rhyme-scheme, but modern traditional versions, surviving in three far-flung lateral areas of the Hispanic world (Salonika, Tangier, and Portugal) preserve a rich variety of assonances and provide ample evidence of the ballad's original strophic versification.

Yoná's closely allied texts contain a number of such parallelistic reliques. Text A makes use of synonyms with differing assonance in many of the repeated hemistichs: *dormí'a-'olgava* (v. 6), *aví'a-'estavan* (v. 7), *'enselava-'enkuvrí'a* (v. 8), *marido-amado* (v. 15), *arivare-vinyera* (v. 18), *kuatro-sinko* (v. 19). Similar parallelistic synonyms are *dezire-kontare* (v. 17; B, v. 16).[1] Version B, in which the repeated second hemistichs—a normal part of any sung rendition of this ballad—have not been printed, sometimes incorporates rhymes belonging to A's repetitions: *'enkuvrí'a* (v. 8), *amađo* (B, v. 12 = A, v. 15). Elsewhere B offers assonances which are unknown to A but have counterparts elsewhere in the Hispanic tradition. The reading *arivara* (v. 17), instead of *arivare* as in A (v. 18), Díaz-Plaja (v. 11), and Attias (v. 36: *allegare*), recalls the *á-a* assonance used at the same point in certain versions from Southern Portugal:

As razões que eram ditas, o pai que chegava.
(VRP 127, 998)

Estando nestas razões, seu pai á porta chegava.
(Athaide Oliveira 93)[2]

Vestiđos (v. 21), instead of *trensados* (A, v. 22), agrees with *Primavera* 170 ("Yo me estaba aquí comiendo, / comiendo sopas en vino; // entró el conde alemán, // echómelas por el vestido."), and *males* for *danyyos* (A, v. 24) occurs in Attias (no. 25.48).

Yoná's v. 6, like Attias and Díaz-Plaja, reads "kon la kondesa dormí'a," but some of our unedited Salonikan texts offer the more satisfactory reading, "reina," which agrees with *Primavera* and most of the Portuguese versions. Cf., however, VRP 108: "com a condessa dormia."

In contrast to *Primavera* and the Portuguese tradition, the Sephardic versions, following a tendency observed in other ballads as well, take pains to attenuate the ballad's more brutal and salacious features.[3] In

[1] Cf. VRP 105.10-11, 122.8, 10, etc. Cf. Alvar, "Paralelismo," pp. 127-130; Asensio, *Poética y realidad,* p. 89.

[2] Cf. also Braga, II, 12, 14, n. 1; Nunes, *RL,* VI, 168, vv. 25-26. Another variant (Braga, II, 25; Rodrigues de Azevedo, pp. 183-184) rhymes the same passage in *á* as in the other Sephardic texts.

[3] Cf. our comments on *Rico Franco* ("Hispanic Balladry," p. 237, n. 24) and *La mala suegra* (DRH, p. 60).

Primavera, when the father claims that the Count's first alleged offense to the daughter was merely an innocent jest, she leaves no room for doubt as to his supposed dishonorable intentions:

—¡Mal fuego quemase, padre, tal reír y tal burlar!
Cuando me tomó en sus brazos conmigo quiso holgar.

The Portuguese versions are even more direct:

—Dou a Deu'lo brincar dele, e o dito do seu brincar,
Ele pegou-me pelo braço, à cama me foi botar.
(VRP 105)

—Malo haia o seu zombar, mais a sua zombaria!
Se lh'eu desse confiança, p'rà cama me levaria!
(VRP 127)

All of this is characteristically reduced to a mere innuendo in the Salonikan texts:

—De detrás de 'estos re'íres akontesen muğos danyyos.
—De detrás de 'estos re'íres akontesen munğos males.

In *Primavera* the Count is evidently doomed without hope of reprieve. The Portuguese versions draw out the scene of his execution in a long series of parallelistic verses in which the daughter taunts the mother by describing the Count's clothing and appearance as he goes to his death. One version from Madeira even specifies a number of horrendous mutilations to be suffered by the unfortunate Count before he is finally put out of his misery:

—Pena tamanha da culpa la culpa tem de pagar;
mandae-lhe vasal los olhos que tão alto vão olhar;
mandae-lhe quebral las pernas com que se foi ao logar;
mandae-lhe quebral los braços com que la quiz agarrar;
mandae-lhe, por derradeiro, la cabeça degolar;
todo lo corpo, n'um feixe, em cinzas se vá tornar.[4]

[4] Rodrigues de Azevedo, p. 180. The verses are a contamination from another ballad involving an accusation of adultery: the extremely rare Azorian ballad of *Las bodas de sangre.* See D. Catalán, "A caza de romances raros," pp. 459-461. On similar punishments as a ballad *topos,* see RoH, I, 271 (on *Primav.* 109

The Salonikan versions present a very different situation. The daughter has made her point: she has disgraced the Count and separated the Queen from her lover. The ballad ends on a note of magnanimity in which the daughter intercedes on behalf of the Count who, she says, is too young to be killed and should only be sent into exile. The ballad's final verses are shared with some Salonikan versions of *Conde Olinos* (no. 12, *infra*):

> —No lo matéx, la mi madre, ni lo quijerex matar.
> El conde es niño y muchacho, el mundo quiere gozar.
> Desterra(r)ldo de estas tierras, de aquí no coma pan.
> (*Conde Olinos*: Benardete 34) [5]

Almost identical verses also occur in *Juan Lorenzo* (MP 12):

> —No matéis a Gian Lorenzo ni lo quijerais matar;
> Desterraldo de sus tierras, que de ellas non coma pan.
> (Coello 2)

The initial verses of Yoná, Attias, and a magnificent unedited text collected by Mrs. Crews constitute a complex and rather bizarre contamination which cannot be related logically to the narrative that follows. [6] Yoná's vv. 1 and 2 are reminiscent of certain phrases in

---

and 171). Cf. also the Moroccan ballad of *El huérfano* (Larrea 190.15-22; Ortega 233*a*; Catalán, "A caza," pp. 456-457). Identical verses occur also in Rodrigues de Azevedos' version of *Conde Claros y la infanta* (p. 74). For the passage's epic antecedents, see *Infantes de Lara,* p. 35.

[5] Cf. also Hemsi, "Sur le folklore," Variant 4 (also from Salonika). In these verses, *Conde Olinos* seems to have borrowed from *Conde Alemán*. The former ballad may also have taken over the idea that the protagonist, who in the Salonikan *Conde Olinos* is known as "Conde Alemán," wishes to deceive or make fun of the Princess: "No es la sirena, mi madre, / si no (*sic*) es el Conde Alimá, // que con mí quiso reír, / que con mí quiso burlar" (Díaz-Plaja 9). More appropriate to the context is Yoná's reading "ke por mí se va akavar" (no. 12.9) or those from other Eastern areas: "que a mí me viene a buxkar" (Galante 2); "que me kere alcanzar" (Danon 19). For other variants, see Hemsi, "Sur le folklore," and no. 12 *infra*. The portion of *Conde Olinos* corresponding to Attias 16.17-26 has apparently suffered from an intrusion of the superficially similar situation in *Conde Alemán* in which a parent also asks a daughter about the intentions of a potential suitor.

For the occurrence of the plea for the Count's life as a contamination in a singular version of *El robo de Dina* from Sérrai (Greece), see no. 8, n. 6 *infra*.

[6] In Díaz-Plaja and in three versions collected from oral tradition in the U.S., these incongruous verses are lacking and the ballad begins with Yoná's

Guiomar (*Primav.* 178). The Moorish Princess Guiomar asks about her father King Jafar and is given the following report by one of his knights:

> —Retraído está, señora, en su palacio real,
> de dentro de siete puertas allá se fuera a encerrar....
> llorando está de sus ojos que es dolor de lo mirar....
> La causa del lloro tan grande yo no la sabré contar;
> mas sé que le han venido cartas de Carlos el emperante,
> lo que contienen aquéllas yo no lo sabré contar.

Guiomar then goes to see the King and finds him engrossed in thought:

> ... allí vido estar al rey en la su silla real,
> su mano tenía en el rostro con un pensamiento grande.

The letters and the "great thought" of which they are the cause recall our Sephardic *Conde Alemán,* although here the mysterious King

---

v. 5, as in *Primavera* and in the Portuguese tradition. The formula used in v. 5 of Yoná's version occurs also in *Valdovinos y Sevilla* (*Primav.* 169): "Tan claro hace la luna / como el sol a mediodía." Numerous *romances* in the modern tradition begin with the same formula:

> Alta vae a lua, alta, mais que o sol ao meio dia. ...
> (*Romera vengadora de su honra*: Braga, III, 438)

> Alta vai a lua, alta, coma o sol do meio día. ...
> (*Oração do dia de juizo*: Carré 105; VRP 766-789)

> Al resplandor de la luna y al sol de mediodía. ...
> (*Boda estorbada*: Larrea 243)

> Que alta que está la luna, más que el sol de al mediodía. ...
> (*Boda estorbada*: MRuiz 69A)

> ¡Qué alta, qué alta va la luna, como el sol por el membrillo! ...
> (*Virgilios*: RPC 125)

> Tan alta estaba la luna como el sol a medio día. ...
> (*Valdovinos y Belardos*: RPM 56-57)

> Tan alta iba la luna como el sol a mediodía. ...
> (*Flérida*: RQDB-II 69)

> ¡O! Qué alta va la luna, como el sol de mediodía. ...
> (*Hermanas reina y cautiva*: Ledesma 170)

For more on this formula, see RVP 95, n. 1. Cf. also J. A. Fernandes, *DL,* IV: v-vi (1951), 126, 137-138.

is worried because he has *not* received letters, while King Jafar's preoccupations stem from letters received. The similarities between the two ballads, of course, could well be coincidental. [7]

Yoná's vv. 3-4 introduce an unknown messenger bearing letters who, we are asked to believe, is 120 years old and whose parents are still alive! These verses are more than likely a borrowing from some early version of *El moro de Antequera* (= *Primav.* 74), in which the protagonist is an aged messenger bearing letters to the King of Granada:

El moro que las [cartas] llevava   ciento y veinte años avía,
ciento y veinte años el moro,   y padre y madre tenía. [8]

BIBLIOGRAPHY

Eastern J.-Sp.: Attias 25; Díaz-Plaja 12; PTJ 30 and 81 (= Attias); UYA 261-263 (= GSA).

Moroccan J.-Sp.: There are no published texts. Menéndez Pidal (Introduction to VRP, p. xvii) mentions unedited versions from Tangier.

Portuguese: Albuquerque e Castro, *DL,* IV:iii-iv (1951), 125-128; Almeida Garrett, II, 81-85; Alves 564-565; Athaide Oliveira, pp. 93-95, 386-387; Braga, II, 1-29; Fernandes Thomás, *Velhas canções,* pp. 5-7; Furtado de Mendonça, *RL,* XIV, 1-2; Gomes Pereira, *RL,* XIV, 138-139; Hardung, I, 168-172, 274-279; Lopes Graça, pp. 77-78; Martins, I, 218; Monteiro do Amaral, *RL,* XI, 102-103; Nunes, *RL,* VI, 168-170; Pereira Monteiro, *DL,* II:i, 71-72; Pires de Lima, *Estudos,* III, 498-499; Id., *RL,* XX, 16; J. A. and F. C. Pires de Lima, *Romanceiro minhoto,* pp. 41-42; Rodrigues de Azevedo, pp. 172-185; Serrano, pp. 30-32; Tavares, *RL,* IX, 311; Thomás Pires, *Lendas,* pp. 50-59; VRP 103-129, 996-999. Cf. also RVP, p. 95, n. 1. For still other versions in publications which we

[7] At least two archaic ballads, like the Salonikan *Conde Alemán,* open with the main character engrossed in deep thought: "Pensativo estaba el Cid ..." (Durán 727); "Pensativo el rey francés ..." (Durán 1140; Rodríguez-Moñino, "Tortajada," no. 32), but neither of these poems is traditional and the parallel is probably coincidental. Cf. also Vicuña, no. 3. In the modern Sephardic tradition, we are reminded of the Moroccan ballad of *El Polo*: "Pensativo está el Polo, / malo y de malenconía ..." (MP 128).

[8] From the British Museum broadside version of "De Antequera salió el moro" edited by F. López Estrada, *La conquista de Antequera,* p. 7 (Text I). Cf. "Dos romances fronterizos," pp. 97-98, n. 23. This aged Moor reappears in a Castilian-Catalan version of *Don Bueso y su hermana*: "El moro que l'ha agafado / ciento y un año tenía ..." (Milá, p. 237, var. P; Aguiló, no. 39.66-70, p. 175). An aged crone is similarly described in a Portuguese text of *Valdovinos y Belardos*: "Ela era tão nova, / cento e um anos tinha ..." (VRP 20).

have not been able to consult, see the bibliography in VRP, I, 154, and Albuquerque e Castro, p. 128.

Archaic Text: Durán 305; *Primavera* 170. For an *a lo divino* adaptation which uses only the first two verses of the archaic version, see Ontañón de Lope, no. 20.

Studies: Braga, III, 498-501; Menéndez Pidal, "A propósito del *Romanceiro português,*" pp. 496-497; Id., "Notícia preliminar" to VRP, I, xvi-xvii; RoH, I, 88, 107, n. 52, 135; II, 331.

8

EL ROBO DE DINA

(The Rape of Dinah)

Se pasean las 12 flores, 'entre 'en medyyo 'una konğá.
Dišo la konğá 'a las flores: —'Oyy 'es dí'a de pasear.
Se pase'a la linda Dînāh por los kampos del rey Ḥămôr.
'A favor de sus 12 'ermanos kaminava sin temor.
Arimóse 'a 'una tyenda, pensando ke non ayy varón.
Visto la 'uvyera visto Šĕḳem 'ižo del rey Ḥămôr.
Ayegóse para 'elyya, tres palavrikas le avló:
—Linda soš, la linda Dînāh, sin afeyte 'i sin kolor.
Lindos son vu'estros 'ermanos; la flor vos yevateš vos.
—Si son lindos 'i non son lindos, a mí ke me los guadre 'el Dyyo.

Source: GSA 5. Variants: RSA 2; LRI 12; BRI 11; GRI 11.

1*a* Se pase'a *GRI* (Se *in boldface*), doğe *RSA* / *BRI* / *GRI*.
1*b* 'entre 'enmedyyo *GRI*, 'en *om. LRI*.
2*b* paseare *GRI*.
3*b* tor (*sic*) los kampos *BRI*, Ḥ'ămôr *GRI*.
4*a* Kon favor *RSA* / *LRI* / *BRI* / *GRI*, 12 om. *RSA* / *LRI*, doğe *BRI* / *GRI*.
4*b* kaminava 'i sin temor *RSA*.
5*a* Arimóse 'en 'una tyenda *LRI* / *BRI*, 'erimos (*sic*) *GRI*.
6*b* Š. 'ižo de 'el rey *RSA*, Š. 'el 'ižo de 'el rey *BRI*, Š. 'el 'ižo del rey *GRI*.
8*a* sos *GRI*, Dînāh *in square letters GRI*.
9*a* son los vuestros *GRI*.
9*b* más ke vos yeváš la flor RSA / LRI / BRI, más ke vos lyeváś la flor *GRI*.
10*a* 'O son lindos 'o non son lindos RSA / LRI / GRI, 'O son lindos 'o no son lindos *BRI*.
10*b* ansí me los guađre *RSA*, a mí me los guadre *LRI* / *BRI* / *GRI*.

Ayegóse más 'a 'elyya, 'izo lo ke non 'es razón.
Se 'esparte la linda Dînāh; se va para ande su se[nyyor],
'a solombra del težado ke non la 'enpanyyara 'el sol.
Su padre deske la vido, 'a resivirla salyyó:
—¿Kyén vos demudó la kara 'i kén vos demudó la kolor?
'O vola demudó 'el ayyre, 'o vola 'enpanyyó 'el sol.
—Ni me la demudó 'el ayyre, ni me la 'enpanyyó 'el sol.
Me la demudó 'un muğağiko, Šĕḳem, 'ižo del rey Ḥămôr.
'Estas palavras dizyendo, kazamenteros le mandó.

11*a* Ayegóse para 'elyya *RSA / LRI / BRI / GRI.*
11*b* no *BRI.*
12*a* Yya se parte *RSA,* Dînāh *in square letters GRI.*
12*b* para *om. GRI,* para 'en del su senyyor *BRI,* ande 'el su senyyor *RSA / LRI / GRI. The abbreviation* se. *is used in GSA.*
13 *Placed between vv. 3 and 4 in LRI / BRI / GRI.*
13*a* de 'el težad̄o *BRI,* del možado *GRI.*
13*b* 'empanyyara *LRI / BRI / GRI.*
14 *om. RSA.*
14*a* 'El padre *LRI / BRI / GRI,* deske lo supo *BRI,* des ke lo supo *GRI.*
15*a* Kén *RSA / LRI.*
15*b* 'i *om. RSA,* kyen *BRI / GRI.*
16*a* 'O *om. BRI / GRI.*
16*b* demud̄ó *RSA / BRI /GRI,* 'empanyyó *LRI.*
17*b* ni me la empanyyó *LRI,* ni me la demud̄ó 'el sol *RSA / BRI / GRI.*
18*a* Šĕḳem *in square letters GRI,* Š. 'el 'ižo *LRI / BRI / GRI.*
19*a* 'Esto ke sintyyó 'el padre *LRI / BRI / GRI.*
19*b* kazamenteros yya mandó *RSA,* kazamyenteros le mandó *GRI.*

Translation:

The twelve flowers go walking, in their midst walks a rose. Said the rose to the flowers: "Today is a day for walking." The beautiful Dinah walks through the fields of King Hamor. Because of the fear inspired by her twelve brothers, she walked without fear. (5) She approached a tent, thinking there was no man within. Shechem had seen her, the son of King Hamor. He drew near to her and spoke a few words: "Beautiful Dinah, you are beautiful without adornment and without rouge. Your brothers are handsome, but you take the flower." (10) "Be they handsome or not, may God protect them." He drew nearer to her and did what was not right. The beautiful Dinah departs;

she returns to her father's house, in the shadow of the eaves, so that the sun would not tarnish her. As soon as her father saw her, he went out to receive her: (15) "What has happened to your complexion? Who has changed it so? Either the wind has changed it or the sun has tarnished it." "Neither the wind has changed it, nor has the sun tarnished it. A youth has changed it, Shechem, the son of King Hamor." (19) As she spoke these words, he sent matchmakers to her.

Motif:

11 T471. *Rape.*

El robo de Dina, which elaborates upon Genesis 34:1-3, 5-8, 25-27, has a sixteenth-century counterpart recently published by P. Ontañón de Lope. In this early text, the schematic biblical narrative [1] has been

[1] Here is the pertinent biblical material as it appears in a medieval Spanish translation:

> [1] E salio Dina fija de Lea, que pario de Jacob, para mirar las fijas dela tierra; [2] e vio la Sequem fijo de Hamor el yneo, prinçipe dela tierra, e tomo la e durmio conella, e afligiola. [3] Et conjuntose su alma con Dina fija de Jacob; e amo ala moça, e fablo avoluntad dela moça. [4] Et dixo Sequem aHamor su padre, diziendo: tomame a esta ninna por muger. [5] Et Jacob oyo que encono aDina su fija; e sus fijos estauan ensu ganado enel canpo; e callose Jacob fasta su venida. [6] Et salio Hamor padre de Sequem a Jacob para fablar conel; [7] e los fijos de Jacob venieron del canpo oyendo lo, e entristeçieron se los omnes, e pesoles mucho. Ca vileza fizo en Ysrrael por yazer conla fija de Jacob; ca asy non deuia ser fecho. [8] Et fablo Hamor conellos, diziendo: Sequem mi fijo enamoro se su alma de vuestra fija; dad gela agora por muger; [9] e consograd con nos; vuestras fijas daredes anos, e anuestras fijas tomaredes para vos. ... [14] Et dixieron les: non podremos fazer esta cosa: dar nuestra hermana aomne que non es çircunçido, ca verguença es anos [15] mas con esto seremos conuenientes a vos: sy fuerdes commo nos otros, que çircunçidedes todo macho; [16] e daremos nuestras fijas avos, e vuestras fijas tomaremos para nos; e poblaremos con vos e seremos vn pueblo. ... [24] ... [e çircunçiaron todo macho, todos los que salieron a conçejo de su villa]. [25] Et enel dia terçero, estando adolorados, tomaron dos fijos de Jacob, Sym[e]on e Leui hermanos de Dina, cada vno su espada, e entraron sobre la çibdat en seguridat, e mataron todo macho; [26] e aHamor e Sequem su fijo mataron a boca de espada, e tomaron aDina de casa de Sequem, e salieron; [27] los fijos de Jacob vinieron sobre los matados e rrobaron la çibdat delos que enconaron a su hermana; [28] e sus ovejas, e vacas, e asnos, e todo lo que era

considerably amplified. Under the influence of a recurrent commonplace of traditional literature, Dinah is represented as going on a hunt ("A caça salía Dina . . ."), [2] but her real purpose seems to be to watch the people of Salén, who are at work building "towns and castles." [3]

> enla çibdat e todo lo que era enel canpo tomaron; [29] e todo su auer, e todas sus criaturas e todas sus mugeres captiuaron; e rrobaron todo quanto era enlas casas.

We quote from *Escorial Bible I.j.4,* ed. O. H. Hauptmann, Vol. I (Philadelphia, 1953), 95-96. Cf. also *Biblias medievales romanceadas,* ed. P. José Llamas, Vol. I (Madrid, 1950), 58-59 (Chap. XXXIII [*sic*]), and *Biblia medieval romanceada,* ed. A. Castro, *et al.,* Vol. I (Buenos Aires, 1927), 45-46.

[2] Cf. N771. *King (prince) lost on hunt has adventures.* Legion are the *romances* both ancient and modern which begin with the protagonist's departure on a hunt: "A cazar va don Rodrigo" (*Infantes de Lara*: *Primav.* 26); "Por los campos de Jerez / a caza va el rey don Pedro" (*Don Pedro el Cruel*: *Primav.* 66-66 *a*); "A cazar va el caballero" (*Infantina*: *Primav.* 151; MP 114); "A caza va el emperador" (*Conde Claros y el Emperador*: Primav. 191); "A caza iban, a caza, / los cazadores del rey" (*Rico Franco*: *Primav.* 119); "A caza salió el gran turco" (ASW 119); "A caça va el rey don Bueso" ("Ensalada de Praga," *Pliegos de Praga,* I, 5; ASW 193); "A caza salió Don Sancho" (Durán 1215); "A caza sale el marqués, / Danés Urgel, el leal" (Wilson-Sage, no. 1); "A caça va el lindo Adonis" (*La muerte de Adonis*: Rodríguez-Moñino, *Suplemento al Cancionero general,* no. 317); "A cazar iba don Pedro" (*Muerte ocultada*: ASW 234-235; MP 75); "A cazar iba el rey moro" (*Hermanas reina y cautiva*: ASW 196); "Don Rodrigo fue a caza" (*Penitencia del rey Rodrigo*: Menéndez Pidal, *Romancero tradicional,* I, no. 14*t* [p. 72]); "Levantóse el rey a casar" (*Landarico*: Bénichou 8; *Pliegos de Praga,* I, 331); "A cazar iba, a cazar / el infante don García" (*Esposa de Don García*: RPM 13); "El señó salió de caza" (*Jesucristo y el incrédulo*: RPE 77; RTCN 80). Lope de Vega, inspired by *La infantina,* uses the same *incipit* in his *romance*: "A caza va el caballero / por los montes de París" (*El villano en su rincón,* Act II, vv. 1252 f., ed. A. Zamora Vicente, "Clásicos Castellanos," no. 157 [Madrid, 1963], p. 51; also Lope de Vega, *Poesías líricas,* I, ed. J. F. Montesinos, "Clásicos Castellanos," no. 68 [Madrid, 1951], p. 64). For further examples and discussion of this motif, see Bénichou, pp. 47, 269; Devoto, "El mal cazador," *passim*; M. R. Lida de Malkiel, *La originalidad artística de La Celestina* (Buenos Aires, 1962), pp. 200-202; Michaëlis, "Estudios," pp. 175-177; NSR, p. 64, n. 15. For related motifs, see the notes to *Rico Franco* (no. 18 *infra*).

[3] The author of the sixteenth-century *romance* used as his source one of many Bible versions in which the Hebrew phrase "Wa-yābō' Yacăkōb šālēm cîr Šĕkem ..." ('Jacob arrived safe in the city of Shechem' [*The Torah,* Philadelphia, 1962, p. 61]) was misunderstood by the translator, the word *šālēm* 'safe, in good health, whole' having been interpreted 'in the city of Shalem', by association with the toponym *Šālēm* (Genesis 14:18), "an earlier, or poetic, designation for Jerusalem" (*The Pentateuch and Haftorahs,* ed. J. H. Hertz [London, 1958], p. 53). Thus the *Biblia medieval romanceada,* edited by A. Castro *et al.,* translates: "Et veno Jacob a Salem villa de Saguem" (p. 44). Cf. the King James

She is seen by Prince Siquén (Shechem), who speaks to her, then seizes her and carries her off to a castle. Dinah complains to her brothers and especially to Zabulón, a personage who does not appear in the modern Sephardic versions, nor in the biblical narrative at this point, where only Simeon and Levi are mentioned. Immediately after her complaint, marriage emissaries arrive from King Emor (Hamor). Zabulón agrees to the marriage, provided it be celebrated at the house of Emor. When all are seated at the wedding feast, Zabulón jumps up and exhorts his brethren to kill Emor and his people. Thus the *romance* ends in typical "fragmentistic" fashion with a dramatic, unresolved climax. This unique sixteenth-century text of *El robo de Dina* reads as follows:

A caça salía Dina, la hija de[l] gran Jacob,
por ver a los de Salén quán bien hazen su lavor;
hazen villas y castillos, qu'es cosa de admiración.
Encontrárala Siquén, el hijo del rrey Emor,
y de aquella sola vista de su amor preso quedó.
—¡O, bendita seas, Dina y bendita tu nación,
y benditos tus hermanos, tanbién tu padre Jacob,
y bendito Dios del cielo que tan bella te crió!
¡O, si te pluguiese, Dina, de tener comigo amor!
Y Dina, muy vergonsosa, nada no le rrespondió.
Tomárala por la mano, a vn castillo la llevó;
más de fuerça que de grado su virginidad gozó,
y Dina muy querellosa del castillo se salió.
Quexávase a sus hermanos, mucho más a Zabulón:
—Si no me vengáis, hermanos, muerte mala muera yo.
Ellos en aquesto estando, el rrey Emor que llegó
a pedilla en casamiento para su hijo el mayor.
Ninguno se la otorgava, si no fuera Zabulón;
Zabulón se la otorgava y avn con la tal condición,
que vayan a hazer las bodas a casa del rrey Emor.

---

version: "And Jacob came to Shālĕm, a city of Shēchĕm." The text edited by Hauptmann translates: "Et vino Jacob paçificamente ala çibdat de Sequem" (p. 94; Llamas, p. 57). Cipriano de Valera renders the phrase correctly: "Y vino Jacob sano a la ciudad de Sichêm."

Todos estando a la mesa, Zabulón se levantó:
22 —¡Aquí, aquí, los mis hermanos, muera esta mala nasción!

The Sephardic ballad is known not only in Salonika, as Attias maintains, but also on the Island of Rhodes (SBS) and in the community of Sérrai (Greece; uned.), which has a tradition largely dependent on that of Salonika (cf. NSR, p. 75, no. 71). Though obviously based upon the sixteenth-century text or some variant thereof, the Judeo-Spanish versions have undergone various elaborations and changes. They possess a number of curious features, some of which approach the biblical narrative more closely than does the Spanish poem.

Except for Bassan, all the Salonikan versions (Attias, Yoná, and four unedited renditions in our collection), as well as our single unedited text from the dependent tradition of Sérrai, are characterized by an allegorical introduction, in which the twelve sons of Jacob are represented as flowers and Dinah as a rose. A similar device is used in Salonikan variants of *Conde Olinos* where, because of his magical singing, the hero is represented as a nightingale:

En el vergel de la reina hay crecido un bel rosal, . . .
en la ramica más alta un rujiol sentí cantar. . . . [4]

[4] Attias 16.1-2, 5-6. Cf. Yoná, no. 12 *infra*. One is reminded of similar allegorical introductions which abound in the balladry of Balkan peoples:

"Two nightingales sang all night,
and they would not let me sleep. ..."
"Those were not two nightingales.
Those were the suitors of Uma Dženetić."

(Bartók-Lord, no. 27*a*)

Two black ravens flew
from Nikšić to Kojrenić.
They were not two black ravens,
but two dear comrades.

(Bartók-Lord, no. 27*c*)

All the little birds began to sing, but one sang not.
"If my mother had wished me to sing,
she would not have given me to an old man, /
that I should always be sad."

(Bartók-Lord, no. 40)

Most of the Salonikan and some Rhodian texts represent Dinah as walking under the shade of roofs so that the sun will not tarnish her complexion. Some renditions (Yoná, variants to v. 13; uned., Rhodes and Salonika) place the verse early in the narrative, between Yoná's vv. 3 and 4; in others, Dinah returns home "'a solombra del težado" (GSA, RSA, Attias, Bassan; uned., Salonika). The expression, which does not occur in the sixteenth-century text, recalls a verse in *Melisenda insomne,* where the protagonist, on a secret midnight sortie to visit Conde Ayruelos, keeps in the shadow of the eaves to avoid being recognized: "a sombra va de tejados / que no la conosca nadie" (Menéndez Pidal, *El Romancero Español,* p. 26; FN 87).

Peculiar to the Sephardic versions is the formulistic dialog concerning Dinah's pallor (Yoná, vv. 15-18), of which there is no trace in the

---

Lo! upon the mountain green
stands a fir-tree tall and thin—
'Tis no fir-tree—none at all—
'tis a maiden thin and tall.
(Stevenson Stanoyevich, no. 66)

For more on such allegorical ballad beginnings, see Bartók-Lord, no. 23*a,* n. 1, and Alexandri, *Ballades ... de la Roumanie,* p. 182, n. 19. Similar devices occur in the Lithuanian ballads (Balys H4, K1). On epic antithesis, the stylistic device *It is not A, it is B,* which is typical of the Slavic and Greek examples, see Bowra, *Heroic Poetry,* pp. 269-272. Cf. also Dozon, *Chansons populaires bulgares,* pp. 228, 333-334; Pernot, *Anthologie,* pp. 46, 50, 53, 54; Petropoulos, *La comparaison,* pp. 120-122; De Grazia, *Canti popolari albanesi,* pp. 178-179; Lambertz, *Die Volksepik der Albaner,* pp. 25, 37, 48.

Could the use of such allegorical beginnings in *El robo de Dina* and *El conde Olinos* constitute yet another Sephardic borrowing from Balkan balladry? (On ballad narratives taken from Greek *tragoúdia,* see NSR, pp. 74-76). The same allegorical presentation is, however, not unknown to Western European ballads. Witness *Brown Robin* (Child 97B):

A featherd fowl's in your orchard, father,
o dear, but it sings sweet!
What would I give, my father dear,
that bonnie bird to meet!

and the Swedish *Liten Vallpiga*:

Och konungen vakna, i höganloft låg.
"Vad är för en fågel, så väl sjunga må?"
"Det är ingen fågel, fast Eder tyckes så,
Men liten vallpiga med getterna små."
(Geijer-Afzelius-2, III, no. 74 [= 60: 1])

Spanish text or in its biblical source. This exchange recalls a dialog in Sephardic versions of *La adúltera* (*ó*):

Abašó la Blankailiña, la puerta le avrió.
Ya le avre la media puerta de kara i no de korasón.
Ya le avre la otra media, su kara se le demudó.
—¿Ké tenéš vos, Blankailiña, ké tenéš vos, Blankaiflor?
Vos tenéš mal de preñada o kovrateš muevo amor.
—Yo no tengo mal de preñada, ni kovrí yo muevo amor.
Es ke a mí me se perdieron las yaves del mi kašón.
(uned., Rhodes)

Al abrir la media puerta la cara se le demudó.
—¿De qué vos se demudó la cara, o del aire o del sol,
o teníais mal preñado o amaríais nuevo amor?
—Me se han pedrido las llaves, las llaves del corridor.
(Attias 12.15-22)

Bajó la niña a abrirle mudadita de color:
—O tú tienes calentura o tú tienes nuevo amor.
—Ni tengo yo calentura ni tengo yo nuevo amor,
que se me han perdido las llaves de mi rico comedor.
(Larrea 109.13-20) [5]

---

[5] The same passage occurs in some Peninsular versions:
Al bajar por la escalera, se la muda la color.
—Tú has tenido calenturas, o has dormido con varón.
—Ni he tenido calenturas, ni he dormido con varón;
se me han perdido las llaves de tu lindo corredor.
(RPC 86-87)

This pattern —a question, generally phrased in terms of two alternate possibilities, followed by an answer which denies both by giving a third, usually false, explanation— is a balladic commonplace:

—¿Qué es aquesto, Melisenda? ¿Esto qué podía estar?
¡O vos tenéis mal de amores, o os queréis loca tornar!
—Que no tengo mal de amores, ni tengo por quien penar,
mas cuando fui pequeña tuve una enfermedad.
Prometí tener novenas allá en San Juan de Letrán:
las dueñas iban de día, doncellas agora van.
(*Melisenda insomne*: *Primav.* 198)

—¿Qué es aquesto, mi señora? ¿Qué es esto, Rosaflorida?
O tenedes mal de amores, o estáis loca sandía.
—Ni yo tengo mal de amores, ni estoy loca sandía,

In line with similar developments already noted in *El conde Alemán y la reina* (no. 7 *supra*), the Sephardic texts all agree in replacing the brutally direct wording of the Spanish version ("más de fuerça que de grado / su virginidad gozó") with an almost ridiculously mild euphemism: "Allegóse para ella / hizo lo que no' [e]s razón" (Attias, vv. 21-22; Yoná, v. 11). And yet the expression may simply echo the

---

mas llevásesme estas cartas   a Francia la bien guarnida;
diéseslas a Montesinos,   la cosa que yo más quería.

(*Rosaflorida y Montesinos*: *Primav.* 179)

—¿De ké yyoráś, kativada?   ¿De ké yyoráś, božagrí'a?
Teníaś mal de amores   'o 'estáś rezín prenyyada.
Ni tení'a mal de amores,   ni 'estava rezín prenyyada. ...

(*La amante abandonada*: Yoná 15.6-8)

Compare *Willie o Winsbury* (Child 100A) where the similarity to *La adúltera* (*ó*) is strikingly close:

'What aileth thee, my daughter Janet,
  Ye look so pale and wan?
Have ye had any sore sickness,
  Or have ye been lying wi' a man?
Or is it for me, your father dear,
  And biding sae lang in Spain?'

'I have not had any sore sickness,
  Nor yet been lying wi' a man;
But it is for you, my father dear,
  In biding sae lang in Spain.'

Telltale changes of color or facial expression as an indication of guilt or of strong emotion are a recurrent device in both ballad and epic. In the *Refundición de las Mocedades de Rodrigo*: "Don Diego cató las cartas / et ovo la color mudado // ... [Rodrigo] desque vio el padre a los tíos muertos, / ovo la color mudado" (ed. *Reliquias*, vv. 389, 678). In prosifications of the *Jura de Santa Gadea*, King Alfonso maintains that he had no hand in the death of his brother Sancho, but he blanches as he swears to it: "Respondió el Rey: 'Amén' e mudógele la color" (*Crónica particular del Cid*, ed. Huber, p. 86; PCG, p. 519*b*.12 and 22). Cf. the following balladic examples: "Reduán le respondía / sin demudarse la cara" (*Primav.* 72); "su manto revuelto al brazo, / demudada la color" (*El infante vengador*: *Primav.* 150); "Montesinos que esto oyera, / la color se le ha mudado" (*Desafío de Montesinos y Oliveros*: *Primav.* 177); "Todos se quedan atentos, / todos les tiembla la barba, // y al que barba no tenía / la color se le mudaba" (*La cena y la Verónica*: RPM 439); "Disse-lhe el rei: —Vós que tendes? / Tendes la côr demudada! // —Das aguas frias, senhor, / que bebo de madrugada" (*Conde Claros fraile*: Braga, I, 397); "mentres la carta llegia / les colors ne trasmudava" (*Conde Claros fraile*: Aguiló, p. 322, vv. 143-144); "Les donzelles que hi havia / tramudaren de color" (*La dama de Aragón*: Macabich 71).

condemnatory understatement in Genesis 34:7: "The men were distressed and very angry, because he had commited an outrage in Israel by lying with Jacob's daughter—a thing not to be done." [6]

In their graphic and phonological character, the names used in the modern texts bespeak the Sephardim's unbroken contact with the Hebrew liturgical language and biblical tradition. In contrast to the Spanish version, where *Jacob, Siquén,* and *Emor* reflect Hispanized graphic pronunciations of transliterated biblical names, the Sephardic texts, to judge by our unedited versions, conserve more authentically Hebraic forms: *Yakov, Šehén, Hamor.* However, the Judeo-Spanish texts are not lacking in onomastic anomalies. Our unedited Salonikan and Sérrai versions change Hamor into "el rey Hevrón" (= Hebron, Salon.-Sérrai) or "Hevrot" (Salon.). Another Salonikan text speaks of both "Hemor" and "el rey Hevrón" and changes Shechem to "Zeher." Aberrant forms such as *Sihén* or *Chehén* for *Šehén* appear in Rhodian renditions.

The Judeo-Spanish versions differ from Genesis 34 in speaking of twelve brothers rather than two. In most Sephardic texts, the brothers remain anonymous, but where they are named their identity differs both from the Simeon and Levi of Genesis 34 and from the early Spanish ballad's Zabulón. The names chosen are, however, within the limits of biblical verisimilitude, since all appear in the list of Jacob's twelve sons in Genesis 49. One version from Salonika names "Rubén i Šimón" as brothers of Dinah (cf. Genesis 49:3, 5; 29:32-33). In texts from Rhodes and Salonika, "Yudá" or "Yeudá" takes the place of Zabulón as the principal agent of the destruction of Schechem's city—an appropriate choice in view of Genesis 49:8: "You, O Judah, your brothers shall praise; your hand shall be on the nape of your foes."

Many of the Judeo-Spanish versions (Yoná, Bassan; uned., Sérrai, Salonika) are evidently closer to the biblical narrative than is the Spanish ballad, in that Dinah, on returning home, speaks first to her father who, in Genesis 34:5 and 7 and in one of our unedited Salonikan texts, subsequently informs the brothers. In other Sephardic texts (Attias, SBS; all uned. Rhodian versions), like the sixteenth-century ballad, Dinah complains directly to the brothers.

---

[6] *The Torah* (Philadelphia, 1962), p. 62. (All subsequent biblical quotations in English are from this edition, unless otherwise identified.) Cf. Hauptmann's ed. of the *Escorial Bible*: "... ca asy non deuia ser fecho" (p. 95).

In Genesis 34:3 Shechem, enamored of Dinah, "spoke to the maiden tenderly" *after* he had assaulted her. In the Spanish ballad, Shechem's speech in praise of Dinah's beauty, an unsuccessful attempt at winning her favors, precedes her being forcibly taken to the castle (Ontañón de Lope, vv. 6-11). In most of the Sephardic texts this speech (Yoná, vv. 8-9) and Dinah's rebuff (v. 10) occur, as is logical, before she is outraged. Yet a number of Rhodian versions (SBS; uned. texts) place the dialog afterward, thus paralleling the biblical text in what is probably a secondary reorganization of the ballad narrative.

Action in the sixteenth-century ballad, like the pictorial recreation of Dinah's abduction in the Escorial Bible, seems to move in a thoroughly medieval milieu. Dinah watches the people of Salén as they build "villas y castillos"; later she is taken to Siquén's own castle. Many Sephardic versions mention no building, while others from Rhodes speak of a cave ("una meará" = H. *meᶜārāh*). Although no structure is specified in Genesis 34, the Salonikan versions, with their allusion to a tent (Yoná, v. 5), stay closer to the pastoral, nomadic ambiance which underlies the biblical narrative: "Jacob arrived safe in the city of Shechem which is in the land of Canaan—having come thus from Paddan-aram—and he encamped before the city. The parcel of land where he pitched his tent he purchased from the children of Hamor, Shechem's father, for a hundred *kesitahs*" (Genesis 33:18-19).

The ballad's dénouement in the Judeo-Spanish texts offers two further details taken from the Bible story which are lacking in the sixteenth-century Spanish version. The latter, obeying the contemporary "fragmentistic" vogue, ends with Zabulón's cry urging the annihilation of Emor and his people. The reader or listener is left to supply intuitively his own dénouement. Yoná's version seems to end happily, by concluding with the arrival of marriage emissaries (cf. Genesis 34:8-12). A unique feature of Attias' text is a verse in which Dinah sends a return message asking if Shechem will convert to Judaism: "Ella le mandó a decir, / si es que se hace jidió." This is apparently a distant echo of the feigned acquiescence voiced by Jacob's sons: "Only on this condition will we agree with you: that you will become like us in that every male among you is circumcised. Then we will give our daughters to you and take your daughters to ourselves; and we will dwell among you and become as one kindred" (Genesis 34:15-16).

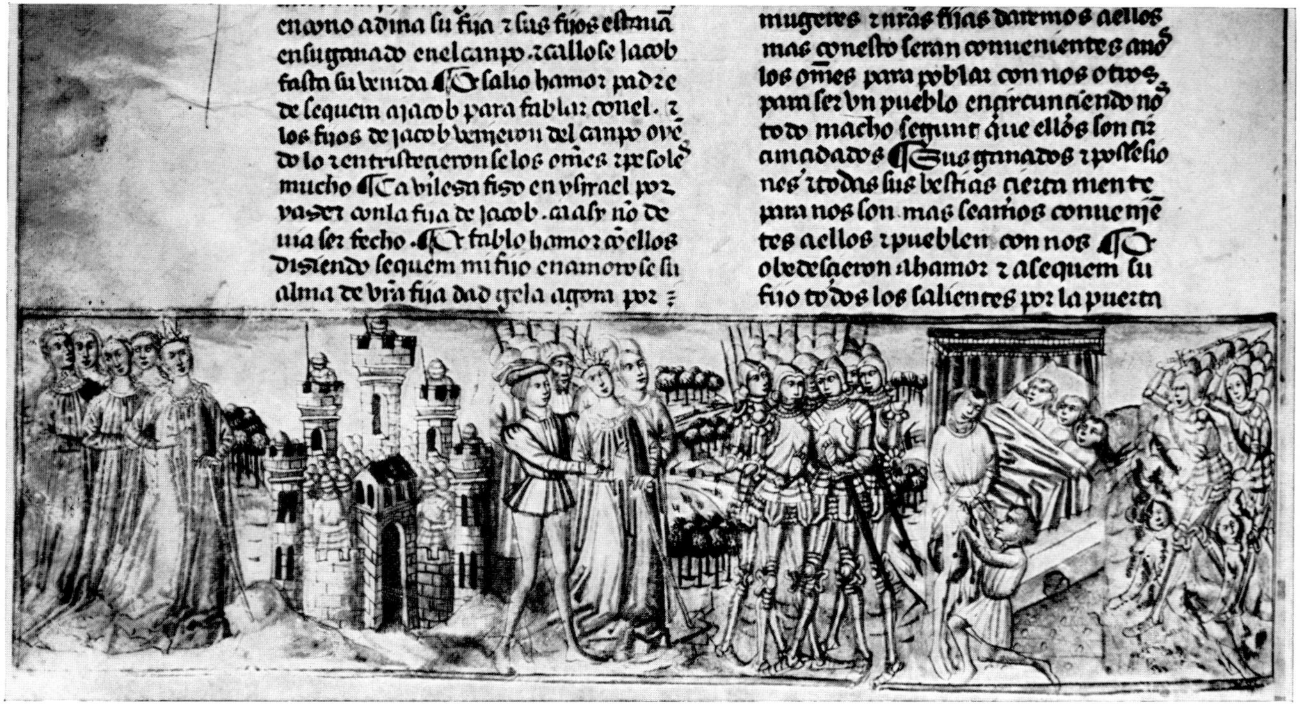

FIG. 4.—A medieval view of the abduction of Dinah (Escorial Bible MS I.j.4, fol. 16*v*).

The final verses of Attias, Levy (SBS), and several of our unedited texts clearly advocate, with interesting variations, what is only implied in the archaic Spanish version, namely, the destruction of Shechem and his people. In some cases only a general destruction is mentioned:

Ya se parten los doče hermanos, ya se van a estruir Hebrón.
(Attias; cf. LSO)

Esto ke sintieron sus doği ermanos, siete sevdades de Šehen ellos
[destroyeron.
(SBS)

Los ermanos ke esto sintieron, Sihén entero se destruyó.
(uned., Rhodes)

Kuando sintieron sus ermanos, grandes sañas se ensañaron.
Tomaron armas i kavalyos, la sivdad de Šehén kon fuersa la derro-
[karon.
(uned., Rhodes)

In others Dinah's brother borrows a tactic from Joshua and levels the city of Shechem with a mighty shout:

Kon un grito ke él echó, Šehén entero lo destruyó.
(uned., Rhodes)

Alsara su mano Yudá, kon un grito lo destruyó.
(uned., Rhodes)

Kon un grito de su boka, la muraya derrogó.
(uned., Salonika)

Two other dénouements result either from contamination or from individual intuitive amplification. In the version from Sérrai the ballad ends on a hopeful note. On hearing what Shechem has done, Dinah's father, here referred to as "the King," orders that he be killed, but Dinah, borrowing lines from the princess in *Conde Olinos* or *Conde Alemán* (see no. 7, n. 5 *supra*), pleads that his life be spared:

El rey ke esto sintió, presto a matar lo mandó.
—No lo matéš, el mi padre, ni lo keréš matar.
El mansevo es ižo i muchacho, el mundo kere gozar.

In one of our Salonikan texts, after the mighty shout brings down the walls, an intimidated "rey Hevrot" delivers Shechem to the avenging brother Yeudá: "El padre le dio en sus manos: / —Azelde de él lo ke kerés vos." [7]

To sum up: In its modern Sephardic form our ballad exhibits a number of extraneous amplifications, most of which are derived from stylistic devices traditional to Hispanic balladry: the allegorical prolog (in the Salonikan versions), the formula of walking under the eaves, the questions and answers concerning Dinah's pallor, as well as the city-destroying shout which doubtless is of biblical origin. At the same time, the Judeo-Spanish *Robo de Dina* offers a number of agreements with the biblical narrative which are lacking in its sixteenth-century Spanish counterpart: Dinah complains first to her father; her demand that Shechem convert to Judaism; the actual, not implicit, destruction of the city. Although the Judeo-Spanish ballad's proper names certainly reflect the continued influence of biblical learning, it seems more logical to derive the Sephardic versions from a more complete sixteenth-century text type than to suppose that their agreements with the Bible reflect later additions taken directly from Genesis. In its dramatic but intuitive ending the unique Spanish text is typically "fragmentistic," having been artfully abbreviated at the culminating moment of its action by some disciple of such masters of fragmentism as the recreators of *El conde Arnaldos* or *El prisionero.* Only the fortuitous discovery of a "complete" text which might have spelled out the vengeance of Jacob's sons could reveal the full dimensions of the ballad and the artistically oriented excisions of the anonymous sixteenth-century poet who reformed it.

BIBLIOGRAPHY

Eastern J.-Sp.: Attias 71; Bassan 18; Benardete 15 (= GSA); Gil 55 (= MP); LSO 113-114 (= Yoná, except for the final verse); MP 32 (= GSA); PTJ 35 (= CBU); SBS 129; UR 3 (= CBU 332; = BRI, with minor variants and errors; omission of v. 5).

Archaic Text: Ontañón de Lope, no. 15. See also M. Frenk Alatorre, "El Cancionero sevillano de la Hispanic Society (*ca.* 1568)," p. 359, no. 1.

---

[7] Cf. Q411.7. *Death as punishment for ravisher*; Q244. *Punishment for ravisher.*

9

EL PASO DEL MAR ROJO

(Crossing the Red Sea)

9A

'En katorze de nîsān, 'el primer dí'a del anyyo,
'el pu'evlo de Yiśrā'ēl de Ayifto salyyó kantando,
ken kon las masas al 'ombro, ken kon los 'ižos 'en brasos;
las mužeres kon 'el 'oro, lo ke 'era lo más livyyano.
Aboltaron la kara atrás, por ver lo ke an kaminađo.
Vyeron venir 'a Par^{c}ōh, kon 'un pendón korolađo.
—¿Ande mos truśites, Mōšeh, 'a mu'erir 'en despovlađo;
'a mu'erir sin sinbultura 'i 'en la mar ser a'ogado?
—Azed θĕfîlāh, ğidyyós, 'i yyo aré por 'el mi kavo.
Tanto fu'e sus 'esklamasyyones, al syelo 'izo burako.
Saltó 'una boz del syelo, kon Mōšeh 'uvo avlađo:
—Toma la vara, Mōšeh, toma la vara 'en tu mano.
Parte la mar 'en 12 kaležas, kita 'a los ğidyyós a nađo.
Ande kaminavan ğidyyós, la mar se 'iva aresekađo.
Ande kaminava miçrî, la mar se 'iva arenovando.

Source: SGM, p. 15.

9B

'En katorze de nîsān, 'el primer dí'a de 'el anyyo,
'el pu'evlo de Yiśrā'ēl de A'ífto salyyó kantando,

ken kon las masas al 'ombro 'i ken kon los 'ižos 'em brasos;
las mužeres kon 'el 'oro lo ke 'era lo más livyyano.
Aboltaron la kara atrás, por ver lo ke an kaminado.
Vyeron venir 'a Par^{c}ōh, kon 'un pendón kolorado.
—¿Ande mos truśites, Mōšeh, 'a morir 'en despovlado;
morir sin sumbultura 'i 'en la mar ser a'ogados?
—Azed 'orasyyón, ğudyyós, 'i yyo aré por mi kavo.
Tanto fu'e la 'esklamasyyón ke al syelo 'izo burako.
Salyyó 'una boz del syelo, kon Mōšeh 'uvo avlado:
—Toma la vara, Mōšeh, toma la vara 'en tu mano.
Parte la mar 'en doğe kaležas 'i kita los ğidyyós a nado.
Ande kaminavan ğudyyós, la mar se 'iva aresekando.
'I ande kaminavan miçrî, la mar se 'iva sobrevyyando.

Source: LRI 1 (pp. 3-4).
The first word of vv. 1, 3, 5, 7, 9, 11, and 14 is in square letters. The first word, first two words, or first three words of vv. 2, 4, 6, 8, 10, and 13 are repeated at the end of these verses, thus indicating repetition of the entire verse in singing. A similar repetition is indicated in González-Llubera's MS version. The repetition of v. 15 is indicated by the words *ande kaminavan.*

3*b* 'embrasos.
5*b* loke.

Translation:

9A-B

On the fourteenth day of Nisan, the first day of the year, [1] the people of Israel went out singing from Egypt. Some carried maces and some held children in their arms; the women carried the gold, which was lightest of all. (5) They all turned their faces to see how far they had come. They saw Pharaoh coming with a scarlet banner. "Where have you brought us, Moses, to die in this barren place, to die without burial, and to be drowned in the sea?" "Pray to God, Jews, and I will do my part." (10) Their outcries were so intense that they pierced the very

---

[1] Nisan is the first month of the Hebrew calendar. The text should read " 'el primer *mes* del anyyo," as in González-Llubera and the Portuguese versions.

heavens. A voice came out of the heavens and spoke to Moses: "Take the staff, Moses, take the staff in your hand. Divide the sea into twelve passages; let the Jews swim to safety." Where the Jews went the sea became dry. (15) Wherever an Egyptian went the sea closed in again (*B* became enraged).

Motifs:

9 V316. *Efficacy of prayer.*

11 A182.3. *God (angel) speaks to mortal.*

13 D1551. *Waters magically divide and close*; N817. *Deity as helper.*

Yoná's texts, which represent a single version, are distinguished by numerous minor variants, most of which are of purely linguistic interest: vv. 6: *korolađo* A, *kolorado* B; 7-8: *mu'erir* A, *morir* B; *sinbultura* A, *sumbultura* B; 9: *θĕfîlāh* A, *'orasyyón* B; *ğidyyós* A (*et passim*), *ğudyyós* B (*et passim*, except v. 13); 11: *saltó* A, *salyyó* B; 15: *arenovando* A, *sobrevyyando* B. Molho's text reflects this same version, except for certain aberrations (omission of v. 1*b*; breaking of assonance in v. 5*b*) and the addition of a repetitive but traditionally authentic verse after Yoná's v. 13 (cf. González-Llubera, vv. 32 ff.). Molho mixes readings characteristic of SGM (*muerir, simbultura, tĕfilá*) and LRI (*salió, sobreviando*). It is impossible to specify the origin of his text. Attias 79*a* is also closely related to the Yoná-Molho version but contains a number of interesting supplementary details: Moses leading the people with a flaming staff in his hand (v. 10); the misplaced allusion to Miriam's well (v. 11; cf. Exodus 15: 20-27); and a slightly more elaborate presentation of Pharaoh, with all his army (*fonsado*), carrying a scarlet banner in his right hand (vv. 15 ff.). By far the most circumstantial version recorded from modern tradition is that of Leo Azose of Marmara (Turkey), recited from a MS and recorded by us in Seattle in 1958 ("Hispanic Balladry," p. 235, n. 19). Its 20 verses rival, if they do not surpass in completeness, the 18 of González-Llubera's early eighteenth-century Venetian MS. [2]

[2] Ultimately related to *El paso del Mar Rojo* are vv. 65-84 of Attias' version of a biblical song concerning Moses (no. 78). Note the association of *El paso del Mar Rojo* with this same song in LRI 1.

The story told in the Sephardic ballad offers a blending of biblical matter (Exodus 14:10-31) with traditions from other Judaic holy writings (cf. González-Llubera, pp. 19 and 27, nn. 33 and 36). The initial scene, in which the people of Israel flee from Egypt laden with a variety of objects, recalls the ballad of *Álora la bien cercada,* where the Moors flee the town, carrying different commodities which are similarly assigned to men, women, and children. However, agreement between the two ballads is very distant and may well be only a coincidence. Compare:

Viérades moros y moras todos huir al castillo:
las moras llevaban ropa, los moros harina y trigo,
y las moras de quince años llevaban el oro fino,
y los moricos pequeños llevaban la pasa y higo.
(*Álora la bien cercada*: *Primav.* 79)

Unos yevavan la leña, otros yevavan el amasado;
los ombres a las kriaturas, de los brazos i de las manos.
Las mujeres yevavan el oro, ke es la koza más liviana.
(*Paso del Mar Rojo*: "Hispanic Balladry," no. 3)

V. 11 of Yoná's texts, which is common to all the Eastern versions of *El paso del Mar Rojo,* also occurs in the Moroccan *Consagración de Moisés*: "Salió una voz del cielo / que a Mosé iba llamando" (Benoliel, XIV, 367, no. 9). See also Larrea, *Canciones,* nos. 83-84, and MRuiz 44. Our Marmara version of *El paso del Mar Rojo* includes the variant "yamando," in contrast to the other texts which read "fablado" or "avlado."

A genetically related counterpart to *El paso del Mar Rojo* is known in Peninsular tradition, but only among the Crypto-Jews of Portugal, where the ballad forms part of a Passover prayer narrating the deeds of Moses and provides dramatic testimony to the common cultural heritage of two otherwise almost totally estranged groups of Sephardim:

Aos catorze de la luna do primeiro mês do ano,
parte o povo do Egito com Israel, seu irmano.
Cantigas iam cantando, ao Senhor iam louvando.
Louvavam o Senhor com todo o seu coração.
—Aonde nos trazes, Moisés? a este despovoado,
onde não há pão nem vinho nem pastor com ganado?
Pede ao Alto Senhor que nos leve a nossas casas.

Moisés, com vara alçada, bateu no mar salgado;
abriram-se doze carreiros para passar o seu povo,
passaram a são e salvo, porque o Senhor o mandou;
passaram o Mar Vermelho para a terra da Promissão. ...
(Morais Machado)

A quatorze da lua do primeiro mez do anno,
parte o Povo do Egypto, Israel meu irmano.
As cantigas que vão cantando ao Senhor vão louvando.
—Aonde nos trazes Moisés, aqui neste despovoado,
onde não ha pão nem lenha, nem nunca pastou o gado?
Louvamos ao alto Senhor que é o Senhor do nosso cabo.
Lá vem Moisés com a sua vara alçada a bater no mar
[selado.
Abriu-se o mar em doze carreiras, passará o meu povo
[em salvo. ...
(Schwarz)

BIBLIOGRAPHY

Eastern J.-Sp.: Attias 79-79*a* (79 = González-Llubera); [3] González-Llubera 3; "Hispanic Balladry," no. 3; Molho, *Usos*, pp. 255-256; PTJ 39-39*a* (= "Hispanic Balladry," Molho).

Portuguese: Morais Machado, no. 56 (p. 39); Schwarz, no. 51 (pp. 72-73; reprinted, with an English translation, in "The Crypto-Jews of Portugal," p. 292). [4]

Studies: NSR, p. 66, nn. 26-28.

---

[3] Cf. the facsimile between pp. 192-193 of Attias' collection.

[4] Amílcar Paulo, *Romanceiro criptojudaico*: *Subsídios para o estudo do folclore marrano* (Bragança, 1969), pp. 10 and 18, reproduces the versions of Morais Machado and Schwarz.

10

LA TORMENTA CALMADA + EL IDÓLATRA

(The Quieted Storm + The Idolater)

10A

Se pase'a pastor fi'el   kon su ganađo ake'a tadre,
kon remolinos 'i tru'enos   'i los relámpagos muyy grandes.
—Senyyor, Senyyor, si pekí,   'el mi ganađo non lo fa'e.
Si 'el mi ganađo pekó,   lo ke non 'es mí'o 'eskapáme.
'Esto ke sintyeron las nuves,   se boltaron por 'otras partes.
Se davan de penyya 'en penyya   'i por agu'a korí'a sangre.
Yyoravan los kapitanes   'i todos los ke 'en la mare.
'Un burlante ayy 'entre 'elyyos   ke 'en 'Elyya non ağetare.
—Senyyora, la mi Senyyora,   de 'esta fortuna 'eskapáme.
Si de 'esta fortuna me 'eskapas,   kon 'oro Vos 'enkoronare.
'Esto sintyyó 'el Patrón del mundo,   las 'olas más sobrevyyare.
—Vate, vate, puta amarí'a,   ke sos falsa 'i mentiroza.

Source: GSA 7. Variants: LRI 11; BRI 10; GRI 10.
The second hemistichs, preceded by the word *'i*, are repeated in all texts. The final hemistich is not repeated.

1*a* Se *in square letters BRI / GRI.*
1*b* de ake'a tadre *LRI / BRI / GRI,* tađre *in repetition GSA.*
7*b* mar *LRI / BRI / GRI.*
11*a* de 'el mundo *LRI / GRI.*
11*b* las aguas más sobrevyyare *BRI / GRI.*
12 Vate, vate, tú, amarí'a, / ke kon ti non atorgare *GRI.*

Tenemos 'un padre raḥămān ke munğas maravías aze.
Molas aga de kontino, de prisa ke non de tadre.
'Él kite la nave de golfo, komo la parida ke pare.
Ansí aga kon los ḥazinos, de prisa ke non de tadre.
Ke ningunos se dezesperen, ni ke pyedran la 'esperansa.
Ke despu'és de la fortuna, 'Él mos mande la bonansa.

13*a* Tenemos 'un padre piadozo *LRI* / *BRI* / *GRI*.
13*b* ke *om. in repetition GRI*, muğas *in repetition GSA*, muğas *BRI*, munğas maravías mos aze *GRI*.
14*a* dekontino *GSA*.
14*b* detadre *GSA*.
15*a* 'Él ke kite la nave del golfo *LRI* / *BRI* / *GRI*.
16*b* deprisa ke non detadre (de prisa *in repetition*) GSA.
17*a* Ke ningunos ke se dezesperen *LRI* / *BRI*, Ke ningunos ke non se dezesperen *GRI*.
18*b* 'Él mos manda *LRI* / *BRI*.

10B

Se pase'a 'el pastor fi'el 'en 'una manyyana tan klara,
kon remolinos 'i tru'enos 'i los relámpagos muyy grandes.
—Senyyor, Senyyor, si pekí, 'en mi ganađo lo fa'e.
Si 'el mi ganađo lo kulpa, lo ke non 'es mí'o apartáme.
'Esto ke sintyeron las nuves; se 'eğaron por 'otra parte.
Se davan de penyya 'en penyya, por agu'a korí'a sangre.
Yyoravan los kapitanes; todos los de la mar yyoran.
Adyentro de ake'a mar yyoran, aví'a 'una senyyora.
—Senyyora, la mi Senyyora, 'eskápame de 'esta fota.
Si de 'esta fota me 'eskapas, de 'oro te visto toda.
'Esto sintyyó 'el Patrón del mundo, más asobrevyyó las agu'as.
—Vate, vate, puta amarí'a, ke sos falsa 'i mentiroza.

Source: RSA 6. Variants: GRA 9.
2*b* + se torna *GRA*.
3*b* 'el mi ganado lo fa'e *GRA*.
6*b* 'i por agu'a *GRA*.
8*a* yyoran *is probably an erroneous repetition from the previous verse.*
11*a* de 'el mundo *GRA*.
11*b* las 'olas *GRA*.
12*a* Vate, vate, kota (*sic*) amarí'a *GRA*.

Tenemos 'un Dyyo bendiğo, ke munğas maravías aze.
Molas aga tan de prisa, de prisa 'i non de tađre.
15 Ansí aga kon los ḥazinos 'i la pariđa kuando pare. (16-15)
Ke ningunos se dezesperen, ni ke pyeđran la 'esperansa. (17)
17 Ke detrás de la fortuna, 'Él mos mande la bonansa. (18)

13*b* muğas *GRA*.
14*a-b* deprisa *RSA* / *GRA*.
14*b* detađre *RSA*.

Translation:

10A

The faithful shepherd is traveling with his stock that afternoon, amid whirlwinds and thunderbolts and great flashes of lightning. "Lord, Lord, if I have sinned, let my property not suffer. If my property was at fault, spare what is not mine. (5) When the clouds heard this they turned in another direction. They struck against cliff after cliff and it poured blood instead of rain. All the captains wept and all who were at sea. There is one blasphemer among them who did not believe in Her. "Lady, my Lady, save me from this storm. (10) If You save me from this storm, I will crown You with gold." When the Ruler of the world heard this He made the waves wilder. "Be gone, be gone, whorish Mary, for you are false and deceitful. We have a merciful Father who does many miracles. May He do them without end, quickly and without delay. (15) May He save the ship from the gulf, as He protects the woman in childbirth.[1] May He do the same for the sick quickly and without delay. May none despair nor lose hope. (18) May He send us fair weather after the storm."

---

[1] The comparison of the woman in childbirth with a ship beset by storms at sea is a traditional commonplace in Sephardic balladry. Cf. *El chuflete* (no. 27 *infra*). On the psychological implications of such imagery, as well as abundant parallels in early mythology, see C. G. Jung, *Psychology of the Unconscious* (New York, 1965), especially pp. 244-246.

10B

The faithful shepherd travels on a morning so clear, amid whirlwinds and thunderbolts and great flashes of lightning. "Lord, Lord, if I have sinned, let my stock not suffer. If You blame my property, set aside what is not mine." (5) When the clouds heard this they headed in another direction. They struck against cliff after cliff; it poured blood instead of rain. The captains were weeping; all who were at sea are weeping. In that sea where they weep there was a lady. "Lady, my Lady, save me from this boat. (10) If You save me from this boat, I will dress You all in gold." When the Ruler of the world heard this He made the waters wilder. "Be gone, be gone, whorish Mary, for you are false and deceitful. We have a blessed God, who does many miracles. May He do them quickly, quickly and without delay. (15) May He do the same for the sick and the woman in childbirth. May none despair nor lose hope. (17) May He send us fair weather after the storm."

Motifs:

3-5 V52.24. *Prayer stops storm at sea* (Bordman); V316. *Efficacy of prayer*; A197. *Deity controls elements.*
6 F960. *Extraordinary nature phenomena—elements and weather*; F962.4. *Shower of blood.*
10 Cf. M266. *Man promises to build church if he is saved at sea.*

Yoná has recorded two rather different traditional versions of a hybrid narrative created from two originally independent ballads: *La tormenta calmada* (vv. 1-6 and 13-18), a unique [2] Eastern Sephardic

---

[2] A curious ballad known in the Catalan tradition, *El pastor deslliurat dels dimonis per la mare de Déu* (mixed *á-a* and *á-e* assonance), shows certain similarities to *La tormenta calmada,* especially in its initial verses:

Si n'hi havia un pastoritu, que en gordava una ramada;
si se'n giren trons i llamps i molta tempestat d'aigues. ...

(OCPC, III, 252)

The similarity is probably coincidental; the rest of the poem bears no relationship to *La tormenta calmada.*

derivative of a late sixteenth-century erudite *romance,* and *El idólatra* (vv. 7-12), a widely distributed traditional ballad which may ultimately be of Hispano-Jewish origin. Yoná's various printings seem to bespeak continued contact with oral tradition, as reflected in certain minor textual alterations. In 10B, the hemistich "más asobrevyyó las agu'as" of RSA, which interrupts the *ó-a* assonance of the interpolated poem, is altered to a more authentic "más asobrevyyó las 'olas" in GRA. In 10A, GSA, LRI, and BRI, all read "Vate, vate, puta amarí'a, / ke sos falsa 'i mentiroza," but GRI, the latest printing of all, alters the second hemistich to "ke kon ti non atorgare," a change which adjusts the assonance to that of the verses of the following fragment of *La tormenta calmada* and which could also be based upon some authentic traditional variant.

La tormenta calmada has enjoyed a rather wide distribution among the Eastern communities. Attias' and Bassan's texts are from the Salonikan tradition, as are two unedited versions in our collection. Levy's fragment (SBS 5) and undoubtedly Galante's version also are from the tradition of Rhodes, whence we have collected seven additional texts. Levy (SBS 4) records a very brief version from Istanbul. In Salonika, the ballad is known both in the contaminated form represented by Yoná and Attias and also in versions which, like the texts from other areas, lack the intrusion of *El idólatra* (Bassan and uned. texts). In Rhodes, *La tormenta calmada* often begins with a set of not inappropriate verses which serve as a stock beginning for numerous ballads in the Eastern tradition: "En el prinsipio de los mis maliz / navegí kon la fortuna . . ." (SBS 5 and uned. versions).[3] Rhodian versions are also variously contaminated by *El falso hortelano* (no. 21 *infra*)—as is Levy's fragment from Istanbul (SBS 4)—by *El robo de Elena* (uned. versions; cf. no. 11 *infra*), and by *La Muerte del duque de Gandía* (SBS 5.6-7).

The Sephardic versions of *La tormenta* exemplify the total metamorphosis and reinterpretation of an erudite ballad which has been absorbed into oral tradition. To our knowledge, the earliest counterpart of the Judeo-Spanish ballad appears in Pedro de Moncayo's *Flor de varios romances nuevos y canciones* (Huesca, 1589). This short muti-

[3] See NSR, p. 68, n. 33, and for more details, *El falso hortelano* (no. 21 *infra*).

lated text (cf. vv. 13-14) is certainly not the source of the Sephardic song. It lacks numerous elements which are present both in a later more extensive rendition and in the latter's Judeo-Spanish derivative. The 1589 version reads as follows:

Tornando las nuues negras   y espessos los claros ayres (1)
con remolinos y poluos   señalando tempestades, (2)
estaua Griseldo solo   *con sus cabras vna tarde,* (6)
y antes quel pastor pudiesse   recogellas y guardarse, (7)
rasgan las nuues sus senos   *y disformes piedras caen,* (8)
mil fieras contrarias suyas   medrosas van a buscalle, (13)
ques esto cielos dezia?   tan grande vengança cabe (9)
en vuestros senos, y vientos   contra humildes animales? (10)
si en algo yo peque   *mi ganado no lo pague,* (11)
y si en el me castigays   *al ques ageno dexadle,* (12)
dexad mi pobre cabilo   medrosas fieras dexadle, (15)
y buscad quien os guarezca   sin que el cielo os escalabre. (16)
En esto passo la nuue   a pesar de sus pesares, (17*a*-20*b*)
a cierta mudança destas   diziendo a su mal que guarde.[4] (20*a*-19*b*)

A much more extensive and coherent version appears in a *Tercera parte de flor de varios romances* (Madrid, 1593). Except for orthographic differences the Valencian printing of the same year is identical, but the text breaks off at v. 13*b* because of a physical lacuna in the only known copy (FRG, III, fol. 214v). The more extensive 1593 version is reproduced with minimal differences in the *Romancero general de 1600* and by Durán:

Tronando las nuues negras   y espessos los claros ayres
con remolinos y poluos   señalauan tempestades, (2*a*)
tinieblas cubren la tierra   sin que la noche llegasse,
y el Sol se escondio huyendo   *de los relampagos grandes,* (2*b*)
entre dos tajadas peñas   junto a vn mõte de arrayhanes,
estaua Riselo solo   *con sus cabras vna tarde,* (1)

[4] Pedro de Moncayo, *Flor de varios romances nuevos y canciones* (Huesca, 1589), fol. 121*r-v* (= FRG, I). Numbers on the right correspond to the text printed in the *Tercera parte* (1593) and the *Romancero de 1600.* Elements present in the Sephardic ballad are italicized.

antes que el pastor pudiera recogerlas, ni guardarse:
rompen las nuues sus senos y disformes piedras caen, (cf. 6)
que es esto cielos dezia, tan grande vengança cabe
en vn pecho tan piadoso contra simples animales?
Si yo soy el que peque mi ganado no lo pague, (3)
y si el mio lo merece, el que es ageno dexalde, (4)
mil fieras contrarias vias huyendo van a buscarme,
que al hõbre acuden los brutos en peligros semejantes,
dexad mi pobre cabrio, medrosas fieras dexadme
y buscad quien os guarezca sin que el cielo os descalabre,
en esto passo la nuue monstrando por otra parte (5)
el Sol sus dorados rayos con muy alegre semblante,
alegre quedo Riselo diziendo a su mal que aguarde (Attias 13)
alguna mudança destas a pesar de sus pesares.[5]

The Sephardic versions pack the essence of the twenty-verse sixteenth-century ballad into seven verses: the shepherd with his flock, the dreadful storm, the plea that the animals —or, in any case, those which do not belong to the shepherd— be spared, the retreat of the storm, and the shepherd's joy at being delivered from danger ("Alegre quedó el pastor / con su ganado aquella tadre": Attias, vv. 13-14). The pious epilog (Yoná, vv. 13-18), on the other hand, seems to be a purely Sephardic creation. The sixteenth-century ballad possesses a minimum of religious overtones: Riselo merely invokes "the Heavens," which are said to have a "merciful heart" (*Tercera parte,* vv. 9-10). The storm clouds seem to disperse only by some happy coincidence. Starting from these essentially non-religious origins, the Judeo-Spanish ballad has come to celebrate in the most fervent terms God's miraculous response to the prayers of a true believer.

Yoná's vv. 7-12 derive from *El idólatra,* a ballad, which from a profoundly anti-Christian perspective seeks to discredit the Virgin's

[5] *Tercera parte de flor de varios romances* (Madrid, 1593), fol. 118*r-v* (FRG, III). Variants: 9*a* cielo *Rom. 1600, Durán.* / 10*a* en vuestro pecho *Durán.* / 13*a* contrarias mías *Rom. 1600, Durán.* / 18*b* y su divino semblante *Durán.* Italics mark correspondences with the Sephardic versions; numbers on the right refer to Yoná's texts or, in the case of v. 19*a*, to Attias.

miraculous intervention in rescuing those in peril on the sea. [6] This uniquely anti-Christian ballad might be described as a miracle in reverse—a rejection of the Virgin in one of her best-known rôles, as *stella maris,* protector of mariners, which can be so abundantly documented in medieval miracle collections. [7] Whoever composed the original version of *El idólatra* did so in violent reaction to sentiments such as those expressed in the following verses of Berceo:

La bendicta Virgen es estrella clamada,
Estrella de los mares, guiona deseada,
Es de los marineros en las cuitas guardada,
Ca quando essa veden, es la nave guiada. [8]

Sparsely documented from widely separated archaic lateral areas of the Hispanic world (Portugal, Galicia, Catalonia, the Canary Islands, and the Sephardic East: Sarajevo, Salonika, Rhodes), *El idólatra,* with its bluntly phrased anti-Mariolatrous sentiments in the Sephardic texts and the Virgin's uncharacteristic rejection of a sinner's pleas in the various Christian versions, has been convincingly supposed by Diego Catalán to have originated among the Spanish Jews. [9]

The hypocritical idolater, who promises exaggerated golden embellishments to a "graven image" in return for some favor, only to blaspheme against the object of his former adoration when his request is denied, recalls the famous *Fuga del rey Marsín,* where the defeated Moorish king cries out in rage against the Prophet:

—Reniego de ti, Mahoma, y avn de quanto hize en ti;
hízete el cuerpo de plata, pies y manos de marfil
y por más te honrar, Mahoma, la cabeça de oro te hiz. [10]

---

[6] Attention might be called to the transparent, euphemistic attenuation of *María* to *amarí'a* (literally 'yellow') in Yoná, v. 12.

[7] See, for example, T. F. Crane, "Miracles of the Virgin," *RR,* II (1911), 235-279: pp. 240-243, 259-260, 263-265 (Miracles, nos. I-III, XVIII, XXI); Gonzalo de Berceo, *Milagros de Nuestra Señora,* ed. A. G. Solalinde (Madrid, 1944), no. XXII: "El náufrago salvado," strs. 583-624.

The situation of *El idólatra* is closely paralleled, but in an atmosphere of Christian piety, in the Catalan *Naufragi* (AFC 2313).

[8] Berceo, *Milagros de Nuestra Señora,* ed. Solalinde, str. 32. Cf. also str. 73 and *Libro de buen amor,* ed. Corominas, str. 1681.

[9] See RCan, pp. 31-32; DRH, pp. 30-31.

[10] *Pliegos góticos,* I, 132; ASW 68. Moors who curse Mohammed also appear in the cyclic ballad of the *Infantes de Lara,* "Ya se salen de Castilla" (*Roman-*

The setting in which the action of Yoná's hybrid text evolves has been completely altered. Galante's and Levy's versions of *La tormenta calmada* from Rhodes and Istanbul begin with a maritime prolog; other texts, contaminated with *El robo de Elena* and *La muerte del duque de Gandía,* likewise evoke a seafaring milieu. The final allusions to *fortuna* and *bonanza,* which occur in most versions of *La tormenta calmada,* are also ultimately from mariners' language. Indeed, the entire poem is aimed at showing how God's power "saves ships from the gulf" (v. 15). In our unedited Rhodian texts, the scene has become altogether maritime:

Se paseó el pastor fidel, ¡Señor del mundo! un día de akeyos días.
I travó gancho i avrió velas i la nave partiría.

---

cero tradicional, II, 97, no. 1*a*.6). An offer to cover the Virgin's image with gold occurs in at least one Peninsular ballad:

Virgem Senhora da Lapa! Ouvi-me, ó Virgem, Maria!
Se me prenderdes o moiro, eu de oiro te vestiria.
(*El moro cautivo*: Vasconcellos, "Bibl. do Povo," p. 28)

In the Catalan *Dida del infant* the negligent nurse, who has caused the baby prince's death, promises:

Verge, si-m torneu l'infant, corona d'or vos faria,
i al vostre fill gloriós un altre de plata fina.
(Avenç, II, 98)

In *El naufragi* the frightened sailors offer the Virgin a crown of gold and precious stones: "Us farem fer una corona, / tota d'or i de brillants" (AFC 2313). Compare also *Valdovinos sorprendido en la caza,* where the hero similarly addresses his sword and promises to cover it with gold if he is successful in battle:

¡Oh mi espada doradina de buen oro y buen metal!
Que de muchas me libraste, désta no me has de fallar.
Y si de ésta me librases, te vuelvo a sobredorar.
(RQDB-II 70)

Cf. also *Conde Olinos* (CVR, p. 138; ASW 203). Analogous verses occur in the Judeo-Spanish and Christian versions of *El idólatra*:

—Valednos, Virgen, valednos, valednos, Virgen señora.
Una vez que me valestes, de oro te di una corona.
Que si de ésta me sacares, de oro os vestiré toda.
(RCan, pp. 31, 29)

I kargada estava la nave de oro i de piedras finas.
¡Ay! Kaminando en mares ondas, fortuna grande él topаría. ... [11]

Similarly some unedited Salonikan versions, though not contaminated by *El idólatra,* also begin by placing the action at sea: "Avía grande fortuna, / ke la nave ya va derrokare" (placed after v. 2 of the Yoná versions). In this context the shepherd's flock must inevitably become the mariner's cargo. Hence, the word *ganado* ('live stock') loses its usual bucolic meaning and takes on the etymologically more primitive sense of 'goods' or 'material wealth,' a semantic archaism which, in any event, can be documented elsewhere in Sephardic balladry. [12] The Judeo-Spanish *romance* has been drawn inexorably seaward and into the orbit of a widely known ballad commonplace: the sea-miracle, wrought in answer to a prayer, confession, or conversion, [13] as exemplified by the Scottish *Brown Robyn's Confession,* its Scandinavian and Slavic relatives, [14] the Greek *Kùr Boriàs,* [15] or the Canarian *Romería del pescador.* [16] This maritime reinterpretation of the once pastoral sixteenth-century ballad undoubtedly facilitated the coalescence of *La tormenta calmada* and the Hispano-Judaic *Idólatra* in the Salonikan tradition.

---

[11] Sung by Rosa Franco, Seattle (Washington), August 25, 1958.

[12] Cf. *Vos labraré un pendón* (no. 22.11 *infra*): "Toparéš syen dukađikos, / los ke 'el mi ganađo son" ('You'll find a hundred ducats, which are all my wealth').

[13] Cf. D2140.3. *Weather changed on confession of deed*; V24.1. *Confession of sins of a pilgrim calms a great storm at sea*; V254.2. *Ship in storm saved because of sailors' "Ave Maria."* On the practice of throwing a sinner to the waves in order to calm a storm, see F. Rodríguez Marín, "Algunas supersticiones de mar y tierra," in his edition of Cervantes' *Viaje del Parnaso* (Madrid, 1935), pp. 493-500: pp. 495 ff.

[14] See Child 57; Bronson 57; Gerould, p. 37, n. 1; DgF, VI, no. 376 (*Hr. Peders Skriftemaal paa Havet*); Arwidsson, II, no. 67 (*Herr Peders Sjöresa*); FSF, no. 38; Prior, II, 225-233; Warrens, pp. 216-223; EEB 337.

[15] Baud-Bovy, *Textes,* pp. 266-270; *Akadēmía,* pp. 472-476; Petropoulos, I, 144-145; Politis, *Eklogaì,* no. 88.

[16] Pérez Vidal, "Romancero tradicional canario," *RDTP,* V, no. 4; RCan 55.

BIBLIOGRAPHY

La tormenta calmada

Eastern J.-Sp.: Attias 59; Castelete;[17] Bassan 19; Galante 6; Gil, pp. xxix and xxx (= Galante, MP); MP 40 (= GSA, with minimal differences: v. 2 "y (los) relámpagos"; v. 5 "partieron" instead of "se boltaron"); PTJ 44-44*a* (= Galante, CBU); SBS 4.13 ff. and 5.8-11; UR 8 (= CBU 337-338; = GRI).

Archaic Texts: Durán 1525; Pedro de Moncayo, *Flor de varios romances nuevos y canciones* (Huesca, 1589), fol. 121*r-v* (= FRG, I); Id., *Tercera parte de flor de varios romances* (Madrid, 1593), fol. 118*r-v* and Felipe Mey, same title (Valencia, 1593), fols. 214*v*-215*r* (FRG, III); *Romancero de 1600,* no. 193.

El idólatra

Eastern J.-Sp.:

Contaminated version: Attias 59 (vv. 15.26); Castelete; RCan, p. 31 (2d text = GSA); Gil 6 (p. xxx; = MP); MP 40 (vv. 7-12 of the *Cultura Española* edition = GSA); PTJ 44*a* (= CBU); UR 8 (vv. 7-12; = CBU 337-338; = GRI).

Autonomous version: Attias, p. 157; RCan, p. 30; DRH 2; PTJ 44b (= DRH).

Canarian: RCan 12.

Galician: Sampedro, no. 271.

Portuguese: Alves 573; Braga, III, 590; Chaves, "O ciclo dos descobrimentos," pp. 143-144; Martins, I, 149; Tavares, *RL,* VIII, p. 74 (no. 8); VRP 616.

Catalan: Milá 34, variant Al (p. 42).

Studies: Armistead-Silverman, "Christian Elements," p. 27; Bénichou, p. 368; DRH, pp. 30-33; RCan, pp. 27-32. Cf. also RoH, II, 337, n. 66.

---

[17] See n. 5 of our Introduction.

II

EL ROBO DE ELENA

(The Abduction of Helen of Troy)

IIA

'Estava la reyna 'Izela   'i 'en su bastidor lavrando, 1
agužika de 'oro 'en mano,   pendón de amor lavrando. 2
Por a'í pasó Parize,   'i 'el su lindo namorado. 5
—Para 'este pu'erpo, Parize,   ¿ké 'ofisyyo avéš tomado?
—Merkader so, mi senyyora,   merkader 'i 'eskrivano.
Tres naves tengo 'en 'el porto   kargadas de 'oro 'i brokado.
De la nave ke yyo vengo,   aví'a 'un riko mansano,
ke 'eğava mansanas de amores   'invyerno 'i 'enverano. 10
—Si 'esto 'es verdad, Parize,   loryya 'es de lo kontare. 11
¿Si vos plazí'a, Parize,   de vos 'ir 'a vižitare? 12
—Vengáś 'en bu'ena 'ora, reyna,   vos 'i 'el vu'estro reynađo. 13
Armó velas 'i 'eğó ganğo;   para 'en Fransyya la lyevaron. 15

Source: GSA 8.
The text bears the following headnote: "Dito romanso se kanta 'en 'el son de 'ôḥîlāh." The second hemistich of each verse, except verse 12, is repeated. The word *'i* precedes each repetition.

11B

’Estava la reyna ’Izela   ’i ’en su bastidor lavrando,
agužika de ’oro ’en mano   ’i ’un pendón de amor lavrando.
Kuando le ka’e la alguža,   ’i kuando le ka’e ’el dedale,
kuando le ka’e la tižera,   non tyene kon ké kortare.
Por a’í pasó Parize,   ’el su lindo namorado.
—Para ’este pu’[e]rpo, Parize,   ¿ké ’ofisyyo avéś tomado?
—Merkader so, la mi senyyora,   merkader ’i ’eskrivano.
Tres naves tengo ’en ’el porto,   kargadas de ’oro ’i brokado.
La nave ke yyo vengo,   aví’a ’un riko mansano,
ke ’eǧava mansanas de amores   ’en ’invyerno ’i ’enverano.
—Si ’esto ’es verdad, Parize,   loryya ’es de lo kontare.
¿Si vos plazí’a, Parize,   de vos ’ir ’a vižitare?
—Vengáś ’en bu’ena ’ora, reyna,   vos ’i ’el vu’estro reynado.
Deske la vido venir[e],   armó velas ’i alevant[ó] ganǧo.
’I armó velas ’i alevantó ganǧo;   de parte [de] Fransyya la yevaron.

Source: LRI 7. Variants: BRI 4; RHP 6; GRI 4.
Headnote: “Dita romansa se kanta ’en ’el son de ’ôḥîlāh lā-’Ēl” LRI. There is no headnote in BRI, RHP, and GRI. The second hemistich of each verse, except v. 15, is repeated in LRI, BRI, and GRI. The word *’i* precedes each repetition. Only v. 1 is repeated in RHP.

1*a* Estava *in boldface BRI / RHP / GRI.*
3*a* kalye *GRI* (3*a et passim*), aguža *BRI / RHP / GRI.*
3*b* ’o kuando *BRI,* ’i *om. RHP.*
4*b* no tyene *BRI / RHP.*
6*a* pu’ rpo *LRI,* pu’erpo *BRI / RHP / GRI.*
7*b* ’i merkader *GRI.*
8*b* kargada *GRI* (kargadas *in repetition*).
10*b* ’i ’en ’enverano *GRI.*
11*a* Ke si ’esto es verdad *GRI.*
11*b* gloryya *RHP,* kontar *RHP.*
12*b* vižitar *BRI* (*but* vižitare *in repetition*) */ RHP.*
13*b* vos ’i vu’estro *BRI / RHP / GRI.*
14*a* Des ke *LRI,* Deske *BRI / GRI,* venir[e]: *end of word hidden by fold in paper. LRI,* venire *BRI / GRI,* venir *RHP.*
14*b* alevant (*sic*) *LRI* (alevantó *in repetition*).
15*a* *We count the repetition of* 14*b as the first hemistich of v.* 15.
15*b* de parte Fransyya *LRI,* de parte de Fransyya *BRI / RHP / GRI,* se la yevaron *RHP / GRI,* lyevaron *BRI.*

Translation (Material from B is in brackets):

11A-B

There was Queen Izela embroidering on a frame, holding a golden needle and making a pennant of love. [First she drops her needle, then she drops her thimble, and when she drops her scissors, she has nothing with which to cut.] (5) Paris passed by, Paris, her handsome lover. "For that fine figure of yours, Paris, what employment have you taken?" "I am a merchant, my lady, a merchant and a scribe. I have three ships at the port, loaded with gold and brocade. In the ship from which I've come, there's a fine apple tree (10) that gives love apples both in winter and in summer." "If this is true, Paris, it is a glorious thing to be told. If it pleased you, Paris, I would come to visit you." "Come, when you will, Queen, you and all your kingdom." [As soon as he saw her aboard,] (15) he raised sails and lifted anchor. [He raised sails and lifted anchor] and they carried her off to France.

Motifs:

5 ff. R12.4. *Girl enticed into boat and abducted*; K775. *Capture by luring merchant to look at supposed bargain*; K775.1. *Capture by taking aboard ship to inspect wares*; K1332. *Seduction by taking aboard ship to inspect wares.*

Versions A and B of *The Abduction of Helen of Troy* testify to Yoná's efforts, similar to those of sixteenth-century *Cancionero* editors,[1] to correct and amplify his printed *romances* by continued reference to oral tradition. Dissatisfied with the brief GSA version (A), Yoná adds the attractive traditional lines in which the fallen scissors provide an excuse for Helen's encounter with Paris.[2] Equally authentic

[1] See n. 17 of our Introduction.

[2] These verses seem to occur only in the Salonikan tradition. The situation is closely paralleled, probably by coincidence, in the Greek song of *The Hundred Words,* where a fallen spindle serves an identical purpose: "Le jeune homme

is v. 14, which supplies an indispensable transition.[3] Text B does not, however, improve upon A's awkward v. 7 by omitting the word *de* (B, v. 9).

Yoná's rendition of the ballad remains truncated in comparison with most other versions, which close with a second dialog between Paris and Helen, where the significance of the apple tree is explained (Attias 6.37 ff.). The verses in question are known to all three branches of the modern tradition.

A sixteenth-century ballad, probably derived in part from some medieval epic poem on the Troy legend,[4] *El robo de Elena* occurs today in oral tradition only in the Canary Islands and among the Sephardim of Morocco and the East, where it has enjoyed very wide diffusion: Attias, Benardete, Díaz-Plaja, and Sciaky reflect the Salonikan tradition; Adatto, Danon, Milwitzky ("versión fragmentaria"), and Romey record versions most likely from Turkey. Our collection includes texts from Salonika, Rhodes, Tekirdağ, Edirne, and Jerusalem. Morocco has yielded renditions from Tetuán (Larrea), Tetuán-Oran (Bénichou), Tangier (MP), Alcázar (MRuiz) and, in our unedited collection, from Larache and Arcila as well.

The modern Judeo-Spanish and Canarian versions preserve only the first half of the ballad which, as printed in the sixteenth-century, consists of two stylistically different segments: the first being in oral

---

souhaite que la chaleur devienne intolérable, que la belle sorte filer à sa fenêtre, que le fil se coupe, que tombe le fuseau, et qu'elle le charge de le lui rapporter" (Baud-Bovy, *Textes,* p. 200). Compare also the following verses from *Hē núfē koumpára* (a Greek congener of *La bella en misa,* no. 24 *infra*): " 'Oh, that the thread might break, that the shuttle might fall, / so that the girl might fall idle and go to the window.' / Then her thread broke, her shuttle also fell, / and the girl fell idle and went to the window. / A horseman saw her and came forward ..." (Argenti-Rose, II, 730-731). All the same, that the Sephardic verses are formulistic and more than likely of Peninsular origin is indicated by the presence of v. 3 of Yoná's text B in at least one version of *A nau Catrineta*:

> Tambem vèjo tres donzellas debaixo de um laranjal;
> uma caíu-lhe a agulha, outra caíu-lhe o dedal;
> ergueu-se a mais mocinha, ergueu-se, foi-lh'os buscar.
>
> (Braga, I, 28)

[3] *Primavera* 109: "Desque todos fueron dentro ..."; Attias 6.33: "Desque la vido venire. ..." Other Eastern texts offer similar verses.

[4] See RoH, I, 353; RCan, p. 23.

traditional style, while the second is a minstrel composition. The modern tradition, divorced from its classical origins, turns Paris into a seafaring merchant and retains only his dialog with Helen and the folkloric theme of the maiden who is abducted after being tricked into boarding a vessel. [5] The Jewish and Canarian versions do not depend directly on the sixteenth-century printed texts, but go back to a common variant source which, unlike the known broadsides, included among other details the marvelous tree bearing "apples of love in both summer and winter." [6]

---

[5] On the motif's occurrence in folktales and in French, Piedmontese, and Catalan ballads, see RoH, I, 353, nn. 35-36, where Menéndez Pidal cites Doncieux, no. 43 (*Le bateau de blé et la dame trompée*; cf. Canteloube, II, 25; III, 200; IV, 305; Davenson 76; Rolland, I, 297-299; Tarbé, II, 230-231; Barbeau-Sapir, pp. 121-124; Gagnon, pp. 39-40), Nigra 44 (*Il marinaro*), and Milá 201 (*El rey marinero*.) See also RoH, I, 285, n. 72, Arbaud, II, 123-127 (*Pierre lou malado*), and Barbeau, *Romancéro*, pp. 55-58 (*Le long de la mer jolie*). Meier offers a German example: A merchant, as the secret marriage emissary of a prince, arrives by ship at the court of a foreign king. "Des Königs Töchter kommen zum Strande und wollen aufs Schiff, um den dort aufgestellten Kram zu besehen. Wie die mittlere [Tochter] rasch das Schiff betritt, stösst der Krämer ab und fährt schnell auf dem Wasser dahin" (DVM 3: *Brautwerbung*; also Meier, *Balladen*, I, no. 4). Kudrun ("Aventiure 7," vv. 442-443), evidently related to this ballad, offers a very similar situation, in which maidens are carried off while inspecting treasures in Wate's ships (cf. DVM, I, 33). For more on the "Kaufmannsmotif als Entführungsmittel," see Kübel, *Das Fortleben des Kudrunepos*, pp. 36 ff., 45 ff., 63 ff. The Scandinavian *Skipper og Jomfru* (DgF, IV, no. 241) embodies the same motif, as also does *Ridderen i Hjorteham* (DgF, II, no. 67) where, however, the stratagem is unsuccessful. For similar situations in Lithuanian, Lettish, Hungarian, and Slavic ballads, see Balys, A27 (*Abduction by Ship*), Bērzkalne, no. 892; Leader, pp. 266, 268; Vargyas, *Researches*, p. 44; Strausz, p. 153; and de Vries, *Heroic Song and Heroic Legend*, pp. 126-127. The marvelous ships and rich cargo promised in *James Harris* (*The Dœmon Lover*: Child 243) exemplify the same *topos*, but with rather different overall implications. Cf. *Le joli tambour* (Davenson 50.10-12; Puymaigre, *Pays Messin*, I, 219; Rolland, I, 269, 273, 274-275; II, 153, 155; Whitfield, *Louisiana-French Folksongs*, p. 57); also D. MacInnes, *Folk and Hero Tales* (from Argyllshire) (London, 1890), pp. 182-187.

[6] See RCan, p. 26. The presentation of the heroine engaged in needle work—a universal ballad commonplace—may, as D. Catalán observes, be a polygenetic development in the Canarian and Salonikan versions.

Bénichou (p. 136) connects the "mansanas de amores" in *El robo de Elena* with the ballad of *El juicio de Paris* (MP 42; cf. H1596.1. *Golden apple as prize in beauty contest*). The courtyard in *La moza y el Huerco* (Attias 85.7-10; Molho, "Cinq élégies," no. 3) includes an apple tree which has surely been borrowed from *El robo de Elena*:

BIBLIOGRAPHY

Eastern J.-Sp.: Adatto 2; Attias 6; Benardete 17; Danon 2; Díaz-Paja 14; Gil 29 (= Danon); Hemsi, "Evocation," pp. 1092-1093 (= Yoná, Text B); Menéndez Pelayo 14 (= Danon); Milwitzky, "El viajero filólogo," p. 326 ("Versión completa" = GSA, with minimal variants); Id., *Encyclopedia,* p. 652 (= GSA); PTJ 46 (= Danon); Romey 16; Sciaky, p. 37; UR 1 (= CBU 330-331 with minor variants = GRI). [7]

Moroccan J.-Sp.: Bénichou 19; Gil, p. lxxiii (= MP); Larrea 47-49; MP 43; MRuiz 48; PTJ 46*a* (= Bénichou); RCan, pp. 24-27.

Canarian: Espinosa, *Romancero canario,* pp. 87-88; RCan 7.

De dientro d'aquel curtijo   había un rico manzano,
qu'echa manzanas d'amores   envierno y enverano.

The apple as a "fruit of love" appears in other Eastern Sephardic ballads as well: "cuando los belos mancebos / servían a sus amores // ... quien los vence con manzanas, / qu'es el fruto de los amores" (*El prisionero*: Attias 8); "Ya le traen *mezetes* [T. *meze* 'appetizer, snack'] / manzanicas d'amor" (*Hero y Leandro*: Attias 61). For similar symbolism in Neo-Hellenic folk poetry, cf. Garnett, I, 58-59, 135, 193, n. *a,* Georgeakis-Pineau, pp. 181-182, and especially Petropoulos, *Comparaison,* pp. 36-37. On the amorous symbolism of apples, see G. de Tervarent, *Attributs et symboles dans l'art profane*: *1450-1600,* II (Geneva, 1959), s. v. *pomme.* Cf. also Meier, *Balladen,* II, 16; Leader, *Hungarian Classical Ballads,* pp. 77-78, 173, n. 255.

The phrase *invierno y enverano,* which really means 'always, at all times,' occurs elsewhere in Hispanic folk poetry: "Aunque no so de alabar / como se alabarán éstos, / que el invierno y el verano / de mí visten los mesquinos" (*Cantar de los colores*: Larrea, *Canciones,* no. 92) and, as "en verano y en invierno," in the Canarian *Dama enamorada de un segador* (Espinosa, *Romancero canario,* p. 31); with *no,* it simply means 'never': "mis ramas non se amurchan en invierno ni en verano" (*Complas de las flores*: LSO, p. 181). The phrase's use in modern traditional poetry reflects the survival of one of many binary expressions current in medieval usage: *moros y cristianos, mozos y ajumados, mancebos y casados, chicos y grandes* 'everyone'; *en yermo y en poblado* 'everywhere.' Compare: "E todo carnicero que mesa posier fora, no la cupra en uierno nen en uerano; e ponga la ala manana e lieuela ala noche" (*Fueros leoneses,* ed. A. Castro and F. de Onís [Madrid, 1916], p. 205.7-8 [Fuero de Salamanca]). For more examples, see Webber, *Formulistic Diction,* pp. 222-223; J. Artiles, *Los recursos literarios de Berceo* (Madrid, 1964), p. 229; and T. A. Perry's important commentary (*Art and Meaning in Berceo's "Vida de Santa Oria"* [New Haven-London, 1968], pp. 160-161 and n. 32).

[7] On the ballad's possible influence upon Hebrew liturgy, see Molho, "Tres romances," p. 66*b*. Molho's information is probably based upon the tune indication at the beginning of GSA and LRI. *'Ôḥîlāh* seems to have imposed its tune on *El robo de Elena* and not vice versa.

Archaic Texts: *Pliegos góticos,* II, 179-181; *Pliegos de Praga,* I, 8, 155-157; II, 245-247; *Primavera* 109; Wolf, *Ueber eine Sammlung,* pp. 264-265. See also Rodríguez-Moñino, *Pliegos de Morbecq,* pp. 50-53; Simón Díaz, III: 2, 2976, 3021.

Studies: M. R. Lida de Malkiel, *Davar,* 10, pp. 13-14, 17; Menéndez Pidal, "El romance tradicional en las Islas Canarias," pp. 5, 7; Puymaigre, "Notes," pp. 270-271; RCan, pp. 22-27; RoH, I, 64, 137, n. 109, 285, n. 72, 353-354; II, 340, n. 74; TRV, II, 364-366.

12

EL CONDE OLINOS

(Count Olinos)

'En 'el verğel dela reyna   'a kresido 'un bel rozale.
La rayyz tyene de 'oro,   la simyente de 'un bu'en kristale.
'En la ramika más alta   'un roši'ó sentí kantar.
'El kantar ke 'iva dizyendo   loryya 'es de lo kantar.
La reyna 'estava lavrando   'i la 'iža durmyendo 'está.
—Alevantéš, la mi 'iža,   de vu'estro dulse folgar.
'O'iređeš kómo kanta   la sirenika de la mar.
—No 'es la sirenika, mi mađre,   no 'es la sirenika de la mar,
sinon 'es 'el konde Alemare,   ke por mí se va akavar.
—Si 'es 'esto, la mi 'iža,   yyo lo mandaré 'a matar.
—No lo matéš, la mi mađre,   ni lo mandéš 'a matar.
Ke 'el konde 'es ninyyo 'i muğağo,   'el mundo kyere gozar.
'I si lo matáš, la mi madre,   a mí kon 'él 'en 'un lugar.
La reyna, ke de mal tenga,   presto los mandó 'a matar.
¿Ande fu'e su 'enteramyento?,   debašo del bel rozal.

Source: GRA 5.
Verse 2 is repeated. Repetition of subsequent verses is indicated by the words *se torna* following v. 3.
2*a* ra'íz *in repetition.*
2*b* bel kristale *in repetition.*
3 + se torna.
4*b* delo.
9*a* si non.
11*b* *or* no (?).

'Él se 'izo 'una grave'ína   'i 'elyya se 'izo 'una konǧá.
La reyna, ke de mal tenga,   presto los mandó arankar.
Arankólos 'i desfožólos   'i 'eǧólos 'a bolar.
'Elyya se 'izo 'una palomba   'i 'él se 'izo 'un gavilán.
La reyna, ke de mal tenga,   presto los mandó 'a kasar.
Kasólos 'i degolyyólos   'i los 'izo ke almorzar.
Los gu'esezikos ke kedaron   los mandó '[e]ǧar ala mar.
'Elyya se 'izo 'una perkyya   'i 'el se 'izo 'un kara sazán.
La reyna, ke de mal tenga,   presto los mandó 'a peškar.
Peškólos 'i 'eskamólos   'i los 'izo ke almorzar.
Las 'espinas ke kedaron   las 'enteró debašo 'el portal.
'Elyya se 'izo 'una kulevra   'i 'él se 'izo 'un alakrán.

---

22 'ǧar; *alternate reading*: mandó a ǧar.

Binyamin B. Yosef's *Sēfer rĕnānôө* ([Jerusalem], 5668 [= 1908]) (abbr. SR) offers, on pp. 13-14, a text which is essentially identical to that of GRA. In *'El bukyeto de romansas* (Istanbul, 5686 [= 1926], pp. 20-22 [no. 12]) (abbr. BdR) B. Yosef apparently copied the *Sēfer rĕnānôө* as he also did in the case of *El falso hortelano* (no. 21 *infra*). The variants from both these booklets vis à vis GRA are as follows:

1*b* rozal *SR* / *BdR*.
2*b* kristal *SR* / *BdR*, bel kristal *in repetition SR*, bu'en kristal *in repetition BdR*.
3*b* + se torna *SR* / *BdR*.
6*b* 'olgar *BdR*.
9*a* si no 'es *SR* / *BdR*, Alemar *SR* / *BdR*.
11*b* no lo mandéś *SR* / *BdR*.
12*b* kere gozar *SR* / *BdR*.
14*b* lo mandó *SR* / *BdR*.
18 los arankó 'i los desfizo / 'i los eǧó 'a bolar *BdR*.
21*a* los kasó 'i los egolyyó (*sic*) *BdR*.
22*b* 'eǧar *SR* / *BdR*.
25*a* los peśkó 'i los 'eskamó *BdR*.
26*b* 'entró *SR*.

Translation:

In the Queen's garden a beautiful rosebush has grown. Its roots are of gold and its base of fine crystal. I heard a nightingale singing on its highest branch. The song that it was singing is glorious to hear sung. (5) The Queen was embroidering, and her daughter is asleep. "Wake up, my daughter, from your gentle sleep. You will hear how the little mermaid sings, the mermaid of the sea." "It is not the mermaid, mother; it is not the mermaid of the sea. It is Count Alemare, who is dying of love for me." (10) "If this is so, my daughter, I will have him killed." "Do not kill him, mother, and do not have him killed, for the Count is a mere youth and wishes to enjoy the world. And if you kill him, mother, put me in the same place with him." The Queen, may ill befall her, quickly had them both killed. (15) Where were they buried? Under the beautiful rosebush. He became a carnation and she became a rose. The Queen, may ill befall her, quickly had them pulled up. She pulled them up and tore off their leaves and threw them to the wind. She became a dove and he became a hawk. (20) The Queen, may ill befall her, quickly had them hunted down. She hunted them and slit their throats and cooked them for a meal. The bones that remained she ordered thrown into the sea. She became a perch and he became a black carp. The Queen, may ill befall her, quickly had them caught. (25) She caught them and scaled them and cooked them for a meal. The bones that remained, she buried under her doorstep. (27) She became a serpent and he became a scorpion.

Motifs:

2 F811.1.1. *Golden tree.* Cf. F811.1.6. *Glass (crystal) tree in otherworld.*
4 D1275. *Magic song.*
13 T80. *Tragic love.*
16 E631. *Reincarnation in plant (tree) growing from grave.*
19 E613. *Reincarnation as bird*; E613.6 *Reincarnation as dove*; E613.3. *Reincarnation as hawk.*
23 E617. *Reincarnation as fish.*
27 E614.1. *Reincarnation as snake*; E629.1. *Reincarnation as scorpion.*

El conde Olinos is one of the most widely known Hispanic ballads. It is abundantly represented in both Sephardic areas, as well as in the Castilian and Portuguese traditions. In Spanish America, variants have been collected in the Antilles, Venezuela, and Argentina. Catalan evidence, however, is sparse and fragmentary.

Among the Eastern Sephardim, the ballad has burgeoned in a number of divergent forms. Attias, Benardete, Coello, Díaz-Plaja, Hemsi (1st text and Vars. 3-4), and Levy (*Chants,* no. 20.1-2) record Salonikan texts much like Yoná's, while Danon, Hemsi (Var. 1), and Romey offer renditions from Turkey. Baruch has collected a radically different Bosnian form, which is paralleled by two unedited texts in our possession. Galante seems to reflect one of several configurations adopted by the ballad in the Rhodian tradition. Unfortunately, Levy's interesting and quite distinctive rendition (SBS 35) bears no geographic identification. Since the early years of this century the ballad's archaic variants, once almost universally distributed among the Eastern Sephardim, have been fighting a losing battle against a radically abbreviated, contaminated version, which probably originated in Istanbul and undoubtedly achieved its present diffusion partly through phonograph recordings. This version, which lacks the lovers' metamorphoses and has suffered successive contaminations from *Hero y Leandro* (cf. Hemsi, Var. 2, final verse), is exemplified by Uziel's Salonikan text (UR 10), by one of Levy's versions from Rhodes (SBS 36), by Hemsi's Variant 2 from Istanbul, and also possibly by the Belgrade *incipit* published by Menéndez Pidal (RoH, I, 401). Our unedited collection includes more than a dozen such texts, all very similar, from such relatively separated areas as Sérrai (Greece), Tekirdağ, Marmara, Istanbul, and Rhodes. Younger singers in the latter tradition, some of whom admittedly learned their texts from phonograph records, invariably proffer this abbreviated version, while two of our aged informants still remembered much more complete, presumably "native" texts, in which the protagonists' multiple transformations are still in evidence.

El conde Olinos also abounds in Morocco. Two different forms, which probably entered the complex North African Jewish tradition at widely separated chronological stages of its development, can be documented.[1] Published versions represent the traditions of Tetuán, Tetuán-Oran, Tangier, Alcázar, and Alexandria (? ; Moya). We have some fifteen unedited texts from Tetuán, Tetuán-Melilla, Tangier, Arcila, Larache, and Alcázar.

---

[1] See BNE 243.

The different branches of Hispanic tradition generally agree as to the essential features of the story: The hero's appearance on the seashore;[2] his magic song (usually presented only allegorically among the Eastern Sephardim);[3] the mother's inquiry concerning the singer's identity; persecution of the hero or of both lovers; their death and subsequent transformation or transformations.

---

[2] Díaz-Plaja's text offers unique Eastern Sephardic evidence of this initial stage of the narrative:

> Se paseaba el Conde Alimá per (*sic*) orillicas de la mar,
> sopletico de oro en boca diciendo va un buen cantar.
> El cantar que va diciendo
> gloria es de lo sentir, gloria es de lo cantar:
> —En el vergel de la reina ha crecido un buen rosá. ...

[3] See *El robo de Dina* (no. 8, n. 3 *supra*). The nightingale (Yoná, v. 3) seems to represent Count Alemare. However, vv. 1-3 are formulistic; vv. 1 and 3 have an exact parallel—even as to rhyme—in the French *Occasion manquée*: "Au jardin de mon père / un oranger il y a; / sur la plus haute branche / un rossignol chantait ..." (Rolland, I, 28). Compare the initial scene of the Danish *Nattergalen* (DgF, II, no. 57) and the introductory verses of *Liebesprobe* (Meier, *Balladen*, II, no. 61).

The rosebush with golden roots and glass base (Yoná, v. 2) apparently occurs only in the Salonikan versions (cf. F811.1.1; F811.1.7; F811.2.1.2). It is related to marvelous trees that appear in other *romances* and elsewhere in European folk tradition. In *La infantina* the protagonist is found sitting in a tree with golden trunk and silver branches or leaves: "el tronco tiene de oro, / las ramas de plata fina" (RoH, II, 415-416 and n. 14; Bénichou 1; Larrea 167; Braga, I, 256). A similar tree, probably borrowed from *La infantina,* appears in Judeo-Spanish versions of *La vuelta del marido* (*í*):

> Arboleras, arboleras, arboleras tan gentil,
> la raíz tiene de oro, la cimiente de marfil.
>
> (Attias 20)

Analogous characteristics are attributed to an orange tree at a different stage of some Portuguese versions of the same ballad:

> —Quanto darieis, vos, senhora, a quem o trouxera aqui?
> —As tres bellas larangeiras que tenho no meu jardim;
> os pés são de fino ouro, as laranjas de marfim.
> (Uma tem o pé de prata, tem outra o pé de marfim.)
>
> (Braga, I, 53, 60)

The ballad's ultimate origins are difficult to determine. There is a definite connection, born out by musical evidence, between *El conde Olinos* and the French *Pernette*. The latter offers the following story:

El maestro, a Catalan ballad which has undergone multiple contaminations from *La vuelta del marido* (*í*), exemplifies the same topos:

Y al mitx d'aquella sala   hi plantarás un pi;
la soca n' es de plata   y la cima d' or fi.
A l' horteta del meu pare   ya n' hi havíe un llessamí,
les rametes son de plata   y 'ls branquets son de l' or fi.
(Milá 532; Var. E)

A l'horta del meu pare,   si n'hi ha un tarongí.
La soca n'és de plata,   les branques són d'or fi;
a la branca més alta,   hi canta el francolí.
(AFC 822)

French balladry informs us of an apple tree with leaves and branches of silver: "Derrière chez mon père, / y a un pommier doux; // d'argent sont les branches, / et les feuilles itou" (*Le pommier doux*: Davenson 58) and the Scandinavian *Linden* evokes a gold-leaved tree (Geijer-Afzelius, no. 71:1.2; Warrens 59). Analogous trees occur in Balkan balladry: A Greek wedding song mentions "a diamond tree, of which the branches are jewels and... roots of precious red stones and pearls for fruit" (Baud-Bovy, *Chansons*, I, 262; cf., also, Marcellus, *Chants du peuple*, II, 380-381):

...δεντρὶ διαμάντι,
πού 'ν' τὰ κλώνια σου περλάντι,
κ' ἔχεις ρίζα σεϊλάνι,
καὶ καρπὸ μαργαριτάρι...

A Yugoslavian ballad speaks of a strikingly similar tree:

An apple tree at Ranko's door was growing,
its trunk was silver, golden were its branches;
its branches golden and of pearls its foliage,
its leaves were pearls, and all its apple[s] corals.
And many dovelets, on the branches seated. ...
(Stevenson Stanoyevich, no. 78)

Other random examples: In the *Coronica troyana* (ed. Norris), the grounds of Priams' palace include "vn grand arbol ... ffecho por arte magica muy sotilmente. ... Todo el arbol era la meatad de oro e la meytad de plata segund representaua. E por esa mesma via eran las flores e foias del arbol e paresçian ser pobladas de djuersas piedras preçiosas e que su fructo del arbol era aquel" (pp. 241-242). Compare also the Mohammedan tree of paradise: "Hay en el paraíso un árbol, llamado *Tūbà*, árbol de deleite y de gozo; de base tan ancha que un hombre más veloz que el más veloz caballo tardaría en rodearle cien

Pernette, while spinning, utters a sigh. Her mother inquires about her sadness and the girl replies that she is sighing for Pierre, who is in prison. The mother answers: "You shall not have Pierre; we will hang him." Pernette wishes to be buried beside her beloved: "Cover Pierre with roses and me with milfoils." [4] Both ballads coincide in the initial topic reference to handwork (though it is the Queen, not the Princess, who is sewing in most versions of *Conde Olinos*); in the mother's question concerning the girl's sentiments; in the mother's desire for and intervention in the beloved's death; in the girl's desire to accompany her beloved to the grave; in the double burial; and in the flowers-from-graves motif.

Entwistle, taking the search for ultimate origins farther afield, sought to connect the French and Spanish ballads to a Greek song, *The Wicked Mother* (*Hē kakè mána*), in which the mother orders her sons to murder their sister, when the latter is courted (perhaps abducted) by a foreign count. He dies of sorrow on hearing of the girl's death; they are buried in the same grave, from which a reed and a cypress grow and entwine. [5] Entwistle suggests that this ballad type—if indeed its agreements with Conde Olinos are not merely coincidental—is ultimately of Eastern origin and must have penetrated Romance balladry along "los caminos por tierra y mar que ligaban Constantinopla a los demás países europeos." [6] He reinforces his theory of an Eastern source by remarking upon Count Olinos' magic song as a reflection of

años. El pie todo es de rubí, y la tierra donde está plantado, de almizcle y ámbar más blanca que la nieve; los ramos todos, de esmeralda; sus hojas, de samit, y las flores, de telas de oro; los frutos, como perlas muy grandes ..." (*La escala de Mahoma*, ed. J. Muñoz Sendino [Madrid, 1949], pp. 217, 364-366 [chap. 39]). For still other instances, see J. H. Philpot, *The Sacred Tree or the Tree in Religion and Myth* (London, 1897), especially pp. 142-143.

[4] See Doncieux's synthetic version (pp. 17-20); also Entwistle ("Second Thoughts," pp. 11-13). *La Pernette* relates ultimately to the Catalan song of *La presó de Lleida* (AFC 3001; Milá 209). Is the Norwegian ballad, *Bendik and Arolilja*, which Pineau translates from Landstad's collection, related genetically to *La Pernette* (*Romancéro Scandinave*, pp. 160-165)? The major features of the narratives are identical. For a possible sixteenth-century Greek analog to *La Pernette*, see Bouvier, *Dēmotikà tragoúdia tēs Monēs tōn Ibērōn*, no. 3 and p. 29.

[5] "El Conde Olinos," p. 241; "Second Thoughts," p. 12. Entwistle's analysis is based upon Passow, nos. 469-470; Tommaseo-Pavolini, pp. 122-123 (no. 106). For other versions, see Dieterich, *Südlichen Sporaden*, no. 10; Lüdeke, *Im Paradies der Volksdichtung*, pp. 215-216; Lüdeke-Megas, nos. 31-33.

[6] Entwistle, "El Conde Olinos," p. 248.

the "bride-stealing by incantation" motif which would somehow relate our ballad not only to *Heer Halewijn* and *Lady Isabel and the Elf-Knight,* [7] but also ultimately to the magic songs and musical instruments by which Digenis Akritas courts his bride in the Anatolian Greek epic and related ballads. The parallels adduced by Entwistle are certainly suggestive of a possible genetic relationship between *El conde Olinos* and some Eastern Mediterranean narrative. Yet the protagonists and the motifs here involved are so universal in nature that the possibility of polygenesis cannot be discounted. [8] We must conclude that in the relationship between *El conde Olinos* and its possible Hellenic congeners much remains to be clarified.

The Pan-Hispanic tradition of *El conde Olinos* has apparently joined a ballad of tragically unsuccessful bride-stealing to another widely known European ballad and tale type: that of *The Transformations,* in which a girl escapes from her suitor by resorting to a series of metamorphoses, only to be pursued by the suitor who undergoes corresponding changes in form. In the *Conde Olinos,* almost all branches of the

---

[7] Entwistle, "Second Thoughts," pp. 13-14. Cf. Nygard, p. 40; DVM 41; Meier, *Balladen,* I, 113, 119; Child 4. Halewijn, the Elf-Knight, and Count Olinos thus appear as supernatural suitors who acquire, possibly only at a certain time of year ("the first morning in May" or "la mañana de San Juan"), special magic powers of song by which they are able to charm and abduct mortal women (F301. *Fairy lover*; F301.2.1. *Elf-knight produces love-longing by blowing on horn*; D1355.1. *Love-producing music*; D1355.1.1. *Love-producing song*; also *El chuflete,* no. 27, n. 16 *infra*). For more on this aspect of the ballad, see Onís, "El celo de los duendes," especially pp. 221, 224-225, nn. 12-13; BNE 243-244; Spitzer, "The Folkloristic Pre-stage," pp. 178, 180-182; Id., "Annex," p. 66.

Entwistle's rather forced attempt to connect the name *Halewijn* with that of Count *Alemán* (*Alimán, Alemare,* etc.) of the Salonikan Sephardic versions of *Conde Olinos* is unacceptable. Cf. "El Conde Olinos," p. 238; "Second Thoughts," p. 14. The name, as well as the dishonorable intentions noted by Onís ("El celo de los duendes," p. 225), and the girl's pleas for her lover's life ("... 'el konde 'es ninyyo 'i muğağo, / 'el mundo kyere gozar") are probably borrowed from *El conde Alemán y la reina* (no. 7, n. 5 *supra*). Cf. also *El robo de Dina* (no. 8, n. 6 *supra*).

[8] For example: Balys' Lithuanian *Poisoned Couple* (C6) contains many of the same components as *Conde Olinos* and its putative Greek analog: young lovers are fatally persecuted by a jealous mother, who poisons them and then attempts to break the branches of the trees that spring from their graves and through which they achieve a kind of immortality. (The poplar pleads: "Let us live as trees at least.") Is this apparent parallel of Child's *Prince Robert* (no. 87) genetically or only coincidentally related to *Conde Olinos*? See also Bénichou's strictures (BNE 244).

tradition agree in including the two stages in which the lovers turn first into plants, trees, or their fruit, and then into birds. In the Salonikan texts, the flowers, *graveína* and *konğá* (or the corresponding plants, *klavinal* and *rozal*) become *palomba* and *gavilán*. One version from the Rhodian tradition (Galante) attests to the transformation: fruit and tree, to flower and plant, to dove and hawk (*toronja-toronjal* > *glavina-glavinal* > *palomba-gavilán*). In Edirne, the metamorphosis from *toronja-toronjal* to birds of some type is evidenced by the verse: "Tomaron mano con mano / y se echaron (*or* se fueron) a volar," which occurs twice in Danon's version. In Morocco, an archaic tradition indicates transformations from *toronja* or *limón-limonar* to *paloma-gavilán*, while a more modern form (Alvar; Larrea 67) has, as in Andalucía (Güéjar), only plants or curative herbs (*rosal, limonar, hierba muy santa*). In the Castilian versions, various plants or their flowers and fruit (*toronja-limonar, naranjo-limonal, oliva-olivar, rosa-rosal, rosal blanco-espino* or *olivo albar, zarcita-zarzal*) are usually followed by birds (*paloma-gavilán, palomar* or *pardal, águila imperial, pichón real*). Similarly, in Argentine versions, *naranjo-parral, naranja-limonar*, or *arbolitos* yield *paloma-gavilán* (Moya, texts III-V; Bayo). Most Venezuelan texts refer only to birds (Monroy; Pardo B), while a lone Canarian version, published in fragmentary form, mentions only plants (*clavel-rosal*, RCan 20). The Catalan versions—contaminations in *Don Lluis de Montalbà* (a distant parallel of *Conde Dirlos*)—include *pino-toronjar, olivera-olivar*, or *taronger-llorer granat* sometimes followed by *coloma-colom* or *colomar*. Innumerable botanical varieties and combinations give way to a somewhat less variable ornithological array in the Galician-Portuguese tradition, where *salgueiro, oliva, oliveira, arvore, acipreste, pereiro, pinheirinho, rosa, lirio, craveiro* and *salgueirae, limoar, pereira real, pinho real, laranjal, canavial, jasminal*, or *rosal*, change to *pomba, -o, pombinha, -o*, and *pombo real* (*trocal, torquaz*), or *gavião real*. There are occasional reversals of this order in various branches of the tradition. An unedited text from Rhodes consecutively turns three youths, who take the place of Count Olinos in courting the girl, into doves, fish, and carnations (*palombas, peškados, glavinas*). Levy's unidentified text (SBS 35) goes from fishes (*peše preto-ermozo sazán*) to plants (*roza-klavinar*). All three versions we have seen from the divergent Bosnian tradition (cf. Baruch) begin with a pearl and coral, go to dove and hawk, and seem to imply a final transformation into a thorn tree (*espino*). The order of birds to plants also occurs sporadically in other areas (cf. VRP 242; Moya, text I), but the consensus of Pan-Hispanic tradition is to begin the various transformations with plants or trees. Such a pattern suggests a single plants-from-graves episode which, as in *La Pernette* and many another ballad, [9] could have constituted the final stage of the *Brautraub* song

---

[9] The "sympathetic plants" motif is little known in Peninsular tradition. It occurs in some forms of the fifteenth-sixteenth-century *Tristán e Iseo* ("Herido está don Tristán": FN 55), doubtless following a French source (cf. Child, I, 98). One text of the Moroccan *Pájaro verde* (Larrea 86), where the girl sometimes changes to a bird out of grief for her dead lover (MP 66), takes over the *gavilán-paloma* transformation from *Conde Olinos.* In another version, the ballad ends with a plant metamorphosis of seemingly independent origin: "De eya sale una azucena / y de él sale un clavel blanco" (Benardete 35). The Castilian *Pastorcita devota* (RPM 389), upon her demise, is transformed into a flower and plants spring from the tomb of an ill-fated knight in the Catalan *Mala nueva* (AFC 2224; Aguiló 222; Capmany 78; Milá 235C).

Examples are legion in the extra-Peninsular traditions: For the English ballads, see Child, I, 96-99; III, 498; V, 481*b*, 491*b* ("Index of Matters . . . ," under *Graves, lovers', plants and trees from* and *Plants from graves*); Hodgart, *The Ballads,* pp. 124, 128-129; Wimberly, *Folklore,* pp. 2, 12, 29, 37-43, 69, 70, 122 (especially pp. 38 and 41, where occurrences are catalogued); Coffin 73, 74, 75, 84, 87; Toelken, "An Oral Canon," pp. 97-100. DVM offers numerous German instances: nos. 9 (*Liebestod*), 45 (*Die entführte Graserin*), 48 (*Graf Friedrich*), 49 (*Die Todesbraut*), 50 (*Die erzwungene Ehe*), 51 (*Das Bauerntöchterlein*), 55 (*Ritter und Magd*), 56 (*Wiedersehen an der Bahre*), 58 (*Der Scheintod*), and especially Vol. I, 83-84; also Meier, *Balladen,* I, nos. 6, 33A.32, 34, 37; II, nos. 53C.11, 58, 71C.12, 73, 87B.14; Taylor, "The Themes Common to English and German Balladry," pp. 27, n. 23, 32, n. 53. For Scandinavian examples, see Child, I, 96; DgF, VIII, no. 482DEI (*Sallemand dør af Elskov*); also Prior, III, 34-35; Pineau, *Romancéro scandinave,* p. 164. The motif is also present in the French *Tristes noces* (Arbaud, II, 144; Davenson 19; Rolland, I, 248; Hodgart, *The Ballads,* pp. 93-94) and the Italian *Due tombe* (Nigra 18). See also Mlotek, "International Motifs in the Yiddish Ballads," pp. 218-220; Doncieux, pp. 38-40; Geijer-Afzelius, nos. 18, 21; Warrens 108, 137. There are numerous instances of the same motif in the Modern Greek tradition. *Charos and the Girl* (Argenti-Rose pp. 722-723; see also DVM, II, 231 f.) adds a comment on the lovers' inseparability which recalls the final verse of certain versions of *Conde Olinos* ("Dos arbolitos crecieron / en aquel mismo lugar: // ni en la vida, ni en la muerte, / los pudieron apartar": Cadilla, *Juegos,* p. 140; VRP 244; Martins; Gomes Pereira):

> The girl became a reed and the young man a cypress,
> and hither and thither they were driven by the air,
> and the reed bent and kissed the cypress.
> "See those unfortunates, see those unhappy ones!
> What they did in life, that they do even in death."

from which the *romance* was derived. Such a plant transformation, as a dénouement, could well have suggested the possibility of linking the bride-stealing ballad to a series of metamorphoses, in imitation of the

---

For other versions of the same ballad containing this motif, see Kind, pp. 110-113 and the note on pp. 210-211; Lüdeke-Megas, nos. 147-148; Pernot, *Anthologie,* pp. 115-116. Cf. also Georgeakis-Pineau, pp. 220-221. For more Greek and Balkan examples, see Baud-Bovy, *Textes,* pp. 192, n. 4, 222, n. 2, 263, 273; Bartók-Lord 31*b,* n. 2; Dieterich, "Die Volksdichtung der Balkanländer," p. 155; Id., "Die neugriechische Volkspoesie," pp. 128-129, 238, n.; Garnett, I, 148 at n. 24; Georgeakis-Pineau, p. 208; Liebrecht, *Zur Volkskunde,* pp. 166-167, 168, 176, 182-183, 188, 189; Lüdeke, "Griechische Volksdichtung," p. 221; Lüdeke-Megas, nos. 19, 49, 54, 90, 107, 109, 121, 144, 169; Petropoulos, *La comparaison,* p. 37; Proust, pp. 34-35; Schmidt, *Das Volksleben,* pp. 250-251; De Grazia, *Canti popolari albanesi,* pp. 102, 260-261; Camarda, *Grammatologia ... albanese,* pp. 112-113; Alexandri, *Ballades ... de la Roumanie,* p. 25; Amzulescu, I, No. 305; Papahagi, p. 54; EEB 276, 342, 353; Dozon, *Chants populaires bulgares,* pp. 291, 334; Strausz, *Bulgarische Volksdichtungen,* p. 268; Járdányi, *Ungarische Volksliedtypen,* p. 75; Aigner, *Ungarische Volksdichtungen,* pp. 92, 132, 138, 160; Leader, pp. 359-360 (s.v. *Plants, sympathetic*); Vargyas, *Researches,* pp. 40, 50, 112-120; Child, I, 97-98; III, 498. A Lithuanian ballad abstracted by Seemann offers a striking example of the "plant-soul." Here a rose springs from the grave of a youth who has died of grief. His sister plucks the flower, but the mother, weeping, explains its true nature: "Das ist keine Rosenblume, sondern der Geist des jungen Burschen, der aus Kummer Starb" ("Deutsch-litauische Volksliedbeziehungen," p. 194 [no. 82: *Der aus Kummer sterbende Knabe*]). See also the Lettish example abstracted by Bērzkalne (no. 23), which is combined with the motif of *The singing bone* (E632. *Reincarnation as musical instrument*; D1610.2. *Speaking tree*). Abundant additional examples of the sympathetic plants are listed by J. Psichari and H. Gaidoz, "Les deux arbres entrelacés," *Mélusine,* IV (1888-1889), 60-62, 85-91, 142; Aarne-Thompson, Type 970: *The Twining Branches,* and the motifs: E631.0.1. *Twining branches grow from graves of lovers*; E631.1. *Flower from grave*; E631.6. *Reincarnation in tree from grave.* See also P. Demetz, "The Elm and the Vine: Notes Toward the History of a Marriage Topos," *PMLA,* LXXIII (1958), 521-532.

Whatever the origin of the "plant-soul" belief, the poetic function of the lovers' metamorphosis in the ballads is abundantly clear in providing a poignant contrast between the continuity and perennial renovation of natural life and the finality of human death. Cf. Hodgart's sensitive observations concerning the similar rôle of seemingly meaningless, irrelevant botanical refrains such as "Fine flowers in the valley" and "The green leaves they grow rarely" (*The Ballads,* pp. 32-33, 166, n. 3, apropos of *The Cruel Mother* [Child 20B]).

Some European ballads coincidentally combine the sympathetic plants with other features known to *Conde Olinos.* In various British, German, and Hungarian ballads, the lovers suffer persecution even in their transformed state and the plants are cut down or pulled up, as in *Earl Brand* (Child 7B.20), *Fair Margret and Sweet William* (Child 74A.20), *Lady Alice* (Child 85), *Der Wirtin Töchterlein, Der todwunde Knabe* (Meier, *Balladen,* II, nos. 58, 73A.14), and the Hungarian *Kate Kádár, Dishonored Maiden,* and *Merika* (Leader, pp. 126,

Pan-European *Transformations* (*Twa Magicians,* etc.), but occasioned, not by a maiden's chaste flight from an ardent suitor, but rather by the mother's homicidal jealousy carried over from the first part of the

---

183, 315; also 360*a*; Vargyas, *Researches,* p. 114). See also Child, III, 498; Wimberly, *Folklore,* p. 40. In Albanian instances, the sympathetic plants have curative properties: De Grazia, p. 102; Camarda, pp. 112-113 (cf. the Peninsular examples cited below at nn. 15, 16, 18). Some forms of *Das Bauerntöchterlein* combine plant and bird transformations much as does *El conde Olinos*: Lilies spring from the lovers' graves, after which two small doves fly together out of the graves toward Paradise (DVM 51). Flowers and doves also appear in the Hungarian *Dishonored Maiden* (Leader, pp. 192, 214; Vargyas, *Researches,* pp. 116, 117). In other Hungarian ballads the plants curse their persecutors (Leader, pp. 325, 355*a*).

Aside from its occurrence in *El conde Olinos,* the "bird soul" is a rarity in the *Romancero*. The motif occurs in the Moroccan *Pájaro verde* (MP 66) and *Gritando va el caballero* (Larrea 219.23). In a version of *La mala suegra* from Santander, three doves—the souls of the dying wife's three sisters—appear to accompany her into heaven (RPM 145). For instances of the "bird-soul" in extra-Hispanic balladry, including combinations with the sympathetic plant motif, see Wimberly, *Folklore,* pp. 48-52. In medieval texts the soul departing for heaven is often represented as a dove. For example: Berceo's "El náufrago salvado" (*Milagros de Nuestra Señora,* ed. A. G. Solalinde, "Clásicos Castellanos," no. 44 [Madrid, 1944], v. 600; cf. T. F. Crane, "Miracles of the Virgin," *RR,* II [1911], 235-279: p. 241 [Chap. II]):

Vidieron palonbiellas essir de so la mar,
más blancas que las nieves contral cielo volar:
credien que eran almas que querie Dios levar
al sancto paraiso, un glorioso logar.

Such is doubtless also the significance of the dove which, in *La Vida de Sancta Oria,* leads Oria to heaven and which she is enjoined to follow at all costs:

Guarda esta palomba, todo lo al olvida:
Tu ve do ella fuere, non seas deçebida,
Guiate por nos, fixa, ca Christus te combida.
(BAAEE, vol. 57, pp. 138*b*-139*a*, vv. 37*b*-*d*)

Cf. Perry, *Art and Meaning in Berceo's "Vida de Santa Oria,"* pp. 96-97, n. 18, 99, 103, n. 32, 104, n. 36, 181. The fourteenth-century *Revelación de un ermitaño* represents the soul as "vna aue de blanca color" (str. 3d). See J. M. Octavio de Toledo, "Visión de Filiberto," *ZRPh,* II (1878), 40-69: p. 63. For more on the meaning of the dove in poetry and iconography, see A. Jacob, "The *Razón de Amor* as Christian Symbolism," *HR,* XX (1952), 282-301: pp. 296-298, especially n. 21. Many additional examples of the dove as spirit may be seen in G. Ferguson, *Signs and Symbols in Christian Art* (New York, 1961), pp. 15-16, 108, 122, 140, 141-142. See also E732.1. *Soul in form of dove*; DVM, no. 23; Meier, *Balladen,* I, 161, 173; Jonsson, *Svenska medeltidsballader,* p. 196

narrative. From the opportune compenetration of these two narratives the myth of the transformations emerges imbued with a new significance by which love, ever resurgent, challenges even the finality of the grave.

Other transformations attributed to the persecuted lovers are less constant in the various subtraditions of *El conde Olinos*. The lovers as fishes seem limited exclusively to the Eastern Sephardim, though the same transmutation may also be implied in certain Azorian versions where the entwined trees are cut down and thrown into the sea, after which fishermen, who fulfill no obvious function in the narrative, suddenly appear on the scene (Braga, I, 274, 276). In the Salonikan texts, plants and birds are followed by fishes which differ from version to version: *perkia* (Yoná, Attias, Benardete, Hemsi, Var. 4), *linguada* (Díaz-Plaja), or *espinato* (Hemsi, lst text) and *kara sazán* (Yoná, Attias, Benardete, Díaz-Plaja), *grande sazán* (Hemsi, Var. 4), or *kiefal* (Hemsi, lst text).[10] Levy's geographically unidentified version (SBS 35) goes from *peše preto* and *ermozo sazán* to *roza* and *klavinar*. The Bosnian versions also imply a sea-change in beginning the transformations with pearl and coral (Baruch). Three mutually divergent texts from Rhodes offer *toronja-toronjal* > *glavina-glavinal* > *palomba-gavilán* > *chapura-kiefal* (Galante)[11]; *torongas* > *mansanas* > *chapuras* (uned.); *palombas* > *peškados* > *glavinas* (uned.). Although the transformation to fishes appears to be absent from all other branches of the Hispanic tradition, we may still wonder if, in the Eastern Judeo-Spanish versions,

(no. 18.16); DgF, II, no. 109, 110; Prior, II, 64-65, 68; M. Haavio, "Der Seelenvogel," *Essais folkloriques* (Porvoo, Finland, 1959), pp. 61-81; Leader, *Hungarian Classical Ballads*, pp. 27, 35, 38, 113, 214.

[10] *Perkia* seems to reflect the influence of T. *perki* 'a voracious freshwater fish' or Gk. *pérkē* 'perch' upon Sp. *perca* 'perch' (itself ultimately of Gk. origin). *Linguada* is Cast. *lenguado* 'flounder.' *Espinato* is not defined by Hemsi beyond stating that it is an "especie de pescado," nor does the form appear in any of the glossaries we have been able to consult. The word's phonology points to an Italian origin. Cf. Ven. *spin* or *spinèlo* 'piccol. pesce d'acqua dolce, a scheletro ossoso ... il quale ha tre spine sul dorso' (G. Boerio, *Dizionario del dialetto veneziano* [Venice, 1856], s.v.), which corresponds to standard It. *spinello*, 'spinel'; also 'dogfish.' *Kara sazán* is T. *kara sazan* 'black carp.' *Kiefal* corresponds to T. *kefal* 'grey mullet.' Cf. Gk. *kéfalos* 'miller's thumb' (a type of fish).

[11] *Chapura* is probably T. *çipura* 'a kind of sea fish' which, in turn, is from Gk. *tsipoũra* 'porgy, flatfish.' Concerning the latter's origin, see N. P. Andriotis, *Etumologikò leksikò tēs koinēs neoellēnikēs* (Athens, 1951), s.v. *tsipoúra*. In J.-Sp. *chapura*, T. *çapa* 'hoe' or perhaps Sp. *chapa* 'sheet, plate (of metal),' may have intruded upon T. *çipura*, as an allusion to the form of the fish in question.

it is the result of some relatively late but widely diffused invention or if, on the other hand, it may in fact go back to an archaic text-type of *Conde Olinos*. The similarities between the Eastern Sephardic texts and the Pan-European *Transformations*, in which the birds often change to fishes or vice versa, seem close enough not to be fortuitous. Compare:

Then she became a turtle dow
  To fly up in the air,
And he became another dow,
  And they flew pair and pair.
    O bide, lady, bide, &c.

She turn hersell into an eel,
  To swim into yon burn,
And he became a speckled trout,
  To gie the eel a turn.
    O bide, lady, bide, &c.
      (Child 44.7-8)

—Je me mettrai anguille, anguille dans l'étang.
—Si tu te mets anguille, anguille dans l'étang,
je me mettrai pêcheur, je t'aurai en pêchant.
—Si tu te mets pêcheur pour m'avoir en pêchant,
je me mettrai alouette, alouette dans les champs.
—Si tu te mets alouette, alouette dans les champs,
je me mettrai chasseur; je t'aurai en chassant.
(Gagnon, *Chansons ... du Canada,* pp. 78-79)

—Un pensament m' ha vingut un pensament á l' istant,
de tornarme palometa pel bosch aniré volant.
—Si tu 't tornes palometa pel bosch anirás volant,
yo 'm tornaré cassadó y t' en aniré cassant.
—Si tu et fas caçador i a mi me véns caçant,
jo me faré l'anguila, l'anguila del mar gran.
—Si tu te fas l'anguila, l'anguila del mar gran,
me faré pescador i t'aniré pescant. [12]

Most versions of *Conde Olinos,* in its various geographic ramifications, end like Menéndez Pidal's synthetic text (FN) at the esthetically

[12] We combine Milá 531 (first four verses) with OCPC, III, 363, See also Milá, Var. B, where the eel is followed by a bird.

satisfying moment when, in the guise of birds, Count Olinos and the Princess succeed in perpetuating their love in defiance of the jealous queen and of death itself. Bénichou, working with the limited and unsatisfactory Eastern Judeo-Spanish evidence available some twenty years ago (Coello, Danon, Galante), saw the lovers' final, vengeful metamorphosis as a relatively modern accretion:

> Algunas versiones modernas imaginan más metamorfosis de los amantes, para llegar al castigo de la reina; por ejemplo, se transforman en una fuente milagrosa, y la reina, al querer beber de su agua, oye una voz que la rechaza ...; o bien los amantes se vuelven ángeles o santos y fundan una ermita donde curan milagrosamente a los enfermos, y acudiendo a ellos la reina, que se ha vuelto ciega, le niegan su ayuda; a veces acaban por perdonarla. ... Pero éstas son, seguramente, adiciones postizas, que disminuyen el valor poético del tema, y se ha de terminar el romance donde termina Menéndez Pidal en la versión sintética de su *Flor nueva,* después de transformarse los amantes en pájaros, como en un desafío final a la persecución y a la muerte.[13]

With the availability of much more abundant and geographically diversified textual evidence, it becomes apparent that the dénouement in which the lovers take vengeance upon their persecutress may well go back to some relatively archaic form of *El conde Olinos.* Although Yoná's text reaches no such vengeful climax, the aggressive animals—serpent and scorpion—of the final metamorphosis clearly indicate the narrative's direction. Other Salonikan texts are more specific:

Ella se hizo una culebra y él se hizo un alacrán.
¿Onde fue sus apozamiento? en el cuello de la reina.
(Attias)

Eya se izo una culebra y él se izo un alacrán.
En el cueyo de la reina se le hue asarrear.[14]
(Benardete)

---

[13] Bénichou, p. 267. A modification of this view is implied in BNE 243.

[14] From T. *sarmak* 'to cling to; to wrap around.' Cf. Wagner, *Beiträge,* p. 165: *sarear* 'knebeln.'

Ella se hiza una culebra, él se hizo un alacrán.
Al cuello de la reina por ahí se fue a posar;
la mató a la madre y tomó al Conde Alimá.
(Díaz-Plaja)

Ella se hizo una culebra, él se hizo un alacrán.
En el garón de la reina ellos se fueron encolgar.
(Hemsi, Var. 4)

Eya se izo una kulevra i él se izo un alakrán.
El meoyo de la reina tomaron a burakar.
(uned., Salonika)

One of our unedited Rhodian versions reserves a different fate for the odious Queen: She catches the fish, cooks them, and then chokes on them:

Ya las peška, ya las toma, ya se meten a gizar.
Ya las giza, ya las kome, i la reina se fue aogar.

In Levy's anomalous version, the Queen dies after smelling the flowers into which the lovers have metamorphosed:

La reina, ke mal tenga, los fue arrankar.
Después de golerlos, las *(sic)* ečó a bular.
Del guesmo ke gulió muerte amarga fue a topar.
(SBS 35)

Peninsular and Moroccan forms also give ample testimony to the lovers' vengeance, though the several means by which it is achieved are at variance with the Eastern tradition. In texts from Santander and Morocco, the plants or trees acquire a capacity to cure infirmities, which they subsequently deny to the wicked Queen:

Donde él nace un alivo (*sic*), donde ella un olivar,
donde curan las heridas y otros males que Dios da.
La reina que ha oído esto un dedo se fué a curar.
—Quítate de ahí, mala reina, que te queremos matar. ...
(RPM 41)

Entre una tierra y otra prezide un limonar
con una hierba muy santa que muchos ciegos curará.

La reina, que se enterara, a su hija ha ido a hablar.
—Hija, si yo me curara, yo te hiciera de festejar.
Y la hija le contesta: —No me haga un festejar,
si de un ojo estás ciega del otro te quedarás:
dos amantes se querían, no les dejaste gozar.

(Larrea 67) [15]

In another dénouement, which occurs in isolated instances in Santander, Galicia, and Northern Portugal, the lovers turn into magic fountains, whose curative powers become famous, but are refused to the cruel Queen (or King), when she (he) becomes ill, is struck blind, etc.:

En la sepultura de ella salió un rico manantial,
donde se curan los dedos y otros males que Dios da.
La reina desque lo supo un dedo se va a curar.
—Vaiga pa allá, mi madre, mi madre, vaiga pa allá.
Que cuando éramos cristianos bien nos mandastes matar.
Y ahora que somos santos no nos vengas a adorar.

(RPM 43)

D'ela volviu unha fonte, correu un limpo cristal,
todol-os coxos e mancos e[n] ela íbanse lavar.
A raiña que tal viu, tamén quixo se lavar.
A fonte lle respondiu: —Ti que vés aquí buscar?
Ti a que vés aquí raiña? a que te vés a lavar?
Que cando eras raiña mandáchesme a min matar,
e cando era oliva mandáchesme a min podar.
A todos darei saude a tí non cha podo dar.

(Carré 19)

Dela nasceu uma fonte, e dele um grande manar;
Curava cegos e mancos, quantos se lá forem lavar. ...
O rei por fim da sua vida ainda chegou a cegar.
—Dá-me água, ó minha filha, para meus olhos lavar. ...
—Não lhe dou água, meu pai, que eu não lha posso dar.
Que mal fazia o conde para o mandares matar?
Que mal faziam as rosas para as mandar cortar?
Que mal fazia o tanque para o mandar atombiar?
Que mal faziam as pombas para as mandar matar?

(VRP 244) [16]

---

[15] Cf. Alvar, "Cinco romances," no. 2.
[16] Compare ASW 204-205; RPM 42, 44; Carré 19; VRP 246.

In various Central Peninsular versions a superficial and inherently self-contradictory Christian overlay turns the lovers into thaumaturgical religious objects or figures—a chapel,[17] an altar, saints, even an image of the Virgin, only so that the pleas of the Queen, placed at their mercy by subsequent misfortunes, may be rejected:

De ella salió una ermita, de él un rico altar,
y los cojos y los ciegos allí se iban a curar.
La reina por su desgracia los ojos llegó a cegar.
—Curármelos, santos míos, si me los queréis curar.
—No te los curamos, reina, no te queremos curar,
que cuando éramos rosales tú nos mandastes cortar.
—Curármelos, santos míos, si me los queréis curar.
—No te los curamos, reina, no te queremos curar,
que cuando éramos palomas tú nos mandastes cazar.
—Curármelos, santos míos, si me los queréis curar.
—No te los curamos, reina, no te queremos curar,
que cuando éramos amantes no nos dejastes gozar,
y ahora que somos ya santos nos vienes aquí a rogar.
(RPM 37)

Ella se volvió una Virgen y el buen conde un pie de altar.
Entre mancos y tullidos a los ciegos luz les da.
La reina se ha quedado ciega y el palacio fatal.
—Por Dios te pido, la Virgen, por Dios te pido, el altar,
que la luz de los mis ojos ya me la podíais dar.
—Cuando éramos olivos me mandó usted cortar;
cuando éramos amantes me mandó usted matar;
cuando éramos palomas me mandó usted matar,
y ahora que somos santos no nos pueden hacer mal,
y la luz de los sus ojos no se la queremos dar.
(RPM 38)[18]

---

[17] The metamorphosis into a chapel or monastery is paralleled in the ballad of *Santa Irene* (RPC 109; Pérez Vidal, "Santa Irene," pp. 525, 527, 543, 552, 559) and in the Catalan *Santa Quitèria* (AFC 72; Milá 25).

[18] Cf. RPM 46, RTR 3, Schindler 4, RPC 8. Berrueta 298, RPM 36 and 45 combine the chapel (*ermita*) and fountain. Some Portuguese texts (Braga, I, 272-276) contain the chapel and altar motif (*ermida-altar*), but nothing is denied to the Queen (or King, in this case) who, in some versions, repents before the altar. Cuban and Venezuelan texts offer *iglesia-rico altar, paloma-cirio del altar,* but without curative properties (Chacón; Montesinos).

In one version from Santander, the magic fountain is of a more aggressive character. Rather than merely refusing to cure, it takes the initiative in killing the Queen just as in the Eastern versions:

Entre medio de los dos   ha nacido un manantial,
en que se lavan los dedos   los condes y los demás.
La reina que se ha enterado   a lavar sus dedos va.
Cuál sería su sorpresa   la fuente ha empezado a hablar.
—Cuando yo era pequeñita   tú me mandaste matar,
y ahora que ya soy fuente   yo te voy a castigar;
tres días tienes de vida   si te quieres confesar;
a otro le he dado la vida   y a ti la voy a quitar.
(RPM 39)

Divine justice is invoked against the Queen and occasions her death in a solitary Moroccan rendition, though this ending is probably an independent invention, since the crucial verse is borrowed from *Las quejas de Jimena* (MP 3, v. 3):

De ella sale una paloma   y de él sale un gavilán;
vola uno y vola el otro,   al cielo van a juzgar:
—Justicia, Señor, justicia,   si me la queréis dar.
Otro día en la mañana   la reina faltó en su lugar.
(Larrea 69)

Both the Sephardic and the Peninsular traditions thus attest in diverse ways to the lovers' vengeance. Such dénouements may have developed independently, although it seems more likely that they were an authentic and deeply meaningful part of some archaic form of the narrative. As Entwistle observed: "Mediaeval narrative poetry is more addicted to justice than to sentiment." [19] Moreover, the presence of the lovers' vengeance in *Conde Olinos* echoes the outcome of *The Transformations,* where the final metamorphosis usually gives mastery to one of the protagonists.

In truth, the two endings represent different artistic preferences, one not necessarily superior to the other. Whereas the felicitous interruption at the metamorphosis to birds is yet another achievement of fragmentistic style, the various conclusions in which the Queen receives her just deserts satisfy — through an inventive array of wish-fulfilling miracles—that traditional Hispanic longing for an art in which virtue and true love are rewarded and evil does not go unpunished.

[19] "Second Thoughts," p. 17.

BIBLIOGRAPHY

El conde Olinos

Eastern J.-Sp.: Adatto 5 (= GRA, with minor variants); Attias 16; Baruch 278; BdR, no. 12 (= SR); Benardete 34; Coello 6; Danon 19; Díaz-Plaja 9; Galante 2; Gil 2 (= Galante, Danon, Coello); Hemsi, "Sur le folklore," pp. 794-795; Levy 20.1-2; Menéndez Pelayo 30 (= Danon); PTJ 54-54*c* (= Coello, Díaz-Plaja, Danon, Baruch); RoH, I, 401; Romey 3; San Sebastián 1 (III); SBS 35-36; SR, pp. 13-14 (= GRA); UR 10 (= CBU 339-340).

Moroccan J.-Sp.: Alvar, "Cinco romances," no. 2; Benardete 33; Bénichou 28; Gil, pp. xx-xxi (= MP); Larrea 67-69; Levy 18 (cf. our review, *NRFH*, XIV [1960], 348-349); Moya, II, 256; MRuiz 66.1-7; MP 55; PTJ 54*d* (= Alvar).

Castilian: ART 247-249; ASW 203-206; Berrueta 298; Córdova y Oña, I, 291; CPE, I, 55-56; II, 19, 21; CPM 75; CVR 25-26; Feito, p. 298; FN 117-118; Gil, "Canciones del folklore riojano," no. 1; Güéjar 5; Gutiérrez Macías, pp. 343-344; Hernáez Tobías, nos. 8-9; Kundert, pp. 90-91; Ledesma, pp. 159-160; Marín, II, 3; Martínez Hernández, no. 186 (pp. 183-184); G. Menéndez Pidal, *Romancero,* pp. 186-188; Morán Bardón, pp. 138-140; Puig Campillo, pp. 107-109; RPC 8; RPE 11-12; RPM 35-46; RQDB-II 3; RTCN 3; RTO 9; RTR 3; Schindler 4; Torner, *Cuarenta canciones,* pp. 133-138; Id., *El folklore en la escuela,* pp. 109-111.[20]

Canarian: RCan 10 and 20.

Spanish American: Aramburu, *El folklore de los niños,* pp. 106-107, 121-123; Bayo, "La poesía popular," p. 47; Id., "Cantos populares," p. 797; Id., *Romancerillo,* pp. 18-19; Cadilla, *Juegos,* pp. 139-140; Chacón, "Nuevos romances en Cuba," pp. 208-209; Deliz, p. 288; Garrido 6; Liscano, pp. 56-57; Monroy Pittaluga, p. 370; Montesinos, "Dos romances viejos," p. 46; Moya, II, 11-14; Pardo 1; Ramón y Rivero-Aretz, I:2, pp. 632-635. See also Menéndez Pidal, "Un recuerdo de juventud," p. 9.

Galician: Carré 18-20; La Iglesia, II, 115; Sampedro 169.

Portuguese: Almeida Garrett, III, 19-21; Athaide Oliveira, pp. 50-51, 300-301; Bellermann, pp. 134-39; Braga, I, 263-276; Chaves, "O Romanceiro e o teatro popular," p. 382; Estácio da Veiga, pp. 65-67; Fernandes Thomás, *Velhas*

[20] The initial scene—Count Olinos singing on the seashore—occurs in the Moroccan and Peninsular tradition as a contamination in various composite narratives: *Conde Olinos* + *Flérida* (MRuiz 66); *Conde Olinos* + *Gerineldo* or vice versa (Fernández Núñez, "Folklore bañezano," pp. 417-418; Id., *Folk-lore leonés,* no. 15; RPM 76-79; Menéndez Pidal, *et al., Cómo vive un romance,* p. 210; Catalán, "Motivo y variación," pp. 172, 175 f., 178); *Conde Olinos* + *Boda estorbada* (Echevarría 87; RPM 95); *Prisionero* + *Conde Olinos* + *Gerineldo* + *Boda estorbada* (Larrea 156; Munthe 2).

canções, pp. 23-24; Gomes Pereira, *RL*, XIV, 130-131; Hardung, I, 216-224; Kundert, p. 91; Martins, I, 181-182; II, 1-5; Neves 136-137; Pires de Lima-Lima Carneiro, *O Romanceiro para o povo e para as escolas*, pp. 49-50; Thomás Pires, *Lendas*, pp. 93-94; Vasconcellos, "Bibl. do Povo," pp. 60-62; VRP 235-248.[21] The reference in VRP, I, 291, to Reis Dâmaso, *Enciclopédia Republicana*, pp. 171-173, is erroneous, since the latter represents *El parto en lejas tierras* (cf. VRP 552-553) and not *El conde Olinos*.

Brazilian: Pereira da Costa, pp. 311-313.

Catalan: AFC 3165; Amades, I, p. 162; Avenç, IV, 74-76; Briz, II, 58; Massot, no. 8.28 ff.; Milá 206.24 ff., Vars. BCDFG; OCPC, I, 281; III, 262; Subirá, pp. 34-35.[22]

Archaic Text: See FN 118; Menéndez Pidal, "Poesía popular ... ," *Los romances de América*, pp. 65-68; H. A. Rennert, *ZRPh*, XVII (1893), 548 f.

Studies: BNE 243-244; Braga, III, 415-423; J. M. Chacón y Calvo, "Figuras del Romancero: *El Conde Olinos*," *AFC*, II (1926), 36-46; W. J. Entwistle, "El Conde Olinos," *RFE*, XXXV (1951), 237-248; Id., "Second Thoughts Concerning *El Conde Olinos*," *RPh*, VII (1953), 10-18; Michaëlis, "Estudos," p. 195, n. 1; J. de Onís, "El celo de los duendes: Una variante americana del romance del *Conde Olinos*," *CuA*, Año XXIII (1964), 219-229; RoH, I, 332, n. 31; II, 13, 16, 302, 324, 351, 396, 397, 398, n. 66, 428, 429; TRV, II, 356-357, n. 1, 412, n. 2; M. Schneider, "Los cantos de lluvia en España," *AnM*, IV (1949), 3-56: pp. 46-47.

La Pernette

French: Arbaud, I, 111-116; Canteloube, II, 57, 128-129; Coirault, *Recherches*, p. 554; Davenson 3; Doncieux 1; Rolland, IV, 20-23; Udry, pp. 213-215.

Italian: *Fior di tomba*: Nigra 19; also Bronzini, II, 23, n. 40, 292-293, n. 28.

Studies: Coirault, *Recherches*, pp. 548-568, 584-596; Doncieux, "La Pernette," *Ro*, XX (1891), 86-135. See also Doncieux 1; Entwistle, "Second Thoughts," p. 11, n. 2.[23]

---

[21] In Galician-Portuguese tradition the lovers' metamorphoses contaminate certain versions of *La novia abandonada*: e.g., Almeida Garrett, III, 38; Bellermann, pp. 140-145; Braga, I, 279, 285, 287, 290-291, 293, 304, 306; Carré, nos. 19-20; Pires de Lima-Lima Carneiro, *Romanceiro para o povo e para as escolas*, p. 77; Serrano, p. 38; Romero, *Brasil*, pp. 79-81.

[22] The Catalan tradition appends *Conde Olinos* to *Don Lluis de Montalbà* (see no. 23, n. 11 *infra*).

[23] Agreements between *Conde Olinos* and the Hungarian *Kate Kádár* and Rumanian *Ring and Veil* (*Inelul şi năframa*) are probably coincidental. However, compare Leader, pp. 125-126, 130; Vargyas, *Researches*, pp. 112-114, 119; Amzulescu, no. 305; Child, I, 97*b*; III, 498*a*.

The Transformations [24]

Catalan: *L'esquerpa*: AFC 2861; Avenç, III, 5-8; Briz, I, 125-128; Capmany 35; Milá 513 (read 531); OCPC, III, 362-363; Sarri, pp. 120-121; Torner, *Cuarenta canciones,* pp. 84-86; Vidal, II, 18.

French: *Les métamorphoses*: Arbaud, II, 128-134; Canteloube, I, 34-36; II, 295-298; III, 201-202, 286-287; Davenson 61; Rolland, IV, 29-33. See also Child 44 (p. 400*a*).

Canadian French: Barbeau-Sapir, pp. 198-203; Gagnon, pp. 78-79, 120-122.

Louisiana French: Whitfield, pp. 34-37.

Breton: Canteloube, IV, 402-403; Udry, pp. 148-150.

Italian: *Amore inevitabile*: Nigra 59.

English: *The Twa Magicians*: Child 44; Bronson 44.

Anglo-American: Bronson 44; Coffin, p. 52.

Scandinavian: *Søster beder Broder*: Dal, no. 35; DgF, VII, no. 437; Prior, III, 94-97; Arwidsson, II, no. 117. Though the parties involved here are brother and sister, the narrative sequence is that of *The Transformations.* Neither Olrik nor Dal remark upon the analogy. *Jomfruen i Fugleham,* with its consecutive transformations of hind to falcon to maid, reflects a similar pattern (see no. 25, n. 7 *infra*). For yet another Danish parallel, see *Dernière ressource* (Pineau, *Le Romancéro scandinave,* pp. 227-229): in this case the transformations are rationalized as a series of vocations.

German: *Thörichte Wünsche*: Erk-Böhme 1083.

Lithuanian: Balys F5; Seemann, pp. 151-152 (no. 7).

Rumanian: *Cucul şi Turturica*: Alexandri, pp. 35-37; Amzulescu 236; Beza, "Balkan Peasant Poetry," pp. 285-287; Cortés, pp. 180-189; Franken, pp. 31-33. Cf. also *Mierla şi Sturzul* (Amzulescu 237) and Vrabie, pp. 458-460.

Serbo-Croatian: Stevenson Stanoyevich, nos. 26, 53. For more Slavic variants, see Child (I, pp. 400-401), Balys, and Seemann.

Greek: Baud-Bovy, *Chansons,* I, 288-289, 385 (no. 14*a*); II, 305-306, 460 (no. 37); Legrand-Pernot, *Précis,* pp. 36-37; Pernot, *Anthologie,* pp. 132, 142; Petropoulos, *La comparaison,* pp. 23, n. 6, 79, n. 1, 112-113, n. 1. In another variant, *Hē rōmaiopoûla,* a Greek girl would adopt various forms to avoid marriage with a Turk: Georgeakis-Pineau, pp. 210-212; Lübke, p. 58; Meyer, p. 20; Passow 574*a* (p. 431); Tommaseo-Pavolini, no. 135 (p. 147). See also Child, I, 400*b*.

---

[24] For folktale analogs, see Aarne-Thompson, Types 313-314, 325; Taylor, "The Parallels between Ballads and Tales," pp. 107, 113. For a Yemenite Jewish song embodying the *Transformations* theme, see S. D. F. Goitein, *Von den Juden Jemens* (Berlin, 1934), pp. 74-75 (*Die Hirtin und ihr Freier*). Cf. also D615.3. *Transformation combat between lover and maid*; D642.3. *Transformation to escape lover.*

13

LA ESPOSA DE DON GARCÍA

(The Abduction of Don García's Bride)

—Yyo me a̯levantí 'un lunes 'i 'un lunes por la manyyana.
Me fu'era 'a kožer tapetes, tapetes 'i almenaras,
para aparentar la tore, la tore ke 'era nombrađa,
la tore de las Saliđas 'i ke la sivdađ la guađra.
'A la tornađa ke atorna, fayyó la tore kemađa;
[fayyó la tore kemađa] 'i 'a la su 'espozada yevada.
—Kavayyo, 'el mi kavayyo 'i 'el mi kavayyo lazare,
tanta sevada te ayy dađo 'i mučo más te [en]tyend[o] dare.
Kyero ke me yeves 'esta noče ande la mi 'esposa royyale.
Saltó 'el kavayyo 'i dišo, kon sensyya ke 'el Dyez le ayy dađo:
—Yyo te yevaré 'esta noče ande la tu 'espoza royya̯le.
'Estrinǧéšme byen la sinǧa 'i aflošéšme 'el mi koyyare.
Dešle sotađas de fyero 'i de 'él no tengáš piađađ.
Por las ka'es ke ayy ǧente, kaminaréš de avagare.
Por las ka'es ke no ayy ǧente, senteas azíaš sa̯ltare.
—¿Si la veríaš a mi 'espoza 'i ala mi 'espoza royyale?
—Por akí pasó 'esta noče, dos 'oras al bel lunare.

Source: GRA 1.
2*b* *repeated.*
3*b* + se torna.
6*a* Cf. Attias 4.13.
8*b* te tyenda 'a dare. *Other known readings*: te vo a dar(e) (*Attias, LSO*), te a de dare (*uned. versions*).

Blanko kalsa 'i blanko viste 'i blanko kavayyo lazare.
Yya se 'esparte 'el kavayero, yya se 'esparte 'i se va.
Por 'en međyyo del kamino, 'enkontró kon 'un personale.
—¿Si la viteš a mi 'espoza, ala mi 'espoza royyale?
Por akí pasó 'esta noğe, tres 'oras al bel lunar.
Preto kalsa 'i preto viste 'i preto kavayyo lazare.

20*a* 'enmeđyyo.

Translation:

"I arose early one Monday, early a Monday morning. I went in search of carpets, carpets and candelabras, to adorn the tower, the tower that was renowned, the tower of Salidas, which stands guard over the city." (5) When he returned homeward, he found the tower burned. He found the tower burned and his bride carried off. "Horse, my horse, my sorrel horse, I have fed you so much barley and I intend to give you much more. I want you to take me tonight to my royal bride." (10) Up jumped the horse and spoke with God-given wisdom: "I'll take you tonight to your royal bride. Tighten my cinch firmly and loosen my collar. Whip me with an iron lash and have no pity on me. Through the streets where there are people, you will ride at a slow pace. (15) Through the streets where there are no people, you should make sparks fly." "Did you by chance see my bride, my royal bride?" "She passed here this night, two hours after moonrise, wearing white shoes, dressed in white, and riding a whitish sorrel." Now the knight departs, now he departs and is gone. (20) Along the way he met a group of people. "Did you by chance see my bride, my royal bride?" "She passed here this night, three hours after moonrise, (23) wearing black shoes, dressed in black, and riding on a blackish sorrel."

Motifs:

1 N128.2. *Monday as unlucky day.*
6 R10. *Abduction.*
10 B211.1.3. *Speaking horse*; B401. *Helpful horse.*
18 Cf. K2112. *Woman slandered as adulteress* (*prostitute*).

The rare, exclusively Salonikan Sephardic versions of *La esposa de Don García* have come down to us in a lamentably fragmentary and contaminated state that obscures the ballad's original sense. Only Yoná and Attias come near to presenting a "complete," though still cryptic narrative. Nonetheless, through comparison with Peninsular evidence, the almost impenetrable Sephardic texts grudgingly yield their story of an abducted bride, who is slandered by her mother-in-law. Attias' version is by far the better preserved. Unlike Yoná (vv. 16 ff.), the *sḥuegra* (= the wife's mother) and García's mother are still distinguished, but both versions tend to obscure the conflicting reports of mother and mother-in-law by indicating the wife's fidelity or lack of it only by the color of her clothing and of her horse. The wife's mother claims that she is dressed in black and rides a black horse (out of sorrow at being abducted); the mother-in-law represents her as dressed in white and on a white horse, indicating the levity with which she accepts the forced separation from her husband. In Attias' version the mother-in-law also represents her as playing a golden *chuflete* (a sort of flute or whistle), as an amorous provocation to her abductors: "chufletico de oro en boca / que mancebos hace quemar." [1] Attias' text strains to clarify the opposition of mother and mother-in-law by appending two not inappropriate proverbial verses borrowed from *La mala suegra*:

La sḥuegra con la nuera   siempre vos quijiteis male
y la madre con la hija   como la uña en la carne. [2]

The presence of these verses in the Sephardic versions of *La mala suegra* indicates that an almost identical verse ("que las suegras y las nueras / siempre se quisieron mal"), found in the ballad's Peninsular counterparts, [3] is probably not, as Cossío maintains (*BBMP*, I, 126), a late and decadent addition. The verses occur also in Moroccan versions of *La mala suegra.* [4] The same sentiments in *La esposa de Don García* may also be of considerable antiquity. Some Portuguese texts observe

---

[1] The instrument, which parallels the *vihuela* or *guitarra* of the Peninsular versions of *La esposa de Don García,* is possibly borrowed from *El chuflete* (no. 27 *infra*). See especially no. 27, n. 9.

[2] Cf. Adatto, p. 51; Benardete 39; Díaz-Plaja 3.

[3] RPM 150, 141, 147; RTR 9 (p. 14).

[4] Larrea 96.45-46; Ortega 224.

that "entre sogras e noras / que a verdade não havia" (VRP 623; cf. Martins, I, 200). However, the expression is proverbial and could also have entered these distant versions separately. [5]

The Sephardic ballad's cryptic narrative is clarified by the Peninsular tradition. Here Don García's wife is carried off by the Moors. When García asks his mother (that is, the wife's mother-in-law) what has happened, she reports that when the girl passed by in the company of Moors three hours before dawn she was dressed in red and was playing a *vihuela* or guitar and singing "Cuernos, cuernos, Don García," "Morra, morra, Dom García," or was talking cheerfully with her abductors. The wife's own mother, on the other hand, exonerates her by stating that she was dressed in black, was disputing angrily with the Moors and, as she played the guitar, cried out to be rescued: "Valme, valme, Don García." The Peninsular texts also supply the ballad's outcome, which is unknown to the Sephardic tradition: Confident in his wife's fidelity, Don García pursues the raiding party and tricks the Moors into letting him ride off with his wife but not before the poor girl's fidelity is again placed in doubt by her abductors.

The Judeo-Spanish texts begin with an explanatory prolog in *á-a*: The action, as in *La adúltera* (*á-a*; no. 16 *infra*) and numerous other *romances,* takes place on Monday — a topic unlucky day in balladry. [6]

---

[5] For similar proverbs, see F. Rodríguez Marín, *Más de 21.000 refranes castellanos* ... (Madrid, 1926), p. 475*b*; *12.600 refranes más* ... (Madrid, 1930), p. 315*a*.

[6] Menéndez Pelayo suggests (TRV, II, 59, n. 1) that this preference for placing balladic occurrences on Monday is based upon an ancient belief in the unlucky character of that day. The archaic versions of *El robo de Elena* (*Primav.* 109) militate in favor of such a conclusion: "Lunes era, caballeros, / lunes fuerte y aciago" or, acording to another variant: "un día fuerte aciago." Similarly, the tragic death of the Duchess of Bragança occurs "un lunes a las cuatro horas, / ya después de mediodía" (*Primav.* 107-107*a*). The murder of the Duke of Gandía is likewise discovered on Monday: "A veinte y siete de julio / un lunes, en fuerte día" (Durán 1251-1252). The three hundred youthful *hidalgos* who, in spite of dire predictions by their elders, go out on a raiding party from Jaén on a Monday morning, seem to gain their resounding victory against the Moors by opposing reckless daring to superstition (*Primav.* 82*a*; Menéndez Pidal, "Poesía popular y romancero," III, 107-109). Compare also the ballad of Don Alvaro de Luna cited by E. M. Wilson, "Samuel Pepys's Spanish Chap-books, Part II," p. 249 (Text G): "Lunes era vn triste día, / al punto de amanecer. ..."

In the modern tradition dreadful events also occur on Monday. The Moroccan *Muerte ocultada* begins: "Levantóse Uezo / lunes de mañana" (MP 75). The

The hero returns home to find that his "tore de las Salid̄as" has been burned down and his wife abducted. The authentic form of the name is undoubtedly *Salinas,* as in Attias, Molho, and one of our unedited texts. It is taken, as Attias has shown, from local Salonikan toponymy: "From old people in Salonika I heard that in fact there was in this city a tower with the name *Salinas,* because of the salt flats around it,

---

happenings narrated in *Sufrir callando* take place on a Monday morning: "Levantíme, madre, / un lunes por la mañana" (Danon 22). Both the *ó* and *á-a* assonant ballads of *La adúltera* (no. 16 *infra*), which almost invariably end in disaster, begin with the migratory verse "Yo me levantara un lunes / un lunes antes de albor" (MP 78; RoH, II, 177) or "... un lunes por la mañana" (MP 80), as also do the North African versions of the thematically analogous *Landarico* (Bénichou 8; Larrea 119-120; MRuiz 63). See also *Abindarráez* (Larrea 20.26). *La nodriza del infante,* in which a baby prince is accidentally burned to death, begins: "Madrugara Teresita / un lunes por la mañana ..." (RQDB-II 60; Larrea 260). The Asturian *Calumnia de la reina,* which ends in the death of an innocent woman, begins "en la mañana de un lunes" (CVR, p. 188). In the Catalan *Presó del rei de França,* the King departs "un dilluns al de matí" only to fall prisoner to the Spanish (AFC 3064; Amades, I, 212, Avenç, III, 49). In *Serrallonga,* unhappy events take place on Monday morning (AFC 3105; Amades, II, 16; Avenç, II, 89), as also in many another Catalan song: *Pau Gibert i Pauleta, La llibertat privada, La desenganyada* (AFC 2380, 2902, 3317). On Easter Monday the Moors capture Don Bueso's sister (Alvar, "Cinco romances," p. 75, n. 60; Benardete 26; FN 210; Larrea 58, 229). *La difunta pleiteada* (M.ª Goyri de Menéndez Pidal, *De Lope de Vega y del romancero,* p. 14; cf. p. 10) contains a baleful prediction:

las bodas se comerán el lunes al mediodía,
que las bodas y la muerte todo ha de ser en un día.

La muerte del Príncipe Don Juan, in the Castilian tradition (RPM 23, also 19, 20, 24-25; ART 224; RPC 77, 79), makes use of the "fatal Monday" motif, sometimes giving it a peculiarly ironic turn:

—¿De dónde viene la mi esposa, tan sola y tan de mañana?
—Vengo de Santo Domingo de oír misa del alba,
de rezar a Dios por ti, te levante de la cama.
—Yo sí me levantaré el lunes por la mañana,
con los pies amarillitos y la cara amortajada.

(RPM 23)

In some Argentine versions of *La adúltera* (*ó*) all three dramatis personae—wife, lover, and husband—are buried "lunes de mañanita" (Moya, I, 454, 457).

Other *romances* that seem to have forgotten the day's once fatal connotations include references to Monday reduced to a meaningless, though recurrent *topos.* There is nothing particularly tragic about *La semana del pretendiente* (MP 137), *Repulsa y compasión* (Larrea 169-171; here the first verse is probably borrowed

which were certainly dug to obstruct the approach to the tower. The said place is on the shore of the sea, near the *Tophana* (= 'arsenal'). In the days of the Ottoman Sultan, a conflagration broke out in the city, the tower went up in flames and its memory was wiped out." [7]

The Sephardic texts, in *á-a* and *á-(e)* assonance, seem to have been completely re-rhymed. The Castilian versions use uniform *í-a* assonance, as do most of the Portuguese (except for a very brief series in *á*). One Portuguese rendition (VRP 625), regrettably unidentified as to geographic origin, seems more closely related to the Salonikan versions in that it includes, among a variety of assonances (*í-a, á, í, í-o, á, í-a, á*), a passage in *á*, in which the hero specifies the proper adjustment of his horse's harness:

Chamou pelo seu criado, por aquele mais liberal:
—Aparelha-me um cavalo, aquele que melhor andar:
Aperta-lhe bem a cilha, alarga-lhe o peitoral.

Almost identical instructions occur in the Salonikan texts, although here they are voiced by the horse itself:

Saltó 'el kavayyo 'i dišo, kon sensyya ke 'el Dyez le ayy dađo:
—Yyo te yevaré 'esta noğe ande la tu 'espoza royyale.
'Estrinğéšme byen la sinğa 'i aflošéšme 'el mi koyyare.
Dešle sotađas de fyero 'i de 'él no tengáš piađađ.
(Yoná, vv. 10-13)

from *La adúltera* [*ó*; MP 78]), or *El pretendiente burlado* (Larrea 246) all of which set their action on Monday, as does *El soldado y la monja* (RPM 261) in the Peninsular tradition. Though no disaster occurs in these ballads, the unlucky nature of the day may possibly be responsible for the fact that in each case the amorous pretensions of the male protagonist are frustrated. For other apparently non-significant uses of the motif, see Larrea, *Canciones*, nos. 4-6; Benarroch, *El indiano*, p. 87. A Peninsular "romance geográfico" collected by Vergara Martín begins with the same commonplace: "Hallándome en el Fondal / un lunes por la mañana ..." ("Algunos romances populares de carácter geográfico," p. 87). That Monday has in general lost its unlucky connotations in the modern Sephardic tradition is apparent from one of Attias' wedding songs which begins "Besimán tob ('in a good sign') me dicen la gente ..." after which the groom says that he will wait for his bride on Monday morning: "Vos espero, dama, / un lunes de mañana" (Attias 100.9-10).

[7] Attias, p. 68. The name applied to the arsenal corresponds to T. *tophane* 'gunnery, arsenal.'

Saltó el caballo y dijo con ḥuerza qu'el Dio le hay dares:
—Apretalde de las cinches, aflojalde el su collare,
deišle sotadas de fierro y no le tengáis piadades.
(Attias 4.21-26)

Saltó el cavallo y le dixo, con gracia que el Dio le dio:
—Apretéx de la mi sincha y afloxéx el mi collar,
dámed cangicadas de fierro, de mí no tengáx piadad.
(LSO, no. 10.10-12)

—Dešme kanǧikadas de fierro, sin pueder apiadarvos.
(uned.)[8]

These verses doubtless derive from the ballad of *Gaiferos y Meliselda,* where the hero is reminded of equestrian advice proffered by Roland at Charlemagne's court:

Muchas veces le oí decir en palacio del emperante,
que si se hallaba cercado de moros en algún lugar,
al caballo aprieta la cincha y aflojábale el petral;
hincábale las espuelas sin ninguna piedad:
el caballo es esforzado de otra parte va a saltar.
(*Primav.* 173, p. 381)

Similar verses survive in modern Catalan and Portuguese versions of the Gaiferos ballad:

Si el cavall fos tan valent com el de l'onclo Roldà,
que en estrènyer-li la cingla i en afluixar-li el pitral,
traspassava set murades i no es feia dany ni mal!
(Macabich 118)[9]

Aperta a cilha ao cavallo, affrouxa-lhe o peitoral....
Finca espóras ao cavallo, que o sangue lhe faz saltar.
(Braga, I, 218)

---

[8] *Kanǧikadas* is certainly based upon T. *kamçı* 'whip.' One would, however, expect **kančiladas* on the basis of T. *kamçılamak* 'to whip.' Perhaps, in the J.-Sp. form, *kamçı* has somehow been contaminated with T. *kancık* 'female animal, she-ass.'

[9] See also Macabich 125-126; Milá 247.27-29.

As formulaic *Wanderstrophen* these verses have migrated to other Carolingian ballads in the Portuguese tradition. Dom Beltrão's horse speaks out to defend his dead master's bravery in battle: "Tres vezes me apertou cilhas, / me alargou o peitoral..." (Braga, I, 209). Conde Claros, riding in haste to rescue Claralinda, makes similar arrangements: "Alarga-lhe a contracilha, / estreita-lhe o atafal" (Braga, I, 312).

The eloquence of Don García's talking horse is probably extraneous to the original narrative. Articulate horses—as in *Búcar sobre Valencia* (*Primav.* 55) or the Portuguese *Muerte de Don Beltrán*[10]—are not unknown to the traditional *Romancero,* but García's steed does no talking in any of the Peninsular texts and the vacillation between first and third person object pronouns at this point in the various Sephardic versions seems to indicate that the harnessing instructions were originally voiced by a human being. One is tempted to ask if the prevalence of speaking horses in Greek tradition may not have suggested a like development in our Salonikan *romance.*[11] The horse's capabilities are

---

[10] Braga, I, 209; VRP 18, 21, 22, 27, 32, 33. A talking horse and talking sword appear in an Asturian version of *Conde Olinos* (CVR, p. 138). Compare also the horse that understands a most elaborate warning in *El rey envidioso de su sobrino* (MP 123; Bénichou 50; Larrea 191-192; MRuiz 94; Ortega 211) and the rider's detailed exhortation of his horse as in *Don García de Padilla* (*Primav.* 69). On talking horses, see TRV, II, 269; Menéndez Pidal, "Poesía popular y romancero," X, 285-286; Entwistle, "El Conde Dirlos," p. 10; Id., "Second Thoughts Concerning *El Conde Olinos,*" p. 16. For British, Scandinavian, and Hungarian examples of the talking horse, see *The Broomfield Hill* (Child 43A.10, B.5); *Hugabald* (Pineau, *Romancéro,* p. 57 [from Landstad]); *Merika* (Leader, p. 316); for intelligent, talking horses in epicry: Bowra, *Heroic Poetry,* pp. 159-170.

[11] For talking horses, other animals, and even objects in Greek and Balkan balladry, see Abbott, *Songs,* pp. 50-51; Baud-Bovy, *Textes,* p. 159, n. 3; Dieterich, "Die neugriechische Volkspoesie," p. 131; Id., "Die Volksdichtung der Balkanländer," pp. 277-282; Firmenich, I, 45-46; Garnett, I, p. 275; Liebrecht, *Zur Volkskunde,* p. 156; Lüdeke, "Griechische Volksdichtung," p. 222; Lüdeke-Megas, nos. 8, 13, 47, 48, 105, 106; Martinengo, pp. 24-28; Tommaseo-Pavolini, pp. 126-127 (no. 109); Strausz, *Bulgarische Volksdichtungen,* p. 202; Lambertz, *Die Volksepik der Albaner,* pp. 34, 51, 118, 141.

One Greek ballad, which includes the talking horse motif, shows other striking but possibly coincidental agreements with *La esposa de Don García.* In *The Abduction of Akritas' Bride* (*Hē harpagḗ tēs gunaikòs toũ Akritē*): The hero's wife is carried off by Moors. Akritas consults with his horses as to which one will carry him in pursuit of the abductors. Only one very old horse answers that it is willing to undertake such an adventure. The hero meets some one (a Moor, a swineherd, shepherd, etc.) along the way and asks if he has seen

so exceptional by Hispanic standards that they must be explained here as a manifestation of divine intervention: "Saltó 'el kavayyo 'i dišo, / kon sensyya ke 'el Dyez le ayy dado . . ." (Yoná, v. 10). In an Asturian *Conde Olinos,* horse and sword become articulate "por la gracia de Dios padre" (CVR, p. 138). Similarly the newborn babe in Moroccan versions of *La mala suegra* acquires speech "con la gracia de Dios guarde" or, undisguised by possible Judaic anti-trinitarian strictures, "con la gracia de Dios Padre" (Larrea 94.48, 95.52). The formula found in *La esposa de Don García* is also used, but without miraculous overtones, to introduce dialog in some Salonikan versions of *La doncella guerrera*: "Saltó la más chica d'eyas [las hijas del rey] / i kon grasia k'el Dio le dio" (uned.). The irregular assonance (. . . *dado,* . . . *dares,* . . . *dio*) of the corresponding verse in *La esposa de Don García* undoubtedly points to its extraneous origin.

The Sephardic *Esposa de Don García* incorporates other formulaic expressions which can be amply documented elsewhere in the Hispanic tradition. In the Castilian versions Don García repeatedly urges his horse to carry him hither and yon in search of his bride, but there is no offer of more fodder as a reward (Yoná, v. 8). The Judeo-Spanish texts share this detail with several other Peninsular ballads:

---

the abductors pass by. In some versions, the wife recognizes the hero's approach by the neighing of his horse (Baud-Bovy, *Textes,* p. 157; cf. ART 215: "ha relinchado el caballo / y le ha conocido la niña"). The wife declares "qu'elle est déjà enceinte du ravisseur" (cf. RPM 15: "que la niña va preñada / de toda la morería"). The hero answers that "l'enfant lui-même est mien, et, belle, tu es mienne" (cf. Don García's similar acceptance of the situation in RPM 15: "Si la niña va preñada / mujer es que pariría; // si pariese hijo varón / será Rey en Castilla, // y si pariese hija hembra / monja en Santa Catalina"). Akritas slaughters the abductors. For texts and discussion of the Greek ballad, see especially Baud-Bovy, *Textes,* pp. 153-162; also: Akadēmía, I, 31-35; Fauriel, I, no. 26; II, no. 11; Fotheringham, p. 29; McPherson, *Poetry,* pp. 34-35; Pernot, *Anthologie,* pp. 32-34; Id., *Études,* nos. 40, 85, 89; Politis, *Eklogaì,* no. 75; Proust, pp. 37-39; Sanders, pp. 10-13. (The ballad is often contaminated with the theme of the husband who returns after a long absence to prevent his wife's remarriage.)

Could a knowledge of the Greek song and recognition of its thematic similarity to the *romance* have suggested the talking horse motif to some Sephardic singer of *La esposa de Don García*?

—Alto, alto, mi caballo, alto más que Gibraltar,
mucha cebada te he dado, mucha más te pienso dar
si me llevas esta noche donde los novios están.
(*Conde Antores*: RPM 48) [12]

—¡Ay mi caballito rojo!, hoy tiene que caminar...
La cebada de tres días hoy te la tengo de dar;
cuatro firraduras nuebas hoy las tienes de gastar.
(*Conde Claros fraile*: Munthe 3.73 ff.) [13]

Bebe, caballo rocío, bebe, caballo rosal;
mucha cebada te he echado pero más te pienso echar,
si me llevas esta noche donde la mi infanta está.
(*Conde Olinos*: Schindler 4)

Corre, corre, meu cavallo, a quanto possas correr;
a' porta da minha ama eu te darei de beber.
Avança, cavallo, avança, quanto puderes avançar;
a' porta da minha ama eu te darei de jantar. [14]

Similarly, the verses in which Don García varies his pace on crowded or empty streets (Yoná, vv. 14-15) are shared with *Conde Claros y el Emperador* and several other Peninsular ballads. [15]

Like the Salonikan versions of *Gaiferos jugador*, the ballad of Don García has apparently replaced much of its original increment with formulaic material borrowed from other sources: the offer of fodder (Yoná, v. 8); the horse that speaks by divine grace (v. 10); the harnessing instructions and cruel spurring (vv. 12-13); and the varied pace of pursuit (vv. 14-15). It is possible that the almost consistent *á-e* assonance of this borrowed material suggested the re-rhyming of the entire latter part of the poem. The Sephardic ballad's *á-a* introduction, however, and the existence of at least one Portuguese version in mixed

[12] Notably these verses are followed in RPM 48 by others which also occur in the Salonikan *Esposa de Don García*: i.e., "Por donde no le ve la gente," etc. Cf. Yoná, vv. 14-15.

[13] Cf. Pérez de Castro, "Nuevas variantes asturianas," no. 1.

[14] The verses occur as an interpolation in a version of *Bernal Francés* + *La aparición* (Braga, II, 41).

[15] See no. 4, nn. 9-10 *supra*. Molho's version of *La esposa de Don García* replaces the entire final portion of the ballad with verses belonging to *Conde Claros y el Emperador*. See LSO 76-77 (no. 10.13 ff.).

assonance (VRP 625) suggest an alternate possibility: *La esposa de Don García,* like *El veneno de Moriana* or *El conde Alemán y la reina,* [16] may have originally consisted of paired couplets. If this were the case, the Castilian and Portuguese versions in *í-a* and the Sephardic texts in *á-a* + *á-(e)* would represent two independent attempts to absorb the ballad into the mainstream of *romance* metrification. But the paucity of textual material now available precludes a definitive decision concerning the ballad's original form.

BIBLIOGRAPHY

Eastern J.-Sp.: Attias 4; Gil 49 (= MP); LSO 76-77 (no. 10.1-12); MP 62; PTJ 62 (= Attias).

Castilian: ART 214-215; ASW 207-209; CVR 27; RPM 13-16; RQDB-I 28; RTO 5. See also TRV, I, 217.

Portuguese: Braga, III, 542-544; Chaves, "O ciclo dos descobrimentos," pp. 110-112; Martins, I, 199-203; Tavares, *RL,* VIII, 74-75; Id., *Ilustração Trasmontana,* I, 143; VRP 623-625.

---

[16] Cf. FN 17-19 and no. 7 *supra.*

14

LA MALA SUEGRA

(The Evil Mother-in-law)

Asentađa 'está la reyna   'en 'el portal de la kalye,
kon dolores de parire,   ke non las pu'eđe somportare.
¡Kén 'estuvyera paryendo   'en 'el sarayy del rey su pađre!
¡Kén la tuvyese por vezina   'i ala konđesa su mađre!
—Kuando me asento a parire,   ke diga: " 'El Dyez la 'eskape."
A'í la 'olyyó la 'esfu'egra   de altas tores de ande 'estare.
—'I andávos, la mi nu'era,   'i a parir ande vu'estra madre.
Si 'el vu'estro mariđo vyene,   yyo le daré ke almorzare.
Le daré ga'ína 'en sena   'i kapones almorzare.
Le daré yerva al kavayyo   'i karne kruda al gavilane.
Le 'eğaré gu'esos al pero   'i ke non vos vayya detraze.
Yya se va Amiral 'i Belyya   'i a parir ande la mađre.
'En kađa paso ke 'elyya dava,   'una dolor le tomare.
'Elyya 'entrando de la pu'erta,   belo 'ižo ke 'elyya pare,
kon 'una fleğa de 'oro 'en mano   'i 'una 'estre'a de diamante.
'Estas palavras dizyendo,   'el bu'en rey ke arivare:
—'A todos ve'o 'en međyyo,   a mi 'espoza non abistare.

Source: GSA 3.
The second hemistich of each verse, except v. 23, is repeated. The word *'i* precedes each repetition, except where *'i* is already present as the first word in hemistich b.

2*b* ke *om. in repetition*; pu'ede *in repetition.*
4*a* tuvyense.

—La tu 'espoza, 'el mi 'ižo,   fu'e a parir ande la madre.
A mí me yyamó "puta",   a ti, " 'ižo de 'un mal padre".
—Kon 'esta 'espada me korten,   si non la vo a matare.
'Estas palavras dizyendo,   ḥaberǧís ke arivare:
—Amiral Belyya paryyó 'un 'ižo,   ke vos se'a 'en bu'en mazale,
kon fleǧa de 'oro 'en mano   'i la 'estre'a de diamante.

18*b* aparir; 'a parir *in repetition*; mad̄re *in repetition.*
20*b* 'a matare *in repetition.*

Translation:

The Queen is seated at the entrance to her palace with birth pangs that she can scarce endure. Oh, that she could give birth at the palace of the King, her father! Oh, that she could have at her side the Countess, her mother! (5) "When I am ready to give birth, may she say: 'May the Lord deliver her.' " Just then her mother-in-law heard her from the lofty towers where she was: "Go on, my daughter-in-law, to give birth at your mother's abode. If your husband comes, I'll prepare him a meal. I'll give him chicken for his supper and capons for his early meal. (10) I'll give fodder to his horse and raw meat to his hawk. I'll throw bones to his dog, so he'll not trail after you." Now Amiral Bella leaves to give birth at her mother's abode. With every step she took she was struck by a pain. Hardly does she cross the threshold when she gives birth to a fair son, (15) with a golden arrow in his hand and a diamond star. As these words were spoken, the good King arrived: "I see all of you about me; my good wife I do not see." "Your wife, my son, went to give birth at her mother's abode. She called me 'whore' and you 'son of an evil father.' " (20) "May I be cut down with this sword, if I do not go and kill her." As these words were spoken, messengers arrived: "Amiral Bella gave birth to a son—may it bring you good fortune—(23) with a golden arrow in his hand and the diamond star."

Motifs:

15, 23 Cf. H71.7.2. *Prince born with bow of gold and string of silver*; H71.7.1.*Girl born with costly jewels: sign of royalty*; H71.7. *Child born with chain around neck: sign of royalty.*

18 K2218.1. *Treacherous mother-in-law accuses innocent wife*; S51. *Cruel mother-in-law.*
20 M113.1. *Oath taken on sword.* Cf. M441.1. *Curse: man's sword will fail in danger.*

The ballad of *La mala suegra* enjoys ample geographic diffusion in the Eastern Sephardic tradition, as well as in Morocco and the Peninsula. Published Eastern texts represent Salonika (Attias; Benardete 39; Coello), Rhodes (Adatto, pp. 52 ff.; Díaz-Plaja; DRH), Jerusalem (SICh), and several Turkish communities (Adatto, pp. 49 ff.; Benardete 40; Danon). Our own fieldwork has yielded versions from Rhodes, Marmara (Turkey), Sérrai (Greece), and Salonika. In Morocco, the ballad is also widely known, in both archaic and more modern Peninsular subtypes. [1] Published and unedited materials attest to the ballad's currency in Tangier, Tetuán, Larache, and Alcázar.

Yoná's version, which has definite affinities with Attias', preserves the ballad's *á-(e)* assonance—with notable use of the paragogic *e* (*somportare, tomare,* etc.)—much more consistently than the rather chaotic Turkish, Rhodian, and Jerusalem texts. [2] Attias' version is more complete than Yoná's, which ends prematurely on a cheerful or at least a noncommittal note, with the arrival of messengers announcing the child's birth. In Attias and numerous other texts the slandered wife is exonerated and the enraged husband repeats his oath (Yoná, v. 20), asking that he be killed with his own sword if he fails to take mortal revenge on his deceitful mother. [3] The Eastern Sephardic versions, in a

---

[1] Compare Larrea 96 and Ortega, with Larrea 94-95 and MRuiz.

[2] Cf. RoH, I, 113; DRH 7; SICh 5.

[3] The oath "may I be killed with my own sword" occurs in differing contexts in the Asturian and Moroccan versions of *Aliarda enamorada en misa*:

Con esta espada me maten, con esta que al lado traigo,
si mujer que me dio el cuerpo nunca con ella me caso.
(ASW 183)

Sacó espada de su sinto, y púzolá a escuentra el día:
—Con ésta me maten moros si en la corte lo diría.
(Bénichou 34; Ortega 220)

In other Castilian versions, the protagonist simply swears by his sword or dagger or on "the cross of his dagger" (ART 218, 219). Attias' text of *Blancaflor y Filomena* uses the same oath: "Con esta espada me corten / o con otra más

typical attenuation, are unanimous in suppressing the wife's death, which occurs under brutal and gory circumstances in the Moroccan and Peninsular traditions. Only one Eastern text (Danon) preserves a remnant of the prodigious Peninsular dénouement, in which the newborn babe speaks out in defense of his dead or dying mother. [4] Yoná

lijera" (no. 37.29 f.). A Rhodian version of *La adúltera* (*ó*) ends with a similar, if less lucid expression: "Estas espadas no mi manken, / ke a vos matí (*read* mati) a los dos" (SBS 87; 'May these swords not fail me,' etc.). Oaths by the sword, "by the cross" of one's sword or dagger, by the point of one's dagger, etc., are a commonplace in the *romances*: "grande jura estaba haciendo / sobre la cruz de su espada" ("En las sierras de Altamira": FN 99); "tienen hecho juramento / en la punta de su puñal" (*Montesinos*: RPM 53); "Tenho feito juramento / nas cruzes da minha espada" or "Juro por esta espada, / affirmo por meu punhal" (*Conde Claros fraile*: Braga, I, 376, 407; VRP 57, 58, 60, etc.); "puso la mano en la espada / y así comenzó a jurar" (*Marqués de Mantua*: Larrea, II, 157, vv. 447 f.); "Juro por mi espada, / mi espada dorida" (*Don Bueso y su hermana*: FN 212; cf. Larrea 59.25; RPM 196, 202; Aguiló 177; Milá, p. 237, Var. Al); "que o noso pai ten xurado / pol-a crus da sua espada" (*Delgadina*: Carré 81 [p. 216]; Braga, I, 449, 453, 457); "Yo le juro a Dios del cielo / y a la mi espada redonda" (*Doña Antonia*: Larrea 128.21 f.). For examples from British balladry, see Wimberly, *Folklore*, p. 92, n. 4. Cf. also Pernot, *Anthologie populaire de la Grèce moderne*, p. 60.

[4] Though in general the *Romancero* is little given to marvels—and its Sephardic branch even less—the Peninsular forms (e.g., ART 211; Echevarría, p. 413; Espinosa; Feito, p. 304; Güéjar 10; Kundert; Marín; QRA 11; RPC 40, 42; RPM 135 ff.; Milá 243; Braga, I, 562; VRP 554 ff.) as well as Moroccan versions (Larrea 94-95) of *La mala suegra* embody the "Sprechende Säuglinge" motif, which also appears in other Hispanic ballads: e.g., *El nacimiento de Montesinos* (Larrea 35.60 f.); *El conde Alarcos* (Carré 72 [p. 197]; Braga, I, 488, 495, 499; *Primav.* 163, n. [p. 332]); also CVR, p. 261; RPC 102, n. 1; RoH, I, 71, n. 15; TRV, II, 418; Menéndez Pidal, "Poesía popular y romancero," X, 285-286. The newborn Christ Child miraculously speaks in a Portuguese Christmas ballad (Serrano, p. 89). Sephardic folk poetry also knows of speaking babes in the biblical song on the birth of Abraham ("Cuando el rey Nemrod": Danon 41; Menéndez Pelayo 52; Attias 127.13). For extra-Hispanic occurrences of this motif, see *L'enfant au berceau parle pour dénoncer un crime* or *Dame Lombarde* (Davenson 10; Rolland, III, 10-11, 13, 14; Barbeau, *Folk-Songs of Old Quebec*, p. 58; Id., *Romancéro*, pp. 98, 102; Id., *Rossignol*, p. 126); *Le miracle du nouveau-né* (Barbeau, *Folk-Songs of Old Quebec*, p. 46; Id., *Rossignol*, p. 311); *Lou pastis* (Arbaud, II, 71); *La nourrice du roi* (Udry, p. 46); *Donna Lombarda* (Nigra 1E.11, etc.); *The Cherry-Tree Carol* (Child 54A.6, 11); *Johnie Armstrong* (Child 169 [III, 367]; cfr. also Child 178A.19; 203A.41); *Frændehævn* (DgF, I, no. 4; Prior, I, 29, 36); *Hævnersværdet* (DgF, I, no. 25-29; Olrik, I, no. 16.28; Prior, I, 273; Smith-Dampier, p. 130); *Valravnen* (DgF, II, no. 60); *Das neue Grab* (DVM 110A); Balys A21; Strausz, pp. 116, 166, 168; Krappe, *The Science of Folklore*, pp. 179 and 188, n. 15; Liebrecht, *Zur Volkskunde*, pp. 210-211; *D1817.4.

and Attias are unique in including another prodigy: the child is born holding a "golden arrow and a diamond star" (Yoná, vv. 15, 23) in cryptic augury of some unknown future greatness.[5] Except for this detail and the version's stable assonance and truncated outcome, Yoná's text offers little of interest to distinguish it from the other renditions current among the Eastern Sephardim.

BIBLIOGRAPHY

Eastern J.-Sp.: Adatto 15 (pp. 49-54); Attias 38; Benardete 39-40; Coello 12; Danon 9; Díaz-Plaja 3; DRH 7; Gil 27 (= Coello, Danon); Menéndez Pelayo 13 (= Danon); MP 70 (= Coello); PTJ 69 (= Díaz-Plaja); SICh 5.

Moroccan J.-Sp.: Larrea 94-96; MP 70 (2d text); MRuiz 54; Ortega 224; PTJ 69*a* (= Ortega). See also Benoliel, "Hakitía," XIV, 225 (no. 79), where the ballad's first verse is used as a proverb.

Castilian: ART 210-213; ASW 221-224, 299-300, 315, 324, 326-327, 330-331; Berrueta, pp. 340-341; Cossío, *BBMP*, I, no. 3; CPE, I, 45; II, 27-28; CPM 74; CVR 35-36; Echevarría, pp. 412-413; Espinosa, "Andalucía," p. 99; Feito,

---

Infant vindicates wrongly condemned mother (Bordman); T575.1-T575.1.1.3. *Child (speaks) in mother's womb (reveals unjust judgment)*; T585.2. *Child speaks at birth*; T585.2.2. *Child speaks prematurely on first birthday*; H. Gaidoz, *et al.*, "L'enfant qui parle avant d'être né," *Mélusine*, IV (1888-1889), 228-232, 272-277, 297, 323-324, 405, 447-448.

[5] We know of few close analogs of this motif in Spanish balladry. It is, of course, ultimately related to the moles or birthmarks which provide identification (H50; H51.1) in various Hispanic ballads: e.g., *La vuelta del marido* (*í*; Díaz-Plaja 1); *La esposa fiel* (Attias 19.38); *Melchor y Laurencia* (Larrea 61.126); *Hermanas reina y cautiva* (Larrea 54-57; RPM 205 ff.; VRP 634, 639; Milá 242D); *La gentil porquera* (Macabich 97); *El renegado reconocido por su hijo* (RTCN 15). For more on this motif, see K. Jaberg, "The Birthmark in Folk Belief, Language, Literature, and Fashion," *RPh*, X (1957), 307-342. One is also reminded of the complicated inscriptions which appear on the throat of a new-born babe in the Eastern and Moroccan ballad of *El augurio*: "... en su gargantita tiene / siete letritas de sangre" (Larrea 259, as well as an uned. text from Turkey). For similar occurrences in *romances vulgares*, see Vicuña, pp. 271, 309-310. Compare also the final verses of *Gil Brenton*: "This lady bare a bonny young son. / An it was well written on his breast-bane / 'Gil Brenton is my father's name'" (Child 5A.73-74). Somewhat closer to the Sephardic ballad is the Bulgarian *Lalo der Metzger*, where a child is born with a little cross on his head, a sword at his side, and a book in his right hand (Strausz, pp. 166-167). In an Albanian epic studied by Lambertz, the hero's marvelous horse is born with moon and stars upon its forehead (pp. 76, 117). A French-Canadian song, *La couronne sur la tête*, tells of a child born crowned and marked with a moon and fleur-de-lis (Barbeau, *Rossignol*, p. 169).

pp. 303-304; *Folk-lore Andaluz,* pp. 40-41 (1st pagination), 76-78; Güéjar 10; Kundert, pp. 94-95; Marín, I, 2; Munthe 7*a,* 7*b*; Poncet, "Entrepeñas," no. 21; QRA 11; RPC 37-42; RPE 32-34; RPM 135-155; RSC 17-18; RTCN 31; RTO 24; RTR 9; Schindler 2.

Spanish American: Henríquez Ureña-Wolfe 2. This text is not of direct tradition but is a broadside reprint of the Asturian version published in ASW 222-223.

Galician: *BTPE,* XI, 262-269; Carré 67-70; La Iglesia, II, 105-113; Sampedro 182.

Portuguese: Almeida Garrett, 53-58; Athaide Oliveira, pp. 55-59; Braga, I, 556-572, 577-582, 584-590; Furtado de Mendonça, *RL,* XIV, 14-15; Hardung, I, 223-243; Kundert, pp. 95-96; Martins, I, 188-192; II, 34; Nunes, *RL,* VI, 177-179; Tavares, *RL,* IX, 293, 319-320; Vasconcellos, "Bibl. do Povo," pp. 38-39; VRP 554-578.

Catalan: AFC 2326; ASW 364; Briz, II, 221-222; Macabich, pp. 79-81; Milá 243.

Studies: BNE 229; Braga, III, 473-478; EEB 182; Menéndez Pidal, *El Romancero Español,* p. 129; Michaëlis, "Estudos," pp. 204-205, 233-235; RoH, I, 71; II, 286, 298, 320, n. 29, 330; TRV, II, 394-395.[6]

---

[6] Though Entwistle (EEB 182) sees *Child Waters* (Child 63) and the Piedmontese *Ambrogio e Lietta* (Nigra 35) as "among the closest parallels to the Spanish *Doña Arbola*" (= *La mala suegra*) they are, in fact, quite remote.

15

LA AMANTE ABANDONADA

(The Abandoned Mistress)

'Un amor tan kerensyyoza   ke 'olvidar non la podí'a.
La manyyanika 'i la tadre   'a vižitar yya la 'í'a.
Si la topava durmyendo,   la kovižava 'i se 'í'a.
Si la topava despyerta,   'a platikar se le metí'a.
La bezava 'i la abrasava   'i 'a yyorar se le metí'a.
—¿De ké yyoráś, kativada?   ¿De ké yyoráś, božagrí'a?
Teníaś mal de amores,   'o 'estáś rezín prenyyada.
—Ni tení'a mal de amores,   ni 'estava rezín prenyyada.
Si volo konto, 'el bu'en rey,   ¿afiaréś mis palavras?

Source: LRI 8. Variants: BRI 5; RHP 5; GRI 5.

The second hemistich of each verse, except 16, is repeated in LRI, BRI, and GRI.

1*a* 'Un *in boldface BRI / GRI.*
1*b* no *in repetition BRI,* no *RHP* (non *in repetition*), pu'edí'a *GRI.*
2*b* 'a vižitar yyo la 'í'a *BRI.*
3*a* durmy ndo *BRI.*
3*b* la ko- / kovižava *GRI.*
4 'i aplatikar *in repetition GRI.*
6*b* 'i de ké *GRI,* boža grí'a *BRI / RHP / GRI.*
7*a* Tenéś *GRI.*
7*b* 'i 'a 'estáš *in repetition BRI,* 'etavaś (*sic*) *GRI* ('estavaś *in repetition*).
8*a* Non tení'a *BRI / RHP / GRI,* damores *GRI.*
8*b* 'i no 'estava *BRI.*
9*a* vo lo *LRI.*
9*b* afiaréś 'a mis palavras *GRI.*

Yyo fu'i kriada 'en su ví'a 'i 'entre bu'ena ǧente 'onorada.
'Un kavayero, Andarleto, ke de mí se namorava,
'eskalerika le 'izo debaśo de sus ventanas,
para ke suva 'i ke abaśe komo si fu'era su kaza.
Tres noǧes durmyyó kon 'elyya, le paresyyó tres semanas.
'A fin de las tres noǧes, se fu'e 'a buśkar mu'eva amada.
'Elyya se fu'e de detrás de 'él, por ver si 'era más galana.

10*a* Yyo volo kriara 'en Sofí'a *GRI,* Seví'a *RHP.*
11*a* 'Un kavalyero Andaleto *RHP,* 'Un kavalyero 'Endarleto *GRI.*
13*a* asuva *GRI.*
15*a* 'A la fin *GRI.*
15*b* 'i fu'e 'a buškar nu'eva amađa *in repetition BRI.*
16*b* fu'e detrás *BRI / RHP / GRI.*

Translation:

It was such an affectionate love that she could not forget it. Early mornings and afternoons, he would go to visit her. If he found her sleeping, he would cover her and leave. If he found her awake, he would enter and talk with her. (5) He would kiss her and embrace her and she would start to weep. "Why are you weeping, my captive? Why are you weeping, my treasure? Were you suffering the pangs of love or are you newly with child?" "Neither did I suffer the pangs of love nor was I newly with child. If I tell you, good King, will you give credit to my words? (10) I was raised in your town, among good and honored people. A knight named Andarleto, who fell in love with me, made himself a ladder beneath the windows to climb up and down, as if the house were his." Three nights he slept with her; to her it seemed three weeks. (15) At the end of the three nights, he went in search of a new mistress. (16) She went after him, to see if she was more beautiful.

La amante abandonada (*í-a* + *á-a* assonance) is apparently restricted to the Salonikan tradition, where it is sung both as an autonomous poem (Benardete 27; LSO 92; uned. versions) and as a prolog to the Pan-Hispanic *Mujer engañada* (Attias 43; uned.) which, in turn, is also known in independent versions throughout the Jewish tradition. To our knowledge, *La amante abandonada* has no counterpart elsewhere in the Hispanic *Romancero,* nor do we find any comparable narrative among the Greek *tragoúdia.* The ballad could be considered a unique Salonikan survival of an otherwise unknown initial episode of *La mujer engañada.* The alternating *í-a* and *á-a* assonance of the strophic sixteenth-century version of *La mujer engañada* (FN 18) [1] might seem to suggest some kinship with the Sephardic *Amante abandonada,* but the story lines of the two poems, though superficially similar, are really difficult to relate. In *La amante abandonada,* the girl seems to be telling her present admirer about her abandonment by an earlier lover. In *La mujer engañada,* the wife secretly follows her deceiving husband and finds him in the company of another woman. The final verses of *La amante abandonada* are, indeed, quite similar to the initial episode of *La mujer engañada.* In both poems the lover, after a short time, goes off in search of another woman and the abandoned girl follows him to ascertain the beauty of her new rival:

'A fin de las tres noǧes, se fu'e 'a buśkar mu'eva amada.
'Elyya se fu'e de detrás de 'él, por ver si 'era más galana.
(*La amante abandonada*: Yoná, vv. 15-16)

Al fin de los diez mezes, nuevo amor tenía.
Un día de los días, me fue detrás onde él ía.
Vide ke entrava en kaza de su nueva amiga. . . .
Ni es más galana, ni es más garida,
su kara enkalada i su seža entenida.
(*La mujer engañada*: uned., Rhodes)

It is questionable whether these similarities are coincidental or respond to some genetic relationship. For now, the origin of *La amante abandonada* remains an enigma.

A few peculiar features of the ballad merit comment: V. 10, "Yyo fu'i kriada en su ví'a / 'i 'entre bu'ena ǧente 'onorada," which in GRI is clumsily revised and contaminated with v. 9a ("Yyo volo kriara 'en Sofí'a . . ." [!]), should, of course, read "Yyo fu'i kriada 'en Seví'a . . . ," as in RHP, Attias, Benardete, LSO 92, and one of our unpublished texts. The protagonist's pride in her noble Sevillian lineage is reminiscent

---

[1] Most Sephardic texts have regularized *í-a* assonance, but Levy's no. 19 and Braga's Azorian text clearly preserve remnants of the poem's earlier form in *coplas pareadas.*

of certain versions of *El forzador,* where the girl rejects her suitor's offers while boasting that:

Más mucho tiene el mi padre, qu'es un duque de Sevilla.
(Attias 52)

Más rico es el mi padre, que es un grande de Sevilla.
(LSO 71)

Andarleto (v. 11), *'Endarleto* (GRI), or *Andarneto,* as in one of our unedited texts, testifies to the influence of the Salonikan version of *Landarico,* where the protagonist, also a deceiver, is so named.[2] Here the name could involve a popular etymology on *andar* as an indication of the lover's restless unfaithfulness.

The little ladder of gold ("Escalerika" or "Escalera de oro" as in Benardete), by which the lover conveniently climbs to the girl's window (vv. 12-13), recalls a Salonikan wedding song:

'Eskalerika de 'oro 'i de marfil,
para ke venga 'el novyyo 'a dar kidûšîn.[3]

There is an intensely amorous quality to this ballad of *The Abandoned Mistress,* beginning as it does *in medias res* with the bittersweet memory of an unforgettably tender and sensuous love. In a few verses, the three-day affair that seemed to last for three weeks is relived with unashamed intimacy by the now captive maiden before the King who is obviously smitten by the charms of his despondent prisoner. With surprising sophistication, this mysterious ballad creates through flashback and evocation a miniature drama of love, rejection, and jealousy. It is as if the girl were some captive Christian in a *novela morisca,* relating to her noble Arabic master, already enamored of her singular beauty and grace, the intimate details of her short-lived relationship with a donjuanesque knight of irresistible charms.

---

[2] See DRH, pp. 57-58, n. 49.

[3] UR, p. 379. Cf. F848. *Extraordinary ladder (stair).*

BIBLIOGRAPHY

La Amante Abandonada (independent form)

Eastern J.-Sp.: Benardete 27; LSO 92.

La amante abandonada + La mujer engañada

Eastern J.-Sp.: Attias 43.

La mujer engañada (independent form)

Eastern J.-Sp.: Bassan 151, 153 (151 = Danon, with minimal differences); Benardete 41; Danon 32; Estrugo, *Los sefardíes,* p. 137; Gil 41 (= Danon); Levy 19; LSO 70 (no. 1.27-33, appended to *Don Bueso y su hermana*); Manrique de Lara, *BN,* 3d and 4th texts; [4] Menéndez Pelayo 43 (= Danon); PTJ 73 (= Danon); SBS 97.

Moroccan J.-Sp.: Bénichou 7; Gil 41 (= MP); [5] Larrea 103-106; MP 74; Ortega 221; MRuiz 57; PTJ 73*a* (= Bénichou); Torner, *Lírica hispánica,* no. 145 (p. 245).

Castilian: BTPE, II, 69-71; Córdova y Oña, I, 151-152; CPE, I, 87; II, 93-94; CVR, p. 349; Montalbán, no. 50; Puig Campillo, pp. 76-78; QRA 8; Rodríguez Marín, *Cantos,* I, 188; RPE 78-80; RPM 298; RTCN 118; RTR 22; Schindler 29; Sevilla 86; Torner, *Lírica hispánica,* no. 145; Id., "Índice de analogías," no. 110.

Spanish American: Cadilla, *Juegos,* pp. 188-190; Chacón, "Contribución," pp. 89-95; Córdova de Fernández, *AFC,* III, 58-60; Deliz, pp. 278-280; Moya, II, 279; Vicuña 83.

Canarian: RCan 30.

Portuguese: Braga, *Archipelago açoriano,* pp. 385-386; Braga, II, 276-277; *Folk-lore Andaluz,* pp. 386-387.

Catalan: Bertrán y Bros, pp. 123-124; Milá 408.

Archaic Texts: Alonso-Blecua 208; Cejador, *Verdadera poesía,* I, 803; II, 1190; FN 18; Pedrell, I, no. 70; p. 316 (no. 58); RoH, I, 387; Torner, "La canción tradicional española," p. 151; Id., "Índice de analogías," no. 110; Id., *Lírica hispánica,* no. 145.

Studies: BNE 223; Menéndez Pidal, *El Romancero Español,* pp. 112-113; Id., "Romances y baladas," pp. 7-8; RoH, I, 387; II, 80, 84, 90, n. 47, 385, 387, n. 54, 409.

---

[4] Reprinted in Mendoza, *El romance español y el corrido mexicano,* p. 37, with unedited indications of geographic origin: i.e., Salonika and Istanbul.

[5] The verses cited on p. xcii ("Pensó el mal villano ...") are not from Tangier, but from a sixteenth-century Peninsular version, as is clearly stated in MP (p. 172).

16

LA ADÚLTERA (á-a)

The Adulteress)

—Yyo me alevantí 'i 'un lunes 'i 'un lunes por la manyyana.
Tomí mi árkol 'i mi fleğa 'i 'en la mi mano dereğa.
¿Ande la fu'era yyo 'a tanyer? 'A pu'ertas de mi namorada:
Avridme, Božú, mi byen, 'i avriđme, Božú, mi vista.
Los pyezes tengo 'en la nyeve 'i la kavesa 'en la yelada.
—¿Kómo vos avriré, mi byen? ¿Kómo vos avriré, mi alma?
Al 'ižo tengo 'en 'el peğo 'i al marido 'en la nêkāmāh.
—¿Kén vos avló, Božú, mi byen? ¿Kén vos avló, Božú, mi alma?
—'El moso del panadero, 'el ke los malos anyyos aga.
Arina non tengo 'en kaza, levadura me demanda.
'Él salyendo de la pu'erta, 'el namorado por la ventana.
Por 'en medyyo del kamino, la kaśika ke 'olvidara.
'Elyya se topó 'en apreto, lo 'entró adyentro la kaśa.
La kaśa 'estuvo de pimyenta, 'el namorado sarnudava.

Source: LRI 9. Variants: BRI 8.

1*a* Yyo *in boldface.*
3*a* Ande se la fu'era yyo.
4*a* Avríšme.
4*b* avríśme ('i *om.*).
8 Kyén.
10*a* no.
10*b* 'i levađura.
12*a* 'enmedyyo *LRI,* 'enmeđyyo *BRI.*

15 —¿Kén sarnuda, Božú, mi byen? ¿Kén sarnuda, Božú, mi alma?
—'El gato de la vezina, 'el ke los malos anyyos ke aga.
Dyyo 'una dada 'en la kaśa, la kaśa la desklavara:
—Vení, veréś, las mis vezinas, las dabašo 'i las dariva;
19 Vení, veréś gato kon barva 'i mostağikos aretorsidos.

15*a* Kyén.
15*b* 'i kyén.
16*b* malos anyyos aga.
17*b* desklavava.
18*a* Venið.
18*b* Las de abašo 'i las de ariva.
19*a* Vnið (*sic*).

Translation:

"I arose early one Monday, early on a Monday morning. I took my bow and pick and carried them in my right hand. And where did I go to play? At my beloved's door: Open the door, Božú, my darling; open the door, Božú, my love. (5) My feet are in the snow and my head in the frosty air." "How can I open the door, my love? How can I open the door, my soul? I have my infant son at my breast and my husband in bed." "Who spoke to you, Božú, my love? Who spoke to you, Božú, my soul?" "It's the baker's boy, may misfortunes befall him! (10) I have no flour in the house and he asks me for leavening." As the husband went out the door, the lover entered through the window. Along the way, [the husband] realized he had forgotten the little box. She found herself in difficulty, so she put her lover into the chest. The chest had been used for pepper, so the lover sneezed and sneezed. (15) "Who is sneezing, Božú, my love? Who is sneezing, Božú, my soul?" "It's the neighbor's cat, may misfortunes befall it!" He struck the chest a blow and broke the chest open: "Come, see, my neighbors, those from below and above; (19) come, you'll see a cat with a beard and curled mustachioes.

Motifs:

1 N128.2. *Monday as unlucky day.*
5-7 Cf. K1212. *Lover left standing in snow while his mistress is with another.*
11 T230. *Faithlessness in marriage*; T481. *Adultery.*
13-16 Cf. K1515. *The animal in the chest*; K1555. *Husband carries off box containing hidden paramour*; K1500. *Deception connected with adultery.*

The *á-a* assonant *romance* of *The Adulteress* is one of the more densely distributed Eastern Sephardic ballads. There are published versions from Salonika (Attias, Hemsi, LSO, no. 19, MP, San Sebastián, SBS 84), Kastoría (LSO, no. 20), Rhodes (SBS 82), Jerusalem (SICh), Turkey (Algazi [?], Danon, Elnecavé), and probably also from Bosnia (Levy 85). Our collection includes texts from Travnik, Sarajevo, Belgrade, Plovdiv (Bulgaria), Istanbul, Izmir, Rhodes, and Jerusalem.

The ballad's Pan-Hispanic development cogently illustrates the crucial importance of archaic lateral areas in ballad criticism and the key position of the Sephardic *romances* in particular. The Eastern Judeo-Spanish communities have preserved *La adúltera* (*á-a*) in a much more complete form than any of the Peninsular traditions or even Morocco which, in this case, must definitely yield its usually preeminent position to its Eastern cousin. In effect, the Eastern texts, in most of their features, provide us with what seems to be an essentially prototypic form of the narrative through which earlier strata of the now diversified and fragmentary Peninsular subtraditions can be perceived.

Except for individual lapses, the Eastern versions agree in including the following narrative stages: (1) The wife's lover rises early on a Monday morning and goes to play his guitar before her door. [1] (2) The lover asks to be admitted to the house. (3) He complains that he is suffering from exposure to snow and frost. (4) The wife answers that she is occupied with her children and that her husband is still at home, asleep. (5) The husband awakes and asks: "With whom are you talk-

[1] Two unedited versions from Rhodes mention floral decorations at this point. See nn. 14-16 *infra*.

ing?" (6) She says it is the baker's boy, who is asking her for leavening, when she does not even have any flour in the house. (7) She sends the husband out, either to market or to go hunting. (8) As he goes out the door, the lover enters through the window. (9) The husband, who has forgotten some object (tobacco pouch, box, lance, guitar), returns unexpectedly. (10) The wife hurriedly hides her lover in a chest containing pepper. (11) He sneezes. (12) The husband asks the identity of the sneezer. (13) The wife answers that it is the neighbor's cat. (14) The husband wants to see the cat, but the wife says she has lost the keys to the chest (only in Adatto; SBS 82, 84; uned. Sarajevo). (15) The husband breaks open the box (usually with an ax). (16) He invites his neighbors in to see a bearded, mustachioed cat. (17) Two unedited Rhodian versions end with a cryptic reference to firewood and dry straw. (18) The husband kills his adulterous wife (only in SBS 84, and possibly in 82, Algazi, and Danon, though in the latter texts it is apparently the lover who is killed). (19) Other texts close with the moral: "Don't neglect your wife; the cat will carry her off and leave you with nothing" (Adatto, Algazi, Danon, Elnecavé, Levy 27, 85; uned. Travnik, Sarajevo).

In most of the Eastern versions the order of narration is that of the above summary. However, in the practically identical versions of Algazi, Danon, Elnecavé, and Zara—all probably of Turkish origin—the narrative sequence has undergone chaotic rearrangement: (1) Morning serenade; (7) husband sent out to do marketing; (8) lover enters through window as husband leaves; (2) lover then asks to be admitted (!?); (3) he is suffering from exposure; (5) husband asks who wife is talking to; (6) baker's boy pretense; (10) lover, hidden in box, (11) sneezes; (12) "Who's sneezing?" (13) "It's the neighbor's cat." (15) Husband breaks box with ax. (16) "Neighbors" (Algazi, Elnecavé) or "Wife (Danon, Zara), come see the bearded cat!" (18) Husband kills lover (?) with ax (Algazi, Danon). (19) Moral: Don't neglect your wife, etc. The ballad's new order results in two glaring nonsequiturs: If the lover has just entered through the window, why does he complain of the cold and beg to be let in? How can the husband possibly ask about the wife's conversation if he has already left for market?

The Moroccan tradition knows the ballad of *La adúltera* principally in an *í-a* re-rhyming which embodies the following features: (1) The

Monday morning serenade; (2) the lover's request for admittance; (3) his sufferings from exposure; (4) the adulteress' excuse that she is occupied with wifely duties which here, as in the Castilian, and especially the Extremeño versions, are multiplied in number, together with other difficulties, such as squeaking doors, which would betray the lover's entry. (5) The husband wakes up. (17) He wishes that he could see his wife tightly bound, burning [2] in a furnace, and her body covered with knife wounds. She answers that she would like to see him in a dungeon, bound hand and foot, and pierced by lances.

The ballad's *á-a* form seems also to be attested in Morocco, but in only one very unsatisfactory fragment (in *ó* plus an *á-a* assonant refrain) which, though we know of no close Peninsular parallel, may be a late borrowing from the Spanish tradition (cf. BNE 223). This lone anomalous Moroccan fragment is particularly important, since it provides a counterpart to the otherwise uniquely Eastern Judeo-Spanish feature of hiding the lover in a chest rather than under the bed, as in the Castilian and Galician-Portuguese versions. Larrea's collection includes the following unique text (no. 270):

Yo me partiera un lunes
de burlas para Aragón,
que yo nunca vidi un gato
con bonete y xabaló.

---

[2] Larrea gives 'arremangado' ('with sleeves rolled up') as the meaning of *jasmeado* (no. 117.26; glossary, Vol. II, 367*b*). This is, in fact, one of the meanings of *ḥazmearse* (Benoliel, "Hakitía," XV, 203: 'ceñirse, arremangarse, prepararse con buena disposición para ejecutar algún trabajo'), although perhaps not the most appropriate. The J.-Sp. verb is from Moroccan Ar. *ḥezzem* 'ceindre, ceinturer, entourer d'une ceinture; sangler' (H. Mercier, *Dictionnaire arabe-français* [Rabat, 1951], s.v.; cf. J. Lerchundi, *Vocabulario español-arábigo del dialecto de Marruecos* [Tangier, 1892], s.v. *ceñir*). The meaning in Larrea's text is probably 'tightly bound with a belt.' A more acceptable reading, given the context, occurs in one of our unedited texts where the verb is *ḥameado* (from Ar. *ḥami* 'chaud; brûlant,' Mercier, s.v.), which Benoliel defines as 'calentar al fuego un metal o cualquier otra cosa hasta ponerla en brasa' ("Hakitía," XV, 201*b*). Given Larrea's defective transcription, it seems impossible to find the origin or meaning of *agchiacados* (no. 117.27), which is spelled *aghiacado* in the glossary, and listed, without definition, as occurring on p. 200 (read 280) of Vol. I.

[*Estribillo*:]
5 Cómo lo madrugaba;
madrugaba la aldeana,
y el mozo en la cama:
pan caliente y carne asada
y el vino de la tinaja....

Según el comunicante, que no recordó más que estos versos, en el cantar se contaba la historia de un cura, cuya amante decía al marido que era un gato lo que tenía encerrado en la alacena.[3]

From Larrea's fragment can be deduced the following narrative stages: (1) The *wife* (not the lover), gets up early one morning (v. 6);[4] (10) the lover, a priest, is hidden in a cupboard (prose summary); (13) he is identified as a cat (v. 3); (16) The husband expresses skepticism: "que yo nunca vidi un gato / con bonete y xabaló" (vv. 3-4). Verses 8-9 may refer to various gifts—sometimes of food and wine—which are provided by the priest, as in the Galician-Portuguese versions.

La adúltera (*á-a*) has been infrequently collected in the Peninsular Castilian linguistic domain. Most published texts are radically abbreviated (cf. CPE; RPM). The best version is Gil's, from Arroyo de la Luz (Extremadura; RPE 29-30). The Central Peninsular texts include the following stages: (1) Monday morning serenade; (2) request for admittance; (4) wife answers that husband is (not) at home and claims that various other inconveniences (squeaking door, barking dog, loquacious maid) would reveal lover's entry; lover suggests ways of obviating

---

[3] The initial verses are remotely reminiscent of the beginning of Moroccan versions of *La muerte del príncipe Don Juan*: "De Burgos partióse el rey, / de Burgos pa Salamanca" (Larrea 17); "De Burlo partió este rey / y ese rey de Salamanca" (Larrea 19); but here also the verse is a contamination, probably from the similar *incipit* of the thematically analogous *Aparición*: "Yo me partiera de Burgos, / de Burgos para París" (MP 56; cf. Morley, "El romance del *Palmero*," p. 308). For the authentic *incipit* of *La muerte del príncipe Don Juan*, see Bénichou 64 and Alvar, *Textos dialectales*, II, 762. What is the meaning of *xabaló*?

The *Adúltera* ballad's refrain (vv. 5-6) is of ancient—at least seventeenth-century—provenance: "Madrugábalo la aldeana, y ¡cómo lo madrugaba!" (Gonzalo Correas, *Vocabulario* [Madrid, 1924], p. 285*a*; Cejador, *La verdadera poesía*, I, no. 305). A similar verse begins an Asturian text of *La calumnia de la reina*: "En la mañana de un lunes / madrugaba la aldeana" (CVR, p. 188).

[4] Cf. Adatto's Eastern J.-Sp. version; also CPE, I, 116; and *La esposa beata*.

obstacles; (8) wife opens door to lover; (9) husband knocks at door (only in RPE 30); (10) lover hidden under bed, (11) makes noise on attempting to escape at midnight; (12) husband: "Who is walking about?" (13) Wife: "It's the neighbor's cat." (16) Husband: "I never saw a cat wearing a hat and cape." [5] (18[?]) Husband threatens to kill lover; wife objects that he helps with household expenses; (17) husband wishes he could see wife burned alive; wife wishes she could attend his funeral.

In the Galician-Portuguese tradition, our ballad has split into two segments which have gone their separate ways, with only occasional secondary cross-pollinations. The first part of the narrative (stages 1-7) has been associated with a different story—*Frei João*—about a wife who sends her husband out hunting so that she can hurry off to an assignation at Friar John's monastery. This massively documented Portuguese ballad—which is known also in Brazil—and the rarer and more schematic *Esposa beata* from Extremadura depend on a common original: (1) Friar John serenades the wife on a cold morning. (2) He begs to be let in, (3) complaining of exposure to ice and snow. Most versions mention freezing only in connection with the morning serenade, but a few (e.g., Braga, II, 108; Neves 30; VRP 424, 1011; Pereira da Costa, p. 328), like the Sephardic texts, preserve a more detailed account of the lover's sufferings *after* the request for entry. (4) The wife objects that she is occupied with her child and husband. (5) The husband asks whom she is talking with; (6) "With the baker's boy"; (7) The husband is sent out hunting and the wife goes off to visit Friar John. At the song's outcome the husband, as in many another Hispanic resolution of problems involving adultery, puts his wife to death, [6] but this dénouement need not be related to stage 18 of *La adúltera* (*á-a*). More rarely the *Frei João* ballad takes over the final recriminations (stage 17), in which the husband would see his wife burned, while she wishes that he be stabbed to death (Braga, II, 107). Similar verses concerning the wife's punishment alone, close at least one version of the

---

[5] In an unedited text, also from Arroyo de la Luz, it is "cape and cassock" ("capa y sotana"): The lover is a curé as in both Galician-Portuguese manifestations of the ballad.

[6] For example, Braga, II, 80-81, 86-87, 89, 97, 100, etc. See also n. 33 *infra*.

Extremeño *Esposa beata* (RPE 31). The latter ballad, a much abbreviated relative of *Frei João,* shares but two narrative stages with *La adúltera* (*á-a*). Here it is (1) the *wife* who rises early on Monday morning, (7) sends her husband out on some undefined errand, and then goes off to visit Fray Miguel at the Franciscan monastery.

In the Portuguese linguistic domain and in Asturias (Torner, *Cancionero musical*), *La adúltera* (*á-a*) also circulates as an autonomous ballad. The song seems to be quite popular in Galicia, but there is only sparse documentation for Portugal, namely, from the extreme north. Torner's lone text in Asturian dialect is the only example we have seen from that region. Except for an initial reference to Monday morning in some variants (= stage 1), this narrative begins at stage 7, precisely where genetic connections between the *Frei João* story and *La adúltera* lapse: (1) The husband gets up early on a Monday morning. (7) He yokes his oxen and goes to the fields, (9) but, forgetting his goading stick or remembering his wife (Torner), (10) he returns to find the door locked. (2) The situation of the lover is here transferred to the husband, who asks to be let in. (4) The wife answers that she is busy. The husband either enters by the back door (perhaps a transference of stage 8), breaks down the door, or threatens to do so and is let in. (12) The husband asks: "What is that under the bed?" (13) Wife: "It's the cat from the monastery" or "the priest's cat." (16) Husband: "I never saw a cat with a shaved head, beard, and cassock." (18[?]) The husband seizes his gun or ax to kill the "cat" who, on hearing this, flees through a window. The wife warns her husband not to kill the priest who has provided them all with clothing, food, and wine. (17) The husband wishes his wife burned; she wishes to attend his funeral. (18) The husband kills his wife (only in VRP 732, as a final remark *hors de texte*).

The Catalan tradition preserves the first part of our ballad in a quite complete form, but the narrative ends before anything really happens: (1) On St. John's day (only in Milá 359) the lover goes to sing before the door of his beloved, (2) asking to be admitted; (3) he complains that his beard and horse are covered with frost. (4) The girl protests that she is occupied with her children and husband, who is asleep. (5) The husband wakes up: "With whom are you talking?" (6) "With the baker's boy (or girl)." (7) The wife sends her children out to do various tasks and sends the husband out hunting. The husband reacts immediately and accuses the wife of unfaithfulness:

> Traydora de ma mullé, quina ya te l'ets pensada,
> de ferm'en aná á n-el bosch, tu tens el galan á casa!
> (Milá)

(17) The wife answers by wishing to attend his funeral; he replies that he would like to see her locked in a burning barn full of hay.

The Catalan tradition knows another song, *Don Ramón y Magdalena* or *El fals mosso de forner,* in *ó* assonance, which is obviously dependent on a Catalan version of *La adúltera* (*á-a*). Metrically *El fals mosso* is not a *romance*; its verses are irregular, having 7-9 syllables in hemistich *a* and 4-5 syllables in hemistich *b* which, in the OCPC version, is repeated. The song tells the following story: (1) The lover, Ramón, rises before dawn and appears at Magdalena's door. (There is no reference to a serenade.) (2) He begs to be admitted. (4) The girl, who is unmarried, answers that she is still in bed, as are her parents, and that the doors of her tower are locked. Ramón threatens to go away. Magdalena answers: "Don't go! I have gotten up, the doors are open, my father is in the garden, my mother in the kitchen." (5) The father overhears their conversation: "Who's talking with you?" (6) Magdalena answers: "It's the baker's boy, asking for bread to be baked." The father, like the husband in the Catalan form of *La adúltera* (*á-a*), reacts immediately, saying that he knows she is talking to Ramón; he accuses Magdalena of lying and threatens her. She answers: "You may beat me, but I will not stop loving my *servidó*[*r*]." *El fals mosso de forner* includes no narrative stage of *La adúltera* (*á-a*) other than those which characterize the ballad in its truncated Catalan form. It ends just as they do, with the father's (= husband's) imprecation, before any action takes place. The song simply uses some essential features of *La adúltera* (*á-a*) (stages 1, 2, 4-6) to describe the plight of an unmarried girl whose lover does not meet with parental approval.

Of all the Hispanic subtraditions, that of the Eastern Sephardim preserves the most complete and cohesive text of *La adúltera* (*á-a*). The following synoptic table facilitates comparison of the ballad's various geographic and linguistic conformations: [7]

TABLE 2

La adúltera (*á-a*): Pan-Hispanic variations

	East. J.-Sp.	Moroc. J.-Sp. (í-a)	Moroc. J.-Sp. (ó + á-a)	Cent. Penin.	*Fr. João*	Gal.-Port.	Catalan	*Fals mosso*
(1) Morning serenade.	X	X	(X)	X	X	(X)	X	(X)
(2) Request for admittance.	X	X		X	X	(X) (applied to husband after stage 9)	X	X
(3) Exposure.	X	X			X		X	
(4) Wife busy.	X	X		X	X	(X) (after stage 9)	X	X
(5) "Who are you talking to?"	X	X			X		X	X
(6) Baker's boy.	X				X		X	X
(7) Husband sent out.	X				X	(X) (Husband goes out)	X	
(8) Lover through window.	X			X (Wife opens door)		(X?) (Husband enters by force, after stage 9)		
(9) Husband forgets something, returns	X			X (Husband knocks at door)		X		

[7] Incomplete or vestigial reflections of a given stage are placed in parentheses. Double parentheses mark extraneous or coincidental features.

	East. J.-Sp.	Moroc. J.-Sp. (í-a)	Moroc. J.-Sp. (ó + á-a)	Cent. Penin.	*Fr. João*	Gal.-Port.	Catalan	*Fals mosso*
(10) Lover in chest.	X		X	X (under bed)		X (under bed)		
(11) Sneezes.	X			X (makes noise)				
(12) "Who's sneezing?"	X			X ("Who's walking about?")		X ("Who's under bed?")		
(13) "Neighbor's cat."	X		X	X		X ("monastery cat")		
(14) Lost keys.	X							
(15) Box opened by force.	X							
(16) "Come see bearded cat."	X		X	X		X		
(17) Burning and funeral.	(X)	X		X	X	X	X	
(18) Wife killed.	(X)			(X) (Lover threatened)	((X))	(X) (Lover threatened; wife killed)		
(19) Moral.	X							

Stages 1-7, 13, 16, and 17—either universally present or attested to in widely separated lateral areas—seem to be prototypic features. Stages 8 and 9, the lover's surreptitious entry and the husband's unexpected return, though clearly attested only in the Eastern Sephardic versions, also seem essential to the story. The lover was doubtless originally identified as a cat (as in Eastern, Moroccan, Castilian, and Portuguese versions, stages 13, 16), but whether this pretense was originally combined with stage 10—the folktale motif of *The animal in the chest* (K1515) and its cognate stage (Breaking the box, stage 15)—remains in doubt. The Eastern Judeo-Spanish versions and the lone Moroccan text in *ó + á-a* could reflect a relatively late intrusion of the *Animal in the chest* motif or, on the other hand, the Castilian and Galician-Portuguese versions might well have exchanged an original box for a more conventional hiding place under the bed. The fact that the Eastern and Moroccan (*ó* + *á-a*) versions, which share the motif of the cat in the chest, differ radically in other features seems to indicate that "the cat in the chest" may have been a prototypic feature of the ballad.

The final moral precept (stage 19), which seems to be limited to the Eastern tradition, could, however, be an original feature of the narrative. Similar sentiments are voiced elsewhere in Sephardic balladry. In *Las bodas en París* (no. 2 *supra*), the husband even takes the blame upon himself:

> No era la vuestra kulpa; sino yo ke lo buškí.
> Ken tiene mužer ermoza nunka ke la deše ansí.
> (uned., Salonika)

Only in the case of stage 17 (burning and funeral wishes) do the Peninsular subtraditions embody a prototypic element which, except for one vestigial allusion, is absent from the Eastern traditions. In two unedited Rhodian versions the ballad ends as the husband addresses the following cryptic words to his wife:

> Ke me adateš, ¡ay, digueña! kon siete chikiles de leña.

> Ke me adateaš, mužer, kon siete chikiles de leña,
> kon siete chikiles de leña i uno de la paža seka. [8]

The bundles of firewood and dry straw which here seem to be destined for the adulteress are obviously a remnant of the public execution by burning with which the enraged husband threatens his faithless wife in the Peninsular texts:

---

[8] The first verse ends a version sung by Rosa Alhadeff, Seattle (Wash.), Aug. 29, 1958; the other verses were sung by Julia Sadis and Bella Alhadeff, Brooklyn (N.Y.), Aug. 18, 1959. The latter informants interpreted *chikiles* as 'karrosas de leña' ('wagon [loads] of firewood'); the form seems to reflect either T. *çıkın* 'a small bundle' or more probably T. *çeki* 'horse load (of firewood, *etc.*).' We can find no meaning for the verb forms *adáteš, adatéaš,* but the context seems to require some form of the verb *dar.* The meaning of the first hemistichs might be rendered in Modern Castilian as: '¡Quién te me diera, mujer ...!'

—Quién te viera, Marianita, en el medio de la plaza,
con un carrito de leña y otro carro de retama,
y un airecito gallego pa que arda mejor la llama.
(RPM 132)

—Quién te pudiera ver en el medio de la plaza
con cien cargas de raíces y otras tantas de retama,
y yo, con el badilito, arrimándote las ascua[s].
(RPE 30; CPE, I, 116 f.)

—Mulher que tal fala dá merece ser queimada
em trinta carros de palha e outros tantos de ramalha.
(VRP 732; Braga, II, 87)

The *romance* evokes a traditional punishment for adulterous or unchaste women: death by fire, a fate suffered by many a wayward ballad heroine. When the disinherited Doña Urraca threatens to take refuge in a life of shameless promiscuity among the Moors, King Fernando answers his daughter's complaints by affirming that "mujer que tal dezía / merescía ser quemada." [9] The Empress of Germany (*Primav.* 162), victim of an unfounded accusation of adultery, like her English counterpart in *Sir Aldingar* (Child 59), is sentenced to be burned, as are also the incontinent princesses in *La infanta deshonrada* (*Primav.* 159; NSR 71) and *Conde Claros vestido de fraile* (*Primav.* 191). [10] In some Portuguese versions of the latter ballad the punishment is described in verses probably borrowed from *La adúltera* (*á-a*):

---

[9] Menéndez Pidal, "Poesía popular y romancero," II, 13; CSA, fol. 158*v*; *Primavera* 36.

[10] See no. 4, n. 7 *supra*. Cf. also the Catalan *Filla del marxant* (Aguiló, p. 303, vv. 73-76) and the French *Infanticide* (Puymaigre, *Pays Messin*, I, 110-111). See also Child, II, 113; Hodgart, *The Ballads*, p. 137; Prior, II, 56-65; A. Taylor, "The Themes Common to English and German Balladry," pp. 30-31 and n. 46; Leader, *Hungarian Classical Ballads*, pp. 231, 233-234 and n. 1, 236, 238-239; Vargyas, *Researches*, pp. 19, 160-163; Lambertz, *Die Volksepik der Albaner*, pp. 53-54; and the motifs: Q414. *Punishment: burning alive*; Q414.0.2. *Burning as punishment for adultery*; Q414.0.3. *Burning as punishment for incest* (*incontinence*) (and the Child ballads there referenced); S112. *Burning to death*. For burning as a punishment for adultery among the West Goths, see Riedel, *Crime and Punishment in the Old French Romances*, pp. 38 and 153, n. 87.

—La filha que tal me fez, disse el-rei, quer ser queimada,
em sete carros de lenha, fogueira bem atiçada.

—Infanta, que tal fizestes, ides, por lei, ser queimada;
fogueira de sete cargas e lenha bem atiçada.

(Braga, I, 394, 397)

Though the Eastern Judeo-Spanish *Romancero* has preserved a more complete text type of *La adúltera* (*á-a*) than has any other branch of the tradition, the Eastern versions also embody a number of probably extraneous elements which appear in none of the other geographic variants of *La adúltera* (*á-a*). Such features are: (11-12) sneezing, (14) the lost keys, (15) forcing open the chest, (18) the wife's death, and possibly also (19) the final pronouncement against the neglect of wives.

In this regard it may be appropriate to compare *La adúltera* (*á-a*) with another thematically identical ballad in *ó* assonance—a Pan-Hispanic congener of *Our Goodman* (Child 274).[11] Such a comparison

---

[11] **Eastern J.-Sp.** versions of *La adúltera* (*ó*): Attias 12; Danon 13; Gil 37 (= Danon); Kayserling, p. xi (2d text); Menéndez Pelayo 25 (= Danon); PTJ 77 (= Danon); SBS 87. We have eight unedited texts from Rhodes and one from Jerusalem. **Moroccan J.-Sp.:** Bénichou 39; Gil 37 (= MP); Larrea 108-113 (nos. 110-113 are of recent Peninsular vintage; cf. BNE 223); MP 78; MRuiz 59; PTJ 77*a* (= Bénichou 39); Pulido, p. 54 (2d text). See also Ortega, p. 195. We have eleven unedited texts from Tetuán, Tangier, Arcila, Larache, and Alcázar.

Espinosa, *Nuevo Méjico,* pp. 66-67, Pérez Vidal, "Romancero tradicional canario," *RDTP,* VII, 270-271, n. 3, and VRP, I, p. 459, offer extensive bibliographies of Peninsular, Latin American, and Portuguese versions, to which should be added the following references: **Castilian:** CPE, II, 24-25; Echevarría, pp. 408-409; Güéjar 12; Micrófilo, pp. 75-78, 108-117; Puig Campillo, pp. 114-115; QRA 1-2; RTCN 55; RTO 21. **Canarian:** Espinosa, *Romancero canario,* pp. 49-50; RCan 4. **Spanish American:** Campa, "Bernal Francés y la esposa infiel," p. 36; Carrera, "Una nueva versión venezolana," pp. 285-286; Córdova de Fernández, *AFC,* III, 77-78; Cuadra, "Horizonte patriótico," p. 23*b-c*; Fernández, "*Romances* from the Mexican Tradition," pp. 36-37; Lucero-White Lea, p. 132; Mejía Sánchez, pp. 41-48; Monroy, p. 371; Montesinos, "Dos romances viejos," pp. 51-52; D. Muñoz, "La poesía popular chilena," pp. 33-34; Pardo 45-50; Ramón y Rivera-Aretz, I:2, pp. 621-623, 630-632; Romero, *Perú,* pp. 109-110; Terrera, *Córdoba,* pp. 340, 350-352; Villablanca, pp. 187-188. A number of Spanish-American ballads on the adulteress theme are conveniently brought together by Bertini under the general title of *La esposa infiel* (pp. 1-15), but there is no further attempt at classification. Nos. 8-12, 16-17, 19-21, and 23 on these pages represent *La adúltera* (*ó*). **Galician:** Carré 64-65 (no. 65 is a verse by verse translation of *Primav.* 136). **Portuguese:** Delgado, *Subsídio,* II, 129; D. Rodrigues, *Ilustração Trasmontana,* I, 53; Schindler, p. 59*a-b*; VRP 399-414,

yields no less than fifteen coincidences between the *á-a* ballad and the various massively documented geographic sub-types of *La adúltera* (*ó*).

1007. **Catalan:** AFC 2294, 2322; Aguiló, pp. 93-100, 239-242 (no. 50.1-100); Amades, II, 126-128; Briz, IV, 185-188; Macabich, pp. 35-38, 137-142; Massot 10, 12. For the ballad's early forms, see Durán 298-299; *Primavera* 136-136*a*; Rodríguez-Moñino-Devoto, *Flor de enamorados,* fols. 48*v*-49*r*; Timoneda, *Rosa de amores,* fols. xxiiij*r*-xxv*r*; for its use in Lopean drama (*La locura por la honra*), see Pérez Vidal, "Romancero tradicional canario," p. 276; RoH, II, 176-177; Frenk Alatorre, "Lope, poeta popular," pp. 260-261. For other important comentary, see RoH, I, 72, 331-332, nn. 29-30; II, 221, 262, 302, 348, 349, 370, n. 11; J. Pérez Vidal, "*Floresvento* y *La esposa infiel,*" pp. 37-40.

Concerning the origin of *La adúltera* (*ó*) in a Medieval French *fabliau, Le chevalier à la robe vermeille,* see Entwistle's fundamental, but sparsely documented study, "Blancaniña," pp. 159-160; also Puymaigre, *Les vieux auteurs castillans,* II, 340-341; J. Bédier, *Les fabliaux* (Paris, 1964), pp. 318-319.

Extra-Hispanic counterparts include *Our Goodman* (Child 274; Coffin 274), *Les répliques de Marion* (Arbaud, II, 152-156; Canteloube, I, 68-69, 252-253; IV, 279; Rolland, II, 208-219; Tarbé, II, 98-100; Udry, pp. 32-33; Barbeau, *Jongleur,* pp. 74-79); and *Le repliche di Marion* (Nigra 85). A song on the Franco-Italian pattern is also known in Catalonia (*La trapassera*: Briz, II, 73). One German form, *Der betrogene Ehemann* (Erk-Böhme 900), is a late translation from English (see Child, V, 89). For Yiddish, Hungarian, and Rumanian versions of this ballad, see Rubin, "Some Aspects of Comparative Jewish Folksong," pp. 244-246; Aigner, *Ungarische Volksdichtungen,* pp. 149-151 (*Das treulose Weib*); Vargyas, "Zur Verbreitung," pp. 63-67; Leader, p. 234, n. 1. On the same theme, but without the series of questions and evasive answers, is *Der Bauer ins Holtz* (Erk-Böhme 149; Meier, *Balladen,* II, no. 100). The husband's questions and wife's excuses ("Mit wem sprachst du?" ... "Wessen Rock liegt auf dem Tisch?" ... "Wer jammert hinter der Türe?" ...) are, however, present in a Lithuanian song and its Slavic analogs analyzed by Seemann ("Deutsch-litauische Volksliedbeziehungen," pp. 201-202, no. 88: *Der betrogene Ehemann*). In the Scandinavian *Hurtige Svar, Thore och hans Syster,* or *Den grymme Brodren* (DgF, V, no. 304; Prior, II, 376-379; Arwidsson, I, no. 55; Geijer-Afzelius, no. 70; Warrens, pp. 153-155), a girl artfully parries her brother's many inquiries concerning a not too secret lover. Child (II, 157) analyzes another Scandinavian ballad, *Father and Daughter,* which embodies a similar repartee. Cf. the Icelandic *Ólöfar kvæði* (Grundtvig-Sigurðsson, no. 34).

According to Entwistle, *Our Goodman* is "de poco interés" ("Blancaniña," p. 164). He cites only the text reproduced by Prior (II, 376-377). *Our Goodman* is certainly a much closer parallel to *La adúltera* (*ó*) than is Entwistle's preference, *Edward* (Child 13), of which the only feature shared with the Spanish ballad is the presence of a series of questions which meet with evasive answers—by no means an exclusive feature, but rather a recurrent pattern in Pan-European balladry: cf., for example, *Clerk Saunders* (Child 69F; II, 157); *The Twa Brothers* (Child 49—by contamination with *Edward*); *Ulinger, Die drei Landsherren, Tod der Braut, Grausame Bruder* (Meier, *Balladen,* II, 120, 133, 135, 276; II, 39); *Le roi Renaud* (Davenson 1; Doncieux 7); *La muerte ocultada* (ASW 235; Amades, I, no. 49); *Morte occulta* (Nigra 21; Vidossi, no. 7);

Some of these agreements are consistent and widely diffused; others are sporadic and occur in but a few geographically restricted variants.

---

the Greek *Constantine and Areté* (Baud-Bovy, *Textes*, p. 165, Section E; Lüdeke-Megas, p. 21) and its cognate, the Albanian *Garentina* (Camarda, pp. 108-109). For abundant additional Pan-European examples, see Leader, *Hungarian Classical Ballads*, pp. 37, 179, 217, 218, 221, 222, 280, 317; Vargyas, *Researches*, p. 136.

Puymaigre (*Les vieux auteurs castillans*, II, 341) noted the similarity between *La adúltera* (*ó*) and a Greek *tragoúdi* (*Máida and Kṓstas*), in which a husband's unexpected return from a hunting trip catches his wife in *flagrante delicto*. Entwistle ("Blancaniña," pp. 162-163) insists on the genetic relationship of the Western European ballads to the Greek song. To the text cited by Entwistle should be added Puymaigre's version; another, translated by Hadjilazaros, pp. 32-33; Lüdeke-Megas, no. 93; Theros, I, no. 371; Akadēmía, I, 367. Cf. also Poncet's analysis ("El romance en Cuba," pp. 290-291). The coincidences between *La adúltera* (*ó*) and the Greek ballad—some of which are not pointed out by Entwistle—are in effect most suggestive of genetic affinity: Kṓstas, the lover, playing a fiddle (cf. n. 22 *infra*), repeatedly passes by the house of the wife, Márō or Máida, -o (= Marion?). He claims to be, or the wife assures him that he should be, unafraid, since the husband, Giánnēs, has gone hunting in the distant mountains (cf. "... el conde es ido a la caza / a los montes de León," *Primavera* 136). Kṓstas hopes that rain, snow, floods will detain Giánnēs and that he will be eaten by bears (cf. the similar imprecations voiced against the husband's hunting animals by the lover in *Primavera* 136-136*a*. In the modern tradition, however, it is the wife who, in some cases, wishes that her husband may be killed and devoured by birds or animals [e.g., ASW 292; CPE, II, 25; Güéjar 12]). These wishes are no sooner uttered than Giánnēs appears, back from the hunt, dragging with him live deer, tamed bears, uprooted trees (!) (in modern traditional versions of *La adúltera* [*ó*], the husband returns from the hunt bringing "un pajarito," "un conejito," "un cervatillo," even "un león vivo." Similar scenes occur in other Greek and Albanian poems: Pernot, *Anthologie*, pp. 111, 116; Lambertz, p. 35). After various other stages which bear no apparent relationship to the *romance*, the husband in the Greek ballad kills the wife (or wife and lover) and grinds her (them) to pieces in a mill. Most striking, though possibly coincidental, is the fact that an identical fate is reserved for the adulterous wife in four—to our knowledge quite solitary—Portuguese texts of *La adúltera* (*ó*). Here the husband returns the wife to her father, specifying that she be ground as fine as salt or as the sands of the sea:

> Que a móa bem moída   como as pedras do sal;
> nem as pombas, que são pombas,   as não possam apanhar!

The text cited is from VRP 400. See also VRP 399; Monteiro do Amaral, *RL*, XI, 102; Thomas Pires, *RL*, VIII, 215. On the punishment in question, see Q414.3.1. *Punishment: crushing in rice mill and scattering ashes*; Q469.3. *Punishment: grinding up in a mill*. For other occurrences in Greek and Albanian balladry: Liebrecht, *Zur Volkskunde*, p. 188 (= nos. 462-467 in Passow); Lüdeke-Megas, nos. 98-99; Pernot, *Anthologie*, p. 112; Camarda, pp. 112-113; De Grazia, p. 171.

Taking all known agreements into account, we find that the two ballads coincide in the following features: in placing the action on Monday morning, in the floral decoration of the wife's door or widow (n. 1 *supra*), and in the lover's serenade (all included in stage 1), as well as in the following details: (2) the lover's request for admittance and (3) his sufferings from exposure; (9) the husband returns unexpectedly; (10) the lover is hidden in a chest; (11-12) the sneeze and the husband's question about it; (13) the lover is identified as a cat or even as a neighbor's cat; (14) the lost keys; (15) the box is forced open with an ax; (16) the neighbors are invited in to see the cat; (17) the burning and funeral imprecations; and (18) the wife's death. A number of these agreements are characteristic of only a few isolated variants of one or the other of the two ballads; some, but not all of these parallels, seem to suggest multiple mutual influences which these two thematically similar narratives, often coexistent in the same geographic area, have exercised upon one another over the centuries.

Both the *á-a* and *ó* forms of *La adúltera* begin with the balladic commonplace of fixing the action on a Monday. Compare:

Yyo me alevantí 'i 'un lunes 'i 'un lunes por la manyyana . . . .
(Yoná)

Estándome levantando un luneh por la mañana . . . .
(CPE, I, 116: Extremadura)

O lunes de feira nova levanteime â madrugada . . . .
(Carré 119: Galicia)

with:

Yo me levantara un lunes, un lunes de la Ascensión . . . .
(Lope, *La locura por la honra*)[12]

Yo me levantara un lunes, un lunes antes de albor . . . .
(MP 78: Tangier)

[12] See RoH, II, 177.

El lunes será por cierto víspera de la Asunción....
(Moya, I, 454: Argentina)

In both ballads the *topos* occurs in versions from widely separated areas. Such geographic diffusion, like the motif's use in Lope's version of *La adúltera* (*ó*), indicates that its presence in both ballads is certainly of considerable antiquity. Here it seems impossible to establish a dependence of either ballad on the other. Both songs may simply reflect coincidental use of a common, formulistic *incipit, Yo me levantara un lunes...*, incorporating the *topos* of Monday as a day of evil import.[13]

In two versions of *La adúltera* (*á-a*) from the Island of Rhodes, the lover wakes to find that his garden has been decorated with sweet basil:

¡Kén se alvantara un lunes, un lunes por la mañana!
Topí la guerta emparrada, yena, yena de alhavaka....

Alvantóse el buen rey, un lunes a la mañana.
Topó la guerta emparrada, yena, yena de alhavaka....[14]

The Rhodian versions reflect the widely practiced custom of decorating the doors and windows of marriageable village girls with garlands on the eve or early morning of various holy days, especially that of St. John. The texts from Rhodes seem to have lost contact with the custom itself, for the floral decorations are placed in the suitor's garden rather than at the house of the girl. All the same, as can be seen by the following quotations, the initial stages of *La adúltera* (*á-a*)—the early morning visit to the girl's door, the floral decorations, perhaps also the serenade, and even the lover's sufferings from cold—coincide with the circumstances surrounding an important amatory folk-custom still widely practiced in rural Spain:

> En casi todos los pueblos de Extremadura, especialmente en los de poco vecindario, celebrábase la Noche de San Juan con parecidas ceremonias, adornando los campesinos, con ramas de flores y frutas, las ventanas de sus novias. En Orellana la Sierra y pueblos limítrofes, después de adornada la reja de

---

[13] See *La esposa de don García* (no. 13, n. 5 *supra*) and also n. 34 *infra*.

[14] The first text was sung by Julia Sadis and Bella Alhadeff, the second by Rosa Alhadeff. See n. 8 *supra*. *Alhavaka* is Cast. *albahaca* 'sweet basil.'

> la novia con todo el arte posible, poniendo en el trabajo sus cinco sentidos, quedábase el enamorado en vela toda la noche guardando la enramada de la dueña de sus pensamientos. Ésta levantábase temprano para acariciar el delicado obsequio y dar las gracias al mozo, que no andaba lejos, aunque no fuera nada más que con una tierna mirada si el joven era de su agrado. En caso contrario, volvíala a cerrar como si nada viera, marchándose él triste y cabizbajo. No solamente ponían allí las enramadas durante la noche de San Juan. Había impacientes que no esperaban su llegada y echaban a sus mozas la enramada a destiempo: en vísperas de la Cruz de Mayo, su fiesta grande, o en la de la Ascensión del Señor. . . . [15]

Similarly in the Alpujarra region of Granada, "on the evening before . . . [Midsummer Day], the young men decorated the doorways of their girls with branches and sang serenades." The custom, which is frequently mentioned in folk poetry, seems to be known throughout Spain. [16]

The garland motif, found only in two Sephardic versions of *La adúltera* (*á-a*), can hardly have been an original feature of the narrative. If not simply an independent reminiscence of the custom itself, it may have been borrowed from the *ó* assonant ballad. Although the latter's

---

[15] I. Gallardo de Alvarez, "El día de San Juan: Un capítulo para el folk-lore fronterizo," *Revista del Centro de Estudios Extremeños* (Badajoz), XVI (1942), 81-110: p. 87. On the custom of "Las enramadas," see especially pp. 87-93.

[16] G. Brenan, *South from Granada* (London, 1963), p. 82. For more on embowering doors and windows, see F. Carrera, "Algo sobre las tradiciones populares en el oriente de Asturias," *BIEA*, X (1956), 290-310: pp. 290-291; V. García de Diego, "Cuestionario sobre la noche de San Juan," *RDTP*, II (1946), 157-160: p. 158, no. 3; B. Gil García, *Las flores en la tradición extremeña* (Badajoz, 1962), p. 14; J. Pérez Vidal, *La fiesta de S. Juan en Canarias* (La Laguna de Tenerife, 1945), pp. 29-31; J. Taboada, "La noche de San Juan en Galicia," *RDTP*, VIII (1952), 600-632: pp. 621-622; J. Romeu i Figueras, *La nit de Sant Joan* (Barcelona, 1953), pp. 21-23, 69-70. On the custom's antiquity, see F. López Cuevillas, *La civilización céltica en Galicia* (Santiago de Compostela, 1953), p. 422. For the practice as reflected in folk poetry: see the above-cited article by Carrera, p. 290; Gallardo de Alvarez, "El día de San Juan," pp. 92-93; CPE, II, 128; Milá, *Romancerillo*, no. 332. The widely known seventeenth-century song, "Si queréis que os enrame la puerta" (Alonso-Blecua 290), which embroiders amply upon the folk custom, is still traditional in Asturias, Logroño, and Miranda do Douro. For texts, see Torner, "Índice de analogías," no. 163; Id., *Lírica hispánica*, no. 220; Cejador, *Verdadera poesía*, VIII, 3225. For additional examples and discussion, see J. T. Reid, "St. John's Day in Spanish Literature," *H*, XVIII (1935), 401-412: pp. 404-406.

Rhodian form lacks the pertinent initial episode, variants from a number of other areas allude to the floral decoration of the wife's door. Central Peninsular, Canarian, Spanish American, and Catalan versions in the modern tradition, as well as the archaic variant used by Lope de Vega in *La locura por la honra,* all embody the motif, usually in combination with that of the morning serenade:

> Mañanita, mañanita, mañana de San Simón;
> hallé mi puerta enramada con ramitos de trebol;
> no me l'ha enramado un sastre ni tampoco labradó:
> que me la enramó don Carlos, hijo del emperadó.
> Con la guitarra en la mano esta copla me cantó:
> —¡Oh, quién dormiera contigo una noche de primó!
> (Extremadura)[17]

> Levantábame yo, madre, mañanita de Ascensión,
> hallé la puerta enramada con tres gajitos de olor,
> no me la enramó villano ni aguililla, ni falcón,
> que me la enramó Don Carlos, hijo del Emperador. ...
> Vigüela de oro en la mano, versos de amor me cantó:
> —Durmiera contigo, alma, una noche, que más no.
> (Canary Islands)[18]

> —Día sábado, en la tarde, por ser día 'e l'Asunción,
> hallé mi casa enramada con ramas de admiración.
> —¡Qué linda eres, niña; eres más linda que el sol!
> ¡quién pudiera dormir contigo una noche y otras dos!
> (Argentina)[19]

> Abans de trencar el dia, abans de sortir el sol,
> li an enramades les portes y les finestres de flors.
> No l'ha feta l'enramada cap pagès ni cap mosson,
> qui l'ha feta es Don Francisco, el fill del Emperador.
> Qui l'ha feta l'enramada se'n va abaix del seu balcó,
> y tocant una viola li canta aquesta cançó:
> —Rosa fresca, rosa bella, ramell de la bona olor....

---

[17] RPE 27. See also RPE 26; RPC 84; Durán 298, n.

[18] We combine RCan 4 (the first four verses) with Pérez Vidal, "Romancero tradicional canario," p. 266.

[19] Laval, *Carahue,* p. 148. Cf. also Moya, I, 453-456, 462; Vicuña 37-39; Bertini, nos. 10-11 (= Vicuña). Moya, I, 458, and Carrizo, *Rioja,* II, no. 3, embody the same motif, but alter *enramada* to "empedrada" and "enrejada" respectively.

Jo pogués dormir, senyora, una nit sense temor
dins una cambra tancada, en un llit de flors amb vos.
(Balearic Islands) [20]

Yo me levantara un lunes, un lunes de la Ascensión....
Hallé mi puerta enramada toda de un verde limón....
No me la enramó escudero, ni hijo de labrador,...
enramómela don Carlos, hijo del Emperador....
(Lope de Vega) [21]

The serenade before the wife's door, which all sub-types of *La adúltera* (*á-a*) share with many variants of *La adúltera* (*ó*), [22] seems to be an essential feature of both narratives rather than a secondary borrowing by either one of them.

Some Eastern Sephardic versions of *La adúltera* (*ó*) have taken over, possibly from the *á-a* ballad (stages 2-3), the recurrent motif of the lover whose nocturnal vigil is beset by rigorous meteorological hazards. [23] In unedited texts from Jerusalem and Rhodes the gallant,

---

[20] Aguiló, no. 50 (joined to *Bernal Francés*). See also Aguiló, nos. 21-22; Milá 254.

[21] *La locura por la honra, Obras de Lope de Vega,* ed. Real Academia Española ("Nueva Edición"), VII (Madrid, 1930), 302*b*. For the text from the *auto* of the same title, see *Obras de Lope de Vega,* ed. Real Academia Española, II (Madrid, 1892), 633*a*.

[22] In *La adúltera* (*ó*), the serenade occurs, for example, in Morocco: Bénichou 39; Larrea 108, 110; in Central Peninsular versions: ASW 291-292; CPE, I, 35; RPE 26-27; in the Canary Islands: Pérez Vidal, "Romancero tradicional canario," p. 266; in Spanish America: Carrizo, *Rioja,* II, no. 2; Chacón, "Contribución," p. 68; Moya, I, 447; Poncet, pp. 285, 287; in Catalonia: Aguiló, nos. 21, 22, 50; Milá 254.

[23] The same motif is present in a fragment of *La mujer engañada* reported by Estrugo (*Los sefardíes,* p. 137), where the errant husband, returning late at night, complains: "Ábrime tú, mi alma, / ábrime tú, mi vida, // que estó en la yelada y la serenada." The proverb listed by A. Galante: "Mi marido en la yelada, y yo también" ("Proverbes judéo-espagnols," *RHi,* IX [1902], 440-454: no. 247) possibly recalls the ballad situation. The lover suffering from exposure appears repeatedly in Lopean dramas:

Toda una noche de enero
estuve al hielo a su puerta,
y al amanecer, abriendo
la ventana, me echó encima,
viéndome con tanto hielo,
una artesa de lejía.

standing before Blancaniña's door, begs to be let in, complaining that the fine rain is soaking his silken jacket:

¿Qué noches habéis dejado
de dormir por este amor?
¿Qué hielos habéis sufrido
en esa puerta? ...

Yo quiero una casadilla,
de cuyos ojuelos negros
saliera el sol más hermoso,
si se acostara con ellos. ...
Fuese el marido a una aldea;
sustituir quise el lienzo
de sus sábanas; volvió;
era riguroso invierno:
escondióme en un tejado,
del marido, y no del cierzo,
donde estuve sin jüicio,
hasta que el alba riyendo,
me tuvo por chimenea;
y con ser tan grande el hielo,
confieso que no ha podido
vencer de mi amor el fuego.

Estas piedras son testigos
de que, cubierto de nieve,
me halló mil veces el sol
antes que el tuyo saliese;
y agora por no aguardar
a que tu nieve me queme,
paso el puerto, temeroso
de que a tu puerta me quede.

The first text is from *El villano en su rincón,* Act II, vv. 1443-1448, ed. A. Zamora Vicente, "Clásicos Castellanos," no. 157 (Madrid, 1963), pp. 57-58; the second, from *Los amantes sin amor,* ed. Real Academia Española ("Nueva Edición"), III (Madrid, 1917), 160*b*; the third, from *¡Si no vieran las mujeres!* ..., ed. Real Academia Española, XV (Madrid, 1913), 161*b*-162*a*; the last text is from Lope de Vega, *Poesías líricas,* ed. J. F. Montesinos, "Clásicos Castellanos" (Madrid, 1951), I, 10-11. Cf. also *La Dorotea,* ed. E. S. Morby (Berkeley—Los Angeles, 1958), pp. 423-424: "Cúlpasme de no verte, y discúlpasme con la aspereza de la noche. Yo fui, Dorotea, a verte; que para mi amoroso fuego no ay en los Alpes nieue. Sentéme en aquella piedra que otras vezes. Salió Celia a la ventana, y quando pensé que me abría, deuía de dezirte que no me hallaua, tanta era la nieue que me cubría. ... Notable fue el frío. ... ¡O, si me vieras mejor que suelo pintarme en los versos, pastor cubierto de nieue, con el ganado de mis pensamientos y el perro al lado!" The motif, a confluence of life and liter-

—Avriméš, la Blankainiña, i avriméš, la Blankaiflor,
k'está'ziendo luvia menuda i me s'amoža el ǧibón.
I el ǧibón era de seda i me se troka la kolor.
(Jerusalem)

---

ature for Lope, can also be found in his mock epic *La Gatomaquia* (ed. F. Rodríguez Marín [Madrid, 1935], pp. 43-44):

¿Qué cosa puede haber con que se iguale
la paciencia de un gato enamorado,
en la canal metido de un tejado
hasta que el alba sale,
que, en vez de rayos, coronó el Oriente
de carámbanos frígidos la frente,
pues sin gabán, abrigo ni sombrero,
Febo oriental le mirará primero
que él deje de obligar con tristes quejas
las de su gata rígidas orejas,
por más que el cielo llueva
mariposas de plata cuando nieva?

The same *topos* is reflected in the following poem from an early *Cancionero* (MS Bibl. Nac. 3913, *apud La poesía castellana: Los primitivos,* ed. F. Gutiérrez [Barcelona, 1950], pp. 506 and 622; also Cejador, *Verdadera poesía,* III, 1787):

Mala noche me diste, casada;
Dios te la dé mala.
Dijiste que al gallo primo
viniese a holgar contigo,
y abrazada a tu marido
dormiste, y yo a la helada.
Dios te la dé mala.

Cf. also Cejador, *Verdadera poesía,* III, no. 2003: "Si desta escapo, / sabré qué contar: / non partiré del aldea / mientras viere nevar. / Una mozuela de vil semejar, / hízome adamán de comigo holgar: / non partiré del aldea / mientras viere nevar."

A Catalan ballad, entitled *Don Joan i Don Ramón* (OCPC, III, 268) offers a variant of the same commonplace, undoubtedly borrowed from *La adúltera* (*á-a*).

The exposed lover is well known to extra-Hispanic balladry. The French song, *Voilà la récompense!,* is built around this motif:

—Je vais à la fenêtre; bell', me l'ouvrirez-vous?
Je suis couvert de neige, dans l'eau jusqu'aux genoux.
Voilà la récompense que je reçois de vous!

See Barbeau, *Romancéro,* pp. 113-116; Id., *Jongleur,* p. 43; Id., *Rossignol,* p. 97; Canteloube, II, 14; Rolland, I, 33; V, 1. In *Sur le pont d'Avignon,* the rejected suitor of a married woman complains: "Comment que j'attendrais! /

—Ávreme, mi Blankailiña, i ávreme, mi Blankaiflor.
K'está aziendo luvia menuda, me se moža el ğibón.
El ğibón era de seda i me se kita la kolor.
(Rhodes)[24]

In a version printed in the Bosnian newspaper *Jevrejski Glas* (*ca.* 1939), it is the returning husband who finds himself out in the rain:

—Ávreme, mi blanka njinja, ávreme, mi ermoza flor.
Ke aze luvia menodika, me se moža el kontor.

The lover as a sneezing cat (stage 11-13), sometimes hidden in a chest (stage 10), appears in certain Sephardic versions of *La adúltera* (*ó*). In a Moroccan text from Alcazarquivir (MRuiz 59) and in essentially identical unedited versions from Larache, the lover, hiding in bed, sneezes and is purported to be a neighbor's cat catching mice:

Eyos en estas palabras, el de la cama estornudó.
—¿Quién es ése, cuál es ése, que en mi cama estornudó?
—El gatito del vesino que el ratonsito cogió.

J'ai la barbe gelée, / la barbe et le menton, / la main qui tient l'épée" (Rolland, IV, 66-67; cf. Canteloube, II, 209, 238, 253; IV, 278, 332; Coirault, *Formation*, III, 412, 414; Tarbé, II, 88-89). In the Italian *Domanda indiscreta* (Nigra 70), a "gentil galant" suffers an identical fate while waiting in vain for his beautiful shepherdess: "tre dì, tre nóit, / fin ch'la barba a j'è geleja, ['si è gelata'] // gelà la barba sül mentun, / gelà la man sla speja ['sulla spada']." In *The Gardener*, a haughty girl predicts the following fate for her rejected suitor: "The new fawn snaw to be your smock, / It becomes your bodie best; / Your head shall be wrapt wi' the eastern wind, / And the cauld rain on your breist" (Bronson 219 [text 5]; Child 219); however, the song is perhaps a bit too contrived to be considered a traditional ballad. The *Schwatzhafte Junggesell* (Meier, *Balladen*, II, no. 69A-B), locked out, complains: "Stehe auf, Herzlieb, und lass mich ein: / Es regnet und schneiet und wehet der Wind." Identical also is the suitor's plight in a Lithuanian ballad abstracted by Balys (A83. *Long Waiting is Annoying*). Compare the situation of Renaut, who waits all night in the wind and rain before his lady's door, in *Le roman du Castelain de Couci et de la Dame de Fayel* (ed. J. E. Matzke and M. Delbouille, Paris: *SATF*, 1936), pp. xl and vv. 2398-2475 (pp. 80-83). See also Boccaccio, *Decameron*, VIII, no. 7 = K1212. *Lover left standing in snow* (*while his mistress is with another*); Matteo Bandello, *Novelle*, I (Turin, 1853), "Parte" I, Novella XXVIII, pp. 332-333.

[24] Cf. also SBS 87.

Asercóse a la cama, con el mansebo s'encontró,
sacó navažita aguda, la cabeza se la cortó.[25]

An unedited text from Jerusalem evokes a similar situation, but again with no mention of the chest as hiding place:

—¡Ay! ¿De kén es este sarnudo, ke akí lo oigo yo?
—Es el gato de la vezina, ke ratones amferó.
Ya kitó él su spada i las kavesas les kortó.[26]

Levy (SBS) has collected a version from Rhodes in which the lover, identified as a cat, is hidden in a closet (stages 10 and 13) and betrays himself by sneezing (11-12):

—¿Kuál es esti bruido, ki akí lo sientu yo?
—Es el gato di la vezina i el ki (él) sarnudó.
Al avrir el armario, al namurado lo tupó.
(SBS 87)

Similarities between the *á-a* and *ó* assonant forms of *La adúltera* are even greater in other Rhodian versions of the latter ballad, which share as many as six narrative stages with *La adúltera* (*á-a*). As in stage 10, the lover is hidden in a chest; (11) he sneezes; (12) the husband asks who it is; (13) the wife identifies the neighbor's cat; (15) the husband seizes a hammer and opens the chest; (16) he invites the neighbors in to see a mustachioed cat and then, in a sanguinary dénouement which need not be related to stage 18 of *La adúltera* (*á-a*), takes out his sword and kills both lovers:

I él entrando más adientro, el del kašón estarnudó.
—¿Kén es éste ke starnuda enderientro del kašón?
—El gatiko de la vezina, ke kedó dientro'l kašón.
Tomó šulik en mano i a desklavar el kašón.
Ve un mostachiko aretorsido i un manseviko del dor.

---

[25] MRuiz 59.29-33. In other Moroccan, Peninsular, and Spanish-American versions, the lover's presence is discovered when he sneezes, but no cat is mentioned. Cf. Bénichou 39; Larrea 109-110; Schindler, p. 59*a* (from Soria); Espinosa, "Puerto Rico," no. 23; Monroy, p. 371; Pardo, p. 47. In Cuban versions, he coughs (Chacón, "Contribución," p. 68; Poncet, p. 288).

[26] Collected by Israel J. Katz, Jerusalem, November 18, 1960.

—Vení, veréš, mis vezinas, el gatiko ke estarnudó,
mostachiko aretorsido i un manseviko del dor.
Él desvainó la su spada, los mató a todos los dos.[27]

In the Sephardic tradition, and especially in the East, *La adúltera* (*ó*) has thus apparently undergone a number of successive contaminations from *La adúltera* (*á-a*), comprising, in the more intensely affected versions, up to six different stages of the narrative (10-13 and 15-16).

In four geographically separated versions of *La adúltera* (*á-a*), from Turkey (?), Rhodes, Salonika, and Sarajevo, the wife claims (stage 14) that she has lost the key to the chest, when the husband demands to know its contents:

—Un día me jui al río, las yaves me olvidara.
(Adatto 8)

—Dami las yaves, hanúm, viré komo los [ratones] alkansa.
—¿Ké le diré, mi marido? Mi kayeron en la balsa.
(SBS 82)[28]

—Dájmi la yave de la kaša, kero ver komo loz [ratones] afara.
—No, no, no, il mi maridu, no tengáš subé de nada.
El día de la kulada, pardí la yave de la kaša.[29]

The lost keys, which are mentioned in the *fabliau* of *Le chevalier à la robe vermeille*,[30] are a constant and prototypic feature of *La adúltera* (*ó*). They are, however, only occasionally related to the lover's hiding place.[31] Many versions are like CPE, II, 25, where the flustered

[27] Sung by Caden Capeluto, 85 years old, Albany (California), June 22, 1958. The informant equated *šulik* with Eng. *hammer* and the Hispanic *esḥuela* 'a tool used for pulling nails' (concerning which, see Wagner, "Espigueo," p. 54, s.v. *ezfwéla*). *Dor* is from H. *dôr* 'generation.'

[28] Text 82 is attributed to a singer from Rhodes. Levy states that no. 84, which contains identical verses, was collected from a Salonikan informant. In both texts, when the husband suggests that the wife use her neighbor's key (!), she makes the additional excuse that she is not on good terms with the neighbor.

[29] From an unedited version collected by Mrs. Cynthia Crews in Sarajevo in 1929. In the excellent, unedited notes which accompany her texts, Mrs. Crews identifies *subé* with T. *şübhe, şüphe,* 'doubt, suspicion, uncertainty.' See Wagner, *Beiträge,* p. 159*a,* who cites the variant *šupé.*

[30] See Entwistle, "Blancaniña," pp. 159-160.

[31] As, for example, in *Primavera* 136a; Aguiló, pp. 94-95; Milá 254.

wife insists that she has lost the keys to the "baúl mayor," but the lover turns out to be hiding under the bed! It is quite possible that the isolated references to the lost keys in Eastern Sephardic versions of *La adúltera* (*á-a*) were borrowed from the *ó* assonant ballad, but it is equally plausible that the very circumstances in which these references occur may independently have suggested the use of such a logical if desperate stratagem.

The mutual imprecations of husband and wife (stage 17) occur in two lone Portuguese versions of *La adúltera* (*ó*), where they are obviously a borrowing from *La adúltera* (*á-a*). Even the original assonance remains intact:

—Quem te agarrara, Filomena, numa praça bem queimada,
com sete carros de lenha e outros sete de palha!
—Quem t'agarrara, homem meu, numa sala bem asseada,
com sete padres à roda, dizendo-te: Saia! saia!
(VRP 406, 407)

The wife's death (stage 18) can, at most, be documented in but four Eastern versions of *La adúltera* (*á-a*). In Algazi, Danon, and SBS 82 (from Rhodes) the verse "Tomó la baltá en su mano / la cavesa le cortava" could apply to the wife, but very probably refers to the "gatiko." One Salonikan version (SBS 84) is more specific, though it is painfully obvious that the final cloyingly moralistic verse is a personal creation of the informant:

Dempraniko [*sic*] en el día la kavesa le kortava.
Por sus pekados desonestos la su vida eya dava.

In the Peninsular tradition, though the lover is often threatened with death or at least a beating in *La adúltera* (*á-a*), the wife's death is mentioned only as an extra-textual comment to a single Portuguese version (VRP 732). In *La adúltera* (*ó*), on the other hand, in contrast to its satirical continental counterparts,[32] the wife's death is an essential feature of the story, which is constantly maintained in the ballad's many and diversified geographic variations. It would be ridiculous,

[32] Cf. RoH, I, 331-332; Menéndez Pidal, "Romances y baladas," pp. 10-11; Gummere, *The Popular Ballad*, pp. 177-178.

however, to assume that the Portuguese and Eastern Sephardic versions of the *á-a* ballad had borrowed this detail specifically from *La adúltera* (*ó*). Punishment by death is practically a *sine qua non* as a conclusion for Hispanic ballads concerned with female adultery.[33] In specifying the wife's death, the Eastern Sephardic version(s) and the lone Portuguese text of *La adúltera* (*á-a*) undoubtedly reflect independent attempts to conform to the normal Hispanic pattern for ending such narratives; a pattern within which *La adúltera* (*á-a*), with its successive deceptions, its cynical repartee, and consistently ironic, mocking tone (stages 3, 4 [*nêkāmāh*], 6, 8, 10, 11, 13, 16, 19), constitutes a notable exception. Only the terrible retribution (stage 17) with which the adulteress is threatened—if not actually punished—rings true to Hispanic balladry's inexorable judicial code.

To summarize: the *á-a* and *ó* ballads of *La adúltera* coincide in the use of several essential and presumably prototypic features which need not reflect borrowing by either ballad. Such are (1) the "fatal Monday" motif and the morning serenade, (2) the lover's request for admittance and (9) the husband's unexpected return. Sephardic versions of *La adúltera* (*ó*), under the influence of the *á-a* ballad, have taken over "the sneezing cat" (stages 11-13), the chest as hiding place (stage 10), forcing open the chest (stage 15), and the husband's ironic invitation to the neighbors (stage 16). From the same source, some Eastern versions of the *ó* ballad may also have borrowed the lover's sufferings from exposure (stage 3). Two Portuguese texts of *La adúltera* (*ó*) have taken over the *á-a* ballad's final imprecatory repartee (17). Borrowing in the

[33] The wife is killed in *La adúltera* (*é-a*) (Larrea 118), *Raquel lastimosa* (Larrea 114; Bertini, p. 15 [no. 22]), *Landarico* (DRH 6), *Bernal Francés* (FN 114; Larrea 170-171; VRP 354-371), *La infanticida* (Bénichou 42; VRP 415), *Celinos y la adúltera* (no. 17 *infra*; some, but not all versions); *La condesa traidora* (uned. version from Tetuán; MP *85bis* and Bénichou 41 leave the ending in doubt.), *Frei João* (see n. 6 *supra*), and *La adúltera* (*á*) (Bertini, pp. 1-2 [no. 2]). There is no punishment, nor, apparently, does the husband even find out, in the cynical *Adúltera y el cebollero* (RQDB-I 48). The modern-sounding *Adúltera arrepentida* (Larrea 232; CPE, II, 55) is narrated by the lover and, of course, no punishment occurs. In notable contrast to the ballads of feminine adultery is *La mujer engañada* (see the bibliography to no. 15 *supra*), where it is the husband who is unfaithful. Here the wife must suffer in patient humiliation; her only revenge is to lock the wayward husband outside when he returns late at night after visiting his "nueva amada."

opposite direction is more difficult to prove. Rhodian versions of *La adúltera* (*á-a*) may well have borrowed the courting garland (nn. 1 and 14-16 *supra*) from *La adúltera* (*ó*) or, again, they may simply preserve an independent if garbled recollection of the folk custom itself. The "lost keys" (stage 14), found in various Eastern *á-a* texts, may have originated in the *ó* ballad but could also have been generated independently by the circumstances described in the *á-a* ballad. The death of the faithless wife (stage 18), only tenuously documented in Eastern and Portuguese versions of *La adúltera* (*á-a*), merely reflects two independent attempts to adjust the dénouement to the classic patterns of Hispanic ballad ethics.

BIBLIOGRAPHY

La adúltera (*á-a*)

Eastern J.-Sp.: Adatto 8; Algazi 62; Attias 58; Danon 43; Elnecavé 6; Gil, p. lix (= MP, Danon); Hemsi 17; Levy 25-27, 85; LSO 85-87 (nos. 19-20); Menéndez Pelayo 54 (= Danon); MP 80; PTJ 79-79a (= Algazi, Hemsi); San Sebastián 7; SBS 82-84; SICh 7; Zara (= Danon).[34] On the music of the Eastern versions, see Katz, *Judeo-Spanish Traditional Ballads from Jerusalem*, I, 242-248; Id., "A Judeo-Spanish Romancero," pp. 76-77.

Moroccan J.-Sp.: Larrea 270.

Castilian: CPE, I, 116-117; II, 25-26; RPE 29-30; RPM 132-133; RQDB-I 47; RQDB-II 32; RTCN 53, 57; RTO 23. Torner, *Cancionero musical de la lírica popular asturiana*, no. 6, in Asturian dialect, is affiliated with the Galician-Portuguese tradition.

Galician: Carré 117-120; La Iglesia, II, 119; Milá, "De la poesía popular gallega," nos. 135-135*a*; Sampedro 79-80.

Portuguese: Alves 565-566; Braga, II, 87; VRP 732-734.

Catalan: AFC 2212; Avenç, III, 19-20; IV, 82-84; Briz, II, 115-116; Milá 359; OCPC, I:1, p. 19 (no. 359); II, 161-162; Tomás i Parés, "L'Hereu Mill," pp. 934-935.

---

[34] The archaic *incipit,* "Yo me (a)levantara un lunes" (ASW 438; Avenary 89 [pp. 385, 388-389]; Danon 101 [p. 107]; RoH, II, 221) may reflect a version of *La adúltera* (*á-a*), but could just as well derive from the *romance* in *ó* on the same theme, from *La esposa de Don García* (no. 13 *supra*), from *Sufrir callando* (Danon 22), or from some other ballad. Avenary (pp. 388-389) indicates various other songs which begin with similar verses. For further documentation, see no. 13, n. 6 *supra.*

El fals mosso de forner

Catalan: AFC 3241; Milá 221; OCPC, II, 331-332.

La esposa beata

Castilian: CPE, II, 26; RPE 30-31.

Frei João

Portuguese: Almeida Garrett, III, 65-68; Alves, pp. 570-571; Athaide Oliveira, pp. 110-112; Braga, II, 78-87, 88-103, 105-110; Fernandes Thomás, *Velhas canções,* pp. 50-52; Furtado de Mendonça, *RL,* XIV, 19-21; Hardung, II, 108-118; Martins, II, 27-28; Neves, p. 30; Nunes, *RL,* VI, 179-183; Pires de Lima, *Romanceiro minhoto,* pp. 39-40; Reis Dâmaso, *Enciclopédia Republicana,* pp. 201-202; Rodrigues de Azevedo, pp. 262-273; Tavares, *RL,* IX, 288-289, 314-315; VRP 417-427, 1011. For texts we have not been able to consult, see VRP, I, 474.

Brazilian: Pereira da Costa, pp. 326-330. Cf. Santos Neves, p. 47 (no. 18).

La adúltera (*í-a*)

Moroccan J.-Sp.: Larrea 117, 121; MRuiz 65.

Studies: BNE 223, 226; Braga, III, 517-522; NSR 73-74, n. 60.[35]

[35] The question of continental counterparts of *La adúltera* (*á-a*) is a difficult one. We know of no very close correspondences, though some of the individual situations are well known to ballads concerned with the adulteress theme. The lover hiding in a chest—of Boccaccian renown—occurs in Anglo-American broadside ballads (*The Boatsman and the Chest*: Laws, *British Broadsides,* Q8) and in the French song of *Le coffre* (Puymaigre, *Pays Messin,* I, 194-196). The pretense that the lover is some type of animal, sometimes locked in a chest, closet, or other hiding place, has several parallels. Such is the Anglo-American *Dog in the Closet* (Laws, *British Broadsides,* Q11), except that here the lover actually is replaced by a dog, to the final confusion of the betrayed husband. In a Lithuanian song, the mother, on hearing her daughter's lover walking about at night, asks who is in the room. She gets the answer: "[It is] a cat, dear Mother." "Why do his steps sound so loud?" "He is shod, dear Mother" (*There was a Cat*: Balys A92). *Der verlorne Schuh* (Meier, *Balladen,* II, no. 76) represents an analogous situation in which the lover is said to be a small dog. In the Provençal *Pris au piège* or *Lou rat* (Arbaud, II, 175-178; Rolland, I, 160-162) the lover is identified with the animal mentioned in the Provençal title. This

ballad also includes other motifs present in *La adúltera* (*á-a*): The husband returns home because he has forgotten something (stage 9); the lover is hidden in the hayloft (stage 10); the neighbors are called in; the lover turns out to be a cleric (stage 16; cf. Peninsular versions of *La adúltera* [*á-a*]). Some of the texts designated by Rolland with the title *Le mari benêt* (Rolland, I, 72-74: texts *c, d, e*; II, 72-73: texts *p, q*), which rhyme in *á*, show a number of striking, though possibly coincidental, agreements with *La adúltera* (*á-a*): (1?) The husband gets up early (text *p*) (7) and goes out to the fields or to the forest (*c, e, q*) or goes hunting (*p*; cf. Eastern J.-Sp. versions), (4) leaving his wife in bed (*c, e, q*). (9) The wife fails to bring him his breakfast and he returns home to find her in bed with the curé (*c, e, p, q*; cf. Peninsular versions, stage 16). (13) There is an allusion to a cat at the end of the ballad (*c, d, q*). For other versions, see Canteloube, I, 147; III, 74, 208; IV, 296; Puymaigre, *Pays Messin,* II, 131-132; Tarbé, II, 133-134; Udry, pp. 201-202; Barbeau, *Jongleur,* pp. 153-156. Whether by coincidence or otherwise, a ballad current in Greece, *Hē ápistos gunaĩka* (*The Faithless Wife*), shares several narrative stages with *La adúltera* (*á-a*): The faithless wife wakes her husband and sends him out on an errand (stages 4 and 7). On the way he realizes that he has forgotten some needed object and turns back (stage 9). He finds the doors locked and his wife with her lover. He kills the wife (stage 18). For texts and comment, see Fauriel, II, 370-373; Firmenich, II, 122-123; Liebrecht, *Zur Volkskunde,* pp. 187-188; Lübke, p. 239; Passow 461; Pernot, *Anthologie,* pp. 101-102. The Albanian *Vendetta d'un marito geloso* (De Grazia, pp. 169-172) follows the Greek ballad closely. Wlislocki ("Zu neugriechischen Volksliedern," pp. 362-363) translates a Slovakian song which also parallels the Greek. The Hungarian ballad, *Barcsai* (Aigner, pp. 102-104, 187-189; Leader, pp. 230-239; Vargyas, *Researches,* pp. 160-163), tells a very similar story. Here and elsewhere the situations are so "universal" that it is most difficult to prove any direct affiliation with the Hispanic ballad.

On the lover hiding in a chest, as a folktale topic, cf. M. R. Lida de Malkiel, *El cuento popular hispano-americano,* p. 30.

17

CELINOS Y LA ADÚLTERA

(Celinos and the Adulteress)

—Ken kere tomar konsežo,   ke venga 'a mí, se lo daré:
Ken kere kazar kon mosa,   non se 'espere ala vežés.
Por mí lo digo, 'el meskino,   ke de syen anyyos kazó 'él.
Kazó kon 'una senyyora,   ke non tyene los dyez 'i seś.
'El dí'a de las sus bođas   'i byen 'o'iréś ké fu'e azer.
Tomó peyne de 'oro 'en mano,   sus kave'os se fu'e a peynar.
'I 'en la su mano dereğa   lyeva 'un 'espežo kristal.
De 'elyyo se mira su pu'erpo   'i 'el su lindo asemežar.
Bendizyendo va del vino   'i bendizyendo va del pan,
bendizyendo al Dyez del syelo,   ke tal linda la fu'e a kriar;
maldizyendo 'a pađre 'i mađre,   ke kon 'un vyežo la fu'e a kazar.
Ke la kazara kon 'un vyežo,   'el vyežo 'es de antigu'eđađ.
La ninyya kere ğugete   'i 'el vyežo kere folgar.
Yyorava la Blankaninyya,   lágrimas de veluntad.
Por a'í pasó Klareto,   kual non la vyera de pasar:
—¿De ké yyoráš, la Blankaninyya,   lágrimas de veluntad?

Source: GSA 12.

Each verse, except v. 24, is repeated.

2b 'a la *in repetition.*

5a bodas *in repetition.*

10b 'a kriar *in repetition.*

12b 'i 'el vyežo de antigu'eđađ *in repetition.*

14a, *16a* Blanka ninyya.

15a 'i por a'í *in repetition.*

—Ke me kazaron kon 'un vyežo, 'el vyežo non 'era mi par 'igua̯l.
—Yyo vos daré 'un konsežo, kua̯l me lo 'uvyeraš de tomar:
azévos de la prenyyada, de tres mezes 'i non más.
—'A los kampos de Alsuma, 'un ḥăzîr vide asar.
Si de akel ḥăzîr non gosto, 'el prenyyado lo vo ağar.
Se alevantó 'el vyežeziko, a ver 'el ḥăzîr ánde 'está.
Arožó 'él la su lansa; la kavesa le 'enfilará:
—Vení, veréš akel ḥăzîre, ke lo viteš asar.

18*b* kual *in repetition.*

Translation:

"Whoever may want advice, let him come to me and I'll give him some: Whoever would marry a maiden, let him not wait for old age. I speak for myself, poor wretch, who married when a hundred years old." He married a young lady who is not quite sixteen. (5) On the day of her wedding, listen well and hear what she did. She took a gold comb in her hand and began to comb her hair. And in her right hand she holds a mirror of crystal. In it she regards her body and her lovely appearance. She blesses the wine and blesses the bread, (10) blessing God in Heaven, who made her so beautiful; cursing her mother and father, who married her to an old man; that they should marry her to an old man, an old and decrepit man. The girl wants to play and the old man wants to rest. Blancaniña was weeping, weeping tears with all her heart. (15) Clareto passed by there; oh, that he had not passed by! "Why are you crying, Blancaniña, tears with all your heart?" "Because they married me to an old man and he was not my equal." "I'll give you some advice, which you should take from me: Pretend that you are with child, three months with child and no more." (20) "In the fields of Alsuma, I saw a roasting pig. If I don't taste that pig, I'll lose the infant." The old man arose, to see where that pig was. He hurled his lance and pierces it through the head. (24) "Come, you'll see that pig, that roasting pig you saw."

Motifs:

3 J445.2. *Foolish marriage of old man and young girl*; T121. *Unequal marriage.*
11 M400. *Curses.*
17 T237. *Old man married to young, unfaithful wife.*
19 ff. K2213.3. *Faithless wife plots with paramour against husband's life*; T230. *Faithlessness in marriage.*
21 H1212.4. *Quest assigned because of longings of pregnant woman.*
22 Cf. N774.3. *Adventures from pursuing animal (not magic).*

Celinos y la adúltera has been collected from oral tradition in a number of widely separated areas, both on the Iberian Peninsula and among the Eastern Sephardim. The texts published to date, however, offer a very incomplete geographic picture of this balladic *rara avis.* Attias' and Yoná's substantial versions and the fragments published by Bassan and Hemsi are from Salonika. In DRH we edited two very brief and divergent texts from the Rhodian MS of Yakov Hazán. Unfortunately, Levy's two-line fragment, like all the texts in his collection, is unidentified as to geographic origin. The Peninsular subtraditions are reflected in print by only two Castilian fragments (RPM 17; RQDB-II 74) and one magnificent and, to our knowledge, unique Portuguese version (VRP 1000) from Campo de Víboras, near Vimioso (Bragança), a few miles from the Spanish frontier.

Thanks to the generosity of Don Ramón Menéndez Pidal, who placed at our disposal his entire file of unedited *Celinos* texts, a total of nineteen Eastern Sephardic and Peninsular versions, we can now provide a much more complete image of the ballad's singular geographic distribution. The following Eastern Sephardic communities are represented in Menéndez Pidal's collection: Sarajevo (3 versions), Salonika (3 versions), Larissa, Sofia, Istanbul, Izmir, Rhodes, and Beirut (one version each). Our own fieldwork in the United States has yielded, aside from the two MS versions of Yakov Hazán, but four fragments, which add only one community—that of Sérrai (Greece)—to those represented in Menéndez Pidal's collection. We collected two other very brief truncated versions from Salonikan informants. Our other text, from Rhodes, consists of seven verses which, like Levy's fragment, serve as a prolog to *Vos labraré un pendón* (no. 22 *infra*). Four verses, which appeared in the Sarajevo newspaper, *Jevrejski Glas*, in the late 30's, are also joined to this same ballad. Menéndez Pidal's Peninsular versions include four from the Province of Burgos and one each from Santander (Valderredible), Zamora (Uña de Quintana), and Ibiza.

Textual evidence available to date thus shows a few locations in Northern Castile, an isolated Leonese mountain town (Uña de Quintana), one village in the extreme north-east of Portugal, a remote corner of the Catalan linguistic domain (Ibiza), and various communities in the Sephardic East, to be the last redoubts of the ballad of *Celinos y la adúltera*. That the massive unedited *Romancero* of Menéndez Pidal, a product of some six decades of intensive fieldwork by a host of collaborators, should contain only nineteen versions is in itself a significant factor in characterizing the ballad's singular and furtive traditional life. In spite of its wide, if spotty geographical range, *Celinos y la adúltera* appears everywhere as a rarity. In whatever subtradition it may occur, it is almost always represented by solitary or ill-remembered fragmentary texts. Throughout the Hispanic world, the ballad of *Celinos* has taken refuge in the most out-of-the-way corners, the most remote lateral areas, where its traditional existence, rooted in the middle ages, has somehow managed to survive into the twentieth century.

The ballad of *Celinos* derives from one of the initial episodes of the widely diffused and much reworked twelfth-century *chanson de geste* of *Beuve de Hantone*.[1] A detailed comparison of the epic's various redactions with all available versions of the ballad must be relegated to a separate study. However, certain details, which elucidate Yoná's version in particular, deserve mention here.

Yoná's text, like many other Eastern Sephardic versions, begins with a series of cautionary verses in *é*. The first verse, "Ken kere tomar konsežo..." which appears in texts from Salonika, Larissa, Sérrai, Sofia, and Rhodes, occurs in practically identical form in Moroccan versions of *Catalina*.[2] In *Celinos* this initial verse is followed by the aphorism "Ken kere kazar kon mosa, / non se 'espere ala vežés," which relates to the ballad *topos* of unequal marriage (see no. 2, n. 4

[1] See RoH, I, 261; II, 406; Menéndez Pidal's introduction to VRP, I, xv-xvi; DRH, pp. 76-79; and our "Romance de *Celinos y la adúltera*," pp. 8 ff.

[2] Cf. MP 67; Larrea 90-91; Ortega 231, which are related to *Primav.* 141.

supra) and, as applied specifically to the husband ("Por mí lo digo, 'el meskino..."), establishes the principal motivation for what is subsequently to occur. Though the maxim, "Ken kere kazar kon mosa..." has no close counterpart in the Sephardic *refraneros* we have seen, it has all the markings of a traditional proverb and its message is well known in both Peninsular and Sephardic paremiology:

Viejo que con moza se casa, de cornudo no escapa.
Ni patos a la carreta, ni bueyes a volar, ni moza con viejo casar. [3]
Casar la moza con el viejo no es buen consejo. [4]
Viejo casado con mujer hermosa es cosa muy dañosa. [5]
La ke toma marido vyežo, toma 'el basín por 'espežo. [6]
Quien cazó y comió temprano, no se arrepintió. [7]

The proverbial nature of the Sephardic ballad's introductory verses helps explain its contamination with *Vos labraré un pendón* (no. 22 *infra*), to which *Celinos* is joined in versions from Rhodes and Sarajevo and in Levy's unidentified no. 67. In several Eastern versions, *Vos labraré,* like its Moroccan and sixteenth-seventeenth-century counterparts, begins with a proverbial observation concerning matrimony, followed by a statement on how the protagonist exemplifies the proverb:

Ken kaza kon amor   siempre vive kon dolor.
Por mí lo digo, el meskino,   ke ansina era yo.
[Yo tomí una muchacha,   iža de un gran señor.]
Mi mužer era pompoza   i yo un ombre gastador.
Gastí lo suyo i lo mío   i lo ke mi padre me dió.
Agora por mis pekados   vine a ser afilador.

(uned., Rhodes) [8]

---

[3] L. Martínez Kleiser, *Refranero general ideológico español* (Madrid, 1953), nos. 1.172, 19.245.

[4] F. Rodríguez Marín, *Más de 21.000 refranes castellanos ...* (Madrid, 1926), p. 71*b*.

[5] J. M. Sbarbi, *Gran diccionario de refranes de la lengua española,* ed. M. J. García (Buenos Aires, 1943), p. 1004.

[6] E. Yehuda, "Mišlê 'espanyoliɵ yĕhûdîɵ," *Zion* (Jerusalem), II (1927), 80-96: p. 87 (no. 60); also reproduced by C. M. Hutchings, *HR,* XX (1952), 315-321: no. 60.

[7] E. Saporta y Beja, *Refranero sefardí* (Madrid-Barcelona, 1957), p. 82. Cf. M. Kayserling, *Refranes o proverbios españoles de los judíos españoles* (Budapest, 1889), p. 9; M. Galimir, *Proverbios* (*Refranes*): *Pocos proverbios del rey Salamon ...* ([New York], 1951), p. 41 (no. 511).

[8] Cf. also Danon 30; SBS 100.

Siempre lo oyí yo dezir en ca de mi padre señor,
que quien por amores caza su vida vive con dolor:
ansí hizi yo, mesquino, por amores cazíme yo;
cazí con una galana, hija era del rey mi señor.
Eya era mujer bien puesta, yo me era hombre gastador;
gastí mi hazienda y suya, cuanto trujo y tenía yo,
y ahora por mis pecados volvíme hombre apropiador.
(Bénichou 9; MRuiz 91)[9]

Here the introductory pattern is identical to that used in the Eastern versions of *Celinos*: (1) A topic phrase which introduces a proverb;[10] (2) a proverbial observation on matrimony; (3) the wretched protagonist's own unfortunate circumstances as a specific illustration.[11] The aberrant assonance of the *Celinos* ballad's paremiological *incipit* seems to mark it as a relatively late accretion. It is worth noting, however, that, in the Castilian tradition, the ballad also begins with a proverb, but whether the cautionary beginning is prototypic or an independent development in the *romance*'s Eastern and Castilian ramifications is difficult to prove. The Castilian versions of *Celinos* incorporate a variant of the ancient proverb, "Casar y compadrar, cada cual con su igual," recorded in the seventeenth century by *Maestro* Gonzalo Correas:[12]

---

[9] Cf. also the archaic version reconstructed by Menéndez Pidal, *El Romancero Español,* pp. 83-84, and RoH, II, 179-180.

For other examples of the use of proverbs in *romances,* see Michaëlis, "Estudos," pp. 198-199. Cf. M. Frenk Alatorre's excellent article "Refranes cantados y cantares proverbializados," *NRFH,* XV (1961), 155-168.

[10] On *Siempre lo oí decir* and other examples of its use in narrative poetry, see Armistead, "Para el texto de la *Refundición de las Mocedades de Rodrigo,*" p. 540, n. 27. Cf. also A. López de Vega, *Paradoxas racionales,* ed. E. Buceta (Madrid, 1935), p. 99.

[11] Stages 2 and 3 occur as an introduction to the Catalan ballad of *La muerta* (Milá 37; AFC 2967):

Valdría mes sé soldat, peleyarne nit y dia
que no posá l'amor ab cap viuda ni cap nina.
Yo parlo per mi mateix l'he posat ab una nina.
M'en ha menat enganyat diguent qu'ab mi's casaría.

[12] *Vocabulario de refranes* (Madrid, 1924), p. 109*b*. For the formulistic pattern reflected in this proverb, see J. Morawski, "Les formules rimées de la langue espagnole," *RFE,* XIV (1927), 113-132: p. 122.

El casar y el comparar cada uno con su igual
y no como pasó a Elena, Elena del Monteadán.
Que se casó con un viejo y no cesaba de llorar.
(uned., Rubena, Burgos Prov.)

El casar es comparar cada uno con su igual
y no casar como Elena, Elena de Montalbán.
La casaron con un viejo y no cesa de llorar.
(uned., Valderredible, Santander Prov.)[13]

The formula *bendiciendo-maldiciendo* (Yoná, vv. 9-10; Attias, vv. 17-22), by which the adulteress expresses dissatisfaction with her aged husband, attenuates the traditional cumulative Pan-Hispanic ballad malediction by substituting 'bless' for 'curse' in the first three instances Similarly phrased but unsoftened curses occur in sixteenth-century Carolingian *romances* and have been perpetuated in the modern traditions of such lateral areas as Catalonia and Galicia. Strikingly similar to the initial scene of the Sephardic *Celinos* is the Catalan *Descontentadiza* and its French congener, "A Paris y a une dame," where a lady combs her hair (before a mirror) while uttering curses against father, mother, and husband:

Catarina s'en pentina ab una pinta d'argent.
S'en pentina y s'en enclenxa sota'l finestral d'argent.
Cada cabell que li queya malehía'ls seus parents.
Malehía pare y mare, son marit primerament.
(Milá 326; AFC 2905; Amades, I, 204; Capmany, no. 41)

A Paris y a une dame qui est belle comme le jour.
Elle se peigne, ell' se mire dans un beau miroir d'argent.
Ell' appelle sa femm' de chambre: —Jeanneton, venez-vous en;
Dites-moi si je suis belle ou si mon miroir me ment.
—Madam', vous êtes un peu brune, ça vous va passablement.
—Si je savais être laide, je maudirais tous mes parents.
Je maudirais pèr' et mère, mon mari premièrement. ...[14]

---

[13] Cf. RQDB-II 74.

[14] Rolland, II, 229; Puymaigre, *Pays Messin,* II, 179. Cf. also the curses of the discontented young nun in Arbaud's *La moungeto* (II, 118-122).

A similar malediction appears in a Galician version of *Silvana,* where the protagonist curses the sun, the day, and the mother who gives birth to a beautiful daughter:

> Maldecindo vai do sol, maldecindo vai do día,
> maldecindo vai a madre que filla hermosa paría.
> (Carré 81) [15]

The name of the ballad's protagonist, who corresponds to the traitorous Doon de Mayence in the *chanson de geste,* [16] varies greatly in the different branches of the Hispanic tradition. The designation *Celinos,* which seems to link the character to the appropriate concepts of *celos* 'jealousy,' *celo* 'sexual ardor' and *celada* 'ambush,' is certainly the most satisfactory and authentic. [17] It can, however, be documented, with a number of minor variations, only in the Peninsular tradition: *Celinos* (Burgos, Santander [RPM], Zamora), *Zelino* (Burgos [RQDB-I]), *Delino* or *Elino* (Burgos), *Cellinos* (Santander), *Selino* (Portugal [VRP]). The name's possible early application to the ballad's central character acquires a degree of confirmation from the sixteenth-century *Conde Dirlos* (Primav. 164), where *Celinos* also designates a wife-stealer: the young Prince who, during Dirlos' absence, attempts to win the hand of the latter's seemingly abandoned bride. [18] *Celinos* is perhaps further confirmed as the protagonist's "authentic" name in that most of the forms used elsewhere in the tradition can be explained as the result of a variety of rather logical secondary borrowings from other thematically analogous ballads. Thus, in the text from Ibiza, Celinos' part is played

---

[15] For more examples of such curses, see DRH, pp. 74-75 and n. 69; AFC 3331. Cf. also CVR, p. 234. On a possible parallel in the epic poem of *El Abad Don Juan de Montemayor,* see Menéndez Pidal, *Historia y epopeya,* pp. 120, 206-207.

[16] On Doon de Mayence's rôle as traitor in the *chansons de geste,* see *Ro,* II (1873), 362 and n. 2.

[17] In one of the English versions of Beves of Hamtoun, Doon de Mayence is appropriately renamed "Sir Mordoure." See *The Romance of Sir Beues of Hamtoun,* ed. E. Kölbing, pp. 4 ff. (vv. 76 ff.).

[18] In the ballad of *Guiomar,* Celinos is mentioned in connection with another unrelated adventure: He had been imprisoned for seven years by the Moorish King Jafar but was secretly liberated by the Princess Guiomar. She hopes that, if he is among the Carolingian forces moving against her father, he may favor her cause out of gratitude. See *Primavera* 178 (p. 405).

by *Condi Grillu*—possibly a variant of *Conde Olinos* or *Conde Niño.*[19] This contamination was perhaps brought about by an association of Celinos' rôle with that of the potential abductor of the Princess in *El conde Olinos.* A similar association may have led one of Menéndez Pidal's unedited Salonikan versions to use the name *Conde Adimar,* which recalls the *Conde Alimán, Alemán, Animar,* etc., of the Salonikan *Conde Olinos.*[20] However, it seems even more probable that the name was taken directly from *El conde Alemán y la reina* (no. 7 *supra*), by equating Celinos with that ballad's adulterous protagonist. Another Salonikan text not illogically replaces *Celinos* with *Virgilio,* thus recalling the latter's amorous escapades as seen in the well-known Sephardic *romance* on Virgil's imprisonment.[21] Such anomalies as *Alguazile* and *Cernetero,* applied to the hero in unedited versions from Larissa and Izmir, defy identification.[22] The name *Klareto,* used by Yoná and Attias, is paralleled by *Clarineto* and *Carleto* in Menéndez Pidal's unedited texts from Beirut and Sarajevo. The latter form in particular suggests the interesting possibility of an association with the extremely rare ballad of *Galiana,* which has so far been documented in but one version (Attias 56). In Attias' text the name *Caloricho* designates Galiana's suitor. S. M. Stern has argued convincingly that *Galiana* is a balladic adaptation of the Galiene episode of the *Mainete* epic. In Spanish prosifications of this *chanson de geste* on the youthful adventures of Charlemagne, Galiana appears as an unwed Moorish princess, who

---

19 The connection between *Grillo* and *Olinos, Niño, Nillo,* is, however, by no means exclusive. *Conde Dirlos* also becomes *Grillo* in *La boda estorbada* (Catalán, "El motivo y la variación," p. 163).

20 See no. 12, n. 7 *supra.*

21 For Eastern versions, see Attias 7; Baruch 277-278; Benardete 23; Bidjarano, p. 24*a*; Danon 15; Gil 50 (= Danon); González-Llubera 1; LSO 73; Menéndez Pelayo 27 (= Danon); PTJ 48*a* (= Baruch); Pulido 296-297. For Morocco: Alvar, "Los romances de *La bella en misa,*" pp. 266-270; Bénichou 25; Gil 53 (= MP); Larrea 51-53; MP 46; MRuiz 49; PTJ 48 (= Alvar). There are rare versions from Castile (cf. RPC 125; RQDB-I 74; RQDB-II 49; RTCN 114) and from Galicia-Portugal (VRP 293; also I, xviii). Cf. RoH, I, 346-348; II, 340, n. 74. For one of the ballad's sixteenth-century forms, see *Primavera* 111.

22 Is the former somehow connected with the *alguaciles* or *alguacel* who appears in certain Eastern Sephardic versions of *Melisenda insomne* (i.e., Danon 7 and Attias 33.61)? He corresponds to "Hernandillo" or "Fernandino, el alguacil" in *Primavera* 198 and Menéndez Pidal, *El Romancero Español,* p. 26.

escapes from Toledo to marry the hero.[23] In the ballad, however, "Galeana" is seen as a married woman who, in spite of her husband's threats, runs off with "Caloricho," whose name is presumably a deformed diminutive of *Carlos* (i.e., *Mainete,* 'young Charlemagne'). Caloricho's rôle as a married woman's suitor is identical to that of Celinos. The names in question—*Caloricho, Clareto, Clarineto, Carleto*—are unknown in Sephardic balladry outside of the *romances* of *Galiana* and *Celinos.* It seems quite possible that, because of obvious analogies between the two narratives, the *Celinos* texts from Sarajevo, Salonika, and Beirut, may have taken over the name *Carleto,* etc., from the ballad of *Galiana.* If so, the Sarajevan *Carleto* offers a better reading, which helps to confirm the identification of *Caloricho* with young Charlemagne[24] and also provides precious additional testimony concerning the diffusion of one of Sephardic balladry's rarest epic survivals.

The meaningless second hemistich of Yoná's verse 15 is patently defective: "Por a'í pasó Klareto, / kual non la vyera de pasar." That the text should read "kual non devyera pasar" is confirmed by an unedited Salonikan version: "Por ahí passó Clareto / que nunca allegara a pasar." The verse, which stresses Clareto's ominous rôle and undesirable character, is, of course, formulistic. Compare the arrival of the telltale hunter in *El conde Claros y la infanta*:

Por ay passó vn caçador, que no deuiera passar,
en busca de vna podenca, que rauia deuía matar.[25]

The type of animal or object specified by the wife's caprice and the name of its habitual retreat or location vary greatly from version to version. In texts from Sarajevo, Burgos, Santander, Zamora, and Traz-os-Montes, the animal is a stag (*ciervo*; *serbo*), while some

[23] See Stern, "A *Romance* on Galiana," p. 230; Menéndez Pidal, *Historia y epopeya,* pp. 270-272. For Galiana's escape from Toledo in Spanish prosifications of the *Mainete,* see PCG, chaps. 597-599; *Gran Conquista de Ultramar,* pp. 184-185; Gómez Pérez, "Leyendas medievales," pp. 28-29, 129-130; id., "Leyendas carolingias," pp. 179-180. Attias' text is reprinted in PTJ (no. 85).

[24] In effect, *Karleto* is the name for young Charlemagne in a Franco-Italian version of *Mainete.* See J. Reinhold, "Karleto," *ZRPh,* XXXVII (1913), 27-56, 145-176, 287-312, 641-678.

[25] *Silva de 1561,* fol. 82*r.* Cf. *Primavera* 190.51-52; Braga, I, 335; Macabich, p. 22.

Salonikan versions mention a pig or boar (uned.: *puerco*; Yoná: *ḥăzîr*; Attias: *quierco*). Both animals occur in variants of the *chanson de geste* and it is difficult to determine which is prototypic in the ballad.[26] In other unedited texts from Salonika and Larissa the animal is a ram (*carnero, carneto*)—evidently a secondary development to avoid the odium of boar's meat.[27] Even more bizarre cravings occur in versions from Rhodes and Ibiza, which respectively call for bramble bush flowers (DRH 10*b*: "flores de sená" [= H. *sĕneh*]) and water from a special fountain (uned.: "aigo de la Font del Rumanar"). The animal's haunt is variously known as *monte* (*de*) *Olivar* (Burgos, Santander), *montes de Celinos* (Zamora), *monte de Selino* (Bragança), and *campos de Algolimbri* or *huertas de Arbolido* (Sarajevo). The Salonikan and Larissan versions show even greater variation: *campos de Clareto* (Attias), *bosques de Castilla* (uned.), *campos de Azumare* (uned.), . . . *de Alzuma* (uned., Larissa), . . . *de Alsuma* (Yoná). The last-named toponym, whatever its origin, is shared with Salonikan renditions of *El sueño de Doña Alda* and *La mujer de Juan Lorenzo*:

Yo por los campos d'Alsume una galza vide volare.
Allí en los campos de Alzmina una garza vi volare.
(*Doña Alda*)[28]

En los campos de Arzuma grande gente vide baxar.
(*Juan Lorenzo*)[29]

---

[26] For a discussion of this problem, see DRH, pp. 80-81, n. 80. The situation involved is a commonplace in folktales: "Ya se comprometió con el gigante la señora y el gigante le decía a ella que cómo podría matarlo [a su hijo]. . . . —Hácete enferma y dile que con el tocino del chancho jabalí puedeh encontrar la salú. Yendo ai, no güelve, lo matan, porque ésas son las fieras más bravas que hay en el mundo" (Y. Pino-Saavedra, *Cuentos folklóricos de Chile,* 3 vols. [Santiago de Chile, 1960, 1961, 1963], no. 70, I, 313); cf. also no. 24, I, 126; S. Thompson, *The Folktale* (New York, 1951), pp. 113-114 (Aarne-Thompson Types 315, 590); and the motif H1212. *Quest assigned because of feigned illness.*

[27] Cf. our "Christian Elements and De-Christianization," pp. 29, 30, 37.

[28] The first text is Benardete 11. The verses are joined to *Melisenda insomne.* The second text is from Menéndez Pidal, "El Romancero y los sefardíes," p. xxii.

[29] Coello 2; MP 12. Cf. also Smyrnian and Rhodian versions of *Las cabezas de los infantes de Lara* (Menéndez Pidal, *Romancero tradicional,* II, 208-211): "En los campos de Ancolores . . ." (4*h*, 4*i*); "Por los campos de Alculantro . . ." (4*n*).

Yoná's text seems to leave the ballad's outcome in suspense. Has Celinos perished, as in most versions, or has the deceived husband fallen victim to the lover, as in the *chanson de geste*? Two Sephardic texts clearly attest to the latter solution, though in both cases the assonance is defective: "En la primera cazada, / al viejo le enfilaría" (uned., Salonika). A Smyrnian version is equally specific:

Namorado que lo vido [al viejo], travó la su espada y lo mató.

Other Judeo-Spanish texts also imply that the hunting expedition has had a fatal outcome for the husband. In one of Yakov Hazán's MS texts from Rhodes the aged husband is said never to have returned from the quest imposed by his adulterous wife: "Tomó armas 'i kavalyo, / 'él más no hu'e 'a tornar" (DRH 10*b*). Attias' version, using two famous ballad formulas, implies an identical dénouement:

Ya s'esparte d'ella el viejo, ya s'esparte ya se va.
Ojos que lo vieron ir, no lo vieron más tornar. [30]

---

[30] Attias 50.49-52. The second formula also appears in Menéndez Pidal's unedited Ibizan version at a different stage of the narrative. As the husband goes off in search of water from the Fountain of Rumanar, the adulteress wishes that she may never see him again: "Es uis que veuen anar-te'n / que no et veiguen tornar." On the formulas used in Attias' version, see no. 1, n. 1 *supra,* and DRH, pp. 36, n. 31; 80, n. 77; "El romance de *Celinos y la adúltera,*" p. 11, n. 14. Add to the above documentation the important discussion of *Ojos que nos* (*me*) *vieron ir* by Michaëlis de Vasconcellos in RVP, pp. 103-105, 188-190, 259, n. 2, 274, 287, n. 4. The verse also figures in Alonso López' *Glosa peregrina*: "Ojos que me vieron yr / nunca me verán en Francia" (*Pliegos góticos,* II, 282*b*). The formula is used to conclude various Portuguese ballads in the modern tradition:

Pegara-lhe pela mão, pousara-a no cavalgar;
olhos que a viram vir não na viram cá voltar!

(*Conde Claros fraile*: Tavares, *RL*, IX, 299*a*)

Espôsa da minha vida, inda te vim resgatar,
olhos que a vêdes ir não na vêdes cá voltar!

(*Gaiferos y Meliselda*: Martins, I, 193)

Acudi-lhe à Milondinha que se vai para além do mar;
olhos que a vedes ir, não na vereis cá tornar.

(*Esposa de Don García*: VRP 625)

Although the final verse of Yoná's text may appear ambiguous in that the speaker remains unidentified and the subject of *'él* in v. 23 is uncertain, there can be little doubt that, in this case, it is the husband who has returned victorious, while the ill-fated Celinos is equated with the adulteress' imaginary boar (*ḥăzîr*). Variants from Sarajevo and from the widely separated Peninsular locations dispell all doubt. In these texts Celinos is made to die at the hands of the outraged husband, who then returns home to confront his wife with the lover's severed head, while equating it with the object of her caprice in a brutally ironic metaphor which clearly parallels the final verse of Yoná's text:

Toma la cabeza de ciervo que me mandabas buscare.
(Zamora)

Toma la cabeza del ciervo que anda en el Monte Olivar.
(Burgos)

Vet ací es desig de s'aigo de la Font del Rumanar.
(Ibiza)[31]

The first part of the phrase is used in various traditional lyric couplets from Castilian-speaking areas:

Ojos que te vieron ir
por aquellos arrabales,
¿cuándo te verán venir
para alivio de mis males?

Ojos que te vieron ir
por esos mares afuera,
¿cuándo te verán venir
para alivio de mis penas?

Ojos que te vieron ir
por el caminito llano,
¿cuándo te verán volver
con la licencia en la mano?

The first two examples are from Restrepo, *El cancionero de Antioquia,* 3d ed., pp. 205-206, 335; the last, from García Matos, *Lírica popular de la Alta Extremadura,* p. 406*a*.

[31] For similar ironic ballad dénouements, see DRH, pp. 81-82, n. 81, and the final vv. of no. 16 *supra*. Compare also the Spanish-American versions of *La adúltera* (*ó*), where the husband receives a metaphoric answer to his question concerning the lover's presence in his house:

Here the story's original outcome has been reversed in accordance with Hispanic balladry's particularly rigorous attitude toward marital infidelity. We might ask, however, if the Sephardic versions ending in the husband's and not the lover's death may not perhaps reflect an archaic variant in which the *romance* has remained more faithful to its epic source or if, on the other hand, we are merely faced with sporadic secondary reversals of the ballad's typically Hispanic dénouement.

BIBLIOGRAPHY

Eastern J.-Sp.: Armistead and Silverman, "El romance de *Celinos,*" p. 12 (= GSA); Attias 50; Bassan 65; DRH 10*a-b*; Hemsi 22; Levy 67.2-4; PTJ 66, 86 (= Hemsi, Armistead-Silverman). Cf. Morley, "A New Jewish-Spanish *Romancero,*" pp. 4-5.

Castilian: ASW 324; RPM 17; RQDB-I 73 (= RPM, except for the variants *Cortárale* and *con la mitad* in v. 3 and the spelling *Zelinos*); RQDB-II 74; RTCN 29.

Portuguese: VRP 1000.

Catalan: Uned., Ibiza. See commentary above.

Studies: Menéndez Pidal, Prolog to VRP, I, xv-xvi, xix; RoH, I, 261, 331; II, 330, 406.[32]

—¿Qué haces por aquí, don Carlos? ¿Qué haces por aquí, traidor?
—Buscando una garza blanca que por aquí se ocultó.
—Esa garza que usté busca por muerta la tengo yo,
y si la fuerza me alcanza, muertos quedarán los dos.

The text quoted is from Pardo, p. 47. Cf. also Bertini, p. 14; Garrido, p. 37; Monroy, p. 371. (The passage also exemplifies the motif of the lost hunting bird that leads the hero to his mistress' chamber [see no. 18, n. 7 *infra*].) The modern Castilian *Infancia de Gaiferos* may have embodied a similar ironic allusion, though the Cossío-Maza version is unclear (RPM 54, pp. 103-104).

[32] Does the *Frau von Weissenburg* (DVM 30; Erk-Böhme 102; Röhrich-Brednich 60), which, Meier claims, depends on a historical incident (DVM, I, 309-310; *Balladen,* I, 217), also derive from *Beuve de Hantone*? Essential features of the two narratives are identical. In the German ballad's dénouement the lover, who has just killed the adulteress' husband, refuses to continue his association with her. Is this, like the death of Celinos in the *romance,* a moralization of the original story's outcome? On the German ballad, see also J. Meier, "Die Ballade von der Frau von Weissenburg," *JVF,* III (1932), 1-34.

On the similarities between *Celinos, Beuve de Hantone,* and Villemarqué's Breton ballad of *Seigneur Nann et la fée* (pp. 40-41), see our article "El romance de *Celinos y la adúltera,*" p. 9, n. 10.

18

RICO FRANCO

(Rico Franco)

Tres falkones van bolando, por las almenas del rey.
Ni topavan ké komere, ni topavan ké bever.
Arimóse 'en 'un kastí'o, kastí'o de 'oro 'es.
Deđyentro de akel kastí'o, ayy 'una mosa pontés.
'El su tokađo 'en klenğa 'i 'el su nyyuđiko ala syen.
Sus kođas ala turkeska, fin a la punta del pye.
'El su kontošiko 'estrego, ke se le areventa 'el bel.
La su kalsika delgađa, ke byen le namora 'el pye.
'El su pađre non la dava, ni por 'oro ni por aver,
sinon la ğugan al ğugo, al ğugo de la šeđré.
La ganara 'el moro franko, moro franko aligorné.
Yya se la tomó 'a brağo 'i la yevó kon 'él.
Yyorava la Blankaninyya, lágrimas de dos 'a tres.
—¿De ké yyoráš, Blankaninyya, lágrimas de dos 'a tres?
Si yyoráš por gu'estro pađre, 'el mi kozinero 'es.
Si yyoráš por gu'estra mađre, la mi lavandera 'es.
Si yyoráš por gu'estros 'ermanos, yyo los matí 'a todos tres.
—Ni yyoro por mis 'ermanos, ni por mi pađre tambyén.
Yyoro por la mi ventura, ke non sé ké a đe ser.
—Yyo sé la vu'estra ventura, de 'un anyyo fin a syen.

Source: RSA 5.
6*b*, 20*b* fina.
19*b* ađeser.

—Moro franko 'i moro franko,   dešme 'el kuğiyo del bel.
Moro franko sin malisyya   le dyyo 'el kuğilyyo del bel.
23 La ninyya kon su malisyya   se lo 'enfinkó 'en el bel.

---

23 'enel.

Translation:

Three falcons go flying, around the battlements of the King. They found nothing to eat, nor anything to drink. He [*read* They] flew near to a castle; a castle made of gold. Within that castle, there is a Pontic(?) maid. (5) She wears her hair parted, with a small bow at her brow; her tresses in Turkish fashion, to the very tips of her toes. Her little waistcoat worn tightly, drawn tightly about her waist. Her stockings are fine and thin and most flattering to her feet. Her father would not give her in marriage for gold nor for goods, (10) except that they wager for her, by playing a game of chess. Moro Franco won her, Moro Franco from Livorno. Now he takes her by the arm and takes her away with him. Blancaniña was weeping, two and three tears at a time. "Why are you weeping, Blancaniña, two and three tears at a time? (15) If you are weeping for your father, he is my cook. If you are weeping for your mother, she is now my laundress. If you are weeping for your brothers, I killed them all three." "I do not weep for my brothers, nor yet for my father. I am weeping for my fate, for I know not what it will be." (20) "I am your good fortune, for the next year and a hundred more." "Moro Franco, Moro Franco, give me the dagger at your waist." Moro Franco, without guile, gave her the dagger at his waist. (23) The girl, with all her guile, thrust it into his side.

Motifs:

3*a* Cf. B582.2.1. *Hero carried by bird to mistress' chamber.*
3*b* F771.1. *Golden castle* (*palace, house*).
10 N2.6.2. *Daughter as wager*; N2.6.3. *Damsel as wager.*
12 R10.1. *Princess* (*maiden*) *abducted.*
15 L410.5. *King overthrown and made servant.*

21 K818.1. *Man killed with sword, which he himself is tricked into passing to captured enemy*; cf. J642.2. *Robbers persuaded to give hero sword with which they are afterwards killed*; K910. *Murder by strategy.*

Yoná's chapbook offers a complete and excellently proportioned version of a Hispanic representative of the Pan-European ballad type exemplified in *Lady Isabel and the Elf-Knight,*[1] *Heer Halewijn,* and *Renaud le tueur de femmes. Rico Franco* is a rather rare ballad in most branches of the Hispanic tradition. Eastern Sephardic variants have been published from Salonika (Attias, Molho, Yoná),[2] from Rhodes—where atypically the ballad is quite common—(DRH, Díaz-Plaja, "Hispanic Balladry," Romey [?]), from Edirne (Danon), and from Bosnia (Baruch). Our unedited collection includes fifteen Rhodian texts and fragments, one text from Tekirdağ (collected by E. Adatto Schlesinger), and one fragment from Athens-Jerusalem (collected by I. J. Katz). The ballad is a rarity in Morocco. In fact, only two autochthonous versions have reached print (Bénichou; MP) and, in over two months of intensive field work during 1962-1963, covering all the Moroccan Judeo-Spanish communities, we were unable to collect a single version. In the center of the Peninsula *Rico Franco* has become a children's play song, whence it has reached the Canary Islands, the Antilles and Morocco (Larrea 269; BNE 225) doubtless through a secondary and quite modern traditional diffusion. Such fringe areas as Portugal, Brazil, and Catalonia conserve more complete and more archaic text-types.

Yoná's version, like Attias' and an unedited text from Tekirdağ, preserves and elaborates upon the rôle of the falcons which introduce the narrative in the lone sixteenth-century rendition. Elsewhere the falcons are either eliminated (Baruch; Danon; Morocco; all Peninsular types) or, by analogy with another traditional *incipit,* are

[1] Curious but probably quite coincidental is the fact that the heroine of *Rico Franco* is known as "Isabel" in the modern Peninsular versions.

[2] Except for two verses added after Yoná's v. 21, a few very minor variants (*se* omitted from v. 7*b*; *hidré* in v. 10; *no* for *non* [*passim*]) and spelling differences, Molho (LSO 75-76) presents the same text as Yoná.

replaced by doves (Danon [variant]; Rhodes).[3] In the sixteenth-century text, the falcons have escaped during an unsuccessful hunting expedition, but it is not clear whether they are really instrumental in leading the hunters, and Rico Franco (> Moro Franko) in particular, to the maiden's castle:

---

[3] Compare: "Tres palomitas / en un palomar ..." (RPM 483); "Tres palomitas volan, / volan y vienen y van" (Larrea, *Canciones,* no. 60); "Tres n'eren les palometes, / palometes n'eren tres; // n'han trencat la voladeta, / s'en van a parâ a la Ignès" (*La missa de Jesucrist*: OCPC, II, 332; AFC 2990). Did the traditional commonplace inspire García Lorca's magnificent vignette, *Cazador* (*Obras completas* [Madrid, 1954], p. 291)?

¡Alto pinar!
Cuatro palomas por el aire van.

Cuatro palomas
vuelan y tornan.
Llevan heridas
sus cuatro sombras.

¡Bajo pinar!
Cuatro palomas en la tierra están.

Such a possibility seems likely in view of the important rôle of popular elements in Lorca's poetic idiom. Cf. Daniel Devoto, "Notas sobre el elemento tradicional en la obra de García Lorca," *Fil,* II (1950), 292-341; Id., "García Lorca y los romanceros," *QIA,* nos. 19-20 (1956), 249-251; Id., "Lecturas de García Lorca," *RLC,* 33 (1959), 518-528; C. Ramos-Gil, "El eco de la *canción añeja* en la lírica de Lorca: Alcance y sentido del popularismo lorquiano," *Romanica et Occidentalia*: *Études dédiées à la mémoire de Hiram Péri* (*Pflaum*) (Jerusalem, 1963), pp. 150-188; G. L. Rizzo, "Poesía de Federico García Lorca y poesía popular," *Clav,* VI, no. 36 (1955), 44-51; also J. F. Montesinos, *NRFH,* II (1948), 295, n. 8. Particularly suggestive of the relationship of Lorca's poem to oral tradition is the following Provençal song:

Très paloumetos au bos, au bos s'en ban,
Très paloumetos mourtos, mourtos seran.
(Coirault, *Formation,* III, 405)

The *Envol de colombes*—sometimes pigeons or even falcons—is a recurrent motif in French balladry. See Coirault, *Formation,* III, 404-414. In some cases, just as in *Rico Franco,* their flight leads to a king's palace and to the discovery of a fair *châtelaine*:

Trois petits pigeons blancs ils ont prins la volée,
Ils ont volé si haut qu'ils ont la mer passée. ...
Sur le château du roi ils se sont reposés. ...
[La dame du château mit la tête en fenêtre:

A caza iban, a caza, los cazadores del rey,
ni fallaban ellos caza, ni fallaban qué traer.
Perdido habían los halcones, ¡mal los amenaza el rey!
Arrimáranse a un castillo que se llamaba Maynés.
Dentro estaba una doncella muy fermosa y muy cortés; . . .
Robárala Rico Franco, Rico Franco aragonés. . . .[4]

Although the nature of the initial episode has become blurred in both the archaic text and its Sephardic derivatives, it apparently embodies three important and intimately inter-related folkloric *topoi*: (1) Adventures while hunting;[5] (2) The "unlucky" hunter who finds no game, but instead encounters a maiden;[6] and (3) animals who lead the hero to the heroine's abode.[7]

—A qui sont ces pigeons qui ont la plume dorée?
—Ils sont à mon aimant qui est dedans la guerre.]
(Coirault, *Formation,* III, 410, 409)

For other instances of this motif, see Canteloube, III, 66; Whitfield, *Louisiana French Folk Songs,* p. 58, v. 7 (in a version of *La courte paille*); Bartók-Lord, nos. 23*a-b*.

[4] *Primavera* 119. See our commentary in NSR, pp. 63-64.

[5] N771. *King (prince) lost on hunt has adventures.* See no. 8, n. 2 *supra.*

[6] The topic occurs plentifully in both Peninsular and Pan-European balladry, as well as in other types of traditional literature. The ballad of *La infantina* (MP 114; Bénichou 1) offers a classic example. For numerous other Hispanic instances, see Devoto's excellent article, "El mal cazador." An additional latter-day example is embodied in *El amor firme* (RPM 315):

Me cogí la carabina y al monte me fui a cazar,
en el monte no cacé porque nada pude hallar;
sólo una blanca paloma [= la amada], en un rico palomar.

The motif penetrates Catalan versions of *Don Bueso y su hermana* (Milá 250, Var. B; Aguiló, p. 174):

Si n'havía un dels moros va cassant per las montillas.
No'n trova cunill ni llebre, sino una trista cautiva.

Compare also the Catalan ballad of *El bon caçador* (Milá 317; AFC 2283; Avenç, I, 121-122; II, 15-16; IV, 71-73; Capmany, no. 31; Briz, I, 79; Bulbena, pp. 22-23; OCPC, I, 140-141; II, 120, 127-128, 333; III, 148-149, 153-155, 387; Sarri, p. 103; Serra i Vilaró, p. 67; Subirá, pp. 74-75; cf. also Briz, III, 51):

Matinadas son fresquetas, yo m'en vaig aná á cassá.
No'n trovo cassa ninguna pera poderli atiná;
Hi ha sino una pastoreta qu'en guardava bestiá.

Several other features of Yoná's text merit comment: The rather elaborate description of the girl and her finery (vv. 5-8), even further developed in Attias, seems limited to the Greek Sephardic versions. It

---

European balladry offers further occurrences, although the unsuccessful nature of the hunt is not always specified:

Allant à la chasse
pensant à l'amour
je rencontrai Climène
plus belle qu'un jour.

(*Allant à la chasse*: Rolland, I, 192)

Il est là-bas dans ces plaines
dans ces jolis champs d'avênes
à chasser le sanglier.
Ce n'est pas le sanglier qu'il chasse,
la belle, ce sont vos amours.

(*Blanche Rose*: Rolland, I, 242)

—Où vas-tu, beau chasseur?
Qué vas-tu donc chassa?
—Je vas chassa la caille
ou lé pigeon ramia,
ou quelque jolie fille
si j'en povais trova.

(*L'occasion manquée*: Rolland, II, 30)

Trois garçons de la ville
à la chasse ils s'en vont.
N'ont pas tiré bécasses,
ni cailles, ni pigeons.
N'ont trouvé qu'une fille
assise sur un pont.

(*Trois garçons de la ville*: Canteloube, II, 84)

Fiöl dël re l'un va a la cassa, a la cassa dël liun,
S'è scuntrà ant üna bargera a l'umbrëta d'ün bissun.

(Il figlio del re se ne va alla caccia, alla caccia del leone,
s'incontrò in una pastora all'ombra d'una siepe.)

(*La fuga*: Nigra 15)

Es blies ein Jäger wohl in sein Horn,
und Alles was er blies, das war verlorn.
—Sol denn mein Blasen verloren sein,
viel lieber wollt ich kein Jäger mehr sein.
Er zog sein Netz wohl über den Strauch,
da sprang ein schwarzbrauns Mädel heraus.

(*Die schwarzbraune Hexe*: Erk-Böhme 19*e*)

also survives fragmentarily in I. J. Katz's text from Athens-Jerusalem. The motif of the wagered daughter (N2.6.2), lacking in *Primavera* 119, appears in both Eastern Sephardic and Castilian texts, though the game

---

Cf. also *Der freche Knabe*; *Der Nachtjäger* (Meier, *Balladen,* II, nos. 79B.1, 92; Röhrich-Brednich 3); *I Rosenslund* (DgF, IV, no. 230); *Tro som Guld* (DgF, IV, no. 254A-B); *Riddaren Tynne* (Geijer-Afzelius, no. 7: I.2). The German *Jäger aus Griechenland* (DVM 5; Erk-Böhme 24; Meier, *Balladen,* I, no. 3; Röhrich-Brednich 15) undoubtedly reflects an adaptation of the same motif, though the person encountered after the fruitless hunt is not a woman. A Lithuanian ballad abstracted by Seemann (p. 184, no. 75) has the unsuccessful hunt but no subsequent encounter with a girl.

The unsuccessful hunter is well known to Greek folk poetry. For examples, see Baud-Bovy, *Textes,* pp. 194, 224; Id., *Chansons,* II, 450 (no. 9); Marcellus, *Chants du peuple,* I, 382-383; Schrader 50. Especially striking is the figure of the hunter who, in one Greek song, discounts from the start all hope of finding game and sets out only to hunt for dark-eyed girls: "Là-bas dans la plaine, dans l'île déserte, le sultan sortit afin de chasser. Il ne chassait pas lièvres et chevreuils, mais il pourchassait les prunelles noires. Mes prunelles noires, lèvres écarlates, paraissez, ma belle, à votre fenêtre" (Pernot, *Anthologie,* p. 144; also Baud-Bovy, *Chansons,* I, 384 [no. 11]; Marcellus, *Chants du peuple,* II, 224-225; Meyer, *Griechische Volkslieder,* p. 16). The hunter's inability to find game is more clearly stated in the Lithuanian *Hunter and the Girl* (Balys L5) and in the following Serbo-Croatian song: "Omerbeg rose early; / he rose early to go hunting in the mountains. / For three years he was in the mountains, / and shot no game, / but he found a beautiful maiden" (Bartók-Lord 10*a*.1-5).

As Devoto has observed, "no deja de ser singular que todos estos encuentros amorosos vayan precedidos del mal éxito del cazador" ("El mal cazador," p. 486). Devoto convincingly argues that the ballad protagonist's failure to find game is ultimately related to his having failed to observe the ritualistic sexual prohibitions incumbent upon hunters in many primitive societies (cf. C119.1.3. *Tabu: Intercourse at hunting season*). Add to Devoto's references, R. Briffault, *The Mothers,* 3 vols. (New York, 1927), III, 353-355; also Th. Kroeber, *Ishi in Two Worlds* (Berkeley-Los Angeles, 1965), p. 194. Such ideas are still very much alive in Greece, as is attested in the monumental Argenti-Rose monograph on the folklore of Chios: "The day after a man has been with a woman, his affairs will go ill, and especially he will have no luck hunting" (pp. 304, 408-409). Perhaps it is also significant that in a possible French parallel to the Hispanic *Adúltera* (*á-a*) the hunter is successful but returns home to find that his wife has deceived him (*Le mari benêt*: Rolland, II, 72.)

[7] For extensive documentation, see M. R. Lida de Malkiel, *La originalidad artística de La Celestina* (Buenos Aires, 1962), pp. 201-202, n. 3; D. Devoto, "El mal cazador," pp. 487-488; NSR 64, n. 15. To the references there offered may be added the following: In a version of *El castigo del sacristán* from Extremadura, the protagonist, who has amorous designs upon three sisters, stumbles at night into their backyard. When they ask him about his presence there, he offers the following excuse:

referred to in v. 10 varies constantly from version to version.[8] The expression "lágrimas de dos 'a tres" (vv. 13, 14), used to describe the girl's grief, is formulaic and occurs in at least one other assonant

---

Iba de caza, señoras, se me perdió un gavilán
y me dieron por noticia que estaba en vuestro corral.

We cite an unedited rendition collected in Arroyo de la Luz (Cáceres), July 1963. CPE, I, 151, documents only a variant of the first verse: "Señorah, vengo de caza / y he perdido el gavilán." CPE, II, 41-42, RQDB-I 68, RQDB-II 47, and RTCN 103 lack the passage in question, as do the fragments published by Braga, I, 155, 166-167. For another example of the same motif in Spanish-American versions of *La adúltera* (*ó*), see no. 17, n. 31 *supra.*

Lope de Vega experiments with the same situation in *La mayor virtud de un rey* (Act I, vv. 510-517 of the autograph MS):

Vienen a ver a señor
el Prínçipe don Manuel
y otro fidalgo con él,
que anda aquí con vn azor
haziendo enredos por veros
bolar al viento suaue;
que como el amor es aue
tiene páxaros terzeros.

Looking farther afield, in the *Volsungasaga,* as in *La Celestina* and many another work, it is an errant hawk that leads the hero to an encounter with his beloved: "It is told that one day Sigurd went riding in the woods with his hawks and hounds and a great number of followers, and when he came home, his hawk flew up to a high tower and settled upon a window. Sigurd went after the hawk, and there within he saw a fair woman, and he knew that it was Brynhild" (Chap. 24, Schlauch trans., p. 113). The medieval English *Corpus Christi* seems to recall the same motif. See Hodgart, *The Ballads,* p. 38. Essentially identical is the initial episode of the modern Greek ballad, *The Fruit of the Apple-tree* (*Ho karpòs tẽs mēlẽās*: Arabantinos, no. 240; cf. the translations of Argenti-Rose 744-747; Garnett, I, 134-135; Georgeakis-Pineau 181-182; Lübke 163; Lüdeke-Megas, no. 34):

Ὁ νειὸς μὲ τὰ λαγωνικὰ ἐβγῆκε 'ς τὸ κυνῆγι
κ' ἐκράτει καὶ 'ς τὸ χέρι του ἕνα μικρὸ γεράκι.
Τὤφυγε, τ' ἀπολύθηκε, σὲ περιβόλι μπῆκε,
καὶ ἀφορμὴ τοῦ γερακιοῦ, μπῆκε κι' ὁ νειὸς κατόπι.
Ἐκ' ηὗρε κόρ' ὁπὤπλενε σὲ γοῦρνα μαρμαρένια....

(The young man with his hunting dogs went out on a hunt.
And he also carried on his arm a small falcon.
It escaped, it freed itself, it entered a garden.
And because of the falcon, the young man followed after.
There he found a maiden washing at a marble basin.)

variation, in *El conde Alemán y la reina* (no. 7 *supra*), where, for prosodic reasons, the Princess sheds tears "in threes and fours" ("lágrimas de tres 'en [*or* 'a] kuatro" [vv. 19-20]). Moro Franco's question

---

A falcon similarly discovers a girl in several Serbo-Croatian ballads. See Stevenson Stanoyevich, nos. 16, 18, 108.

The falcon or eagle as a symbol for the suitor is widespread in folk poetry. To the numerous examples given by M. R. Lida de Malkiel add the following: "¡Madre, un caballero, / blanco lleva el sayo, / saltó de la torre / vino al mi palacio! ... / —¿Qué bušcáis, falcone, / por el mi palacio? / —Bušco a la novia, / que me se hay bolado" (Attias 94). Identical is the central motif of the Danish *Ridderen i Fugleham* (DgF, II, no. 68; Prior, III, 206-211), its French and French-Canadian analog *Je me suis habillé en plumes* (Barbeau-Sapir, pp. 171-174; Barbeau, *Rossignol,* p. 13), and *The Earl of Mar's Daughter* (Child 270). Cf. also the Bulgarian ballad *Stoïan changé en aigle* (Dozon, no. 10).

Meier's *Die schöne Magdalena* (*Balladen,* II, no. 80A) begins as follows:

Wer ich ein wilder Falke,
Ich wolt mich schwingen aus
Und wolt mich niderlassen
Für eines reichen Burgers Haus.
Darinnen ist ein Meidlein,
Magdalena ist sie genannt....

The Danish *Bortfløjne falk* (Dal, no. 56) uses the same image (there is no genetic relationship with DgF, no. 68). The bridegroom and bride as falcon and dove or partridge respectively appear in the wedding songs of many Balkan peoples. See Abbott, *Macedonian Folklore,* pp. 93, 180; Chianis, nos. 10 and 14; Dieterich, "Die Volksdichtung der Balkanländer," p. 406; EEB 317, 340, 347; Georgeakis-Pineau, p. 228; Montesanto, "La città sacra," p. 72; Pernot, *Anthologie,* p. 257 (nos. CXXXVIII and CXLII); Petropoulos, *La comparaison,* pp. 60-61; Bartók-Lord, no. 23*a*, n. 1; Dozon, *Chansons populaires bulgares,* p. 335; Camarda, *Grammatologia ... albanese,* pp. 120-123; Lambertz, *Die Volksepik der Albaner,* p. 110; Reinhard, *Süd-Türkei,* pp. 199, 235.

More brutally direct are the hunting and fowling metaphors applied to amorous activities in various Romance ballads. Count Claros' words to Claraniña are unequivocal (*Primav.* 190; cf. Larrea 33.31 ff., 49.43 f.; Macabich, p. 15; Braga, II, 34):

—Bien sabedes vos, señora, que soy cazador real;
caza que tengo en la mano nunca la puedo dejar.

When Gerineldo is questioned by the King concerning where he has spent the night, he claims, in certain Portuguese versions, to have been hunting for a turtle dove on the other side of the river: "Venho de caçar a rola / do lado d'além do rio." The King answers: "A rola que tu caçaste / dormiu na cama contigo" (VRP 1004; cf. Braga, I, 180, 185, 186, 204; Menéndez Pidal, *et al.,* *Cómo vive un romance,* pp. 173-174). In the Italian *Monacella salvata,* a hunter, whose amorous advances are frustrated by a nun, is described as having allowed

concerning the girl's weeping, which in many versions embodies an iterative pattern much used in balladry,[9] is absent from the sixteenth-century version but consistently crops up in the various branches of the modern tradition and must be of respectable antiquity:

---

a quail to escape from under his feet: "Voi avevate la quaglia dinanzi ai piedi, ve la lasciaste volar via" (Nigra 72); so also in *L'occasion manquée*:

Moun beou moussu, quand l'on la ten,
fau plumar la gallino.
(Arbaud, II, 92)

—Sire chevalier rassemblez,
à l'espervier vous resemblez
qui tient la proye emmy ses pieds
et puis la laissez enfuire;
ainsi faictes vous, sire.
(Rolland, II, 36)

Quand vous teniez l'alouette,
il fallait la plumer.
Quand vous teniez la fillette,
il la fallait baiser.
(Rolland, I, 28; II, 30; Canteloube,
II, 106; Tarbé, II, 139 f.)

A Greek ballad translated by Proust (pp. 51-52) offers an identical conceit. Cf. also *La Celestina,* II (Madrid: "Clásicos Castellanos," 1949), 181. For similar imagery in learned poetry of the fifteenth and sixteenth centuries, see Carrizo, *Antecedentes hispano-medioevales,* pp. 801-805; D. Alonso, *De los siglos oscuros al de Oro* (Madrid, 1958), p. 254 ff.; M. D. Triwedi, "A Possible Source for Cetina's Heron Sonnet," *RN,* X (1969), 359-361.

Ultimately related to such imagery is the sexual symbolism of the bird—well known to the slang of many European speech communities (cf. the references provided by Wagner, *Caracteres,* pp. 37-38 and 41, n. 2; also *RPh,* XX [1966-67], 357)—as well as the bird as a symbol of fertility (see H. Friedmann, *The Symbolic Goldfinch* [Washington, D.C., 1946], pp. 28-32). Concerning the falcon motif, see now R.E. Barbera, "Medieval Iconography in the *Celestina,*" *RR,* LXI (1970), 5-13.

On the more general topic: *Adventures from pursuing (enchanted) animal* (N774, N774.3), see E. G. Gardner, *The Arthurian Legend in Italian Literature* (London, 1930), pp. 322-324; Laiglesia, *Tres hijuelos había el rey,* pp. 8-10, 28-30; our "Romance de *Celinos y la adúltera,*" pp. 9-10, n. 10; Keller, "The Hunt and Prophecy Episode of the *Poema de Fernán González,*" pp. 253-254. Other examples: Partinuples' adventures begin when he becomes lost on a hunt while pursuing an enchanted boar (*Libros de caballerías,* ed. A. Bonilla y San Martín, vol. II [*NBAE* 11], 579). The action of *El marqués de Mantua* is likewise initiated by the protagonist's pursuit of a stag (*Primav.* 165). See also *Sir Gawain and the Green Knight,* trans. B. Stone (Baltimore, 1959), p. 89, n. 1. Cf. *Poema de Fernán González,* ed. *Reliquias,* vv. 226 ff. In the prosification of a lost

¿De ké yyoráš, Blankaninyya, lágrimas de dos 'a tres?
(Yoná) [10]

¿Por qué lloras, hija mía, por qué lloras, Isabel?
(RPM 182-183) [11]

Cantar de Fernán González absorbed by the *Crónica de 1344*, the evil Archpriest discovers the hiding place of the fugitive Count and the Navarrese Princess while hunting "con su açor e lançolo a una perdiz, e fue dar con ella en aquel lugar dondellos hyazian, e quando alli metio los podencos, començaron a ladrar," etc. (ed. *Reliquias*, p. 165). Cf. *Poema de Fernán González*, vv. 651-652. Similarly, Count Claros and the *Infanta* are discovered by a hunter "en busca de una podenca [*var.* un azor], / que rabia debía matar" (*Primav.* 190.52, p. 436, n. 10). Compare also motifs B582.2.1. *Hero carried by bird to mistress' chamber*; B151.2. *Bird determines road to be taken*; B563.2. *Birds point out road to hero*; B455.2. *Helpful falcon.*

[8] See "Hispanic Balladry," pp. 237-238, n. 25; DRH, p. 67.

[9] Note the following examples:

¿De qué lloras, blanca niña? ¿De qué lloras, blanca flor?
(*Vuelta del hijo maldecido*: Hemsi 27)

¿De ké yoras, blanka niña? ¿De ké tienes ke yorar?
(*La niña de los siete enamorados*: uned., Jerusalem)

¿Por qué lloras, alma, por qué lloras, vida?
(*Don Bueso y su hermana*: RPM 192, 193)

Por que choras, minha mãe, por que choras, ó mãe minha?
(*Jesús y la Virgen*: Vasconcellos, "Bibl. do Povo," p. 32)

¿Perque plorau vos, la bella, perque plorau vos, l'amor?
(*Don Blasco*: Milá 223; Aguiló, p. 28)

¿Por qué no cantáis, la flor? ¿Por qué no cantáis, la bella?
(*¿Por qué no cantáis?*: MP 57)

¿En qué lo conoces, hijo, en qué lo conoces, flor?
(*Doncella guerrera*: RPM 266)

¿Dónde va la blanca flor, dónde va la blanca niña?
(*La doncella vengadora*: RPM 180)

Many versions of *Rico Franco* (e.g., "Hispanic Balladry," no. 4; Díaz-Plaja 4; Romey 1) replace Yoná's v. 14 with an *ó* assonant line which coincides with the example cited above from *La vuelta del hijo maldecido*. See our remarks in DRH, pp. 67-68.

[10] Also Attias 9; LSO 76.

[11] The verse occurs regularly in the Central Peninsular versions and their analogs of recent diffusion. Cf. RPE 46; RPM 182-183; Córdova y Oña, I, 130; also RCan 25; Larrea 269; Cadilla de Martínez, *Juegos*, p. 154, etc.

¿De qué ploreu, la dama, dama, de qué ploreu?
(Aguiló 9.23 f.) [12]

Qu'estás tu ahi chorando? Cal-te, calt', em que te pêz.
(Rodrigues de Azevedo, p. 61) [13]

The girl who obtains her abductor's knife through some artifice [14] —in other versions of *Rico Franco* often more specifically developed than in Yoná—is known to various Romance ballads. [15] Some Eastern Judeo-Spanish texts attenuate the narrative's sanguinary ending, [16] but Yoná's rendition brings the ballad's compact drama of family honor to its traditional and satisfactorily vengeful conclusion.

BIBLIOGRAPHY

Eastern J.-Sp.: Attias 9; Baruch 286; Danon 11; DRH 9; Díaz-Plaja 4; Gil 36 (= Danon); "Hispanic Balladry," no. 4; LSO 75-76; Menéndez Pelayo 23 (= Danon); PTJ 87-87a (= Baruch, Díaz-Plaja); Romey 1.

Moroccan J.-Sp.: Bénichou 37; Larrea 269; Gil, p. lxxxv (= MP); MP 85; PTJ 87*b* (= Bénichou).

Castilian: BTPE, III, 98-99; Córdova y Oña, I, 130; CPE, I, 82, 88.1-6; CPM 155; CVR 350; P. García de Diego, "Siete canciones infantiles," pp. 113-115; Montalbán, no. 29; RPC 24-25; RPE 46; RPM 182-183; RTCN 45.

Canarian: RCan 25.

---

[12] Also no. 10.27-28; Bulbena, p. 31; OCPC, I, 88; II, 322.

[13] Also Braga, I, 151, 152, 154.

[14] Motifs: K818.1; K910; cf. also K1218.5. *Girl asks importunate lover for weapon to use against her father. Instead, she uses it to defend herself against suitor.*

[15] Cf. "Hispanic Balladry," p. 238. In *Melisenda insomne,* the Princess asks the luckless constable Hernandillo for his dagger and then stabs him with it: "Prestásesme, dijo a Hernando, / prestásesme tu puñal. ... // Diérale tal puñalada / que en el suelo muerto cae" (*Primav.* 198). Cf. Nigra 13 (*Un'eroina*), 14 (*Il corsaro*), and 15 (*La fuga*); Bronzini, I, 115, 120; II, 199, 219; Doncieux, p. 449 (*L'embarquement de la fille aux chansons*); also Canteloube, II, 381; Barbeau, *Jongleur,* pp. 135-136; Id., *Rossignol,* pp. 394, 395; Vargyas, *Researches,* pp. 44, 46, 88.

[16] See DRH, pp. 68-69. Cf. also "Hispanic Balladry," p. 237, n. 24.

Spanish American: Cadilla de Martínez, *Juegos*, pp. 153-154; Chacón, "Contribución," pp. 74-75; Córdova de Fernández, p. 67; Poncet, p. 249.

Portuguese: *Braga*, I, 148-155; Id., *Archipélago açoriano*, nos. 48-49; Id., *RL*, I, 103-104; Fernandes Thomás, *Canções*, pp. 14-15; Hardung, II, 61-63; Rodrigues de Azevedo, pp. 57-62; VRP 478.

Brazilian: Pereira da Costa, pp. 309-311; Santos Neves, p. 47 (no. 17).

Catalan: AFC 2207; Aguiló, pp. 35-40; Amades, I, 207-210, 262; Bulbena, pp. 30-31; Milá 551; OCPC, I, 88-89; II, 322, 399; Serra i Vilaró, pp. 82-83; Tomás i Parés, "L'Hereu Mill," p. 929.[17]

Archaic Text: Durán 296; CSA, fol. 191*r-v*; *Primavera* 119. See also CSA, pp. xxxii f., RoH, II, 316, n. 22.

Continental analogs:

French: *Renaud le tueur de femmes*: Canteloube, IV, 46; Davenson 7; Doncieux, pp. 351-365; Puymaigre, *Pays Messin*, I, 140-145.

French-Canadian: Barbeau-Sapir, pp. 22-28; Barbeau, *Rossignol*, pp. 143-145.

Italian: *Un'eroina*: Nigra 13; Vidossi, no. 4. Cf. Bronzini, I, 42, n. 38.

English: *Lady Isabel and the Elf-Knight*: Child 4; Bronson 4.

Anglo-American: Bronson 4; Coffin 4.

German-Dutch: *Der Mädchenmörder, Heer Halewijn, Ulinger*: DVM 41; Erk-Böhme 41-42, 195; Meier, *Balladen*, I, no. 17; Röhrich-Brednich 1.

Yiddish: Mlotek 215.

Scandinavian: *Kvindemorderen, Ulver og Vænelil, Den Falske Riddaren, Röfvaren Rymer*: Dal, no. 29; DgF, IV, no. 183; Olrik, II, no. 3; Smith-Dampier 253-255; Arwidsson, I, no. 44; Geijer-Afzelius, no. 66-67; FSF, no. 39; Warrens 128-132.

Lithuanian: *The Jewish Girl Enticed and Drowned*: Balys C18; Seemann 77.

Hungarian: *Anna Molnár*: Aigner, pp. 120-121; Járdányi, I, 102-103; Leader, pp. 107-125, 319, 321; Vargyas, "Rapports," pp. 85-88, 98; Id., *Researches*, pp. 129-157.[18]

Studies: EEB 84-85, 182, 260; Menéndez Pidal, *El Romancero Español*, p. 124; Puymaigre, "Notes," p. 272; RoH, I, 141, n. 117, 330; II, 316; TRV, II, 389-390. On *Rico Franco's* European analogs, see Entwistle "Second Thoughts Concerning *El Conde Olinos*," pp. 13-15; Taylor, "The Parallels between Ballads and Tales," pp. 105-106; for in-depth studies: I. Kemppinen, *The Ballad of Lady Isabel and the False Knight* (Helsinki, 1954); H. O. Nygard, *The Ballad*

---

[17] The Catalan ballad of *La Pepa* seems to have certain points of contact with *Rico Franco*, though the similarities may be coincidental. See AFC 816; Briz, I, 233; Canteloube, I, 213; Capmany, no. 43; Milá 277; OCPC, I, 131.

[18] Vargyas, *Researches*, pp. 129-134, includes massive additional bibliographical references to the various European linguistic groups, as well as to Slavic and Rumanian analogs which we have not yet seen.

of 'Heer Halewijn,' Its Forms and Variations in Western Europe: A Study of the History and Nature of a Ballad Tradition, FF Communications, no. 169 (Helsinki, 1958). Incredibly, Kemppinen confuses *Rico Franco* with numerous quite unrelated Hispanic ballads: *Isabel de Liar* (Milá 253), *Don Bueso y su hermana* (Durán, I, lxv-lxvi; Milá 250, etc.), *La venganza de honor* (CVR 38-41), *La hija de la viudina* (CVR 42), as well as various other folk poems (cf. Kemppinen, pp. 78-83, 177-178). Nygard's analysis does not extend to *Rico Franco.*

19

EL TRISTE AMADOR

(The Forlorn Lover)

'En akel verğel pekenyyo,   pekenyyo de gran valí'a,
ande ayy rozas 'i flores,   alḥavaka 'i grave'ínas,
ande krese la naranğa   'i 'el limón 'i la sidra,
ande ayy ruda menuda,   ke 'es guadri'a de paridas,
ande kanta la le'ona   'i 'el le'ón ke respondí'a,
a'í 'está 'el triste amadore,   'el ke de amores morí'a.
Yya se parte 'el amadore,   yya se parte 'i se 'í'a.
Topó las pu'ertas seradas,   ventanas ke no se avrían.
Kon palavras de 'enkantamyento   de par 'en par se avrían.
Topó ala ninyya durmyendo,   kon konğás 'i grave'ínas.
—Vate, vate, 'el amadore,   vate, vate kon tu vida.
Si de akí 'eğo 'un grito,   yya trago 'a toda Seví'a.
Ke mi padre 'i mis 'ermanos   dezpozada me tenían
kon akel duke de Fransyya,   ke no ayy 'otro 'en la ví'a.
Yya se parte 'el amadore,   yya se parte 'i se 'í'a.
De los sus 'ožos yyorava   'i de la su boka dezí'a:
—¡Malanyyo 'a akel 'ombre   'el ke de mužeres se fí'a!
Falsas son 'i mentirozas   'i kriadas ala malisyya.

Source: GRA 4.

2 *repeated*; *preceded by* 'i.

3*b* se torna.

Translation:

In yonder little garden, little but of great worth, where there are roses and flowers, sweet basil and carnations, where the orange grows, the lemon and the citron, where there is fine rue, guardian of mothers who have just given birth, (5) where the lioness sings and the lion answers, there stands the sad Lover, who was dying of love. Now the Lover departs, he departs and is gone. He found the doors locked and windows that would not open. With words of enchantment they were opened wide. (10) He found the maiden sleeping among roses and carnations: "Away, away, Lover, be off while you have the chance! If I cry out, all Seville will answer my call; for my father and my brothers have pledged my troth to that Duke of France, without equal in all the town." (15) Now the Lover departs, he departs and is gone. His eyes were weeping and from his mouth he spoke these words: "Accursed be the man who puts his trust in women. (18) They are false and deceitful and nurtured in cunning."

Motifs:

4 D965.16. *Magic rue.* Cf. D1385.2.2. *Rue, when burned, keeps evil spirits at a distance.*

5 B214.1.5. *Singing lion.*

9 D2088. *Locks opened by magic.*

Discussion of this extraordinary poem must begin with a *romance* of very different tenor: the Pan-Hispanic ballad of *El forzador* (*The Ravisher*). Though it seems to have once known a relatively wide diffusion among the Eastern Sephardim, *El forzador* is not easily come by in the modern tradition. Published texts represent the communities of Salonika (Attias, Benardete, Molho, Uziel, Yoná), Sérrai (DRH 3*b*), Rhodes (DRH 3*a*), and Jerusalem (?)(SICh). Our unedited collection includes but a single fragment from Salonika and another more complete version from Jerusalem (collected by Israel J. Katz). The ballad is somewhat more frequently encountered in Morocco, whence texts have been published from Oran-Tetuán, Tetuán, Tangier, and Alcazarquivir. Our unedited versions include five from Tetuán and one from Tangier.

The Eastern Sephardic *Forzador*'s connections with other branches of Hispanic tradition, though indisputable, are somewhat less than transparent. Versions published to date seem to indicate that on the Peninsula the *Forzador*'s counterparts have taken refuge in two fringe areas, where somewhat divergent subtypes have evolved. Such are the Asturian *Hija de la Viudina* (CVR-Munthe) and an apparently more modern Leonese-Extremeño-Portuguese *Soldados forzadores* (Kundert-RPE-VRP), the latter being more closely linked to the ballad's North African form. All the same, the cleavage between the Peninsular *romance*'s two geographic varieties is probably more apparent than real. Menéndez Pidal mentions unedited versions from Castile (Riaza, Malpartida, Santander) which will doubtless help to establish a continuum between the geographic subtypes. The ballad's various conformations —*El forzador, La hija de la Viudina,* and *Los soldados forzadores*— are compared in detail in DRH (pp. 37-47).

Except for a number of minutiae, the poem printed by Yoná is identical with Molho's text (LSO 89). This Yoná-Molho variant stands apart from all other versions of *El forzador*. It has been radically shortened and profoundly but artfully modified; its initial verses are quite extraneous to the rest of the narrative. Yet it is precisely because of these developments that the Yoná-Molho version has achieved an original and esthetically pleasing transformation of the *Forzador* ballad. Yoná's version which, under the guise of Molho's essentially identical publication, can be said to have been included in our DRH analysis (pp. 37-38), comprises only six of the 20 narrative stages which characterize the Eastern Sephardic *Forzador*. All belong to the latter part of the ballad: (11) The Lover finds his beloved's doors and windows locked (v. 8); (12) he opens them by means of magic words (v. 9) (14) and discovers the maiden sleeping "among roses and carnations" (v. 10). (17) She threatens to cry out for help (vv. 11-12), (18) claiming that she is betrothed to the powerful Duke of France (13-14). (19) The Lover then flees, lamenting the fickle nature of women (15-18). The Yoná-Molho text replaces the entire first part of *El forzador* with a long lyrical introduction (vv. 1-6) taken from the rare ballad of *El enamorado y la Muerte* (Attias 42) though, in fact, only v. 6 can be said to be uniquely characteristic of this ballad, since vv. 1-5 constitute a stock prolog which, with a number of variations, occurs in many other Eastern Judeo-Spanish *romances*: that is, *El falso hortelano, La choza del desesperado, El encuentro del padre, La muerte del duque de Gandía, La tormenta calmada,* and *La fuerza de la sangre.*[1]

The juxtaposition of this lyrical description of a garden and the material derived from *El forzador* was doubtless suggested by the latter's initial verse which in most Eastern versions is also concerned with flowers: "En mis huertas crecen flores, / en mis saksís gravellinas" (Attias). The locked doors and windows of v. 8, found in most texts of *El forzador,* occur also in some Eastern versions of *La muerte del duque de Gandía* (MP 14),[2] which is likewise in *í-a* assonance, but their inappropriateness to the latter narrative suggests a borrowing from *El forzador,* rather than any extensive use as a formulaic element. The incantation by which the Lover opens the doors and gains entrance to the maiden's abode occurs also in Attias, Benardete, DRH 3*b,* and SICh. It is a genial innovation, paralleled in the ballad of *Melisenda insomne* (*Primav.* 198).[3] It was probably calculated to attenuate the violence of the forced entry which survives in Sephardic versions from Rhodes (DRH 3*a*) and Morocco and is characteristic of a majority of the Peninsular variants:

Dyó 'el punyo 'en la pu'erta, la pu'erta se avrirí'a. . . .
(DRH 3*a*)

Sin aguardar más razón, la puerta en el suelo tiran. . . .
(Kundert, p. 99; Munthe 8)

Deitaram a porta a dentro, em procura da menina. . . .
(VRP 477)

---

[1] See the commentary to *El falso hortelano,* no. 21 *infra.*

[2] "Vide puertas ceradas; / ventana que no se abría" (Sánchez Moguel, "Un romance español," p. 500); "Topí yo puertas seradas / i ventanas ke non s(e) 'avrían" (SBS 42.17-18).

[3] "Las puertas halló cerradas, / no sabe por do entrar: // con arte de encantamento / las abrió de par en par" (*Primav.* 198). See DRH, p. 43. The fourth hemistich, which is an assonantal variant of Yoná's v. 9*b,* occurs also in one of the Gaiferos ballads ("Media noche era por filo," *Primav.* 174): "las puertas que están cerradas / abriólas de par en par," in *Mora moraima* (*Primav.* 132): "fuérame para la puerta / y abríla de par en par," as well as in everyday speech.

Con el puñal que ha traído, la puerta desquisiaría. ...
(Bénichou 38.39-40) [4]

In most Eastern versions of the *Forzador,* the protagonist's approach to the girl, once he has entered the house, is direct and daring in the extreme. Attias, Uziel, Molho (p. 72), DRH 3*a-b,* and Benardete all record a verse such as: "Metió la mano en su pecho / por ver si se konsentía" (DRH 3*b,* v. 11 = stage 15 of our analysis, p. 38). Only the Jerusalem version from S. I. Cherezlí's MS softens the verse: "Kon palavras de amores / la ninyya se despertaría" (SICh 2.17). In the Yoná-Molho version, this stage of the narrative, which is altogether out of tone with the new direction taken by the poem as a whole, has simply been omitted.

Among the Eastern Sephardim, *El forzador* can have two radically divergent dénouements. In one the Lover threatens the girl with his sword (Attias, vv. 45 ff; DRH 3*b*; LSO, p. 72) and she consents to accompany him (Attias, vv. 49-50). [5] This outcome is doubtless a weakened survival of the ballad's "authentic" traditional ending, where in all probability the girl was forcibly carried off, as in the Moroccan and Peninsular texts and in our unedited version from Jerusalem. In Attias (vv. 35 f.), Uziel, DRH 3*a*, and Yoná-Molho, the ballad ends on a completely different note. Here the frustrated, rejected Lover simply abandons his purpose and tearfully withdraws, voicing bitter imprecations against womankind. The addition of these misogynistic observations to *El forzador* is certainly the work of some Sephardic balladeer, though the verses themselves are widely known *Wanderstrophen,* deeply rooted in Pan-Hispanic oral tradition. [6] Together with other innovative

[4] Cf. stage 12 of our analyses in DRH, pp. 38, 40, 41, 42-43.

[5] See DRH, pp. 37, 46-47. Cf. R18. *Abduction by rejected suitor.*

[6] A number of variations on the same formula occur in the Portuguese hybrid ballad of *El caballero burlado* + *Don Bueso y su hermana*:

Arrenego eu de mulheres mais de quem n'ellas se fia!
(Almeida, II, 38)

Mal o hajam as mulheres, mais de quem n'ellas se fia!
(Braga, I, 231)

Mais tolo é o menino que de meninas se fia!
(Braga, I, 261)

elements present in the Yoná-Molho text they help to bring about a radical alteration in the tone and direction of the entire narrative.

Compare also Braga, I, 233; VRP 204, 220-223. Similar formulas are sometimes applied to mothers or to mothers-in-law:

Malditas sean las suegras y quien en ellas se fía.
(*Muerte ocultada*: RPC 81)

Desgraçados são os homens que em suas mães se fiam.
(*Mala suegra*: Braga, I, 572)

Mal haja quem se cofia em palavras de su madre.
(*Mala suegra*: Braga, I, 570)

Alonso López' sixteenth-century *Glosa peregrina* provides an early instance: "Mal houiesse el cauallero / que de las mugeres fía" (*Pliegos góticos*, II, 283*b*). Identical misogynistic sentiments, variously expressed, occur in numerous ballads from Morocco, from all the major branches of the Peninsular tradition, and from Spanish America:

Malhaya y a las mujeres que tienen tanta razón.
(*Sancho y Urraca*: Larrea 4-5)

Malditos sean los hombres que de mujeres se creen.
(*Mala suegra*: RPC 42, 40)

... que ningún casado haya confianza en mujer.
(*Adúltera* [*ó*]: Bertini, p. 14)

Perde quem tem seus amores quando em donzellas se fia.
(*Dom Aleixo*: Braga, I, 171, 165)

L'homo qui de dones fia de mort no pot defallir.
(*Bernal Francés*: Aguiló 243, vv. 151 f.)

Fadrins que veniu al mon no's fieu de las donzellas.
(*Tristeza* and *Desengaño*: Milá 368, 370)

Other and more specific negative judgments of womanhood also abound in the *Romancero*:

que firmeza de mujeres no puede mucho durar.
(*Pésame de vos, el conde*: *Primav.*, p. 442, n.)

que el seso de las mujeres no era cosa natural.
(*Quejas de Jimena*: FN 123)

¿No sabes que las mujeres son como el aire que vuela,
delicadas como el vidrio, que sin tocarle se quiebra?
(*Vuelta del marido* [*é-a*]: RPM 110, 108-9, 112)

The initial evocation of the small garden, with its bounty of flowers and fruits, its beneficent herbs [7] and unreal singing animals, and the figure of the love-sick *Amadore*, all borrowed from *El enamorado y la*

Malditas sean lah mujereh   que todito se lo cuentan.
(*Blancaflor y Filomena*: CPE, II, 30)

Malhaya sean las mujeres   que a dos hombres les dan cara.
(*Los dos rivales*: RPC 92)

que no hay mujer en el mundo   que tenga el sezo cumplido.
(*Gerineldo*: Bénichou 4A)

The latter verse originates in the ballad *Sufrir callando* (MP 71; RTCN 116), whence it has also migrated to *La malcasada del pastor* (Larrea 100.27 f.).

Verses similar to those used in *El forzador* also occur in Eastern Sephardic versions of *Andarleto* (Pulido 399; Wiener 11) and *La vuelta del marido* (*á-a*) (Baruch 280; NSR 68, n. 31), but here it is masculine unfaithfulness which is decried:

Maldición en las mojeres   que en los hombres van (?) se creien.
Que los hombres son muy falsos,   si los altos, si los bajos.
(Pulido)

A mal vaygan las mužeris   ke en ombri si an kunfiadu.
(Wiener)

Un mal hay a las mujeres   que en los hombres se confían.
Falsos son y mentirosos   echados a la malicia.
(Baruch)

The same formula with minimal variations enjoys a certain currency in ballads and songs from the Peninsula and Spanish America:

¿Quién se fía de los hombres,   quién de los hombres fiar?
(*Boda estorbada*: RPM 82)

Malhaya quien se fía   de hombre ninguno.
(*Me vine sola*: Güéjar 34)

Malhayan sean las mujeres   que de los hombres se fían.
(*Mi tía tiene un peral*: CPM 156)

¡Qué tontas son las mujeres   que de los hombres se fían!
(Id.: RPM 340)

For more examples, see Menéndez Pidal, *et al.*, *Cómo vive un romance*, p. 235; RPM 83, 85, 88, 89, 96. For other occurrences of the two latter verses which, as in RPM 340, are sometimes appended to *Las hijas del merino*, see BTPE, II, 69; Sánchez Fraile, no. 144; DRH, p. 47, n. 43; Carré 87. Compare

Muerte, impose upon the narrative as a whole a melancholy, dreamlike quality, which contrasts completely with the importunate scheming of the rejected but stubborn and daring suitor (or suitors) of the other

---

also "Mal hubiese el caballero / que de escuderos se fía" (*Romancero general de 1600,* no. 79; Durán 1713), as well as the sixteenth-century song "De velar viene la niña":

—Mas maldita sea la hembra
que de los hombres se fía,
porque aquella es engañada
la que en palabras confía.
(Alonso-Blecua 75)

Yoná's v. 16, which introduces the Lover's final embittered comment, is also formulistic. Cf. *Cancionero general de 1511,* fol. cxxxviij*v* II: "lloraua de los sus ojos / de la su boca dezía" (from the ballad, "Triste estaua el cauallero"; also in Thomas, *Trece romances,* p. 25).

[7] References to rue—usually called "fine rue" (*ruda menuda*)—as a protector of infants and recently delivered women occur in a number of traditional Sephardic poems. In the *Complas de las flores,* where various plants and flowers dispute their respective qualities and worth, the rue boasts:

Saltó la ruda y dixo: "Grandes son las mis famas,
yo so roza de paridas, me meten en las sus camas,
y todo el ojo malo lo quemo con las mis plantas,
le guadro la su alma del que lleva a mí."
(LSO 181)

An unedited Rhodian birth song (*cantiga de parida*) from the MS of Yakov Hazán begins with a joyous invocation of the rue's beneficent power: "¡Saksís de ruda menuda! / ¡Ke biva 'esta kriatura!" ('Flower pots of fine rue! May this child prosper!'). An unedited version of *La doncella guerrera* (from Izmir) alludes to the aromatic rue's habitual use in reviving persons who have fainted:

Ni kon rudas, ni kon uezmos, él no se aretornó,
sino kon tres palavrikas de eya ke al oído le avló.

For other references to rue in Sephardic balladry, see Danon 4 (n. 4), 12, 34; Menéndez Pelayo 24, 38. Is the allusion to rue in MP 107 (*Una ramica de ruda*) related to the plant's use as an erotic charm in Argentina as documented by F. Coluccio, *Diccionario folklórico argentino,* 2d ed. (Buenos Aires, 1950), p. 331?

The rue's curative properties are well known to folk medicine. A. Danon summarizes the Eastern Judeo-Spanish beliefs in the rue's uses and properties: "*Rue.*—Préserve surtout du mauvais oeil, de la peste et de plusieurs autres maladies. Cette plante facilite aussi l'accouchement, guérit de l'épilepsie et sert comme antidote contre le venin du serpent" ("Les superstitions des juifs ottomans," *Actes de l'Onzième Congrès International des Orientalistes* [Paris, 1899], pp. 259-270: p. 267, no. 26. For a much more detailed discussion, see

Sephardic and Peninsular variants. At the same time, the flowers mentioned in the prolog—roses, sweet basil, carnations—anticipate the roses and carnations which surround the sleeping maiden in the second

---

the article with the same title in *Mélusine,* VIII [1896-1897], 265-281: pp. 277-278). In Jerusalem, rue was used by both Sephardim and Ashkenazim, but in the latter's local form of Yiddish the plant is referred to as *rúde,* obviously a loanword from Judeo-Spanish. M. Kosover quotes a text from Jerusalem illustrating the belief in rue's protective powers following childbirth: "My bed was ornamented with ... branches of 'ruda' so that an evil eye, God forfend, should not acquire power over the baby and the woman in confinement (Sephardim and Ashkenazim alike used this scenty plant against an evil eye)" (M. Kosover, "Ashkenazim and Sephardim in Palestine: A Study in Intercommunal Relations," *Homenaje a Millás-Vallicrosa,* I [Barcelona, 1954], 753-788: p. 782 and n. 69; also Id., *Arabic Elements in Palestinian Yiddish* (Jerusalem, 1966), pp. 290-291 [no. 456]). For an identical practice among Bosnian Sephardim, as well as other uses of rue, see L. Glück, "Skizzen aus der Volksmedicin und dem medicinischen Aberglauben in Bosnien und der Hercegovina," *Wissenschaftliche Mittheilungen aus Bosnien und der Hercegovina,* II (Vienna, 1894), 392-454: p. 447. Eastern Mediterranean Sephardim in the U.S., recalling folk cures still current during the early decades of the twentieth century, allude frequently to rue. In Izmir the plant had the following applications: "La ruda se uzava mucho por ainarah. Se ponían las mužeres matas de ruda, para ke uno vea la ruda, ke no la vea a eya; el ožo malo vaya a la ruda, ke se seke la ruda, ke no vaya a la mužer. La ruda la uzavan las mužeres kuando estavan kon iñervos. Komían ruda i las ayudava a regoldar. Uzavan un poko de rakí kon ruda, bevían rakí, maškavan la ruda i eso les traía los regoldos i el rakí las azía dormir i se sentían buenos." ('Rue was used a great deal against the evil eye. Women would pin on little bunches of rue, so people would look at the rue and not at them; thus, the evil eye would go to the rue and wither it, but not harm the woman. Rue was used by the women when they felt nervous. They would eat rue which helped them to belch. They used a little bit of arrack with rue. They drank arrack and chewed the rue and this made them sleep and they felt well.') Rhodian informants recall the following practices: "A los niños los vestían ruda, para ke, kuando va venir alguna señora para ver al bebi, ke no le tokara nazar. Es guardia de las kriaturas. I kuando sakan al niño a la kaye, le ponen un ramo de ruda i un enkolgaže kon piedras presiozas kolor azul, para ke no le echen nazar, ainará, o ožo malo. I la ǧente ke lo veyen, le ponen una dedala de saliva en la frente i le dizen ansí: '¡Pu, pu, mašalá! / ¡Guadrado de nazar! / Mi ožo ke no le aga mal.' " ('They made the children wear rue, so that, when some woman came to see the child, the evil eye would not touch him. Rue is the protector of children. When they take a child out into the street, they put a bunch of rue on him and an amulet of precious blue stones, so that people will not give him the evil eye. And the people who see him put a dab of saliva on his forehead with the tips of their fingers and say: 'Pu, pu, mašallá! / Safe from the evil eye! / May my eye do him no harm.') For still other uses of rue among Eastern Sephardic immigrants in the U.S., see M. M. Firestone, "Sephardic Folk-Curing in Seattle," *JAF,* 75 (1962), 301-310: p. 308.

part of the song and thus help to unite what were originally two independent and quite heterogeneous fragments. The tone set by the borrowed prolog is further maintained by the innovative features of the ballad's later stages. Contrary to tradition, the Lover does not force his way into the house but gains entrance instead by means of some magic power, generated perhaps by the overwhelming intensity of his hopeless love, which has come to define his very existence: " 'el triste

---

Quite similar beliefs are current on the Iberian Peninsula and in Spanish America. See J. A. Sánchez Pérez, *Supersticiones españolas* (Madrid, 1948), pp. 19, 261-262 ("En casa donde hay ruda, no se muere criatura"; many other beliefs are listed); Pereira, "Fafe," *RPF,* IV, 375; P. de Carvalho-Neto, *Diccionario del folklore ecuatoriano* (Quito, 1964), p. 370*a*; Coluccio, *Diccionario, loc. cit.* There are also numerous references to the rue's medicinal properties in early Spanish literature. See Lope de Vega, *La Dorotea,* ed. J. M. Blecua (Madrid, 1955), pp. 572-573, n. 6 (Act V, scene vii); Fernando de Rojas, *La Celestina,* 2 vols., ed. J. Cejador y Frauca ("Clásicos Castellanos," nos. 20 and 23, Madrid, 1951, 1949), I, 251 (Aucto VII). Other important and more specific references are recorded in S. Cirac Estopiñán, *Los procesos de hechicerías en la Inquisición de Castilla la Nueva: Tribunales de Toledo y Cuenca* (Madrid, 1942), pp. 89-90, 154, 186, 192. The medicinal qualities of rue are also mentioned in the Catalan song *Varios oficios* (Milá 490).

Sephardic and Pan-Hispanic beliefs in the virtues of rue, either as an amulet or as a medicine, correspond closely to those of other European peoples—especially to the plants's use as an amulet in Southern Italy. See S. Seligmann, *Der böse Blick und Verwandtes,* 2 vols. (Berlin, 1910), I, 285, 386, 388 (no. 10), 389, 396, 397, n. 122; II, 78, 80-83, 98, 100, 102; F. Th. Elworthy, *The Evil Eye* (New York, 1958), pp. 21, 344-349; E. Hoffmann-Krayer and H. Bächtold-Stäubli, *Handwörterbuch des deutschen Aberglaubens,* 10 vols. (Berlin-Leipzig, 1927-Berlin, 1942), VII, 542-548; X, s.v. *Raute*; O. A. Erich and R. Beitl, *Wörterbuch der deutschen Volkskunde,* 2d ed. (Stuttgart, 1955), s.v. *Raute*; H. Marzell, *Zauberpflanzen-Hexentränke: Brauchtum und Aberglaube* (Stuttgart, 1963), pp. 55-56; J. G. Frazer, *The Golden Bough,* 12 vols. (London, 1932-1935), I, 281; IX, 158; X, 213; W. Carew Hazlitt, *Faiths and Folklore of the British Isles,* 2 vols. (New York, 1965), s.v. *rue*; *The Frank C. Brown Collection of North Carolina Folklore,* Vols. VI-VII: *Popular Beliefs and Superstitions of North Carolina,* ed. W. D. Hand (Durham, N. C., 1961-1964), nos. 331, 426, 1441; *Standard Dictionary of Folklore, Mythology, and Legend,* ed. M. Leach, 2 vols. (New York, 1949-50), s.v. *rue.* Rue is likewise considered a protective herb among Moroccan Moslems (M. Ibn Azzuz Akím, *Diccionario de supersticiones y mitos marroquíes* [Madrid, 1958], p. 47). For more on rue in Moroccan folklore, see E. Westermark's monumental treatise *Ritual and Belief in Morocco,* 2 vols. (New Hyde Park, N.Y., 1968), II, 608 (s. v. *rue*). For the uses of rue in Iran, see B. A. Donaldson, *The Wild Rue: A Study of Muhammadan Magic and Folklore in Iran* (London, 1938), pp. 20-21, 22, 23, 26, 29-30, 51, 146, 201, 204. Cf. also A2611.7. *Origin of rue: from drops of Christ's blood* and Aarne-Thompson, Type 713A. **Garland* (*Wreath*) *of Rue.*

amadore." In accord with the poem's new direction, the Yoná-Molho version simply omits the Lover's crass importunity, usually seen in stage 15 of the narrative. Again, contrary to the ballad's original story, the Lover, once rejected, does not seek to impose his will by force but meekly withdraws, bitterly decrying the defects of womanhood. Each of these changes in the narrative's original conformation—the addition of the lyrical prolog, the entrance by enchantment, the omission of stage 15, and the Lover's resignation to rejection—enjoys a different distribution in the Eastern Judeo-Spanish tradition and each was undoubtedly realized at a different moment in the ballad's history. But all illustrate the consistent tendency of Sephardic singers to attenuate the more violent details of their Hispanic ballad heritage. In their present context all these innovations seem directed toward achieving the same poetic goal. The Yoná-Molho ballad thus offers an excellent illustration of collective authorship—the diachronic collaboration of an untold number of individual singers, each of whom, during the ballad's multisecular trajectory, has imposed his own creative criteria upon the inherited poem and each of whom, in some measure, has contributed with his individual esthetic choices and decisions to what the ballad was eventually to become. The combination of these decisions has changed what was once, to judge by the Moroccan and Peninsular versions, a horrendous tale of abduction, rape, mutilation, and murder, into a melancholy, but esthetically balanced lyrical evocation of hopeless, unrequited love, and ultimate disillusionment. The final result of this gradual collaborative process can perhaps best be described as a new poem, a distinct ballad type, which might well bear the title of *El triste amador.* [8]

BIBLIOGRAPHY

Eastern J.-Sp.: *El forzador*: Attias 52; Benardete 47; DRH 3*a*-*b*; LSO 71-72, 89; PTJ 97-97*a* (= DRH, Uziel); SICh 2; UR 9 (= CBU 338-339).

---

[8] Another distinctive feature of *El triste amador* is the allusion to the Duke of France (v. 14 = stage 18). To our knowledge there is no other mention of this figure in the Eastern Sephardic ballads. Concerning the widely used formulistic v. 7 ("Yya se parte 'el amadore," etc.), which, uniquely in the Yoná-Molho version, anticipates the identical v. 15, see no. 1, n. 1 *supra*.

Moroccan J.-Sp.: *Los soldados forzadores*: Bénichou 38; Larrea 144-145; MP 96; MRuiz 79; PTJ 96 (= Bénichou).

Castilian: *La hija de la Viudina*; *Los soldados forzadores*: ASW 228-230; CVR 42; Kundert, p. 99; Munthe 8; RPE 110; RTCN 85. See MP 96 for references to unedited Castilian and Extremeño versions.

Portuguese: *Los soldados forzadores*: Alves, pp. 579-580; Braga, I, 590-593, 594-596; Hardung, I, 116-117; Martins, II, 38-39; Michaëlis, "Estudos," pp. 205-206; Monteiro do Amaral, *RL*, XI, 99-100; Tavares, *RL*, IX, 277-278; VRP 464-477. See also DRH, pp. 40-41, n. 38. We have not been able to locate the version listed for Daniel Rodrigues—without further bibliographical information—in VRP, II, 42.

Catalan, Basque, French, Italian: The question of the ballad's possible analogs in Catalonia and on the Continent remains unclear. There are several Catalan songs concerning one or more knights, soldiers, or gallants who abduct a maiden from within her house (R10.1.1. *Maiden abducted by soldiers*), but the similarities between these ballads and *El forzador* and its other Hispanic relatives seem to be coincidental. Cf. *Isabel* (AFC 2468; Amades, I, 106-108; Avenç, II, 55-57; IV, 108-112; Briz, I, 111-112; Capmany 53; Milá 284; OCPC, III, 277-278), *La venjansa* (Briz, I, 227-228), *Pau Gibert* (Briz, III, 127-128), *La noia robada per soldats* (OCPC, II, 144), *Lo rapte del Empordà* (Bulbena, pp. 21-22) and *La donzella robada que es fingeix morta* (AFC 3031; OCPC, II, 292-293). The last two have Basque, French, and Italian relatives: *Arrosa xuriaren* (*Rosal blanco*: Azkue, *Literatura popular*, IV, 175-176; Lecuona, pp. 161-163), *La fille qui fait trois jours la morte pour son honneur garder* (Arbaud, I, 143-147; Canteloube, I, 43-44; Davenson 51; Puymaigre, *Pays Messin*, I, 131-136; II, 151-153; Rolland, III, 58-63; Barbeau-Sapir, pp. 40-44; Barbeau, *Jongleur*, pp. 22-26; Id., *Rossignol*, pp. 231-232), and *L'onore salvato* (Nigra 53). A girl abducted from her house by three "gentlemen" also appears in *Der Wirtin Töchterlein* (Meier, *Balladen*, II, no. 58). The Hungarian *Anna Biró* embodies the same *topos*. See Leader, pp. 284-287, 340-341; Vargyas, "Rapports," pp. 70-72; Id., *Researches*, pp. 12-14. In its initial stages, the Catalan *Tres cavallers* (Briz, V, 55-56), in *í-a* assonance, is distantly reminiscent of *Los soldados forzadores*, but the rest of the story is totally different: The girl is more than willing, unlocks the door for the gentlemen, and welcomes them in. Canteloube's tragic *Fill' dedans Paris* (III, 163), which tells of the girl's death after being abducted by three soldiers, agrees coincidentally with the Hispanic *Forzadores*.

Studies: BNE 222-223; J. Amador de los Ríos, *Historia crítica de la literatura española* (Madrid, 1865), VII, 443-444; Braga, III, 478-483; DRH, pp. 35-47; Michaëlis, "Estudos," pp. 205-206; TRV, II, 390-391.

20

SILVANA

(Silvana)

Se paseava Silvana por 'un koral ke tení'a,
vigu'ela de 'oro 'en su mano ¡'i tam byen ke la tanyí'a!
Mežor tanye 'i mežor dize, mežor romanso tení'a.
De a'í la 'oyyó su pađre, de altas tores de a'í ariva:
—¡Ké byen pareséś, Silvana, kon sayyos de seđa fina,
más ke la reyna tu mađre, ke de 'oro se vestí'a!
¿Si vos plazí'a, Silvana, de ser vos la mi amiga?
—Plazer me azéś, mi pađre, plazer 'i deskortezí'a.
Déśeme 'ir 'a los banyyos, 'a los banyyos de agu'a frí'a,
'a lavarme 'i 'a trensarme 'i 'a muđar 'una kamiza,
komo se 'iva la mađre kuando kon 'el rey dormí'a.
Yya se 'espartí'a Silvana, yya se 'espartí'a 'i se 'í'a.
De los sus 'ožos yyorava 'i de la su boka dezí'a:
—¡'Oyygaméš, 'el Dyyo del syelo, 'i 'atambyén la mađre mí'a!
De a'í la 'olyyó su mađre, de altas tores de a'í ariva.
—'Esta boz de akí syento de Silvana me paresí'a.
Se aparó por la ventana, 'a Silvana la verí'a:
—Suviréš akí, Silvana, suviréš akí ariva.

Source: RSA 1.

2*b* tambyén.
9*a* Deśe me.
11*b* + 'i kuando kon 'el rey folgava.
14*b* 'a tambyén.

Kontaréš vu'estros 'enožos,   la vu'estra mala 'enkonyí'a.
—¿Ké vos kontaré, mi mađre?   Vergu'ensa me paresí'a:
'un pađre ke a mí me 'a kriađo   de amores me akometí'a.
—Para todo ayy remeđyyo,   para la mu'erte non aví'a.
Mandalde vos 'a dezir   ke non asyenda kandelerí'a.

Translation:

Silvana was walking through her courtyard with a gilded guitar in her hand. How well she played it! How well she is playing and singing a ballad that she knew! From above her father heard her, from his towers on high: (5) "How beautiful you look, Silvana, in your dress of fine silk, even better than the Queen your mother, who wore garments of gold! Would it please you, Silvana, to be my mistress?" "You flatter me, my father, with flattery and discourtesy. Let me go to the baths, to the baths of cold water, (10) to bathe and braid my hair and to change my chemise, as my mother would do when she slept with the King." Now Silvana departed, now she departed and was gone. From her eyes she was weeping and she uttered these words: "Hear me, God in Heaven, and you also, my mother!" (15) From above her mother heard her, from her towers on high: "This voice I perceive from here seemed to be Silvana." She drew near to the window and saw Silvana. "Come up here, Silvana, come up here to me. You will tell me your troubles and your dreadful grief." (20) "What shall I tell you, mother? It seemed shameful to me: that a father who raised me should pursue me with love." "There is a remedy for everything, for death there is none. (23) Send word to him to say that no candles should be lit."

Motifs:

7 T410. *Incest*; T411. *Father-daughter incest*; T411.1. *Lecherous father. Unnatural father wants to marry his daughter.*
9 K1227.1. *Lover put off till girl bathes and dresses.*

The ballad of *Silvana* does not seem to be particularly popular in current Sephardic tradition. Published versions originate only in

Salonika (Attias; Benardete 29; Uziel [UYA]) and Bosnia (Baruch). Levy's text is unidentified. Our unpublished collection includes three versions from Salonika, two from Tekirdağ, and a single fragment from Rhodes. MS Heb. 8° 2946 of the Jewish National and University Library (Jerusalem) contains an extensive eighteenth-century Bosnian rendition. [1] In the Moroccan tradition the ballad is quite rare. Menéndez Pidal and Larrea record lone texts from Tangier and Tetuán. During our 1962-1963 field work we were unable to find a single version in the North African communities.

The ballad's central theme—incest—is given repeated and varied treatment in the *Romancero.* [2] Most ballads of incest, such as *Delgadina,* [3] *Tamar y Amnón,* [4] and *La incestuosa,* [5] end in tragedy. In *La romera perdonada* [6] and the *romancillo* of *Los peregrinitos de Roma,* [7] on the other hand, incest between cousins is tolerated. In the *romance* of *Silvana* disaster is circumvented by means of feminine sagacity. Yoná's version is truncated. In more complete texts the father's incestuous designs are frustrated when mother and daughter put into practice the well-known artifice of the substitute bed-partner. [8] The

---

[1] See our "Christian Elements," pp. 30 (sec. 4), 32.

[2] On incestuous ballads in Hispanic tradition, see M. R. Lida de Malkiel, "El romance de la misa de amor," p. 32; also Câmara Cascudo, *Vaqueiros e cantadores,* pp. 187-189, 269, and Rodrigues de Carvalho, *Cancioneiro do Norte,* pp. 53-56, on the Brazilian ballad *O pai que queria casar com a filha.* Cf. such British ballads as *Sheath and Knife, The Bonny Hind, Lizie Wan, The King's Dochter Lady Jean,* and *Brown Robyn's Confession* (Child 16, 50-52, 57). For the theme's infinite ramifications in traditional narrative, see O. Rank, *Das Inzest-Motiv in Dichtung und Sage* (Leipzig-Vienna, 1926), especially pp. 312 ff.

[3] MP 99; Attias 45; Bénichou 43. For abundant additional bibliography, see the Spanish-American collections of Bertini, Section C; Espinosa, *Nuevo Méjico,* nos. 26-36; Romero, *Perú,* pp. 79-80; and nos. 55, 113, 191, 193, 254, 365, 367, 537, 717, 730, 791, 952, 1037, 1041(?), 1076, 1135, 1304, 1320, 1386, 1486, 1544, 1926-1927, 1934, 2045, 2053 of Simmons' *Bibliography.* Cf. also M. R. Lida de Malkiel, *El cuento popular hispano-americano,* p. 15.

[4] MP 37; Bénichou 68; Alvar, "Amnón y Tamar en el romancero marroquí"; Güéjar 2; VRP 515-516, 1014; Amades, I, no. 32.

[5] CVR 63; RPM 175-176; RQDB-II 42; RTCN 58.

[6] RPM 295-296; RTO 43.

[7] CPE, I, 23-24; II, 47; Echevarría, pp. 401-402; Ledesma, pp. 161-162; Pedrell, *Cancionero,* I, no. 32 (p. 28); Schindler 86. See also Córdova y Oña, IV, no. 262.

[8] In the late Castilian ballad of *La incestuosa* (see n. 5 *supra*), the substitute bed-partner motif leads to incest rather than preventing it. In the Moroccan and

King is persuaded to leave all candles in the palace unlit and the mother, dressed in Silvana's clothes, enters the King's chamber in her daughter's stead.[9] The ballad ends as follows:

—Por la muerte no hay remedio, por la vida mucho había.
Trocávos vuestros vis(i)tidos, los míos vos meteríais,
y dicilde a vuestro padre, que no acienda candelería,
al escuro a la entrada, al escuro a la salida.
A la fin de la media noche, las honras demandaría.
—Madre que parió a Silvana, ¿qué honras le quedaría?
—Beata a tala hija que de pecado me quitaría.

(Attias 41.39-52)[10]

Castilian *Capitán burlado*, a servant girl is substituted for the heroine to foil the importunate Captain (Bénichou 55; Larrea 176-177; MP 117; RPM 277). For other balladic examples of this commonplace, see Child, nos. 5 (*Gil Brenton*; also the commentary on pp. 66*b*-67*a* of Vol. I) and 268 (*The Twa Knights*; V, 21-25); P. G. Brewster and G. Tarsouli, "Two English Ballads and Their Greek Counterparts," *JAF*, 69 (1956), 41-46; Pernot, *Anthologie*, p. 89; Lüdeke-Megas, nos. 36-38 (*Mavrianos and His Sister*). For German and Scandinavian instances, see *Herr und Graserin* (Meier, *Balladen*, II, no. 65); *Stolt Elselille* (DgF, IV, no. 220A.45 ff.; Prior, III, 98-112 [vv. 43 ff.]); *Brud ikke Mø* (DgF, V, no. 274; Prior, III, pp. 347-352; also Child's commentary to his no. 5); *Terkel Trundesøn* (DgF, VIII, no. 480A.97 ff.; Prior, II, 447-468 [vv. 75 ff.]; Arwidsson, I, no. 36.87 ff.). Cf. also K1223.2.1. *Chaste woman sends man's own wife as substitute*; K1223.5. *King's daughter deceives king by substituting her maid*; K1843. *Wife deceives husband with substituted bedmate* and other examples under K1223-K1223.5, K1317 ff., K1843.1-K1844.3, K1911.1.5; Aarne-Thompson, Type 1441* *Old Woman Substitute*: *The master wants to come at night to a young girl. She substitutes an old woman*; M. de Riquer, "Les gestes catalanes," *Història de la literatura catalana*, I (Barcelona, 1964), 386.

As a ballad heroine, Silvana is not lacking in stratagems. Earlier in the story, her temporary disengagement from the King is accomplished by means of another traditional pretext: "Déšeme 'ir 'a los banyyos ..." (v. 9). This excuse is also used, but to no avail, in *Conde Claros y la infanta*, where the Princess tries to effect a postponement of her encounter with Claros:

Mas dejáme ir a los baños, a los baños a bañar;
cuando yo sea bañada, estoy a vuestro mandar.

(*Primav.* 190)

Cf. also such modern versions as Braga, I, 314; Aguiló, p. 309 (vv. 43-46); Macabich, p. 15. The same delaying tactics are employed in the Moroccan wedding ballad, *El hallazgo del esposo* (Larrea, *Canciones*, no. 4; Benarroch 87-88).

[9] Cf. K1317.5. *Woman substitutes for her daughter in the dark.*

[10] We alter the punctuation of vv. 49-50.

That Yoná would print such an obviously truncated version of *Silvana* suggests at least two possible explanations. The ballad might already have been such a rarity that a more complete text was simply not available to him. However, this was probably not the case, for Yoná himself used a verse—corresponding to the crucial hemistichs 49-50 of Attias' text—in a poem of his own composition included in GSA (p. 24): "Madre ke paryyó 'a Silvana / ¿ké 'onra le kedarí'a?" [11] On the other hand, the dénouement of the ballad may well have been considered such a commonplace that nothing more was needed to remind the listener (or reader) of the felicitous outcome than the verse "Mandalde vos 'a dezir / ke non asyenda kandelerí'a." In our field work with singers of both the Moroccan and Eastern traditions nothing was more common than to hear the rendition of a ballad that would end on a note of suspense, with a quality of seeming incompleteness for us. When we would question the informants about the dénouement, they would often provide the banal details of a happiness-forever-after ending in a singsong voice that almost mocked us for our need to have spelled out what to them was so completely obvious from the tenor of the ballad itself. Such an attitude on the part of the singers may help to explain one of the most attractive features of Hispanic ballad esthetics, that is, "saber callar a tiempo." [12]

BIBLIOGRAPHY

Eastern J.-Sp.: Attias 41; Baruch 286-287; Benardete 29; Levy 2; PTJ 98 (= Baruch); UYA 172 and 175. Yoná includes a verse from *Silvana* in an *ensalada* of his own composition appended to GSA. See n. 27 to our description of GSA.

Archaic J.-Sp. Incipit: "Paseábase Silvana": Aguilar-De Sola, p. 13, n. 12; ASW 438; Avenary 63 (pp. 384, 387, 390); Danon, p. 103, n. 4 (no. 3); Kayserling, p. xi; RoH, II, 220.

Moroccan J.-Sp.: Larrea 147; MP 98. See also Benoliel, "Hakitía," *BAE*, XIV (1927), 157 (no. 37), who lists the traditional imprecation: "¿Va a pasear? ¡Paseábase Silvana . . . !"

Castilian: CVR, p. 242, n.; Kundert 100 (H 31); RPC 26-28; RPM 162; RQDB-I 26; RTCN 59; RTO 25; Schindler 12.

---

[11] See n. 27 of our Introduction.

[12] Cf. Menéndez Pidal, "Romances y baladas," pp. 12-13.

Canarian: Espinosa, *Romancero canario,* pp. 31-33; RCan 18. We have not been able to consult A. Espinosa, "Sildana-Delgadina," *La Rosa de los Vientos,* 1927, no. 2 (see García Blanco, "El Romancero," p. 47).

Spanish American: Silvana contaminates some Spanish-American versions of *Delgadina.* See our remarks below concerning the Portuguese versions. The story is preserved in mixed verse and prose in Puerto Rico: Espinosa, "Romances de Puerto Rico," nos. 7-9; Mason, pp. 78-79.

Galician: Carré 80; La Iglesia, II, 114-115; Sampedro, 186.

Galician-Portuguese-Brazilian: In the Galician-Portuguese linguistic domain, *Silvana,* in various stages of preservation ranging from only the initial verses to practically the entire narrative, serves as prolog to two other ballads: *Delgadina* and *Conde Alarcos.* The obvious thematic affinity between *Silvana* and *Delgadina* easily explains the coalescence of these two songs. For examples of *Silvana* + *Delgadina,* see Almeida Garrett, II, 115-120; Athaide Oliveira, pp. 40-45; 324-327; Braga, I, 447-451; 455-468, 475-477, 480-483; Id., *Archipélago açoriano,* pp. 197-200; Fernandes Thomás, *Velhas canções,* pp. 12-15; Hardung, I, 128-134, 138-141; Michaëlis, "Estudos," pp. 234, 235; Nunes, *RL,* VI, 171-173; Serrano, pp. 39-41; Thomás Pires, "Entre-Douro-e-Minho," no. 2; VRP 482, 483, 486, 489, 491, 501-503, 506, 507, 513, 514; for Galicia: Carré 81; for Brazil: Boiteux, "Poranduba catarinense," pp. 23-24; cf. also Câmara Cascudo, *Historia,* pp. 225-228. Similar hybridization of the two ballads occurs independently in Castilian, Spanish American, and Canarian versions (cf. ASW 249, n. 1; Bertini, no. XVI [p. 36]; Fernández, "*Romances* from the Mexican Tradition," p. 38; RTA 22; NSR, p. 64, n. 16) and in at least one Eastern Sephardic text (Levy 2.13; cf. *NRFH,* XIV, 347, no. 2). In the Catalan tradition, the initial verses of Milá's no. 272 are also affected by *Delgadina.* In Portugal, the two ballads have become so intimately related that the combination *Delgadina* + *Silvana* + *Delgadina* can also be documented: Azevedo, pp. 112-115; Braga, I, 473-475; 477-480; Hardung, I, 134-138. For *Silvana* + *Conde Alarcos,* see Athaide Oliveira, pp. 60-64; Basto, *RL,* XVII, 55-56; Braga, I, 483-488, 496-499, 503-506, 513-524, 539-543, 551-556; Id., *Archipélago açoriano,* pp. 259-264; Dias, *RL,* XIV, 41-44; Furtado de Mendonça, *RL,* XIV, 6-9; Gomes Pereira, *Ilustração Trasmontana,* I, 176; Id., *RL,* XIII, 99; Kundert, p. 100 (G32); Martins, I, 209-211; Michaëlis, "Estudos," p. 234 and n. 2; Pereira, "Fafe," pp. 393-396; J. A. and F. C. Pires de Lima, *Romanceiro minhoto,* pp. 19-24; A. C. Pires de Lima, *RL,* XVII, 292-294; Id., *Estudos,* III, 483-489, and IV, 207-209; Pires de Lima-Lima Carneiro, *O Romanceiro para o povo e para as escolas,* pp. 69-72; Tavares, *RL,* IX, nos. 79, 100; Thomás Pires, "Entre-Douro-e-Minho," no. 3; Vasconcellos, "Bibliotheca do Povo," pp. 39-41 (this text is also affected by *Delgadina.*); VRP 130-182, 1001; for Galicia: Carré 71-73; Milá, "Poesía popular gallega," pp. 390-391; for Brazil: Pereira de Mello, *A música no Brasil,* pp. 118-122; Romero 6. Braga (I, 579-582) records a lone Azorian example in which the initial verses of *Silvana* introduce *La mala suegra.* For an uncontaminated Portuguese version of *Silvana,* see Martins, II, 37-38.

Catalan: Milá 272.

Archaic Documentation: Although no complete texts have come down to us, *Silvana* must have been well known in the archaic tradition. There is a sixteenth-century Eastern J.-Sp. *incipit* (see above). The initial verse, "Passeava-se Silvana / por hum corredor hum dia . . . ," also appears in a seventeenth-century Portuguese drama. See RVP, pp. 142-144; Menéndez Pidal, *El Romancero Español,* p. 109; RoH, I, 160; II, 408, n. 5; TRV, II, 395. The discussion in RVP confuses *Silvana* and *Delgadina.*

Studies: Braga, III, 453; RoH, I, 160; II, 220, 324, 344, 408, 435.

21

EL FALSO HORTELANO

(The False Gardener)

21A

—'Indome por 'estas mares,   navegí kon la fortuna.
Ka'í 'en tyeras aženas,   ande non me konosían,
ande non kantava gayyo,   ni menos pero ma'úlyya,
ande brame'a 'el le'ón   'i la le'ona arespondí'a;
¡aḥ! ande krese la naranğa   'i 'el limón 'i la sidra,
ande krese yerva sidrera   'i konğás 'i grave'ínas,
ande krese ruda menuda,   guadri'a de las kriaturas.
¡Aḥ! Yyulyyo, falso 'i tra'idor,   kavzante de los mis males,

---

Source: LRI 2. Variants: BRI 2, RHP 2, GRI 2.
BRI bears the following, highly gratuitous headnote, in parentheses: 'Esta romansa aremira 'el pasaže de los mansevos ke / 'estuvyeron 'en la gera. *GRI reads*: 'Esta romansa admira 'el pasaže delos mansevos ke 'es-/tán sirvyendo al servisyyo militar (*no parentheses*).

1*a* ¡Aḥ! 'Indome *RHP*, 'Indome *in boldface LRI*. Aḥ *in boldface precedes* 'Indome, *which, like the rest of the text, is in rashi letters BRI / GRI*.
2*a* Kalyí *RHP*.
3*b* pero ma'úlyyan (*sic*) *GRI*.
4*b* respondí'a *GRI*.
5, 8, 12, 16 Aḥ *in boldface LRI / BRI / GRI* (*GRI omits* Aḥ *in v. 5; puts* Ande *in boldface followed by an exclamation mark*).
6*a* krese la yerva *GRI*, sindeda (*sic*) *RHP*.
7*b* guadrias *GRI*.
8*b* kavzantes *GRI*.

'entrates 'en mi ğadir   'un dí'a de 'enverano.
Akožites la flor de mí;   la kožites 'a grano 'a grano,
kon tus avlas delikadas   'i me 'enganyyates.
¡Aḥ! ¿Damas, ké dirán de mí   las ke a mí me konosían?
Ke kon mí se konortavan   muğağikas.
Syendo 'iža de ken so,   me kazateś kon 'un vilano.
'Iža 'era de 'un gu'ertelano   'i de la mi gu'erta.
¡Aḥ! Yyulyyo, vamos de akí,   de 'este árvol sin flores.
Luvyya kayyga de los syelos   'i mos amože.

10*b* la akožites *GRI*.
11*b* 'a mí me 'enganyyates *RHP*, 'enganyyastes *BRI* / *GRI*.
14*a* kyen *RHP* / *GRI*.
14*b* kazates *BRI*, kon 'un fulano *GRI*.
15*a* 'Ižo *GRI*.

21B

—¡Aḥ! 'Indome por 'estas mares,   navegí kon la fortuna. (1)
¡Aḥ! Ka'í 'en tyeras aženas,   ande non me konosían,
ande non kantava galyyo,   ni menos pero ma'úlyya,
ande brame'a 'el le'ón   'i la le'ona arespondí'a,
ande krese la naranža   'i 'el limón 'i la sidra, (5)
ande krese yerva sidrera   'i konğás 'i grave'ínas,

Source: GRA 11.
13*a* demí.

Binyamin B. Yosef's *Sēfer rĕnānôə* ([Jerusalem], 5668 [= 1908]) (abbr. SR) contains, on p. 12, a text of *El falso hortelano* which agrees essentially with GRA's. In *'El bukyeto de romansas* (Istanbul, 5686 [= 1926], p. 24 [no. 16]) (abbr. BdR) B. Yosef seems to have copied the *Sēfer rĕnānôə*, though with several notable alterations. SR and BdR differ from GRA in the following details:

2*b*, 3*a* no *SR* / *BdR*.
3*b* ni menos amanesí'a *BdR*.
4*b* respondí'a *BdR*.
5*a* naranğa *BdR*.
5*b* si 'el limón si la sidra *SR*.

ande krese ruda menuda, guardyya delas kriaturas.
Yyulyyo, falso 'i tra'idor, kavzante delos mis ma̯les, (8)
'entrastes 'en mi ğadir 'i me 'enganyyastes. (x)
'Entrastes 'en mi ğadir 'un dí'a de 'enverano. (9)
Akozites la flor de mí; la kožites 'a grano 'a grano. (10)
Kon tu avlar delikado, me 'enganyyastes.
¿Damas, ké dirán de mí, las ke a mí me konosían?
Ke kon mí se konortavan muğağikitas.
Syendo 'iža de ken so, me kazateš kon 'un vilano.
'Ižo 'era de 'un gu'ertelano, de la mi gu'erta. (15)
Yyulyyo, vamos de akí, de 'este árvol sin flores.
Luvyya kayyga de los syelos 'i mos amože. (17)

9*a*, 10*a* 'entrates *BdR*.
9*b*, 12*b* 'enganyyates *BdR*.
11*a* akožites *SR* / *BdR*.
14*b* muğağikas *BdR*.
18*b* 'i lágrimas de mis 'ožos *BdR*.

Translation:

21A-B

Traveling upon these seas, I sailed before the storm. I was thrown upon foreign shores, where no one knew me, where no rooster crowed, nor even less a dog howls, where the lion roars and the lioness answered; (5) where the orange grows and the lemon and the citron, where citrus plants (?) grow and roses and carnations, where fine rue grows, which is guardian of small children. Oh, Julio, false and treacherous, author of all my woes, [*B* you entered my tent and you deceived me]! (10) You entered my tent on a summer's day. You plucked my flower; you plucked it petal by petal.[1] With your fine talk, you deceived me.

---

[1] For similar imagery, see Menéndez Pidal, *et al.*, *Cómo vive un romance*, pp. 17-18, 39, 171-172 (*Gerineldo*); Coirault, *Formation*, III, 389; Davenson, p. 353 (no. 56); Rolland, I, 197-205; IV, 72 (*En revenant des noces*); Rolland, II, 148-152 (*Les trois tambours*); Toelken, "An Oral Canon for the Child Ballads," pp. 93-97; Meier, *Balladen*, II, 13-16 (*Der Muskatenbaum*, no. 45).

Oh, what will they say of me, the ladies who knew me well? For many young maidens took comfort in me. (15) Though I was a daughter of high lineage, you married me to a peasant, son of a gardener and of my own garden. Oh, Julio, let us leave this place, this tree without flowers! (18) May rain fall from the heavens and drench us.

Motifs:

1 Cf. N781. *Hero embarks in rudderless boat*; R131.15. *Children abandoned in a boat survive storm*....

7 D965.16. *Magic rue*. Cf. D1385.2.2. *Rue, when burned, keeps evil spirits at a distance*. See no. 19, n. 7 *supra*.

9-16 Cf. K1816. *Disguise as menial*; K1816.1. *Gardener disguise*; K1323. *Man disguised as gardener enters convent and seduces nuns*. See nn. 4 and 6 *infra*. T91. *Unequals in love*.

14 T121. *Unequal marriage*; T121.3.1. *Princess marries lowly man*; L161. *Lowly hero marries princess*.

The False Gardener seems to have been well known among the Salonikan Sephardim, to judge by the number of published versions originating in that tradition: that is, Attias, Díaz-Plaja, Molho (LSO), San Sebastián, Yoná, Sciaky's translation, as well as two unedited texts and a fragment in our collection.[2] The song's traditional life seems to have been less vigorous in other communities. Danon's text, presumably from Edirne, and Levy's fragment (SBS 4, prefixed to *La tormenta calmada*), from Istanbul, bespeak a certain diffusion in Turkish tradition. Other than the Salonikan versions mentioned above, our fieldwork in the United States has produced only a very brief fragment from the Greek town of Sérrai (Šeres), whose tradition depends upon that of Salonika. The versions in *Bukyeto de romansas* and *Sẽfer rĕnānôθ*, though published in Istanbul and Jerusalem (?) respectively, agree essentially with GRA.

---

[2] Molho's text is so close to Yoná's versions that it seems to have been adapted from one of them. Except for various insignificant details, Díaz-Plaja agrees with the *Bukyeto de romansas*.

All of Yoná's texts are editorial arrangements of a single traditional rendition although, as in the case of other ballads, [3] some of these later emendations may reflect authentic traditional readings. Thus GRI's seemingly ridiculous variant of v. 14*b* "me kazateś kon 'un fulano" approximates Danon's important "me casaron con Juliano," which offers a more pristine form of the protagonist's name, in place of the usual "vilano." Verse 9 of text B, " 'entrastes 'en mi ǧadir / 'i me 'enganyyastes," which seems a mere anticipation of v. 12*b*, is authenticated by v. 7 of Danon's version. The reading " 'Ižo" (v. 15), as in GRI and GRA, corrects LRI-BRI-RHP " 'Iža."

The ballad's story is, on the face of it, somewhat less than transparent. The speaker has been seduced by false, treacherous Julio and is obliged, despite her noble lineage, to marry a peasant, the son of her gardener. As Menéndez Pidal suggests, the ballad's source is the sixteenth-century Portuguese playwright Gil Vicente's *Tragicomedia de Don Duardos,* where the English prince, Duardos, takes the pseudonym *Julián* and disguises himself as a lowly peasant, the son of a gardener, to test the affection of his beloved Princess Flérida. [4] The motives for Duardos' disguise are altogether noble: If Flérida's love for him is sincere, his high estate should be of no importance to her, since true worth is an essential attribute of the person and does not depend on rank:

FLÉRIDA. ¿No fuera mejor que fueras
a lo menos escudero?
DON DUARDOS. ¡Oh, señora!, ansí me quiero:
hombre de bajas maneras;
que el estado

[3] Cf. our commentary to *El conde Alemán* (no. 7), *La tormenta calmada* (no. 10), and *El robo de Elena* (no. 11).

[4] RoH, II, 216 and n. 27. The *Tragicomedia* is based, in its turn, upon the romance of chivalry of *Primaleón y Polendos.* See Menéndez Pelayo, *Orígenes de la novela,* 4 vols. (Madrid, 1961), I, 417-421; H. Thomas, *Las novelas de caballerías españolas y portuguesas* (Madrid, 1952), pp. 70-73. For the portion of *Primaleón* pertinent to Don Duardos' disguise as a gardener, see *Primaleón*: *Los tres libros del muy esforcado* (*sic*) *cauallero Primaleon et Polendos su hermano hijos del Emperador palmerin de Oliua* (Venice, 1534), fols. cxiv*v*-cxvii*r* (= Book II, Chaps. X and XI [Chap. XI is numbered "X" by mistake]). For other sixteenth-seventeenth-century Spanish instances of the gardener disguise, see Gil Vicente, *Tragicomedia de Don Duardos,* ed. D. Alonso (Madrid, 1942), p. 24. The gardener disguise also occurs in the French ballad of *L'enlèvement* (Puymaigre, *Pays Messin,* I, 80-81).

no es bienaventurado,
que el precio está en la persona.
... ...
Quien tiene amor verdadero
   no pregunta
ni por alto ni por bajo
ni igual ni mediano.
   Sepa, pues,
que el amor que aquí me trajo,
aunque yo fuese villano,
   él no lo es. [5]

Inevitably such subtleties are lost upon the traditional muse. In balladry, disguise—usually, and more logically, in girl's clothing—is a frequent adjunct to seduction. [6] Although it is no longer a factor in the Sephardic texts of *El falso hortelano,* Julián's disguise must have been present in the ballad at an earlier stage of its development. The traditional association of disguise and seduction doubtless underlies the ballads' profound transformation of Don Duardos' once nobly motivated deception. With the disappearance of the disguise motif, the ballad also lost all knowledge of Julio's true identity. At the end of the play, when Flérida departs for England to marry Duardos, she is fully aware

[5] *Tragicomedia de Don Duardos,* ed. D. Alonso, vv. 1040-1046, 1521-1528.

[6] Cf. *Disfrazado de mujer* (*í-a*; MP 116; Larrea 172-175); *La apuesta ganada* or *A tecedeira* (*á*; ART 199; RPC 14-15; RPM 278-281; RQDB-I 72; RTO 39; Carré 85; Braga, I, 356-357, 414-418; VRP 75-91, 987-993); the Catalan *Sileta* (AFC 3207; Amades, I, 48-50; Briz, III, 207-208; OCPC, III, 159-160). There are many parallels in Continental balladry: *Galant en nonne* and *Le Comte Ory* (Coirault, *Formation,* I, 167-169; II, 266-269; Davenson 79); *La falsa monaca* (Nigra 79; Bronzini, II, no. 8, especially p. 86, n. 36); *Brown Robin* and *The Holy Nunnery* (Child 97B.6-7; 303); *Der verkleidete Markgrafensohn* (DVM 6; Erk-Böhme 140; Meier, *Balladen,* I, no. 44; Röhrich-Brednich 16); *Hagbard og Signe* (DgF, I, no. 20 and p. 271; III, 796; Dal, no. 22; Olrik, I, no. 1; FSF, no. 31; Jonsson, no. 40; Prior, I, 205-240; Smith-Dampier, pp. 75-83); *Ho Chartsianês kaì hē Aretḗ* (Baud-Bovy, *Textes,* pp. 176, 180, 194-195; Legrand, *Recueil,* no. 138; Liebrecht, *Zur Volkskunde,* pp. 204-205; Lüdeke-Megas, nos. 105-106; Politis, *Eklogaì,* no. 74; Pernot, *Anthologie,* pp. 84-87), and *Márō kaì Giánēs* (Liebrecht, *Zur Volkskunde,* pp. 189-190; Passow, no. 478; Theros, no. 372). See also K1310. *Seduction by disguise ...* ; K1321. *Seduction by man disguising as woman*; K1321.1. *Man disguised as woman admitted to women's quarters*: *seduction*; K1349.1. *Disguise to enter girl's room*; K1836. *Disguise of man in woman's dress.* Disguise as pilgrim or beggar for purposes of seduction occurs in *Der Pilgrim* and *Der Bettler* (Meier, *Balladen,* I, no. 43; II, no. 81).

of his princely rank. The *romance,* on the other hand, evokes the traditional figure of the highborn lady who is seduced and then married to a lowly churl—"un vilano"—though he too may turn out to be a king's son after all. [7] The exotic *ğadir* (= [čadír]), from T. *çadır* 'tent,' which Yoná's versions (A, v. 9; B, vv. 9-10) share with Attias and an unedited fragment from Sérrai, is undoubtedly based upon an earlier *jardín,* still present in Danon's "te entrates en mis jardines" and Molho's "entrates en mi vergel" (LSO 72). In spite of such radical departures from its source, the ballad has faithfully preserved Don Duardos' pseudonym *Julián,* which comes down through tradition as *Julio* (= [žúljo] or [ğúljo]?; Attias 10.15; Díaz-Plaja; LSO), *Yyulyyo* (Yoná), *Julio* (with a velar spirant, as in Modern Castilian; uned., Salonika), *Ğuño* (uned., Salonika), *Juliano* (Attias 10.31; Danon 4.10), or even unchanged, as in Danon 4.6 and 12.

The ballad's final verses, perhaps its most cryptic feature, paradoxically embody the closest verbal coincidence with Gil Vicente's text. In the *Tragicomedia,* Flérida, impatient to know Julián's identity, tells her companion, Artada, that they must leave the garden, intimating that she will carry out an earlier threat [8] to have it destroyed by fire:

Vámonos de aquí, Artada,
de esta huerta sin consuelo
para nos,

[7] Compare the final verses of *Tiempo es el caballero* (*Primav.* 158), where the girl's seducer announces:

Hijo soy de un labrador y mi madre pan vendí.
La infanta desque esto oyera comenzóse a maldecir:
—¡Maldita sea la doncella que de tal hombre fue a parir!
—No vos maldigáis, señora, no vos queráis maldecir,
que hijo soy del rey de Francia, mi madre es doña Beatriz:
cien castillos tengo en Francia, señora, para os guarir,
cien doncellas me los guardan, señora, para os servir.

For British and Danish examples of the same motif, see Child, V, 500, s.v. *Unequal marriages,* and Prior, III, 147. Cf. *T123. *Supposedly unequal marriage (princess and supposed commoner)* (Bordman). *Gerineldo* (MP 101) usually ends with the protagonist's marriage to the *infanta,* though he is apparently not of noble birth.

[8] Referring to Flérida, Artada had stated earlier: "Llorando le oí decir / que ha de mandar quemar / luego la huerta" (ed. D. Alonso, vv. 1505-1507).

¡de fuego seas quemada,
y sea rayo del cielo:
plega a Dios! [9]

The closing verses of Yoná's texts have a regularized *ó-e* assonance ("... flores," "... amože") and seem to have little recognizable relationship to the above-cited passage. The *Bukyeto* and Molho's version (LSO) replace the irregular and rather pointless final hemistich with an octosyllabic verse which seeks to relate the protagonist's emotions to the tempestuousness of nature:

Yyulyyo, vamos de akí, de 'este árvol sin flores.
Luvyya kayyga delos syelos 'i lágrimas de mis 'ožos.

Other Sephardic texts have remained closer to their source:

Juliano, vamos d'aquí, d'este huerto sin provecho.
Luvia caiga de los cielos y mos amoje.
(Attias 10.31-34)

I vamos, Ǧuño, de akí, d'este guerto sin provecho.
Ke luvia kaiga de los sielos i mos amože.
(uned., Salonika)

With the inevitable replacement of the secondary character Artada by Juliano or Julio and the variant *provecho* for *consuelo,* the ballad's vv. 16-17 offer a recognizable evolution of vv. 1763-4 of the play, even maintaining the vowels of the original *-elo* rhyme, which is also faithfully preserved in *syelos* (v. 17*a*). Likewise the *ó-e* assonance of v. 17*b* seems to echo the *-ós* rhyme of the *Tragicomedia*'s vv. 1765 and 1768. The replacement of fire by rain is more difficult to justify. Perhaps the implications of the drama's vv. 1767-8, "... y sea rayo del cielo: / plega a Dios!," were too daring—even blasphemous—for traditional tastes, especially those of Sephardic Jewry. The transformation of the drama's destructive fire into a rather ambivalent rain seems to constitute yet

[9] Ed. D. Alonso, vv. 1763-1768. *Fuego* was often used figuratively to indicate great emotional distress, particularly in matters of love. See M. L. Radoff and W. C. Salley, "Notes on the *Burlador,*" *MLN,* XLV (1930), 239-244: pp. 239-240, and C. E. Anibal, "The Historical Elements of Lope de Vega's *Fuente Ovejuna,*" *PMLA,* XLIX (1934), 657-718: pp. 660-661, n. 14.

another example of the attenuation of violence so characteristic of the Judeo-Spanish *Romancero.* [10]

The ballad's peculiar, irregular metrical structure offers another possible analogy with its Vicentine source. Several of the song's second hemistichs are inordinately short, consisting of but six, five, or even four syllables: "('i) me 'enganyya(s)tes" (A, v. 11*b*; B, vv. 9*b*, 12*b*), "muğağikas" or the bizarre "muğağikitas" (A, v. 13*b*; B, v. 14*b*), "('i) de la mi gu'erta" (A, v. 15*b*; B, v. 16*b*), " 'i mos amože" (A, v. 17*b*; B, v. 18*b*). Gil Vicente's play is written in rather irregular *coplas de pie quebrado*: that is, two octosyllabic verses, followed by a single half-verse of four syllables. [11] Viewed as *pie quebrado* half-verses, the above-cited hemistichs suggest the possibility that our ballad may descend from a now lost narrative poem, based upon the Vicentine drama and, like it, written in *coplas de pie quebrado.* Such a hypothetical intermediary might help to explain some of the radical differences in tone and content between the drama and its balladic derivative. Parallel treatments of the Don Duardos theme, such as the Moroccan-Asturian-Portuguese *romance* of *Flérida* [12] and the Portuguese *Hortelão das flores* (in assonant couplets), [13] which are still current in oral tradition, add a measure of credence to the possible existence of such a *pie quebrado* poem. Like the *coplas pareadas* of *El conde Alemán y la reina* (no. 7 *supra*) and *El veneno de Moriana* or the *romancillo*

---

[10] Perhaps the rain motif, which appears often in Judeo-Spanish wedding songs, has had some influence here. Cf. Attias 105; Alonso-Blecua 500; Alvar, "Cantares de boda," p. 22*b*; id., "Paralelismo," pp. 138, 147 (nos. 3.6-7, 27.15); Larrea, *Canciones,* nos. 32-34.

[11] On the play's metrical irregularity, see D. Alonso's ed., pp. 15-16.

[12] MP 105; Larrea 157; MRuiz 37C.1-6, 66.8-18; PTJ 104 (= MP); RQDB-II 69; RTCN 9; Almeida Garrett, III, 145-147; Alves, p. 563; Bellermann, no. 24; Braga, *Archipélago açoriano,* nos. 56-57; Braga, I, 442-446 (as well as various contaminations in other ballads: e.g., pp. 428, 435, 438, 442, 495, 512, 519, 542; II, 136); Hardung, I, 12-15; Tavares, *RL,* VIII, 78-79; Vasconcellos, "Bibliotheca do Povo," no. 10; VRP 276-280, 1001 (p. 502); CSA, fol. 253*v*-254*v*; Durán 288. For studies on *Flérida,* see Michaëlis, "Estudos," p. 220 (no. 10); RVP, pp. 14, 115-134, 236, 272, n.; Menéndez Pidal, "Los *Estudos sobre o Romanceiro peninsular* de Doña Carolina," pp. 496-500; RoH, II, 216-217; TRV, II, 360; I. S. Révah, "Edition critique du *romance* de don Duardos et Flérida," *BHTP,* III (1952), 107-139.

[13] See Braga, I, 426-428, 432-442; Rodrigues de Azevedo, pp. 191-201; VRP 275. Most versions of the *Hortelão* couplets are followed by verses from the *romance* of *Flérida.*

of *Don Bueso y su hermana,* [14] the *pie quebrado* verse of our hypothetical poem would have gradually succumbed to the ascendant octosyllabic *romance* pattern, leaving in the Judeo-Spanish versions but a few vestiges of its original metric structure.

The initial verses of Yoná's text, which occur in similar form in all known versions of *El falso hortelano,* evoke the desolation of some uninhabited wilderness. They provide an ominous, strangely unreal setting for the maiden's complaint. Whether intentionally or not the tempestuous initial scene parallels the stormy invocation of the ballad's final verse. These predominantly *í-a* assonant lines exhibit little of the syllabic irregularity characteristic of vv. 8 ff. They are, in fact, quite unrelated to the Don Duardos story. The prolog to *El falso hortelano* embodies the following features: (1) The stormy sea voyage (SBS carries the variant "En prinsipios de los mis maliz / navigí," etc.); (2) the arrival in foreign lands (*tierras aženas* or *sevdades aženas,* as in SBS), where the protagonist is unknown, (3) where no roosters crow, (4*a*) or dogs howl. (4*b*) Danon, SBS, Sciaky, and an unedited Salonikan version read "ni menos canta gallina." (4*c*) *Bukyeto* and Díaz-Plaja replace the verse in question by "ni menos amanesí'a." (5) Where the lion roars and the lioness answers; (6) the presence of oranges, lemons, and citrons, (7*a*) of citrus plants (?) (*yerva sidrera*), roses (*konğás*), and carnations (*grave'ínas*); (7*b*) Attias: "rosas y flores, / alhabaca y gravellina"; and (8) of fine rue, protector of infants.

In a variety of combinations, the prolog's several components reappear in at least seven other Eastern Sephardic *romances.* [15] A lone version of *La choza del desesperado,* from Sofia, Bulgaria (Wiener 28), absorbs (1) the stormy sea voyage, (2) the arrival in foreign lands, and a telescoping of stages 3-5 in which the rooster's silence is reciprocated by the lioness:

> Andandu pur estas maris, navigí kun grandi fortuna.
> Kayí in tyeras aženas, andi no mi kunusían.
> Andi no kantava gayo, ni la leona arespondía. ...

---

[14] On *Moriana,* see Menéndez Pidal, *El Romancero Español,* pp. 125-128; FN 18-19. On *Bueso,* see FN 214; Menéndez Pidal, "Supervivencia del *Poema de Kudrun*" ("Austral"), pp. 103-104, 141; DRH, p. 63, n. 55. See also *La galana y su caballo* (no. 25 *infra*).

[15] Cf. our remarks in NSR, p. 68, n. 33; "A New Collection of Judeo-Spanish Ballads," nos. 3 and 22.

The rare, enigmatic *Encuentro del padre,* which seems to be known only in Bosnia, begins with essentially identical verses. Wiener's text (no. 12) knows only stages 1 and 2 ("Yo kaminí por altas maris, / navigí por las fortunas. // Kayí mi en sivdat ažena, / ondi non mi kunosían..."), but an eighteenth-century MS version and another, printed in the newspaper *Jevrejski Glas* (*ca.* 1939), include other typical features: (3-4*b*) the absence of roosters and chickens and (5) the roaring lion (or wolf) and answering lioness, as well as a unique reference to cold and freezing water:

Kaminí por altas tores, navigí por las fortunas.
Kají en tjeras aženas, onde no me konosijan,
onde no kantavan gajos, ni menos kantan gajinas.
Ají el león abramava, la leona respondía. ...
(*Jevrejski Glas*)

Kaminand[o] por altaš mareš, navegí kon 'una fortuna.
Kayí 'en tyeraš aženaš, 'onde non me konosíyan,
'onde non kantava gayyo, ni menoš kanta gayina,
'onde 'el lovo brameava 'i la le'ona respondiy'a,
'onde no ayy aguaš friyaš ni menoš aguaš yeladaš. ... [16]

On the Island of Rhodes the migratory prolog has been joined to the ballad of *La muerte del duque de Gandía* (= MP 14). Levy's anomalous fragment (SBS 5) joins stages 1 and 2 to a single verse of that ballad and then continues with material belonging to *La tormenta calmada.* An unedited Rhodian version of *El duque de Gandía* includes also the allusion to rooster and dog:

Un día de los días, navegando en mi fortuna,
kaí en sivdades aženas, ande a mí no me konesían.
Ni gayo kanta, ni perro maúya. ...

The use of such verses in connection with *El duque de Gandía* is quite exceptional. Much more characteristic is their occurrence as a prolog to Rhodian renditions of *La tormenta calmada,* such as Galante's no. 6 and three unedited versions in our collection, where the absence of cock-crowing suggests, as in the *Bukyeto* (see variants to text 21B,

[16] Jewish National and University Library MS Heb. 8° 2946, fol. 20*r*.

v. 3*b*) and Díaz-Plaja texts of *El falso hortelano,* a strange, benighted land in which dawn never comes. Like Levy's Istanbul text of *El falso hortelano* (SBS 4), which is joined to *La tormenta calmada,* most of these Rhodian versions of the latter ballad prefer the formula *En principio de mis males*... to the usual participial clause, though one of our unedited texts begins: "Naviegando en las mares...":

De principio de mis males, naviguí con la fortuna:
Cayí en civdades ajenas, onde dinguno me conocía,
ni onde gallo canta, ni menos amanesía. ...
(Galante 6)

¡I galeas, las mis galeas, i las ke en la mar galean!
Yo en principio de mis males i navegí en la fortuna.
Kaí en sivdates aženas i onde no las konosía.
Ni sé kuando anochesía i ni menos amanesía.
Ni onde gayo kanta, ni menos pero mauyava. ...
(uned., Rhodes)[17]

The unique version of *El enamorado y la Muerte* (Attias 42) shares certain botanical references (7*b*: "rosas"; "alhabaca") and (8) the child-protecting rue with the prolog of *El falso hortelano.* The additional allusion to *menta romana* 'spearmint' as a protector of recently delivered women appears only in *El enamorado y la Muerte*:

Ande hay conjás y rosas, alhabaca y gravellinas;
onde hay menta romana, guardia para las paridas;
onde hay ruda minuda, guardia de las criaturas;
y en aquel vergel chiquito, chiquito, que gran valía,
ahí estaba Testadore, que por amor se muría. ...

The Yoná-Molho version of *El triste amador* (no. 19 *supra*), which borrows its introductory verses from *El enamorado y la Muerte,* is more

---

[17] The first verse, which also occurs in Attias' version of *La vuelta del hijo maldecido* (no. 24.35-36: "¡Gáleas, las mis gáleas, / galeando por la mar!" [accentuation *sic*]), recalls the mariner's song in *El conde Arnaldos*: "Galera, la mi galera, / Dios te me guarde de mal, // de los peligros del mundo, / de fortunas de la mar" (Menéndez Pidal, "Poesía popular y poesía tradicional," *Los romances de América,* p. 65; cf. MP 143; Bénichou 29). The narrator's inability to distinguish night from day suggests the plight of *El prisionero*: "ni sé cuando es de día, / ni menos cuando es de noche" (Attias 8.11-12; FN 194).

elaborate than Attias' unique text of the latter ballad and includes (5) a *singing* lion and answering lioness, (6) the orange, lemon, and citron, as well as (7*b*) roses, flowers, sweet basil and carnations, and (8) the beneficent rue which, in this case, protects women in childbirth. Finally, (3-4*b*) rooster and hen, (5) lion and lioness, have entered the enigmatic ballad of *La fuerza de la sangre,* which, as a prolog to Bosnian and Salonikan versions of *El caballero burlado,* develops a typical heroic exposure myth, in which the protagonist is nurtured in the forest by a lioness:

Pariérame la mi madre   en una oscura montiña,
onde no cantava gallo,   ni menos canta gallina,
onde bramavan leones,   la leona respondía,
siete años me dio de leche   de una leona parida,
siete años me dio de pane   del pane que él comía. ... [18]

A strange, anomalous fragment collected by Romey (no. 8), which seems in part to be related to *La fuerza de la sangre,* alludes to (3) roosters, (4*c*) the absence of dawn, and (2) the arrival on foreign shores:

¿Ande me parierex, madre?   ¿Ande me parierex, madre?
Ande gallos no cantavan,   ni menos amanecían (*sic*).
Cayí en tierras ajenas,   ande no me conocían.
A los ajenos haze parientes   y no te hagas aborecer. [19]

An anisosyllabic funeral dirge, replete with traditional elements, printed in the booklet *'Endeğas de θiš^{c}āh bĕ-'Āb* ([Izmir], n.d.) begins with verses embodying stages 1 and 2:

De prinsipyyo de sus males,   navegó por la fortuna.
Deśó 'el Dyyo de su ventura   ke kayeron 'en despovlados.
Se les rompyeron las velas   'en 'el golfo dela mar. ...
('*Endeğas,* p. 7)

---

[18] We cite the synthetic Judeo-Spanish text published by D. Catalán, in "A caza de romances raros," p. 451. Cf. Attias 17; Wiener 7. The Portuguese versions studied by Catalán (pp. 452-454) elucidate the Sephardic fragment: "él" in the fifth verse refers to a hermit who shelters the exposed infant. Cf. S. Thompson's cross-references under B535. *Animal nurse*; R131.10. *Hermit rescues abandoned child.*

[19] The final verse, suggested by the word *ajenas* in v. 3*a*, is from the wedding song, "Dicho me habían dicho." See Elnecavé 9; Danon 12; Menéndez Pelayo 24; Molho, *Usos,* p. 44; Wiener 1; and other variants listed under Attias 64.

The following table details the relative diffusion of the prolog's various components in the Eastern Sephardic tradition:

TABLE 3

Diffusion of the migratory prolog's components in the Eastern Sephardic tradition

	Falso hortelano	Choza del desesperado	Encuentro del padre	Duque de Gandía	Tormenta calmada	Enamorado y la Muerte	Triste amador	Fuerza de la sangre	¿Ande me parierex?	Endecha
1) Stormy sea voyage	X	X	X	X	X					X
2) Arrival in foreign lands	X	X	X	X	X				X	X
3) No cocks crow	X	X	X	X	X			X	X	
4*a*) nor dogs howl	X			X	X					
4*b*) nor chickens crow	X		X	X				X		
4*c*) nor does it dawn	X				X				X	
5) Lion and lioness	X	X	X				X	X		
6) Orange-lemon-citron	X						X			
7*a*) *Yerva sidrera-konğás-graveínas*	X									
7*b*) *Rosas y flores-alhavaca-graveínas*	X					X	X			
8) Child-protecting (or mother-protecting) rue	X					X	(X)			

El triste amador certainly borrows its introduction from *El enamorado y la Muerte.* The apparent preference of *La tormenta calmada* for the formula "En principio de mis males . . ." may have occasioned the same formula's use in Levy's version of *El falso hortelano* (SBS 4) which, in fact, is joined to *La tormenta.* The very infrequent occurrence of the prolog in connection with *La muerte del duque de Gandía* in the Rhodes tradition might indicate a contamination from *La tormenta calmada,* where the prolog also occurs sporadically but with somewhat greater frequency. However, such relatively transparent borrowings are exceptional. In most instances it is impossible to establish any order of dependence among the above-cited ballads as far as the material in question is concerned. The prolog might best be characterized as a cluster of *Wanderstrophen,* a migrant formulaic complex, which has attached itself to a number of very different ballad narratives as a convenient suspense-creating introduction. In its present rather elaborate form, the prolog is probably largely the work of Eastern ballad singers, for several of its components, especially those referring to plants, have to our knowledge no parallels in other branches of the tradition. Other features of the prolog are well known to the Pan-Hispanic *Romancero.* The initial participial pattern occurs very frequently in ballad *incipits*: "Durmiendo está Parisi" (MP 42), "Saliéndome a pasear" (RPE 29), "Dormiendo está el conde Claros" (ASW 73), "Caminando va la Virgen" (ASW 260), "Estándose doña Arbola" (ASW 221), "Yo me estando en Giromena" (*Primav.* 104), etc.[20] The Moroccan Sephardic *Mal encanto* (Bénichou 30; MP 108 *bis*) uses the combination "rozas y flores / claveyinas y alḥabacas," as in stage 7*b* of Attias' version of *El falso hortelano, El enamorado y la Muerte,* and *El triste amador.* The dark forest (as in *La fuerza de la sangre + El caballero burlado*), singing lions (cf. stage 5 of *El triste amador* and other ballads) and chill waters (as in the eighteenth-century Bosnian *Encuentro del padre*) occur in Moroccan versions of *La infantina*:

> ¿Ánde le cogió la noche? Y en una oscura montiña,
> ande canta la leona y el león la respondía,
> ande cae el añebe a copo, y corría el ahua fría.
> (*La infantina*: Bénichou 1B)[21]

Similar elements are present in various Peninsular ballads, except that here serpents take the place of the lions:

---

[20] For more examples, see Michaëlis, "Estudos," p. 212 (no. 1).

[21] Essentially identical readings in Alvar, *Textos dialectales,* II, 765; Larrea 167-168; MP 114; Ortega 235. Cf. B214.1.5. *Singing lion.*

Allá arriba en aquel monte, allá en aquella montiña,
do cae la nieve a copos y el agua muy menudina;
donde canta la culebra, responde la serpentina. ...
(*Infantina* + *Caballero burlado*)[22]

Cuando me parió mi madre, me parió en alta montina,
donde cae la nieve a copos, agua menudita y fría,
donde canta la culebra, la serpiente respondía. ...
(*Penitencia del rey Rodrigo*)[23]

Agárrala de la mano, monte arriba la subía,
donde canta la culebra, la sierpe la respondía. ...
(*Devota del rosario*: ART 258; RPM 381)

Mándeme dejar a una montaña 'onde no vive gente viva,
'onde la culebra grita, la serpiente respondía. ...
(*Devota del rosario*: Vicuña 87)

In the Canarian tradition, the introductory verses borrowed from *La infantina* by *El caballero burlado* allude not only to singing snakes, but also to the absence of domestic fowl as in various Eastern Sephardic *romances*:

---

[22] CVR, p. 156; ASW 217. The snow and cold water are found in Poncet, "Entrepeñas," no. 5; RPM 62; RTO 15, and in *Jesu Cristo y el incrédulo* (Schindler 57) which is an *a lo divino* adaptation of *La infantina.* Snow, cold water, and snakes appear as a contamination in *La esposa de Don García* (RPM 13). The verse: "caía la nieve a copos / y el agua menuda y fría" also occurs in *La muerte ocultada* (G. Menéndez Pidal, *Romancero,* p. 201, v. 5). Singing snakes appear in *Don Bueso y su hermana* (FN 214), in *¡Ay! un galán de esta villa* (Caso González, "Ensayo de reconstrucción," pp. xiv, xvi-xviii, xxv-xxvi; Torner, "Índice de analogías," no. 191; Id., *Lírica hispánica,* no. 254; Llano Roza de Ampudia, *Del folklore asturiano,* pp. 257-259), and in at least one version of *Delgadina* (CVR, p. 240). Cf. B214.1.10. *Singing snake*; Lambertz, *Die Volksepik der Albaner,* pp. 72, 155. See now D. Devoto's study of this motif (*Ábaco,* I [Madrid, 1969], pp. 22-44).

[23] Menéndez Pidal, *Romancero tradicional,* I, p. 67 (no. 14L). The verses quoted may have been borrowed from *La fuerza de la sangre* (cf. D. Catalán, "A caza de romances raros," pp. 450-455); however, the singing snakes, snow, and icy water appear in other versions, at different stages in the narrative, without the reference to birth in the wilderness: e.g., nos. 14LL, 14M, 14o, 14R, 14S. See also p. 88; ASW 167 (no. 2); Braga, II, 312. No. 14G would seem to have been influenced by *La devota del rosario.*

Se le oscureció la noche en una escura montiña,
donde no cantaban gallos, ni menos cantan gallinas,
sólo cantan tres culebras, todas tres cantan al día. . . .
(RCan 1)

¿Dónde lo cogió la noche? En una oscura montiña,
donde no cantaba gallo, ni menos canta gallina,
sólo cantan tres culebras, tres horas antes del día;
una canta a la mañana, otro canta al mediodía,
otro cantaba la noche (*sic*) cuando el sol ponerse ía.
(Cuscoy, *Folklore infantil,* p. 88)

At least two elements present in the Eastern Sephardic prolog have documentable sixteenth-century counterparts. The silence of roosters (3) and the absence of barking dogs (4*a*) contribute to the somber circumstances surrounding the ill-fated protagonist's birth in an *endecha,* printed in 1562, which was to merit various literary adaptations and allusions, as well as consecration in the North African Jewish tradition as a funeral dirge:

Parióme mi madre
vna noche escura
cubrióme de luto
faltóme ventura
quando yo nascí
era hora menguada
ni perro se oya
ni gallo cantaua
ni gallo cantaua
ni perro se oya
sino mi ventura
que me maldezía. . . .
(*Flor de enamorados*) [24]

Parióme mi madre,
crióme mi tía,

---

[24] *Cancionero llamado Flor de enamorados* (Barcelona, 1562), ed. A. Rodríguez-Moñino and D. Devoto, fol. 63*r*. On the date of the first edition, see pp. xv ff., xlviii. This *endecha* is cited in the Prague *Ensalada* (*Pliegos de Praga,* I, 5). For other early texts and parallels, see Alvar, *Endechas,* pp. 115-122; Alonso-Blecua, no. 73 and p. 229; RVP, pp. 150-151; Cf. also PTJ, pp. xlviii-xlix; Cejador, *Verdadera poesía,* II, 1189.

púsome por nombre
niña y güena dicha.
Parióme mi madre
y una noche escura;
ni gayo que cante,
ni pedro que ladre,
más que una aguiliya,
que sus bozes daba. . . .
(Tetuán-Xauen)[25]

In the early Castilian song: "Caminad, señora, / si queréis caminar, / que los gallos cantan, / cerca está el lugar,"[26] the crowing of roosters imparts a feeling of renewed hope and a sense of the proximity of homely comforts and security to the foot-weary travelers. By contrast, the absence of crowing is used, just as in the migratory Judeo-Spanish prolog, to epitomize transoceanic remoteness and desolation in various heretical incantations preserved in Inquistorial records of the sixteenth-century:

Allá vayas, mal, de la parte del mar
donde no canta gallo ni gallina,
que no pares en esta casa ni en este hogar.

. . . a las ondas de la mar te echaré,
donde ni gallo canta,
ni buey ni vaca brama.
Fuye, mal, allende el mar.[27]

---

[25] Uned. MS version collected by Professor Américo Castro in Tetuán, 1922. For other modern texts, see Alvar, *Endechas*, nos. 11*a-b*; MP 141; PTJ 253-253*a*.

[26] Alonso-Blecua, no. 218. See also p. lxvi-lxvii, nn. 66-69; Frenk Alatorre, *La lírica popular*, p. 66; Cejador, *Verdadera poesía*, I, no. 932.

[27] S. Cirac Estopiñán, *Los procesos de hechicerías en la Inquisición de Castilla la Nueva* (Madrid, 1942), pp. 89, 100. For another sixteenth-century Castilian instance of the same formula, see J. Roque, *Rezas e benzeduras populares* (*Etnografia alentejana*) (Beja, 1946), pp. 7-8, n. 7. Being out of earshot of cockcrowing clearly has magical significance in one of the accounts, published by Cirac Estopiñán, of a sorcerer's ritual designed to cure a child of the effects of the evil eye (*desaojamiento*): "E fuemos todos tres juntos con el niño *fasta donde non sonase gallo ni gallina,* e que en el camino fablásemos a la yda a persona ninguna. Et fezimos en el campo un hoyo, e metimos dentro el moçuelo con sus envolturas," etc. (p. 91; italics ours). Cockcrowing would presumably have nullified the efficacy of the rite in question. Cf. D791.1.7. *Disenchantment at cockcrow.*

The same concept lives on in modern incantations from Catalonia, Galicia, and Portugal:

Agafeu la trencadura
d'aquesta pobra criatura
i tireu-la en una vall de llàgrimes,
on no se'n canti gall ni gallina,
ni record de criatura viva. ...[28]

Aire malino,
de todos los males, ...
aquí te desterro,
pro mar coallado,
donde non oias cantar
galina nin galo,
nin pita acacarear. ...

Yo te bendigo, *Dicipela* maligna;
la que bendice no soy yo,
que es la Virgen María.
Que vayas a los mares altos
donde no oigas cantar gallo ni gallina. ...

—Rosa cabalare, ¿qué ves aquí buscare?
—Cinza ou carbón de tras d'o lare.
—Vaite aló, as ondas d'o mare,
onde non oias galo cantare,
nin galina cacarexare. ...[29]

—Assim como tu és rosa ponçonhosa, esmasolosa, ...
P'ràs ondas do mar t' ê' hê-de dêtar,
Donde nã' oiças galo cantar,
Nem pinto piar,
Nem pai p'lo filho bràdar. ...[30]

---

[28] AFC 3491; Collected by Joan Amades in Lérida (1930).

[29] V. Lis Quiben, *La medicina popular en Galicia* (Pontevedra, 1949), pp. 58-59, 138, 163; other examples: pp. 149, 150, 170, 276. *Dicipela* and *rosa* are popular Galician terms for erysipelas.

[30] Roque, *Rezas e benzeduras*, p. 8; other examples: pp. 9, 10, 11, 24, 29, 36. Strikingly similar to the Hispanic verses is the following Rumanian incantation against the evil eye which we cite together with Cortés' Spanish translation (*Antología de la poesía popular rumana*, pp. 146-147, vv. 33-40):

BIBLIOGRAPHY

Eastern J. Sp.: Attias 10; Babani (= SR); BdR, no. 16 (= SR); Danon 4; Díaz-Plaja 13; LSO 72; Menéndez Pelayo 16 (= Danon); San Sebastián 6; SBS 4.1-12; Sciaky, pp. 37-38; SR, p. 12 (= GRA).

Study: RoH, II, 216 and n. 27.

Eşi deochi,/ Dintre ochi!
Să te duci/ şi să fugi
Unde cocoşul nu cântă
Unde codrul nu 'nverzeşte,
Unde cioban nu chiuişte
Unde popa nu citeşte.

(Sal, mal de ojo,/ De los ojos.
Vete, / Escapa
Donde el gallo no canta,
Donde el bosque no reverdece,
Donde el pastor no alboroza.
Adonde el cura no lee.)

22

VOS LABRARÉ UN PENDÓN

(I shall weave you a pennant)

'Era 'una mužer pompoza 'i 'él 'un 'ombre gastađor.
Gastó lo sulyyo 'i lo mí'o, lo ke 'el mi pađre me dyyó.
Agora, por mi pekađo, vine a ser 'un kađrađor.
'El kađrava la 'okita: —Mi mužer, filalda vos.
Filalda muyy byen delgađa, ke ansí kere 'el patrón.
Si non la filáš delgada, non vos paga 'el patrón.
—Yyo ke tengo manos blankas de lavrar al bastiđor.
—Yyo las tení'a más blankas de meldar la ley del Dyyo.
—Vení, vos daré 'un konsežo; mi mariđo, tomaldo vos.
'Éndavos para la kaša, ala kaša del kašón.
Toparéš syen dukađikos, los ke 'el mi ganađo son.
Merkaldos de sirma 'i perla; yyo vos lavraré 'un pendón.
Por 'un kavo las 'estreas, por 'otra 'el 'ožo del sol;
'en međyyo meto mis ansyyas, las ke 'estó pasando yyo.
Yya lo kitan a vendere, por la sivdađ de Aragón.
Todos 'ivan dizyendo: —¡'O, ké bu'enas manos son!
—¡Akél 'era 'el rey mi pađre, akél 'era 'el mi senyyor!

Source: RSA 4.

Translation:

She was an extravagant woman and he a spendthrift man. He spent his money and mine: all that my father gave me. And now, for my sins, I came to be a carder of wool. My husband carded it by the pound: "Wife, you must spin it. (5) Spin it nice and fine, for the master wants it so. If you don't spin it fine, the master will not pay you." "As for me, my hands are white from sewing on the frame." "And mine were whiter still from reading the Law of God." "Listen, my husband, take counsel from me: (10) Go to the cash box, the cash box in the chest. You'll find a hundred little ducats, which are all my wealth. Spend them on silver thread and pearls; I will weave you a pennant. On one side I'll embroider the stars, on the other the sun's eye; in the middle I'll put the anguish that I am enduring now." (15) Now they take it out to be sold through the city of Aragón.[1] Everyone kept saying: "Oh, what skilful hands!" (17) "That was the King, my father; that was my lord!"

Motifs:

1-2 W131.1. *Profligate wastes entire fortune. . . .*
3 L113.1.0.1. *Heroine endures hardships with menial husband.*
13 Cf. D1051. *Magic cloth.*
16-17 H110. *Identification by cloth or clothing.*

The popularity and wide diffusion of *Vos labraré un pendón* in both branches of the Judeo-Spanish tradition—attested in the East since the seventeenth-century—contrasts radically with the extreme paucity of texts in the Peninsular collections. Published Eastern Sephardic versions

[1] The toponym's use is formulistic and implies no local reference, nor can it be used to determine the ballad's origin. Concerning this problem, see our study on *Los siete hermanos y el pozo airón* (in preparation) and M. R. Lida de Malkiel, "El romance de la misa de amor," pp. 31-32, n. 1, in the light of which Entwistle's statements ("*La Dama de Aragón,*" p. 191; "La chanson populaire française en Espagne," p. 256) are unacceptable. On the unreal nature of ballad geography, see also RoH, I, 76, n. 24.

are from Salonika (Attias; LSO), Edirne (?) (Danon), Tekirdağ (?) (Adatto), Rhodes (Hemsi 1; SBS 98 and 100), and Bosnia (?) (Levy). Our collection comprises eight texts from Rhodes, three from Salonika, and one each from Istanbul and Jerusalem. William Milwitzsky's MSS have yielded a Ladino fragment from Sofia (Bulgaria). The ballads published in the Bosnian newspaper, *Jevrejski Glas,* include a version which, like Levy's unidentified text, is preceded by verses from *Celinos y la adúltera.* The Moroccan tradition, counting nine versions gathered on our 1962-63 field trips, has provided texts from Oran-Tetuán, Tetuán, Tangier, Larache (uned.), and Alcázar. By contrast, the Peninsular *Romancero* can so far boast only eleven texts, all from the northeastern corner of Portugal, though the ballad seems also to have been known in Algarve, if we credit it with having imposed the motif of the marvelous pennant upon the cyclic ballad of *La muerte del Príncipe Don Juan + El testamento de Fernando El Magno + Afuera, afuera, Rodrigo.* [2]

Like *El falso hortelano* (no. 21 *supra*), the destiny of *Vos labraré un pendón* is closely linked to early Hispanic drama. Here, however, it is the ballad that gives its subject matter to the theatre, not the reverse. Menéndez Pidal relates the *romance* to two seventeenth-century *comedias*: Luis Vélez de Guevara's *El príncipe viñador* (or *podador*) and Agustín de Castellanos' *Mientras yo podo las viñas.* Using these texts and an incidental quote in Reyes Mejía de la Cerda's *Famosa comedia de la Zarzuela,* Menéndez Pidal has reconstructed the first part of an archaic form of the ballad. [3] The *comedias,* and all but one of the modern Portuguese texts, take the narrative only up to the weaving

[2] For the text, see Estácio da Veiga, pp. 19-22; ASW 342-343; Braga, II, 308-311; for commentary, ASW 340; Menéndez Pidal, "Poesía popular y romancero," II, 17, n. 1 (cf. RoH, I, 215). Braga's remarks (III, 569) are worthless.

[3] See Menéndez Pidal, *El Romancero Español,* pp. 82-83; RoH, II, 178-179. That *Vos labraré un pendón* was already well known in the sixteenth century can be deduced from a certain Gothic-type *glosa* by Alonso López which includes the verse: "Mientras yo podo las viñas, / vida, sarmentaldas vos." See *Glosa peregrina: la qual glosando muchos Romances antiguos narra la eterna perdiciõ de Lucifer ...,* reproduced in *Pliegos góticos,* II, 281-292; the verse in question is on p. 284*a.* On Castellanos' *Mientras yo podo las viñas,* see also F. de B. San Román, *Lope de Vega los cómicos toledanos y el poeta sastre* (Madrid, 1935), pp. c-cvi.

of the pennant ("de un cabo porné la luna / y del otro porné el sol . . ."; cf. Yoná, v. 13).

The Judeo-Spanish traditions provide the *romance* with two rather different dénouements. In the East, the weaving of the marvelous pennant leads to a reunion of father and daughter, when "the King" recognizes the pennant's distinctive embroidery and presumably rescues the unfortunate couple from their lowly condition. As far as the Eastern tradition is concerned, Yoná's v. 16*a*, "Todos 'ivan dizyendo . . . ," must be considered defective, since in this context it is meaningless that everyone should praise the pennant's artistry and the hands that created it; for the exclamation signifies not only admiration but also recognition which could be voiced only by the King, since he alone was able to see in the pennant's perfection his own daughter's inimitable handiwork. Other Salonikan versions supplement Yoná's text and carry an important additional verse, in which the wife specifies that the pennant must not be sold at any price until it has been seen by the King:[4]

Volo yevarėš a vendere por la sivdá de Aragón.
Ni por oro, ni por plata, i no lo deš este pendón,
sino a'kél ke vos dize: —¡Bendichas manos ke tal lavró!
Akél es el rey mi padre i akél es el mi señor.
(uned., Salonika)

In Morocco, as in the *comedias* and Portuguese texts, the couple have become vine growers. In the Moroccan dénouement the pennant is simply taken to the *zoco,* where it is sold to the highest bidder and brings such a price as to free the couple from their menial trade. The ballad ends: ". . . con labor de sus manos / a su marido enriquesió" (Bénichou 9A). Here there is no sudden anagnorisis and the text can "correctly" read: "Todos dizen a una boca: / —¡Bendita la que te bordó!" (Larrea 183; cf. 184, Bénichou 9A-B). Martínez Ruiz's version from Alcazarquivir adds a curious detail, which strangely enough is echoed at the other extreme of the Mediterranean in Danon's text from

[4] Danon 30, Hemsi 1, SBS 98, and our unedited Rhodian versions blur the dénouement: the pennant or *tovaža* is merely sent to the girl's father (or uncle, as in SBS 98).

Yoná's text also lacks the ballad's usual proverbial *incipit,* concerning which see no. 17, nn. 8-10 *supra.*

Edirne (Turkey) and in an unedited fragment collected by Israel J. Katz from an *Istanbulí* informant in Jerusalem. In Alcázar the husband, who goes out to sell the pennant, is enjoined not to identify his wife as having embroidered it lest her father and other relatives grieve concerning her fate.[5] In Danon's version and the fragment from Istanbul the pennant is sent to the family, with the inexplicable warning that the brothers must not be told their sister made it:

y a la sibdad donde fuere, no digáis quien lo bordó,
no sea que lo oiga mi padre lo vivá (*sic*) con mucho dolor,
que no sea que lo oya mi madre y tenga ansia en su corasón,
no sea que lo oyan mis hermanos de su culpa y nuestra no. ...
(MRuiz)

Que se lo mandéis donde mi padre, que sepa de mi dolor.
Si preguntan mis hermanos, les decís que no lo hize yo.
Si pregunta mi madre, le decís que lo labrí yo. ...
(Danon)[6]

Si lo viteš al mi padre, no digáš ke lo lavrí yo.
Porke los padres son kruweles, ya m'echan la maldisión.
Si ves a los mis ermanos, no digáš ke lo lavrí yo.
Porke los ermanos son selozos i me echan la maldisión.
Si la viteš a mi madre, dizilde ke lo lavrí [yo].
Ke las madres son piadozas; m'echan la bindisión.
(uned., Istanbul)

Only one of the Portuguese texts goes beyond the description of the pennant to hint—ambivalently—at the narrative's outcome. Vasconcellos' version (VRP 716) from Argozelo (Vimioso, Bragança) ends with the following obviously traditional but essentially uninformative verses:

---

[5] It would be risky to see in this secrecy some distant reflection of the play *Mientras yo podo las viñas,* where the protagonists *go into hiding* as vine growers.

[6] Danon's verses are closely paralleled in *Los siete hermanos y el pozo airón* (Attias 83; NSR, pp. 75, 78) and could conceivably be an independent borrowing from that ballad. Such incremental, formulistic listings of relatives are frequent in Sephardic balladry. Compare *David llora a Absalón* (Attias 86), *El cautiverio del príncipe Francisco* (MP 52), and *El culebro raptor* (MP 93). Cf. also *El duque de Bernax* (Larrea 66). For a detailed discussion of the device in question, see our study on *Los siete hermanos y el pozo airón* (in preparation).

Na procissão onde ele [o pendão] for, não irá outro melhor;
p'ra que diga a gente toda: —Quem seria o bordador?

Given the documentation at hand, it seems impossible to award definitive priority to one or another of the Sephardic dénouements: the Eastern *Identification by cloth* motif or the fortune-making pennant of the Moroccan versions. The latter outcome seems, perhaps, almost too facile. It could well be a late rationalization of the pennant's original rôle. [7] The Eastern *romance*'s ending, with its joyous reunion of daughter and parent, is certainly more satisfying to the ballad esthetic than is the Moroccan form's rather insipid tale of "rags to riches." In using the pennant as a means of identification the Eastern *romance* exemplifies, moreover, a favorite device of Hispanic balladry. The Catalan song of *Los dos aymadors nats a un mateix dia* (*í-a*), for example, reunites Don Bertrán and Doña María when he identifies a beautiful shirt which she has woven. [8] The abandoned wife in *La boda estorbada* is recognized in many versions because of some garment that she is wearing. [9] In an early prototype of the ballad of *Espinelo* (= *Primav.* 152) the hero was presumably reunited with his mother when she recognized a richly embroidered cloak in which he had been wrapped when an infant. [10] In short, both esthetically and philologically

[7] See, however, M. R. Lida de Malkiel's comment in *Davar,* X, 23.

[8] AFC 3246; Aguiló, pp. 67-76; Amades, II, 62-68; Avenç, III, 50-54; Briz, IV, 223-225; Bulbena, pp. 45-51; Milá 219; OCPC, II, 157-158. RQDB-II 37 and RTCN 8 offer a version in Castilian from Aragon. The ballad even attributes similar astral decorations to the marvelous shirt: "Al davant hi broda'l sol, / al faldar l'estel del dia" (Aguiló, p. 74; Briz; Milá; cf. Yoná, v. 13). The verse is formulistic and occurs in various Hispanic ballads: "a un cap hi té sa lluna / i a s'altre hi té es sol pintat" (*En Rodriguet*: Macabich 147); "en un lado lleva el Sol, / en otro la Luna llena" (*La Virgen buscando a Cristo*: RCan 42); "Numa ponta tinha a lua, / na outra o sol arraiado" (*A pastora*: VRP 718). Compare also the marvelous seamstresses who appear in an Aegean Greek song: "... Il y avait les trois filles du roi: /L'une brode le ciel, /l'autre la lune, / et l'autre, la plus jeune, / brode les étoiles" (Georgeakis-Pineau 245; cf. also p. 191).

[9] See Catalán-Galmés, "La boda estorbada," p. 92; Menéndez Pidal, *et al.*, *Cómo vive un romance,* pp. 231-234; Bénichou, p. 130; M. R. Lida de Malkiel, *Davar,* X, 8-9. In a Basque song on *The Husband's Return,* he is identified by a silk handkerchief (Azkue, *Literatura popular,* IV, 186).

[10] See RoH, I, 336-337; for texts which mention the cloak: MP 104; RQDB-II 68; RTCN 26. For still other examples of the motif, *Identification by garment* (H111), see Child, II, 68; K. Warnke, *Die Lais der Marie de France* (Halle, 1900), 2d ed., p. lxxxiv (*Le Fraisne*); DVM, IV, 21.

the Eastern dénouement, whether prototypic or not, is certainly the most satisfactory.

Neo-Hellenic balladry provides us with evidence which may, perhaps, elucidate the *romance's* clouded final episode while adding a measure of support to the contention that the *Identification by cloth* motif may be a prototypic feature of *Vos labraré un pendón.* The Greek song of *Hē xepesménē archontopoûla* (*The Impoverished Nobleman's Daughter*) tells the following story: Helen, a king's daughter, brings a rich dowry to her marriage with a young man in a distant land. However, the couple falls upon hard times and gradually consumes both his riches and her dowry. They are finally reduced to working at menial tasks. The husband becomes a shepherd (or a swineherd); his wife must beat flax (or spin cotton). After the day's work the flax is weighed and, if it is found insufficient, the girl is scolded by "her lord." She is seized with a longing to see her native land and asks her husband to return her to her family. He replies that when he married her she was white and beautiful (or rich); now she is ugly (or poor) and he would be fearful and ashamed to face her parents and relatives. She therefore sets out alone and finally encounters her father's forty servant girls washing at a fountain. They bring her unrecognized to her mother who inquires if the "foreign girl" is skilled at any craft. She answers that she knows no menial work but is a king's daughter and was taught to weave "fine silken damask." They seat her before a loom and, as she weaves, she sings a dirge which tells the story of her misfortunes. Her mother embraces her and welcomes her home.

The Greek ballad shows a striking number of agreements with our *romance*: The rich dowry, gradually expended by husband and wife; the menial tasks the couple must perform including, in both the Greek and Judeo-Spanish songs, duties involving early stages in the manufacture of cloth (flax beating or wool carding); the threatened or actual dissatisfaction of "the lord" with the girl's work (cf. "Si non la filáš delgada, / non vo paga 'el patrón": Yoná, v. 6); the emphasis placed on the girl's fair complexion and the adverse effects, either actual or projected, that her labors may have upon her physical appearance (cf. "que tengo las manos blancas / y me las quemará el sol": *comedias* and Morocco); the husband's (in the Greek ballad) or the wife's shame (implied in MRuiz; Danon; uned., Istanbul) at the prospect of her family's discovery of her ill fortune; the girl's claim of inability to perform menial tasks, as contrasted with her pride and confidence in the well-learned art of weaving or embroidery (cf. "No quiero, señor, ni puedo, / mi padre no me lo enseñó . . .": Bénichou 9.17-18); and finally the fact that the girl's knowledge of weaving (or embroidery) leads, in one way or another, to a reunion with her parents.[11]

Clearly there is an ultimate genetic relationship between the two ballads. The association of weaving with the Princess' return in the Greek song lends strong credence to the Eastern Sephardic *Identification by cloth* motif as a prototypic feature of *Vos labraré un pendón.* All the same, given the multiple known contacts between Romaic and Eastern Sephardic balladry, the possibility that this feature, as well as the replacement of the vine growers (Morocco; Portugal; *comedias*) by wool carders, may have been borrowed by the Eastern versions from *The Impoverished Nobleman's Daughter,* on the strength of the two songs' other obvious analogies, cannot be altogether discounted. A thorough comparative study of the Hispanic and Greek ballads, in view of a much more extensive sampling of the latter's versions, is a desideratum.

BIBLIOGRAPHY

VOS LABRARÉ UN PENDÓN

Eastern J.-Sp.: Adatto 13.18 ff.; Attias 47; BdR, no. 18 (= Danon); Danon 30; Gil 19 (= Danon); Hemsi 1; Hemsi, "Evocation," p. 1057*b*; Levy 67.5-8; LSO 70-71; Menéndez Pelayo 41 (= Danon); PTJ 123-123*a* (= Danon, Hemsi); SBS 98 and 100.

[11] The Greek ballad prefers another widely used device: H12. *Recognition by song* (*music*). The same motif occurs in some versions of *Tà kakà peθeriká* (*The Evil Parents-in-law*), a Greek analog of *La gentil porquera* (Lüdeke-Megas, no. 86.95 ff.). For other balladic instances, see *Hermanas reina y cautiva* (MP 48; Attias 11) and its British counterpart *Fair Annie* (Child 62); the Catalan *Don Lluis de Montalbà* (see no. 23, n. 11 *supra*); *Le retour du soldat* (Barbeau, *Folk-Songs of Old Quebec,* p. 38); *Red the Rose and White Lily* (Child 103C); and *The Famous Flower of Serving-men* (Child 106); *The Lord of Lorn and the False Steward* (Child 271A.72 ff.); *Der edle Moringer* (DVM 12; Meier, *Balladen,* I, no. 8). The Greek ballad's Bulgarian analog (*Die arme Neda*) combines *Recognition by song* with *Recognition by cloth.* Cf. also Leader, *Hungarian Classical Ballads,* pp. 242-243.

Archaic J.-Sp. Incipit ("Quien casa con amores / sienpre vive con dolor"): Avenary 66 (pp. 384, 389). The song "Si las manos tiengo blandas" (Avenary 71 [p. 384]) treats the same theme. See Frenk Alatorre 316; Cejador, *Verdadera poesía,* III, no. 1948.

Moroccan J.-Sp.: Bénichou 9; Gil 19 (= MP); [12] Larrea 183-184; MP 120; MRuiz 91; PTJ 123*b* (= Bénichou).

Portuguese: Alves, pp. 573-574; Kundert, p. 108*b* (no. G49); Martins, II, 70; Tavares, *RL, IX,* 316; VRP 711-717. See also n. 2 *supra.*

Archaic Texts: Menéndez Pidal, *El Romancero Español,* pp. 82-85; RoH, II, 179-180. A "Glosa sobre quien casa por amores" by Martín de la Membrilla is listed in the *Abecedarium B* of Fernando Colón, edited by Rodríguez-Moñino, *El Cancionero general: Noticias bibliográficas,* p. 124 (no. 205). See also n. 3 *supra.*

Studies: Menéndez Pidal, *El Romancero Español,* pp. 82-85; *La epopeya castellana,* pp. 200-203; RoH, II, 173, 178-180, 338.

Hē xepesménē archontopoûla

(The Impoverished Nobleman's Daughter)

Greek: Garnett, I, 186-191; Jeannaraki, no. 272; Liebrecht, *Zur Volkskunde,* pp. 187, 216; Lüdeke, "Griechische Volksdichtung," p. 219 (type 3); Lüdeke-Megas, nos. 79-84; Passow 459; Pernot, *Anthologie,* pp. 112-115; Petropoulos, I, 128-130; Politis, *Eklogaì,* no. 85; Theros, I, nos. 375-376; Tommaseo-Pavolini 101. [13]

Bulgarian: *Die arme Neda:* Wlislocki, "Zu neugriechischen Volksliedern," pp. 361-362.

---

[12] Gil's inexplicable mania for "Orientalizing" his very sloppily edited collection leads him to falsify many of the geographic attributions of his texts, all of which are "secondhand" versions. In the present case the second text (= MP) under no. 19 is not from Adrianople but from Tangier.

[13] Worthy of further investigation are the multiple agreements between the Greek ballad and a crucial scene of *Los dos aymadors nats a un mateix dia* (*Don Bertran i Donya Maria*): Maria sets out in search of Bertran; she encounters seven washerwomen at a fountain; inquiry as to what tasks she can do; her knowledge of embroidery; she is brought unrecognized to the Queen's palace; she is given hand work to do; recognition by embroidery (cf. texts listed in n. 8 *supra*). Similarly in the British *Blancheflour and Jellyflorice* (Child 300.10-13), Blancheflour arrives at the gates of a castle; is brought before the Queen; inquiry as to what tasks the girl can do; "... I can neither card nor spin, / Nor cows I canno milk, / But sit into a lady's bower / And sew the seams o' silk."

De Två Konungadöttrarne
and
Marsk Stigs Døttre

Scandinavian: Certain Norse ballads show distant but clear similarities to the Spanish and Greek songs. In the Swedish *Två Konungadöttrarne* (Arwidsson, II, no. 114; FSF, no. 41; Geijer-Afzelius-2, III, no. 73) and most of the Danish texts included under DgF, no. 146 (AD ff.), two Princesses are stolen from their parents in childhood, but later return to offer their services to the Queen, their mother. She asks: "What work can you do?" They answer: "We can neither brew nor bake, but we can sew." They weave the sun, heaven and earth, and the stars into the silver and gold fabric of a marvelous garment. The Queen's delight at seeing their handiwork leads to a revelation of the girls' identity. Another form of this story, *Marsk Stigs Døttre* (DgF, III, no. 146BC; Olrik, II, no. 19; Prior, II, 213-216; Smith-Dampier 295-298), has been drawn into the cycle of the great Danish hero (cf. Dal's note to nos. 13-16). Here, since the girls are apparently orphaned, there is no reunion; the embroidery leads to their adoption at the Norwegian court; one girl dies of grief all the same, while the younger marries the King's son. [14] Are the Scandinavian songs genetically related to their Greek and Hispanic parallels?

---

[14] Though it embodies a quite different motif, the Scandinavian ballad of *Esbern Snare,* where little Kirstin's marvelous needlework wins her the protagonist's promise of marriage, perhaps deserves mention here. At the end of this ballad, as in *Vos labraré,* the girl's expert embroidery calls forth a blessing upon the hands that wrought it. For texts, see DgF, III, no. 131; Olrik, I, no. 20; Smith-Dampier 141-142; Prior, II, 182-185; Arwidsson, II, no. 116; Jonsson, no. 26. On the motif of the marriage shirt and sewing as a prerequisite to marriage, see DgF, III, 182, 918-919. Cf. also H383.2.2. *Bride test: weaving magic cloth, sewing magic shirt*; T61.3. *At betrothal maid makes shirt for her lover.* For another perspective on related beliefs, see O. H. Green, *Spain and the Western Tradition,* 4 vols. (Madison, Wisconsin, 1963-1966), I, 117-118, n. 159.

23

LA VUELTA DEL HIJO MALDECIDO

(The Accursed Son's Return)

—Dulse 'eraš, la mi madre,   'i 'atan dulse 'en 'el avlar.
Dos bezikos aš pedrido   'i tres 'i kuatro 'entyendo a dar.
Los dos 'eran de amores   'i los dos de veluntad.
Yyorava la Blankaninyya   lágrimas de veluntad.
—¿De ké yyoráš, Blankaninyya,   lágrimas de veluntad?
—Yyoro por vos, kavalyero,   ke voš vaš 'i me dešáš.
Me dešáš ninyya 'i muǧaǧa   'i ǧika de la poka 'edađ.
Me dešáš 'ižos ǧiketos,   yyoran 'i demandan pan.
'Esto sintyyó 'el kavalyero,   dešó todo 'i tornó atrás.
Metyyó la mano 'en su peǧo,   syen doblones le dará.
—¿Para ké me basta 'esto,   para vino 'o para pan?
—Si 'esto no vos abasta,   venderéš medyya sivdad.
Venderéš los mis vestidos,   sin manǧar 'i sin sudar.
Fin a tres anyyos me 'esperáš,   alos kuatro vos cazáš.

Source: GRA 6.

2 *repeated.* 'I 2 bezikos *in repetition.*
3*b* + se torna.
4, 5 Blanka ninyya.
14 Fina.

Translation:

"You were sweet, my mother, and so sweet in your speech. You've lost two kisses and three and four I intend to give you. Two were for love and two with all my heart." Blancaniña was weeping tears with all her heart. (5) "Why are you weeping, Blancaniña, tears with all your heart? "I am weeping for you, my lord, for you are departing and leaving me. You leave me a young girl, only a child in years. You leave me with little children, who weep and beg for bread." When the knight heard this, he left everything and turned back. (10) He put his hand in his pocket and gives her a hundred doubloons. "What good will this do me, for wine or for bread?" "If this is not enough for you, you can sell half the city. You can sell my clothes, those without stains and sweat. (14) Wait for me three years, marry in the fourth."

Motifs:

14 Cf. T61.2. *Parting lovers pledge not to marry for seven years*; H387.1. *Bride's constancy tested by seven years' mourning over supposed dead lover.*

La vuelta del hijo maldecido, a ballad of intricately mixed ancestry and complex affiliations elsewhere in Hispanic tradition, enjoys wide popularity in the Sephardic *Romancero.* In the East, geographically identifiable published versions originate in Salonika (Attias, UR[?], UYA [?], Yoná), Bosnia (Baruch), Edirne (Danon), Izmir (Hemsi), Rosiori ([Rumania] Pulido), Milas-Rhodes (SBS), and Jerusalem (?) (SICh). Unedited texts in our possesion include twelve from Rhodes and one each from Çanakkale, Tekirdağ, and Bucharest (collected by Wm. Milwitzky). The ballad is much less satisfactorily documented in Morocco, where the texts encountered are either rather short or confused. Larrea's versions are, as always, from Tetuán; Martínez Ruiz's, from Alcazarquivir. We have a number of brief unedited fragments from Tetuán and Tangier and one very ample version from Larache.

Except for vv. 1-3, an impertinent contamination from *Conde Claros y la infanta,* [1] Yoná's ballad derives in its entirety from the early sixteenth-century *Conde Dirlos* (*Primav.* 164), a Spanish representative of the Pan-European narrative of the long-absent husband who returns to reclaim his wife at the very moment of her marriage to another man (i.e., *Hind Horn, Edle Moringer*). In other Hispanic traditions outside of the Eastern Sephardic domain, the old minstrel ballad of *Dirlos* is the ancestor not only of a *Hind Horn-Moringer*-type *Conde Antores* (recluded today in various conservative fringe areas: Morocco, Santander, León, Zamora, Extremadura, Orense, Tras-os-Montes, Algarve), but also of a more recent and more widely diffused ballad, *Conde Sol,* in which, as in *Young Beichan* and *Stolt Ellensborg,* it is the abandoned wife who searches out her husband just in time to interrupt his marriage to a foreign rival. [2]

Yoná's text, like SICh, UR, and a number of our unedited renditions, is but a fragment. Many Sephardic versions offer a much longer and more detailed narrative which attests to a complex intertwining of traditional materials derived from both Hispanic and Neo-Hellenic balladry. They continue with a story based upon the Greek ballad, *Hē kakḕ mána* (*The Evil Mother*) where, as in the *romance,* a mother curses her son at the moment of his departure for foreign lands. [3] The son

---

[1] Cf. Attias' version of *Conde Claros y la infanta* (no. 30.1-8):

> Dulce erais, la mi siñora, y a tan dulce en el hablar.
> Con dulzor de vuestra boca a la gente hacéis pecar.
> Dos besicos has pedrido, cuatro vos entiendo dar,
> que los dos eran d'amores, los otros dos d'amistad.

The allusion to the mother at the beginning of Yoná's text surely anticipates her crucial rôle in later stages of the narrative not included in Yoná's truncated version. *Conde Claros y la infanta* contaminates a number of unedited versions to be published by Menéndez Pidal in *Romancero tradicional,* III (see nos. III. 3-5). This monumental volume brings together all known versions of *Conde Dirlos, Antores, Sol, La vuelta del hijo maldecido* and *El navegante.*

[2] Cf. H1385.4. *Quest for vanished husband.*

[3] Cf. M411.1. *Curse by parent.* Such parental curses are an important feature of Balkan folk belief; once pronounced, the curse must inevitably come true (though such is not the case in *La vuelta del hijo maldecido*). For curses in Balkan balladry, see Stevenson Stanoyevich, *An Anthology of Jugoslav Poetry,* p. 155. For other instances of parental cursing, see Pernot, *Anthologie,* pp. 60, 95; Lüdeke-Megas, nos. 14, 15 (*Saránta kléftes*; *Constantine and Aretḗ*); Leader, *Hungarian Classical Ballads,* pp. 307, 310; Amzulescu, *Balade populare romî-*

then describes how she will later regret her actions and yearn for his presence. She will ask for news of him from passing sailors, pilgrims, travelers, or a sea captain, only to learn that they have seen his body being devoured by birds, lying upon some foreign shore. The text from Chios edited and translated by Argenti and Rose is representative of the Greek narrative:

Μιά μάννα, μιά κακόμαννα τοῦ γυιοῦ της καταριέται.
«Ἄντε γυιέ μου στὸ δαίμονα, ἄντε μὲ τὰ καράβια,
ὅλοι νὰ πᾶν καὶ ν' ἀρθοῦνε καὶ σὺ νὰ μὴ γυρίσῃς.»
«Διώχτεις με μάννα διώχτεις με μάννα θὰ φύγω, θέλω.
Μάννα θ' ἀρθῇ τοῦ 'Αγιοῦ Γιωργιοῦ ἡ πρώτη γιορτὴ τοῦ κόσμου,
μάννα θὰ πᾷς στὴν ἐκκλησιὰ νὰ κάμῃς τὸ σταυρό σου,
θὰ 'δῇς τοὺς νηούς, θὰ 'δῇς τὶς νηές, θὰ 'δῇς τὰ παλληκάρια,
θὰ 'δῇς τὸν τόπον ἀδειανόν, θὰ θυμηθῇς νὰ κλάψῃς:
Θὰ κατεβῇς καὶ στὸ γυαλὸ τοὺς ναῦτες νὰ 'ρωτήσῃς:
‹Ναῦτες μου καλοναῦτες μου δὲν εἴδατε τὸ γυιό μου;»
«Γιὰ 'πές μας τὰ σημάδια του καὶ ἴσως καὶ τον ἐξεύρω.›
‹'Ελιὰ 'χενε στὸ μάγουλα κι' ἐλιὰ στὴν ἀμασχάλη
κι' ἀφ' τὴ δεξιά του τὴν μεριὰ εἶχε περίσσια χάρη.›
Μάννα, οἱ ναῦτες θὰ σοῦ 'ποῦν κι' οἱ μοῦτσοι θὰ λαλήσουν.
‹'Εχτὲς προχτὲς τὸν εἴδαμε στὴν ἄμμο ξαπλωμένο,
εἶχε τὸ κῦμα πάπλωμα, τὴν θάλασσα σεντόνι,
καὶ τὰ βωλάκια τοῦ γυαλοῦ τά 'χενε προσκεφάλι,
μαῦρα πουλιὰ τὸν τρώγανε κι' ἄσπρα τὸν τριγυρίζαν....

---

neşti, nos. 7, 307, 317 (*Şarpele*; *Fata blestemată*; *Blestemul mamei*); Comişel, pp. 36-37; Cortés, pp. 218-221 (*Blestemul*); Vrabie, pp. 122-123, 139, 150-153; Dozon, *Chansons populaires bulgares,* pp. 275, 283, 320, 338; Gesemann, p. 97 (*Der Mutter Fluch*); Strausz, pp. 261-263. The motif is not lacking in Hispanic folk poetry. Cf. *La maldición de la madre* (CPE, II, 30-31 [nos. 41-42]; Menéndez Pidal, *El Romancero Español,* p. 105); *La maldición* (CVR 85); *La maldiciente* (RQDB-I 18), and the famous *Lanzarote y el ciervo del pie blanco* (*Primav.* 147; RCan, pp. 6-8 and no. 6). In "A North Mexican Ballad: *José Lizorio,*" pp. 245-247, F. Goodwyn compares the Greek *Kakē̂ mána* with yet another Hispanic manifestation of the same motif. See also Espinosa, *Nuevo Méjico,* No. 97.

Compare also Nigra's *Maledizione della madre* (no. 23; concerning which see Bronzini, I, 74, 190, 195-197; Vidossi, no. 8) and Child's *The Mother's Malison* (no. 216).

(A mother, a wicked mother, cursed her son,
"My son, go to the devil, go with the ships;
may all go and come back but may you not return."
"You chase me away, mother, you chase me away; I will go. I wish to go.
Mother, the feast of St. George will come, the foremost feast of the world;
you will go, mother, to the church to cross yourself;
you will see the young men, you will see the young women, you will see the brave youths,
you will see my place empty, you will be moved to tears.
You will go down also to the shore to ask the sailors:
'Sailors, good sailors, have you not seen my son?'
'Tell us his signs and perhaps I have met him.'
'He had a mole on his cheek and a mole in his armpit,
and on his right side he had peculiar loveliness.'
Mother, the sailors will speak to you and the ship-boys will call out:
'Yesterday or the day before we saw him lying on the sand;
he had the wave for his coverlet and the sea for his sheet,
and the shingle of the shore he had for his pillow.
Black birds were eating him and white birds went around him. . . .)

What is usually only an imaginative projection on the part of the son in the Greek ballad actually takes place in the Judeo-Spanish song: The rejected son like Count Dirlos really does depart, but later returns, unrecognized, as a sailor or as the captain of a ship. When the mother begs him for news of her son he deceives her into thinking him dead by describing in detail the scene of his demise upon a distant shore. On hearing this news, the mother attempts suicide but is dissuaded when the son reveals his true identity. Attias' version, supplemented with details from our unedited Rhodian texts, exemplifies the Judeo-Spanish ballad:

Esto que oyó la madre, maldiciones l'echará:
—Las naves de todo el mundo, vayan y tornen en paz,
y las naves de mi hijo, vayan y no vengan más.
Pasó tiempo y vino tiempo, escariño [le fue a dar].
S'asentó a la ventana, a la ventana de la mar.
Vido venir unas galeas, galeando por la mar:
—¡Gáleas, las mis gáleas, galeando por la mar!
[*or*: Así vivaš, marinero, si me digaš la verdad.]

Romance del conde
Dirlos: y delas grandes ven=
turas que vuo. Nueuamente
añadidas ciertas cosas que
fasta aqui no fueron pue=
stas. Y vna canciõ de
nuestra Señora.
Año. 1538.

FIG. 5.—The departure of Count Dirlos according to an early broadside (Bibl. Nac., Madrid).

¿Si es que viteis al mi hijo, al mi hijo caronal?
—Ya lo vide, mi bolisa, a la orilla de la mar,
las piedras por cabecera, l'arena por almadrak,
la onda que va y viene por cubierta le será,
[i un burako en la su tripa, k'entra i sale el gavilán.]
Esto que oyó la madre, de arriba s'echará.
—No vos echéis, la mi madre, ni vos quijerais echar,
yo so el vuestro hijo, el vuestro hijo caronal.

This Judeo-Spanish narrative borrows heavily from the *Romancero* heritage into which it has been absorbed: the son's imaginary death scene is paralleled in *La muerte de Don Beltrán* (*Primav.* 185-185*a*) and other Hispanic ballads, while the final verses depend again on *Conde Dirlos*. However, the Sephardic song's numerous similarities in structure and detail to *Hē kakē mána* clearly point to an intrusion of the Greek ballad upon an Eastern Sephardic form of *Conde Dirlos*. We must assume the mixed narrative's subsequent migration to Morocco.[4]

Hidden as it is within a thematically alien narrative, the Eastern Sephardic *Dirlos* fragment has escaped the notice of those who have studied the traditional derivatives of *El conde Dirlos* in the Pan-Hispanic *Romancero*. Exiguous though it may be, the Judeo-Spanish fragment is not without importance, for it has preserved several features of the sixteenth-century *Dirlos* which have survived nowhere else in that ballad's traditional derivatives. The Sephardic fragment embodies the following narrative stages (E = Eastern J.-Sp. versions; M = Moroccan J.-Sp. versions; D = *Dirlos*; A = *Antores*; S = *Sol*):

(1) Blancaniña is weeping (E/M/D/A/S). (2) The knight asks: "Why are you crying?" (E/M/A/S). (3) "Because you are leaving me" (E/M/S). (4) Blancaniña is "niña y muchacha / chica de poca edad" (E/M/D/S). (5) She has small children who are crying for bread (E/M). (6) "If they

[4] Larrea 193 (vv. 17-20) alludes briefly to the mother and to the boat in which the son will presumably return. MRuiz 95 is more complete and includes the mother's curse, her questioning of a returning "cabayero," and the scene of the son's supposed death. Unedited versions in our collection parallel the Eastern form even more closely. Agreement between the North African and Eastern Mediterranean texts of *La vuelta del hijo maldecido* is much closer than is normally the case with ballads occurring in both traditions.

The question of the relationship of *La vuelta del hijo maldecido* to the Greek *Evil Mother* is discussed in detail in our review article "A New Collection of Judeo-Spanish Ballads," no. 18.

ask for their father, I will not know what to tell them" (Attias; Levy; uned., Rhodes). (7) The knight turns back (Yoná; Attias). (8) He tells her not to grieve (Attias; UR/D/S) and (9) offers her money (E/M/D). (10) She claims it will be insufficient (E/M). (11) In that case, says he, she may pawn or sell "vineyards, fields, and half of the city" (E/M/D). (12) She asks him when he will return (Baruch/D/A/S). (13) He will be absent for seven (one, two, three, eight, nine, thirty [!]) years (E/D/A/S), (14) after which she should marry another (E/D/A/S), (15) who must be the knight's equal (E). (16) She should give him her first husband's clothing, possessions, and half of the city (E) or his lands (D). (17) The knight then departs (UR/D/A/S).

Several stages of the narrative (2, 3, 7, 10) have no parallel in the archaic *Dirlos,* but all such stages embody rather obvious features which might logically have been added to the story in the course of its transition from minstrel to traditional style. Parallels to stages 2-3 do, in fact, appear in *El conde Sol,* while a Portuguese version of *Antores* includes stage 2. The emotion-charged stages 5-6 (the starving, fatherless children, whose presence contradicts the abandoned wife's tender age) and the aristocratizing stage 15 (the stipulation that the new husband be the knight's equal) must count as more radical innovations. However, the major features of the Sephardic ballad echo the archaic *Dirlos* with notable fidelity:

---

[5] Cf. also *Dirlos,* p. 345: "Dejaste mujer hermosa, / moza y de poca edad."

[6] Composition: Stage 1 is from Yoná and Attias; stages 2-4 from Attias; stage 8 from Attias and UR; stage 9 from Yoná; stage 11 from uned. (Rhodes) and Attias; stage 12 from Baruch and uned. (Bucharest); stages 13-14 from Levy and Baruch; stage 16 from an uned. version (Rhodes); stage 17 from UR.

[7] Except for stage 2, we follow the synthetic text published in "El tema," pp. 70-72, which has been compared with the versions listed in our bibliography below. For stages 12-14 and 17, cf. also "El tema," p. 84. Stage 2 occurs in Martins, I, 203.

[8] Composition: Stages 1-3 are from *Cómo vive,* p. 241. Cf. also Catalán, "Motivo y variación," pp. 161-162; RPM 87, 90, 91, 94, 97, 103; Schindler 1; Aguiló 117; Milá 244. Stage 4 is from *Cómo vive,* p. 243; stage 8 from Larrea 156.114-115; stages 12-14, 17 from "El tema," p. 84. The resultant synthetic text has been checked against all versions listed in our bibliography. As in *Conde Antores* (cf. MP 60), stage 17 normally occurs as the first verse of some subtypes of *El conde Sol.* Cf. RPM 88, 89, 93; "El tema," p. 84, n. 1; " Motivo y variación," p. 165.

(1)	La condesa que esto vido, llorando empezó de ha- [blar. ... (v. 27)	Yorava la Blankaniña lágrimas de veluntad.	A todo esto la condesa no cesaba de llorar.	La condesa que lo supo no cesaba de llorar.
(2)	*(lacking)*	—¿De ké yoráš Blancaniña, mi alma de ké yoráš?	—Que tendes, ó minha espôsa, não te posso afagar?	—¿Por qué lloras, ¡ay! condesa? ¿Por qué es tanto suspirar?
(3)	*(lacking)*	—Yoro por vos, kavayero, ke vos vaš i me dešáš.	*(lacking)*	—Porque me han dicho que ibas de capitán general.
(4)	...mas tiene mujer hermosa, mochacha de poca edad. ... [(v. 18)[5]	Me dešáš niña i muchacha, chika de poka edad.	*(lacking)*	...Y a su esposita la deja pequeña y de poca edad.
(8)	—No lloredes vos, condesa, de mi partida no hayáis pe- [sar, (v. 41)	—No vos sikliéš ['preocupéis'], mi iža [!], ni vos kiéraš siklear. *or* —No yores tú, Blankaniña, no yores tú, Blankaflor.	*(lacking)*	—No llores tú, la princesa, ni te quieras hacer mal.
(9)	que antes que yo me parta, todo vos lo quiero dar. [(v. 43)	Metió la mano en su pecho, sien doblones le dará.	*(lacking)*	*(lacking)*
(11)	Podéis vender cualquier villa y empeñar cualquier ciudad. [(vv. 44, 95)	—Venderéš viñas i kampos i media parte de sivdad. *or* Empeñéš kualkier kastiyo, empeñéš kualkier sivdad.	*(lacking)*	*(lacking)*
(12)	—¿Cuántos años, el buen con- [de, hacéis cuenta de tardar? [(v. 32)	—Si ya vos vaš, kavayero, desidme kuándo tornáš.	—¿Cuántos años, el buen conde, cuánto tiempo has de tardar?	—¿Para cuántos años, conde, para cuántos años vas?
(13)	—Siete años, la condesa, todos siete me esperad; [(v. 52)	—Vos asperaréš a los siete, si no, a los ocho vos kazáš. *or*	—Siete años, la condesa, siete años me esperad;	—Si a los siete años no vuelvo, a los ocho casarás.
(14)	si a los ocho no viniere, a los nueve vos casad. (v. 53)	—Si a los ocho no torno, a los nueve vos kazáš.	si a los ocho no viniere, a los nueve vos casáis.	Y si eres mujer de bien, a los nueve aguardarás.
(16)	El que con vos casare, señora, mis tierras tome en ajuar. [(v. 55)	Le darás todos mis bienes i una parte de sivdad.	*(lacking)*	*(lacking)*
(17)	Ya se parte el buen conde de París esa ciudad. (vv. 104, [64)	Se espartió el kavayero, se esparte i ya se va.	Ya se sale el conde Antores, ya se sale, ya se va.	Ya se marcha el conde Sol, ya se marcha, ya se va.

The Sephardic ballad shares stages 1-4, 8, 12-14, and 17 with one or another or both of *Dirlos*' modern Peninsular derivatives, but stages 9 (the Count's offer of money), 11 (the selling or mortgaging of properties), and 16 (the gift of the Count's belongings to the new husband), which in the modern tradition occur only in the Judeo-Spanish fragment, mark it as a notably conservative relique and entitle it to a place of importance beside *Dirlos*' other traditional descendants.

Another problem concerns the characteristics of the hypothetical later stages of the Eastern Sephardic *Dirlos* underlying *La vuelta del hijo maldecido.* The *Dirlos* verses "¡No fuyades, la condesa, / ni os queráis espantar, // que yo soy el conde Dirlos, / vuestro marido carnal!" [9] are echoed at the end of *La vuelta del hijo maldecido*: "No vos echéis, la mi madre, / ni vos quijerais echar, // yo so el vuestro hijo, / el vuestro hijo caronal." [10] Except for this detail other features of *Dirlos,* subsequent to his departure, have all been replaced by material taken over from the Greek *Evil Mother.*

Many of the Peninsular versions of *Conde Antores* have been influenced in varying degrees by the ballad of *El navegante,* another Hispanic treatment of the interrupted wedding theme. [11] One of the

---

[9] *Primavera* 164, p. 343.

[10] Attias 24.47-50. See also our review article, "A New Collection of Judeo-Spanish Ballads," no. 18.

[11] For the geographic range of this *romance,* its characteristics, and a synthetic version representing all branches of the tradition, see Catalán-Galmés, "El tema de la boda estorbada," pp. 76-77, n. 1. **Eastern J.-Sp.:** No text available. "El tema," p. 76, n. 1, reports an unspecified number of unedited versions from Sarajevo (Bosnia). See also the map on p. 68. **Archaic J.-Sp. incipit:** "La vida de las galeas / yo os la quiero contar": ASW 437; Avenary 383 (no. 44); Danon 107 (no. 63); RoH, II, 221. **Castilian:** No text available. See "El tema," p. 76, n. 1, where a version from Zamora is alluded to. Sampedro's geographically Galician text (no. 173), from Orense, is in Castilian. **Portuguese:** *A noiva arraiana:* Almeida Garrett, III, 121-123; Athaide Oliveira, pp. 397-399; Braga, I, 73-79, 85-86; III, 353-354; Bellermann, no. 23; Chaves, "O ciclo dos descobrimentos," pp. 108-110; Id., "O Romanceiro e o teatro popular," pp. 369-371; Estácio da Veiga, pp. 108-111; Hardung, II, 97-102; Pires de Lima-Lima Carneiro, *Romanceiro para o povo e para as escolas,* pp. 63-64; Tavares, *RL,* IX, 311-312; VRP 97-102, 994. **Brazilian:** *A noiva roubada:* Braga, I, 86-87; Romero, pp. 72-73; Santos Neves, p. 48 (no. 26). **Catalan:** *Don Lluis de Montalbà:* AFC 3165; Amades, I, 160-162; Avenç, IV, 74-76; Briz, II, 57-59; Massot, no. 8; Milá 206 (also OCPC, I: 1, 18); OCPC, I, 281; II, 152-153, 187; III, 261-262; Subirá, pp. 34-35. On the *Navegante*'s influence upon *Antores,* see "El tema," pp. 76-79, and nn. 12-13 *infra.*

Navegante's most characteristic intrusions upon *Antores* involves a scene in which the protagonist, returning after a long absence, meets and talks with his mother (aunt or aunts), before continuing on to the wedding feast to prevent his wife's second marriage. [12] The presence of such a borrowed allusion to the returning husband's encounter with his mother in some archaic form of the Judeo-Spanish *Dirlos* would certainly have heightened that narrative's similarity to the Greek *Evil Mother* and would have greatly facilitated the formation of the hybrid ballad of *La vuelta del hijo maldecido.* The fusion of *Dirlos* and *Hē kakḕ mána* may have been further helped along by certain maritime allusions, already implied in the old *Dirlos,* which, in some versions of *Antores,* are probably reinforced by interference from *El navegante.* [13] Such a possibility may explain the first verse of Pulido's Rumanian V*uelta del hijo maldecido*: "Naviguero, naviguero, / ¿ónde vais y mi dešáis?" (p. 397), though this mariner could simply have been transposed from a later stage in the narrative (i.e., Pulido, v. 16). Certain phrases found in *El navegante,* or taken by *Antores* from *El navegante,* seem to be echoed in *La vuelta del hijo maldecido.* In a Santander version of *Antores* (RPM 49) the aunt (< *El navegante*) evokes the figure of the hero's mother, who has gone blind gazing out to sea in hope of his return:

> —Tu madre ya estaba ciega   amirando pa la mar,
> por un hijo que tenía   y nunca le vio asomar.

Here the mother's rôle is analogous to that of the mother in *Hē kakḕ mána* and *La vuelta del hijo maldecido*:

---

[12] The mother appears as a contamination in *Antores* in RPM 48; Braga, III, 352, 355; Martins, I, 205; Tavares, *RL,* IX, p. 302, and in some versions of *El navegante:* e.g., Sampedro, no. 173; Braga, III, 353; VRP 100. For the aunt, see, for example, RPM 47, 49 (*Antores*) and Almeida Garrett, III, 121; Athaide Oliveira, p. 397; Braga, I, 73, 75, 77, 85, 86; VRP 97-99, 101-102; Romero, p. 72 *(Navegante).*

[13] Cf. in *Antores* such verses as "marinero soy, señora, / que navego por la mar" ("El tema," p. 75) or "No me llame marinero / nunca navegué en la mar" (RPM 47), which reflect *Dirlos*' voyage from "allende el mar," but may also be an echo of *El navegante,* which has imposed the aunt upon this same text (RPM 47).

Pasó tiempo i vino tiempo   i eskariño le fue a dar.
Aparóse a la ventana,   la ke da para la mar.
Vido venir naves frankas,   navegando por la mar.
(uned., Rhodes)

The formulistic term *hijo carnal*, which echoes similar constructions in *Dirlos* ("sobrino carnal," "marido carnal," "primos carnales": *Primav.* 164, pp. 341, 343, 347) and is so important in *La vuelta del hijo maldecido,* is also used for the protagonist's self-identification in at least one versión of *El navegante:* "que soy su hijo, señora, / que soy su hijo carnale" (Sampedro, no. 173). Compare the final verses of *La vuelta del hijo,* which at the same time are evidently calked from *El conde Dirlos:* [14]

No vos echéis, la mi madre,   ni vos quijerais echar,
yo so el vuestro hijo,   el vuestro hijo caronal.
(Attias 24.47-50)

An early *incipit* ("La vida de las galeas," etc.) and the unedited Bosnian versions of Catalán-Galmés vouch for *El navegante*'s presence in the tradition of the Eastern Sephardim. The above-mentioned similarities between *El navegante* and *La vuelta del hijo maldecido* seem to indicate that, either in exile or already on the Peninsula, *El navegante*'s influence was probably brought to bear upon a Judeo-Spanish form of *Dirlos.* Contaminations from *El navegante* doubtless helped to encourage *Dirlos*' union with the Greek ballad of *The Evil Mother.*

BIBLIOGRAPHY

La vuelta del hijo maldecido

Eastern J.-Sp.: Attias 24; Baruch 284; Cantera Ortiz, p. 28 (= Danon or Menéndez Pelayo); Danon 8; Elnecavé 1; Estrugo, *Los sefardíes,* p. 128; Id. "Reminiscencias," p. 71; Gil 32 (= Menéndez Pelayo, MP, Pulido); Hemsi 27; Levy 3; LSO 85 (= Molho, "Tres romances"); Menéndez Pelayo 21 (= Danon); Molho, "Tres romances," p. 69*b* (= UR, with minimal variants); MP 124; PTJ 128-128*b* (= Gil, CBU, Baruch); Pulido 397-398; Romey 6-6*a*; SBS 55; SICh 10; *Spomenica,* p. 322 (= Baruch); UR 7 (= CBU 335-336); UYA 176-177. All Eastern and Moroccan texts published to date, as well as abundant unedited

[14] See nn. 9-10 above.

versions, are brought together in R. Menéndez Pidal, *Romancero tradicional,* III (in press). Cf. also Rubiato, "El repertorio musical," p. 457.

Moroccan J.-Sp.: Larrea 193-194; MRuiz 95; PTJ 128*c* (= MRuiz).

Studies: Armistead-Silverman, "A New Collection of Judeo-Spanish Ballads," no. 18; Morley, "A New Jewish-Spanish *Romancero,*" p. 5 (on Hemsi 27); Puymaigre, "Notes," p. 271 (on Danon 8).

El conde Antores

For the text-type's geographic distribution and a synthetic version, see Catalán-Galmés, "El tema de la boda estorbada," pp. 67-80.

Archaic J.-Sp. Incipit: "Los ojos de la blanca niña / no hacen sino llorar": ASW 437; Avenary 383 (no. 47); Danon 106 (no. 11); RoH, II, 221. Cf. also p. 339.

Moroccan J.-Sp.: MP 60. Also: Catalán-Galmés, "El tema," p. 67.

Castilian: Menéndez Pidal, *El Romancero Español,* pp. 117-119; RPM 47-50; RQDB-II 54; RTCN 95; RTO 10. Also: Catalán-Galmés, "El tema," pp. 67-74.

Portuguese: Athaide Oliveira, pp. 266-267; Braga, I, 71-72; III, 351-353, 354-356; Chaves, "O ciclo dos descobrimentos," pp. 106-108; Id., "O Romanceiro e o teatro popular," pp. 364-369; Martins, I, 203-206; Reis Dâmaso, *Enciclopédia Republicana,* p. 173; Tavares, *RL,* IX, 302-303, 317-318; VRP 92-96. The later stages of Braga (= Tavares), Chaves, "O ciclo" and "O Romanceiro" (= Tavares), Martins, Tavares, and VRP are greatly influenced by *El navegante.* See "El tema," pp. 76-79 and nn. 11-13 *supra.*

El conde Sol

For the text-type's range and characteristics, see Menéndez Pidal, et al., *Cómo vive un romance,* especially pp. 53-108, 219-268; Catalán-Galmés, "El tema de la boda estorbada," pp. 80-95. Contaminated texts, in which *Conde Sol* is preceded by *Gerineldo,* are accompanied below by the indication "G+" in parenthesis.

Moroccan J.-Sp.: Alvar, "Gerineldo," pp. 139-140 (G+); Bénichou 16; Larrea 156.108 ff (G+), 240-243; MRuiz 69A-B; PTJ 60-60*a*; (= MRuiz, Alvar). See also: PHP 445-446, n. 2 (G+).

Castilian: Amador de los Ríos, "Romanzen Asturiens," pp. 290-291; ART 202-205; ASW 176-179, 278-279; Berrueta 343-345; Córdova y Oña, IV, nos. 213, 270, 272-273 and pp. 239-240; Cossío, *BBMP,* II, no. 12; CPE, I, 37-38 (G+); II, 21-22 (G+), 22-23; CPM, I, 42-43; CVR 5 (G+); Durán 327; Echevarría, pp. 416-417; Estébanez Calderón, *Escenas andaluzas,* pp. 250-252; FN 190-194; González Palencia, "El romance de Gerineldo en Albarracín," p. 24 (G+); Güéjar 17.79 ff. (G+); Hernáez Tobías, nos 3-5; Ledesma, pp. 165-166 (G+), 168-169, 180; Menéndez Pidal, et al., *Cómo vive un romance,* pp. 241-245, 248-249, 251-252, 255-256, 264-265 (G+); Micrófilo, pp. 93-97 (G+), 145-149;

Munthe 2 (G+); Pedrell, *Cancionero,* I, no. 51 (pp. 44-46); *Primavera* 135; RPE 17-20; RPM 82-96, 97-102 (G+), 103; RQDB-II 2; RSC 1-3 (G+); RTCN 2; RTO 17; RTR 6; Schindler 1; Torner, "La canción tradicional española," pp. 135-137 (G+).

Spanish American: Castro Leal, "Dos romances tradicionales," pp. 243-244 (G+); Chacón y Calvo, "Nuevos romances en Cuba," pp. 201-202 (G+). See also Catalán-Galmés, "El tema," p. 81; *Cómo vive un romance,* pp. 218-268.

Portuguese: Braga, III, 357-359; Chaves, "O Romanceiro e o teatro popular," pp. 362-364; Tavares, *RL,* IX, 320-321; VRP 995. See also "El tema," p. 81.

Catalan: AFC 2295; Aguiló, pp. 117-122; ASW 365-366; Massot 6; Milá 244; OCPC, II, 148.

El conde Dirlos [15]

Archaic Texts: Castañeda-Huarte, I, 153-175; CSA, fols. 6*r*-28*v*; Durán 354; *Pliegos góticos,* IV, 253-275, 325-344; *Pliegos de Praga,* I, 89-110; *Primavera* 164; Rodríguez-Moñino, "Campo de Alanje," no. 47; Id., *El Cancionero general*: *Noticias bibliográficas,* p. 116 (no. 4045); Id., "Tortajada," no. 22; *Silva de 1561,* fols. 11v-33v; Thomas, *Romance del conde Dirlos,* pp. 11-26. See also Simón Díaz, III:2, nos. 3011, 3040, 3042, 3054, 3056.

Studies:

Dirlos-Antores

Beatie, "Oral-traditional Composition," pp. 95, 107-108; Id., "Oral-traditional Themes"; Braga, III, 347-362; Catalán-Galmés, "El tema de la boda estorbada," *passim,* but especially pp. 66-80; CSA, pp. x-xi; EEB 25, 85-86, 103-104, 154, 176-177, 257-258, 384; Entwistle, "El Conde Dirlos," *passim*; Id., "French Epic Cycles," p. 208; Id., "La *Odisea,*" *passim*; Id., "New Light," pp. 379, 380; Id., "The Noble Moringer," pp. 3-4, 9; Menéndez Pidal, *El Romancero Español,* pp. 21, 116-119; Id., et al., *Cómo vive un romance,* pp. 53, 220-221 and n. 3; Id., "Poesía popular y Romancero," VIII, 266-267; X, 283, 284, 286; RoH, I, 77, 275-285; II, 67, 174, n. 8, 207, 221, 231, 246, 339, 419, n. 22; TRV, II, 253, 316, 383, 416.

---

[15] The story of *Conde Dirlos,* doubtless based upon some late broadside printing of the minstrel version, is well known to Philippine folk literature. On the 1,252 quatrain *corrido* of *Conde Irlos,* written in the Pampango language, see Fansler, "Metrical Romances," pp. 213-215, and the exhaustive treatment by Eugenio, *Awit and Korido,* pp. 95-111.

El conde Sol

BNE 224-225, 237, n. 13, 240, n. 15, 242-243; Catalán, "El motivo y la variación," pp. 158-166; Catalán-Galmés, "El tema de la boda estorbada," *passim,* but especially pp. 81 ff.; EEB 89; Entwistle, "El Conde Sol," *passim*; Id., "New Light," p. 379; FN 19; M. R. Lida de Malkiel, *Davar,* X (1947), pp. 8-9, 20; Michaëlis, "Estudos," p. 196; RoH, II, 379, 388-396, 399, 400-401.

Continental Analogs:

We can add little to Child's magnificently documented headnotes for *Hind Horn* (no. 17) and *Young Beichan* (no. 53); however, a few very basic indications may help to place *Dirlos* and its derivatives within the broader context of Pan-European balladry.

Dirlos-Antores

English: *Hind Horn*: Child 17; Bronson 17. Other English ballads on the interrupted wedding: *The Kitchie-Boy*: Child 252; *Lord William* or *Lord Lundy*: Child 254.

Anglo-American: Bronson 17; Coffin 17. Cf. Coffin 252.

Scandinavian: *Unge Hr. Tor og Jomfru Tore*: DgF, II, no. 72; Prior, III, 151-159. *Herr Lagman och Herr Thor*: Arwidsson, I, no. 24; Prior, II, 441-446. *Henrik af Brunsvig*: DgF, II, no. 114; Arwidsson, II, no. 168; Prior, II, 69-75.

German: *Heimkehr des Ehemannes*: DVM 11; Meier, *Balladen,* I, no. 7. *Der edle Moringer*: DVM 12; Erk-Böhme 28; Meier, *Balladen,* I, no. 8; Röhrich-Brednich 19; also Butzmann, "Eine neue Handschrift"; Entwistle, "The Noble Moringer." *Heinrich der Löwe-Der Herzog von Braunschweig*: Erk-Böhme 26-27; see Child, I, 195-197. Cf. also *Der heimkehrende Bräutigam*: DVM 102.

Rumanian: *Moşneagul*: Amzulescu, no. 290; Fochi, pp. 540-547; Vrabie, pp. 468-472.

Macedo-Rumanian: Fochi, pp. 561-563; Weigand, nos. 61-62.

Slavic: See Child, I, 200; EEB 11-12, 86, 104, 258, 357, 364, 367-368, 385; Fochi, pp. 550-558; Lüdeke, "Griechische Volksdichtung," p. 252; Schirmunski, pp. 109-110 (no. 14).

Greek: *Ho niópantros sklábos* (*The Recently Married Galley Slave*): Arabantinos, nos. 2 and 462; Baud-Bovy, *Textes,* pp. 158-160; Dawkins, "Tragoúdia tõn Dōdekanēsōn," no. 25; Fochi, pp. 563-567; Jeannarakis, nos. 264-265; Legrand, *Recueil,* pp. 326-329 (no. 145); Liebrecht, *Zur Volkskunde,* pp. 167-168 (no. 13), 185-186 (nos. 439, 448-449), 207 (no. 145), 216 (no. 264-265); Lüdeke, "Griechische Volksdichtung," pp. 218-219, 252; Lüdeke-Megas, nos. 67-70; Passow, nos. 439, 448-449; Sakellarios, I, 37-38 (no. 13); Sakellarios, II, 58-61 (nos. 15-16). For more bibliography, see Child, I, 199-200. As Entwistle observes, this Greek ballad is probably related genetically to *El navegante* (*Don*

Lluis de Montalbà). See "El Conde Dirlos," pp. 9, 11, 12; "The Noble Moringer," pp. 3-4, 9; "La historia del cautivo," *RFH*, II (1940), 387-388; n. 11 *supra* and *La esposa de Don García* (no. 13, n. 10 *supra*).

Albanian: *Konstantíni i bógeliə* (*Constantino il piccolo*); *Aga Ymeri*: Camarda, pp. 90-97; De Grazia, pp. 118-125, 263-265; Fochi, pp. 558-561; Skendi, p. 47. Also: Child, I, 198-199, and the epic, *Ali der Bajraktar*, discussed by Lambertz, pp. 64, 107.

El conde Sol

Italian: *Moran d'Inghilterra*: Nigra 42. See also Bronzini, I, 40.

English: *Young Beichan*: Child 53; Bronson 53.

Anglo-American: Bronson 53; Coffin 53.

Scandinavian: *Stolt Ellensborg*: DgF, IV, no. 218; Olrik, II, no. 27; Smith-Dampier, pp. 318-322.

Hungarian: A ballad of this type contaminates *Clement Mason*: Leader, pp. 27 (text *O*), 31, n. 1.

Slavic: Schirmunski, p. 110.

Hē kakè mána (The Evil Mother)

Greek: Abbott, *Macedonian Folklore*, p. 195 and n. 2; Argenti-Rose 736-737; Dawkins, "Tragoúdia tōn Dōdekanēsōn," no. 4; D'Istria 626; Fauriel, II, 202-205 (no. 23); Hadjilazaros, pp. 23-25; Haxthausen, no. 15.19 ff. (pp. 116-119); Jeannarakis, no. 195; Kind, *Anthologie*, pp. 124-127; Klaar, no. 54; Legrand, *Recueil*, pp. 248-251 (no. 123); Lübke, pp. 241-242; Lüdeke-Megas, nos. 26-29; Michaelides Nouaros, pp. 216-217, 262; Pappadopoulos, *Pandōra*, p. 416b; Passow, nos. 343-349; Pellegrini, *Cargese*, pp. 15-16; Pernot, *Études*, nos. 32, 114; Politis, *Eklogaì*, pp. 197-198 (no. 165); Sanders, pp. 44-47; Schmidt, *Griechische Märchen*, nos. 67-68; Schrader, pp. 54-55; Theros, II, no. 558; Tommaseo-Pavolini, pp. 79-80; Tozer, "Modern Greek Ballads from Corsica," no. 1. A sixteenth-century fragment of this song appears in the Mount Athos MS discovered by Bouvier (*Dēmotikà tragoúdia tēs Monēs tōn Ibērōn*, no. 11). Cf. also "Treize chansons populaires du XVIe siècle."

Macedo-Rumanian: *Blăstemlu di mumă*: Papahagi, pp. 61-63.

24

LA BELLA EN MISA

(The Beauty in Church)

Tres damas van ala misa 'a azer la 'orasyyón.
'Entre medyyo mi 'espoza, la ke más kerí'a yyo.
¡Mi Se[nyyor]!
Kamiza de 'olanda yeva, sirma 'i perla al kavesón.
¡Kara de flor!
Sayyo yeva sovre sayyo, 'un śiboyy de altornasyyón.
¡Mi Se[nyyor]!
Su kavesa 'una torong̃a, sus kave'os briles son.
¡Kara de flor!
La su sežika 'enarkada árkol de tirar yya son.
¡Mi Se[nyyor]!

Source: GSA 4. Variants: LRI 6, BRI 6, GRI 6.
In GSA, the refrain to vv. 2, 4, 6, 10 is abbreviated *mi se'*. LRI and BRI do not abbreviate. LRI omits the refrain following v. 2. GRI lacks all refrains. In GSA, LRI, and BRI, vv. 2-10 are repeated following their respective refrains. GRI repeats hemistichs *a* and *b* of v. 2, but only hemistich *b* of subsequent verses. LRI, BRI, and GRI introduce repetitions with *'i*.

1*a* ala milsa *LRI* / *GRI*, 'a la milsa *BRI*.
2*a* 'Entre medyyo la mi 'espoza *in repetition* GSA. 'Entre 'enmeđyyo (la) mi espoza *BRI* (la *in repetition only*) / *GRI*.
3*a* lyeva *in repetition BRI*, 'el kavesón *in repetition LRI*.
4*a* sayyo yeva sovre salyyo *GRI*, sóvere *in repetition GSA*.
4*b* 'en śiboyy *in repetition BRI*.
5*a-b* kavelyyos *BRI* / *GRI* (*In BRI the repetition is completely vitiated*: 'i sus kave'os 'una torong̃a / sus kavelyyos briles son).

Los sus 'ožos ğiketikos, 'espežikos de 'Istambol;
¡Kara de flor!
las sus karas koloradas mansanas de 'Eskopyya son.
¡Mi Senyyor!
Su nariz aporfilada péndola de 'eskrivir yya son.
¡Kara de flor!
10 La su boka ğiketika, ke non le kave pinyyón.
¡Mi Se[nyyor]!
11 Sus dyentes tan menudikos perla de 'enfilar yya son.
¡Kara de flor!

7*b* 'espežos *BRI* ('espežikos *in repetition*) / *GRI*.
8*a* raras *GSA* (karas *in repetition*), koreladas *BRI* (koroladas *in repetition*), koroladas *GRI*.
9*b* naris *LRI* / *BRI*, aperfilada *LRI* / *BRI* / *GRI*.
10*b* ke *om*. *GRI*, 'un pinyyón *GRI*.

Translation:

"Three ladies are going to Mass, to say their prayers. One of them is my betrothed, the one who is dearest to me. *Oh, my Lord*! She is wearing a blouse of Holland cloth, with a neckpiece of pearls and silver thread. *Her face like a flower*! She is wearing many pleated skirts and her best waistcoat. (5) Her head is a round grapefruit; her hair is golden thread. Her arched eyebrows are taut bows. Her little eyes are small mirrors from Istanbul. Her pink cheeks are apples from Skoplje; her fine nose is a writing pen; (10) her mouth so small that not even a rosebud can fit between her lips. *Oh, my Lord*! (11) Her tiny teeth, so fine, are pearls for a necklace. *Her face like a flower*!

The famous Pan-Hispanic ballad of *La bella en misa* has been substantially documented in the major Eastern Judeo-Spanish communities: Salonika (Attias, "Hispanic Balladry," G. Menéndez Pidal, Yoná), Edirne (Danon), Izmir (Hemsi), Rhodes (DRH), and Jerusalem (?) (SICh). In addition, we have four other unedited versions from Rhodes. The *romance* is rare in Morocco, where its attachment to another ballad—a development which is paralleled in some Castilian versions—offers an index of its tenuous traditional life.[1] The three known versions are all from Tetuán, but we could find none there or elsewhere in Morocco during our 1962-63 fieldwork. Representation from Portugal (an area, in this case, dependent on the Castilian tradition), the center of the Peninsula, and Spanish America (Argentina only) is equally spotty, though Schindler's version from Avila, Magaña's from La Rioja, and Echevarría's Manchegan fragment give the ballad a slightly wider range than is indicated by Menéndez Pidal: "Cáceres, Salamanca y Segovia" (FN 189). Only in Catalonia, whence a relatively large number of versions of *La dama de Aragón* have been published, do we find a vigorous modern tradition.

Yoná's printings are all essentially identical and reveal no attempt at subsequent editing in view of the oral tradition. Yoná's version, which offers an excellent example of the usual metaphoric catalog of the girl's personal attractions,[2] is incomplete as regards the ending. Other Salonikan texts supply at least four essential verses following Yoná's v. 11:

---

[1] Cf. Alvar, "Los romances de *La bella,*" pp. 270-271. The ballad may, however, have enjoyed a more vigorous existence in the fairly recent past, for it seems to have left its mark on at least one other Moroccan ballad: i.e., *El capitán burlado*: "El que sopla la candela / la barba se le quemaba" (Larrea 177.37-38).

[2] On the ballad's use of traditional imagery paralleled in other Sephardic songs (*Melisenda sale de los baños* and the wedding song *Ansí dize la nuestra novia*), see our remarks in "Hispanic Balladry," p. 239, and DRH, pp. 26-27. The following publications are also germane to this problem: Menéndez Pidal, "Un viejo romance cantado por Sabbatai Ceví," pp. 186, 188; RoH, II, 222-226; M. R. Lida de Malkiel, *NRFH,* III (1949), 84-85; Alvar, "Patología y terapéutica rapsódicas" and "Interpretaciones judeo-españolas del árabe *ġabba*"; our review articles NSR, pp. 65-66, and "Sobre unos romances del Cid recogidos en Tetuán," p. 390, nn. 10-14; and I[saac] R. M[olho], "Similitud de la nariz a la péndola," in *Tesoro de los judíos sefardíes,* II (Jerusalem, 1959), 116.

On the popular Spanish expression *boca de piñón* (cf. Yoná, v. 10), see F. Rosselli, "Alcune integrazioni ai glossari del *Diablo cojuelo,*" *Miscellanea di studi ispanici,* Vol. 6 (Pisa, 1963), 178-222: pp. 221-222. See also the erudite ballad "Hizo calor una noche" (*Romancero general de 1600,* I, no. 614.61-62), which mentions "Una boca, chica era, / que con un piñón se mide"; extraneous verses in a text of *La mujer engañada* from Cartagena: "... Adiós, María, / boca de piñón" (Puig Campillo, p. 78); the Catalan ballads, *Francisca:* "Sí té el cabell ros y fi / la trena gruixada y llarga, // la boqueta de pinyó, / la dent menudeta y blanca" (Milá 387.6-7), *El indeciso*: "Te la boca de pinyó / la dent menudeta y blanca" (Milá 432), and *Montanyas del Canigò*: "Té la cara be feta, / la boca de pinyó" (Canteloube, I, 184).

Eya entrando a la misa, la misa s'arrelumbró.
El papás k'está meldando, de meldar ya se kedó.
—Melda, melda, el papaziko, i ke por ti no vengo yo.
Vine por el ižo del reyes, ke de amor v'a muerir yo.[3]

Combining evidence provided by the various Eastern Sephardic texts, we can piece together the following brief course of action which is, in part, corroborated in other geographic subtraditions: a marvelously beautiful girl, bedecked in the most exquisite finery, attends mass and by her presence throws the priest and lesser officiants into a state of confusion, disrupting the service and bringing it to a halt.[4] The girl then tells the priest to continue praying, for she has not come to church for him, but for the King's son, of whom she is enamored.

In his articles on *La dama de Aragón,* Entwistle convincingly argues that the Spanish ballad is only a fragment of a much larger narrative. He demonstrates that the *romances* (the Catalan *Dama* and the Castilian *Bella*) correspond exactly to the culminating scene of a Pan-Hellenic

---

Apples from Skoplje (Üsküb) (cf. Yoná, v. 8) are used with reference to a girl in a Bulgarian ballad: "Meglena, Mädchen, du schönes, / Meglena, Apfel von Skopje ..." (Gesemann, *Zweiundsiebzig Lieder,* p. 21). On imagery similar to that used in *La bella, Melisenda,* and *La nuestra novia,* in Balkan folk poetry, see Dieterich, "Die Volksdichtung der Balkanländer in ihren gemeinsamen Elementen," p. 406; Petropoulos, *La comparaison,* p. 41, n. 5.

[3] The first three hemistichs are from Attias 14.29-31; the rest, from "Hispanic Balladry," no. 5.13-15. Attias, Hemsi, and Danon seem to have been influenced by some treatment of *The Husband's Return.* Compare Attias, vv. 37-40 ("Siete años hay que l'aspero," etc.) with *La esposa fiel* (Attias 19.29-32), *La vuelta del marido (é)* (Attias 18.15-18), and *La vuelta del hijo maldecido* (LSO 85, no. 18.11-12). These versions also suffer incremental amplifications involving who is to be the girl's future husband—the Pope of Rome, the Duke of Istanbul, or the lute player (*tañedor*)—in case the girl's beloved "does not return." Cf. M. R. Lida de Malkiel, "El romance de la misa de amor," pp. 38-39, n. 1; Entwistle, *HR,* VIII, 159, at n. 6.

[4] Cf. V5. *Negligence in religious exercise*; X434. *The parson put out of countenance.* On the medieval *topos* of the priest whose wandering fancy leads him to inject secular matter into the mass, see M. R. Lida de Malkiel, "El romance de la misa de amor," p. 41. Compare the French *Confesseur* (Arbaud, I, 166-169 [*Lou Pero blanc*]; Rolland, I, 162-163):

Se lou Pero blanc s'en vai, s'en vai dire la grand messo.
Toutes les mots que disie: Alleluia! par ma mestresso.

On the gallant who goes to mass better to contemplate his beloved and on analogous *topoi,* see our forthcoming study on *De-Christianization,* s.v. *mass.*

ballad, *Hē núfē koumpára* (*The Bridesmaid Who Became a Bride*). The Greek song tells the following story:

> A young lord proposes to desert his beloved and marry another woman. He orders the former to attend on the latter at the wedding. Taking her mother's advice, the discarded lady dresses herself exquisitely, and her entry into the chapel completely disorganizes the ceremony. The bridegroom swoons and, when he recovers consciousness, orders the service to be begun again and the bridal crown to be given to his former mistress. [5]

The Greek verses that parallel the *romances* have the following import:

> Then she bedecked herself three days and three nights. She put on heaven for her mantle, and the sea on her gown, the sun on her face, the moon on her breast, and the raven's feather on her arched brows, an embroidered viper as ribbon for her tresses, and cast on pearls unmeasured, like sand. She takes (a ring) and goes to the church to plight and crown the bride. Handmaids go before her, handmaids behind, and two handmaids at her sides to keep the sun from falling on her. Along the way she passed, the footpaths burst into flowers. And when the church saw her, it shook from end to end. The priest saw her and stumbled, the deacon quite forgot. The choir and precentors forgot their psalters. [6]

Entwistle is altogether correct in relating the *romances* and the *tragoúdi,* but he has seen relatively few Greek texts and fewer Hispanic ones and he overlooks an important French song, *Les atours de Marie-Madeleine,* an *a lo divino* reworking of the Catalan *Dama de Aragón* which shares certain important archaic features with the Judeo-Spanish tradition. A comparison of Greek, Hispanic, and French texts unavailable to Entwistle, or not consulted by him, reveals a mass of features on which the Western-European and Greek ballads agree. These agreements deserve individual consideration, for such a procedure greatly clarifies the relationship of the Romance songs to one another

---

[5] We adapt Entwistle's summary ("*La Dama de Aragón,*" p. 187). On the Greek ballad's wide geographic range, see also Baud-Bovy, *Textes,* p. 214.

[6] Entwistle, "*La Dama de Aragón,*" p. 187.

and to their ultimate source, the Greek *Bridesmaid Who Became a Bride.*

The Greek, Catalan, and French-Provençal songs coincide in evoking a scene in which the girl puts on elaborate adornments before leaving for mass. In the Castilian ballad, and in its Portuguese and Judeo-Spanish derivatives, these preparations are usually combined with the description of the girl's breathtaking beauty at the moment of her entering the church. However, Attias' singular text begins with the usual "Tres damas van a la misa ... ," etc., goes through the entire description corresponding to Yoná's vv. 3-11, and then includes the following verse:

Ya se viste, ya se endona, para la misa partió.

The text then continues "Ella entrando a la misa, / la misa s'arrelumbró," etc. Does Attias' version recall a previous stage of the Castilian-Judeo-Spanish tradition in which the girl's *toilette* was separated from the description of her entrance into the church? The verse in question is formulistic and may well be a mere borrowing from *La expulsión de los judíos de Portugal, Blancaflor y Filomena,* or some other ballad:

Ya la visten, ya la endonan, y al caballo ya la han subido.
(*Expulsión*: Attias 57.15-16)

Ya la viste, ya la endona, encima el caballo la subiera.
(*Blancaflor y Filomena*: Attias 37.31-32)

Ya se viste y se atacana, a la nave a yegado.
(*Robo de Elena*: Adatto 2)

Se vistió y se atacanó, en cavayo se suvería.
(*Don Bueso*: Adatto 1) [7]

In the Greek texts (e.g., Passow, no. 436), aunts and cousins help to adorn the bridesmaid, just as various relatives perform the same task

[7] The last case is itself obviously a contamination. *Atacanar* is from T. *takınmak* 'put on, wear'. Cf. C. Crews, "Miscelanea Hispano-Judaica," *VR,* 16 (1957), 224-245: pp. 229-230.

in Catalonian and Provençal forms of the Western ballad. Metaphoric descriptions of the girl's beauty or adornments occur in both the Greek song and the Eastern Sephardic form of *La bella en misa* though the latter has certainly been influenced by similar formulistic descriptions in other *romances.* [8] The solar imagery with which the description of the girl begins in the Greek texts ("Bázei tòn hēlio prósōpon kaì tò feggári stēθos") [9] also appears, though not metaphorically, in *Les atours*: "Iéou voou quèré ma queifuro / que lou choulel rayo dedzou" ('Je vais chercher ma coiffure où le soleil rayonne dessous'); "La coiffure qui la coiffe / les quatre soleils y son." [10] In Catalonia the girl is "bonica com un sol"; [11] in *La bella en misa,* she enters the chapel "relumbrando como el sol." [12] Some Eastern texts are even closer to their Greek

[8] See n. 2 above.

[9] 'She put on her the sun for a face and the moon for a bosom' (Argenti-Rose 730-731). Cf. Politis, *Eklogaì,* no. 83.28. The Greek verse is formulistic. It occurs, for example, in an apparently unrelated ritual song traditional among the nomadic Saracatsans: "Mets le soleil sur ton visage / et pose la lune sur ta poitrine" (Kavadias, *Les saracatsans,* p. 260) and in a Chian "Praise song" published by Argenti and Rose: "poú'cheis tòn hēlio prósōpo kaì tò feggári stēθeia" ('You have the sun for a face and the moon for a bosom': pp. 646-647). Legrand records a variant of the same formula: "Pour visage elle prend le soleil, pour collier la lune" (*Recueil,* no. 109); cf. Georgeakis-Pineau, pp. 264, 317. Essentially identical verses occur in *St. George and the Dragon* (Jeannaraki, no. 1; Pernot, *Anthologie,* p. 91), *Mavrianos and his Sister,* and *The Sold Wife* (Lüdeke-Megas, nos. 36, 37, 77). For similar imagery in Hungarian ballads, see Leader, p. 291; Vargyas, *Researches,* p. 159.

[10] Rolland, VI, 7-8 and 3. Cf. also pp. 9-10 (Text G); Doncieux, p. 169, v. 9.

[11] For example: Briz, I, 63; Milá, OCPC, III, 241.

[12] *Primav.* 143; FN 189. The girl's resplendent beauty is sometimes mentioned as part of her description; in other cases it is alluded to at the moment of her entering the church.

Cf. F574.1. *Resplendent beauty.* The motif appears elsewhere in Hispanic traditional poetry: "Dimés k'es vuestra figura / k'alelumbra más k'el sol" (*Torongal* [wedding song]: SBS 150); "Cuando tú entras, / la iglesia se ilumina ..." (*seguidilla*: CPM, no. 459); "Blanca y rubia como el sol / que relumbra de una legua" (*La Virgen romera*: RPM 356-360; RTO 57). For Hispano-Arabic and medieval European instances, see A. Castro, *La realidad histórica de España* (Mexico City, 1954), pp. 420-422; cf. also J. T. Monroe, "*The Muwashshaḥāt,*" *Collected Studies in Honour of Américo Castro's Eightieth Year* (Oxford, England, 1965), pp. 335-371: 341-342; H. Pérès, *La poésie andalouse en arabe classique au XI*[e] *siècle* (Paris, 1937), pp. 404, 406; E. García Gómez, *El libro de las banderas de los campeones de Ibn Saʿīd al-Maġribī* (Madrid, 1942), pp. 130, 140; Id., *Poemas arábigoandaluces,* 3rd ed. (Buenos

and French analogs: "'I su firente ['frente'] reluzyentre, / ke arelumbra más ke 'el sol." [13] In some Catalan texts, just as in the Greek ballad, the mother intervenes to suggest that the girl go to church. [14] In the Greek song, the girl is accompanied by handmaidens ("bágies"); [15] in the Eastern Sephardic versions she is one of three, or even a hundred damsels (Hemsi, DRH); in Morocco and the Central Peninsular tradition she is said to be "entre todas la mejor"; [16] in Catalonia she is escorted by servants ("criats" [Briz, I, 6]). Along the way the girl's beauty causes the very footpaths to burst into bloom ("Stò drómon ópou pḗgaine, tà monopátia anθoûsan" [Politis, v. 37]). Likewise, flowers, bushes, or trees bloom along the way or at the font in the church itself in the French, Provençal and Catalan ballads:

Les chemins par où qu'all's passent, les bussons fleurissaient tous.
(Rolland, VI, 6)

Lo camin per ont el passa, los albres florisson tos.
(Doncieux, v. 13)

Con vol pendre aigua beneita, les piques tornaren flos.
(OCPC, III, 241) [17]

The Greek bridesmaid, upon approaching the church, causes it to shake from end to end: "Ki' hōsàn tȇn eîde hē ekklēsiá, ap' ákrē s'ákrē seístē" (Politis, v. 38). Similar seismic phenomena are produced—in one case with exact verbal correspondence ("ap' ákrē s'ákrē" = "bout pour bout")—in the Provençal and French *Atours de Marie-*

Aires—Mexico City: "Austral," 1946), no. 73; Id., *Las jarchas romances de la serie árabe en su marco* (Madrid, 1965), no. 26.2 ("šamsiyya l-muḥaiyā" ['un sol es su rostro']); also no. 31.3; Ibn Quzmān uses the Romance metaphor "maḫšallu du šul" ('mejilla de sol') in one of his *zajals* (A. R. Nykl, *El cancionero de Aben Guzmán* [Madrid-Granada, 1933], p.116 [no. 49.6*b*]).

[13] DRH 1.6. The Italian song collected by Casetti and Imbriani may also recall this solar imagery: "Pari 'na luna ...," etc. The Greek ballad evokes both sun and moon. See n. 9 *supra.*

[14] Camps y Mercadal 182; Milá 218F; Rolland, VI, 9-10.

[15] Politis, no. 83.35-36. Concerning this aspect of the Greek ballad, see Romaios, "*Le retour de l'expatrié,*" pp. 50-51. Cf. Baud-Bovy, *Textes,* p. 215, where the "slaves" are stones which move, animated by the beauty of the girl.

[16] Alvar, Larrea; *Primav.;* FN, CPE.

[17] Cf. also Rolland, VI, 4; Briz, I, 63; Milá 218H and B1; Segura 110.

Madeleine: "Quant metèt ginol en terra, / los autars tremblavon tos" (Doncieux, v. 17); "Quand elle prit d'l'eau bénite, / l'autel trembla bout pour bout" (Rolland, VI, 4).[18] In one of the Greek texts, a deacon goes mad[19] and the same happens to an acolyte in one of the Catalan versions: "escolà que li ajuda, / ha perduda la raó" (OCPC, I, 106). In the Greek ballad the bridegroom faints; in Morocco this mishap may have been transferred to "el que toca la vigüela / en un desmayo cayó" (Larrea 202.25-26).

The confusion experienced by the priest and other officiants is universally attested in the Hispanic and French traditions and is closely paralleled in the Greek. However, in this connection, many Eastern Judeo-Spanish texts add another important detail. When the priest and his helpers stop to gawk at the beautiful girl, she admonishes them to continue their prayers:

El papás k'está meldando i de meldar ya se kedó.
—Melda, melda, el dezdichado, ke por ti no vengo yo. . . .
El ke tañe la laúta, de tañer ya se kedó.
—Tañe, tañe, el dezdichado, ke por ti no vengo yo. . . .[20]

Though it is not included in Politis' composite text used by Entwistle, the girl's admonition to priest and helpers is also a common feature of the Greek versions:

Παπᾶς τὴν εἶδε κι' ἔσφαλε καὶ διάκος κι' ἐξηλώθη
καὶ τὰ μικρὰ διακόπουλα ἐχάσαν τὰ χαρτιά τως.
«Ψάλλε παπᾶ σὰν πού 'φαλες, διάκο σὰν ποὺ 'λειτούργας
καὶ σεῖς μικρὰ διακόπουλα εὑρᾶτε τὰ χαρτιά σας.»

---

[18] The same motif occurs also in the Italian song collected by Casetti and Imbriani, which must be related to the other Romance ballads: "E quandu pigghi l'acqua beneditta, / parsi ca tutta la chiesa tremau." See n. 26 *infra*.

[19] See the Argenti-Rose text cited below (n. 21).

[20] Uned., sung by Leah Huniu, from Rhodes, in Los Angeles, July 31, 1958. Cf. DRH, p. 29, n. 26. Compare also Danon, Hemsi, SICh. The presence of the *tañedor* and other minor figures, in addition to the priest, is surely a prototypic feature of *La bella en misa,* since they also appear in the Greek ballad. Concerning the minor officiants and their relationship to the Judeo-Spanish lute player, guitar player, etc., see our forthcoming study on *De-Christianization,* s.v. *priest.*

(The priest saw her and slipped, and the deacon [saw her] and went mad,
and the little choir-boys lost their papers.
"Chant, father, as you chanted and you, deacon, as when you conducted the service,
and you little choir-boys, find your papers.")[21]

Were further corroboration of the authenticity of this stage of the *romance* necessary, it could be found in both *Oc* and *Oïl* versions of *Les atours de Marie-Madeleine,* which here parallel exactly the Judeo-Spanish ballad and its Greek counterpart:

Loous prèchtés quittoun lour mécho, maï loous clergués lours [leïchous.
—Atsabas, prèchtres, lo mécho, et clergués, vochtras leïchous.
('Les prêtres quittent leur messe et les clercs leurs leçons.
—Achevez, prêtres, la messe, et clercs, vos leçons.')

(Rolland, VI, 8)

Le clerc qui disait la messe au Kyrie demeura court.
Et l'clergé qui lui répond en oublia sa leçon.
N'y eut que le grand saint Pierre qui n'fit pas attention:
—Tout beau, tout beau, Madeleine, abaissez votre grandour!
—Prêtres, continuez la messe, je n'l'abaiss'rai pas pour vous.

(Rolland, VI, 5)[22]

The Galician version of *La bella en misa* seems to have kept some memory of what the church service is all about. In the other Hispanic texts the girl's opulent finery serves no apparent purpose, but here we are told that a peasant's daughter has put on her Sunday best to marry a high-born gentleman:

Sube al alto, sube al alto, ao mais alto corredor,
que verás como vai guapa a filla do labrador. . . .
Casa c'un Conde galán, casa c'un rico señor.

(Sampedro-Carré)

---

[21] Argenti-Rose 730-731. Similar verses occur in Abbott; Arabantinos; Baud-Bovy, *Chansons,* II, 253; Fauriel; Garnett; Lagarde; Lüdeke-Megas, nos. 56, 59-62; Passow, nos. 436, 438; Pernot, *Études,* no. 110.40; Petropoulos, text B, v. 30; Proust.

[22] See also Rolland, VI, 10-11.

Though the allusion may be a coincidence, Extremeño versions seem still to recall the girl's lover. Here, the rings which form part of her finery were brought to her from the fair at León. In other words, the rejected fiancée seeks to use a gift from her former lover to help regain his affection:

Y en sus manos blancas lleva anillos de gran való[r],
que se los trajo su amante, que se los trajo su amó[r],
que se los trajo su amante de la feria de León. [23]

Lastly, though it is impossible to tell for certain whether or not they are simply coincidental "reconstructions," it is worth noting that, in our Salonikan text of *La bella* ("Hispanic Balladry"), the girl is enamored of a "King's son," just as in Legrand's and Pellegrini's versions of *Hē núfē koumpára* and that, in Attias, as in all the Greek texts, the girl seems to have won "the King's" love as the ballad ends:

Estas palabras diciendo, que el buen rey que allegó.
Se tomaron mano con mano y juntos se ḥueron los dos. [24]

---

[23] RPE 90, vv. 5-7. Cf. CPE, II, 40. The girl's brother replaces the lover in Catalan versions, but an "aymadó[r]," who is apparently waiting for brother and sister at church, is referred to in Milá 218G. The quasi-incestuous intervention of the brother in the Catalan ballad, of which there is no trace in the Greek texts we have seen, seems to be a contamination, though of respectable antiquity, since certain Bragançan versions also hint at the same motif: "Tamen una irmana mia / das mais guapas que lá vão" (Alves 577; VRP 744). The motif of the fair (*d'Aragó, de León,* etc.), though extraneous to the Greek original, must be quite archaic, since it appears in both Catalonia and Extremadura. The girl's being sold at the fair (OCPC, III, 241) is also impossible to reconcile with the Greek texts at our disposal. Could the Catalan ballad have been based upon a Greek version somehow contaminated by the story of *The Sold Wife* (Lüdeke-Megas, nos. 76-78, 84.22 ff.)? Here a long-lost sister is unknowingly purchased by her brother. See also Lüdeke "Griechische Volksdichtung," pp. 219, 253.

[24] Attias 14.47-50. Needless to say these are simply formulistic filler verses. Their use here satisfies an obvious need to bring the narrative to some definite conclusion. But, all the same, might they not also conceal some "authentic" memory of a more extensive narrative? The second verse, which is also present in Danon and Hemsi, is used to conclude many other Eastern Sephardic *romances*. See M. R. Lida de Malkiel, "El romance de la misa de amor," p. 39, n. In Larrea 202 the girl goes off with a "caballero," who appears to be identical with "el que toca la vigüela" (v. 25). The ending of SICh and an unedited Rhodian version might also distantly echo the original story: "Yyo no vine por 'el Papa de Roma, / ni por 'el Duke de 'Istambol. // Vine por 'el mi marido, / telas de

The following table brings together the features shared by the Greek and Romance ballads. The order of presentation follows the Greek narrative. Parentheses enclose dubious or sporadically attested features:

TABLE 4

Hē núfē koumpára and its Romance congeners

	Koumpára	*Dama de Aragón*	*Atours*	*Bella en misa*	"Pari 'na luna ..."
Mother suggests girl go to church	X	X			
Adornment scene	X	X	X	(X)	
Girl helped by relatives	X	X	X		
Metaphoric description of adornments or beauty	X			(X)	
Solar imagery	X	X	X	X	X
Girl accompanied by attendants	X	X		(X)	
Beauty causes flowers to bloom	X	X	X		
Church shakes	X		X		X
Priest confounded	X	X	X	X	X
Lesser officiants confounded	X	X	X	X	
Lesser officiant goes mad	(X)	(X)			
Fainting	X			(X)	
"Continue praying"	X		X	X	
Marriage service	X			(X)	
Lover mentioned	X	(X)		(X)	
Lover is King's son	X			(X)	
Girl regains lover's affection	X			(X)	

In short: Although Entwistle has perhaps tended to over-stress the possible rôle of Greece—Akritic Anatolia in particular—as a fountainhead of balladic themes, in this particular case we can only applaud his scholarly acumen. A host of details in *La bella en misa, La dama de Aragón,* and *Les atours de Marie-Madeleine,* [25] like similar enigmas

mi corazón" (v. 12). Cf. also Entwistle's observation concerning Danon's version in *HR,* VIII, 159, at n. 6.

[25] In *Textes,* p. 217, n. 1, Baud-Bovy perceives the relationship between *Les atours* and *Hē núfē koumpára,* but envisions a French source for the Greek ballad rather than the reverse. Doncieux (pp. 171-172) connects *Les atours* with

present in those Spanish ballads which broke away from the more complex structures of medieval epicry, only take on full significance when seen as part of the more extensive narrative of the Greek *Bridesmaid Who Became a Bride*. Of the numerous additional, sometimes very close, agreements adduced here between the Western European and Greek texts, some may well be coincidental later developments (e.g., the presence of the lover [Extremadura; Catalonia]; recollection of the wedding [Galicia]; the deranged acolyte; the *topos* of the King's son; formulistic Judeo-Spanish dénouements), but taken as a whole they cannot but help to confirm vigorously Entwistle's contention that *La bella en misa* must depend on the Greek ballad. That the *romance*'s prototype reached the Western Mediterranean as a Catalan ballad (*La dama de Aragón*) —undoubtedly subsequent to the Catalan presence in Greece during the fourteenth century— is borne out by various correspondences between the latter, its French derivative (*Les atours*), and the Greek song, which, on the other hand, do not come over into the Castilian *Bella en misa* (*toilette*; intervention of mother and relatives; blooming flowers). This Catalan source text was, however, sensibly more detailed than any Catalan version known today, a fact that is confirmed by the Greek features (shaking church; "Continue praying"), which are known to *Les atours* and *La bella*, but which do not appear in *La dama*.

BIBLIOGRAPHY

La bella en misa

Eastern J.-Sp.: Attias 14; BdR, no. 14 (= Danon); Danon 29; DRH 1; Gil 34, 44 (= MP and Menéndez Pelayo); "Hispanic Balladry," no. 5; Hemsi 29; Hemsi, "Evocation," p. 1056*b* (= Hemsi 29.23-25); Menéndez Pelayo 40 (= Danon); G. Menéndez Pidal, *Romancero*, pp. 191-192; MP 133 (= GSA,

---

La dama de Aragón. In 1878 Liebrecht referred to *Primav*. 143, in connection with Legrand's version of the Greek *Bridesmaid to Bride*. See *Zur Volkskunde*, p. 218, first published in *ALG*, VII (1878), 236-253. In RoH, I, 332, Menéndez Pidal mentions the relationship of *La dama de Aragón* to "ciertas canciones griegas y *francesas*" (italics ours.) We cannot agree with Entwistle's attempt (*HR*, VIII, 156-159) to connect *La dama de Aragón* with the French *Dame mariée nouvellement* (Rolland, II, 227-233) and the Catalan-French-Italian *La vella* (Briz, II, 143 ff.; Milá 566)—*Noces de la Vieille* (Rolland, II, 219-227)—*Vecchia sposa* (Nigra 86) mainly on the basis of musical evidence and the use of similar formulas and refrains.

completed with two verses at the end of the text, which agree essentially with G. Menéndez Pidal, vv. 9 and 11); PTJ 136-136*a* (= Danon, "Hispanic Balladry"); SICh 1.

Moroccan J.-Sp.: Alvar, "Los romances de *La bella,*" p. 266 (vv. 1-30); Larrea 201-202; PTJ 136*b* (= Alvar). The ballad serves as a prolog to *Virgilios* (= MP 46).

Castilian: CPE, II, 39-40; Echevarría, p. 416 (no. 89.9-12; as part of *El enamorado en misa* [= RTCN 12]); FN 188-189; Magaña, "Notas," pp. 459-460 (prefixed to *El testamento del enamorado*); RPE 90; RQDB-I 46; RQDB-II 31; RTCN 112; RTR, pp. 32-33; Schindler 23 (prefixed to *El testamento del enamorado*). Milá 47 embodies a fragment of a Castilian version of *La bella en misa.*

Spanish American: M. R. Lida de Malkiel, "El romance de la misa de amor," pp. 28-29, n. 1; Moya, II, 56-57.

Galician: Carré 116; Sampedro 194 (I, 129).

Portuguese: Alves, p. 577; VRP 743-744.

Archaic Text: *Pliegos de Praga,* II, 268-270; *Primavera* 143; Wolf, *Ueber eine Sammlung,* p. 267.

La dama de Aragón

Catalan: AFC 3129; Amades, I, 199-202, 260-262; Avenç, I, 21-23; Briz, I, 63-66; Camps y Mercadal 182-183; Canteloube, I, 192-193; Capmany 48; Macabich, pp. 71-72; Milá 218; cf. also 47 (music, pp. 443-444); OCPC, I, 105-106; II, 374; III, 241; Pedrell, *Cancionero,* I, no. 66; Pujol, *Cançons populars,* pp. 18-19; Segura, pp. 109-110; Serra i Pagès, p. 14; Serra i Vilaró, pp. 73-74; Subirá, pp. 52-53.

Les atours de Marie-Madeleine

French-Provençal: Canteloube, III, 159-160; Doncieux, pp. 166-173; Rolland, VI, 2-11. For additional versions, see Doncieux, pp. 166-167.

Pari 'na luna quandu va a la missa...

Italian: The Southern Italian song, with alternate verses in *-au,* published by Casetti and Imbriani, *Canti popolari delle provincie meridionali,* I, 200, and cited by Liebrecht, *Zur Volkskunde,* p. 218, strongly suggests some genetic relationship to *La bella-La dama-Les atours.*[26] We have no other examples of these Italian verses.

---

[26] The complete text as published by Casetti and Imbriani reads as follows:

Pari 'na luna quandu va a la missa,
lu populu di tia s'annamurau.
E quandu pigghi l'acqua beneditta,

Hē núfē koumpára

(The Bridesmaid Who Became a Bride)

Greek: Abbott, *Songs,* pp. 202-207; Arabantinos, no. 215; Argenti-Rose 730-733 (also n. 2); Baud-Bovy, *Chansons,* II, 251-253, 457 (no. 16); Id., *Textes,* pp. 213-217; Dawkins, "Tragoúdia tōn Dōdekanēsōn," pp. 67-70 (no. 24-24A); Fauriel, II, 376-379; Garnett, I, 148-150, 250-252; Georgeakis-Pineau, pp. 214-216; Jeannaraki, no. 292; Lagarde, pp. 24-25 (no. 19); Legrand, *Recueil,* pp. 300-303 (no. 135); Liebrecht, *Zur Volkskunde,* pp. 184-185 (no. 436), 217-218 (no. 292); Lüdeke, *Im Paradies,* pp. 94-95; Lüdeke-Megas, nos. 56-63, 218.26-49; Passow, nos. 436, 438; Pellegrini, pp. 17-18; Pernot, *Études,* III, nos. 16, 60, 80, 110; Petropoulos, I, 107-109; Politis, *Eklogaì,* no. 83; Proust, pp. 11-12; Theros, I, pp. 315-316 (no. 360); Tommaseo-Pavolini, no. 94. Documentation for the Greek ballad reaches back to the sixteenth century at least. Key verses of *Hē núfē koumpára* contaminate an Akritic ballad in the Mount Athos MS discovered by Bouvier (*Demotikà tragoúdia tēs Monēs tōn Ibērōn,* no. 4 and p. 33). On the MS's discovery and date, see also "Treize chansons populaires du XVIe siècle."

Bulgarian: "Marko Dafini govori": Dozon, no. 45. The Bulgarian ballad seems to be based upon the Greek.

——— · ———

Continental Analogs: Various distant analogs of the Greek ballad and its Western Romance derivatives are known to European balladry: **English:** *Lord Thomas and Fair Annet*: Child 73; Bronson 73; *Thomas o Yonderdale*: Child 253. **Anglo-American:** Bronson 73; Coffin 73.

Scandinavian: *Herr Peders Slegfred*: DgF, IV, no. 210; Olrik, I, no. 45; Prior, III, 361-365; Smith-Dampier, pp. 229-231; *Liten Kerstins Hämd* or *Herr Peder och liten Kerstin*: Arwidsson, I, no. 45 (pp. 305-307); FSF, no. 62; Geijer-Afzelius, I, no. 9 (pp. 51-54; II, 51-54). For more versions, see Child, II, 180*b*. The English and Norse ballads end tragically, as do the **French** and **Italian** songs, *Les tristes noces* (Arbaud, II, 139-144; Canteloube, I, 52-53; III, 168-169; Davenson 19; Doncieux, pp. 338-350; Udry, pp. 63-65) and *Danze e funerali* (Nigra 20), analyzed by Child (II, 181) and Hodgart (*The Ballads,* pp. 88-95, 105-108). The French song has crossed into **Catalonia:** *La boda* (Milá 262). The initial stages of these Romance ballads vaguely recall the Eastern Sephardic *Venganza de la novia rechazada* (Levy 62; see our review, *NRFH,* XIV, p. 349). The English and Scandinavian ballads include the rejected girl's elaborate adorn-

---

parsi ca tutta la chiesa tremau;
lu sacerdoti chi dicia la missa,
vitti tanta bellizza e si votau;
dicendu: —O chi bellizza! o chi bellizza!
Sia benedettu diu chi la criau!—

ments and the essential contrast between her beauty and the plainness of the "nut-browne bride" (cf. DgF, no. 210B.20, where the bride herself makes the comparison). The British ballad even embodies the resplendent beauty motif: "And whan she came to Mary-kirk, / And sat down in the deas, / The light that came frae Fair Annie / Enlightend a' the place" (Child 73E.24); "And whan she cam into the kirk, /She shimmerd like the sun..." (Child 73A.20). Brewster and Tarsouli, in "Two English Ballads and their Greek Counterparts" (p. 41), allude to the similarity of *Lord Thomas and Fair Annet* and the Greek *Núfē koumpára.* Vargyas has attempted to link *Les tristes noces* to the Hungarian *Girl Danced to Death* (*Researches,* pp. 36-42; Leader, pp. 292-295).

Studies (on *La bella en misa* and *La dama de Aragón*): ASW 349, 461; BNE 220, 245-248; Castro, *La Celestina como contienda literaria,* pp. 96-98; EEB, pp. vi, 51-52, n. 3, 87-88, 181-182, 316; Entwistle, "*La Dama de Aragón*"; Id., "A Note on *La Dama de Aragón*"; Id., "New Light," p. 380; Id., "La chanson populaire française en Espagne," pp. 257-258, 259-260, 266; M. R. Lida de Malkiel, "El romance de la misa de amor"; Menéndez Pidal, *El Romancero Español,* p. 129; Pons, "Poésie courtoise ... La Dame d'Aragon"; RoH, I, 63, 325, 332-333; II, 416; TRV, II, 409-410.

25

LA GALANA Y SU CABALLO

(The Beauty and Her Horse)

'Estávase la galana siyando 'el su kavalyyo.
Si'ólo 'i byen si'ólo; yevólo 'a bever aguas.
Kon amores.
Las aguas 'eran truvyyas; se sobrevyyó 'el kavalyyo.
Kon amores.
Ravyyóse la galana; lo 'eğó dyentro 'el baro.
Kon amores.
—¿Ké te 'ize, galana, ke me 'eğates al baro?
Kon amores.
—De kuando tú nasites, fu'ites mi lindo amado.
Kon amores.
Lo tomó por 'el braso; se lo yevó al palasyyo.
Kon amores.
Lyya metyeron las mezas 'i a komer se asentaron.
Kon amores.
Lyya le azen la kama; para 'eğar 'elyyos andaron.
Kon amores.

Source: GSA 9. Title: *Kantiga de novyya.*
The second hemistich of vv. 2 ff. is repeated after each occurrence of the refrain.

1*a* 'Estávanse.
2*b* Yevóla. Yevólo *in repetition.*

10 La fin de međyya noğe, 'un ğugo mu'evo kitaron.
Kon amores.
11 Ganó 'el novyyo ala novyya; ¡ke le se'a para muğos anyyos!
Kon amores.
Kon amores, mi novyya, kon savores.

Translation:

The beautiful maiden was saddling her horse. She saddled it and saddled it well and led it to drink water. *With love.* The water was turbid. The horse became unruly. The maiden became angered; she threw him into the mud. (5) "What did I do to you, maiden, that you should throw me into the mud?" "Since the day you were born, you have been my handsome lover." She took him by the arm and led him to the palace. Now they set the tables and sat down to eat. Now they make the bed for her; they went to lie down. (10) After midnight, they discovered a new game. (11) The groom won the bride. May it be for many years! *With love. With love, my bride, with pleasure.*

Motifs:

6 B611.3. *Horse paramour*; B621.7. *Horse as suitor*; H62.0.1. *Recognition of man transformed to horse.*
7 D332. *Transformation*: *equine animal* (*domestic*) *to person*; cf. D131. *Transformation*: *man to horse.*
9 Cf. B641.6. *Marriage to person in horse form.*

To judge by the versions collected to date, *La galana y su caballo* is an exclusively Salonikan song. Published "original" texts total only four: Attias, Bassan, Hemsi, and Yoná. Our unedited collection adds but one six-verse fragment to this list. To our knowledge the song has no counterparts elsewhere in Hispanic tradition.

As its content and Yoná's title indicate, *La galana y su caballo* was intimately associated with the traditional preparations for Salonikan weddings. A similar refrain: "¡Con amores, con amores, galana, con sabores!" occurs in *El sueño profético,* a ballad which also has nuptial connotations.[1] *Galana* is a habitual designation for the bride in Judeo-Spanish wedding songs.[2]

Yoná's and Attias' texts appear to be a *romance* in *á-o* assonance. However, Bassan and Hemsi offer clear indications that such a pattern must be a relatively late development and that the poem originally consisted of parallel assonant couplets or perhaps tercets. Both Bassan and Hemsi include an *í-o* parallel to Yoná's vv. 4-6:

Raviόse la galana, lo echó adientro el vado.
—¿Qué te hize, galana, que me echates al vado?
—De cuando tú nacites, fuetes mi lindo amado.

Raviósa (*sic*) la galana, lo echó adientro el río.
—¿Qué te hize, galana, que me echates al río?
—De cuando tú nacites, fuetes mi lindo amigo.
(Bassan 46, vv. 4-9)

The alternations *río* / *vado* and *amigo* / *amado* are well known to Hispanic lyric poetry.[3] Yoná's *baro* (= Cast. *barro*) and Attias' *varo* (< *vado* + *barro*?) are certainly parvenus, while Bassan's *vado* clearly offers the better reading, conserving in fact a notably archaic alternate which has largely died out in Hispanic traditional poetry.[4]

The song's central motif—the horse which apparently metamorphoses into the girl's lover—reflects a widely known *topos*: the horse as a symbol both of fertility and of unbridled sexuality.[5] Though

---

[1] See Moya, II, 257.

[2] Cf. Molho, *Usos,* pp. 24, 26, 32, 314; Attias 98, 99, 101, 104, 106, 109, 112, 115, 117, 119; Alvar, "Cantos de boda," p. 22*a*; Id., "*Paralelismo,*" pp. 144, 151; Larrea, *Canciones,* nos. 27, 45.

[3] For examples, see Asensio, *Poética y realidad,* pp. 87-88, 90; Alvar, "Paralelismo," pp. 125-126, 132-133; id., "Cantares de boda," p. 20*b*; Alonso-Blecua 498. Cf. also Frenk Alatorre, *La lírica popular,* p. 36, n. 111.

[4] See Alvar, "Paralelismo," p. 133 at n. 37. *Varo* (< *vado*?) also invades the ballad of *Melisenda sale de los baños* as a replacement for a more authentic *vae* (= Cast. *valle*). See Attias 13.8.

[5] For abundant documentation, see Th. R. Hart, *La alegoría en el Libro de buen amor* (Madrid, 1959), pp. 70-71, n. 4; A. Valbuena Briones, "El simbolismo en el teatro de Calderón," *RF,* 74 (1962), 60-76; P. Calderón, *La vida es sueño,* ed. E. W. Hesse (New York, 1961), p. 47, n. 7; C. G. Jung, *Psychology of the Unconscious* (New York, 1965), pp. 308, 310-312, 316. See also Devoto, "El mal cazador," p. 490 and n. 19; G. Ferguson, *Signs & Symbols in Christian Art* (New York, 1961), p. 20. On the horse as a symbol of fertility, see *Standard Dictionary of Folklore, Mythology, and Legend,* ed. M. Leach, 2 vols. (New

ultimately the same connotation no doubt underlies the ballad commonplace defined by Bronzini as "rapimento in groppa al cavallo,"[6] we know of no close parallels to the transformation undergone in the *Galana* ballad, which in this magical feature seems altogether un-Hispanic.[7]

York, 1949-50), s. vv. *Aśvamedha, horse,* and *October horse*; M. O. Howey, *The Horse in Magic and Myth* (London, 1923), p. 101. We might also recall García Lorca's insistent symbolic use of the horse in *Bodas de sangre* and *La casa de Bernarda Alba* (*Obras completas* [Madrid, 1954], pp. 1092-1094, 1097, 1101, 1112, 1118, 1122, 1147, 1160, 1162, 1166, 1178, 1416, 1423). See also J. Villegas, "El leitmotiv del caballo en *Bodas de sangre*," reprinted from *Hispanófila,* no. 29 (1966), pp. 21-36, especially pp. 30, 34-35; J. Palley, "Archetypal Symbols in *Bodas de sangre*," *H,* L (1967), 74-79: pp. 75-76. Note the horse symbolism in the poems of William of Aquitaine (*Les chansons de Guillaume IX Duc d'Aquitaine,* ed. A. Jeanroy [Paris, 1927]), Nos. I. 7 ff., II. 18, and probably v. 81. See also R. E. Barbera, "Medieval Iconography in the *Celestina*," *RR,* LXI (1970), 5-13: pp. 9-10.

[6] Bronzini (I, 187) lists a number of Italian examples. In Hispanic balladry, compare *Los soldados forzadores* (cf. VRP 465.11; bibliography at no. 19 *supra*), *El caballero burlado* (MP 114; Wiener 7), *Santa Irene* (J. Pérez Vidal, *RDTP,* IV [1948], 518-569), *La esposa de Don García* (ASW 207-208; no. 13 *supra*), *Blancaflor y Filomena* (MP 100), and *Don Bueso y su hermana* (MP 49). Again, compare Devoto, "El mal cazador," p. 490, n. 19, and N721. *Runaway horse carries bride to her lover.*

[7] Compare, however, *Lanzarote y el ciervo del pie blanco* (*Primav.* 147; RCan, pp. 6-11 and no. 6). Transformation of a maiden to a deer occurs in certain Catalan versions of *La infantina* (AFC 2284; Avenç, I, 88-89; Milá 212-213). Cf. the French *Blanche biche* (Canteloube, III, 355-356; Davenson 8; Decombe, pp. 270-274; Doncieux, pp. 233-242; Barbeau, *Rossignol,* pp. 141-142). A serpent metamorphosis is mentioned in Catalan texts of *La inocente acusada* (AFC 2321; Aguiló, p. 43; Avenç, III, 61; Briz, V, 17). Such metamorphoses are much more characteristic of British, German, and Scandinavian disenchantment ballads: e. g., *Kemp Owyne* (Child 34), *The Laily Worm and the Machrel of the Sea* (Child 36), *Tam Lin* (Child 39); *Die Rabenmutter* (Meier, *Balladen,* II, no. 96C.17-18); *Jomfruen i Ulveham* (DgF, II, no. 55); *Jomfruen i Fugleham* (Dal, no. 5; DgF, II, no. 56; Olrik, I, 140-143; FSF, no. 16); *Nattergalen* (DgF, II, no. 57); *Jomfruen i Hindeham* (DgF, II, no. 58; Olrik, I, 139-140; Jonsson, no. 6), *Jomfruen i Ormeham* (DgF, no. 59; Olrik, II, 38-40), *Lindormen* (DgF, II, no. 65; Olrik, II, 48-49; Arwidsson, II, no. 139; Jonsson, no. 7), and probably also *Bedeblak* (DgF, II, no. 63; cf. Greverus, p. 116). A particularly close coincidence with our Sephardic song is the Faroese ballad of *The White Horse,* translated by Pineau from Hammershaimb, where the horse metamorphoses into a knight upon being kissed by a maiden (*Le romancéro,* p. 88). On Scandinavian transformation ballads, see A. Olrik, *Nordens Trylleviser* (Copenhagen, 1934).

BIBLIOGRAPHY

Eastern J.-Sp.: Attias 102 (= "Marriage Customs," with minimal differences); Id., "Marriage Customs," pp. 34-35; Bassan 46; Gil 43 (= MP); Hemsi 20; LSO 89-91 (= GSA); MP 136 (= GSA); PTJ 138 (= Hemsi). Attias' version ("Marriage Customs") is translated into English by R. Patai, "Sephardi Folklore," pp. 29-30.

26

EL VILLANO VIL

(The Peasant of Low Degree)

26A

'En la sivdad de Manselyya
aví'a 'una linda dama.
Se tokava 'i se afeytava
'i se asentava ala ventana.
Por a'í pasó 'un muğağiko
vestido 'entero de gala.
—De avlar me davaš gana.
Le dišo al Selví:
—Lyyo kon mi galana
me kero 'ir.
—¡Aḥ! ¡Suve ariva, pastor lindo!
Gozarás delos mis byenes.

Source: GRA 10. Variants: BRI 1, RHP 3.
The refrain *Lyyo kon mi galana,* etc., each occurrence of the exclamation *Aḥ,* and the words *'En* and *Vate, vate* in vv. 1 and 28 are in boldface in BRI. In RHP the refrain *Yyo kon,* etc., and the words *Vate, vate* are in boldface. There is no boldface printing in GRA.

1 Marselyya *BRI / RHP.*
4 'en la ventana *RHP.*
6 mayya *BRI / RHP.*
7 De kantar *RHP,* le dava *BRI / RHP.*
Refrain to v. 7 Le dišo 'el Selví *BRI / RHP,* Yyo *RHP,* kyero *RHP.*

—Lyyo non avlo kon mužeres,
le dišo 'el Selví.
—Yyo kon mi galana
me kero 'ir.
—¡Aḥ! ¡Suve ariva, pastor lindo!
Komerás 'i beverás
'i gozarás de mis kave'os,
atan lindos 'i atan belyyos.
Kuando los kito 'a peynare,
'el sol 'espunta 'en 'elyyos.
—¡Tú va 'enkólgate kon 'elyyos!,
le dišo 'el Selví.
—Yyo kon mi galana
me kero 'ir.
—¡Aḥ! ¡Suve ariva, pastor lindo!
Komerás 'i beverás
'i gozarás de las mis karas,
'atan lindas, koloradas.
—¡'En 'el fu'ego sean kemadas!,
le dišo 'el Selví.
—Yyo kon mi galana
me kero 'ir.
—¡Aḥ! ¡Suve ariva, pastor lindo!
Komerás 'i beverás,
gozarás de los mis dedos,
'atan lindos, alḥenyyados.
—¡'En 'el fu'ego sean kemados!,
le dišo el Selví.

---

10 Yyo *RHP*, no *BRI*.
Refrain to vv. 10, 17, 22, 27 Lyyo *BRI*.
13 'i *om. BRI* / *RHP*, kavelyyos *BRI*.
14 yya tan *BRI* (*both cases*) / *RHP*, 'i tan belyyos *RHP*.
15 los tomo *BRI*, 'a peynar *BRI* / *RHP*.
17 Va 'enfórkate *BRI* / *RHP*.
20 'i *om. BRI* / *RHP*.
21 yya tan *BRI* / *RHP*, koreladas *BRI*.
26 yya tan *BRI* / *RHP*.
Refrain to v. 27 kyero *RHP*.

—Yyo kon mi galana
me kero 'ir.
—¡Aḥ! ¡Vate, vate, pastor negro!
Peros koman tus 'ovežas.
Tu mužer se kaze kon 'otro.
Tus 'ižos vengan 'en mi meza.
—¡Maldisyyón de mužer mala
no me alkansa a mí!
Lyyo kon mi galana
me kero 'ir.

---

28 ¡Aḥ! *om. BRI.*
29 pero koman (*sic*) *BRI.*
31 'i tus 'ižos *BRI / RHP.*
33 non me *BRI.*
Refrain to v. 33 Yyo *RHP.*

26B

'En la sivdad de Marselyya
aví'a 'una linda dama.
Se tokava 'i se afeytava
'i se asentava ala ventana.
Por a'í pasó 'un muğağiko (5)
vestido 'entero de malyya.
De avlar le dava gana. (7)
Le dišo 'el Selví:
—Yyo kon mi galana
me kero 'ir.
—¡Aḥ! ¡Suve ariva, pastor lindo! (11)
Komerás 'i beverás, (12)
gozarás de mis kave'os, (13)
'atan lindos 'i 'atan belyyos. (14)
Kuando los tomo 'a peynare, (15)
'el sol 'espunta 'en 'elyyos. (16)
—¡Va, 'enfórkate kon 'elyyos!, (17)
le dišo 'el Selví.
—Yyo kon mi galana. . . .

—¡Aḥ! ¡Suve ariva, pastor lindo! (18)
Komerás 'i beverás, (19)
gozarás de las mis karas, (20)
yya tan lindas koloradas. (21)
—¡'En 'el fu'ego sean kemadas!, (22)
le diśo 'el Selví.
—Yyo kon mi galana. ...
—¡Aḥ! ¡Suve ariva, pastor lindo! (23)
Komerás 'i beverás, (24)
gozarás de los mis dedos, (25)
yya tan lindos 'i alḥenyyados. (26)
—¡'En 'el fu'ego sean kemados!, (27)
le diśo 'el Selví.
—Yyo kon mi galana. ...
¡Aḥ! ¡Suve ariva, pastor lindo! (8)
Gozarás de los mis byenes. (9)
—Yyo non avlo kon mužeres, (10)
le diśo 'el Selví.
—Yyo kon mi galana. ...
—¡Vate, vate, pastor negro! (28)
Peros koman tus 'ovežas.
Tu mužer se kazó kon 'otros (30)
'i tus 'ižas vengan 'en mi meza.
—¡Maldisyyón de puta vyeža
non me alkansa a mí! (33)
Y[y]o kon mi galana
me kero 'ir.

Source: GRI 1.
The words *Yyo kon mi galana* / (*me kero 'ir*) in the refrain, each occurrence of *Aḥ*, and the words *Vate, vate* in v. 28 are in boldface.

Translation (The order is that of Text A):

26A-B

In the city of Marseilles there was a beautiful lady. She combed her hair and adorned herself and sat at her window. (5) A young fellow passed by, dressed all in finery (GSA; in a coat of mail BRI / RHP /

GRI). She had a strong desire to speak with him (to sing RHP). *The young man said to her: "I have my own girl and I'll go with her."* "Oh, come up, fine shepherd! You'll enjoy my possessions." (10) "I don't speak with women," *the young man said to her. "I have my own girl," etc.* "Oh, come up, fine shepherd! You will eat and drink and enjoy my beautiful tresses. (15) When I comb them, they glisten in the sun." "Go, hang yourself with them!" *the young man said to her. "I have my own girl," etc.* "Oh come up, fine shepherd! You will eat and drink (20) and enjoy my cheeks, so beautiful and red." "May they be consumed by fire!" *the young man said to her. "I have my own girl," etc.* "Oh, come up, fine shepherd! You will eat and drink (25) and enjoy my fingers, so beautiful and painted with henna." [1] "May they be

---

[1] Medieval Hispanic texts allude to the use of henna as a dye: "cabellos amariellos, non sean de alheña" (*Libro de buen amor,* ed. Criado de Val-Naylor, v. 432 [MS *G*]); "las uñas alheñadas" (A. Martínez de Toledo, *Arçipreste de Talavera* [*El Corbacho*], ed. M. Penna [Turin, 1955 (?)], p. 94); "Nin aqui [in Navarre] cura la dueña / de afeytes nin de alfeña" (*El Cancionero de Juan Alfonso de Baena,* ed. P. J. Pidal [Madrid, 1851], no. 305, p. 339*a*). For other early references, see *DCELC,* s.v. *alheña.* Covarrubias attributes to Moslems the custom of using henna to dye the finger nails: "Con las raízes desta planta tiñen en Turquía y otras partes ... los moros y moras los cabellos y uñas" (*Tesoro,* s.v. *alheña*). Hispano-Arabic poetry also alludes to the custom. In a composition from Ibn Zaidūn's *Dīwān,* the poet's beloved beckons with "le bout du doigt teint au henné" (H. Pérès, *La poésie andalouse en arabe classique au XIe siècle* [Paris, 1937], p. 413 at n. 2). The practice of applying henna, not only to the nails but to hands and feet as well, continues among Islamic and Sephardic women today, especially in connection with traditional adornment of the bride before a wedding. See Adatto, p. 73, n. 3; Attias, p. 164; Molho, *Usos,* p. 25; E. Saporta y Beja, *Refranero sefardí* (Madrid-Barcelona, 1957), p. 252 ("Pleito de hermanos, alhenia de manos"); H. Cohn, *Mœurs des juifs et des arabes de Tétuan (Maroc),* 2d ed. (Paris, 1927), p. 18; J. Goulven, *Les mellahs de Rabat-Salé* (Paris, 1927), pp. 46-47; N. Slouschz, *Travels in North Africa* (Philadelphia, 1927), p. 437; E. Wm. Lane, *The Manners and Customs of the Modern Egyptians* (London-Toronto, 1923), pp. 39-40, 172; J. Bourrilly, *Éléments d'ethnographie marocaine* (Paris, 1932), p. 62; E. Arques, *Tierra de moros: Estampas de folklore,* I (Ceuta-Tetuán, 1938), p. 249 and plates, pp. 258 f., 260 f., 264 f.; E. Westermarck, *Ritual and Belief in Morocco,* 2 vols. (New Hyde Park, N. Y., 1968), II, 587 (s.v. *henna*). Cf. also R. Dozy and W. H. Englemann, *Glossaire des mots espagnols et portugais dérivés de l'arabe,* 2d ed. (Leiden, 1869), s.v. *alheña.* The custom is often evoked in Near Eastern folk poetry: "Unten im Bach habe ich eine Spur entdeckt, / Ich hab ein mit Henna gefärbtes Mädchen gefunden..." (Reinhard, *Volksliedtexte aus der Süd-Türkei,* pp. 278-279; also pp. 35, 141, 145, 157, 161, 175, 177, 227, 349, 375); B. Sidky Rasheed, *Egyptian Folk Songs* (New York, 1964), p. 9. An identical wedding custom is current among the

consumed by fire!" *the young man said to her.* "*I have my own girl,*" *etc.* "Off with you, bad shepherd! May dogs eat your sheep; (30) may your wife marry another and your children come serve at my table." "An old whore's curse (33) doesn't affect me! *I have my own girl and I'll go with her.*"

Motifs:

8 ff. T55. *Girl as wooer: Forthputting woman*; T55.1. *Princess declares her love for lowly hero*; T91. *Unequals in love.*
17 ff. Cf. T232.4. *Woman enamored of repulsive and abusive lover.*

El villano vil derives from an early *villancico* adaptation of *La gentil dama y el rústico pastor,* a *romance* which is preserved in a MS copy of 1421—the oldest known text of a Spanish ballad. [2] *La gentil dama* and its strophic derivative entail a reversal of the topic situation in which a noble gentleman attempts to seduce a rustic shepherdess. [3] The two poems also exemplify another theme that is dear to the *Romancero*: the forthputting woman, who woos a lowly paramour. [4]

Greeks of the Island of Lesbos (see Georgeakis-Pineau, p. 315; *knás* is from T. *kına* 'henna'). Cf. also Lüdeke-Megas, no. 90.38.

[2] See E. Levi, "El romance florentino" and "Poesie catalane."

[3] E.g., the Catalan *Pastora y caballero* (AFC 2368); *La bergère et le monsieur* (Davenson 43; Puymaigre, *Pays Messin,* I, 176-177; Rolland, I, 34-36; II, 44-45; Barbeau, *Romancéro du Canada,* pp. 179-182). Cf. EEB 134. See RoH, I, 339, where possible Old French antecedents of the Spanish songs are discussed. Arbaud's *Bargiereto de Mestre André* (II, 182-183), where the suitor offers the shepherdess a series of material benefits, is strongly suggestive of relationship to the Spanish song, though the dénouement is different to say the least. For a thorough study of the theme, see Wm. P. Jones, *The Pastourelle* (Cambridge, Mass., 1931); for additional bibliography: M. de Riquer, *La lírica de los trovadores* (Barcelona, 1948), pp. lii-lv, nn. 16-20.

[4] Cf. *Gerineldo* (MP 101), *La princesa y el segador* (MP 108; SICh 9), and, exclusively in the Eastern tradition, the theme of *La princesa y el bozağí* (Attias 62; "Hispanic Balladry," no. 7; SICh 8); also *La consulta del paje* (CVR 54; RTCN 6) and *El burlador* (RTCN 17). The lady's wishes are sometimes complied with, as in *Gerineldo, La consulta,* and *El segador,* but in other cases are rejected, as in *La gentil dama, El villano vil,* and *El bozağí.* For the peasant as reluctant lover, compare the rôle of the bashful bumpkin in the following very popular sixteenth-century song:

Besábale y enamorábale
la doncella al villanchón;

Both the *é* assonant *romance* and the *villancico* were known to the sixteenth-seventeenth-century Sephardic tradition. Avenary's *Baqašoth* (Text A), which uses the *incipit* "Estaba la gentil dama," was printed around 1525. Danon's Edirne MS (text D2), which records "Ea, llamábalo la doncella," was put together some time before 1641. [5] Both songs have also survived in the modern Sephardic tradition, though the life of the ballad is much less vigorous than that of the derivative song. Menéndez Pidal uses unedited versions from Sarajevo, Larissa, Izmir, Rhodes, and Tetuán to construct a synthetic version of the *romance* (RoH, I, 341 f.). In our field work in the United States and in Morocco, we have been able to find no complete texts, though several very brief fragments were collected from Rhodian singers. In the same tradition, isolated verses of the *romance* survive as contaminations in *El villano vil* and occasionally as an *incipit* to *El robo de Elena.* The unedited ballad collection of William Milwitzky includes an extensive, geographically unidentified Ladino MS text.

Among the Eastern Sephardim, the tradition of *El villano vil,* which also embraces Castilian and Catalan speaking areas of the Peninsula, reaches the Canary Islands, and extends to the farthest reaches of Spanish America, is much more alive than is the tradition of its *romance* antecedent. Geographically identified or identifiable Eastern versions or fragments are from Salonika (Attias, Yoná), Sofia (or more precisely, Plovdiv; SBS 70), Edirne (Danon), Anatolia (?) (Hemsi), Milas-Rhodes (SBS 69), and Rhodes (Granell, MacCurdy). Molho's text (LSO) is probably from Salonika; Díaz-Plaja's, from Rhodes. We have eight unedited texts from Rhodes and one each from Marmara and Plovdiv (by the same informant as SBS 70). In Morocco, the song's traditional life is at best precarious. It is known in Tetuán as a recent importation but must also have formed part of a more archaic repertoire, since the refrain, "Digo yo ansí: / yo al ganado me quiero ir" (or "a mi ganado

---

besábale y enamorábale,
y él metido en un rincón.
(Alonso-Blecua 164)

On this theme, see also Michaëlis, "Estudos," pp. 206-207. Cf. also *The Kitchie-Boy* (Child 252A.4); *Der treue Dienstknecht, Der hübsche Schreiber,* and *Der Bettler* (Meier, *Balladen,* I, nos. 25, 42B.3-4; II, no. 82; p. 196).

[5] See Avenary, pp. 380 and 381; Danon, pp. 104-105, especially n. 1 on p. 105.

yo quiero ir"), is preserved as part of the wedding song, "Ay mi padre, ay mi madre" (Larrea, *Canciones,* no. 28).

Unlike many of the non-*romance* songs that have been incorporated into the Judeo-Spanish *Romancero, El villano vil* has managed to escape being forced into the almost universally dominant *romance* mold. It preserves its *villancico* rhyme scheme reasonably well, a circumstance that fully justifies its being printed in short verses.

The importunate lady's insistent self-praise constitutes, if we combine the readings of all known texts, a catalog of Oriental feminine beauty which merits comparison with similar enumerations in *La bella en misa, Melisenda sale de los baños,* and *Dize la nuestra novia.* There has very probably been some cross-pollination among these songs. For example, a variant of Yoná's vv. 15-16, "Kuando los tomo 'a peynar(e), // 'el sol 'espunta 'en 'elyyos," occurs in *La bella en misa*: "Kuando los tomó a peinare, / en eyos despuntó el sol." [6] All the same, the lady's self-description in the Judeo-Spanish *Villano vil* must count as a relatively archaic survival. While most modern traditional texts tend to take advantage of another of the song's inherent potentialities by incrementally multiplying the material benefits the lady offers in hopes of tempting the evasive shepherd, [7] the Judeo-Spanish versions, as well as certain Peninsular and Spanish American forms, [8] still stress the lady's physical attractions, thus echoing the unabashed self-portrait of the song's *romance* source:

—Vete con Dios, pastorcillo, no te sabes entender,
hermosuras de mi cuerpo yo te las hiciera ver:
delgadica en la cintura, blanca soy como el papel,
la color tengo mezclada como rosa en el rosel,
el cuello tengo de garza, los ojos de un esparver,

[6] "Hispanic Balladry," no. 5.6. Attias 14.11-12 carries the variant "quita" as in RHP's and GRA's version of *El villano vil,* which read "kito." Similar references to the sun shining upon the girl's hair occur in some American versions of *El villano*: "Mira qué lindos cabellos / y llevarás que contar; // el sol se enamora de ellos / cuando me siento a peinar" (Espinosa, *Nuevo Méjico,* no. 19; also nos. 21, 24; Id., "Romancero nuevomejicano," nos. 10, 13; Id., "California," no. 12).

[7] Cf. FN 217-218 and Martínez Ruiz's remarks (Güéjar, p. 522).

[8] See, for example, CPE, II, 115; RPM 312; Espinosa, *Nuevo Méjico,* nos. 19-21, 24, 25.

las teticas agudicas   que el brial quieren romper,
pues lo que tengo encubierto   maravilla es de lo ver.
—Ni aunque más tengáis, señora,   no me puedo detener.
(*Primav.* 145)

Several other features of Yoná's texts deserve comment. There seems to be little justification for the revised verse order of GRI. Attias, Danon, Díaz-Plaja, Elnecavé, Granell, Molho, and an unedited version from Rhodes all support the sequence of BRI-RHP-GRA. Verse 7 in all of Yoná's texts and the BRI-RHP-GRA reading of v. 32 are clearly euphemistic. In the latter case the rhyme words *ovežas* and *viežá* provide the clue which authenticates GRI's variant, known to many other versions as well. Such readings as "de besar me dabais gana" (Attias; cf. Danon, SBS 70), "de amaldo [= Cast. *amarlo*] le daba gana" (Díaz-Plaja, Granell) or the formulistic "ke de él se namorava" (Elnecavé) for v. 7 are obviously closer to the lady's intentions than Yoná's readings "de avlar..." (shared with Idelsohn and Molho) and "de kantar...," Hemsi's "de llamarlo le daba ganas," or the ridiculous "de comer (no) le daba gana" as in MacCurdy and an unedited Rhodian text. [9]

A confluence of factors is involved in the problematic form *Selví*. In the sixteenth-century versions of the *villancico*, the reluctant peasant is simply called "el vil." This designation is amplified in certain modern texts to "villano vil," [10] "grande vil," [11] or "infame vil." [12] The Moroccan version reflected in Larrea's wedding song alters the refrain to "Digo yo ansí." Many of our Rhodian renditions have also obviously encountered difficulty with the original designation and have replaced it with such clumsy readings as "le izo dezir," "le (*or* se) dešó dezir," or "se dešó sentir." MacCurdy's very lame "Le dijo, le dijo" is a product of the same tendency. The form *Selví* or *el selví*, which occurs in Attias, Danon, Díaz-Plaja, Elnecavé, Granell, Idelsohn, Yoná, and unedited versions from Rhodes, is apparently based upon a variant in

---

[9] Cf. also SBS 69: "De komer no tenía gana."

[10] See, for example, ASW 290, n. 1, 301; Echevarría; Güéjar; RPE; RSC; Campa, *Folk-Poetry*, p. 44; Espinosa, "California," nos. 10-12; id., "Romancero nuevomejicano," nos. 10-12; id., *Nuevo Méjico*, nos. 20-23. Olivares Figueroa's Venezuelan text converts the designation into a proper name: "Villanovil."

[11] Espinosa, "Traditional Spanish Ballads," p. 97; id., "Romancero nuevomejicano," no. 13; id., *Nuevo Méjico*, no. 19.

[12] CPE, II, 114-115.

which "el vil" was known as "el ser vil." The readings *Serví* (uned., Rhodes), a metathesized *Selvir* (SBS 69, 70; uned., Rhodes), and an unaltered *Servil* (Plovdiv; alternating with *Selvir* in Marmara) confirm this supposition. The designation seems, however, to have completely lost its original pejorative connotation. Attias simply translates *el selví* as 'hā-ᶜelem' ('youth, lad'; no. 15.8 ff., pp. 86-87). What then has happened to the sixteenth-century song's infamous *vil*? The abstract verbal noun *ser* and the semi-literary *vil,*[13] especially in combination, must have become quite meaningless to speakers of Judeo-Spanish, both in Morocco and the East. However, in the latter communities, another hitherto unnoticed factor, which depends on a coincidental phonetic similarity to an item in the poetic lexicon of a neighboring speech group, was brought to bear upon the poem and helped to dissipate any unsavory implications that might have lingered on in connection with "el ser vil." In Turkish, *selvi* means 'cypress tree.' The ballad thus makes use of a metaphor which, if not unknown to Hispanic traditional poetry,[14] is certainly more favored in that of the peoples of the Balkan Peninsula: the comparison of a girl's or young man's stature to the form of a slender cypress tree.[15] Danon's version of *La bella en misa* (no. 29) confirms the originally metaphoric connotations of the name *Selví* in *El villano vil.* The beauty, as she enters the church, is described, in a thoroughly Turkish verse, as having a figure like a cypress tree: "Su bel, muy delgado, / y su boy, selvi boy" 'Her waist, very slender, and her stature, the stature of a cypress'). The metaphor implicit in

---

[13] Cf. *DCELC,* s.v. *vil.* A similar transmogrification involving the word *ser* takes place in Moroccan versions of *La mujer engañada,* where "este ser villano" (Larrea 104, 105; Ortega 221) can alternate with "es(t)e sevillano" (Bénichou 7; Larrea 103; Torner, *Lírica hispánica,* no. 145; MP 74). See Bénichou, pp. 70-71.

[14] In *La vuelta del marido* (*é*), the husband is sometimes said to be tall like a cypress: "Mi marido es blanco y rubio, / alto como un aciprés" (Levy 15, a text of Moroccan origin); "... alto como un asifrés"; "... un arciprés" (Larrea 75-77); "Es un rubio, guapo, curro / y alto como los ciprés" (Massot 5.4). See also NSR, p. 69, n. 34. The bride in a series of wedding couplets collected by G. M. Vergara is said to be "como el ciprés, / que al cielo llega la copa" (*Cantares populares,* p. 124).

[15] Examples abound in Greek and Albanian balladry. For just a few, see Petropoulos, *La comparaison,* pp. 33-35; also Dieterich, "Die Volksdichtung der Balkanländer in ihren gemeinsamen Elementen," p. 406; Garnett, I, 400-401, n. 24; De Grazia, pp. 105, 261.

selví offers yet another instance of the influence of Balkan folk poetry upon the Eastern Sephardic *Romancero.* [16]

BIBLIOGRAPHY

EL VILLANO VIL

Eastern J.-Sp.: Attias 15; Danon 25; Díaz-Plaja 6; Elnecavé 3; Gil 42 (= MP, Menéndez Pelayo); Granell, p. 290; Hemsi, "Évocation," p. 1056*b*; Idelsohn 500; LSO 79-81; MacCurdy, text D; Menéndez Pelayo 36 (= Danon); MP 139 (= Danon); PTJ 141 (= Danon); SBS 69-70.

Archaic J.-Sp. Incipit: "Ea, llamábalo la doncella": ASW 438; Avenary, p. 383 (no. 25); Danon, p. 108 (no. 109); Frenk Alatorre, pp. 314-315, n. 7; RoH, II, 221.

Moroccan J.-Sp.: Larrea 210. Cf. Torner, "La canción tradicional española," p. 29. Our collection includes an unedited text of this type from Tetuán. All of these versions seem to be of recent Peninsular origin. However, an archaic "autochthonous" text-type of *El villano vil* has contaminated a wedding song from Tetuán: Larrea, *Canciones,* no. 28.

Castilian: Acevedo y Huelves, *Los vaqueiros de alzada,* p. 365; ASW 290, n. 1, 301; CPE, I, 67; II, 114-115; Chacón y Calvo, "Romance de la dama y el pastor," pp. 294-295; Echevarría, pp. 420-421; Fernán Caballero, *¡Pobre Dolores!*, pp. 266-267; FN 217-220; Gil, "Folklore musical extremeño," pp. 59-61 (nos. 8, 17); Güéjar 23; Ledesma, pp. 18-19; Nuevo Zarracina, pp. 112-113; RPE 93-94; RPM 311-313; RSC 4; RTCN 127; RTO 49; Torner, "Del folklore español," pp. 65-70, 99-100; Id., *Cancionero musical de la lírica popular asturiana,* nos. 403-408; Id., "Índice de analogías," no. 118; Id., *Lírica hispánica,* no. 155; Id., "La canción tradicional española," pp. 29, 48, 51-53. Llano Roza de Ampudia (*Esfoyaza,* no. 1016) records a version in the Asturian dialect in which a shepherdess plays the rôle of the *villano.* Cf. Torner, *Cancionero,* no. 405, "Índice," *Lírica,* and "La canción," pp. 52-53.

Canarian: Pérez Vidal, "Romancero tradicional canario," *RDTP,* VII, 439-444.

Spanish American: Campa, *Folk-Poetry,* pp. 43-44; Id., *Folksong,* pp. 23-24; Carrizo, *Jujuy,* p. 137; Id., *Salta,* nos. 14-14*c*; Id., *Tucumán,* I, no. 12; Chacón y Calvo, "Romance de la dama y el pastor," pp. 289-290; Di Lullo, pp. 14-15 (no. 4); Draghi Lucero, p. 181; Espinosa, "California," nos. 10-13; Id., *Nuevo Méjico,* nos. 19-25; Id., "Romancero nuevomejicano," nos. 10-13; Id., "Traditional Spanish Ballads," pp. 97-98; Laval, "Nuevas variantes," pp. 18-19; Id., "Sobre dos cantos chilenos," pp. 41-42; Lummis, "New Mexican Folk-songs,"

---

[16] For a more detailed discussion of this aspect of the ballad, see our article "*Selví*: Una metáfora oriental en el Romancero sefardí," *Sef,* XXVIII (1968), 213-219.

pp. 245-246; Moya, II, 77-83; Olivares Figueroa, *Folklore venezolano,* pp. 71-72; RTA 14; Vicuña 51-54.

Catalan: AFC 2352; Amades, I, 43-45.

Archaic Texts: "Llamábalo la doncella": Alonso-Blecua, no. 378 and pp. 236-237; Castañeda-Huarte, I, 177-180; Cejador, *Verdadera poesía,* VII, 2766-2769; Foulché-Delbosc, "Prague," pp. 390-391; Gallardo, *Ensayo,* I, nos. 91, 92, 585; *Pliegos góticos,* I, 205-210, 245-251; II, 135-136, 224; *Pliegos de Praga,* I, 32; II, 303-304; Porębowicz, pp. 25, 62-68; Rodríguez-Moñino, *Segunda parte del Cancionero general,* pp. 253-270; Id., "Campo de Alanje," nos. 18 and 19; Simón Díaz, III:2, nos. 2972, 3004, 3285, 3292, 3301; TRV, II, 405-406, n.

La dama y el pastor

Eastern J.-Sp.: RoH, I, 341-342.

Archaic J.-Sp. Incipit: "Estaba la gentil dama": Avenary, pp. 383 (no. 35), 386; Frenk Alatorre, p. 317 (no. 35).

Moroccan J.-Sp.: RoH, I, 341-342.

Archaic Texts: "Estáse la gentil dama" or "Gentil dona, gentil dona": ASW 465; *Cancionero de obras de burlas,* p. 239; Cejador, *La verdadera poesía,* II, no. 1302; E. Levi, "El romance florentino de Jaume de Olesa," pp. 140-144; Id., "Poesie catalane," pp. 164-165 (Plate); *Pliegos góticos,* I, 283-284; *Pliegos de Praga,* I, 8*b* (*Ensalada*); II, 209-212; *Primavera* 145; Rodríguez-Moñino, *Cancionerillos góticos,* pp. 59-60; Id., *Cancionero general*: *Noticias bibliográficas,* p. 120 (no. 78); Id., *Pliegos de Morbecq,* p. 340; Simón Díaz, III:2, no. 2940; Thomas, *Trece romances,* p. 32; Wolf, *Ueber eine Sammlung,* pp. 268-269.

Studies: EEB 178; E. Levi, "El romance florentino"; Massot, "El romancero tradicional español en Mallorca," pp. 159-160; S. G. Morley, "Chronological List," p. 273, n. 2; RoH, I, 339-343; II, 13, 16, 89-90, 204, 221, 239, 346, 357; Spitzer, "Notas sobre romances españoles," pp. 153-158; TRV, II, 404-406.

27

EL CHUFLETE

(The Magic Flute)

Salir kere 'el mez de mağyyo 'i 'entrar kere 'el mez de april,
kuando 'el trigo 'está 'en grano 'i las flores kere salir,
kuando 'el Kondalemare para Fransyya kižo 'ir.
Konsigo 'él se yevava 'onra 'i fama 'i tan ğentil.
Konsigo 'él se yevava, konde, 'i 'un ğuflete de marfil.
'I lyya lo mete 'en la su boka, non lo saví'a dezir.
—'I lyyo malanyya tal ğuflete, las doblas ke di por ti.

Source: GSA 10.
Variants from: LRI 5; BRI 7; RHP 7; GRI 7.
Vv. 2, 3, 6-14 are repeated in GSA / LRI / BRI. Vv. 2, 3, 6-12 are repeated in GRI. GRI omits vv. 13-15. GRI writes a̯l for *'el* or *'él* throughout.

1*a* Salir *in boldface RHP / GRI,* kyere *GRI,* mayyo *LRI / BRI / RHP / GRI.*
1*b* kyere *GRI,* 'el de april *RHP.*
2*b* keren *LRI / BRI / RHP / GRI.*
4*a* kon sigo *GSA / LRI / BRI / RHP / GRI.*
4*b* tal ğentil *BRI.*
5 'I konsigo a̯l se yevava 'onra 'i fama 'i tan ğentil / 'i 'un ğuflet de marfil *GRI.*
5*a* 'I konsigo *LRI / RHP,* konde *om. LRI / BRI / GRI.*
5*b* ğuflet *LRI / BRI / RHP.*
6*a* Yya *LRI* ('I yya *in repetition*) / *BRI* ('I lyya *in repetition*) / *RHP / GRI,* se lo mete *BRI / RHP,* selo mete *GRI,* su *om. GRI.*
6*b* no *RHP,* 'i non *GRI* (*in repetition*).
7*a* Yyo malanyyo tal ğuflet *LRI,* Yyo malanyyo tal ğuflete *BRI* ('I lyyo *in repetition*) / *RHP,* Yya malanyyo tal ğuflete *GRI* ('I yya; ğuflet *in repetition*).
7*b* kedí *GSA* (ke di *in repetition*).

'I 'otras tantas lyyo les dyera   ke me lo kiten de akí.
'I lyya lo kitan 'a vendere   por plasas 'i por ğarśíś.
Ningunos le davan presyyo,   ni 'un aspro ni suvir.
'I tanto fu'e de boka 'en boka,   fu'e 'en la boka de Amadí.
—'I 'otras tantas le dyera,   ke me lo trayygan akí.
'I yya lo meten 'en la su boka   'i yya lo 'enpensan 'a retenyir.
Las naves ke 'están 'en porto,   presto las azen venir.
La parida ke 'está paryendo,   presto las azen parir.

8*a* yyo *LRI* / *BRI* / *RHP* / *GRI*, le *GRI*.
9*a* yya *LRI* / *BRI* / *RHP* / *GRI*, avendere *GSA* (*in repetition*), 'a vender *LRI* / *BRI* / *RHP*.
9*b* ğarśís *GSA* (*in repetition*) / *LRI* / *GRI*, ğarš s *BRI* (ğarśís *in repetition*), ğaršís *RHP*.
10*a* 'I ningunos *RHP*.
10*b* 'i 'un aspro *BRI* (ni 'un *in repetition*).
11 'I tanto fu'e de 'en boka 'en boka / fu'e 'en boka de Amadí *GSA* (*repetition*).
11*a* 'I *om*. *LRI* / *BRI* / *RHP* / *GRI*.
11*b* la *om*. *LRI* / *BRI* / *RHP* / *GRI*, deAmadí *LRI*.
12 *This verse, which is uttered by the Count, belongs at the end of the ballad. Cf. the Bosnian texts studied below.*
12*a* 'I 'otros tantos *LRI* / *BRI*, yyo le dyera *LRI* / *BRI* / *GRI*, yya le dyera *RHP*.
13 'I 'a lo meten 'en la su boka / 'i 'a lo 'enpesan aretenyir *GSA* (*repetition*).
13*a* 'i *om*. *LRI* / *BRI* / *RHP*.
13*b* 'empesan *LRI* ('enpesan *in repetition*) / *BRI* / *RHP*, aretenyir *GSA* (*in repetition*) / *LRI*.
14*b* los azen *BRI* (las *in repetition*).
15*b* la azen *LRI* / *BRI* / *RHP*.

Translation:

The month of May is going out and April is coming in, when the wheat is in the grain and flowers begin to bloom; when Count Alemare wished to set out for France. He took with him honor and fame and gallantry; (5) and with him the Count took a flute of ivory. Now he puts it to his mouth, but he could not make it play. "Oh, accursed be such a flute and the coins I paid for thee! And I would give them as much again that they might take it away from here." Now they take it to be sold, through markets and bazaars. (10) No one would give a penny, much less offer more. It went so long from mouth to mouth, till it came to Amadí. "And I would give him as much again that they might bring it here to me." Now they put it to his mouth and he begins to make it ring. It makes boats on their way to port come quickly to the shore; (15) women in the throes of labor, it makes them quickly give birth.

Motifs:

5 D1223.1. *Magic flute*; D1224. *Magic pipe* (*musical*); D1224.1. *Magic flageolet*; D1225. *Magic whistle.*
14 D1275.1. *Magic music*; D1275.2. *Magic melody*. Cf. D1523.2.6. *Boat guided by magic songs.*

El chuflete closes our edition of Yoná's *romances* on an enigmatic note. The ballad seems very old and authentically traditional but has been reported from no area other than the Eastern Judeo-Spanish domain, where it appears in two rather different forms in widely separate communities. Even among the Sephardim the ballad is rare. We have never found it in our field work. In reality there are but four extant "original" texts and one fragment with which to work. Attias and Yoná, whose versions are quite similar, represent Salonika, while Baruch and a version published in the newspaper *Jevrejski Glas* record the tradition of Bosnia. Menéndez Pidal's text (MP 142) is synthetic: vv. 1-11 follow GSA with only one important emendation (*mağyyo* > *Marzo*); vv. 12-15, presumably from Vienna, agree in essence with Baruch and *Jevrejski Glas,* and must ultimately be of Bosnian origin. This Viennese version probably provided Menéndez Pidal with the more logical reading *Marzo,* which also appears in the Bosnian texts.

Attias' version supplements Yoná's in certain details. Here we learn that Count Alemare bought the flute for a hundred gold coins "in the fairs at Paris," a detail which is confirmed by the Bosnian texts: "Cien doblas y más le costa / de las ferias de París" (Attias 49.11-12). Attias' rendition also improves upon the description of the Count's dissatisfaction with the flute, as he morosely stuffs it into his pocket and begins cursing: "Ya lo echa en la su falda, / ya lo empeza a maldicir: // —Ya malaño..." etc. (vv. 15-17). Yoná, on the other hand, supplies an authentic verse (v. 12) lacking in Attias, which, as the Bosnian texts show, is misplaced in Yoná's version and should be voiced by Count Alemare at the end of the ballad: " 'I 'otras tantas le dyera, / ke me lo trayygan akí."

The two texts from Bosnia and the Viennese fragment tell a somewhat different story: The King of Germany owns a flute, purchased at the fairs of Paris (Baruch) or Budim (*Jev. Glas*). He passes it around to his knights (Baruch) or gives it to one of his servants (*Jev. Glas*), but they are unable to make it sound. The King curses the flute (Baruch), but takes it back and begins to play it. Whereupon: all the boats in the world come to dry land (Baruch) or boats sailing before the storm (*Jev. Glas*) or on the gulf (MP) are brought to port; women in labor are delivered painlessly; crying children fall asleep without nursing; doors open without the use of keys (*Jev. Glas*); and young lovers are brought together (Baruch; *Jev. Glas*). The King calls down blessings upon the flute and considers as well spent the money invested in it.[1] Two of the three pertinent texts are difficult to obtain and merit being reprinted here, along with Menéndez Pidal's Viennese verses:

Salir quere el mes de marzo, entrar quere el mes de abril
cuando el trigo está en grano y las flores por abrir.
Entonces el rey de Alemania a Francia se quiso ir.
Con sí trujo gente mucha caballeros más de mil.
Con sí trujo un chuflete de las ferias de París.
Lo dio el rey de boca en boca, ninguno lo supo sonergir.
—Que mal haya tal chuflete, los doblones que por él di.
Lo tomó el rey en boca y lo supo sonergir.
Todas las naves del mundo a seco las hizo venir.
La parida que está pariendo sin dolores la hizo parir.
La criatura que está llorando sin teta la hizo dormir.
La novia que a su novio ama a su lado la hizo venir.
—Que bien haya tal chuflete que tantos doblones por él di.
(Baruch)

Salir kere el mez de mart, entrar kere el mez de april,
kuando el rej de Alemanja a Francija se kižo ir.
Kon sí jeva đente munća, kavajeros más de mil.

[1] Cf. D1523.2.6. *Boat guided by magic songs*; D2088. *Locks opened by magic*; D1426.1. *Magic flute compels woman to come to man.*

Djo el ćuflet a uno de sus mosos, no lo supo sanergir.
Lo tomó el rej en su boka, lo enpesó a sanergir.
La barka ke está en fortuna, el porto la izo venir.
La parida ke está pariendo, sin dolor la izo parir.
La kreatura ke está en kama, sin tetar la izo dormir.
La puerta ke está serada, sin jave la izo avrir.
El novjo ke a la novja ama, a su kaza la izo venir.
—O, bien aga tal ćuflet i los dublones ke di por ti,
sien dublones más me kosta de las feridas de Budim.

(*Jevrejski Glas*)[2]

... ...

la parida que está pariendo sin dolor la hizo parir,
la criatura que está llorando sin tetar la hizo dormir,
la nave que está en el golfo al porto la hizo salir.
—¡Oh bien haya tal chuflete, las doblas que di por ti!

(MP)

The first verse of Attias and Yoná, with what seems ridiculous reverse chronology, exemplifies the famous "May song" *incipit* with its invocation of the delights of Spring:

Por el mes era de mayo cuando hace la calor,
cuando canta la calandria y responde el ruiseñor. ...

(*El prisionero*: *Primav.* 114*a*)

En el mes era de abril, de mayo antes vn día,
quando los lirios y rosas muestran más su alegría. ...

(*Flérida*: CSA, fol. 253*v*)

Ara ve lo mes de mayo que n'es temps de grans caloris,
quant la civada n'esgrana, els trigos quedan en floris.
El comte de l'Alamanya enamorat d'una senyora. ...

(*El enamorado y la Muerte*: Milá 240C)[3]

---

[2] The bottom two-thirds of the letters of the first three words in the final hemistich ("de las feridas") have been cut off or otherwise rendered illegible in the original. Rabbi Gaon was kind enough to provide us with two different photographic copies of this page. The words are obscured in the same way in both, but our reading almost certainly is correct. The form *feridas* should probably be read *féridas*.

[3] Given the mention of May and April and the graining of the wheat, followed by the intervention of "el comte de l'Alamanya," it would be tempting

Mes de maig y mes d'abril, regalada primavera,
floriran los atmetllers, [los] que en fan la fló vermella. ...
(*Constancia*: Milá 361 + text Al)

Entra mayo y sale abril,
tan garridico le vi venir.
Entra mayo con sus flores,
sale abril con sus amores. ...
(*Cancionero musical,* ed. Barbieri, no. 61)[4]

Given the prevalence of *Entra mayo-sale abril* as a ballad introduction we might wonder if the rather exceptional Bosnian variant —*Sale marzo-entra abril*— may not be an innovation and the aberrant Salonikan *Sale mayo-entra abril* a mere reversal of the ballad's original *incipit*. However illogical, the Salonikan verse bears no tampering with, for in a ballad world where, as in *La venganza de Montesinos* (*Primav.* 176), both Paris and the River Duero can be sighted from the same mountain top, it is perhaps not inappropriate that time should be allowed to move in reverse![5]

As well as a period of joyous florescence spring was also a time for war—a circumstance frequently mentioned in medieval poetry.[6] At

---

to relate these verses somehow to the Sephardic ballad. But the similarity is a coincidence. The first two verses are clearly a borrowing from *El prisionero*. How the Count of Germany entered this Catalan version of *El enamorado y la Muerte* remains a mystery.

[4] For other occurrences of these verses in poems of both known and anonymous authorship, see Alonso-Blecua, nos. 457 and 467; Wilson-Sage, no. 67; Cejador, *Verdadera poesía,* I, 466; II, 1389; III, 1720.

For more on the May song, see F. Hanssen, "Las coplas 1788-1792 del *Libro de Alexandre,*" pp. 21-30; Menéndez Pidal, "La primitiva poesía lírica española," pp. 242-244; Catalán, *Poema de Alfonso XI,* pp. 78-79; Cintra, *Crónica Geral de Espanha de 1344,* I, 249, n. 17, 294 at n. 383; EEB 88, 105, 179, 191, 320; RVP, pp. 155-157; Torner, "Índice de analogías," no. 84; Id., *Lírica hispánica,* no. 110. Cf. also the initial verses of Attias' version of *El conde y la condesa* (no. 55):

En el mes de sanjiguale cuando las ovejas paren,
cuando el conde y la condesa se pasean por la mare. ...

See also no. 4, nn. 1-3 *supra.*

[5] On the unreality of ballads, see RoH, I, 75-77. Sephardic versions of *Flérida* also have reversed chronology: "Entrar quiere el mes de Mayo / y el de Abril antes de un día" (MP 105). Cf. Michaëlis' commentary (RVP, p. 118, n.).

[6] See Michaëlis, "Estudos," p. 222, n. 3. On the military practice, see Menéndez Pidal, *La España del Cid,* I, 357; Id., *La Chanson de Roland y el neotradi-*

least one ballad, the seemingly modern, though widely distributed, *Quintado* begins with a similar allusion: "Mes de mayo, mes de mayo, / y mes de la primavera, // cuando los pobres soldados / marchaban para la guerra . . ." (RPM 250). We might wonder then, if Count Alemare's (or the King of Germany's) springtime departure for France, in the company of more than a thousand knights, is a peaceful venture, or if perhaps it is some sort of military expedition. The enigmatic *Chuflete* gives us no answer.

The exact nature of the musical instrument represented by the word *chuflete* is itself a problem. In Modern Judeo-Spanish, *chuflet* means 'whistle'. Both Crews (*Recherches* 395: "sintimos el čuflét del ƀaporiko") and Cherezli (*Dictionnaire,* s.v. *ğuflet*) define it as Fr. 'sifflet'. On the Peninsula, forms in *u,* instead of *i* as in Castilian, are characteristically Navarro-Aragonese and usually pertain to the general semantic area of whistling. Thus: *chuflete* 'chiflete; chiflo, silbato',[7] 'silbo';[8] *chuflet* 'silbato, pito' (Borao); *chuflé* 'silbato' (Pardo Asso); *chufleta* 'silbo, flauta rústica' (Iribarren; cf. Pardo Asso), 'especie de chiflo' (Llatas); *chuflaina* 'dulzaina' (Borao), 'cornetilla o trompetilla, generalmente de una sola nota ..., gaita, flauta, o instrumento rústicos ..., chiflato, silbato' (Iribarren), 'flauta, silbato con varios agujeros; dulzaina' (Pardo Asso); *chuflar* 'silbar' (Borao; Pardo Asso; Llatas), 'chiflar, silbar con fuerza' (Iribarren); *chuflido* 'silbido, chiflido' (Borao; Pardo Asso; Llatas); *chuflo* 'silbato, pito' (Pardo Asso); *chuflada* 'acción de chiflar o silbar' (Pardo Asso); *chuflato* 'chiflato, silbato, *chuflaina*' (Iribarren); *chuflador* 'el que chifla o silba' (Iribarren). We have, however, translated *chuflete* as 'flute.' It seems unlikely that magical properties such as those mentioned in the ballad would be attributed to a mere whistle. More likely the thaumaturgical music of the Judeo-Spanish *romance* is produced by some kind of flutelike

---

cionalismo, p. 181, n. 20. In *Las Mocedades de Rodrigo,* a battle is planned for "el día de Santa Cruz de Mayo" (*Crónica particular del Cid,* ed. Huber, Chap. IX, p. 17; *Reliquias,* p. 276, v. 638). In *Beves of Hamtoun,* Sir Guy is ambushed on the first of May. See *The Romance of Sir Beues of Hamtoun,* ed. E. Kölbing, p. 6 (vv. 91-92, 103-104), and, for other instances in medieval literature, the note on p. 225.

[7] J. Borao, *Diccionario de voces aragonesas* (Zaragoza, 1908), s.v.; J. Pardo Asso, *Nuevo diccionario etimológico aragonés* (Zaragoza, 1938), s.v.; V. Llatas, *El habla del Villar del Arzobispo y su comarca,* 2 vols. (Valencia, 1959), s.v.

[8] J. M. Iribarren, *Vocabulario navarro* (Pamplona, 1952), s.v.

instrument such as the Aragonese *chufleta* or *chuflaina* or the *chuflete* 'chiflo' illustrated in Llatas' monograph on the geographically Valencian dialect of Villar del Arzobispo (p. 202).[9]

If the immediate ancestry of the ballad of *El chuflete* remains obscure its ultimate thematic connections with Hispanic and Pan-European balladry are patently clear. Like *El juicio de Paris* (no. 1 *supra*), with its marvelous mills, or *El conde Olinos*' transformations and sympathetic plants (no. 12 *supra*), *El chuflete* shares its central motif with several Hispanic *romances* and with numerous ballads from other linguistic groups. Marvelous singing, piping, or harp playing and their thaumaturgical effects are Pan-European in distribution. The Hispanic examples embodied in *El conde Arnaldos, El conde Olinos,* and the Canarian *Poder del canto* have a common origin:

¡Quién hubiera tal ventura sobre las aguas del mar
como hubo el infante Arnaldos la mañana de San Juan!
Andando a buscar la caza para su falcón cebar,
vio venir una galera que a tierra quiere llegar. ...
Marinero que la guía, diciendo viene un cantar,
que la mar ponía en calma, los vientos hace amainar;
los peces que andan al hondo, arriba los hace andar;
las aves que van volando, al mástil vienen posar.
(FN 185)

Conde Niño por amores es niño y pasó la mar;
va a dar agua a su caballo la mañana de San Juan.
Mientras el caballo bebe él canta dulce cantar;
todas las aves del cielo se paraban a escuchar,
caminante que camina olvida su caminar,
navegante que navega la nave vuelve hacia allá.
(FN 117)

¡Quién yo tuviera la dicha o la pudiera alcanzar,
la que tuvo el Conde Luna, la mañana de San Juan!

---

[9] Note also Attias' translation—*ḥalîl* 'flute, fife' (no. 49.10, 17). However, in no. 4.47 (*La esposa de don García*), he translates *chufletico* by *çafçēfāh* 'whistle.'

'*El Chuflete* was the title of a humorous weekly magazine ("semanal 'umorístiko") published in Istanbul in 1909. See Moshe David Gaon, *A Bibliography of the Judeo-Spanish* (*Ladino*) *Press* (in Hebrew) (Tel Aviv, 1965), p. 43 (no. 90). Molho translates the variant title *El Chuflet* as 'Pito' (LSO, p. 335).

que fue a bañar sus caballos, a las orillas del mar.
Mentres mi caballo bañas quiero cantar un cantar,
ni muy alto ni muy bajo, que al cielo deba llegar,
los niños que están de cuna, los haciya dispertar,
los pescaos del mar jondo, los haciya sobreaguar,
los naviyos que están lejos, puerto le jacen tomar.
(RCan 10)[10]

Count Olinos' song, or its effects, has migrated sporadically to other ballads as well: for example, *La fratricida por amor* and *Gerineldo + La boda estorbada.*[11] The Catalan *Canción del huérfano* links the Iberian Peninsula with Italy and *Il poter del canto,* in that the protagonists of both ballads win freedom from prison by their singing[12] and produce marvelous side effects the while:

—Posa esta viguela als braços i trempa-la con primor
i quan la n'hauras trempada canta, canta una canço.
—Quina cantaria, mare, quina cantaria jo?
—La que cantava el teu pare a la nit de l'Ascensió.
Los aucells que van en l'aire, no podien volar, no;
els infants per les bressoles, se adormien de dolçor;
tamben los patges del rei caminar no saben, no.[13]

---

[10] On these ballads, see Menéndez Pidal, "Poesía popular y poesía tradicional," pp. 68-69; TRV, II, 411-412; RCan, p. 35. Cf. D1355.1. *Love-producing music*; B767. *Animals attracted by music*; B767.1. *Fish follow sound of music*; D1523.2.6. *Boat guided by magic songs.*

[11] See, for example, Larrea 133-136; Amador de los Ríos, "Romanzen Asturiens," p. 291b; Menéndez Pidal, et al., *Cómo vive un romance,* p. 210. The same verses occur also in the Portuguese religious ballad of *Os reis magos* (Braga, II, 423). Andrés Ortiz's *Floriseo y la reina de Bohemia* adapts the magic song from *Conde Arnaldos* (ASW 57; Durán 287).

[12] Cf. K606. *Escape by singing song,* as well as the Hispanic ballad of *El moro cautivo* (Larrea 221-222; RQDB-I 15; RQDB-II 12; RTCN 72; ASW 266; Vasconcellos, "Bibliotheca do Povo," p. 28; VRP 617-622); the Scandinavian Sir Verner, who escapes after lulling his captors to sleep with a song (*Verner kommer af Fangetaarn*: DgF, VI, n. 383; Olrik, I, no. 47; Prior, III, 353-355; Smith-Dampier, pp. 233-234); *Allebrand Harpspelaren* (Arwidsson, I, no. 65); *Der Spielmannssohn* (DVM 62; Meier, *Balladen,* I, no. 12); cf. also Schirmunski, p. 105 (no. 5). The Greek *Nióपantros sklábos* (See no. 23 *supra*) in many versions wins his freedom with a song.

[13] We cite D. Catalán's synthetic text ("A caza de romances raros en la tradición portuguesa," p. 464). For the versions upon which this text is based, see the bibliography on pp. 463-464, n. 16. Add to these references, AFC 74; Amades, I, 188-189; Avenç, III, 67-69. *La canción del huérfano* is entitled *El*

—O fradei, me car fradei, o cantè d'üna cansun.
Ël pi cit l'à comensà-la, j'áutri dui a 'l l'àn cantè.
Marinar ch'a marinavo s'a n'i'n chito d'marinè;
siadur cha' na' siavo sa' n'i'n chito de siè;
sapadur ch'a n'a sapavo s'a n'i'n chito de sapè;
la serena ch'a cantava s'a n'i'n chita de cantè.

(—O fratelli, miei cari fratelli, oh! cantate una canzone.
Il piú piccolo l'ha cominciata, gli altri due l'hanno cantata.
Marinai che navigavano cessano di navigare;
falciatori che falciavano cessano di falciare;
zappatori che zappavano cessano di zappare;
la sirena che cantava cessa di cantare.)
(*Poter del canto*)[14]

In Modern Greek balladry magic singing also plays an important rôle. The heartrending lament of *The Maiden on the Bridge* produces cataclysmic results:

Κόρη ξανθὴ τραγούδαγε στῆς Τρίχας τὸ γεφύρι,
φιλὰ τραγούδια νἔλεγε καὶ παραπονεμένα,
κι' ἀπὸ τὸ χλιβερὸ σκοπό, τὸ χλιβερὸ τραγούδι,
καὶ τὸ γεφύρι ἐράγισε καὶ τὸ ποτάμι στάθη,
καὶ τὸ Στοιχειὸ τοῦ ποταμοῦ στὴν ἄκρια νἐπετάχτη.
Κ' ἕνας διαβάτης φώναξε 'πὸ πέρα ἀπὸ τὴ ράχη:
«Ἄλλαξε, κόρη, τὸν ἠχό, καὶ πὲς ἄλλο τραγούδι,
γιὰ νὰ κινήση ὁ ποταμός, νὰ σμίξη τὸ γεφύρι,
και τὸ Στοιχειὸ τοῦ ποταμοῦ στὸν τόπο του νὰ πάη.

(A fair-haired girl was singing by the bridge of Tricha,
singing high pitched songs and lamentations
and from the sad tune, from the sad song,
even the bridge cracked and the river stopped
and the river spirit was thrown out upon the bank.
And a traveler from the distant hillside called out:

poder del canto by Milá (no. 207). Magic singing is also mentioned in the Catalan song, *L'afillada d'Organyá* (Serra i Vilaró, pp. 88-89).

[14] Nigra 47.4-9. The song is related to the French *Prisonniers sauvés par une chanson* ("Dans les prisons de Nantes": Rolland, I, 285-287; Nigra, p. 333, n. 1). Cf. also Decombe, pp. 319-320. The girl's request that the prisoners sing also figures in *La presó de Lleida* (AFC 3001; Milá 209).

"O maiden, change the tune and sing a different ballad,
that the river may move and the bridge may mend
and the river spirit may go to his proper place." [15]

In other Greek ballads, songs of lamentation bring ships to land or stop them upon their course:

Μιά κόρη πικροτραγουδάει ἀπὸ κρουσταλλένιον πύργο,
κι' ἀγέρας πῆρε τὴ φωνή, κι' ὁ ἄνεμος τὸ τραγοῦδι,
καὶ σέρνει το καὶ πάει το ἀνάμεσα πελάγου.
Κι' ὅσα καράβια τ' ἄκουσαν, ὅλ' ἄραξαν καὶ δένουν....

(A girl was singing a bitter song from atop a crystal tower.
The air seized the voice and the wind took the song
and they drew it along and went out to sea
and as many ships as heard it, all anchored and made fast
[their moorings].) [16]

The balladry of Germanic peoples is also replete with examples of magic music. In some versions of *The Twa Brothers,* Lady Margret pipes or harps her dead lover from the grave and causes small birds to leave their resting places as well:

She put the small pipes to her mouth,
And she harped both far and near,
Till she harped the small birds off the briers,
And her true love out of the grave.
(Child 49B.10) [17]

[15] Politis, *Eklogaì,* no. 129B. Cf. Arabantinos, no. 473; Edwards, "Greek Popular Poetry," p. 9; Garnett, I, 100; Kerr, "Greek Folk-songs," pp. 238-239; Theros, I, 169-170 (nos. 85-86); Akadēmía, p. 416 (no. D.[a]) .

[16] Politis, *Eklogaì,* no. 129A. For other texts, translations, and commentary, see Arabantinos, no. 457; Garnett, I, 61-62; Jeannarakis, no. 296; Liebrecht, *Zur Volkskunde,* pp. 180-181; Lüdeke-Megas, no. 101; Marcellus, *Chants du peuple,* I, 378-379; Id., *Chants populaires,* p. 169; Passow 337. Cf. also Entwistle, "El Conde Dirlos," pp. 9, 11.

[17] In no. 49C.18, her weeping produces similar but more extensive effects, bringing small birds from the tree, stars from the sky, fish out of the sea. Cf. D1224. *Magic pipe* (*musical*); D1231. *Magic harp*; B767. *Animals attracted by music*; B767.1. *Fish follow sound of music*; E55. *Resuscitation by music.*

Glasgerion or Glenkindie produces magic effects with his harping, which also earns him the love of a young noblewoman:

> Glenkindie was ance a harper gude,
>   He harped to the king;
> And Glenkindie was ance the best harper
>   That ever harpd on a string.
> He'd harpit a fish out o saut water,
>   Or water out o a stane,
> Or milk out o a maiden's breast,
>   That bairn had never nane. [18]

Scandinavian balladry is especially fond of the motif. In the Danish *Harpens Kraft,* William's grief inspires him to harp his bride out of the arms of a Troll, while birds remain enraptured on the branch, bark springs from oak and birch, horns from the kine, and the vane from Mary's Church. Or, in a Swedish version, birds dance on the branch, bark separates from the hardest tree, bairns forsake their mother's knee, water leaves the brook, and the water nix's eyes spring from its head:

> Villemand tog Harpen i Hænde,
> han gaar for Strømmen at stande.
>
> Han legte alt saa liste,
> der rørtes ikke Fugl paa Kviste.
>
> Han slog Harpen saa saare,
> det hørtes over alle de Gaarde.
>
> Barken sprak ud af Egetræ,
> og Hornet af det bøvende Fæ.

---

[18] Child 67B.1-2. These verses migrate to text K of *Child Waters* (no. 63). See Child, V, 220*b*. Cf. F301.2.1. *Elf-knight produces love-longing by blowing on horn*; D1355.1. *Love-producing music*; D1355.1.1. *Love-producing song.* On magic singing or horn blowing as a bride-stealing stratagem in *Lady Isabel and the Elf-Knight* and *Heer Halewijn,* see Entwistle, "El Conde Olinos," pp. 239-240; "Second Thoughts Concerning *El Conde Olinos,*" pp. 13-14; and no. 12, n. 7 *supra.* Cf. also *The Elfin Knight* (Child 2) and *Hind Etin* (Child 41A.1). Compare *Hr. Oluf og hans forgyldte Ljud* (DgF, II, no. 73; Olrik, II, no. 9; Prior, III, 34-38; Smith-Dampier 268-271) and also *The Gypsy Laddie* (Child 200) where, however, the singing is apparently not magical. A baron's daughter is similarly captivated by the persistent flute playing of a shepherd boy in a Hungarian ballad (Járdányi, I, 186).

For a thorough discussion of magic elfin music in British balladry, see Wimberly, pp. 293-298, 332-335.

Barken sprak af Birke,
og Knappen af Marri-Kirke.

Saa slog han Harpen af Harme,
hans Brud ud af Troldens Arme.

Herr Peder han spelade så ljufvelig,
Så foglarne på qvistarne de dansa dervid.

Han spelade barken af hårdaste träd,
Han spelade barnet ur moderens knä.

Han spelade vattnet ur bäcken,
Han spelade ögonen ur necken. [19]

---

[19] The first text is from Olrik, I, no. 8.19-24; the second, from Arwidsson, II, 314, stanzas 21-23. Other versions: Dal, no. 1; DgF, II, no. 40; III, 820*b*-822*b*; Arwidsson, II, 310-319 ([no. 149]); FSF, no. 5; Geijer-Afzelius, no. 75; Jonsson, no. 4. Translations: Greverus, pp. 42 ff.; Smith-Dampier, pp. 106-108; Prior, II, 283-287; Warrens, pp. 240-244. See B82.1.2. *Harp music makes merman restore stolen bride.* Compare also the Icelandic *Gauta kvæði* (Grundtvig-Sigurðsson, no. 3), which has a tragic ending. In the Danish *Hr. Tønne af Alsø* or the Swedish *Riddaren Tynne,* little Ulfva, an elf maid, paralyzes all nature with her golden harp and bewitches Tynne, the knight (DgF, II, no. 34; Prior, III, 10-11; Geijer-Afzelius, no. 7; Warrens, pp. 46-58). Similar phenomena are produced by the singing of an elfin maid in *Elvehøj* (*The Elf-mound*: Dal, no. 3; DgF, II, no. 46; Arwidsson, II, no. 147). In *Venderkongens Jomfrurov,* little Kirsten and proud Karen win the favor of their abductor, the King of the Wends, by singing a ballad that gladdens all beings of the earth and sea—fish, animals, birds (DgF, IV, no. 240; Olrik, II, no. 16; Smith-Dampier, pp. 286-288). Cf. D1359.3.1. *Magic music causes joy.* In *Krybskyttens Sang* (DgF, VI, no. 384), a poacher sings a ballad that gladdens small birds upon the branch and wins him the favor of Denmark's King. For yet another Scandinavian instance of magic singing and harping, see *Den fortryllende Sang* (DgF, IV, no. 243; Arwidsson, I, nos. 62-64; Geijer-Afzelius 60; Warrens, pp. 234, 238; also Bénichou's analysis, "La belle qui ne saurait chanter," pp. 271-272).

For additional instances of magic music in European traditional literature, see Child, II, 137, 511*b*-512*a*; to which may be added the following random gleanings: Cortés, *Antología de la poesía popular rumana,* p. 249*b*, vv. 220 ff. (*Mihu copilul*); Amzulescu, *Balade populare romîneşti,* III, 271 (vv. 56 ff.) (*Ghiţă cătănuţă*); Vargyas, "Rapports," p. 77; Id., *Researches,* p. 19; EEB 222-223; Entwistle, "El Conde Olinos," pp. 244-245; Id., "Second Thoughts Concerning *El Conde Olinos,*" pp. 15-16; Fuks, *The Oldest Known Literary Documents of Yiddish,* II, 69, vv. 689 ff. (*Ducus Horant*); *Sir Orfeo,* vv. 270-280, in K. Sisam, *Fourteenth Century Verse and Prose* (Oxford, 1946), p. 22; Apollonius of Rhodes, *The Voyage of Argo,* trans. E. V. Rieu (London, 1959), p. 51; de Vries, *Heroic Song and Heroic Legend,* p. 122; S. Baring-Gould, *Curious Myths of the Middle Ages* (London, 1881), pp. 430-446.

In most of the above-cited ballads, the magic music serves some clearly defined purpose: Count Olinos sings a courting song; *La canción del huérfano* and *Il poter del canto* win the singers their freedom; the Greek songs are lamentations; the British and Scandinavian examples wake the dead, inspire affection, effect a rescue from an otherworldly being, or place mortals under elfin power. Everywhere such miraculous effects are merely ancillary to the music's major purpose. In *El chuflete,* on the other hand, the magic flute's *raison d'être* in itself constitutes one of the ballad's mysteries. Apparently the flute sounds forth and works its joyous miracles upon the ambient world just for the sheer marvel of it and that is, perhaps, the very best purpose of all.

BIBLIOGRAPHY

Eastern J.-Sp.: Attias 49; Baruch 287; Gil 26 (= MP); MP 142 (= GSA + 4 vv.); PTJ 143 (= Attias); UYA 75-76 (= CBU 328; = GRI).

THE CHAPBOOKS

I.
SĔFER GĔDÛLAΘ MŌŠEH
(n.p., 1891)
(abbr. SGM)

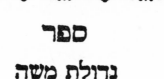

ספר
גדולת משה

אין דיטה נוב׳לה קונטייני לאס גראנדיזאס די משה רבינו ע״ה די טודו לו קי ב׳ידו אה לוס סיילוס , אי לו קי סי אפאריסייו איל סאנטו בינדיג׳ו איל אין מונטי די סיני .

די מאס טופאראן לה סינייוריאס דיטראס אומוב רומאנסוס באסטאנטיס אגראדאב׳ליס טוקאנטי אה משה רבינו ע״ה , קי ב׳אן אטומאר מוג׳ו פלאזיר טאנטו אומב׳ריס קומו מוז׳יריס .

טרזאידה אין לה איסטאמפאריאה סור מאנו די איל סי׳ יעקב יונה הי״ו .

תחת ממשלת אדונינו המלך סולטן עבדול חמיד חאן יר״ה

שנת ויעקב איש תם יושב אוהלים

(2)

גדולת משה

כתפוח בעצי היער כן דודי בין הבנים, איסטי איס משה רבינו ע״ה און לה אורה קי לי דישו איל ש״ית אין הר חורב אנדה אי קיטאלוס אה איז׳וס די ישראל די מצרים פורקי ייא אויי קון ג׳ימידוס אי מימברי אה איל פ׳ירמאמיינטו אי לה מירקיד אי לה ג׳ורה קי ג׳ורי אה אברהם אבינו מי קירידו, דישו משה רבינו ע״ה קין סו ייו קי אנדארי אנדי פרעה אי קי קיטי אה איז׳וס די ישראל די מצרים, דישו איל ש״ית אה משה טו סי אבלאשטאש אנטי מיזמו אי דישיטיס קין ייו קי אנדארי אה פרעה ייו טי דארי כבוד שנאמר ושפל רוח יתמוך כבוד אי דארי אה טודו מצרים אין טו מאנו אי סובירי אסטי סירקה סיאה די מי אונרה אי טי אמוסטרארי אה טודוס לוס מלאכים די לוס סיילוס די אריבה דיספואיס אנסי אינקומינדו איל ש״ית אה מי״ט שר הפנים קי איס איל מלאך מאס גראנדי אי לי דישו אנדה אי טראיי אה משה קון טודוס די קאנטאדורס אי אליגריאה אי גאו, דישו מי״ט רבונו של עולם כון פואידי משה סור קוביר אי סור ציר אה לוס מלאכים פורקי קין די פואיגו אי איל איס בשר ודם, דישו אה איל אנדה אי בולטה אסו קארני פור טיזון די פואיגו, בינו איל מלאך מי״ט סירקה משה, קואנדו לו בידו משה אה מי״ט סי איספאנטייו, דישו אה איל קין טו, דישו ייו סו חנוך בן ירד פאדרי די טו פאדרי, מי מאנדו איל קב״ה בינדיג׳ו איל פור קי טי סובה סירקה סיאה די סו אונרה, דישו משה אה מי״ט ייו בשר ודם אי כון פואידו מיראר אה לוס מלאכים קי סאלבו אי בולטו אסו קארני פור טיזון די פואיגו אי פוס

(3)

אטום קומו גלגלי מרכבה, אי סו פ׳ואירסה פ׳ואירסה די מלאכים אי סו אילגואינסה קומו פ׳למה די פ׳ואיגו אי סוב׳ייו אה איל אה לוס סיילוס אי סי ספאראראון לוס מלאכים קימי מיל די לאס דירינג׳ה אי קימי מיל די לה איסקיירדה אי מ״ט אי משה אין מידייו, אי סוב׳ייירון אה משה אה לוס סיילוס.

קואנדו סוב׳ייו משה אה איל סיילו פרימירו קי אב׳יזה אה איל דיאה פרימירו די לה סימאנה, אי ב׳ידו לאס אגואס ריגלאס ריגלאס אי איל סיילו טודו ב׳ינטאנאס אי אין קאדה ב׳ינטאנה אב׳יאן אלייי מלאכים, דישו משה אה מ״ט קי סון איסטאס ב׳ינטאנאס, לי דישו ב׳ינטאנה די תפלה, ב׳ינטאנה די תחינה ב׳ינטאנה די בושקאר פיאדאד, ב׳ינטאנה די ייורו, ב׳ינטאנה די אליגריאה, ב׳ינטאנה די ארטורה, ב׳ינטאנה די אמברי, ב׳ינטאנה די עניות, ב׳ינטאנה די ריקיזה, ב׳ינטאנה די גירה, ב׳ינטאנה די פאס, ב׳ינטאנה די פריניים, ב׳ינטאנה די פארידה, ב׳ינטאנה די לוב׳ייה, ב׳ינטאנה די עון, ב׳ינטאנה די תשובה, ב׳ינטאנה די רייו, ב׳ינטאנה די ב׳ידאס, אי ב׳ינטאנה די מגפה בר מינן, אי אוטרה די מגפה די בהמה, ב׳ינטאנה די אזינורה, ב׳ינטאנה די רפואה, אי ב׳ידו משה קוזאס די מאראב׳ייאס קין אמנון.

סוב׳ייו משה אה איל סיילו סיגונדו, קי אב׳יזה אב דיאה סיגונדו די לה סימאנה, ב׳ידו אלייי און מלאך קי סו לארגורה קינייינטאס מיאס אי סינקואינטה מילארייאס די מלאכים ב׳אן טודוס די פ׳ואיגו אי אגואה, אי סון קאראב׳ פארה לה קבינה אי דיזין שירה דילאנטרי איל ש״ית גדול ה׳ ומהולל מאוד דימאנדו משה אה מ״ט קי סון איסטוס מלאכים, לי דישון איסטוס סון ממונים סוברי איל איירי אי לה לוב׳ייה אי אזין קומאנדו די איל ש״ית אי טורנאן אסו לוגאר אי אלאבאן אה איל דיו ב״ה, דישו משה פורקי איסטאן לה קארה פ׳לאמה לה

(4)

נבינה, ג'י דישו די'ל דיאה קי לוס קריאו איל דייו ב"ה אנסי
איקסואן אי נון סי מיניאן די סו לוגאר.

קונ'ייו משה אה'ל סייל טריסירו אי בידו אלייי און מלאך
קי סו אלטורה סינקואנטה אנייוס, אי טינייאה סינקואנטה מיל
קאביסאס, אי קאדה קאביסה אי קאביסה סינקואנטה מיל בוקאס
אי און קאדה בוקה סינקואנטה מיל לינגואיגואס, אי קון איל
סינקואנטה מיל מילאריאס די מלאכים טודוס די פואיגו בלאנקו
אי ברודוס אלאבאן אל ש"ית אי דיזין לך ה' הגדולה
והגבורה כו', דימאנדו משה קי סון איסטוס מלאכים אי
קי סון נומברים, לי דישו איסטוס סון אראלים ונומבריס קואטרי
לאס ייראנסאס אי איל פואיגו אי לוס אראלים אי לאס פואירטאס
אי טודוס אזין קומאנדו די איל פאטרון די איל מונדו.

קונ'ייו משה אל סייל קוארטינו בידו אלייי איל בית המקדש
פראגואדו קון פילאריס די פואיגו קוריבאדו אי לאס קאביסאס
די פואיגו אמארייו, אי סוס אלמיניזים די פואיגו בלאנקו אי
סוס פואירטאס די פיידראס די קריסטאל, אי איל היכל די
קארבונקאל, אי בידו מלאכים קי אלאבאבאן אה איל סי' דיל
מונדו קומו דישו דוד המלך ע"ה, ברכו ה' מלאכיו
גבורי כח עושי דברו, דימאנדו משה אה מט"ט קי סון
איסטוס מלאכים, לי דישו איסטו סון מזלות קונטרי לה טיירה
אי קונטרי איל סול אי לה לונה, אי לאס איסטרילייאס אי לוס
מזלות אי לוס גלגלים, אי טודוס דיזין שירה אה איל ש"ית
אי בידו מאס דוס איסטריילייאס גראנדיס, אי קאדה איסטרילייה
קואטר די און מונדו, אי סי נומבריי די לה אונה נוגה אי
לה אוטרה מאדים. לה אונה איגריסאה דיל סול אי לה אוטרה
איגריסה די לה לונה, דישו משה פורקי איגסה איגריסה די
איגסה, לי דישו לה איסטרילייה די נוגה איגסה אינסירנסי
איל סול די אינבירנו פארה אסיריקאר אל סול די לה קאלור

(5)

אי לה אוטרה קי איס מאדריס אינפֿרינטי לה לונה, אין אינבֿיירנו פור קאליינטאר אל מונדו דיל ייִלור די לה לונה.

סובֿייו משה אל סיילו קינטו ביֿדו אלײ כיתות די מלאכים קון קאשאש די פֿואיגו אי די ניבֿי, לה ניבֿי אינריבֿה איל פֿואיגו אי נון סי אמאטאבֿה, אי איל שי״ת מיטייו פאס אינטרי אילייוס, שנאמר עושה שלום במרומיו, דישו משה קי אין איסטוס אי קומו סי מאנטיינאן, לי דישו איסטוס סי ייאמאן אישים שנאמר אראלים אישים אקרא.

סובֿייו משה אה איל סיילו די שש אי בֿידו מלאך סו לונגורה קיניינטוס אנייוס, אי סו בֿינטה קולור דיל פידריסקו אי קון איל מלאראייאס די מלאכים סין קואינטו אי טודוס אלאבֿאנדו אה איל פאטרון די איל מונדו, דימאנדו משה קומו סי יאמאן, דישו עירין קדישין.

סובֿייו משה אל סיילו די סייטי בֿידו אלײ און מלאך טודו די פֿואיגו אי דוס מלאכים אטאדוס קון קאדינאס די פֿואיגו פרייטו אי קולוראדו, אי קאדה אונו אנדאדורה די קיניינטוס אנייוס, דימאנדו משה אה מי״ט קי סון איסטוס מלאכים, לי דישו אף וחמה לוס קרייו איל שי״ת די ששת ימי בראשית פור אזיר סו בֿולונטאד, דישו משה יו מי איספאנטו די איסטוס מלאכים אי נון פואידו פור מיראר סוס קאראס, לואיגו סי אבֿ׳י בֿאנטו מי״ט אי אבראסו אה משה אי טומו אה איל אין סו סינו אי לי דישו, משה נביא אמיגו די איל שי״ת נון טי איספאנטיס לואיגו סי אריפוזו סו דעת די משה, דיספואיס בֿידו און מלאך דימודאדו סו פֿיגורה מאס קי טודוס לוס מלאכים, סו אלטורה 560 אנייוס אי איל קואשאדרידו די קוארינטה לוגאריס אי מודו איל לינו די אזוב די פֿואיגו די לה פונטה דיל פיי אסטה לה קאבֿיסה אי טודו איל קי לו בֿיאה קאלייאבה די צוקה מאנגו די איל איספאנטו, דימאנדו משה קון איל אינבֿי, דישו אה

(6)

איל סיסטי איס סמאל איל קי טומה לאס אלמאס די לה ג'ינטי
דישו אה איל מגדי זה, לי דישו אה טומאר לה אלמה די
איסטי צדיק, דישו משה יהי רצון מלפניך וכו', קירי דיזיר קי
איזו תפלה אי דישו סיאה בולונטאד דילאנטרי די טי די מי
דייו אי די מיס פאדרים קי נון מי אינטריגיס אין סו מאנו,
אי ביידו משה מלאכים דילאנטרי איל שיית אי קישו אבלאר אה
קאדה אונו קון דוס קוראזון סוס אוג'וס סור נון מיראר פני
השכינה אי קון דוס קוראזון סוס פייס, אי קון דוס אבולאן
אי אלאבאן אה איל פאטרון דיל מונדו, אי קאדה אלה סו
לונגורה קינייטוס אנייוס, אי לה אנג'ורה די קאבו דיל מונדו
אסטה איל אוטרו קאבו, דימאנדו משה קי סון נומברים, לי
דישו סון חיות הקדש, דישירון חכמים ז"ל קואנדו דישו נבוכדנצר
סוביירי אינסימה לאס נובים אי מי אסימיז'ארי אה איל אלטו,
לי ריספונדייו רוח הקודש אי דישו טפה פרוחה קואנטוס
אנייוס סון לוס דיאס די טו בידה 70 אנייוס אי דיסיירטו די
לה טיירה אסטה איל סיילו קון 500 אנייוס, אי די רקיע
אסטה שחקים 500 אנייוס, אי די שחקים אסטה זבול 500
אנייוס, אי די זבול אסטה מעון 500 אנייוס, אי די מעון
אסטה ערבות 500 אנייוס, אי פייס די לאס חיות נגד די
טודוס, אי לאס רודיאס נגד די טודוס, אי אלאס די לאס
חיות נגד די טודוס, אי סוס פיגוראס אינסאלסינטי די טודוס
אי אינסימה די איליוס כסא הכבוד אי איס כעין הקרח
הנורא, אינסימה איסטה אסינטאדו מלך מלכי המלכים הקב"ה
רם ונשא, אי טו דיזיס סוביירי אין אלטוראס די לאס נובים
מי אסימיז'ארי אה איל אלטו? גואיי פור טי אי פור טו אלמה
אבאשאראס ביין אין גהינם אבאשאראס אין לוגאר די סוביר אי אלסי
ירה טו אורגולו. אין 7 מוראדאס די גהינם איסקאבראס פארה
סיימפרי.

(7)

דיספואיס סוביו משה און מלאך אל סיילו קי סי ליאמה ערבות אי אסי איל סיילו די 7 אי איסטי מלאך סי אסינכה אי אימביזה אמילדאר אה לאס נשמות קי קריאו איל ש״ית די ששת ימי בראשית אי לוס מילדה אין 70 לשונות אין לה ישיבה די ארינבה אי טודוס דיזין הלכה למשה מסיני קי איסטה איסקריטו דינא יתיב וספרין פתיחו ואין דינא אל פי, כמלאך קי אסי איל שר די לה ליי אי לה חכמה אי איי כומבריי אוטרו קי כון כי פואידי כומבראר.

אי אין איל זוהר דיזי רבי שמעון בן יוחאי ע״ה אין לה אורה קי סוביו משה אה איל סיילו סי אסיזרו דילאנטרי סמאל מלאך אי לי אימביזו 370 סיקריטוס די לה ליי, דישו משה אאיל דיין ב״ה ייו כון מי אבלאשו די אקי אקטה קי מי דיש מתנות בואינאס, דישו איל ש״ית אה משה, משה נאמן די מי קאזה לייה עי די לה ליי מיאה קי אין איליאה איסטאן לאס מתנות בואינאס קי דיזי איל פסוק כי לקח טוב נתתי לכם, אי איסטאן מצות עשה ומצות לא תעשה אי כון מאס סאלבו קי סי דיזין די סו כומבראדו קומו דיזי איל פסוק זכרו תורת משה עבדי, אי די אנדי טומאמוס קי סוביו משה אה איל סיילו קי דישו איל פסוק ומשה עלה אל האלהים, אי אוטרו פסוק עלה אלהים בתרועה, אי אימבזאמוס קי משה סי ייאמו אלהים קימו כומבריי די סו רבי קי אנסי דישו איל פסוק ראה נתתיך אלהים לפרעה, אי פור איסטו סואי דיגו כתפוח בעצי היער קי אירס משה גראנדי מאס די טודוס לוס נביאים אי סירבו די מי אסימיזאנסה אל מאכשאכאל אין גואיזו אי אין מאצור, אין אקיאה אורה סאליו בת קול דיזיאנדו די כסא הכבוד אי דישו משה סירבו די מיל דיין סו סן פי איספאנטים די איליוס אי איסטה איסקריטו עיר גבורים עלה חכם וירד עוז מבטחה. אי כון איס מאס

(8)

באשה לה ליי, קומו דישו איל פסוק ה׳ עז לעמו יתן ,
דישו איל ש״ית, אה משה מי קירידו טו ב׳יניסטים אי אוטוגטים
זוכה אי ב׳יסטיס טודו איסטו, אי קונוסי אסטי אה סײלוס אי אבאשאסטי
אסטי מונדוס אים סריוורוס, אי די אסטי מי ליי, אבאשי סירחס
זוכה אי ב׳ירחס דוס ב׳ירג׳ילים קי קריאי אין איל מונדו אוטו
מארה לוס צדיקים אי אוטו מארה לוס רשעים קי סון גן עדן
אי גהינם.

אין אקילה אורה מאנדו איל ש״ית אה גבריאל אי לי דישו
אנדה קון משה אי קײרדו מי אורדג אי אמוסטרילי גהינם
לי דישו משה יו נון פואידו איכטראר אין גהינם אד ינערו די
איל פואיגו קי אינסײינדי, דישו גבריאל אה משה איי אוטרו
פואיגו קי אינסײינדי אי קימה ומאס די איסטי אחון קי פואידאס
קון טו פיי נון טי קימאראס, אין לה אורה קי איניטרו משה
פולײו איל פואיגו די גהינם פור מודרי משה קינײנטאס פרסאות
דישו איל שר די גהינם קין טו, דישו אה איל יו משה בן
עמרם, דישו אה איל נון איס טו לוגאר אקי; דישו אה איל
ביי פור ביר לום ב׳זראגאסיאס דיל קאנטו ב׳ינדיגו איל, דישו
איל ש״ית אה איל שר די גהינם אנדה אמוסטרה אה משה
אה לוס רשעים קי מאנירה איסטאן אין גהינם, לוגו אנדובו
קון משה קומו תלמיד דילאנטרי סו רבי אי איניטרו אין גהינם אי
בידו אײי ג׳ינטי קי מאלאכי חבלה ליס איסטאן דאנדו . זיסים ,
אײאן ג׳ינטי קולגאדוס פור לאס פאלפאראס די לוס אוגוס, אי
קון פור סוס פיים קין פור סוס מאנוס, קין פור סוס אילגואינגאס
אי איסקלאמאן, אי בידו מאירים קולגאדאס פור סוס קאביאוס
אי קין פור סוס פיגוס אי טודוס קון קאדינאס די פואיגו,
דימאנדו משה אה איל שר די גהינם פורקי מודרי די קי איסטאן
קולגאדוס פור סוס אוגוס, אי אוטרוס פור לה אילגואינגה,
אי ליס דאן טודו איסטי לאנסר אי לה פינה לה גראנדי לה

(9)

איסטה , דישֿו אה איל פור ראזון קי פארלאן מינטיס אין
מוז׳ירים אירמאנאס , אי אין מאיר קאזאדה , אי אין אזייגדם
די סו חבר פארה מאל ; אי דאנזאן עדות אין מינטירוזאס , אי
ז׳ידו אין גהינם ג׳ינטי קולגאדוס פור לאס ערלות אי לאס מאנוס
אטאדאס , דישֿו אה איל מה פורקי איסטאן אנסי דישֿו אה
איל פורקי איראן זנים אי רובאבאן אי מאטאבאן , אי לוס
אוטרוס פורקי איסטאן קולגאדוס פור לאס אוריזאס אי לאס
איגלאזינגאס , פורקי סי באלאבאזאן די לה ליי אי קונטאבאן
לשון הרע אי דברים בטלים , אי לאס מוז׳ירים קי איסטאבאן
קולגאדאס פור סוס פיגוס אי סוס קאבֿילייוס , פורקי דיס•
קוברייאן סוס פיגוס אי סוס קאבֿילייוס דילאנטרי לוס מאנסיבוס
אי קודדיסיאבאן אי דיזיאבאן אה אילייוס אי ביניאן על ידי די
עבירה , דיספואיס די איסטו איסקאלאנו גהינם קון בוז אמארגה
אי דיזיאה איל סר די גהינם דאמי אה מי רשעים פארה
קומירלוס קי איסטו אונבריינטו אי כון סי ארטה אי איסקלאמה
סייעמפרי פור קומיר רשעים , ומה לדיקים כון אה אילייה רשות
הכדוזו אי ז׳ידו לוגאר אוטרו קי לוס רשעים קולגאדוס לה
קאביסה אין באשו אי לוס פיים אין אלטו אי איסקאמאבאן גרי•
טאנדו די לער די גהינם אי לייבוס די גאנאנוס פריטוס די
פלאנטה די סו פיי אסטה איל מיאולייו אי קאדה גאנאנו 500
גייאס , איסקלאמאבאן אי דיזין גואיי אמוס די לה פינה לה איבטה
דאמוס לה מואירטי אי מואירירימוס פור ריפאזאר אי כון טיין
פרוביגו קי אנסי דיזי איל פסוק , לוס איספירהנסים זה נה
מואירטי אי כון איל , דימאנדו מאה קי איראן בוס ומעש ס ד
איסטוס לי דישֿו גוראנזאן אין פאלבו אי איבבינזאזאן שבת
אי דיזוכראנזאן תלמידי חכמים , אי מיטיאן כומברי מאלו אסו
חבר , אי דאנאן לער אה יתומים ואלמנות , פור איסטו לוס
איממינגו איל ש״ית אין פודיר די לוס גאמטס פור ז׳ינגאנסי

(10)

די אילייוס, דימאנדו משה אל שר די גיהנם קומו איס איל
מספר די איסטי לוגאר, דישו אה איל עלוקה שמאונר. לעלוקה
שתי בנות. פואי אה לוגאר אוטרו אי בידו רשעים די קארה
אין.פיירה אי דוס מיל מאלאקראכים אפיגאדוס אין אילייוס אי
מודרין אי פונגאן אה אילייוס אי איסקלאמאן דיל לזער, אי
קאדה מאלאקראן טייני 70 מיל בוקאס, אי קאדה בוקה טייני
די 70 מיל פונגונים, אי קאדה פונג'ין לייני די 70 מיל קאנ״
סארוס' די אדיפלה אי לוס אברינצאן אה אילייוס, אי ב'
דיריטין לוס אוזוס די לוס רשעים די איספאנטו אי איסקלאמאן
גואיי אה נוס די נואיסטרוס עונות אי די איל דיאה דיל דין,
דימאנדו משה קי איזיאן קון מעשים די איסטוס, דישו אה
איל איסטוס איסטריגאבאן אזיינדה די ישראל אה אומות העולם
אי קי טומאבאן גאנה אי אברגואינסאבאן פאנים די קון חברים
אין לוס מונגוס, אי איסטריגאבאן אזיינדה אה אומות העולם
אי קאפראבאן אין פאלאבראס די חכמים, אי דיזיאן כון קריאו איל
ש״ת אל עולם, איסטו איס סוס פינאס אי כי איסטריגארון
אין פודיר די לוס מאלאקראכים, בידו אוטרו לוגאר קי סי גאנאן
די איל אומבליגו פארה אבאשו אי אקיל לוגאר כי ייאמה
טיט היון. אי מלאכי חבלה אפאראבאן קון קאדינאס די פיירו
אי מלקות די פואיגו אי קון פיידראס די פואיגו רומפין קום
דיינטים די לה מאנייאנה אסטה לה טאדרי אי לה נוגי לוס
אריגאלאן אי לוס רומפין קומו דישו איל פסוק. שיני רשעים
שברת. אי גריטאן אי דיזין גואיי די מאוטרוס קי נון איי פיאדאד
דימאנדו משה קי איזיאן סוס מעשים די איסטוס, לי דישו
איסטוס קומיאן נבלה וטרפה אי דאבאן אה קומיר אה אוטרוס
קומו דיזי איל פסוק ירבעם חטא והחטיא את הרבים, אי
דאבאן מונידה אה רבית, אי איסקריביאן שם המפורש אלגוס
גוים, אי פיזאבאן קון באלאנסה פאלסה, אי רובאבאן די

(11)

לה נ̃ינטי, אי קונטאן אין דיאה די כפור אי קונטאן סאנגרי אי
גואיסוס די לאס פ̃רוטאס פור איסטו סי גואנגאן אין סאליר די
מלאכי חבלה, מאס ב̃ידו ג̃ינטי קי סי גואנגאב̃אן מיטאד אין
איל פ̃ואיגו מיטאד אין לה כייב̃י, לי דישו איל שר די גיהנם
אה משה ב̃ין אי ב̃יראס קומו איסטאן לוס רשעים אין איסטי
לוגאר, לי דישו משה מי איספאנטו די פ̃יגור אליי, לי דישו
נון טי איספאנטיס קומו דישו איל פסוק. גם כי אלך בגי
צלמות לא אירא רע כי אתה עמדי. אי ב̃ידו משה קי לה
שכינה אנדאב̃ה דילאנטרי די איל פורקי נון סי איספאנטארה
אי ב̃ידו מלאכי חבלה ייכוס די אוזוס אי אטראב̃אסאדו קון קא.
דינאס די פ̃ואיגו אי קאדה מלאך לונגורה די 500 אנייוס אי
פ̃ואיגו אי כייב̃י אי גואנגוס קוב̃יאן אי אבאשאב̃אן אין לוס
פואירפוס די לוס רשעים אי פילאר די פ̃ואיגו אין איל גארון
אי כון הניאה ריפוזו אה אילייוס אפואירה די שבת אי מועד
אי פור איסטו דישו איל פסוק אי כאלאן אי ניראן אין פואירה.
פוס די לוס ב̃ארונים לוס ריב̃יאנטיס אין מי, קי סו גוזאנו
נון מואירירה אי סו פ̃ואיגו נון סי אמאטארה וכו', דימאנדו
משה קי קון קוס מעשים, דישו איסטוס ב̃יניאן סוב̃רי מוזיר
קאזאדה אי סוב̃רי גויה אי סירב̃ייון עבודה זרה אי דיזונראב̃אן
אה פאדרי אי מאדרי, אי איל קי דיזי יו דיו קומו נמרוד,
אי פרעה אי נבוכדנצר אי אוטרוס רשעים קומו איסטוס פור
איסטו לוס איספריגי איל דיו ברוך הוא אין מאנו די מלאכי
חבלה פור ב̃ינגארסי די אילייוס, דימאנדו משה אה איל מלאך קי
סו נומברי די איסטי לוגאר דישו אבדון דישו משה קיאה ב̃ילונטאד
דילאנטרי די טי הי מי דיו אי דיו די מי פאדרי קי מי איס.
קאפים האי אי אה מודו מו פואידב̃י קאזה די ישראל די איסטוס
לוגארים קי ב̃ידי אין גיהנם, דישו אה איל איל דיו ביב משה
מי אינו יו קריאי דוס ב̃ירג̃ילים גן עדן אי גיהנם קון האי ב̃ין

(12)

אנדה אה גן עדן קון אי מאל אנאשה אה גהינם קומו דישו
איל פסוק, "אי תוקר כליות" וכו' קירי דיזיר קי איל ש"ית
סאבי איל קוראסון די איל בן אדם פארה פאגאר אה קאדה
אונו קומו סוס מעשים.

דיספואיס אנסי זֿידו משה אל מלאך גבריאל אי כי אינ,
קורזֿו אה איל, לי דישו זֿיקטיב גהינם זֿין סי אמוסטרארי
גן עדן קון ליסינסייה די איל דיו ב"ה, אנדוזֿו משה קון איל
מלאך אי איינטרו אין גן עדן לי דישירון לוס מלאכים די גן
עדן יא אלייגז טו טיאמפו פור איספארטירטי די איל מונדו?
דישו אה אילייוס נון, סי כין זֿיני פור זֿיר לאס בארגאנסיאס
דיל דיו ב"ה, אי לה פאגה די לוס צדיקים אין גן עדן קי
מאנירה איסטאן, סי אפארארון לוס מלאכים אי אלאבארון
אה משה אי דישירון ביאטה טו משה סיירבו די ה', ביאטה
לה בידו די מוזֿר קי שואיסים זכה פור קוזֿיר אה סייטי סילום
ביאטה איל פואיזֿלו קי אנסי אה איל שבכה, קי לי אימפורטה
אבנון די משה, אין לה אורה קי איינטרו אין גן עדן זֿידו
און מלאך קי איסטאבה דיבאשו די איל ארבול די לאס זֿידאס
דימאנדו משה אה גבריאל קון איסטי מלאך, לי דישו איסטי
איס מאיוראל די גן עדן קי סו נומברי אנשי, לי פריגונטו
איל מלאך אה משה קין נו, לי דישו ייו סו משה בן עמרם,
לי דישו פארה קי ביניטיס אקי, דישו פור זֿיר לה פאגה די
לוס צדיקים אין גן עדן, לי פראשו איל מלאך אה משה אי
שואירון לוס דוס אה לורה אי זֿידו משה אלזיי סיטינטה קיאם
ארגאלאדאס הונה קון אוברה אי טודאס די פיידראס בואינאס
אי קארבונקאל, קאשירה אי דיאמאנטי אי גולייאס, אי טודוס
סום פיים די אורו די אופז, אי קאדה סייה סיטינטה מלאכים
דיאנאן, אי אנזֿייה אונה סייה גראנדי אי עאנבום מלאכי בשרת
זֿיקליאנדו, דימאנדו משה אל מלאך איסטה סייה די קין

(13)

סים לי דישו די אברהם אבינו ע״ה, אגורה משה פירקה אברהם
לי דישו אה איל קין סו, דישו יו משה בן עמרם, דישו פור
קומו אלייגו סו טיימפו פור איספארטירסי דיל מונדו לי דישו
בין אלייגו מי טיימפו פארה ביני קון ליסינסייה די איל סאנטו
בינדיגו איל פור ביזיר לה פאסה די לוס צדיקים אין גן עדן
אינטונסים דישו אברהם ״הודו לה׳ כי טוב כי לעולם חסדו,
ביטו משה פירקה לה קארה די יצחק אי אנסי לי דישו אה איל
אי אנסי לי ריספונדייו אה איל, דימאנדו משה אאיל מלאך
איל שר די גן עדן קואנטו איס סו לונגורה אי סו אנגורה די
גן עדן, דישו אה איל קין פואידי אקאנסידיאר אה איל, נון
מלאך אי נין סרף נון פואידי קאבזיר לה אנגורה ני לה לונגורה
קי נון איי אה איל שיעור ני חשבון אוסרו קי קאדה קיאה
אי סיאה מלאכי השרת לה גואדרה אה איליה, אי נון אונה
אסינטה אה לה אוטרה פאלבו אי די איליאס די פלאטה,
אי די איליאס די אורו אי די קריסטאל.

אין אקיאה אורה סאלייו בת קול די לוס סיילוס אי לי דישו
אה משה רבינו ע״ה משה קירינו די איל סאנטו בינדיגו איל
נאמן די בו קאזה אל מודו קי פואיטיס זוכה אי ביסטים לוס
פריבייוס די לוס צדיקים קי איסטה גואדראדו לעתיד לבא,
אנסי סיראס זוכה אי בירהס לאס בידאס די עולם הבא טו
אי טודוס לוס ג׳ידייוס, אי אין לה פראגואה דיל בית המקדש
קי אין ביבדה די איל מלך המשיח פור ביזיר אין אירמוזורה
די ה׳ אי פור בזיטאר אל פאלאסייו, קיאה בילונטאד דילאנטרי
די טי ה׳ מואיסטרו דייו אי דייו די מואיסטרוס פאדרים קי
סיאמוס זוכה מוזוטרוס אי טודו סו פואיבלו קאזה די ישראל
פור ביזיר אין נואיסטרוס דיאס די משיח אי אין לה
פראגואה די איל בית המקדש אי אה תחיית המתים אי אה
בידאס די עולם הבא אמן כן יהי רצון.

ת׳ ו׳ ש׳ ל׳ ב׳ ע׳

(14)

רומאנסום די משה רבינו

אה משה משה אין לה סארסה מורה, איל לי ריספונדיין
פריסטו אין איסטה אורה, קומאנדי מי סינייור ריי די מי קורונה.

אזמי טו משה אזמי אינביטי מאנדאדו, ג'ס אנדי פרעה קיסה
אה מי פואיבלו אה סאלבו.

פידון מי סי די לו קי הם אבלאדו, קי אמי מי הם קריאדו
קון לה אילגואינגה טרטאבאדו, קאדה ביז קי אבלו קון פינה
אי פאסיון, קומו משה רבינו עליו השלום.

קאייאדו משה כון אבלים לוקורה, קי ייו אה קריאדו אל
סול אי אה לה לונה, אי אה לאס איסטריאס אה אונה פור
אונה.

באטי טו משה באטי קון איספאנטו, אדילאנטרי ייבאס איל
מי נומברי איל סאנטו.

סי איספאנטי משה סי איספאנטי, אי סי איאה, אה פואירי
מאם די פרעה אאי סי מאמיסיאה.

לו טומו אה פרעה אין לה מיזה אסינטאדו, קון סוס דוזי
רייס סיש די קאדה לאדו, אבלאנדו אי פלאטיקאנדו מאל די
לוס ג'ודיוס.

קי זיניים משה אין איל מי פאלאסייו, מי מאנדו מי דייו
אה קיטאר אמי פואיבלו אה סאלבו.

קין איס איסטי דייו קי אטי טי אה מאנדאדו, ייו כון לו
קונוסקו ני קון איל אבלאדו, ני און פיסקיסיקו אביסטו די סו
מאנו.

(15)

סי איספארטי עסה ארינייה אב לוס סיילוס אה דארלי לה ריספואיסטה לו קי דישו אקיל פירו .

קי סי דישו עסה קי סי דישו אקיל פירו , ייו נון לו קונוסקו ני קון איל אנ׳לאדו . ני און פישקישיקו אנ׳יקסו די סו מאנו .

ייו לי מאנדארי פישקישיס אי פישקישיקו , לי מאנדארי לאנ׳גוסטה קון און בואין מוסקיסו , קי לי קומה לה קאנ׳סה קון איל גיאורייקו .

אין קאמפוטי די כיבן , איל פרימיר דיאה דיל אנייו , איל פואיבלו די ישראל די אייפ׳טו קאלייו קאנטאנדו .

קון קון , לאס מאנאס אל אומברו , קון קון לוס איזוס אין בראסוס , לאס מאדריס קון איל אורו , לו קי איראה לו מאס ליב׳ייאנו .

אבולטארון לה קארה אטראס פור ביר לו קי און קאמינאדו , ביירון ביניר אה פרעה קון און סינ׳דון קורולאדו .

אנדי מוס טרוסיטים מאס אה מואיריר אין דיספובלאדו , אה מואיריר כין סינבולטורה אי אין לה מאר סיר אוגאדו .

איזו תפילה ג׳ידייוס , אי ייו אדי פור איל מי קאבו , עדבטו פואי קום איסקלאמאבייוכים אל סיילו אזו בוראקו .

סאלטו אונה בת דיל סיילו , קון מאס אוזו אבלאדו , טומה לה באירה מאס טומה לה באירה אין טו מאנו , פארטי לה מאר אין 12 קאלייזאס , קיטה אה לוס ג׳ידייוס אנאדו .

אנדי קאמינאבאן ג׳ידייוס , לה מאר סי איבה אריסקאדו , אנדי קאמינאבה מיצרי לה מאר סי איבה אריבוזאנדו .

II
GU'ERTA DE ROMANSOS 'IMPORTANTES
(Salonika, before 1905)
(abbr. GSA)

גואירטה

די רומאנסוס

אימפורטאנטים

דישה גוארטה קונטייני אונוס רומאנסוס אירמוזוס, אי
ביין אנסיקאדוס, אי אימפורטאנטיס, קי כון סי אספה„
ריסיירון די אנטיס, קי פריגואין סור קאנטארסן אין
נוג׳אדאס די ביאולה אי נוג׳אדאס די בואינו די בילאר,
קי איל קאנטאדור קי ז׳ה נאמוראר.

סי טאמביין קונטייני אונוס בליגדים פארה קאנטאר
אין פייסטאס אי זיאפיטים די בריט מילה טודוס אין
פואיזיאה.

סראדה אה לה איסטאמפאריאה פור מיזו די

יעקב אברהם

יונה ס״ט

סאלוניקו

—2—

רומאנסו 1

אי איל קונדי אי איל קונדי, קי אין לה מאר סיאה
סו פ̃ין :

אי קי אין לה מאר סיאה סו פ̃ין, ארמו ארמאס אי גאליראס ;
אי פארה פ̃ראנסייה קיזו איר :

אי פארה פ̃ראנסייס קיזו איר, לאס ארמו די טודו סונטו
אי לאס איג̃ו דיינטרו איל קאנג̃יר :

אי לאס איג̃ו דיינטרו איל קאנג̃יר, איל קאנג̃יר קומו אירה
איסטריג̃ו, אי נון לאס פודיאה ריזיר :

אי נון לאס פודיאה ריזיר, אטראס אפראס לוס פ̃ראנסיזיס,
נון לי דיש צ̃ירגואילה אקי :

אי נון לי דיש צ̃ירגואילה אקי, קי איל גראן דוקי לו מאנדי,
אה פ̃ראנסייה נון צ̃וס דיש̃ה איר :

אי אה פ̃ראנסייה נון צ̃וס דיש̃ה איר, ני צ̃וס דאן פאן אה
קומיר, ני קון לאס דאמאס דורמיר :

אי ני קון לאס דאמאס דורמיר, אין לה טורנאדה קי אטורנה ;
מאטארון קיטינטה מיל :

אי מאטארון קיטינטה מיל, אפארטי די ג̃יקיטיקוס, קי נון
איי קואינטה ני פ̃ין :

אי קי נון איי קואינטה ני פ̃ין, גראנדים בודאס איי אין
פ̃ראנסייה, אי אין לה קאלי די פאריס :

אי אין לה קאלי די פאריס, קי קאזו לה איז̃ה דיל ריי,
קון לה איז̃ה די אמאדי :

אי קון לה איז̃ה די אמאדי, באיילאן דאמאס אי דומיאס,
קאב̃אייירוס מאס די מיל :

אי קאב̃אייירוס מאס די מיל, לה קי אגינ̃ה לה מאייסה,
אירה אונה דאמה ג̃ינטיל :

—3—

אי אירה אונה דאמה ג'ינטיל , מיראנדו לה איספאדה איל
בואין קונדי, אי אקיל קונדי די אמאדי :
אי אקיל קונדי די אמאדי , קי מיראש̆ אקי איל בואין קונדי ,
קונדי קי מיראש̆ אקי :
אי קונדי קי מיראש̆ אקי , או מיראב̄אש̆ אלה טאייפה , או
מי מיראב̄אש̆ אמי :
או מי מיראב̄אש̆ אמי , ייו קון מירו אלאס טאייפה , כי נינוס
סי̆ מירו אטי :
אי כי מינוס טי נירו אטי , מירו אה איסטי ליינדו פואירטו ,
טאן גאלאנו אי טאן ג'ינטיל :
אי טאן גאלאנו אי טאן ג'ינטיל , סי ב̄וס אגראדו איל קונדי ,
קינסיגו ייב̄יש̆מי אמי :
אי קון סיגו ייב̄יש̆מי אמי , מאדרידו אין ב̄יאז'י סיגנו , לונג'י
איסטה פארה ב̄יניר :
אי לונג'י איסטה פארה ב̄יניר , אונה איספואיגרה ב̄ייז'ה
סיגנו, מאלה איסטה פארה מוריר :
אי מאלה איסטה פארה מוריר , דוס איז'יקוס ג'יקוס סיגנו ,
קי נין פי לו סאב̄ין. דיזיר :
אי קי נון סי לו סאב̄ין דיזיר , לאס אימזראו אין און מאנטיל
די אורו , די אספואירה דישו איל ג'אפין :
אי די אספואירה דישו איל ג'אפין , פור אין מיליין דיל קאמינו ,
איסקונסרו קון אמאדי :
אי איסקונסרו קון אמאדי , קי ייב̄אש̆ אקי איל קונדי , אי
קונדי קי ייב̄אש̆ אקי :
אי קונדי קי ייב̄אש̆ אקי , ייב̄ו און פאס'יקו די אורו , קי
אינדה אויי מי לו מירקי :
אי קי אינדה אויי מי לו מירקי , איסטי פאס'יקו קונדי ,
סמי מי איספואילי אה סירב̄יר :

— 4 —

אי אמי מי איספּוזאלי אה קירֵיר , איל דיאס פארה לה
מ׳יזה , אי לה נוג׳י פארה איל דורמיר :
אי לה נוג׳י פארה איל דורמיר , כון לה קוזוסי אין איל
גארדי , כי מינוס אין איל ב׳יסטיר :
אי כי מינוס אין איל ב׳יסטיר , קומוכי איל ג׳אפין די אורו ,
אאיכדה אבייר סי לו מירקי :
אי אאיכדה אבייר סי לו מירקי , איסטו קי סינטייו איל
קונדי , לה דישו אי סי איגו אה סואיר :
אי לה דישו אי סי איגו אה סואיר , בון ב׳וס פריגאד׳ איל
בואין קונדי , כי ב׳וס קיזירד׳ סואיר :
אי כי ב׳וס קיזירד׳ סואיר , איסטו נון איס לה ב׳וסיסטרה
קולפה , קי נון איס ייו קי לו בושקי :

רומאנסו [2]

פור לוס פאלאסייוס די קארלו , נון פאסאן קי נון ג׳ואארי :

נון פאסאן קי נון ג׳ואארי , נון ג׳ואאן פאלאסיו די אורו , קי
נון ב׳יאס אי סיב׳דאדים :
אי קי נון ב׳יאס אי סיב׳דאדים , גאנו קארלו אה גאייפירו ,
סוס ב׳יאס אי סוס סיב׳דאדים :
אי סוס ב׳יאס אי סוס סיב׳דאדים , גאנו גאייפירה אה קארלו ,
אי אלה סו מאיר ריאלי :
אי אלה סו מאיר ריאלי , מאס ב׳אליאה אה פידרילאס ;
פידרילאס קי נון גאנארי :
אי פידרילאס קי נון גאנארי , סופ׳רינו איל מי סופ׳רינו ,
איל מי סופ׳רינו קארונאלי :

—5—

אי איל מי סוב'רינו קארונאלי, יו ב'וס קריאי צ'יקיטו, איל דיאה טי איזו באראגאני :

אי איל דיין טי איזו באראגאני, איל טי דיו באראב'יקה רוסה, אי אין סו פואירטו פ'ואירסה גראנדי :

אי אין סו פואירטו פ'ואירסה גראנדי; לייו ב'וס די אה באלאנקה ביניס, פור מאטיר אי פור איגואלי :

אי פור מאטיר אי פור איגואלי, פ'ואיטיס און הומברי קאב'אלו, ב'ולה דיספואיס ייב'ארי :

אי ב'ולה דיספואיס ייב'ארי, און דיאה איסטאנדו אין לה מיסה, אין איל ב'ירג'יל די ב'ואיסטרו פאדרי :

אי איניל ב'ירג'יל די ב'ואיסטרו פאדרי, קואנדו רואה אי פ'לורים, מאנייאנה די סאנג'ואני :

אי מאנייאנה די סאנג'ואני, טאלדיסיין ב'וס איג'ו איל מי סוב'רינו, קי נון לה ב'אס אה בוסקארי :

אי קי נון לה ב'אס אה בוסקארי, פור לוס קאמינוס קי ב'אס, נון סוס ב'ינו ני פאני :

אי נון סוס ב'ינו ני פאני, ני מינוס דינירו אין טולסה, פארה איל קאמינו גאסטארי :

אי פארה איל קאמינו גאסטארי, נון דיס סיב'אדה אה לה מולה, ני קארני קרודה אל גאב'ילאנו :

ני קארני קרודה אל גאב'ילאני, לה מוג'יר קיב'וס טוב'ייריס, נון ב'וס גואדרי קראילדאדי :

אי נון ב'וס גואדרי קראילדאדי, לוס אוג'וס קי ב'וס פאריירי, בין ב'וס קונוסקאן פור פאדרי :

רומאנסו 3

אסינטאדה איסטה לה ריינה, אין איל פורטאל די לה קאליי;

—6—

קון דולוריס די פארירי, קי נון לאס פואידי קונפורטארי:

אי נון לאס פואידי קונפורטארי, קון איסטוזֿיירה פארייאנדו,
אין איל פאלאסייו דיל ריי סו פאדרי:

אי אין איל פאלאסייו דיל ריי סו פאדרי, קון לה ווזֿייאנסי
פור זֿיזינאס אי אלה קונדיסה סו מאדרי:

אי אלה קונדיסה סו מאדרי, קואנדו מי אסינטו אפארירי,
קי דיגה איל דיין לה איסקאפי:

אי קי דיגה איל דיין לה איסקאפי, אאי לאס אולייו לאס
איסקזֿואיגרה, די אלטאס טורים די אנדי איסטארי:

אי די אלטאס טורים די אנדי איסטארי, אי אנדאזֿום לה
מי מואירה, אי אפארייר אנדי זֿואיסטרה מאדרי:

אי אה פארייר אנדי זֿואיסטרה מאדרי, קי איל זֿואיסטרו
מארידו זֿייני, ייו לי דארי קי אלמוזארי:

אי ייו לי דארי קי אלמוזארי, לי דארי גאליננה אין סינה,
אי קאפונים אלמוזארי:

אי קאפונים אלמוזארי, לי דארי יירבה אל קאבאייו, אי
קארני קרודה אל גאבילאני:

אי קארני קרודה אל גאבילאני, לי איגֿארי גואיסים אל
פירו. אי קי נון זֿום זֿאייה דיטראזֿי:

אי קי נון זֿום זֿאייה דיטראזֿי, ייא סי זֿה אמיראנד אי ביילייה,
אי אפארייר אנדי לה מאדרי:

אי אפארייר אנדי לה מאדרי, איז קאדה פאסו קי איבייה
דיזֿה, אונה דולור לי טומארי:

אי אונה דולור לי טומארי, איילייה איניטראנדו די לה
פוארטה, ביֿלו אייזו קי איילייה פארי:

אי ביֿלו אייזו קי איילייה פארי; קון אונה פֿלינגֿה די אורו
אין מאנו, אי אונה איסבֿריאה די דיאמאנטי:

אי אונה איסבֿריאה די דיאמאנטי, איסטאס פאלאבֿראס

—7—

דיזיינדו , איל בואין ריי קי אריב̃ארי :

אי איל בואין ריי קי אריב̃ארי , אה טודוס ב̃יאו אין ג׳ודייו ,
אמי איספוזה נון אביסטארי :

אי אמי איספוזה נון אביסטארי , לה טו איספוזה איל מי
איזו , פ̃ואי אפארי׳ר אנדי לה מאדרי :

אי פ̃ואי אה פאריר אנדי לה מאדרי , אני ני ייאנו פונה ,
אטי איזו די און מאל פאדרי :

אי אטי איזו די און מאל פאדרי , קון איסטה איספאדה
מי קורטין , קי נון לה ב̃ו אמאטארי :

אי קי נון לה ב̃ו אה מאטארי , איסטאס פאלאב̃ראס דיזיינדו ,
אאב̃ירג̃ים קי אריב̃ארי :

אי אאב̃ירג̃ים קי אריב̃ארי , אמירא ב̃יליה סאלייו און איזו
קי ב̃וס סיאה אין בואין מאזאלי :

אי קי ב̃וס סיאה אין בואין מאזאלי , קון פ̃ליג̃ה די אורו
אין מאנו , אי לה איסטריאה די דיאמאנטי :

רומאנסו [4]

טריס דאמאס ב̃אן אלה מיסה , אה אזיר לה אוראסייון ;
אינטרי מידייו מי איספוזה , לה קי מאס קיריאה ייו , מי ק׳י :

אינטרי מידייו לה מי איספוזה , לה קי מאס קיריאה ייו , קאמיזה
די אולאנדה ייב̃ה , סירמה אי פירלה אל קאב̃יסון , קארה
די פ̃לור :

קאמיזה די אולאנדה ייב̃ה , סירמה אי פירלה אל קאב̃יסון ,
סאייו ייב̃ה סוב̃רי סאייו , און שיבויי די אלטורנאסיון מי ק׳י :

סאייו ייב̃ה סוב̃רי סאייו , און שיבויי די אלטורנאסיון , סו
קאב̃יסה אונה טורונג̃ה , סוס קאב̃יאוס ברילים סון , קארה
די פ̃לור :

—8—

סו קאב׳יסה אונה טורונג׳ה, סוס קאב׳ילייוס ג׳ריליס סון,
לה סו פ׳יאיקה אינארקאדה, ארקו די טיראר ייה סון, מי סי:
לה סו פ׳יאיקה אינארקאדה, ארקו די טיראר ייה סון,
לוס סוס אוג׳וס ג׳יקיטיקוס, איספיז׳יקוס די איסטאמבול, קארה די פ׳לור:
לוס סוס אוג׳וס ג׳יקיטיקוס, איספיז׳יקוס די איסטאמבול,
לאס סוס ריזאס קולוראדאס, מאנסאנאס די איסקופייה סון, מי סינייור:
לאס סוס קאראס קולוראדאס, מאנסאנאס די איסקופייה סון, סו נאריז אפורפ׳ילאדה, פינדולה די איסקריב׳יר ייה סון, קארה די פ׳לור:
סו נאריז אפורפ׳ילאדה, פינדולה די איסקריב׳יר ייה סון,
לה סו בוקה ג׳יקיטיקה, קי נון לי קאב׳י פינייון, מי סי:
לה סו בוקה ג׳יקיטיקה, קי נון לי קאב׳י פינייון, סוס דיינטיס טאן מינודיקוס, פירלה די אינפ׳ילאר ייה סון, קארה די פ׳לור:

רומאנסו 5

סי פאסיאן לאס 12 פ׳לורים, אינטרי אין מידייו אונה קונג׳ה:
דיזו לה קונג׳ה אה לאס פ׳לורים, אויי אים דיאה די פאסיאר:
סי פאסיאה לה לינדה דינה, פור לוס קאמפוס דיל ריי חמור:
אה פאסאר די סוס 12 אירמאנוס, קאמינאב׳ה סין טימור:
אריטוקי אה אונה טיינדה, פינסאנדו קי נון סי ב׳אזון:
ב׳ידו לה אב׳ייה ליסטו, סאבס איז׳ו דיל ריי חמור:
אייגוקי פארה סיליאה, טריס פאלאב׳ריקאס לי אב׳לו:
לינדה בוז לה לינדה דינה, סין אפ׳ייטי אי סין קולור:

—9—

ליינדוס סון ב'ואיסטרוס אירמאנוס, לה פ'לור ב'וס ייב'אשיש ב'וס:

סי סון ליינדוס אי נון סון ליינדוס, אשי קי מי לוס גואדרי איל דייו:

אייגוזי אשטה לה אילייה, אזו לו קי נון איס ראזון:

סי איספארטי לה ליינדה דינה, סי ב'ה פארה הנדי סו סיי:

אה בולומבדס דיל טיזאדו, קי נון לה איספאנטייארה איל סול:

סו פאדרי דיסקי לה ב'ידו, אה רימיב'יר לה סאלייו:

קי'ן ב'וס דימודו לה קארה, אי קי'ן ב'וס דימודו לה קולור:

או ב'ולה דימודו איל איירי, או ב'ולה איספאנטייו איל סול:

ני מי לה דימודו איל איירי, ני מי לה איספאנטייו איל סול:

מי לה דימודו און מוג'אג'יקו, שכס אזו דיל ריי אמור:

איסטאס פאלאב'ראס דיזיינדו, קאזאמינטירוס לי טאזדו:

רומאנסו 6

לה דיל דייה אי קאלאבידאד, קי איל דייה מי דאב'ה איל סול, אי לה טוב'י קאלאבו לונגאר:

אי לה טוב'י קאלאבו לונגאר, לה מאנייאנה לאס איסטרייאס, קואנדו קירי אלב'וריאר:

אי קואנדו קירי אלב'וריאר, סי פאסיאן טיאו אי סוב'רינו, ג'וגאנדו ב'אן און באראנגאר.

אי ג'וגאנדו ב'אן און באראנגאר, קי קאב'אייוס ייב'אן די און פריסייו, אי פור ב'יר קואל קוריאס מאס:

אי פור ב'יר קואל קוריאה מאס, קי קורי אונו אי קורי אוטרו, ג'וגאנדו ב'אן און באראנגאר:

אי ג'וגאנדו ב'אן און באראנגאר, אב'לאנדו אי פלאטיקאנדו, לו קי לים אימפורטס מאס.

—10—

אי לו קי ליס אימפורטה מאס, אונה מירסיד לי רוגו מייו,
קירו יר אה לה בודאש די אסטורגאר:
אי קירו יר אה לה בודאש די אסטורגאר; קי מי דיש לה פראנקה
ביניה, פור מאר אי פור איגואל:
אי פור מאר אי פור איגואל, איקבה מירסיד איל מי
ביזרינו, קון לה פואידו אג'ינאר:
אי קון לה פואידו אג'יטאר, קואנדו ייו לה אביאה דאדו,
קון לה קיטיש טומאר:
אי קון לה קיטיש טומאר, קי דאדו לה טינגו אין פראנסייה,
פור קיין דיבלאס אי אלגו מאס:
אי פור קיין דובלאס אי אלגו מאס, קי דיספוזאדה לה
טינגו אין פראנסייה, אי קון איל קונדי אליגורנאר:
אי קון איל קונדי אליגורנאר, גירירו קון איל מי סוברינו,
אי לה ביזיטיש מויי ביין גאנאר:
אי לה פיאידיש מויי ביין גאנאר: דיזמי קאמיזה דילגאדה,
ביריטה אי פירלה אין סו קויאר:
אי ביריטה אי פירלה אין סו קויאר, ייא סי איספאזרטי איל
קאבאיירו, ייא סי איספאזרטי אי ייא סי בה:
אי ייא סי איספאזרטי אי ייא סי בה, פור קאמיס קי אביאה
ג'ינטי, קאמינאבה די אבלגאר:
אי קאמינאבה די אבלגאר, פור לאס קאמיס קי כון אביאה
ג'ינטי סינטיאס אזיאה קאלנטאר:
אי סינטיאס אזיאה קאלנטאר, קין איס איסטי מורו פראנקו,
קי לה קיבדאד בה דירוקאר:

—11—

רומאנסי [7]

סי פאסיאה פאסטור פ׳יאיל, קון סו גאנאדו אקיאה טאדרי:
קון סו גאנאדו אקיאה טאדרי, קון רימולינוס אי טרואינוס,
אי לוס רילאמפאגוס מויי גראנדים:
אי לוס רילאמפאגוס מויי גראנדים, סינייור סי פיקי,
איל מי גאנאדו כון לו פ׳אאי:
אי איל מי גאנאדו כון לו פ׳אאי, קי איל מי גאנאדי פיקו,
לו קי כון איס מיאו איסקהפאמי:
אי לו קי כון איס מיאו איסקאפאמי, איסטו קי סינפיירון
לאס נוב׳יס סי בולטארון פור אוטראס פארטיס:
אי סי בולטארון פור אוטראס פארטיס, סי דאב׳אן די ביבייה
אין פינייה, אי פור אגואה קוריאה סאנגרי:
אי פור אגואה קוריאה סאנגרי, יוראב׳אן לוס קאפיטאניס,
אי טודוס לוס קי אין לה מארי:
אי טודוס לוס קי אין לה מארי, און בורלאנטי אי אינפרי
סיליוס, קי אין איליה כון אג׳יטארי:
אי קי אין איליה כון אג׳יטארי, סינייורה לה מי סינייורס,
די איסטה פ׳ורטונה איסקאפאמי:
אי די איסטה פ׳ורטונה איסקאפאמי, סי די איסטה פ׳ורטונה
מי איסקאפאס, קון אורו ב׳וס אינקורונארי:
אי קון אורו ב׳וס אינקורונארי, איסטו סינפייו איל פאדרון
דיל מונדו, לאס אולאס מאס קורריב׳ייארי:
אי לאס אולאס מאס קורריב׳ייארי, ב׳אסי ב׳אשי פוסה
אמאריאה, קי סום פ׳אלסה אי מינטירוזה:
אי קי סום פ׳אלסה אי מינטירוזה, פ׳יזימוס און פאדרי רחמן,
קי מוג׳אס מאראב׳יאס אזי:
אי קי מוג׳אס מאראב׳יאס אזי, מולאס לוגה דיקופסיטו

—12—

די פריסה קי כון דיסאדרי :
אי די פריסה קי סון דיסאדרי , איל קיטי לה כאלי די גולפו ,
קומו לה פארידה קי פארי :
אי קומו לה פארידה קי פארי , אנסי אגה קון לוס אאזינוס ,
דיפריסה קי כון דיסאדרי :
אי די פריסה קי כון דיסאדרי , קי כינגונוס כי דיזקפירין ,
כי קי פידראן לה איספיראנסה :
אי כי קי פידראן לה איספיראנסה , קי דיספואים די לה
פורטונה , איל מוס מאנדי לה בונאנסה :

רומאנסו 8

דיטו רומאנסו סי קאנטה אין איל סון די אוחילה

איספאנייה לה ריינה איזאבלה , אי אין סו באסטידור לאבראנדו :
אי אין סו באסטידור לאבראנדו , אגוזיקה די אורו אין מאנו ,
סידרון די אמור לאבראנדו :
אי סידון די אמור לאבראנדו , פור אאי פאסו פאריזי ,
אי איל סו לינדו נאמוראדו :
אי איל סו לינדו נאמוראדו , פארה איסטי סואירטו פאריזי ,
קי אוביסיין אנייוס טומאדו :
אי קי אוביסיין אנייוס טומאדו , מירקאדיר סו מי קיריודה ,
מירקאדיר אי איסקריבאנו :
אי מירקאדיר אי איסקריבאנו , סרים כאנים טינגו אין איל
פורטו , קארגאדאס די אורו אי ברוקאדו :
אי קארגאדאס די אורו אי ברוקאדו , די לה כאלי קי יו
ביגו , אגיאה און ריקו מאנסאנו :

—13—

אי אב'יאה און ריקו מאנסאנו, קי איג'אב'ה מאנסאנאס די
אמוריס, אינב'יירנו אי אינב'יראנו:

אי אינב'יירנו אי אינב'יראנו, סי איסטו איס ב'ירדאד פארי,
בורייס איס די לו קונטארי:

אי בורייס איס די לו קונטארי, סי ב'וס פלאזיאה פאריזי
די ב'וס איר אה ב'יספארי:

אי די ב'וס איר אה ב'יספארי, ב'ינגאס אין בואינה אורה
ריינה, ב'וס אי איל ב'ואיסטרו ריינאדו:

אי ב'וס אי איל ב'ואיסטרו ריינאדו, ארמו ב'ינאס אי_איגו
באנייו, פארה אין פ'ראנקייה לה לייב'ארון:

רומאנסו 9

קאנטיגה די נובייה

איסקאב'אנסי לה גאלאנה, סאלידו איל סו קאב'אלייו, סאלודו
אי בין סאלודו, ייב'ולה אה ב'יב'יר אגואס, קון אמוריס:

ייב'ולו אה ב'יב'יר אגואס, לאס אגואס איראן פ'רוב'ייאס; קי
סוב'ריב'ייו איל קאב'אלייו, קון אמוריס:

קי סוב'ריב'ייו איל קאב'אלייו, ראב'ייוסי לה גאלאנה, לו איגו
דיינטרו איל_באנייו, קון אמוריס:

לו איגו דיינטרו איל באנייו, קי טי אאי גאלאנה, קי מי
איב'אסים אל באנייו, קון אמוריס:

קי מי_איב'אסים אל באנייו, די קואנדו מי נאסיסים, פואיטים
מי_לינדו אמאדו, קון אמוריס:

אי פואינים מי לינדו אמאדו, לו סומו פור איל בראסו קי
לו ייב'ו אל פאלאסייו, קון אמוריס:

—14—

סי לו ייבֿו אל פאלאסייו, ייה מיטיירון לאס ארמאס, אי אקומיר סי אסינטארון ׳ קון אמוריס :

אי אקומיר סי אסינטארון, ייה לי אזין לה קאמה. פארה איג׳אר אילייוס אנדארון, קון אמוריס :

אי פארה איג׳אר אילייוס אנדארון, לה פֿין די מילייה נוג׳י, און ג׳וגו נואיבֿו קיטארון, קון אמוריס :

אי אין ג׳וגו נואיבֿו קיטארון, נאסו איל טוֿייו אלה נוג׳ייה, קי לי קיאה פארה מוג׳וס אנייוס; קון אמוריס :

קון אמוריס אי נוג׳ייה, קון סאבֿוריס.

רומאנסו 10

סאליר קירי איל מיז די מאייו, אי אינטראר קירי איל מיז די אבריל :

קואנדו איל טריגו איספיגה אין גראנו, אי לאס פֿלוריס קירי סאליר :

קואנדו איל טריגו איספיגה אין גראנו, אי לאס פֿלוריס קירי סאליר, קואנדו איל קונדאלינארי, פארה פֿראנסייה קיזו איר :

קואנדו איל קונדאלינארי, פארה פֿראנסייה קיזו איר, קון סיגו איל סי ייבֿאבֿה מוזירה, אי פֿאמה אי טאן ג׳ינטיל :

קון סיגו איל סי ייבֿאבֿה קונדי, אי און גופֿליטי די מארפֿיל, אי לייבֿה לו מיטי אין לה סו בוקה, כון לו סאביאה דיזיר :

אי לייבֿה לו מיטי אין לה סו בוקה, כון לו סאביאה דיזיר, אי לייו מאלאנסייה טאל גופֿליטי, לאס דונזלאס קידי פור סי :

אי לייו מאלאנסייה טאל גופֿליטי, לאס דונזלאס קי די פור טי, אי אירמאס טאנטאס לייו ליס דייבֿה, קי מי לו קיטין די אקי :

אי אורמאס טאנטאס לייו ליס דייבֿה, קי מי לו קיטין די

—15—

אקי, אי לייא לו קיטאן אה בֿינדירי, פור פלאסאס אי פור
גֿארסיס:

אי לייה לו קיטאן אבֿינדירי, פור פלאסאס אי פור גֿארסיס,
נינגונוס לי דאבֿאן פריסייו, ני און אספרו ני פֿוזיר:

נינגונוס לי דאבֿאן פריסייו, ני און אספרו ני פֿוזיר, אי טאנטו
פֿואי די בוקה אין בוקה, פֿואי אין לה בוקה די מאדרי:

אי טאנטו פֿואי די אין בוקה אין בוקה, פֿואי אין בוקה
די מאדרי, אי אוטראס טאנטאס לי דירה, קי מי לו טראיי
גאן אקי:

אי אוטראס טאנטאס לי דירה, קי מי לו טראייגאן אקי,
אי ייא לו מיטין אין לה סו בוקה, אי ייא לו אינפינסאן אה
ריטינייר:

אי אה לו מיטין אין לה סו בוקה, אי אה לו אינפיסאן
אריטינייר, לאס נאבֿיס קי איסטאן אין פורטו, פריסטו לאס
אזין בֿיניר:

לאס נאבֿיס קי איסטאן אין פורטו, פריסטו לאס אזין בֿיניר:
לה פארידה קי איסטה פארייינדו, פריסטו לאס אזין פאריר:

רומאנסו 11

פֿינקאטיבֿלי איסטה איל בואין ריי, אי אונוס פינסירייוס
מויי גראנדיס:

אי אונוס פינסירייוס מויי גראנדיס, קי נון לי אבֿינידו
קארטאס, קארטאס די לה סו סיבֿדאדיס:

קארטאס די לה סוס סיבֿדאדיס, אי איל קי טראאיאה נאס
קארטאס, סיין אי בֿינטי אנייוס טיניאה:

סיין אי בֿינטי אנייוס טיניאה, אי נון בֿוס טומיש די מאראבֿיאה,
קי פאדרי אי מאדרי טיניאה:

—16—

קי פאדרי אי מאדרי טיניאה , אי לה פאן אלבה ב'ה לה לונה , קואנדו איל סול סאליר קיריאה :

קואנדו איל סול סאליר קיריאה , אי קואנדו איל קונדי אלימארי , קון לה קונדיסה דורמיאה :

קון לה קונדיסה אולגאב'ה , כון סי לו סאפ'י נינגונוס , קואנטוס אין איל קורטי אב'יאה :

קואנטוס אין איל קורטי איסטאב'אן , סי טון אירה לס סו איזה , קי לו ב'יאה ״ לו איכסילאב'ה :

קי לו ב'יאה אי לו איכקוב'ריאה , סי אלגו ב'שיש לה מי איזה , אין קיב'רילו אי איכסילאדו :

איכקוב'רילדו אי איכסילאדו , ב'ים דאמי אל קונדי אלימארי , קון סאיוס די סילו דאמאסקו :

קון סאיוס די סילו דאמאסקו , אי יו מאלאחיה לוס סוס כאיוס , אי לה טאמביין קון לוס קיריאה :

אי לה טאמביין קון לוס קיריאה , אין ב'ידה דיל ריי מי פאדרי , יו מאס מוגו איסטרואיאב'ה :

יו מאס מוגוס איספרואיאה , אארען ב'וס סי אגה איזה , לה ליג'י קי יו סי דיירה :

לה ליג'י קי יו סי דיירה , אארען ב'וסי אגה מאדרי , איל פאן דיל מי פאדרי קומייראש' :

איל פאן דיל מי פאדרי קומייראש' , אין ב'ידה דיל ריי מי פאדרי , טומאטיש' מוזיב'ו מארידו :

טומאטיש' מוזיב'ו מאראדו , דישה קי אב'אש'י איל ריי מי פאדרי , דישה קי אב'אש'י די לה מיסה :

דישה קי אב'אש'י די לה מיסה ; יו סי לו ב'ו אה דיזירי , יו סי לו ב'ו אה קונטארי :

יו סי לו ב'ו אה קונטארי , איסטאס פאלאב'ראס דיזיינדו , איל בואין ריי קי ייא אריב'ארי :

— 17 —

אי איל בואין ריי קי יש ג'יריס , טודה לה נוג'י יוראנדו ,
לאגרימאס די טריס אין קואטרו :
לאגרימאס די קואטרו אין סינקו , די קי יוראב'ה לה מי אלמה ,
לאגרימאס די טריס אין קואטרו :
לאגרימאס די טריס אין קואטרו , יו איסטאנדו אין לה מי
פואירטה אי אין מי באסטידור לאב'ראנדו :
אי אין מי באסטידור לאב'ראנדו , פור אהי פאסו איל קונדי
אלימאני , לה טראב'ו פור לוס טרינסאדוס :
לה טראב'ו פור לוס טרינסאדוס , אנסי ריאין לה מי אלמה ,
אנסי ריאין לוס מוג'אג'וס :
אנסי ריאין לוס מוג'אג'וס , די דיטראס די איסטוס ריאירים ,
אקונטיסין מוג'וס דאנייוס :
אקונטיסין מוג'וס דאנייוס , סי ב'וס פלאזי לה מי אלמה ,
יו לו מאנדארי א מאטארי :
יו לו מאנדארי א מאטארי , קון לו מאטיש' איל מי פאדרי ;
ני לו קיראש' מאטארי :
ני לו קיראש' מאטארי , קי איל קונדי איס ניניו סי אינגאנייו ,
איל מונדו קירי גאנארי :
איל מונדו קירי גאנארי , דיספירטאנדו די איספאדאס פ'ייראס ,
קי די אקי טאן קומו פאני :

רומאנסו 12

קון קיין טומארי קונסיז'ו , קי ב'ינגה א מי סי לו דארי ,
קון קיין קאזאר קון מוסה , טאן סי איספירי אה לה ב'יז'יס :
קון קיין קאזאר קון מוסה , טאן סי איספירי אה לה ב'יז'יס ,
פור מי לו דיגו איל מיסקינו , קי די סיין אנייוס קאזו איל :
פור מי לו דיגו איל מיסקינו , קי די סיין אנייוס קאזו איל ,

—18—

קאזי קון אונה סינייורה, קי נון טייני לוס דייז אי סיס :
קאזי קון אונה סינייורה, קי נון טייני לוס דייז אי סיס,
איל דיאה די לאס סוס בודאס, אי דייז מוזיריס קי פואי אזיר :
איל דיאה די לאס סוס בודאס, אי דייז מוזיריס קי פואי אזיר,
טומו פייני די אורו אין מאנו, סוס קאבֿיאוס סי פואי אפייניאר :
טומו פייני די אורו אין מאנו, סוס קאבֿיאוס סי פואי אפייניאר,
אי אין לה סו מאנו דיריג̃ה, לייבֿה און איספיז'ו קריסטאל :
אי אין לה סו מאנו דיריג̃ה, לייבֿה און איספיז'ו קריסטאל,
די אילייו קי מירה סו פואירטו, אי איל סו לינדו אסימיז'אר :
די אילייו קי מירה סו פואירטו, אי איל סו לינדו אסימיז'אר,
בֿינדיזיינדו בֿה דיל בֿינו, אי בֿינדיזיינדו בֿה דיל פאן :
בֿינדיזיינדו בֿה דיל בֿינו, אי בֿינדיזיינדו בֿה דיל פאן,
בֿינדיזיינדו אל דייו דיל סיילו, קי טאל לינדה לה פואי אקריאר :
בֿינדיזיינדו אל דייו דיל סיילו, קי טאל לינדה לה פואי א קריאר; מאלדיזיינדו אה פאדרי אי מאדרי, קי קון און בֿייז'ו לה פואי אקאזאר :
מאלדיזיינדו אה פאדרי אי מאדרי, קי קון און בֿייז'ו לה פואי אקאזאר, קי לה קאזארה קון און בֿייז'ו, איל בֿייז'ו איס די אנטיגואילאד :
קי לה קאזארה קון און בֿייז'ו, אי איל בֿייז'ו די אנטיגואילאד,
לה ניניה קירי ג'וגיטי, אי איל בֿייז'ו קירי פולגאר :
לה ניניה קירי ג'וגיטי, אי איל בֿייז'ו קירי פולגאר, ייוראבֿה לה בלאנקה ניניה, לאגרימאס די בֿילונטאד :
ייוראבֿה לה בלאנקה ניניה, לאגרימאס די בֿילונטאד, סול אסי פאסו קלארינו, קואל נון לה בֿיירה די פאסאר :
אי פור אאי פאסו קלארינו, קואל נון לה בֿיירה די פאסאר,
די קי ייוראש לה בלאנקה ניניה, לאגרימאס די בֿילונטאד :
די קי ייוראש לה בלאנקה ניניה, לאגרימאס די בֿילונטאד,

—19—

קי מי קאזארון קון און ביז'ו, איל ביז'ו כון אירה מי פאר איגוש:
קי מי קאזארון קון און ביז'ו, איל ביז'ו כון אירה מי פאר
איגוש, ב'ום דאמי און קונסיז'ו, קואל מי לו אוב'יירה'ש די טומאר:
ב'ום דאמי און קונסיז'ו, קואל מי לו אוב'יירה'ש די טומאר,
איב'ום די לה פריסייאדה, די טרים מיזים אי כון מאם:
איב'ום די לה פריסייאדה, די טרים מיזים אי כון מאם, אה
לום קאמפום די אלסוטה, און חזיר ב'ידי אסאר:
אה לום קאמפום די אלסוטה, און חזיר ב'ידי אסאר, קי די
אקיל חזיר כון גוסטו, איל פריסייאדו לו ב'ו אג'אר:
קי די אקיל חזיר כון גוסטו, איל פריסייאדו לו ב'ו אג'אר,
קי אליב'אנטו איל ב'יז'יקו, אב'יר איל חזיר אנדי איסטה:
קי אליב'אנטו איל ב'יז'יקו, אב'יר איל חזיר אנדי איסטה,
ארחו איל לה סו לאנסה; לה קאב'יסה לי אינפ'ילארה:
ארחו איל לה סו לאנסה, לה קאב'יסה לי אינפ'ילארה,
ב'יני ב'יריש אקיל חזירי, קי לו ב'יטיש אסאר

ברינדים

אימפורטאנטים פארה פ׳ייסטאם

סינייורים, טודו מודו די קידושין, כון קי דה קון נינגון מיטאל
סולאמינטי קון אנילייו, אי דיש'י די סיר די אורו
פ'ינו אם קולור די איל לידייו; אי ב'יב'ה לה משפחה
פ'ולאנה, קי קונסוגרו קון משפחה די ף אמילייו:
סינייורים, לום ברינדים סי סאלודאן סיגון לה פואיזיאה קי
אפטה, אי טודו מודו די מאנסיב'ו קואנדו קאזם

—20—

אס קי אריפאה, אזֿייגה לה פאלוסה די לוס קי
גֿונסו איל איספאו אי לה איספאה :

סינייוריס, נונקה צֿוס אינגלאנ ייו אמיר דיספאן די אינדייזֿינוס
אי איסטריאירוס, קי לוס נאיס קי ומס אוי איל
דייו סון פור סיגורו צֿירוס; אזֿייגה אלב פאלאבראס די
לוס סי, אין גֿונסו לוס סינייוריס קיפשאיגרוס :

סינייוריס, לאס פֿיסטאס די אגורה, סי אואן קון גֿאלגי אי
טרופה, אי אין איסבי בֿירנדי קי עומן קארה מונ
אי מונו סו קופה, אזֿייגה איל איסאו אי איספאה,
קי איל קאמאנייכעו לים זֿאייב איםפואה :

סינייוריס, טודו מונדו די בֿירנדי קי פאלודו אימפירעירו לו
איסמירו אי לו מונדו, אי לה פריסונה דינזֿי פינה
טימוי די ך פאסרון דיל מונדו, אזֿייגה לה קאוסה
די פֿולאנו, אלוס אי יירכס פרימירו אי סיגונדו :

סינייוריס, איל פאראש קואנדו סומה אלגון דוקאדו אימפיריעירו
לו פיה, אי אין איסטי מונדו פֿאלנסו אה ריקו אי
אה פרוזֿי נון איי שֿירמיה, אזֿייגה בה פאלוסה דיל
סי פֿולאנו, אין גֿונטו לה סינייוריאה די לה מזֿוז :

סינייוריס, לה גירה אין ליגואה טורקה סי ייאמה מזֿידיאזֿי
אלסין, אי פודו לו קי גֿאנאמוס לה סימאנה, גֿואזֿיים
לאס קונסינייאמוס אב סי אלאסין, סיזֿייגה מספפה
שֿולאנה, קי קונסוגרו קון מספאה די שֿוריגלין :

סינייוריס, לה פריסונה פור לו קי סי פוסה, דינזֿי די איסמאר
גוסטאו אי נון טריספי, אי איל קיספאס אין נוסיספרה
סיזֿדאר איי טיימפו קי איגזיסני, אזֿייגה מספאס
שֿולאנה, קי קונסוגרו קון מספאה די ך צֿיניסי :

סינייוריס, אל טיימפו די אנניס אידה פרואיבֿיטו די קאמינאר
לה נוגֿי סין פֿינל, אי איל קי זֿימאה אין קופאן

— 21 —

טייני גוסטו די קאמינאר פור דיבאשו איל סול,
איסטה משפחה פולאנה, קי קונסוגרו קון משפחה
די אבראבאנאל:

סינייורים, לה פריקונה אין איסטי מונדו, דישי די סיר דינייו,
אי איל איגאדור די ברינדים סי מיטי סיינפרי
אין גראנדי אימפינייו, איסטה משפחה פולאנה, קי
קונסוגרו קון משפחה די גאטינייו:

סינייורים, לוס ברינדיס קי יו באלודו אלה סינייוריאה איס
פינה אנדי אלקאנסה מי בראסו; אי סיינפרי לוס
סינייורים קי מוס פוסימוס אין פראנסו אי נון אין
אינבאראסו, איסטה משפחה פולאנה קי קונסוגרו
קון משפחה די קאראסו:

סינייורים, טודו איל פישקאדו סי אפירה קון בואין דיטי, אי
פריזאלי סיינפרי פארה פיסטאס אי קומביטי,
איסטה משפחה פולאנה, קי קונסוגרו קון משפחה
די ארדיטי:

סינייורים, אל טיימפו עודים לוס טראטוס איראן אין סימן
די פיר אי פינאר אי מטון, אי אגורה נון מוס קידו
נינגון איגו אפילו אין איל קוטון, איסטה משפחה
פולאנה, קי קונסוגרו קון משפחה די מטון:

סינייורים, לוס פירקונאלים קי איגאן סו מונידה אין לה באנקה
נוסה, אקיל אים סיגורו קי קומי פישקאדו מונוקוס
אי אוספיטאה, איסטה משפחה פולאנה, קי קונ-
סוגרו קון משפחה די קאסורסו:

סינייורים, אין סו אוטיסיין לה פירקונה דישי די סיר מאאבסרו
קי אים טומו, קומו סלוס ססח היליבדי; קי פאשי
פראזאר סו פליגה אין סו קישאן, איסטה משפחה
פולאנה, קי קונסוגרו קון משפחה די נחמן:

—22—

שינייוריס, בֿאס שאמאראס אבֿאבֿאדאס קין, איל שאמור, אי
איל שינגאס, אי לה קאפֿה, אי און לה איבֿיבֿה לוס
שי שיגורו קי טון אראן ג׳יפֿב, איבֿיבֿה לה שאלוטה
די פֿולאס, ג׳ונטו שודה לה טאייפֿה :

שינייוריס, שור שיר בֿירדאד קי קון לאס בֿיראס איסטו שיליאדו
אי נון קירו אזיר באריש, מה קון לוס גרושיקוס
איספירו די לוס שינייוריס קימי אראן און בואין
אלבֿישבֿיריס, שיינדו שו ליין און בֿיזינו אין איל
קוארטייר דיל בארון פירמ :

שינייוריס, קון טודו שירו לאס פואיזיאס אין דימאנדובֿוס די
לה שינייוריאה לה איסקאקאה, שיינדו איל גאסטי די
פסח מיאו קי טראטה די איסטאס גימאראב איכטאכסו
כון מי אגאס לה ריפֿאה, איבֿיבֿה לייו יעקב יונה
קון טודה לה כינייוריאה אינקלאה :

ברינדים

פארה זאפיטים די ברית מילה

שינייוריס, נואיסטרו דייו איס שיימפרי אל מלא רחמים, אי
איל קי די אברהם אבינו שי פריבֿו עשרה פעמים,
איבֿיבֿה לה שאלוטה דיל קיטאדור אי איל פאריזו
אין ג׳ונטו טודוס לוס שינייוריס חכמים :

שינייוריס, קי אליגריאה טומאמוס טודוס קואנדו מוס אינטרה
לה פרימה בֿירה, אי איל דייו קי אקונטיסי אה
אקיאה מאיר דיאאה קי שיאה שאלידירה, איבֿיבֿה

—23—

לה סאלוטה דילוס קי ג׳וסטו קיטה״ר אי קיפאדירה :

סיניורים, סיימפרי דימאנדאמוס דיל דייו קי מוס מאנדי אליגרייה קומפלידה, אי טודו מודו די מוזיר פארה סו מארידו איס קירידה, אישיטה לה סאלוטה די לוס סיניורים ג׳וסטו איל פאדרידו אי לה מאדרה :

סיניורים, לה מאס פארטי די לוס סיניוריס די לה מיזה סון קרובים; לאס פ׳ייסטאס אי זיאפיטים סי איסקאפאן קון גאסטאר בואינאס זהובים, אישיטה לה סאלוטה דיל פאדרידו אל מודו קי לו אייגו אל איזו א לה ברית, אנסי קי לו אייגי א לה חופה אי א לה מצות אי א מעשים טובים :

סיניורים, איל פוסטירו סיימפרי דישי די קי אזיר אין לה מיזה איכדילינו, אי לה פירקונה אין איסטי מונדו פור אזיר מצות אי מעשים טובים איס לו קי צ׳ינו, אנסי קי לו אייגי איל דייו א לה פולאנו אה דיזיר ברכה

להכניסו בבריתו של אברהם אבינו :

דיטה קאנטיגה סי קאנטה אין איל טן די שבועות

סימן אני יעקב יונה

אין איסטי טיימפו איספירו די סיר שנטוראדו; איספיראנדו לה בונדאד דיל דייו נואיסטרו ארימאו, איל דייו איס מאדריאדו אי כון איס אוליבידאדו .

נון דישארי איל דייו די קונסיליר דיאוס די מואיסטרה אלמה, סיינדו די טאנטוס סינסיירוס כון דורמימוס אין לה קאמה, בושקה סיגנו פור אלמה, כון סיגנו שאזי די דראמה .

יו שו סיימפרי גיראנדו אי נון מוסטרו אלגונוס מיריקאה, מה

—24—

אין סופיטו בֿו אפּארטיר פור בֿיאז׳ די פּראטיקאס, סיינדו
דיזי איל פרובֿירבֿייו, אמה נון מואירי די פיקיאס.
דיו דודון אנוס אמי מוז׳יר לה ייאמאריאס, פינין דולסים אי
אינספארוני קון איליה אלה בירדיאס, מאדרי קי פארייז
אה פילזאנה קי נונקה לי קידאריאס.
אליגרים אי קונטינטים איסטאמוס אינבוטיסו מי מינטה, סיינדו
אים מי אמור פריזידו לה קירו קומו מי ביניאס, מה פייני
אונה מאנקורה קי קואנדו קאי נון איזה ביודו אלה זיסה.
קואנדו מי זי ספאראר לה נוג׳י איל אלמה סי לי ארנקה, מי
ארישבֿי קומו און ג׳ילידי קי איספה אין לה באנקה, סינגו
ספפק איספה אמיקסטאר נון מי מיסה דיבאשו לה פלאקה.
באסטאשי מיריקיאה טומה קואנדו מי בֿו אין קאזה און שיניל,
אין בֿינג׳י די ג׳ילידי מי ייאמה אים אניל, קומו קירי אבראזאניל
אנסי קירי זאמבראניל.
ייה מי דיזי מונג׳אס בֿיזים קי טינגו טאין פארימיר, אי ליין
לי דו הבטחה דזיינדו קי לייה בֿו אה אינריקיסיר; קאנטאס
גאייו קאנטה, קי ייה בֿה אמאנסיר.
דיינדוני פור אוראס סין פאראס מי פראגה פור אמאל, אי
סיימפרי בֿו קוריינדו מאס ניגרו די און אינימאל, סון מילדו
מאמה הי דיבֿאנטאל טאפה מונג׳ו מאל.
נון מי קידו פאראס פור מירקאר אשׁילו און פאטיר, ליין לי
אבֿלו בואינו איליינה איבֿסטה קון באטיר; די נוס מיאוס קירו
דיזיר מה נון קירו ליניר.
דיקונה מוז׳יר מיאה מי טראשטה אמי פור ריקו, מה סון מירה
דינירוס קי נון טינגו באסטון די פירו, קון דה איל
אספריקו לי טאפיין איל גוליטיקו.

III
GU'ERTA DE ROMANSAS ANTIGUAS DE PASATYEMPO
(n.p., before 1908?)
(abbr. GRA)

GÜERTA
DE
ROMANSAS ANTIGUAS
DE PASATIEMPO.

En dita guimará contiene tres artículos presentes.

I.—Once romansas, las más brillantes que puede ser por pasatiempo de los señores en todas las horas de alegria y de nochadas de velar.

II.—Una cantiga moral al ceder del alfabet(o) y se canta en todo modo de son que les plaze à los señores, si tambien en el son de *Xeborlimi mané*.

III.—Un cante del Felek que se canta en el son de las coplas de Xabuot.

Yo el autor
Jacob. Abraham Joná.

(Title page of GRA according to the transcription of M. Manrique de Lara.)

גואירטה
די
רומאנסאס אנטיגואס
די פאסאטיימפו

רומאנסה א

ייו מי איסטאבה אין טורים, אי און טורים פור לה מאנייאנה.
אין פואירה דה קאזר פאשאריס, פאשאריס די אלמוגאבאראס
אי פאשאריס די אלמינאראס, פארה אפארינסאר לה טורי,
לה טורי קי איירה מוראדה די סונה
לה טורי די לוס קאבאלייוס, אי קי לה קיאמאן לה
גואדרה
אה לה סוראדה קי אסוטה, פאזיר לה טורי קימאדה
אי אה לה קון אספאדה ייאדה
קואנדו ייו מי קאזארי, אי איל מי קאזאר לאמארי
פולגה קיאדה אין איי דאדו, אי מוגו מאס אין פיידה
אה דארי
קידו קי מי ייאמאן איסטה נוג'י, אנדי לה מי איספאדה
דוראדה
סאלטו איל קאזאר די דיגו, קון פיגורה קי איל דין
לי איי דאדו
ייו מי ייאמו איסטה נוג'י, אנדי לה סו איספאדה דוראדה
איסקורינג'אזו דין לה פינייה, אי אפאלואשו איל מי קייארי
דישלי קוצאלאש די פיירו, אי די איל נו ערנגאש פיאדה.
פור לאס קאזאס קי איי ג'ינטי, קאמינארים די אזנגארי.
פור לאס קאזאס קי נו איי ג'ינטי, סינטיאס איאש קאנטארי.
קי לה זיראש אנגי איספאדה, אי אלה מי איספאדה דוראדה

— 2 —

פ׳ור אקי פאסו איסטה נוג׳י, דוס אוראס אל ב׳יל לונארי.
בלאנקו קאלבה אי בלאנקו ב׳יסטי, אי בלאנקו קאב׳אייר
לאזארי
יא קי איספארטי איל קאב׳איירו, יא קי איספארטי אי קי ב׳ה.
פ׳ור אינמידייו דיל קאמינו, אינקונטרו קון און פירקונטי.
קי לה ב׳יזיש און איספאדה, אלה מי איספאדה רוייאלי.
פ׳ור אקי פאסו איסטה נוג׳י. טריס אוראס אל ב׳יל לונאר.
פ׳ריטו קאלבה אי פ׳ריטו ב׳יסטי, אי פ׳ריטו קאב׳אייו לאזארי.

רומאנסה 2

פ׳ור לוס פאלאסייוס די איל ריי. קי פאסייאה אונה דונזיאה.
בלאנקה איס אי קולוראדה, אירמוזה קומו לאס איסטרייאס.
בלאנקה איס אי קולוראדה, אירמוזה קומו לאס איסטרייאס.
ב׳יסטו לה אוב׳ו איל בואן ריי. נאמוראר קי אוב׳ו די אייה:
קי מורנה.
דימאנדו איל ריי אה סו ג׳ינטי, קין אירה איסטה דונזיאה.
קי אירה די אלטה ג׳ינטי. פ׳ואירה לה מי מאדרי פרימירה.
קי אירה די באשה ג׳ינטי, אירה אונה די מיס דונזיאס.
ב׳ואיסטרה אירמאנה איס איל בואן ריי, ב׳ואיסטרה איר-
מאנה לה פיקינייה.
סיינדו קי איס לה מי אירמאנה. גראן פיאגה ני איי-
און אייה.
אקי אקי מיס קאב׳אייריס. לוס קי די לה מי פאן קומיראש.
מאטאדה לה איסטה דונזיאה. אי אראנקאדי קין קאזיטאס.
מזדו איל אומברי קי לה אינפ׳ינה, די דאדיב׳אס קי יו לי דירה.
מזדו איל אומברי קי ני לה איספ׳ינה. דאראלי יו קון ייליוור פ׳ינה.

— 3 —

די אמי קאטיבו איל גראן קידי, כי אגאש מאל אה איספוזה דונזילה.

קי אטורגאש בוס איל גראן קידי, בואיסטרה קאמאראדה פואירה.

כי איס מי קאמאראדה איל בואין ריי, איס לה מי מאס פרימירה.

קי מי לה דייו איל ריי בואיסטרו פאדרי, מוגו אנטיס קי מורייירה.

יא כי פארטי איל גראן קידי. יא כי פארטי אי כי פואירה,

איל בואין מורו איל בואין מורו, איל די לה באראבה אינבילייוטאדה.

בוס מאנדו אה יאמאר איל בואין ריי, קי בוס קירי אונה פאלאבּרה.

קי פאלאבּרה אירה איסטה, טאן סיקריטה אי טאן קונטאדה.

קורטאר בוס קירי לה קאבּיקה, אינגאראלה אין אונה מונטאנייה.

אנדה דיזילדי אל בואין ריי, קי ייו נו לי קולפו נאדה

די קולגדו פואירון מיס גירראס, פידרי מי אובירה אי מי קאמה,

פידרי אזום אי מאדריס, אי אונה קאזה קי ייו מאנדאבה

פידרי אונה אלמה דונזילה, קי נו אבילה אין גראנאדה

פידרי מאל אי קינייאטוס מאלינוס, קי סוליאן קומי אי דיאה

לוס קינייאטוס מאליאן אורו, אי לוס קינייאטוס פלאטה פינה.

לוס קינייאטוס מוליאן פולבו, פארה איל ריי סי איספארטיאה,

יא כי פארטי איל בואין מורו, יא כי פארטי אי סי איבה,

רומאנסה 3

אין פאריז איסטה דונייאלדה, אי לה איספוזה די רולדאני.
טריזיינטאס דאמאס קון אילייה, קי טודאס סון די און לינאזי.
אי טריזיינטאס דאמאס קון אילייה, קי טודאס סון די און לינאזי.
לאס סיינטו איראן די בורגו, אי לאס סיינטו די פורטוגאלי.

(סי טורנה)

לאס סיינטו איראן די פראנסייה לה סיבדאד די גראן קודאלי

נו פינסיש קי איסטאן דיבאלדיס, קי טודאס אופיסייו אאן
לאס סיינטו פילאבאן פירלה, אי לאס סיינטו טישאן קאנדאלי
לאס סיינטו טאנייין ביגואילה, פארה דונייאלדה פולגארי
אי דונייאלדה קון גראנדי ביסייו. מאל אדורמיסידה קאאי
טריס דיאס קון לאס טריס נוג׳יס, נו לי אוזו אריפולגארי
אה פין די לאס טריס נוג׳יס, סי דיספירטו קון פאבור גראנדי
ביני אקי מיס דונייאס, לאס קי אין מי קונאנדי איסטאריש
איספואינייו קוניי דונזיאס, אין ביין מי לו אסולטאריש
קי אירה מוקה סולטירה, יו לה דיבו די קאזארי
סי טאל אירה קאזאדה, אנדי קו מארידו אבאלארי
ני סי קונאבאן קאבאליירוס, ני סי קונאבאן סיבדאדיס
סי לים קונאבאן לאס בארבאס, אי לה קודורה ריאלי

רומאנסה 4

אין אקיל ביגג׳יל פיקינייו, פיקינייו די גראן באלייה
אנדי איי ראמאס אי פלוריס, אלמאנזאקה אי גראנאדינאס
אי אנדי איי ראמאס אי פלוריס, אלמאנזאקה אי גראנאדינאס

— 5 —

אנדי קירי לה נאראנג׳ה, אי איל לימון אי לה סידרה. ב׳ טורנה:
אנדי איי רודה מנודה, קי איס גואדריאה די פארידאס .
׳ אנדי קאנטה לה ליאונה , אי איל ליאון קי ריספונדיאה .
אאי איסטה איל טריסטי אמאדורי, איל קי די אמוריס מוריאה.
ייא סי פארטי איל אמאדורי , ייא סי פארטי אי סי איבה .
טופו לאס פואירטאס סיראדאס, ב׳ינטאנאס קי נו סי אב׳ריאן.
קון פאלאב׳ראס די אינקאנטאמיינטו, די פאר אין פאר סי אב׳ריאן.
טופו אלה נינייה דורמיינדו, קון קאנאס אי גראב׳יאנאס .
ב׳אטי ב׳אטי איל אמאדורי , ב׳אטי ב׳אטי קון מי ב׳ידה .
סי די אקי איגו און גריטו , ייא טראגו אה טודה סיב׳יאה .
קי מי פאדרי אי מיס אירמאנוס , דיספידאדה מי ב׳ירן .
קון אקיל דוקי די פראנסייה, קי נו איי אוטרו אין לה ב׳ילה .
ייא סי פארטי איל אמאדורי , ייא סי פארטי אי סי איבה .
די לוס סוס אוזוס ייוראב׳ה , אי די לה סו בוקה דיזיאה .
מאלדיג׳ו סיאה אקיל מאדרי , איל קי די אמוריס סי פ׳יאה .
שאפאטאס קון אי מיטיראס , אי קריאדאס זה שיב׳יה .

רומאנסה 5

אין איל ב׳ירג׳יל די לה ריינה, אה קריסידו און ב׳יל רושי .
לה ראיז טייני די אורו לה סימיינסי די און בואין קריסטאל.
לה ראאיז טייני די אורו, לה סימיינסי די און ב׳יל קריסטאל .
אין לה ראמיקה מאס אלטה, און רוסינייו סינטי קאנטאר. ב׳ טורנה.
איל קאנטאר קי איב׳ה דיזיינדו , לוגו איס דינו קאנטאר .
לה ריינה איספאב׳ה לאב׳אנדו, אי לה אזה דורמיינדו איסטה.
שבאשיש לה מי אזה , די ב׳וסקוזו דולסי פולגאר .

אוליר'דיש קומו קאנטה, לה סירינקה די לה מאר.
נו איס לה סירינקה ני נאדה, נו איס לה סירינקה די
לה מאר.
קי סון איס איל קונדי ג'ינאר. קי סוס ני? די ספה אקאבאר.
כי איס איסטו לה ני איזה, יו לו מאנדארי א מאטאר,
נו לו מאטיש לה מי מאדרי. כי לו מאנדיש א מאטאר.
קי איל קונדי איס נינייו אי מוג'אג'ו. איל מונדו קירי גאנאר,
אי קי לו מאטאש לה מי מאדרי, אונדי קון איל אין און לוגאר.
לה ריינה קי די מאל טינגה, פריסטו לוס מאנדו א מאטאר,
אנדי פואי און אינטירמוריגטו, דיזאשו דיל ציל ראאל.
איל קי איזו אונה גראנדיינה, אי איליה קי איזו אונה קונגה,
לה ריינה קי די מאל טינגה, פריסטו לוס מאנדו ארראנקאר,
ארראנקאדוס אי דיספאוזוס, אי אינגלוס א בונאר.
איליה קי איזו אונה פאלומה, אי איל קי איזו און גאביאן,
לה ריינה קי די מאל טינגה, פריסטו לוס מאנדו א קאזאר,
קאזאדוס אי דיגולייאדוס, אי לוס איזו קי אלמוראר.
לוס גואיסיקוס קי קדארון, לוס מאנדו אמאר אלה מאר,
איליה קי איזו אונה סירקייה אי איל קי איזו און קארה באזאן,
לה ריינה קי די מאל טינגה, פריסטו לוס מאנדו א פישקאר,
פישקאדוס אי אינקאמוטאדוס. אי לוס איזו קי אלמוראר.
לאס אינספינאס קי קדארון, לאס אינסירו דיזאשו איל פורטאל.
איליה קי איזו אונה קולינדרה, אי איל קי איזו און טאבראן.

רומאנסה 6

דולסי איראש לה מי מאדרי, אי אה פאן דולסי אין איל אזוקאר.
דיס בזיקוס אש פידרידו, אי מיס לוס קוארינו אינטיינדו אדאר.

— 7 —

אי 2 בזיקוס אס̃ פידרדו, אי טריס אי קואטרו איבטיינדו אדאר
בוס דוס איראן די אמוריס, אי לוס דוס די ב̃ילונטאד: קי סורנה.

ייוראבה לה בלאנקה נינייה, לאגרימאס די ב̃ילונטאד.
די קי ייוראש̃ בלאנקה נינייה, לאגרימאס די ב̃ילונטאד.
ייורו פור בוס קאב̃אלייירו, קי בוס ב̃אש̃ אי מי דישאש̃.
מי דישאש̃ נינייה אי מוג̃אג̃ה, אי ג̃יקה די לה פוקה אידאד.
מי דישאש̃ איז̃וס ג̃יקיטוס, ייוראן אי דימאנדאן פאן.
איסטו סינטייו איל קאב̃אלייירו, דישו טודו אי טורנו אטראס.
מיטייו לה מאנו אין סו סינו, סין דובלונים לי דארה.
פארה קי מי בוסקה איסטו, פארה בינו או פארה פאן.
סי איסטו נו בוס אבאסטה, בינדירש̃ מידייה סיבדאד.
בינדירש̃ לוס מיס ב̃יסטידוס, סין מאנג̃אר אי סין קודאר.
סינה טריס אנייוס י׳ איספיראש̃, אל קואטרו בוס קאזאש̃.

רומאנסה 7

גראנדים בודאס אי אין פראנסייה, אין לה קאזה די פאריס.
קי קאזו איל איז̃ו די איל ריי, קון לה איז̃ה די אונאדי.
קי קאזו איל איז̃ו די איל ריי. קון לה איז̃ה די אמאדי.
באיילאן דאמאס אי דונזיאס, קאבאלירוס מאס די מיל: סינודנה.
איל קי גיאה לה מאייפ̃ה. אים אונה דאמה ג̃ינטיל.
מיראנדו לה איספאדה איל קונדי, אי אקיל קונדי די אמאדי.
קי מיראש̃ אקי איל קונדי, אי קונדי קי מיראש̃ אקי.
או מיראב̃אש̃ לה סאייה, או מי מיראב̃אש̃ אמי.
ייו נון מירו אלה סאייה, ני מינוס מי מירו אמי.
מירו אה איסטי נינייו קואירפו, קי אים גלאנו אי מאן ג̃ינטיל.
קי בוס פלאזיאה איל בואין קונדי, קון סיגו ייב̃ישו אמי.

— 8 —

מאדרי אין ביאֵי טינגו, אי לונג'י איסטה פארה ביניר.
דוס אִיז'יקוס ג'יקוס טינגו, קי נון סי לו סאבֿין דיזיר.
אונה איספוזיגרה ביאה טינגו, אי נואֵה איסטה פארה מוריר.
אינבולואֵלה אין און מאנטיל די אורו, אי די אספואירה דישו
איל ג'אפין.
לה סאלידה דילה פואירטה, אינקונטרו קון מאמאדי.
קי יבֿאמוש אקי איל בואין קונדי, אי קונדי קי יבֿאמוש אקי.
ייבֿו און פאז'יקו די אורו, קי אאינדה אבֿייר ייו לו מירקי.
איסטי פאז'יקו איל קונדי, קי אמי מי איספואזי אה סירביר.
איל דיאה פארה לה מיזה, אי לה נוג'י פארה דורמיר.
איסטו קי סינטייו איל בואין קונדי, לו דישו אי סי איג'ו אספואיר.
כון בֿוס פֿייגאמוש איל בואין קונדי, אי נו בֿוס קיזיראמוש סואיר.
קי מי אים לה בֿואיסטרה קאלפה, סי נון ייו קי לו בושקי.
אקיל קונדי אי אקיל קונדי, אי אין לה מאר סיאה סו פֿין.
ארמה נאבֿים אי גאליאס, אי פארה פֿראנסייה קיזו איר.
לאס ארמאס די טודו טינטו, אי לאס איג'ו דיינטרו איל פאלאג'יר.
איל פאלאג'יר קומו אירה איסטריג'ו. נו לאס פודיאה ריזיר.
אטראס אטראס לוס פֿראנסיזיס כון לי דיש בֿירגואינסה אסי.
סי איל גראן דוקי לו סאבֿי, לה פֿראנסייה כון מוס דישה איר.
ני בֿוס דאן פאן אה קומירי, ני קאן לאס דאמאס דורמיר.
לה סורנאדה קי אסוראן, מאטארון סיסינטה מיל.
אפארטי די ביקיקוס, קי נון אי קואינטה ני פֿין.

רומאנסה 8

לה דיל דיאה אי קלארידאד, קי איל דיאה לי דירה איל סול.
אי לה נוג'י איל קלארו לונאר.
אי לה נוג'י איל קלארו לונאר, לה מארינירקה לאס איסטריאס.
מי קואדו קירי אבֿלאר. סי סונה

— 9 —

סי פאסיאה טיאו אי סוב'רינו, ג'ונטוס ב'אן אה און באראבאר.
קי קאב'איוס ייב'אן די און פריסייו, פור ב'יר קואל קוריאה מאס.
קי קורי אונו אי קורי אוטרו, ג'ונטוס ב'אן אאון באראבאר.
אב'לאנדו אי פלאטיקאנדו, נו קי ליס אימפורטה מאס.
אונה מירסיד לי רוגו טיאו, קואל מי לה אב'יש די אטורגאר.
קי מי דיש אה קאבאלירה נינייה, פור מוז'יר אי פור איגואל.
איסטה מירסיד איל מי סוב'רינו, נו ב'ו לה פואידו אג'יטאר.
דיספוזאדה לה טינגו אין פ'ראנסייה, קון איל קונדי טיגורנאר.
גירירו קון איל מי סוב'רינו, סיפאש לאס ב'יין גאנאר.
לאס ארמאס טינגו אינפינייאדאס, פור קיין דובלאס אי אלגו מאס.
דאדי קיין דובלאס אל קונדי, פארה לאס ארמאס קיטאר.
אוטראס טאנטאס יו לי דייה, פארה איל קאמינו גאסטאר.
דאדיש קאמיזה די סידה, סירמה אי פירלה אין סו קוייאר.
דאדיש ג'אקיטה די סירמה, קי לה לאב'רו אל ביל לונאר.
ייה סי איספאנטי איל קאב'אליירו, ייה סי איספאנטי אי סי ב'ה.

רומאנסה 9

סי פאסיאה איל פאסטור פ'ייל אין אונה מונטאנייה סאן קלארה.
קון רימולינוס אי טרואינוס, אי נוס רילאמפאגוס מויי גראנדיס.
סי טורנה.
סינייור סינייור סי פיקי איל מי גאנאדו נו פאזי.
סי איל מי גאנאדו נו קולפה, נו קי נון איס מיאו אפארטאר.
איסטו קי סינטיירון לאס נוב'יס, סי אג'ארון פור אוטרה פארטי.
סי דאב'אן די פינייה אין פינייה, אי פור אגואה קוריאה סאנגרי.
יוראב'אן לוס קאפיטאניס. טודוס לוס דילה מאר יוראן.

אדיינטרו די אקיאה מאר ייוראן, אבֿיאה אונה סינייורה.
סינייורה לה מי סינייורה , איסקאפאמי די איסטה פֿוטה.
סי די איסטה פֿוטה מי איסקאפאס, די אורו טי ב֯יסטו טודה.
איסטו סינטייו איל פאטרון די איל מונדו, מאס אבוטריב֯ייו
באס, אולאס .
שאטי לאשי קוטה אמאריאה, קי סון פֿשטה אי מינטירה .
סינטום און דייו ב֯ינדיגֿו , קי מונגאס מאראב֯יאס אזי .
מי לאס אגה טאן דיפריקה, דיפריקה אי כון די טאדרי.
אנסי אגה קון לוס אזינוס, אי לה פארידה קואנדו פארי.
קי נינגונוס סי דיספירן , ני קי פירדאן לה איספיראנסה.
קי דיטראס די לה פֿורטונה, איל טוס מאנדי לה בונאנסה.

רומאנסה 10

אין לה סיבֿדאד די מארסילייה , אבֿיאה אונה לינדה דאמה.
סי מוקאבֿה אי סי אשֿייטאבֿה , אי סי אסינטאבֿה אה בֿינטאנה .
פור איי פאסו און מאנסיבֿיקו, בֿיסטידו אינטירו די באלה.
די אבֿלאר מי דאבֿאש גאנה לי דישו אל בינטי .
לייו קון מי גשאנה מי קידו איר .
אה ! סובי אריבֿה פאסאדור לינדו. גאנאראס דובלוס מאס ב֯ייניס .
לייו מון אבֿלו קון מאדירים , לי דישו איל סינייי .
ייו קון מי גאנאנגה מי קידו איר .
אה ! סובי אריבֿה פאסאדור לינדו . קומיראס אי ביב֯יראס.
אי גאנאראס די מיס קאבֿיאוס אטאן לינדוס אי אטאן ביילייוס.
קואנדו לוס קיסו אה פיינאר, איל סול איסקורינסה אין איילייוס.
סו בֿה אינקולגאסי קון איילייוס , לי דישו איל סינייי.
ייו קון מי גאנאנגה מי קידו איר .

— 11 —

אה ! קוז׳י ארינ׳ה פאסטור לינדו, סוניראס אי ב׳יב׳יראס,
אי גוארדאס די לאס מיס קאראס אה טאן לינדאס קולוראדאס.
אין איל פ׳ואיגו ב׳ין קימאדאס, לי דישו איל ב׳ינב׳י.
יו קון מי גאלאנה מי קירו איר.

אה ! קוז׳י ארינ׳ה פאסטור לינדו, סונירא אי ב׳יב׳ירה.
גוארדאס די לוס מיס דידוס אה טאן לינדוס אנאב׳ייאדוס.
אין איל פ׳ואיגו ב׳ין קימאדוס, לי דישו איל ב׳ילב׳י.
יו קון מי גאלאנה מי קירו איר.

אה ! ב׳אטי פאסטור ניגרו, סירוס קומאן מוס אוב׳יאס,
טו מאליר די קאזי קון אוטרו, מוס אוזוס ב׳ינגאן אין מי מיזה.
מאלדיסייון די מאליר מאלה, נו מי אלקאנסה אמי.
יו קון מי גאלאנה מי קירו איר.

רומאנסה 11

אה ! אנדוני פור איסטאס מאריס, נאב׳יגי קון לה פ׳ורטונה,
אה קאאי אין טיירה ז׳ינאס אנדי נון מי קונוסיאן.

אנדי נון קאנטה גאייו, ני מינוס פירו מאולייה,
אנדי בראמה איל ליאון, אי לה ליאונה אריספונדיאה.

אנדי קריסי לה נאראנז׳ה, אי איל לימון אי לה סידרה,
אנדי קריסי ייר׳בה סידרירה, אי קוג׳אס די גראב׳יאינאס.

אנדי קריסי רודה מינודה, גוארדייה די לאס קריאטוראס.

יולייו פ׳אלסו אי ספאראדור קאב׳זאנטי די לוס מיס אוז׳וס,
אינטראסטיס אין מי גואדיר אי מי אינגאנייאסטיס.

אינטראסטיס אין מי גואדיר , און דיאה די אינבֿיראנו ,
אקאבֿיס לה פֿלור די מי , לה קאיטיס אה גראנו אה גראנו :
קון טו אבֿלאר דיליקאדו , מי אינגאנייאסטיס .

דאמאס קי דיראן די מי , לאס קי אמי מי קונוסיאן ,
קי קון מי סי קונדינאבֿאן , מוג׳אג׳יקיטאס .

סיינדו איזה די קון סו . מי קאזאסטיש קון און בֿילאנו ,
איזו אירה די און גוארפֿאנו , די לה מי גוארטה .

יולייו בֿאמוס די אקי , די איסטי ארבֿול סין פֿלוריס .
בֿוזייה קאייגה די לוס סיילוס , אי מוס אמאי .

קאנטיגה מוראל די לה ליי קון לה אלמה

אלמה מיאה מי קירידה , אסטה קואנדו באס פירדידה .
טורנה אין תשובה קומפלידה , אי סיראס טו מי אמור . סי טורנה .

ביוס מי פאדרי איל מי אמיגו , פורקי נון איסטאש קון מיגו .
קי איסטו אינטרי אינימיגוס , אינטרי סיטינטה אומות .

גראנדיס פינאס איזיטיס , קי פור איסטו סי פירדיטיס , סי
אים קי סי ארפינטיטיס , אי טורנאריס אמי .

דארי קודיס אין טו מאנו , אסטה טסו סי ארמאנו . סי
קיריס ביביר טו סאנו , קיטי אסקוג׳אר אמי .

הון פיוס לייו טו פינאדו . דיזיר טו סונברי איסקיבֿלאדו .
פורקי מי בֿאן דיזמאנדאנדו . סגדי דייו די מוס פאדריס .

— 13 —

וין טו מי אזה איסקאלידה , לייה ייצ׳אסטיס מואה צ׳ידה ,
פריסטו ייא סירא ריגמידה , אין סירב׳יינדו טו עמי .

זכות די מיל פאדריס מירה , אי אבאשי לה טו אירה .
ולא תעביר גזירה , די זרע של ישראל .

חסדים די בוס איספירו, קי די טי נון מי דיזיספירו , טו
פירדון אי פרוספירו , אפיאדה קוב׳רי מי .

טומה איל קאמינו דיריג׳ו, אי טירנאס מונג׳ו פרוב׳יג׳ו . כון
ב׳יראס ביגון דיספיג׳ו , אין סירב׳יינדו טו עמי .

ייה איסטו אין איסטי טינו. די סירב׳ירטי די קורטינו. כון
דישאה איל איספינו , קי מי פונגה איל אמי .

בואנדו איל איספינו טי פונגה, אה איל ניגרו נו סי איסקוג׳ה,
מילדיטי אה. איל ביי מונג׳ה , אי דיספידאשאלו אה איל .

לה קאזה אים מויי פואירטי, אי די מי מויי דיפירינטי , ייא
ני איסמינטי לה מואירטי, בון מי דישה איל אמי .

מה קי דיזים כון לו ג׳יאו , איל און אלו טייני פיאו, בון
איס קואנטו און קאב׳יאו, פור ג׳ינסירלו טו אה איל .

נון מי קוקוקו מי מאלייה , פורקי איל אמי מי איגאלייה .
מי פארסי אוגה מוכאלייה, פור ג׳יכסירלו לייו אה איל.

סאג׳יס קי איסטאס איגקאנאדו, איל שבע טייניס טאפאדו,
סי קיריס סיר איסקאפאדו, אי קי פואידאס טו קון איל .

עניים טינגאס אב׳ירטוס, די נון סינטיר פינסאמיינטוס .
אי נון דיסקוב׳ריר סיקריטוס , אה קי ג׳ינקאס טו אה איל .

פינגה ביין אין איסטי ריאו , אימפיזארלו אה טו איאו. בודו
איס איל איספיקאו , אל קאבו ביירבי איל אמי .

צער גראנדי יו בו טוביינדו, דילו ביגרו בו פירינדו, אי די
איל מיבו איסקונדיינדו , פין קי פירגה איל די מי .

— 14 —

קון איסטו מוס פאס קאידה, סיימפרי מי טופאס פירדידה; קי קיריס גאנאר לה בידה, איסטי מונדו אי איל ב׳ינין.

ראוס מי איריס ייאמאדו, דייו אלטו אי אינשאלשאדו, איספירו סיר אייודאדו. אפיגאטי טו קון מי.

שלום דיגאן אין מי ב׳ינידה, די מי סיאה ריסיב׳ידה, אה טו אורה לה קירידה. טורנארלה אה סו לוגאר.

תמונה אי נון אינקונאדה, קון צדיקים סו מוראדה, קון קורונה אינקורונאדה, די סיכן ערך העליון.

קומפלאס דיל פ׳יליק

קי קאנטאן אין איל סון די לאס קומפלאס די שבועות.

אלאב׳ימוס אה איל דייו קון אב׳לאס די אלאב׳אסייון, קון טודה מואיסטרה בואינה אינטינסייון, די איסטימאר אי די אונראר, אה איל דייו די לה קריאסייון.

באסטאנטיס סומוס נוס אזי קי נון סי ב׳ינין אקונטאר, סיינדו איסטה אב׳יאדה נוס ב׳ינו אקאבאנטאר. לו קי פאסו, אי טריספאסו, לו דירימוס קון ביין קאנטאר.

גראן דייו טינימוס קי נון אי אוטרו קומו איל, קי נון מוס דישו קאאיר אין מאנו די קרואיל. קומו איסטה דיג׳ו הנה לא ינום ולא יישן שומר ישראל.

די ב׳יר קי אי לארגו טיימפו קי אפריטו איל קי׳קאב׳, קי אה גראנדים אי אה צ׳יקוס מוס פואי גראן סיקאב׳, קי אפריטו באסטאנטיס טאנטו אילייוס קומו איבקאב׳.

הוי אין איסטי אנייו אבייני סינסי אי אדר, קי איל פ׳ירה פואירטי בין מוס דישו קאנסאר. לה מאס פואירטי אפריטו די לה צ׳אגה דיל באדאר.

IV
LIVRIKO DE ROMANSAS 'IMPORTANTES
(Sofia, 1908)
(abbr. LRI)

ליב׳ריקו
די
רומאנסאס אימפורטאנטיס

סינייורים,

איסטה דיג׳ה ברושורה קי ייו בֿוס פריזינטו קונטייני אונאס קואנטאס רומאנסאס אימפורטאנטיס.

1 — פרימירו לה קאנסינה די משה רבנו עי׳ס קואנדו סא-לימוס לוס ג׳ודייוס די אאיפטו;

2 — דוז׳י רומאנסאס אונה מיז׳ור די אוטרה פור קאנטארסין אין אונאס אוראס די אליגריאס;

בֿוס רוגו סינייורים די טומאר קאדה אונו אונאס גמרס, סיינדו כון קוססה מונג׳ה פארה אי טודס מי פֿאמילייה בֿו לו רינגראסייארה, אי איל דייו דימאנדאס די בֿואיסטרו קוראסון בֿום קומפלירה.

שנת וירבו ימי יעקב יונה למות ויקרא!!!

רומאנסה 1.

קאנטיגה פור משה רבינו ע״ה די חג־הפסח.

אה משה, אין לה סארזה מורה, איל לי אריספונדיין
פריסטו אין אקיאה אורה, קימאנדי מי סינייור ריי די מי
קורונה: קימאנדי.

—

אזמי טו משה, אזמי איסטי מאנדאדו ב׳ה אנדי פרעה, ק טם
אם מי פואיב׳לו אה סאלב׳ו: ב׳ה.

—

פארדון מי סינייור, דילו קי אס אב׳לאדו קי אמי מיאס
קריאדו, קון לה אילגואינגה טראב׳אדו, קאדה ב׳יס קי אב׳לו
קון פינה אי פאסייון. קומי משה רבינו ע״ה: קומו.

—

קאייאדן משה, : נון אב׳לים לוקירה, קי ייו אה קריאדו אל
סול אי אה לה לונה, אי אה לאס איסטריאס אה אונה פור
אונה: אי אה לאס.

—

ב׳אטי טו משה, ב׳אטי סין אי פאנטו, אדילאנטרי ייב׳אס מי
נומברי איל סאנטו: אדילאנטרי.

—

סי איספארטי משה, סי איספארטי אי־סי איאה, אה פואירטאס
די פרעה אאי סי אמאניסיאה: אה פואירטאס.

—

לן טופו אה פרעה, אין לה מיזה אסינטאדו. קון סוס דוג׳י
רייס סיס די קאדה לאדו, אב׳לאנדו אי פלאטיקאנדו מאל די
לוס ג׳ודייוס: אב׳לאנדו.

—

3

קי ב׳יניטיס מצה, אין איל מי פאלאסייו, מי מאנדו מי דייו
קיטאר אמי פואיב׳לו אה סאלב׳ו: מי מאנדו.

—

קין איס איסטי דייו, קי אטי טי אה מאנדאדו, ייו נון לו קונוסקו
ני קון איל אה אב׳לאדו, ני און פישקישיקו, אב׳יסטו די סו
מאנו: ני און פישקישיקו.

—

סי איספארטי מצה, אריב׳ה אלוס סיילוס, אה דארלי לה ריפו-
איסטה לו קי דישו אקיל פירו: אה דארלי.

—

קי טי דישו מצה, קי טי דישו אקיל פירו, ייו נון לו קונוסקו
ני קון איל אה אב׳לאדו, ני און פישקישיקו אב׳יסטו די ב׳ואיסטרה
מאנו: ני און פישקישיקו.

—

ייו לי מאנדארי פישקיס אי פישקישיקו, לי מאנדארי לאנגוסטאס
קון און בואין מוסקיטו, קי לי קומה לה קאב׳יסה קון איל
מיאוייקו: קי לי קומה.

—

אין קאטורזי די נסן, איל פרימיר דיאה די איל אנייו, איל
פואיב׳לו די ישראל, די אאיפטו סאלייו קאנטאנדו: איל פואיב׳לו.

—

בין קון לאס מאסאס אל אומברו, אי קן קון נוס אזוס
אימבראסוס, לאס מוז׳יריס קון איל אורו, לו קי אירה לו
מאס ליב׳ייאנו: לאס מוז׳יריס.

—

אבולטארון לה קארה אסראס, פור ב׳יר לוקי אן קאמינאדו,
ב׳יירון ביניר אה פרעה, קון און פינדון קולוראדו: ב׳יירון ב׳יניר.

—

אנדי מוב טרושיטיס מצה, אה מוריר אין דיספוב׳לאדו, מוריר
סין סומבולטורה, אי אין לה מאר ביר אאוגאדוס: מוריר.

—

4

אזיד אוראסייון ג׳ודייוס, אי ייו אירי פור מי קאזו, טאנטו
פואי לה איסקלאמאסייון, קי אל סיילו איזו בוראקו: טאנטו.

סאלייון אונה בוז דיל סיילו, קון משה אובו אבלאדו, טומה
לה ב׳ארה משה, טומה לה ב׳ארה אין טו מאנו, פארטי לה
מאר אין דוג׳י קאליז׳אס, אי קיטה לוס ג׳ודייוס אנאדו: פארטי לה
מאר.

אנדי קאמינאב׳אן ג׳ודייוס, לה מאר סי איב׳ה אריפ׳יקאנדו, אי
אנדי קאמינאב׳אן מצרי, לה מאר סי איב׳ה סוב׳ריב׳ייאנדו: אנדי
קאמינאב׳אן.

רומאנסה 2.

אינדומי פור איסטאס מאריס, נאב׳יגי קון לה פ׳ורטונה, קאאי
אין טיירס אז׳נאס אנדי נון מי קונוסיאן, אנדי נון קאנ-
טה גאייו, ני מינוס פירו מאאולייה, אנדי ברמאב׳אן איל
ליאון, אי לה ליאונה אריספונדיאה:

אה — אנדי קריסי לה נאראנג׳ה, אי איל לימון אי לה סידרה,
אנדי קריסי יירב׳ה סידירה, אי קונב׳אה אי גראב׳ינאס,
אנדי קריסי רודה מינודה, גואדריאה די לאס קריאטוראס:

אה — ייולייו פאלסו אי טראאידור, קאבזאנטי די לוס מיס
מאלים, איטראאטיס אין מי גואדיר, און דיאה די איב׳יירנו,
אקוזיטיס לה פ׳לור די מי, לה קוזיטיס אס גראנו אה גראנו,
קון טוס אב׳לאס דיליקאדאס אי מי אינגאנייאטיס:

אה — דאמאס קי דיראן די מי, לאב קי אמי מי קונו-
סיאן. קי קון מי כי קינורטאב׳אן מוגאג׳יקאס סיינדו איזה

5

די קין סו, מי קאזאטיס קון און בֿילאנו. איזה אירס די און
גואירטילאנו, אי די לה מי גוארטה:
אה -- ייוליין בֿאמוט די אקי, די איפטי ארבֿול סין פֿלוריס,
לובֿייס קאיינה די לוס סיילוס. אי מוס אמוזי:

רומאנסה 3.

פור לוס פאלאסייוס די קארלו, נון פאסאן ני נון גֿונאר,
אי נון פאסאן ני נון גֿונאר, נון גונאן פלאטה ני אורו, סי נון
בֿיאס אי סיבֿדאדים:
אי ני נון בֿיאס אי סיבֿדאדים, נאנו קאיירו אה גאפֿיירו, סוס
בֿיאס אי סוס סיבֿדאדים:
אי סוס בֿיאס אי נוס סיבֿדאדים, נאנו גאייפֿירו אה קאיירו,
אי אלה סו מוזיר ריאלי:
אי אה לה סו מוזיר דיאלי, מאס בֿאלייה אה פידרירלה,
פידרירלה קי נון גאנארי:
אי פידרירלה קי נין גאנארי, סובֿרינו איל מי סובֿרינו, אי איל מי
סובֿרינו קארונאלי:
אי איל מי קונדינו קארונאלי, ייו בֿוס קריאי ניקיטו, איל דיין טי
איזו בארהגאני:
אי איל דיין שי איזו בארהנאני, איל טי דייו בארבֿיקס רוסה,
אי אין טו פואירפו פֿואירסה גראנדי:
אי אין טו פואירפו פֿואירסה גראנדי, ייו בֿוס די אה בלאנקה
נינייס, פור מוזיר אי פור איגואלי:
אי פור מוזיר אי פור איגואלי, פֿואיטיס און אומברי קונבֿאדו,
בֿו לה דישאטיס ייבֿארי:
אי בֿו לה דישאטיס ייבֿארי, און דיאה אין לה מילסה,
אין איל בֿירגֿיל די בֿואיסטרו פאדרי:

6

אי אין איל ב'ירג'יל די ב'ואיסטרו פאדרי, קוז'ינדו רוזאס אי פ'לוריס,
מאנייאנה די סאנג'ינואארי:
אי מאנייאנה די סאנג'ינואארי, מאלדיסייון ב'וס איג'ו איל מי קוז'רינו,
סי נון לאס ב'אש א בושקארי:
אי סי נון לה ב'אש א בושקארי, טור לוס קאמינוס קי ב'אש.
נון טופיס ני ב'ינו ני פאני;
אי נון טופיס ני ב'ינו ני פאני, ני מינוס דינירו אין בולסה.
פארה איל קאמינו גאסטארי:
אי פארה איל קאמינו גאסטארי, נון דיס סיב'אדה אלה מולה,
ני קארני קרודה אל גאב'ילאני:
אי ני קארני קרודה אל גאב'ילאני, לה מוז'יר קי ב'וס טוב'ייראש,
נון ב'וס גואדרי קרואילדאדי:
אי נון ב'וס גואדרי קרואילדאדי, לוס איז'וס קי ב'וס פאריירי,
נון ב'וס קונוסקאן פור פאדרי:

רומאנסה 4.

איסטה נוג'י מיס קאב'אליירוס, דורמיר קון אונה סינייורה, אי
דורמיר קון אונה סינייורה, און דיאה די לוס מיס דיאס, נון
טופי אוטרה קומו אילייה:
אי נון טופי אוטרה קומו אילייה, בלאנקה איס אי קולוראדה,
אירמוזה קומו לה איסטריאה:
אי אירמוזה קומו לה איסטריאה, אלה באשאדה די און ריאו,
אי אלה סוב'ידה די און ב'איי:
אי אלה סוב'ידה די און ב'איי, איסקונטרי קון מי לינדה, לה
איז'ה דיל אימפיראדור:
אי לה איז'ה דיל אימפיראדור, קי ב'יניאה די לוס באנייוס, אי
די לוס באנייוס די לאב'ארסי:

7

אי די לוס באנייוס די לאבֿארסי, די לאבֿארסי אי אינטרינסארסי,
אי די מודארסי אונה דילגאדה:
אי דימודארסי אונה דילגאדה, דישו לה קונדיסה אל קונדי,
אי קונדי פור קי כון קאזאטיס:
אי קונדי פור קי כי קאזאטיס, קאזארי סי איל דייו קירי,
קאזארי כי אה איל לי פלאזי:
אי קאזארי סי אה איל לי פלאזי, טומארי מוזיר צ׳יקיטה, אי ג׳יקה
די לה פוקה אידאדי:
אי צ׳יקה די לה פוקה אידאדי, קי סיאה צ׳יקה די אנייוס,
אי די איל אינטינדימיינטו גראנדי:
אי די איל אינטינדימיינטו גראנדי, קי כיאה אלטה סין ג׳אפינים,
אי אירמוזה סין אפֿייטארסי:
אי אירמוזה סין אפֿייטארסי, לוס אוז׳יקוס קי מי פאריירי,
מי אסימיז׳ין אה לה מאדרי:
אי מי אסימיז׳ין אה לה מאדרי, פוקו מאס און פוקו מאנקו,
קי מי אסימיז׳ין אל פאדרי:

רומאנסה 5.

סאליר קירי איל מיז די מאייו, אי אינטראר קירי איל מיז די אפריל
קואנדו איל טרינו איסטה אין גראנו, אי לאס פֿלוריס קירין
סאליר:
אי קואנדו איל טרינו איסטה אין גראנו, אי לאס פֿלוריס קירין סאליר,
קואנדו איל קונדאלימארי, פארה פֿראנסייה קיזו איר:
אי קואנדו איל קונדאלימארי, פארה פֿראנסייה קיזו איר,
קון סיגו איל סי ייבֿאבֿה, אונרה אי פאמה אי טאן ג׳ינטיל:
אי קון סיגו איל סי ייבֿאבֿה, אי און ג׳ופֿליט די מארפֿיל,
ייה לו מיטי אין לה סו בוקה, נון לו סאבֿיאה דיזיר:

8

אי ייה לו מיסי אין לה סו בוקה, נון לו סאב׳יאה דיזיר,
יין מאלאכייו טאל גופ׳ליט, לאב דובלאס קי די פור טי:
אי יין מאלאכייו טאל גופ׳ליט, לאס דובלאס קי די פור טי,
אי אוכראס סאנטאס יין לים דיירה, קי מי לו קיטין די אקי:
אי אוטראס טאנטאס יין לים דיירה, קי מי לו קיטין די אקי,
אי ייה לו קיטאן אה ב׳ינדיר, פור פלאסאס אי פור ג׳ארסים:
אי ייה לו קיטאן אה ב׳ינדיר, פור פלאסאס אי פור ג׳ארסים,
כינגונוס לי דאב׳אן פריסייו, ני און אספרו ני סוב׳יר:
אי כינגונוס לי דאב׳אן פריסייו, ני און אספרו ני סוב׳יר,
סאנטו פ׳ואי די בוקה אין בוקה, פ׳ואי אין בוקה דיאמאדי,
אי טאנטו פ׳ואי די בוקה אין בוקה, פ׳ואי אין בוקה דיאמאדי,
אי אוטרוס טאנטוס יין לי דיירה קי מי לו טראייגאן אקי:
אי אוטרוס טאנטוס יין לי דיירה, קי מי לו טראייגאן אקי,
ייה לו מיטין אין לה סו בוקה, אי ייה לו אימפיסאן אריטינייר:
אי ייה לו מיטין אין לה סו בוקה, אי ייה לו אינפיסאן אריטינייר,
לאס לאב׳ים קי איספאן אין פורטו, פריסטו לאס אזין ב׳יניר:
אי לאס לאב׳ים קי איספאן אין פורטו, פריסטו לאס אזין ב׳יניר,
לה פארידה קי איבטה פארייגדו, פריסטו לה אזין פאריר:

רומאנסה 6.

טרים דאמאס ב׳אן אלה מילבה, און אזיר לה אוראסיון,
אינטרי מידייו מי איבפאה, לה קי מאס קיריאה ייו: מי סינייור
אי אינטרי מידייו לה מי איספוזה, לה קי מאס קיריאה ייו,
קאמיזה די אולאנדה ייב׳ה, בירמה אי פירלה אל קאב׳יבון:
קארה די ב׳לור
אי קאמיזה די אולאנדה ייב׳ה, בירמה אי פירלה איל קאב׳יסון,

9

סאליו ייג'ה קוב'רי סאייו, און שיבויי די אלטורנאסייון: מי
סינייור

אי סאליו ייג'ה סוב'רי סאייו, און שיבייי די אלטורנאסייון,
כון קאמ'יסה אונה טורונג'ה, סוב קאב'יאוס ברילים סון: קארה
די פ'לור

אי סו קאמ'יסה אונה טורונג'ה, סוס קאב'יאוס ברילים סון,
לה סו פ'יזיקה אינקארקאדה, ארקול די טיראר ייה סון: מי סינייור
אי לה סו פ'יזיקה אינקארקאדה, ארקול די טיראר ייה סון,
לוס סוס אוזוס צ'יקיטיקוס, איספ'יזיקוס די איסטאמבול: קארה
די פ'לור

אי לוס סוס אוזוס צ'יקיטיקוס, איספיזיקוס די איסטאמבול,
לאס סוס קאראס קולוראדאס, מאנסאנאס די איסקופייס
כון: מי סינייור

אי לאס סוס קאראס קולוראדאס, מאנסאנאס די איסקופייס סון,
סו נאריס אפירפ'ילאדה, פינדולה די איסקריב'יר ייס סין:
קארה די פ'לור

אי סו נאריס אפירפ'ילאדה, פינדולה די איסקריב'יר ייה סון,
לה סו בוקה צ'יקיטיקה, קי נון לי קאב'י פינייון: מי סינייור
אי לה סו בוקה צ'יקיטיקה, קי נון לי קאב'י פינייון,
סוס דיינטים טאן מינודיקוס, פירלה די אינפ'ילאר ייה כון:
קארה די פ'לור.

רומאנסה 7.

ד׳ה רומאנסה סי קאנטה אין איל סון די אוחילה לאל:

איטאב'ה לה ריינה איזילה, אי אין סו באסטידור לאב'ראנדו:
אי אין יו באסטידור לאב'ראנדו, אגוזיקה די אורו אין מאנו,
אי א פינדון די אמור לאב'ראנדו:

10

אי און פינדון די אמור לאב̃ראנדו, קואנדו לי קאאי לה אלגוזה,
אי קואנדו לי קאאי איל דידאלי:
אי קואנדו לי קאאי איל דידאלי, קואנדו לי קאאי לה טיזירה,
נון טייני קון קֵי קורטארי:
אי נון טייני קון קי קורטארי, פור אאי פאסו פאריזי,
איל סו לינדו נאמוראדו:
אי איל סו לינדו נאמוראדו, פארה איסטי פוארפו פאריזי,
קי אופ̄יסייו אב̃ים טומאדו:
אי קי אופ̄יסייו אב̃ים טומאדו, מירקאדיר סו לה מי סינייורה,
מירקאדיר אי איסקריב̃אנו:
אי מירקאדיר אי איסקריב̃אנו, טריס נאב̃ים טינגו און איל פירטו,
קארגאדאס די אורו אי ברוקאדו:
אי קארגאדאס די אורו אי ברוקאדו, לה נאב̃י קי ייו ב̃ינגו,
אב̃יאה און ריקו מאנסאנו:
אי אב̃יאה און ריקי מאנסאנו, קי איגואב̃ה מאנסאנאס די אמוריס,
אין אינב̃יירנו אי אינב̃ירנו:
אי און אינב̃יירנו אי אינב̃ירנו, סי איסטו אים ב̃ירדאד פאריזי,
לורייה אים די לו קונטארי:
אי לורייה אים די לו קונטארי, קי ב̃ום פלאזיאה פאריזי,
די ב̃ום איר אה ב̃יזיטארי:
אי די ב̃ום איר אה ב̃יזיטארי, ב̃ינגאם און בואינה אורה ריינה,
ב̃ום אי איל בואיסטרו ריינאדו:
אי ב̃ום אי איל ב̃ואיסטרו ריינאדו, דים קי לה ב̃ידו ב̃ינירי,
ארמו בילאס אי אליב̃אנטו גאנגו:
אי ארמו בילאס אי אליב̃אנטו גאנגו די פארטי פ̄ראנסייס לה יב̃ארון:

11

רומאנסה 8.

און אמור טאן קירינסייוזו, קי אולב֗ידאר נון לה פודיאה,
אי קי אולב֗ידאר נון לה פודיאה, לה מאנייאניקה אי לה טאדרי,
אה ב֗יזיטאר ייה לה איבה:
אי אה ב֗יזיטאר ייה לה איבה, סי לה טופאב֗ה דורמיינדו,
לה קוב֗יזאב֗ה אי סי איבה:
אי לה קוב֗יזאב֗ה אי סי איבה, סי לה טופאב֗ה דיספיירטה,
אה פלאטיקאר סי לי מיטיאה:
אי אה פלאטיקאר סי לי מיטיאה, לה ביזאב֗ה אי לה אבראסאב֗ה,
אי אה יוראר סי לי מיטיאה:
אי אה יוראר סי לי מיטיאה, די קי יוראש קאטיב֗אדאס,
די קי יוראש בוזאגריאה:
אי די קי יוראש בוזאגריאה, טיניאש מאל די אמוריס,
או איסטאש ריזין פרינייאדה:
אי או איסטאש ריזין פרינייאדה, ני טיניאה מאל די אמוריס,
ני איסטאב֗ה ריזין פרינייאדה:
אי ני איסטאב֗ה ריזין פרינייאדה, סי ב֗ו לו קונטו אל בואן ריי,
אפ֗יאריש מיס פאלאב֗ראס:
אי אפ֗יאריש מיס פאלאב֗ראס, ייו פ֗ואי קריאדה אין סו ב֗יאה,
אי אינטרי בואינה ג֗ינטי אונוראדה:
אי אינטרי בואינה ג֗ינטי אונוראדה, און קאב֗איירו אנדארליסו,
קי די מי סי נאמוראב֗ה:
אי קי די מי סי נאמוראב֗ה, איסקאלירקה לי איזו,
דיבאשו די סוס ב֗ינטאנאס:
אי דיבאשו די סוס ב֗ינטאנאס, פארה קי סוב֗ה אי קי אבאשי,
קומו סי פ֗ואירה סו קאזה:
אי קומו סי פ֗ואירה סו קאזה, טריס נוג֗יס דורמייו קון אילייה,
לי פאריסייו טריס סימאנאס:

12

אי לי פאריסייו טריס קימאנאס, אה פ׳ין די לאס טריס נוג׳יס,
כי פ׳ואי אה בושקאר מואיב׳ה אמאדה:
אי סי פ׳ואי אה בושקאר מואיב׳ה אנאדה, אילייה כי פ׳ואי די
דיעראס די איל, פור ב׳יר כי אירה מאס גאלאנה:

רומאנסה 9.

ייו מי אליב׳אנטי אי און לונים, אי און לונים פור לה מאנייאנה:
טומי מי ארקול אי מי פ׳ליג׳ה, אי אין לה מי מאנו דיריג׳ה:
אנדי לה פ׳ואירה ייו אה טאנייר, אה סואירטאס די מי נאמוראדה:
אב׳רידמי בוזו מי ביין, אי אב׳רילדמי בוזו מי ב׳יסטה:
לוס פייזיס טינגו אין לה נייב׳י, אי לה קאב׳יסה אין לה יילאדה:
קומו ב׳וס אב׳רירי מי ביין, קומו ב׳וס אב׳רירי מי אלמה:
אל איז׳ו טינגו אין איל פיג׳ו, אי אל מארידו אין לה ניקאמה:
קין ב׳וס אב׳לו בוזו מי ביין, קין ב׳וס אב׳לו בוזו מי אלמס:
איל מוסו דיל פאנאדירו, איל קי לוס מאלוס אנייוס אנה:
ארינה נון סינגו אין קאזה, ליב׳אדורה מי דימאנדה:
איל סאלייינדו די לאס פואירטאס, איל נאמוראדו פור לאס ב׳ינטאנאס:
סור אינמידייו דיל קאמינו, לאס קאש׳יקה קי אולב׳ידארה:
אילייה כי טוסו אין אסריטו, לו אינסרו אדיינטרו לאס קאשה:
לה קאשה איסטוב׳ו די פימיינטס, איל נאמוראדו כארנודאב׳ה:
קין סארנודה בוזו מי ביין, קין כארנודה בוזו מי אלמה:
איל גאטו די לה ב׳יזינה, איל קי לוס מאלוס אנייוס קי אנה:
דיין אונה דאדה אין לה קאשה, לה קאשה לה דיסקלאב׳ארה:
ב׳ייני ב׳יריס לאס מיס ב׳יזינאס, לאס דאבאסו אי לאס דארייב׳ה:
ב׳ייני ב׳יריס גאטו קון בארב׳ה, אי מוסטאג׳יקוס אריטורסידוס:

13

רומאנסה 10.

לא דיל דיאה אי קלארידאד, קי איל דיאה מוס דאס איל סול,
אי לה נוג׳י קלארו לונאר:
אי לה נוג׳י קלארו לונאר, לאס מאנייאניקאס לאס איסטריאס,
קואנדו קירי אלב׳וריאר:
אי קואנדו קירי אלב׳וריאר, סי פאסיאה טיאו אי סוב׳רינו, ג׳ונטוס
ב׳אן אה און באראבאר:
אי ג׳ונטוס ב׳אן אה און באראבאר, קי קאב׳אייוס ייב׳אן די און
פריסיין, אי סור ב׳יר קואל קוריאה מאס:
אי סור ב׳יר קואל קוריאה מאס, קי קורי אונו אי קורי אוטרו,
ג׳ונטוס ב׳אן אה און באראבאר:
אי ג׳ונטוס ב׳אן אה און באראבאר, אב׳לאנדו ב׳אן אי פלאטיקאנדו,
לוקי לים אימפורטה מאס:
אי לוקי לים אימפורטה מאס, אונה מירביל לי רוגו טיאו,
קואל מי לה אב׳ים די אטורגאר:
אי קואל מי לה אב׳ים די אטורגאר, קי מי דים אה בלאנקה
ניניה, סור מוז׳יר אי סור איגואל:
אי סור מוז׳יר אי סור איגואל, איסטה מירסיד איל מי סוב׳רינו,
כון ב׳ו לה פואידו אג׳יטאר:
אי כון ב׳ו לה פואידו אג׳יטאר, קואנדו ב׳ו לה אב׳יאה דאדו,
כון לה קיז׳יטים טומאר:
אי כון לה קיז׳יטים טומאר, קי דאדה לה טינגו אין פ׳ראנסייה,
פור סיין דובלאס אי אלגו מאס:
אי פור סיין דובלאס אי אלגו מאס, קי דיספוזאדה לה טינגו
אין פ׳ראנסייה, אי קון איל קונדי אלינורנאל:
אי קון איל קונדי אלינורנאל, גירידו סוס איל מי סוב׳רינו,
אי לה פואידים מויי ביין גאנאר:

14

אי לה פואידיס מויי ביין גואר, דימי קאמיזה דילגאדה,
סירמה אי פירלה אין סו קוייאר:
אי סירמה אי פירלה אין סו קוייאר, ייה סי איספארטי איל קאב׳אליירו,
ייה סי איספארטי אי ייה סי ב׳ה:
אי ייה כי איספארטי אי ייה סי ב׳ה, פור קאמים קי אב׳יאה ג׳ינטי,
קאמינאב׳ה די אב׳אגאר:
אי קאמינאב׳ה די אב׳אגאר, פור לאס קאמים קי נון אב׳יאה ג׳ינטי,
סינטיאה אזיאה סאלטאר:
אי סינטיאה אזיאה סאלטאר, קון איל איסטי מורו פ׳ראנקו,
קי לה סיב׳דאד לה אדירוקאר:

רומאנסה 11.

סי פאסיאה פאסטור פ׳יאיל, קון סו גאנאדו די אקיאס טאדרי,
אי קון סו גאנאדו די אקיאה טאדרי, קון רימוליכוס אי סרואיכוס,
אי לוס רילאמפאגוס מויי גראנדים:
אי לוס רילאמפאגוס מויי גראנדים, סינייור סי פיקי,
איל מי גאנאדו כון לו פ׳אאי:
אי איל מי גאנאדו כון לו פ׳אאי, סי איל מי גאנאדו פיקו, לו
קי כון אים מיאו איסקאפאמי:
אי לוקי כון אים מיאו איסקאפאמי, איסטו קי כינטיירון לאס
נוב׳ים, סי בולטארון פור אוטראס פארטים:
אי סי בולטארון פור אוטראס פארטים, סי דאב׳אן די פינייס
אין פינייס, אי פור אגואה קוריאה סאנגרי:
אי פור אגואה קוריאה סאנגרי, יורדאב׳אן לוס קאפיטאנים. אי
טודוס לוס קי אין לה מאר:
אי טודוס לוס קי אין לה מאר, און בורלאנטי איי אינטרי איליוס,
קי אין איליה כון אג׳יטארי:

15

אי קי אין איליאה נון אב׳יטארי, סינייורה לה מי סינייורס, די
איסטה פֿורטונה איסקאפאמי:
אי די איסטה פֿורטונה איסקאפאמי, סי די איסטה פֿורטונה
מי איסקאפאס, קון אורו בֿוס איינקורונארי:
אי קון אורו בֿוס איינקורונארי, איסטו סינטייו איל פאטרון די
איל מונדו, לאס אולאס מאס סובריב׳ייארי:
אי לאס אולאס מאס סובריב׳ייארי, באטי באטי פוסה אמאריאה,
קי סוס פֿאלסה אי מינטירוזה:
אי קי סוס פֿאלסה אי מינטירוזה, טינימוס און פאדרי פיאדוזו,
קי מונגאס מאראב׳ייאס אזי:
אי קי מונגאס מאראב׳ייאס אזי, מולאס אגה די קונטינו,
די פריסה קי נון דיטאדרי:
אי די פריסה קי נון דיטאדרי, איל קי קיטי לה נאב׳י דיל גולפֿו,
קומו לה פארידה קי פארי:
אי קומו לה פארידה קי פארי, אנסי אגה קון לוס מאזינוס,
די פריסה קי נון דיטאדרי:
אי די פריסה קי נון דיטאדרי, קי נינגונוס קי סי דיזיספירין,
כי קי פיידראן לה איספיראנסה:
אי כי קי פיידראן לה איספיראנסה, קי דיספואיס די לה פֿורטונה,
איל מוס מאנדה לה בונאנסה:

רומאנסה 12.

סי פאסיאן לאס 12 פֿלורים, איינטרי מידייו אונה קונגֿה:
דישו לה קונגֿה אלאב׳ פֿלורים, אויי אים דיאה די פאסיאר,
סי פאסיאה לה נינדה דינה, פור לוס קאמפוס דיל רייי חמוד:

16

אס קולומבראס דיל טיז׳אדו, קי נון לאס איספאנטייארס איל. סול;
קון פ׳אב׳ור די סוס דוז׳י אירמאנוס, קאמינאב׳ה סין טימור;
ארימוסי אין אונס טיינדה, פינסאנדו קי נון איי ב׳ארון;
ב׳יסטו לה אוב׳יירה ב׳יסטו, שכם איז׳ו דיל ריי חמור,
איינוכי פארה איליה, טריב פאלאב׳ריקאס לי אב׳לו;
לינדה סוש לה לינדה דינה, סין אפ׳ייטי אי סין קולור:
לינדוס סון ב׳ואיסטרוס אירמאנוס. מאס קי ב׳וס ייב׳אש לה פ׳לור:
או סון לינדוס או נון סון לינדוס, אמי ני לוס גואדרי איל דייו:
איינוסי פארה איליה, איזו לוקי נון איס ראזון;
כי איספארטי לה לינדה דינה, סי בה פארה אנדי איל סו סינייור;
איל פאדרי דיסקי לה בידו, ארסיב׳יר לה סאלייו;
קין ב׳וס דימודו לה קארה, אי קין ב׳וש דימודו לה .ולור;
או ב׳ו לה דימודו איל איירי, או בו לה איספאנייו איל כול;
כי מי לה דימודו איל איירי, כי מי לה איספאנייו איל כול;
מי לה דימודו און מונאג׳יקו, שכם איל איז׳ו דיל ריי חמור;
איסטו קי סינטייו איל פאדרי, קאמינטירוס לי מאנדו;

סוף ייד״ה
לימפרינטיריאה די רחמים סינונוב׳ גי קונפי
1908.

V
ROMANSOS
(n.p., before 1909)
(abbr. RSA)

רומאנסוס

אין דיג'ה גאזיטה קונטייני אונוס רומאנסוס מואי אירמוזוס
קי פריזאלאן פארה קאנטאר, טאנטו אומברים קומו
מוז'ירים.
אי אונוס ריפראנים קי טומאראן פלאזיר לוס סינייורים
אין איספאנייול אי אין טורקו מואי גראסיוזוס,

אי איספירו קון איאודה דיל דייו אי דיספואיס לוס
אמיגוס קי די אוי אי אידילאנטרי סון אפארישירי
מונג'אס גימאריקאס, קון קי סון קוסאס פוקאס פאריקאס.

אי טודו סולו טראייגו קון נואיבה הכנה, יו איל קומ׳
פונידור יעקב אברהם יונה הי"ו

תמ"ה שולטן עבדול חמיד חאן יר"ה

לאס דיג'אס גאזיטאס סי טופאן אין לה איסטאמפאריאה
די נון הח"ס פור ג'ינדירמאן.

(2)

רומאנסו פרימו

ס׳ פאסיאב׳ה סילב׳אנה, פור און קוראל קי טיניאה.
ב׳יגואילה די אורו אין סו מאנו, אי טאמביין קי לה טאנייאה.
מיז׳ור טאניי אי מיז׳ור דיזי, מיז׳ור רומאנסו טיניאה.
די אאי לה אוייו סו פאד׳רי, די אלטאס טוריס די אאי אריב׳ה.
קי ב׳יין פאריסיש סילב׳אנה, קון קאייוס די סיד׳ה פ׳ינה.
מאס קי לה ריינה טו מאד׳רי, קי די אורו סי ב׳יסטיאה.
סי ב׳וס פלאזיאה סילב׳אנה, די סיר ב׳וס לה מי אמיגה.
פלאזיר מי אזיש מי פאד׳רי, פלאזיר אי דיסקורטיזיאה.
דיש׳י מי איר אה לוס באנייוס, אה לוס באנייוס די אגואה פ׳ריאה.
אה לאב׳ארמי אי אה טריספארמי. אי אה מוד׳אר אונה קאמיזה.
קומו סי איב׳ה לה מאד׳רי, קואנדו קון איל ריי דורמיאה אי קואנדו קון איל ריי פ׳ולגאב׳ה.
ייא סי איספארטיאה סילב׳אנה, ייא סי איספארטיאה אי סי איאב.
די לוס סוס אוז׳וס ייוראב׳ה, אי די לה סו בוקה דיזיאב.
אב׳ייגאמיש איל דייו דיל סיילו, אי אה טאמביין לה מאד׳רי מיאה.
די אאי לה אולייו סו מאד׳רי, די אלטאס טוריס די אאי אריב׳ה.
איב׳ה בה די אקי סיינטו, די סילב׳אנה מי ספאריסיאה.
קי אספארו פור לה ב׳ינטאנה, אה סילב׳אנה לה ב׳יריאה.
ב׳ינירש אקי סילב׳אנה, ב׳ינירש אקי אריב׳ה.
קונטאריש בואינטרוס אינוזוס, לה בואינטורה מאלה אינקוב׳ייאה.

(3)

קי ב֞וס קונטארי מי מאדרי, ב֞ירגואינסה מי פאריסיאה.
און פאדרי קי מי מי הא קריאדו, די אמוריס מי אקונטיסיאה.
פארה טודו איי רימידייו, פארה לה מואירטי נון אב֞יאה.
מאלאב֞לאדי ב֞וס אה דיזיר, קי נון אסיינדה קאנדיליראה.

דומאנסו סיגונדו

סי פאסיאן לאס דוג׳י פ֞לוריס, אינטרי אין מידייו אונה קונג׳ה.
דישו לה קונג׳ה אה לאס פ֞לוריס, אויי איס דיאה די פאסיאר.
סי פאסיאה לה לינדה דינה, פור לוס קאמפוס דיל ריי אמור.
קון פ֞אב֞ור די סוס אירמאנוס, קאמינאב֞ה אי סין טימור.
ארימוסי אה אונה טיינדה, פינסאנדו קי נון איי ב֞ארון.
ב֞יסטו לה אוב֞יירה ב֞יסטו, שכם איז׳ו די איל ריי חמור.
אייגוסי פארה אילייה, טריס פאלאב֞ריקאס לי אב֞לו.
לינדה סוס לה לינדה דינה, סין אפ֞ייטי אי סין קולור.
לינדוס סון ב֞ואיסטרוס אירמאנוס, טאם קי ב֞וס ייב֞אש לה פ֞לור.
או קון לינדוס או נון סון לינדוס, אנסי מי לוס גואדרי איל דייו.
אייגוסי פארה אילייה, איזו לו קי נון איס ראזון.
ייה סי פארטי לה לינדה דינה, סי ב֞ה פארה אנדי איל סו קינייור.
לה סולומברה דיל טיזאדו, קי נון לה אינפאלייארה איל קאל.
קין ב֞יס דימודו לה קארה, קין ב֞וס דימודו לה קולור.
או ב֞ולה דימודו איל איירי, או ב֞ולה דימודו איל קאל.
נו מילה דימודו איל איירי, נו מי לה דימודו איל קאל.

(1)

מי לה דימודו און מוג׳אג׳יקו, שנס איזו דיל ריי אמור
איסטאס פאלאבֿראס דיזיינדו , קאזאמינטירוס ייא מאנדו

רומאנסו טירסייו

פינסאטיבֿלי איסטה איל בואין ריי , אין אונוס פינסירייס מויי גראנדיס .

קי נון לי אבֿינדו קארטאס , קארטאס די לה סו סיבֿדאד .
איל קי טראאיאה לאס קארטאס , סיין אי בֿינטי אנייוס טיניאה .
נון בֿוס טוניש די מאראבֿיאה , קי פאדֿרי אי מאדֿרי טיניאה .
אה טאן אלטה בֿה לה לונה , קואנדו איל סול סאליר קיריאה .
קואנדו איל קונדי אלימאני , קון לה קונדיסה דורמיאה .
נון לו סאבֿיאה נינגונוס , קואנטוס אין לה קורטי אבֿיאה .
סי נון אירה לה סו איזה , קי לו בֿיאה אי לו אינקובֿריאה .
סי אלגו בֿיטיש מי איזה , אינקובֿרילדו אי אינסילאלדו .
בֿוס דארה איל קונדאלימאני , קון סאייוס די פֿילו דאמאסקו .
ייו מאלאנייו לוס סאייוס , אי אה טאמביין קין לוס קיריאה .
אין בֿידה דיל ריי מי פאדֿרי , טומאטיש מואיבֿו אמאדו .
אוראן בֿוסי אגה איזה , לה ליג׳י קי ייו טי דיירה .
אוראן בֿוסי אגה מאדֿרי , איל פאן דיל מי פאדֿרי קומייראש .
בֿה קי לו סאבֿי איל ריי מי פאדֿרי , ייה קי סאבֿי די לה מילכה .
ייו סי לו אה דיזירי , ייו סי לו אדֿי קונטארי .
איסטאס פאלאבֿראס דיזיינדו , אי איל בואין ריי קי אריבֿארה .
טאנטו פֿואי יוראנדו , לאגרימאס די טריס אה קואטרו .
די קי יוראש לה מי איזה , לאגרימאס די טריס אה קואטרו .
ייו איסטאנדו אין מי פואירטה , אי אין מי באסטידור לאבֿראנדו .
קיאנדו איל קונדי אלימאני , מי נראבֿו פור לוס ביסטייס .

אנסי דישו לה מי איז'ה, אנסי דישו לה מי אלמה.
די ד'יגראס די איסטוס דישיריס, אקונטיסין מונג'וס מאליס.
סי בֿוס פלאזי לה מי איז'ה, יו לו מאנדארי אה ייאמארי.
נון לו ונאטיש איל מי פאדרי, ני לו קיז'יראש מאטארי.
קי איל קונדי נינייו אי מוג'אג'ו, איל מונדו קירי גאנארי.
דיסטיראלדו די איסטה טיירה, קי די אקי נון קומה פאני.

רומאנסו קוארטו

אירה אונה מוז'יר פומפאה, אי איל און אומברי גאסטאדור.
גאסטו לו סוייו אי לו מיאו, לו קי איל מי פאדרי מי דייו.
אגורה פור מי פיקאדו, ביני אסיר און קארגאדור.
איל קארגאבֿה לה רוקיטה, ני מוז'יר פֿילאנדה בֿוס.
פֿילאנדה מויי ביין דילגאדה, קי אנסי קירי איל פאטרון.
סי נון לה פֿילאש דילגאדה, נון בֿוס פאגה איל פאטרון.
יו קי טינגו מאנוס בלאנקאס, די לאבֿראר אל באסטידור.
יו לאס טיניאה מאס בלאנקאס, די מילדאר לה ליי דיל דיין.
בֿיני בֿוס דארי און קונסיז'ו, מי מארידו טומאלדו בֿוס.
אינדאבֿוס פארה לה קאשה, אלה קאשה דיל קאשון.
טופאריש סיין דוקאדיקוס, לוס קי איל מי גאנאדו סון.
מירקאלדוס די סירמה אי פירלה, יו בֿוס לאבֿרארי און סינדון.
פור און קאבֿו לאס איסטריאס, פור אוטרו איל אאו דיל סול
אין מידייו מיטו מיס אנסייאס, לאס קי איסטו פאסאנדו יו.
ייה לו קינאן אבֿינדירי, פור לה סיבֿדאד די אראגון.
טודוס איבֿאן דיזיינדו, או קי בואינאס מאנוס סון.
אקיל אירה איל ריי מי פאדרי, אקיל אירה איל מי סינייור.

(6)

רומאנסו קינטו

טריס פ̄אלקוניס ב̄אן בולאנדו, פור לאס אלמינאס דיל ריי.
ני טופאב̄אן קי קומירי, ני טופאב̄אן קי ביב̄יר.
ארינוסי אין און קאסטיאו, קאסטיאו די אורו איס.
דילייכטרו די אקיל קאסטיאו, איי אונה מוסה פונטיס.
איל סו טוקאדו אין קלינגה, אי איל סו ניודיקו אלה סיין.
סוס קודאס אלה טורקיסקה, פ̄ינה לה פונטה דיל פיי.
איל סו קונטוש̄יקו איסטריג̃ו קי סי לי ארישינטה איל ביל.
לה סו קאלסיקה דילגאדה, קי ביין לי נאמורה איל פיי.
איל סו פאדרי נון לה דאבה, ני פור אורו ני פור אב̄יר.
סי נון לה ג̃וגאן אל ג̃וגו, אל ג̃וגו די לה ש̄ידרי.
לה גאנארה איל מורו פ̄ראנקו, מורו פ̄ראנקו אליגורני.
יא סי לה טומו אה בראג̃ו, אי לה ייב̄ו קון איל.
יורארה לה בלאנקה ניניה, לאגרימאס די דוס אה טריס.
די קי יוראש̄ בלאנקה נינייה, לאגרימאס די דוס אה טריס,
סי יוראש̄ פור ב̄ואיסטרו פאדרי, איל מי קאיינדו איס.
סי יוראש̄ פור ב̄ואיסטרה מאדרי, לה מי לאב̄אנדירה איס.
סי יוראש̄ פור ב̄ואיסטרוס אירמאנוס, יו לוס מאטי אה טודוס טריס.
ני יורו פור מיס אירמאנוס, ני פור מי פאדרי טאמביין.
יורו פור לה מי ב̄ינטורה, קי נון סי קי אב̄יסיר.
יו סי לה ב̄ואיסטרה ב̄ינטורה, די און אנייו פ̄ינה סיין.
מירו פ̄ראנקו אי מורו פ̄ראנקו, דיש̄מי איל קונג̃ייו דיל ביל.
מורו פ̄ראנקו סין עגליסייה, לי דייו איל קונג̃יליו דיל ביל.
לה ניניה קון סו עגליסייה, סי לו אינש̄ינקו אינאל ביל.

(7)

פרוב׳ירב׳ייוס איספאנייוליס

איל דייו איס טאדריאוזו , נון איס אולב׳ידאדיזו .
איל מונדו קי מיניאה , ונה נון קאאי .
אין לה מיזה דיל ריי , ביין פאריסי אונה בוגאג׳ה .
- אקילייה מאדרי פאריו קולייב׳רוס , איני פריגונטו פור איליוס
- איל סילו , פודרי לוס גואיסוס .
איל פאדרי קון איל איז׳ו , קומו לה פיידרה אין איל אניאו
איל איז׳ו קון איל פאדרי , קומו לה אונייה אין לה קארני .
איל איספואיגרו קון איל יירנו , קומו איל סול דיל אינ
ב׳יירנו , קי סאלי טאדרי אי סי אינוב׳לה פריסטו .
אינטרי לה איספואיגרה אי לה נואירה , דישארון לה קאזה
סין באריר .
- אינטרי לה קומאדרי אי לה פארטירה . אינטיניירון אה לה
קריאטורה .
איל דוקאדו אי איל פרינייאדו , נון פואידי איסטאר גואדראדו .
אנדי איי ביין קיריר , נון קאב׳י מאל מיטיר .
- איל אירמאנו פארה איל דיאה מאלו .
אין בוקה סירראדה נון אינטרה מושקה .
- אשוגאר אי קונטאדו טי פואידו דאר , לה ב׳נטורה ב׳אילה
אבושקאר .
אנטיס קי קאזיס מירה לו קי אזיס .
איז׳ו בואינו פארה קי סי קירי איל ביין .
איז׳ו נייגרו פארה קי סי קירי איל ביין .
איז׳ו פואיטיס פאדרי טי אראס , סיגון אזיריס טי אראן .
אל מארידו בואינו און קואירנו , אל מאלו טרים אי קיבראדו .
אוגוס לאזדראן אל קאנדיל , אוטרוס ב׳ייאן אזיר מזיל :
- איל ביין די ישראל , אין חאצ׳ירא נבה איס .

(8)

אנדי נון סי אונדיאה סאלי .
אימבֿיזאלה איסטה לה קאמרה, אדורמיר אל קירידו
איל קומיר נון פאריסי, ביין סאבֿי אנדי סי מיטי .
אין קאזה דיל גֿוגאדור, פוקו טורה לה אליגריאה .
איספאנטאטי די אקיל קאיאדו, קי ארוזה לה פיידרה אי
איסקונדי לה מאנו .
אל לוקו אי אל בֿובֿו, סיגון לי דה .
אזנו נון מואירי די טיקיאה .
איל באנייו לו טייני אקומפאנייאדו, לו פריטו נון לו אזי בֿלאנקו .
אל מינטירוזו, און קארנודו לי איס און אייודו .

בֿוטיקה טיינגו פור פֿאמה, נון טיינגו בֿאני ני דראמה .
בֿיסטים אל אומברי, פריגונטה פור איל נומברי .
בֿיסטיר אה און ליניו, פאריסי און גֿינטיל מאנסיבֿו .
בֿיסטים אל אזנו, ני פריטו ני בֿלאנקו .

גֿואיסו קי טי קאלייו אין פארטי, ייבֿאטילו קון ארטי .
גֿובֿו מי גֿובֿו, קון מי מוזיר מי טומו .
גאנה גאנאנדון, אינה גואיסום אל קאנטון :
גֿואיבֿי פואי אלה פֿיירייה, אין לוגאר די גאנאר פירדייו .
גֿואה אנטים די קאזאר, איסקומינדו לה קונה .

די איל דייו אי דיל בֿיזינו, נון סי פואידי איסקונדיר .
די לה קאבֿיסה פֿיידי איל פישֿי .
די לה מאדרי אלה איזה, די לה פארה אלה בֿיזייה .
די אנדי סאלייו איסטה איסטיאה, די אקיל מאל נאדירו .
די לה רואה, סאלי איל איספינו .
די איל אל סיילו, נון איי און דידו

(9)

די לוס מיאוס קירו דיזיר, מאס נון קירו סינייר.
די לה מאנייאנה, קי בֿי איל בואין דיאה.

הזין קורטאדו, איס מידייו פאגאדו.
טודו לו קי אזין די לוס סיילוס, איס פור בֿין.
טו הבאס יו מירקאדיר, בואינו טינגאמוס איל פאריקיר.
טי דאן טומה, טי אחארבֿאן פֿויי.
טינים קאזאס קון די מואיריר, איספירדאר אי נון בֿיביר, מיטיר
לה מיזה אי נון קומיר, איגֿאר אין קאמה אי נון דורמיר.

-ריכו דיל מיליקו, בֿילונטאד דיל דייו.
ייא מי בֿינו איל אמיגו, קי לו קירו מאס די מי מארידו.
לה דיל דייו סי אזי.
לה מוזיר סאבֿייה פֿראגואה לה קאזה, לה לוקה קון סוס מאנוס לה דירוקה.
לה לימפייזה, איס מידייה ריקיזה.
לו קי נון אקונטיסי אין און אנייו, אקונטיסי אין און פונטו.
לה מאדרי אי לה איזה, פור דאר אי טומאר קון אמיגאס.
לה מאדרי גאלאנה, קריה אה לה איזה אראגאנה.
לה מאדרי פיאדוזה, קריה אלה איזה טינייוזה.
לה מאדרי קי איס פאזידירה, קי סיאה סאפאנירה.
לה איספואיגרה קון לה נואירה, סיימפרי סי קיזירון מאל.
-לה נואירה טראאי אבֿוגאר די אורו אי די מארפֿיל, לה איספואיגרה טייני קי דיזיר.
לה נוזייה פור סי אבֿזנטאר, סי קוזייו אל מוסקאדארה.
לה טינזה לי דיזי אלה קאלדירה, באטי נאטי קי סוס פריטה.
לה בֿינטורה, פור קין לה פירקורה.
-לו קי אטי נון טי אגראדה, אה אוטרו נון לו אגאס.

(10)

מאנה אי דיב̈אנטאל, טאפה מונג̈ו מאל .
מיז̈ור קאלייר אין און ריאו פ̈וריינטי, אי נון אין בוקאס
די לה ג̈ינטי .
- מי נואירה אלה איסקונדידב̈, מי איספ̈ואיגרה אלה מיש̈קיטה
מא̈יר טי קירו דיש̈אר, קריסימי לה כתובה .
מי מוסו, טייני אוטרו מוסו .
- מאס סירקה סון דיינטיס, קי פאריינטיס .

נון ב̈אייאס אנדי איל מידיקו, סי נון אה קין לו פאסה .
נון טי פ̈יאיס די איל איסטריאד̈ו, ני דיל מארידו דיל לאד̈ו .
נון אי ביין קומפלידו, ני מאל אקאב̈אד̈ו ׳
נון אגאס פלאזיר אל מאלו, ני מודקיד ני גראד̈ו .
ני פאלאב̈רה ני פיילדראד̈ה . נון טורנה אטראס .
ני פור מונג̈ו מאדרוגאר . אמאניסי .
ני קאב̈יאו ני קאנטאר, נון קאב̈י אין המ̈וגאר, ב̈יין קאב̈י
אנדי איסטה .
ני אלה נוב̈ייה, ני אלה סימולה, נון לה מירים אלה קאנדילה .
נון אי מיירקולים סין סול, ני מוסה סין אמור, ני ביב̈דה
סין דולור .
- נינגונוס מואירין, סי איל דייו נון קירי .

סי ניגרה פ̈ואי לה איג̈ה, מאס ניגרה איס לה דיזאיג̈ה .
סידאסיקו מואיב̈ו, טריס דיאס אלה פארי .

פרימוס אי הירמאנוס קירינוס, אין לה בולסה נון טוקימוס .
- פור מאס גודרה קי סיאה לה גאינה, לייני טייני מיניקטיר
די לה ב̈יזינה .
פארה קין ב̈ינו איל ומיא, פארה בוטון אי ונליא .

(11)

- פארה קאדה אולייה, איי סו טאפאדירה :
  פארה סיקריטו, נון דיס פארתס .
- פארה לאקירדי׳, נון סי קירי קאנדיל .
  פארה חאזינה, נון סי פיידרי .
  סוקו אזנאר, סאבור פארה איל פואירפו .

- קאדה אונו פור סי, אי איל דייו פור אילייוס .
  קומי קון קין קומים, אי אבלה קון קין טי אינטיינדי .
  קריסי אין לה גואירטה, לו קי נון קירי איל פאטרון .
  קוראמוס, קי ליס פאריסקה אלה ג׳ינטי קי גאנאמוס .
  קואנדו ייא פ׳וייו איל קאמאיו דיל אמיר, פ׳ואירון אה סיראר לה פואירטה .
  קומו סי איסטאנייה איל קוב׳רי, ארילומברה .
- קוג׳יאדאס אין פואירפו אזינו, נון דואילי .
  קונב׳יאה קון לוס בואינוס, אי פיראס טו אונו די אילייוס .
  קואנדו סוב׳ירה איל אזנו די לה איסקאלירה, טירנה אמיסטאד איספ׳ואיגרה קון נואירה .

פרוב׳ירב׳יוס טורקוס

אטילאן טאש, יירי דונמיס .
אוקלו אדאמה, זאביט ייוק .
אידי קיי איסאפ, פאזארה אויימאס .
אג׳ילי אישלאט, ייא קייור ייא סאקאט :
איכמי ג׳ומירט, קייארמי ג׳ומירט .
אל דידיכלה מורדאר אולור .

---

(12)

באליק , באשטאן קוקאר .
ביר ג'יג'יקלאן , ייאז אולמאס .
בוייוכו באק , מ'ירינ'יט איט .

גאמסיס אדאם , אולונאס .
גוק דוש'ונמיק , אקילינה זארר .

דינזדין דוש'ין , קיליג'י סארילר .
דוב'ליטין ייג'. דילדיר .
דוכייה טוקייולור . איכייל טוקייולמיס .
דומאדאן קיל קופארמאק , סיבאפטיר .

הולמאדי טאש' , באש' ייארר .

וור דידיליר , אולדור דימידיליר .

זינה , בינה ייקאר .
זורלה , ייתיליק אולמאס

חירסיזין יילדיזי , אלג'אקטיר .
חירכים אוג' , חיכאפטאן דיש'ארי ג'יקמאס .

טאוק סו איג'יר , אללה באקאר .
טאש' יירינדי , אגירדיר .

יהודי אקיל , סונראדאן ייליר .
יילאב יילנה , דוכנה דוכמה .
ייג' אולסון , ייוג' אולונאסין .
ייאזילאן , בוזולונאס .
ייול ייוכוילה , אולונאבי בזלטיילה .
ייאלאן ש'איט , באש'י אוג'ונדאן .
ייאלאנים טאש' , דוג'אר אולונאס .
ייאת יורי , קולאוז איכטיניס .

(13)

כון קולה, סינים.

ליביליבי דיינג̈ה, פאזאר קאוש̈טו.

מאנדי פ̈ירמאן יאזילאן, ג̈ינימידי ביבי אוקומאם.
מאראזאדאן פ̈יידה ג̈יקאר.

נ̇י סו אדאייאן, כי קארי אה אינאן
כירדי ג̈וקלוק, אורדה בוקלוק.

סאראוש̈טאן ייולונה, זירי באש̈ינה ייליר.
סיניק אולדורמים, בולאנדיריר.
סיבאסטאן קאג̈, ייוכאה יילמיאיבין.

ע̇יינאה באקאן, זאמפארה יידיר.

פאראי צ̈ירין, דודו צ̈אנאר.

צוראן לוראן, קייאבי יידיר.

קורקאן באזירייאן, כי קייאר, כי זאראר.
קורקו, באגלארה ביקליר.

תותולאן קיסטראק, ארנאן דוייר.

(14)

רומאנסו סיזינו

סי פאסיאה איל פאסטור פ̄יאיל, אין אונה מאנייאנה טאן קלארה, קון ריוולינוס אי טרואינוס, אי לוס רילאמפאגוס מויי גראנדים.

סינייור סינייור סי פיקי, אין מי גאנאדו לו פ̄אגי, קי איל מי גאנאדו לו קולפס, לו קי כון אים מיאו אפארטאוני.

איסטו קי סינטיירון לאס נוב̄יס, סי איג̄ארון פור אונדה פארטי,
סי דאב̄אן די פ̄יגייה אין פ̄יגייה, פור אגואה קוריאה סאנגרי.

ייוראב̄אן לוס קאפיטאנים, טודוס לוס די לה מאר ייוראן, אדיינטרו די אקיאה מאר ייוראן, אב̄יאה אונה סינייורה.

סינייורה לה מי סינייורה, איסקאפאמי די איסטה פ̄ורטונה,
סי די איסטה פ̄וטה מי איסקאפאס, די אורו טי ג̄יסטו כודה.

איסטו סינטייו איל פאטרון דיל מונדו. מאס אקודיזייו לאס אגואס, ג̄אטי פוטה אמארייאה, קי קום פ̄אלבה אי מינטירה.

טינימוס און דייו ב̄ינדיג̄ו, קי מונג̄אס מארב̄ילאס אזי, מולאס אגה טאן דיפריסה, דיפריסה אי כון דיטאדרי.

אנסי אגה קון לוס מאזינוס, אי לה פארידה קואנדו פארי, קי כינגונוס סי דיזיספירין, כי קי פ̄ידראן לה איספירנסה, קי דיטראס די לה פ̄ורטונה, איל בוס מאנדי לה בונאנסה.

VI

BROŠURA DE ROMANSAS 'IMPORTANTES

(Salonika, 1913)

(abbr. BRI)

ברושורה
די
רומאנסאס אימפורטאנטים

סינייוריס, איסטה ברושורה קונטייני לוס ארטיקולוס סיגואינטיס:

1—אונאס רומאנסאס ביין אימפורטאנטיס.

2—לאס ברכות די ברית מילה אין פ̄ראנסיס אי אין איספאנייול פארה טודה לה צ̈ידא דיל אומברי קי נו פיכין לוס סינייוריס.

3—אונה קאנטיגה די איל פ̆יליק די נו קי איגזיסטי אגורה.

טראאידה אלה אימפרימיריאה מיזו איל אאוטור
יעקב אברהם יונה.

סאלוניקו 5673

ברושורה
די
רומאנסאס אימפורטאנטים

רומאנסה אונה

אין לה סיב׳דאד די מארסילייה, אב׳ייה אונה לינדה דאמה,
קי טוקאב׳ה אי קי אפ׳ייטאב׳ה אי קי אינקנטאב׳ה אלה ב׳ינטאנה,
פור איי פאסו און מוג׳אג׳יקו ב׳יסטידו אינטירו די מאייה,
די אב׳לאר לי דאב׳ה גאנה לי דישו איל סיב׳די,
לייו קון מי גאלאנה מי קירו איר:

———

אה! סוב׳י אריב׳ה פאסטור לינדו, גוארדאס די לוס מיס ב׳יינים,
לייו נו, אב׳לו קון מוזירים לי דישו איל סיב׳די,
לייו כון מי גאלאנה מי פירו איר:

———

אה! סוב׳י אריב׳ה פאסטור לינדו, קומיראס אי ב׳יב׳יראס
גוארדאס די מיס קאב׳ילייוס ייה טאן לינדוס אי ייה טאן ב׳ילייוס,
קואנדו לוס סומו לה פיינאר, איל סול איספונטה אין אילייוס,
לה אינפ׳ורקאסטי קון אילייוס לי דישו איל סיב׳די,
לייו כון מי גאלאנה מי כירו איר:

———

— 2 —

אה! סובֿי אריבֿה פאסטור לינדו, קומיראש אי בֿיבֿיראש,
גוזאראש די לאש מיש קאראש, ייה טאן לינדאש קורילאדאש
אין איל פֿואיגו סיאן קימאדאש, לי דישו איל סילבֿי.
לייו קון מי גאלאנה מי קירו איר:

———

אה! סובֿי אריבֿה פאסטור לינדו, קומיראש אי בֿיבֿיראש,
גוזאראש די לוס מיש דידוס ייה טאן לינדוס אנילייאדוס,
אין איל פֿואיגו סיאן קימאדוס, לי דישו איל סילבֿי:
לייו קון מי גאלאנה מי קירו איר:

———

בֿאטי! בֿאטי! פאסטור ניגרו, פירו קומאן טוס אובֿיזאש,
טו מוזיר סי קאזי קון אוטרו, אי טוס איזוס בֿינגאן אין מי מיזה
מאלדיסייון די מוזיר מאלה נון מי אלקאנסה אמי,
לייו קון מי גאלאנה מי קירו איר:

———

רומאנסו דוס

(איסטה רומאנסה אריפֿירה איל פאסאזי די לוס מאנסיבֿוס קי
איספוזיירון אין לה גירה.)

———

אה! אינדומי פור איסטאש מארים, נאבֿיגי קון לה פֿורטונה,
קאאי אין טייראש אזינאש, אנדי נון מי קונוסיאן,
אנדי נון קאנטאבֿה גאייו, ני מינוס פירו מאאולייה,
אנדי בראמיאה איל ליאון, אי לה ליאונה אריספונדיאה:

———

אה! אנדי קריסי לה נאראנגֿה, אי איל לימון אי לה סידרה,
אנדי קריסי יירבֿה סידרילה, אי קונגֿאש אי גראבֿיאינאש,
אנדי קריסי רודה מינודה, גואדריאה די לאש קריאטוראש:

— 3 —

אה! ייולייו פ׳אלסו אי טראאידור, קאב׳זאנטי די לוס מיס מאליס,
אינטראטיס אין מי ג׳אדיר, און דיאה די אינב׳יראנו,
אקוז׳יטיס לה פ׳לור די מי, לה קוז׳יטיס אס גראנו אה גראנו,
קון טוס אב׳לאס דיליקאדאס, אי מי אינגאנייאסטיס:

———

אה! דאמאס קי דיראן די מי, לאס קי אמי מי קונוסיאן,
קי קון מי סי קונורטאב׳אן מוג׳אג׳יקאס, סינדו איז׳ה די קין סו,
מי קאזאטיס קון און ב׳ילאנו, איז׳ה אירה די און גואירטילאנו;
אי די לה מי גואירטה:

———

אה! ייולייו ב׳אמוס די אקי, די איסטי ארב׳ול סין פ׳לוריס,
לוב׳ייה קאייגה די לוס סיילוס אי מוס אמוז׳י:

———

רומאנסה טרים

איסטה נוג׳י מיס קאב׳אליירוס, דורמיר קון אונה סינייורה,
אי דורמיר קון אונה סינייורה, און דיאה די לוס מיס דיאס,
נון טופי אוטרה קומו אילייה:

———

אי נון טופי אוטרה קומו אילייה, בלאנקה איס אי קורילאדה
אירמוזה קומו לה איסטריאה:
אי אירמוזה קומו לה איסטריאה, אה לה אבאשאדה די און ריאו
אי אלה סוב׳ידה די און ב׳אליי:
אי אלה סוב׳ידה די און ב׳אליי, אינקונטרי קון ני ליזילדה
לה איז׳ה דיל אימפיראדור:

— 4 —

אי לה איז'ה דיל אימפיראדור, קי ב'יניאה די לוס באנייוס,
אי די לוס באנייוס די לאב'ארסי:
אי די לוס באנייוס די לאב'ארסי, די לאב'ארסי אי אינטרינסארסי,
אי די מודארסי אונה דילגאדה:
אי די מודארסי אונה דילגאדה, דישו לה קונדיסה אל קונדי,
אי קונדי פורקי נון קאזאטיש:
אי קונדי פורקי נון קאזאטיש, קאזארי סי איל דייו קירי,
אי קאזארי סי אה איל לי פלאזי:
אי קאזארי סי אה איל לי פלאזי, טומארי מוז'יר ג'יקיטה,
אי ג'יקה די לה פוקה אידאד;
אי ג'יקה די לה פוקה אידאד, קי סיאה ג'יקה די אנייוס,
אי די איל אינטינדימיינטו גראנדי:
אי די איל אינטינדימיינטו גראנדי, קי סיאה אלטה סין ג'אפינים.
אי אירמוזה סין אפ'ייטארסי:
אי אירמוזה סין אפ'ייטארסי, לוס איז'יקוס קי מי פאריירי;
מי אסימיז'ין אלה מאדרי:
אי מי אסימיז'ין אלה מאדרי, פוקו מאס או פוקו מאנו,
קי מי אסימיז'ין אל פאדרי:

———

רומאנסה כואטרו

איסטאב'ה לה ריינה איזיבלה, אי אין סו באסטידור לאב'ראנדו:
אי אין סו באסטידור לאב'ראנדו, אגוז'יקה די אורו אין מאנו,
אי און פינדון די אמור לאב'ראנדו:
אי און פינדון די אמור לאב'ראנדו, קואנדו לי קאאי לה אגוז'ה,
אי קואנדו לי קאאי איל דידאל:
או קואנדו לי קאאי איל דידאל, קואנדו לי קאאי לה טיז'ירה,
נו טייני קין קי קולטארי:

— 5 —

אי נו טייני קון קי קונטארי, פור אאי פאסו פאריזי,
איל סו לינדו נאמוראדו:
אי איל סו לינדו נאמוראדו, פארה איסטי פואירפו פאריזי,
קי אופֿיסייו אבֿיש טומאדו:
אי קי אופֿיסייו אבֿיש טומאדו, מירקאדיר סו לה מי סינייורה,
מירקאדיר אי איסקריבֿאנו:
אי מירקאדיר אי איסקריבֿאנו, טריס נאבֿיס טינגו אין איל פורטו,
קארגאדאס די אורו אי ברוקאדו:
או קארגאדאס די אורו אי ברוקאדו, לה נאבֿי קי ייו בֿינגו,
אבֿיאה און ריקו מאנסאנו:
אי אבֿיאה און ריקו מאנסאנו, קי איגֿאבֿה מאנסאנאס די אמוריס,
אין אינבֿיירנו אי אינבֿיראנו:
אי אין אינבֿיירנו אי אינבֿיראנו, סי איסטו איס בֿירדאד פאריזי,
בורייה איס די לו קונטארי:
אי בורייה איס די לו קונטארי, סי בֿוס פלאזיאה פאריזי,
די בֿוס איר אה בֿיזֿיטאר:
אי די בֿוס איר אה בֿיזֿיטארי, בֿינגאס אין בואינה אורה ריינה,
בֿוס אי בֿואיסטרו ריינאדו:
אי בֿוס אי בֿואיסטרו ריינאדו, דיסקי לה בֿידו בֿינירי,
ארמו בֿילאס אי אליבֿאנטו גאנגֿו:
אי ארמו בֿילאס אי אליבֿאנטו גאנגֿו, די פארטי די פֿראנסייה
לה לייבֿארון:

רומאנסה סינכו

און אמור טאן קירינסייוזה, קי אולבֿידאר נון לה פודיאה:
אי קי אולבֿידאר נו לה פודיאה, לה מאנייאניקה אי לה טארדי,
אה בֿיזֿיטאר ייו לה איאה:

— 6 —

אי אה בֿינטאר יין לה מאר , סי לה סופאבֿה דולסי נדו ,
לה קובֿיזאבֿה אי סי איאה :

אי לה קובֿיזאבֿה אי סי איאה , סי לה סופאבֿה דיספיירטה ,
אה פלאטיקאר סי לי מיטיאה :

אי אה פלאטיקאר סי לי מיטיאה, לה ביזאבֿה אי לה הבראסאבֿה,
אי אה יירלאר סי לי מיטיאה :

אי אה יירלאר סי לי מיטיאה , די קי יירלאש קאטיבֿאדה ,
די קי יירלאש בוזה גריאה :

אי די קי יירלאש בוזה גריאה , טיניאש מאל די אמוריס ,
או איסטאש ריזין פרינייאדה :

אי אה איסטאש ריזין פרינייאדה, נון טיניאה מאל די אמוריס,
ני איסטאבֿה ריזין פרינייאדה :

אי נו איסטאבֿה ריזין פרינייאדה, סי בֿו לו קונטו איל בואין ריי,
אפיאריש מיס פאלאבֿראס :

אי אפיאריס מיס פאלאבֿראס , יין פואי קריאדה אין סו בֿיאה,
אי אינטרי בואינה ג'ינטי אונוראדה :

אי אינטרי בואינה ג'ינטי אונוראדה, און קאבֿאיירו אנדאראליטו,
קי די מי סי נאמוראבֿה :

אי קי די מי סי נאמוראבֿה , איסקאלירינה לי איזו ,
דיבאשו די סוס בֿינטאנאס :

אי דיבאשו די סוס בֿינטאנאס , פארה קי סובֿה אי קי אבֿאשי ,
קומו סי פואירה סו קאזה :

אי קומו סי פואירה סו קאזה, טריס נוג'יס דורמייו קון איליה,
לי פאריסייו טריס סימאנאס :

אי לי פאריסייו טריס סימאנאס, אה פֿין די לאס טריס נוג'יס,
סי פואי אה בושקאר נואיבֿה אמאדה :

אי פואי אה בושקאר נואיבֿה אמאדה, איליה סי פואי דיטראס די איל
פור בֿיר סי איירה מאס גאלאנה :

———

רומאנסה סיש

טריס דאמאס ב'אן אה לה מילסה, אה אזיר לה אוראסייון,
אינטרי אינמידייו מי איספוזה, לה קי מאס קיריאה ייו: מי סינייור

אי אינטרי אינמידייו לה מי איספוזה, לה קי מאס קיריאה ייו,
קאמיזה די הולאנדה ייב'ה, סירמה אי פירלה אל קאב'יסון: קארה די פ'לור

אי קאמיזה די הולאנדה לייב'ה, סירמה אי פירלה אל קאב'יסון,
סאיין ייב'ה סוב'רי סאייו, און ש'ידויי די אלטורנאסייון: מי סינייור

אי סאיין ייב'ה סוב'רי סאייו, אין סידויי די אנטורנאסייון,
סו קאב'יסה אונה טורונג'ה, סוס קאב'ילייוס בריליס סון: קארה די פ'לור

אי סוס קאב'יסה אונה טורונג'ה, סוס קאב'ילייוס בריליס סון,
לה סו סיז'יקה אינארקאדה, ארקול די טיראר ייה סון: מי סינייור

אי לה סו סיז'יקה אינארקאדה, ארקול די טיראר ייה סון,
לוס סוס אוז'וס ג'יקיטיקוס, איספיז'וס די איסטאמבול: קארה די פ'לור

אי לוס סוס אוז'וס ג'יקיטיקוס, איספיז'וס די איסטאמבול,
לאס סוס קאראס קוראלאדאס, מאנסאנאס די איסקופייה סון: מי סינייור

אי לאס סוס קאראס קורולאדאס, מאנסאנאס די איסקופייה סון,
סו נאריס אפירפ'ילאדה, פינדולה די איסקריב'יר ייה סון: קארה די פ'לור

אי סו נאריס אפירפ'ילאדה, פינדולה די איסקריב'יר ייה סון,
לה סו בוקה ג'יקיטיקה, קי נון לי קאב'י פינייון: מי סינייור

אי לה סו בוקה ג'יקיטיקה, קי נון לי קאב'י פינייון,
סוס דיינטיס טאן מינודיקוס, פירלה די אינפ'ילאר ייה סון: קארה די פ'לור

רומאנסה סייטי

סאליר קירי איל מיז די מאייו, אי אינטראר קירי איל מיז די אפריל,
קואנדו איל טריגו איסטה אין גראנו, אי לאס פ'לוריס קירין סאליר:

אי קואנדו איל טריגו איסטה אין גראנו, אי לאס פ׳לוריס קירין סאליר,
קואנדו איל קונדאלימארי, פארה פ׳ראנסייה קיז׳ו איר:

אי קואנדו איל קונדאלימארי, פארה פ׳ראנסייה קיז׳ו איר,
קון סיגו איל סי ייב׳אב׳ה, אונרה אי פ׳אמה אי תאל ג׳ינטיל:

אי קון סיגו איל סי ייב׳אב׳ה, אי און ג׳ופ׳ליט די מארפ׳יל,
ייה קי לו מיטי אין לה נו בוקה, נון לו נאב׳יאה דיזיר:

אי לייה לו מיטי אין לה סו בוקה, נון לו סאב׳יאה דיזיר,
ייו מאנאנייו תאל ג׳ופ׳ליטי, לאס דונלאס קי די פור טי:

אי לייו מאלאנייו תאל ג׳ופ׳ליטי, לאס דונלאס קי די פור טי,
אי אוטראס תאנתאס ייו ליס דיירה, קי מי לו קיטין די אקי:

אי אוטראס תאנתאס ייו ליס דיירה, קי מי לו קיטין די אקי,
אי ייה לו קיטאן אה ב׳ינדיר, פ׳יר פלאסאס אי פור ג׳ארב׳ ס:

אי ייה לו קיטאן אה ב׳ינדיר, פור פלאסאס אי פור ג׳ארסיס,
נינגונוס ליס דאב׳אן פריסייו, אי און אספרו ני סוב׳יר:

אי נינגונוס לי דאב׳אן פריסייו, ני און אספרו ני סוב׳יר,
תאנטו פ׳ואי די בוקה אין בוקה, פ׳ואי אין בוקה די אמאדי:

אי תאנטו פ׳ואי די בוקה אין בוקה, פ׳ואי אין בוקה די אמאדי,
אי אוטרוס תאנטוס ייו לי דיירה, קי מי לו טראייגאן אקי:

אי אוטרוס תאנטוס ייו לי דיירה, קי מי לו טראייגאן אקי,
ייה לו מיטין אין לה סו בוקה, אי ייה לו אימפיסאן אה ריטינייר:

אי ייה לו מיטין אין לה סו בוקה. אי ייה לו אימפיסאן אה ריטינייר,
לאס נאב׳יס קי איסתאן אין פורטו, פריסטו לוס אזין ב׳ינייר:

אי לאס נאב׳יס קי איסטאן אין פורטו, פריסטו לאס אזין ב׳יניר,
לה פארידה קי איסטה פאריינדו, פריסטו לה אזין פאריר:

רומאנסה איג׳

ריך מי אליב׳אנטי אי און לונים, אי און לונים פור לה מאנייאנה:
סומי מי ארקוב׳ אי מי פ׳ליג׳ה, אי אין לה מי מאנו דיריג׳ה:

אנדי סי לה פֿואירה ייו אה טאנייר, אה פואירטאס די מי נאמוראדה:
אבֿרישמי בוזו מי ביין, אבֿרישמי בוזו מי בֿיקטה :
לוס פייזיס טינגו אין לה נייבֿי, אי לה קאבֿיסה אין לה ייגֿאדה :
קומו בֿוס אבֿרירי מי ביין, קומו בֿוס אבֿרירי מי אלמה :
אבֿ איזו טינגו אין איל פיגֿו, אי אבֿ מארידו אין לה ניקאמה :
קיין בֿוס הבֿלו בוזו מי ביין, קיין בֿוס אבֿלו בוזו מי אלמה :
איל מוסו דיל פאנאדירו, איל קי לוס מאלוס אנייוס אגה :
אירינה נו טינגו אין קאזה, אי ליבֿאדורה מי דימאנדה :
איל סאלייגדו די לה פואירטה, איל נאמוראדו פור לה בֿינטאנה :
פור אינמידייו דיל קאמינו. לה קאשיקה קי אולבֿידארה :
איליים סי טופו אין אפריטו, לו אינטרו אדיינטרו לה קאסה :
לה קאשה איקטושו די פימיינטה, איל נאמוראדו סארנודאבֿה :
קיין סארנודה בוזו מי ביין, אי קיין סארנודה בוזו מי אלמה :
איל גאטו די לה בֿיזינה, איל קי לוס מאלוס אנייוס הגה :
דיין אונה דזדה אין לה קאסה, לה קאסה לה דיקקלאבֿאבֿה :
בֿיניד בֿיריס לאס מיס בֿיזינאס, לאס די אבאשו אי לאס די אריבֿה:
בֿניד בֿיריס גאטו קון בארבֿה, אי מוסטאגֿיקוס אריטורסידוס :

———

רומאנסה מואיב'י

לון דיל דיאה אי קלארידאד, קי איל דיאה מוס דאשׁ איל סול ,
אי לה נוגֿי קלארו לונאר :

אי לה נוגֿי קלארו לונאר, לאס מאנייאניקאס לאס איסטריאס
אי קואנדו קירי אלבֿוריאר :

אי קואנדו קירי אלבֿוריאר , סי פאסיאה טיאו אי סובֿרינו ,
גֿונסוס בֿאן אה און באראבאר :

אי גֿונסוס בֿאן אה און באראבאר, קי קאבֿאייוס ייבֿאן די און פריסייו,
אי פור בֿיר קואל קוריאה מאס :

אי פור בֿיר קואל קוריאה מאב, קי קורי אונו אי קורי אוטרו,
גֿונסוס בֿאן אה און באראבאר :

—10—

אי ג̈ונטוס ב̈אן אה און באראבאר, אב̈לאנדו ב̈אן אי פלאטיקאנדו,
לו קי ליס אימפורטה מאס :

אי לו קי ליס אימפורטה מאס , אונה מירסיד לי רוגו טיאו ,
קואל לה אב̈יש די אטורגאר :

אי קואל מי לה אב̈יש די אטורגאר, קי מי דיש̈ אה בלאנקה ניניה,
פור מוזיר אי פור איגואל :

אי פור מוזיר אי פור איגואל, איסטה מירסיד איל מי סוב̈רינו,
כון ב̈ו לה פואידו אג̈יטאר :

אי נו ב̈ו לה פואידו אג̈יטאר , קואנדו ב̈ו לה אב̈יאה דאד̈ו ,
כון לה קיז̈יטיס טומאר :

אי נו לה קיז̈יטיס טומאר, קי ד̈אד̈ה לה טינגו אין פ̈ראנסייה ,
פור סיין דובלאס אי אלגו מאס :

אי פור סיין דובלאס אי אלגו מאס, קי דיספוזאדה לה טינגו אין פ̈ראנסייה,
אי קון איל קונדי אליגורנאל :

אי קון איל קונדי אליגורנאל, גירירו סוס איל מי סוב̈רינו ,
אי לה פואידיס מויי ביין גאנאר :

אי לה פואידיס מויי ביין גאנאר , דישמי קאמיזה דינגאד̈ה,
סירמה אי פירלה אין סו קוייאר :

אי סירמה אי פירלה אין סו קוייאר, ייה סי איספארטי איל קאב̈אליירו,
אי ייה סי איספארטי אי ייה סי ב̈ה :

אי ייה סי איספארטי אי ייה סי ב̈ה, פור קאליים קי אב̈יאה ג̈ינטי,
קאמינאב̈ה די אב̈אגאר :

אי קאמינאב̈ה די אב̈אגאר, פור לאס קאליים קי נון אב̈יאה ג̈ינטי,
סינטיאס אזיאה קאנטאר :

אי סינטיאס אזיאה קאנטאר , קיין איס איסטי מוכו פ̈ראנקו ,
קי לה פ̈ידאד̈ ב̈ה אה דירוקאר :

———

—11—

רומאנסה דייז

סי פאסיאה פאסטור פֿיאיל, קון סו גאנאדו די אקיאה טאדֿרי,
אי קון סו גאנאדו די אקיאה טאדֿרי, קון רימולינוס אי טרואינוס,
אי לוס רילאמפאגוס מויי גראנדיס :

אי לוס רילאמפאגוס מויי גראנדיס, סינייור סינייור סי פיקי ,
איל מי גאנאדו נון לו פֿאאי :

אי איל מי גאנאדו נון לו פֿאאי , סי איל מי גאנאדו פיקו ,
לו קי נו איס מיאו איסקאפאמי :

אי לו קי נו איס מיאו איסקאפאמי, איסטו קי סינטיירון לאס נובֿיס,
סי בולטארון פור אוטראס פארטיס :

אי סי בולטארון פור אוטראס פארטיס, סי דיאבֿאן די פינייה אין פינייה
אי פור אגואה קוריאה סאנגרי :

אי פור אגואה קוריאה סאנגרי , ייוראבֿאן לוס קאפיטאניס ;
אי טודוס לוס קי אין לה מאר :

אי טודוס לוס קי אין לה מאר, און בוראנטי: איי אינטרי אילייוס,
קי אין אילייה נון אגֿיטארי ·

אי קי אין אילייה נון אגֿיטארי , סינייורה לה מי סינייורה ,
די איסטה פֿורטונה איסקאפאמי :

אי די איסטה פֿורטונה איסקאפאמי, סי די איסטה פֿורטונה מי איסקאפאס
קון אורו בֿוס אינקורונארי :

אי קון אורו בֿוס אינקורונארי, איסטו סינטייו איל פאטרון דיל מונדו
לאס אגואס מאס סובריבֿייארי :

אי לאס אגואס מאס סובריבֿייארי, בֿאטי בֿאטי פוטה אמאריאה ,
קי סוס פֿאלסה אי מינטירוזה :

אי קי סוס פֿאלסה אי מינטירוזה, טיניימוס און פאדֿרי פיאדוזו,
קי מואג׳אס מאראבֿיאס אזי :

אי קי מואג׳אס מאראבֿיאס אזי , נו לאס אגה די קונטינו ,
די פריסה קי נון די טאדֿרי :

—12—

אי די פריסה קי נון דיטארדי, איל קי קיטי לה כאבֿי דיל גולפֿו,
קומו לה פארידה קי פארי :
אי קומו לה פארידה קי פארי, אנסי אגה קון לוס מאזינוס ,
די פריסה קי נון דיטארדי :
אי די פריסה קי נון דיטארדי, קי ניגונוס קי סי דיזיספירין ,
ני קי פיידראן לה איספיראנסה :
אי ני קי פיידראן לה איספיראנסה, קי דיספואיס דילה פֿורטונה,
איל מוס מאנדה לה בֿונאנסה :

———

רומאנסה אונזי

סי פאסיאן לאס דוג׳י פֿלוריס , איינטרי אין מידייו אונה קונג׳ה :
דישו לה קונג׳ה אלאס פֿלוריס , אויי איס דיאה די פאסיאר :
סי פאסיאה לה לינדה דינה, פור לוס קאמפוס דיל ריי חמור :
לה קולונדרה די איל טיזארו, קי נון לה איספאנייארה איל סול:
קון פאבֿור די סוס דוג׳י אירמאנוס, קאמינאבֿה סין טימור :
אריינוס· אין אונה טיינדה, פינסאנדו קי נון איי בֿארון :
בֿיסטו לה אובֿיירה בֿיסטו , שכם איל איזו די איל ריי חמור :
איינגוסי פארה איליייה , טריס פאלאבֿריקאס לי אבֿלו :
לינדה סוש לה לינדה דינה, סין אפֿייטי אי סין קולור :
לינדוס סון בֿואיסטרוס אירמאנוס. מאס קי בֿוס ייבֿאש לה פֿלור :
או קון לינדוס או נו סון לינדוס , אמי מי לוס גוארדי איל דייו :
איינגוסי פארה איליייה, איזו לו קי נו איס ראזון :
סי איספאנטי לה לינדה דינה, סי בֿה פארה אין דיל סו סינייור:
איל פאדרי דיסקי לו סופו, אריסיבֿיר נו קאלייו :
קיין בֿוס דימודו לה קארה, אי קיין בֿוס דימודו לה קולור :
בֿונה דימודו איל איירי, או בֿו לה דימודו איל סול :
ני מי לה דימודו איל איירי, ני מי לה דימודו איל סול :
מי לה דימודו און מוג׳אג׳יקו, שכם איל איזו דיל ריי חמור :
איסמו קי סינטייו איל פאדרי, קאזאמינטירוס לי מאנדו :

———

קומפלאס מואיב'אס
פור
איל פ'יליק די אגורה

(סי קאנטאן אין איל סון די לאס קומפ'לאס די **שבועות**)

או דייו! מאנדאליס פאס אין טודוס לוס ריינאדוס,
אי קי איסטין טודוס אה און קוראסון אאונאדוס,
אי טודוס לוס פואיב'לוס איסטארימוס אריקינטאדוס:

בסורות בואינאס סינטאמוס טודאס לאס נאסייוניס,
אי די אויי אי אינדילאנטרי נון טיניר מאס פאסייוניס,
אי פור מוזוטרוס אינטאנטו איס טומאר ליאיסייוניס:

גירה אין איסטי פ'יליק אזימוס אויי לה ג'ינטי,
אנקי סיאה און מיליק איסטה דיסקונטינטי,
איל קי סאב'י קיטאר סו פאן אקיל איס מויי ב'אליינטי:

דיב'ימוס קומפורטארנוס אין לה איקונומיאה,
פורקי נון טינגה דיזפלאזיר איל אי סו פ'אמיאה,
קון לה פארטי קי איל דייו מוס דה איסטימוס קון אליגריאה.

הים אוגאנייו קי לה פאסימוס מויי דיסקונטינטי לה אינב'יירנאדה,
די פאס אי אליגריאה קי מוס אינטרי לה אינב'ירנאדה.
אי פור אינדילאנטרי קי נון אייגה מאס גיראס נאדה:

ואיי דילוס קי סי מוריירון אל פ'ריאו אי לה יילור,
די ב'ירלו אה קונטארלו מוס דה גראן טימבלור,
אי איל דייו קי מוס גואדרי די אזינוראס אין לה קאלור:

—14—

זורטו מונג'ו טראבאחרון די סיד אי די אמברי,
אי די מונג'ו פריאו מורייירון ג'ינטי קי לים אבאשו קאנאמברי,
אי די מוג'ידומברי דילוס מאטאדוס אבאשאבה ריאו די סאנגרי:

——

חשבון דילוס מאטאדוס נון סי אסומה אין איסטה גירה,
סי קונטינטאבאן מיזור מורירסין אין לה חולירה,
כון סוז̈ייירון מאל די איגטיראסין אין לה טיירה :

——

טודאס לאס 10 מכות די פרעה מאס סי מיטייירון אין לוס אוזוס:
טודאס מואיסטראס מוראדאס מו סי איניג'ירון די פיאוזוס:
די וונגאס סופריינסאס כון ביימוס כי קון איבטוזוס :

——

ייה אזי 6 מיזים איסטה מכה אאינדה קי מום טורה,
די שאנטה אראסקאטינה מום דה קאזינטורה.
טי רוגאמוס דייו סאנלאמוס די איסטה סיקאטורה:

——

כנל דילה קוזה איס, קי כון ביימוס און דיאה די בונדאד,
כון איס סולו אין סאלוניק אי אין טודה לה סיבדאד,
איסטה גזרה קאזי ייה סי פואי פינה באגדאד :

——

לה ליבירטאד קי פוזימוס פואי טודו די מינטיראס,
דיזגראסייאדוס דילוס מאנסיבוס קי דיילון שאנטאב ליראס,
אילייום אלה מונטאנייה אי אוטרוס ביבייינדו ביראס :

——

מאנדארון אלוס מאנסיבוס אין פאגאנדו איל בידיל אלה גירה,
דימאנדאבאן אוטראב 40 ליראס קי לים דיירה,
פור כון טינירלאס טראבאראן שאנטה גאלירה :

——

נון סי סאבי נאביר די אונוס קואנטוס קי סי פואירון,
כון דאן דינגון דימאלייו איסטוס קי ביינייירון,
פור פיגורו קי אלגון לוגאר לונגי סי איסקונדייירון :

——

—15—

סיגורו קי איל דייו מוס ב׳ה אה קיטאר אה סילאניק,
מה לאס אוראס איסטאן טראב׳אנדו גראנדי ז׳אמאס,
אין אגורה קי איספיראן טיניר בואין קיסמיט :

——

עניין דינה קוזה אים דישאר לאס איג׳אס אה איל דייו,
סיינדו איסטה גירה פור סו מאנו מו סי דייו,
קי מאנדי ריפוזו אה טודוס לוס פואיב׳לוס אי אל ג׳ידיין :

——

פורים די אוגאנייו לו פאסימוס מויי דיזגראסייאדו,
טאנטו ריקו קומו פרוב׳י איסטוב׳ימוס אנסייאדו,
מה פסח קון בואינו איסטארימוס טודוס טודוס אינב׳יסייאדו:

——

צער ב׳אמוס פאסאנדו טודוס אין מויי דיפ׳ירינטי,
כון קי איסקאפה אונה קוזה קי לה אוטרה ייה איסטה אינפ׳רינטי,
מירנדו קי טאן ב׳אראטו איסטה אוגאנייו לה מואירטי :

——

קרוב ה׳ אים אל קי לו ייאמה די קוראסון ,
רוגאמוס קי מוס קומפלה אה טודוס מואיסטרו רצון ,
מואיסטראס פורטונה אב׳ולטים די טריסטיזאס אה ששון :

——

רחום וחנון סוב ליב׳ראמוס די טאנטה קריזה קי מוס איסטריגה,
קי נו מוס קידו אין מואיסטראס קאזאס ני רוב׳ייאדור ני פ׳ליג׳ה,
מאנדאמולה אה איסטה אינב׳ירנאדה דיריג׳ה :

——

שאקה מוס פאריסי לה אינב׳יירנאדה קי פאסימוס,
מויי פוקוס סומוס קי אה סילאניק סאלימוס,
מה אים מוזוטרוס פור סיגורו קי נו לו קולפימוס:

——

תפילה אזימוס אה איל דייו די ישראל ,
קי נו מירי מואיסטרוס פיקאדוס אי מוס מאנדי אה איל גואל,
סיאמוס אקומפאנייאדוס די אליהו אי גבריאל :

——

פ״ז

—16—

אין איסטה אוז׳ה קונטייני לאס ברכות די **ברית מילה**
אין בואינה קומפוזיסייון פורקי כון פיני איל פאדרידו אה דיזירלאס :

איסטוס סינקו ביירבוס דיבי׳ה דיזיר איל פאדרידו :

אש:י תיבחר ותקרב ישכון חצריך

איסטוס סינקו ביירבוס דיראן לוס סינייורים פריזינטיס :

נצבעה בטוב בתיך . הדוש הכליך

אי דיספואיס דירה איל פאדרידו איסטאס דוס ברכות :

ברוך אתה ה׳ אלהינו מלך העולם אשר הידשנו במצותיו וציונו להכניסו בבריתו של אברהם אבינו :

ברוך אתה ה׳ אלוהינו מלך העולם שהחיינו וקיימנו והגיענו לזמן הזה

קאנטאלדו אה פאדרידו קון **בסימן טוב**

Achré tivhar vetikarev yichcon hassereha.

Barouh ata Adonaï éloénou meleh aolam acher kidéchanou bemisvotav vessivanou léahnisso bivrito chel Abraam avinou .

Barouh ata Adonaï éloénou meleh aolam chééhiyano vekiyémano véigianou lazeman azé :

VII

'UN REMORSO POR LA HAGĀDĀH DE ḤAG HA-PESAḤ

(Salonika, 1915)

(abbr. RHP)

Bonne Fête מועדים לשמחה

און רימורסו
פור לה
הגדה די חג הפסח

(אין איסטה ברושורה קונטייני 5 ארטיקולוס)

1—און רימורסו די אונוס קוזנטוס ב׳ירנוס טוקאנטי

אה לה הגדה.

2—אונה קאנטיגה דיל פ׳יליק קי איגזיסטי אגורה.

3—אונאס רומאנסאס אימפורטאנטיס

4—לאס ברכות די ברית מילה אין פ׳ראנסיס אי

אין איספאנייול, פורקי נו ב׳יני איל פארידו אה

דיזירלאס

5—איל נומברי דיל אאוטור יעקב יונה

סאלוניקו

שנת ואת לחצנו זה הדחק

און רימורסו די אונוס קואנטוס בי׳רבוס

אינדיקאדה אלה הגדה די חג הפסח

הא לחמא עניא

איסטי איל פאן די לה אפליסייון, קי קומימוס איסטי אנייו אין טיירה די סאלוניק, אין טאנטו אפליטו, מוס טרושו איל דייו אה קומיר פאן פריטו, טודו איל קי טוטו דימאניבאנד פונגו, מירקימוס אה 5 גרושים, איסטי אנייו מוס פואי איזה אינגינה, אה איל אנייו איל ביניין איסקאפאר די טאנטה קימאסינה, איסטי אנייו אקי אבולבאדוס, אה איל אנייו איל ביניין טודאס באר לאס ביוניס אריבינטאדוס.

מה נשתנה

קואנטו פואי דימודאדו, איל אנייו איל איסטי מאס קי טודוס לוס אנייוס, קי אין טודוס לוס אנייוס, נוזוטרוס קומימוס לה קארני אה 6 גרושים, אי איל אנייו איל איסטי אה 15, קי אין טודוס לוס אנייוס מוזוטרוס קומיאמוס איל קודרירו אפארטאר, אי איל אנייו איל איסטי זה אסיר אגוקטאר, קי אין טודוס לוס אנייוס בו קומיאמוס אה 8 גרושים, אי איל אנייו איל איסטי אה 15 אבוגאר.

עבדים היינו לפרעה

סיירב'ום פ̄ואימוס אוגאנייו א באקאליס אי משטראפאזיס, אי סאליירון טודוס ק̄ורנאזיס, לאס רופאס קי סי ליס פ̇אלייו א קומו קירין לה ג'אן ג'ינדיירו, אין אנוס פרוג'יס קי מוס איסג'אן אשינדיירו, דילוס באקאליס מוס ג'ינו מאס מוג'ו לוס מאלים, נו קוג'יירון איליוס טודו איל ז'איירי, נו אונ'ו נינגונוס קי בושקארן א- גון ג'ארי; לוס קארנישירוס טיינין ראזון, קי ליס אי- ג'אן לאס באקאס אלה מאר סי ליס קורטו איל מזון, לוס פישקאדוריס קי ליס ג'ייני איל סאזון די לוגאר לונג'י, לו ג'ינדין א 10 אי א 12.

מעשה

אקונטיסייו מעשה אין לוס ז'איריג'יס, מוס טומארון א לה זולה קומו ייאבאנג'יס, קואלוס די לה פלאסה אי קו- אלוס דילה מעלי, קוג'יינדו לאס רופאס די דיאה אין דיאה ייולי, טאנטו דיל גאס אי דיל שאבון אינג'יטרי, די סינטיר לוס פריבייוס מוס דה דולור די ג'ייניטרי, א מוזוטרוס קי מוס שאלגה אי א: איליוס קי ליס איינטרי.

אמר

דישו רבי פולאנו, קי אים איסטה שוג'ידורה, די לה באלאנ- קורה די אוגאנייו, א סיין גרושים איל סיינטו קון מיטאד די פיסקו קון טאנטו אינגאנייו, ג'ינו איל דיין איל אינג'יירנו נו לו איזו אינג'ירנאנו, אים קימאר אב פרוג'י סולאמינטי, קי מודו סיבטונסים קי נו מינטי, איל ריקו לו מירקה באראטו סי בוליינו. ג'ינו איל דיין לו מאנדו פור אונטראס פארטיס איל אינג'יירנו.

ברוך המקום

בינדיג'ו איל קריאדור בינדיג'ו איל, קי אל פרובֿי נוס דה לה פאסינסייה, קי סי סינבאמוס אלגונוס קאבֿוס פיד־ריאמוס לה פאסינסייה, די ביר קי לאס רופאס קוזין אי נו אבֿאסטה, אל פרובֿי צ'אזייאמוס לה בֿאלסה אי איליוס אינג'ין לה קאשה, איספירהמוס די אבֿאשאר קואטרו קוזאס, איל פאן, לה בֿלאנקורה, איל זאייטי, לה קארני אי איל פיסקאדו אי טודוס לוס פואיבֿלוס אריסינבֿאדו.

חכם

סאביו קי איל דיזיין, קי אים איסטה קאריסטיאה די איל גולבֿו אי דיל פאן, נו נוס איסטאמוס ארטאנדו די קון ארינה די קאפאן, איל סאן ג'יקו אה 7 מיטאלי־קיס, נוס סי איזו טודו פראנקוס אין לוגאר די אל־טיליקיס, פור נואס דיזגראסייה איל פאן פריטו, דיס־פואיס די קומיר טאנטו אפריטו, טודו איסטו אים אמארגאסיון די איל דייו, חכמי טו די אה איל, נוסוטרוס נו לו קונפיאמוס, אולבידימוס לה ליי אי פור איסטה ראזון נוזוטרוס לה טופימוס.

רשע

מאלו קי איל דיזיין, קי איס איסטאס דוס אנייאדאס קי בֿוס דייו איל אה בֿוס, אה בֿוס אי נו אה איל סאבֿיין טו די אה איל, דה אה איל אה לוס דיינטיס, אה קי נו אלבֿין נואס קוזאס דיפירינטיס.

תם

פריגיזמו קי איל דיזיין, קי איס איסטו די אוגאנייון, פור אנ-
די מוס אבולטאמוס טודו איסקורו אי אינבאלאנייון,
טאמביין טו די לה איל, אנסי טו לו איזו איל דיין
אי אה מוזוטרוס טאמביין מוס פלאזייר.

ושאינו

א׳ איל קי נו סאבי לאס אנייאדאס פ׳ורטונוזאס קי פא-
סימוס, טאמביין טו די לה איל, גראסייאס אל דיין
קי איסטאמוס ביבוס אי נו מוס מורימוס, פארה טודו
סי קירי לה פאסינסייה, איסטה אורה איס די נו פי-
דריל לה קונסינסייה, טי דאן אה קומיר קומי, סי לי
דאן פאראס קי טומי, אי סי לו אארבאן קי סי פ׳ויינה.

מתחילה

די פריסיפיין סירב׳יינטיס אה איל דיין אילה די ב׳ירדאד
אי אגורה איסטאמוס אוזאדוס לה מאס פארטי אין
לה מאלדאד, קומו אנסי דיזי מואיסטרה לייי, טודו
איל קי טורנה אין תשובה איל דיין לו פירדונה.

וארא

א׳ טומי דיספואיס די איסטו לוס «דיינוס» די סאלוניק,
ב׳יינדו קי פור טודאס לאס פארטיס איסטה טודו בו-
לאניק, איספירחמוס אגורה. קי טודאס לאס גיראס קי
סי קידין אינבונורה, אי פור אינדילאנטרי טיניר בו-
אינה לה אינב׳ירנאדה, די טודאס לאס אנגוסטייאס
אי לאס גיראס קי נו קידין נאדה.

שורה מוס אירטי פאלויייר, כיי פיראסי טו האיימונה

לוס דיינוס

קואנטוס גראדוס בואינוס א־איל קריאדור סוב'רי נוס

סי סי איסקאפארה לאס גיראס, אי מאנדארה איל דייו
פאס אין לוס ריינאדוס : מוס אבאסטארה

סי מאנדארה איל דייו פאס אין לוס ריינאדוס, אי סי
אבריאן טודוס לוס פורטוס : מוס אבאסטארה.

סי סי אבריאן טודוס לוס פורטוס, אי מוס מאנדארה
איל דייו אינביירנאדה בואינו : מוס אבאסטארה.

סי מוס מאנדארה איל דייו אינביירנאדה בואינה, אי נו
סי סינטיירה נינגונה אזינורה : מוס אבאסטארה.

סי נו סי סינטיירה נינגונה אזינורה, אי מוס מאנדארה
איל דייו אה טודוס לאס נאסייוניס איג'וס בואינוס: מוס אבאסטארה.

סי מוס מאנדארה איל דייו איג'וס בואינוס, אי סי מוס
מאנדארה איל דייו פולבו אה בולג'יליק : מוס אבאסטארה

סי מוס מאנדארה איל דייו פולבו אה בולג'יליק, אי כון
מוס סוב'יאה לה מצה אה אוג'ו אי מידייו : מוס אבאסטארה.

סי מוס סוב'יאה לה מצה אה אוג'ו אי מידייו, אי נו
מוס טומאראן אה לוס פרוב'יס אה סיס מיטאליקים: מוס אבאסטארה.

סי מוס טומאראן אה סיס מיטאליקים לה אוקה, אי נו
מוס סוב'יאן איל פאן אה סייטי מיטאליקים: מוס אבאסטארה.

סי מוס סוב'יאן איל פאן אה סייטי מיטאליקים, אי נו מוס
סוב'יאן איל זאיירי לוס באקאלים : מוס אבאסטארה.

סי מוס סוב'יאן איל זאיירי לוס באקאלים, אי מוס איס-
קאפארה איל דייו די טודוס לוס מאלים : מוס אבאסטארה.

קומפלאס די איל פ׳יליק קי איגזיסטי אגורה

אורדיני איסטי קאנטאר, קון גראן זוק אי בראמה, סיינדו קוזה די איגקאנטאר, איסטי פ׳ואיגו סין פ׳לאמה, טודו איל פואיבלו איסקאלאמה, סין אב׳יר פיאדאד, די איסטי מאל אין קאנטידאד, די איסטה מיזירייה, מוס בולטי איל דיין לה איסטריאה.

ב׳ינו לאס גיראס אזיר, אה טודוס איסקלאבוס, טודוס איסטאמוס ביזיר, אי די לה ב׳ידה קאנסוס, טודוס לוס איגב׳אראסוס, ב׳ינו אל עולם, קידימוס טודוס זולאס, גראנדי קומו ג׳יקו, פרוב׳י טאמביין ריקו:

גיראס אין איסטי פ׳יליק, אזימוס אויי לה ג׳ינטי, אנסי סיאה און מיליק, איסטה דיסקונטינטי, איל קי איס ב׳אלייינטי, אה קיטאר סו פאן, קון אריסה דיל קאפאן, קיין פאסה אנסי לה ב׳ידה, לה גאנה לה פארטידה.

דיב׳ימוס אויי די אזיר, לה איקונומיאה, פור נו טינירדיספלאזיר, איל קון סו פאמיליאה, אין קאמה נו דורמיאה, אין טיימפו קייאנט, קונפ׳יסאנדו אין פ׳יסאט, אי מאטאר נו · פואירפו, פור פאסאר איל טיימפו.

היוס ב׳ינימוס אין און דור, די קידאר איסקלאב׳וס, מירקאדיר ני קורידור, נינגונוס סומוס סאלב׳וס, טודוס טינימוס קלאב׳וס, אין מואיסטרה אופיניון, קי מוס בוראקה איל ריניון, פור נוס גאסטים טיריב׳לים, סיינדו אימפוסיב׳לים.

וידאד איס קי איל זמן, מונו איסטה קאב׳זאנדו, קאלי בוסקאר אלגון דירמאן, די איל פיסקוזאנדו, נו קי ב׳אמוס אוזאנדו, איסטי קיאפ׳יט, מונו אזין פור מאראפ׳יט, ב׳יסטיר לוסוס אי מודאס, פור אירסין אה לאס בודאס.

זוכ׳ט מוס אים אין קאנטידאד, איל גאנאר די אגורה, מו סי איסב׳ריינו לה פרוב׳ידאד, פור נון סינסאר אונה אורה, דאר לה איסבוכורה, לאס מודאס סין מינישטיר, מוסי אימפיסו אה ריב׳ירטיר לאס קוזאס דימאזיאה, מוס פאריסי מאנזיאה.

תאל מוס ב׳ינו אין ג׳ינירﬡל. פור מואיב׳ראס מאנקוראס, סי איזו
לוס לוקוס נאטוראל, סין ב׳וסקאר לאס קוזאס, טודו קאנ׳זאס
איסקוראס, סין אב׳יר קונסינטיר, טודו קאמינה קון אאטיר, לה
ב׳אמוס פאסאנדו, מוס איב׳ספאמוס אסאנדו.

טודוס ייב׳אמוס איסטי מאל, אי נו סומוס קריאידוס, לאזדראמוס
קומו חאמאל, מויי אב׳יגיאידוס, קי טאפאן אואידוס, סי ב׳אמוס
אה קונטאר, די לאס מודאס קי אינב׳ינטאר. איס גראנדי אימ-
פורטו, פארה דאר ראפורטו.

ייה כבוד נו ב׳ה אה קידאר, קונטאנדו לוס דירטיס, נון סון קוזאס
די אולב׳ידאר, סיינדו סון מויי פואירטיס. מוס קאייו איספואירטיס,
אין קואלקיר פודיר, אפילו איל מירקאדיר, קי טראטה אי באר-
טה, סיימפרי ב׳ייני אין פלאטה.

סימן יעקב יונה הי״ו

ייה איס אורה די סיר קון איל דייו נאמורוזו,
אה גראנדיס אי אה צ׳יקוס נון מוס קידו ריפוזו,
איל דייו איס טאדריהוזו, אי נון אולב׳ידאדוזו.

עין די טאנטוס פינסידייוס נון דורמימוס אין לה קאמה,
די טודאס לאס פארטיס איסטה אין אונה פ׳לאמה,
בוטיקה טינימוס פור פ׳אמה, נון טינימוס ב׳יזני ני דראמה.

קומו די אפאנניס מוס ב׳ינו איסטאס אנייאדאס
די טודאס לאס פארטיס איסטאן אבאראב׳אדאס,
קי ניגרו לאס אינב׳יירנאדאס, קומו לאס אינב׳ירנאדאס.

בשורות פור אינדילאנטרי סינטיר די ב׳ירדאד,
די טודאס לאס נאסייוניס קי טינגה איל דייו פיאדאד,
קי מוס סי אינריינו באסטאנטי לה פרוב׳ידאד.

ייו סיימפרי סירי ב׳ואיסטרו ג׳ינירוזו אמיגו.

נונקה סיקריטו די ב׳וזוטרוס אה נינגונוס נון לו דיגו,

הים אגורה קי אדיאו אה טודוס אין ג׳ינירﬡל ב׳וס דיגו

גואירטה
די
רומאנסאס אימפורטאנטיס

רומאנסה אונה

אקיל קונדי, אי אקיל קונדי, אין לה מאר סיאה סו פ׳ין;
אין לה מאר סיאה סו פ׳ין, ארמו ארמאדאס אי גאליראס אי פארה
פ׳ראנסייה קיזו איר. די טורנה
לאב ארמו די טודו פונטו, אי לאס איגו דיינטרו איל סאנגיר,
איל סאנגיר קומו אירה איסטריגו, אי קון לאס פואידיאה ריזיר:
הטראב אטראס לוס פ׳ראנסיזים, קון לי דיש ג׳ירגואינסה אסי;
כי איל גראן דוקי לו סאבי, אה פ׳ראנסייה קון ג׳ום דישה איר;
כי ג׳ום דאן פאן אה קומיר, כי קון כאס דאמאס דורמיר,
אין לה טורנה קי אטורנה, מאטארון סיטינטה מיל;
הפארטי די ג׳יקיטיקוס. קי קון איי קואינטה כי פ׳ין,
גראנדים בודאס איי אין פ׳ראנסייה, אי אין לה קאבה די פאריס;
קי קאזה לה איזה דיל ריי, קון לה איזה די אמאדי,
באיילאן דאמאס אי דונזיאס, קאב׳אליירוס מאנג׳די מיל,
לה קי ג׳יאבה לה טאייפה, אירה אונה דאמה ג׳ינטיל,
מיראנדו לה איסטאבה איל קונדי, אי אקיל קונדי די אמאדי;
קי מיראש אקי איל בואין קונדי, אי קונדי קי מיראש אקי,
לו מיראבאש אלה טאייפה, או מי מיראבאש אמי,
ייו כון מירו אלה טאייפה, כי מינוס טי מירו אטי,
מירו אה איקסטי לינדו פואירפו, טאן גראנדו אי טאן ג׳ינטיל,
כי ג׳ום אגראדו איל קונדי, קון סיגו ייב׳ימאר אמי;
מאדידו אין ב׳יאז׳י טינגו, לונג׳י איסטה פארה ב׳יניר,
אונה איספוזיגרה ב׳יילה טינגו, מאלה איסטה פארה מוריר,

דוס איז'יקוס ג'יקוס טינגו, אי נון סי לו סאב'ין דיזיר,
לה אינב'רוזו אין און מאנטיל די אורו, אי די אפואירה דישו איל ג'אפין,
פור אינמידייו דיל קאמינו, אינקונטרו קון סמאדרי,
קי ייב'אס אקי איל קונדי, אי קונדי קי ייב'אס אקי;
ייב'ו און פאסאזיקו די אורו, קי אינדה אויי מי לו מירקי,
איסטי פאסאזיקו קונדי, אמי מי לו איס פ'יאיל אה קירב'יר,
איל דיאה פארה לה מיזה, אי לה נוג'י פארה דורמיר,
נון לה קונוסי אין איל גארב'י, ני מינוס אין איל ב'יסטיר,
קונוסי אין איל ג'אפין די אורו, אאינדה אאייר סי לו מירקי,
איסטו קי סינטייו איל קונדי, לה דישו אי סי איגו אה פ'ואיר,
איסטו נון איס לה ב'ואיסטרה קולפה, סי נון ייו קי לו קולפי:

רומאנסה דוס

אה! אינדונדי שול איסטאס מארים, נאב'יגי קון לה פורטונה
קאליי אין טיירה אז'ינה, אנדי נון מי קונוסיאן,
אנדי נו קונטאב'ה נאדייז, ני' מינוס פירו מאאולייס.
אנדי בראמאב'ה איל לאון, אי לה לאונה ריספונדיאה;
אה! אנדי קריסי לה נאראנג'ה, אי איל לימון אי לה סידרה,
אנדי קריסי ייירב'ה ב'ינדידה, סי קאנג'אס מי גראב'יאינאס,
אנדי קריסי רודה מינודה, גואדריאה דילאס קריאטוראס,
אה! ייוליין פאלנו אי סראאידור, קונזאנטי דילוס מיס מאלים,
אינטראטים אין מי גאדריר, און דיאה די אינב'יירנו,
אקוזיפים לה פ'לור די מי, לה קוזיטים אה גראנו אה גראמו,
קון טוס אב'לאס דיליקאדאס, אה מי מי אינגאנייאטים;
אה! דאמאס קי דיראן די מי, נאס קי אמי מי קונוסיאן,
קי קון מי סי קונורטאב'אן מוג'אג'יקאס, סיינדו איזה די קיין פור
מי קאזאטים קון און ב'ילאנו, איזה אירה די און גואירטילאנו,
אי דילה מי גואירטה;
אה! ייוליין ב'אמוס די אקי, די איסטי ארב'ול סין פ'לוריס,
נוב'יס קאייגה דילוס סיילוס, אי מוס אמוזי:

רומאנסה טרים

אין לה סיב'דאד די מארסילייה, אב'יאה אונה לינדה דאמה,
קי טוקאב'ה אי קי לאב'ורב'ה, ני קי סינטאב'ה אין לה ב'ינטאנה
פור אאי פאסו און מוג'אג'יקו, ב'יסטידו אינטירו די מאייה,
די קאנטאר לי דאב'ה גאנה, לי דישו איל סינב'י,

ייו קון מי גאלאנה מי קיירו איר

אה! סוב'י אריב'ה פאסטור לינדו, גואדראס די לוס מיס ב'ינייס,
ייו כון אב'לו קון מוזיקס, לי דישו איל סינב'י:

ייו כון מי גאלאנה מי קירו איר

אה! סוב'י אריב'ה פאסטור לינדו, קומיראס אי ב'יב'יראס,
גואדראס די מיס קאב'יאוס, ייה טאן לינדוס אי טאן ב'יליוס,
קואנדו לוס קיטו אה פיינאר, איל סול איספונטה אין איליוס,
ב'ה איספורקאטי קון איליוס, לי דישו איל סינב'י:

ייו כון מי גאלאנה מי סירו איר

לה! סוב'י אריב'ה פאסטור לינדו, קומיראס אי ב'יב'יראס,
גואדראב' די לאב' מים קאראס, ייה טאן לינדאס קולוראדאס,
אין איל פואיגו סיאן קימאדאס, לי דישו איל סינב'י:

ייו כון מי גאלאנה מי קירו איר

אה! סוב'י אריב'ה פאסטור לינדו, קומיראס אי ב'יב'יראס,
גואדראס די לוס מים דידוס, ייה טאן לינדוס אלאסינייאדוס,
אין איל פואיגו סיאן קימאדוס, לי דישו איל סינב'י:

ייו כון מי גאלאנה מי כיירו איר

ב'אטי, ב'אטי, פאסטור ניגרו, פירוס קומאן טוס אוב'יזאס,
טו מוזיר קי קאזי קון אוטרו, לי טוב' ליזוב' ב'ינגאן לין מי מיזר
מאלדיסייון די מוזיר מאלה, נו מי אלקאנסה אמי:

ייו קון מי גאלאנה מי קירו איר

רומאנסה קואטרו

איסטה נוג'י מיס קאב'אייירוס, דורמיר קון אונה סינייורה;
או דורמיר קון אונה סינייורה, און דיאה די לוס מיס דיאס,
נו טופי אוטרה קומו אילייה,
בלאנקה איס אי קולוראדה, אירמוזה קומו איס, לה איסטריאה;
אלה אבאשאדה די און ריאו, אי אלה סוב'ידה די און ב'אליי,
אינקונטרי קון מי ליזילדה, לה איז'ה דיל אימפיראדור,
קי ב'יניאה די לוס באנייוס, אי די לוס באנייוס די לאב'ארסי,
די לאב'ארסי אי אינטרינסארסי, אי די מודארסי אונה דילגאדה,
דישו לה קונדיסה אל קונדי, אי קונדי פורקי נון קאזאטיש,
קאזארי סי איל דייו קירי, אי קאזארי סי אל דייו לי פלאזי;
טומארי מוז'יר ג'יקיטה, אי ג'יקה דילה פוקה אידאד,
קי סיאה ג'יקה די אנייוס, אי די איל אינטינדימיינטו גראנדי,
קי סיאה אלטה סין ג'אפינים, אי אירמוזה סין אפ'ייטארסי,
לוס איז'יקוס קי מי פארייירי, מי אסימיז'ין אלה מאדרי,
פוקו מאס או פוקו מאנקו, קי מי אסימיז'ין אל פאדרי.

רומאנסה סינקו

און אמור טאן קירינסייוזה, קי אולב'ידאר נו לה פודיאה;
קי אולב'ידאר נון לה פודיאה, לה מאנייאניקה אי לה טאדרי,
אה ב'יז'יטאר ייה לה איאה !
סי לה טופאב'ה דורמיינדו, לה קוב'יז'אב'ה אי סי איאה;
סי לה טופאב'ה דיספיירטה אה פלאטיקאר סי לי מיטיאה;
לה ביז'אב'ה אי לה אבראסאב'ה, אי אה ייוראר סי לי מיטיאה,
די קי ייוראס קאטיב'אדה, די קי ייוראש בוז'ה גריאה;
טיניאס מאל די אמוריס, או איסטאש ריזין פרינייאדה;
נון טיניאס מאל די אמוריס, ני איסטאב'ה ריזין פרינייאדה;
סי ב'ו לו קונטו איל בואין ריי, אפ'יאריש מיס פאלאב'ראס;
ייו פ'ואי קריאדה אין סיב'יאה, אי אינטרי בואינה ג'ינטי אונוראדה,
און קאב'אלייירו אנדאלוזו, קי די מי סי נאמוראב'ה;
איסקאב'יריקה לי איזו, דיבאשו די סוס ב'ינטאנאס,

פארה קי סופה אי קי אבאשי, קומו סי ייב'ארה סו קאזה,
טריס נוג'יס דורמייו קון איליה, לי פאריסייו טריס סימאנאס;
אה פין די לאס טריס נוג'יס, סי פואי אה בושקאר מואיצ'ה אמאדה;
איליה סי פואי דיטראס די איל, פור ב'יר סי אירה נואיס גאנאנסה.

רומאנסה סייש

איסטאב'ה לה ריינה איזאבילה, אי אין סו באסטידור לאב'ראנדו;
אי אין סו באסטידור לאב'ראנדו, אגוז'יקה די אורו אין מאנו ,
אי און פינדון די אמור לאב'ראנדו;
קואנדו לי קאאי לה אגוז'ה, קואנדו לי קאאי איל דידאלי,
קואנדו לי קאאי לה טיז'ירה, נו טייני קון קי קורטארי,
פור אאי פאסה פאריזי, איל סו ליינדו נאמוראדו;
פארה איסטי פואירטו פאריזי, קי אופיסייו ב'יש טומאדו;
מירקאדיר סו לה מי סינייורה, מירקאדיר אי איסקריב'אנו ;
טריס נאב'יס טינגו אין איל פואירטו, קארגאדאס די אורו אי ברוקאדו;
לה נאב'י קי ייו ב'ינגו, אב'ייה און ריקו מאנסאנו;
קי איגואלה מאנסאנאס די אמורים, אין איב'יירנו אי אינב'יראנו ;
סי איסטו איס ב'ירדאד פאריזי, גוזארייה איס די לו קונטאר;
סי ב'וס פאזיאה פאריזי, די ב'וס איר אה ב'יזיטאר;
ב'ינגאש אין בואינה אורה ריינה, ב'וס אי בואיסטרו ריינאדו;
דיסקי לה ב'ידו ב'יניר ארמו ב'יאס אי אב'יב'אנטו גאנגו,
די פארטי די פראנסייה, אה איליה סי לה ייב'ארון.

רומאנסה סייטי

סאליר קירי איל מיז די מאייו, אי איסטראר קירי איל די אפריל.
קואנדו איל טריגו איסטה אין גראנו, אי לאס פלורים קירין סאליר,
קואנדו איל קונדאלימארי, פארה פראנסייה קיזו איר,
קון סיגו איל סי ייב'אב'ה, אורה אי פאמה אי טאן גינטיל ,
אי קון סיגו איל סי ייב'אב'ה, אי און גופ'ליט די מארפ'יל,
ייה סי לו מיטי אין לה סו בוקה, נו לו סאב'יאה דיזיר ,
יין מאנאנסייו טאל גופ'ליטי, לאס דונזיאס קי די פור טי,
אי אוטראס טאנטאס יין לים דיירה, קי מי לו קיטין די אקי,

חי ייה לו קיטחן חה צ̈ינדיר, פור פלחסחס חי פור ג̃חרשים,
חי ביכגוכום לי דחצ̈חן פריקיין, כי חון חקפרו כי קוצ̈יר,
נחכטו פ̈וחי די צוקה חין צוקה, פ̈וחי חין צוקה די חמחדי,
חי חוטרחס טחכטחס ייה לי דיירה, קי מי לו טרחייגחן חקי;
ייה לו מיטין חין לה כו צוקה, חי ייה לו חימפיקחן חה ריטיבייר,
נחב נחצ̈יב קי חיקטחן חין פורטו, פריקטו לחב חזין צ̈יניר.
לה פחרידה קי חיקטה פחריכדו, פריקטו לה חזין פחריר

רומאנסה אוג'ו

לון דיל דיחה חי קלחרידחד, קי חיל דיחה מוס דחש חיל ...
חי לה כוג̈י קלחרו לונחר,
חי לה כוג̈י קלחרו לונחר, נחב מחנייחניקחב נחב חיקטריחב
חי קוחנדו קירי חלצ̈וריחר;
כי פחקילה טיחו חי קוצ̈רינו, ג̃ונטוס צ̈חן חה לון בחרחבחר.
קי קחצ̈חייוס ייצ̈חן די חון פריקיין, חי פור צ̈יר קיחל קוריחה ייחב.
קי קורי חונו חי קורי חוטרו, ג̃ונטוס צ̈חן חה חון בחרחבח-
חצ̈לחנדו צ̈חן חי פלחטיקחנדו. לו קי ליס חימפורטה מחב
חונה מירקיד לי רוגו טיחו, קוחל לה חצ̈יש די מטורגחר.
קי מי דים חה בלחנקה ניניה, פור מוזיר חי פור חיגוחל.
חיקטה מירקיד חיל מי קוצ̈רינו, לו צ̈ולה פוחידו חג̈יטחר.
קוחנדו צ̈ולה חצ̈ימה דחדו, לו לה קיזיטיש טומחר.
קי דחדה לה טינגו חין פ̈רחנסייה, פור סיין דובלחס חי חלגו מחב
קי דיספוזחדה לה טינגו חין פ̈רחנסייה, חי קון חיל קונדי חליגודחר.
גירילו סוש חיל מי קוצ̈רינו, חי לה פוחידים מויי ביין טומחר.
דים מי קחמיזה דילגחדה, סירמה חי פירלה חין לו קוייחר.
ייה כי חיקפחרטי חיל קחצ̈חיילו, חי ייה כי חיקפחרטי חי ייה כי לה.
פור קחיים קי חצ̈יחה ג̈יכטי, קחמינחצ̈ה די הצ̈חגחר:
פור נחם קחלייס קי לו חצ̈יחן ג̈ינטים, סינטילייחב חזיחה קחלנטחר.
קיין חים חיקטי מוכו פ̈רחנקו. קי לה סיבדחד צ̈ה חה דירידחר

פרוב׳רבייום אימפורטאנטים

א קיין אל דייו ייאמה, נונקה איסקלאמה,
קיין אל סיילו איסקופי, אין לה קארה לי קאיי,
קיין אינגלוטי אמארגו, נו איסקופי דולסי,
קיין אסיד לי אזי, אגואה דיל קאנייו ביבֿי,
קיין אטראס בֿייני, פור ראבֿו סי מיטי,
קיין אקומיטי, אין דיבֿדה סי מיטי,
ב קיין בֿה אי בֿייני, אלמה טייני,
ג קיין גאסטה אין לו סיקו, קומי אין לה מאר,
קיין גאסטה בֿיירנים, קומי שבת,
ד קיין דה אלה פואירטה, סיינטי סו ריפואיסטה,
קיין דה איל ביין אין סו בֿידה, מיריסי אפידריאדו,
קיין די אוטרו בֿיסטי, אינמידייו דילה קאליי לו דיזנודאן,
קיין דואירמי, נון אלקאנסה פיסקאדו,
קיין דה איל אספריקו, ני טאניין איל גֿופֿליטיקו,
קיין די לה מייל מאניאה, אלגו סי לי אפיגה,
ה קיין היס פאגאדור, איס פאטרון אין בולסה אז׳ינה,
קיין איס ריי, אין לה קארה סי בֿי.
קיין היס טינייוזו, איס בֿינטורוזו,
קיין היס לאדרון, קי סיאה די לוס פייזיס ליז׳ירוס,
ט קיין טייני טיז׳אדו די בֿידרו, קי נו ארוז׳י פיידרה אל בֿיזינו,
קיין טייני מארידו די סירבֿיר, נו דיבֿי די דורמיר,
קיין טייני מאניאס מיטי, קיין נו מירה די אינפֿריינטי,
קיין טייני קאבֿאייו אל אזיר , נו איס בֿירגואינסה די קאמינאר אה פיי,
קיין טראטה אי באראטה, סובֿי אי אבאשה,

קיין טי דייו ליג׳י טי דייו פ׳ייל, אי קיין טי דייו ספאנ׳אקי
טי דייו מ׳ייל,
קיין טי איזו קוזינירה, לה אספאראן אי לה פימיינטה,
קיין טודו בינאגרי ביב׳ייו, אי קיין טודו פאן מורייו,
קיין טוקה סאנגרי, נו מואירי אלה אמברי,
י קיין ייגה איל מאל, סי איגה איל מזראמאן,
ל קיין לי דיגואילי לה מואירה, קי סי ג׳אייה אנדי איל בירביר,
קיין לאזדרה, אלקאנסה,
קיין לאג׳ה לה קאג׳יסה דיל אמור, פיידרי לה ליש׳יאה א
איל שאג׳ון
מ קיין מירה אלה ג׳ינטי, נון ביג׳י קונטינטי,
קיין מאל פינסה, פארה סי סי לו פינסה,
נ קיין נו פיגה קון ישראל, פיגה קון ישמעאל,
קיין ניגרה סינה קירי סינאר, די נוג׳י אי אליסקורו קי לה
ג׳אייה אה בושקאר,
קיין ניגרו נאסי, ג׳אמאיי סי אינדיריגה,
קיין ניגרו ג׳ה אליגורנה, ניגרו ג׳ה פיאור טורנה,
ס קיין סי אזארג׳ה קון סוס מאנוס, קי נו ייורי,
קיין סארנודה, איל דייו לו איידה,
פ קיין פיידרי איל קאמינו ג׳ייזו, פיידרי איל ג׳ייזו אי איל מואיג׳ו,
קיין פ׳יניי אי אמאסה, נו לי רוג׳ים לה מאסה,
קיין פ׳ולי דילה מאלה הורה, ביג׳י קיין אנייוס,
ק קיין קירי ביג׳יר סאנו, קי קומה אי קי ביג׳ה אנדי **יוסף**
וארסאנו ,
קיין קומי אי איניגה, סי לי אזי מזראס,
קיין קומי דימאנייאנה, נו סי אינגאנייה,
קיין קיירי לו אג׳ינו, פיידרי לו פוקו אי לו מוג׳ו,
קיין קירי קאזאר קון מוסה, קי נו סי איספירי אלה ג׳יזים.

חיקטוק 5 בייׄנׄוׄק דילה חׄיל פחׄכידו

Achre tivhar outkarev yichkon hasséréha.

Barouh ata Adonaï éloénou meleh aolam acher Kidechanou bemisvotav vessivanou léahnisso bivrito chel Avraam avinou.

Barouh ata Adonaï éloénou meleh aolam chééhiyanou vekiyemanou veigianou la zeman azé

אשׁרי תיבחר ותקרב ישׁכון חציריך

דיקפוחׄים דילה דיטחׄק דוק ברכות

ברוך אתה ה׳ אלוהינו מלך העולם אשר
קדשׁנו במצותיו וציונו להכניסו בבריתו
שׁל אברהם אבינו
ברוך אתה ה״ אלהינו מלך העולם
שׁהחיינו וקימנו והגיענו לזמן הזה.

VIII
GU'ERTA DE ROMANSOS 'INPORTANTES
([Salonika], 1920)
(abbr. GRI)

גואירטה

די

רומאנסוס אינפורטאנטיס

אין דיטה ברושורה קונטייני לוס דיטוס ארטיקולוס

1 — אונזי רומאנסוס אינפורטאנטיס

2 — לאס ברכות די ברית מילה אין פ׳ראנסיס
אי אין לשון הקודש

3 — לאס קאנטיגאס אלאבאנסאס די טבריה

4 — איל נומברי דיל אאוטור יעקב יונה

אנייו — ליהודים היתה אורה ושמחה

פריסייו 1 פ׳י.

גואירטה

די רומאנסאס אימפורטאנטיס

רומאנסה אונה

אין לה סיב̃דאד די מארסילייה, אב̃ייה אונה לינדה דאמה, קי טוקאב̃ה אי סי אפֿייטאב̃ה אי סי אסינטאב̃ה אלה ב̃ינטאנה, פור אאי פאסו און מוג'אג'יקו, ב̃יסטידו אינטירו די מאלייה, די אב̃לאר לי דאב̃ה גאנה לי דישו איל סילב̃י:

ייו קון מי גאלאנה מי קירו איר

אה! סוב̃י אריב̃ה פאסטור ליגירו, קומיראס אי ב̃יב̃יראס, גוזאראס די מיס קאב̃ייוס, אס טאן לינדוס אי אס טאן ב̃יליוס, קואנדו לוס טומו אה פיינארי, איל סול איספונטה אין איליוס, ב̃ה אינ-פורקארטי קון איליוס, לי דישו איל סילב̃י:

ייו קון מי גאלאנה.....

אה! סוב̃י אריב̃ה פאסטור ליגירו, קומיראס אי ב̃יב̃יראס, גוזאראס די לאס מיס קאראס, ייה טאן לינדאס קולוראדאס, אין איל פואיגו סיאן קימאדאס, לי דישו איל סילב̃י:

ייו קון מי גאלאנה.....

אה! סוב̃י אריב̃ה פאסטור ליגירו, קומיראס אי ב̃יב̃יראס, גוזאראס די לוס מיס דידוס, ייה טאן לינדוס אי אלמינייאדוס, אין איל פואיגו סיאן קימאדוס, לי דישו איל סילב̃י:

ייו קון מי גאלאנה.....

קומפואיסטה אין לה אימפרימיריאה נוב"יל קאליי קאלאמין נו' 2 (אל פורטו)

— 2 —

אה! סובי חריבֿס ספחקטור נוכלו. גוחרדחם די לוס מיס בייזיס. ייו כון חבֿלו קון מוזירים, כי טיבנו חיל קילבֿי:

ייו קון מי גאלאנה.....

ב׳אטי! ספחקטור כיגרו. פירום קומחן טוס חוביזחס, טו מוזיר קי קחזו קון חוטרוס, חי טוס חיזום ביבנחן חין מי מיזם מחליסיון די פוטה בֿיזוס, כון מי חלזחנקס חמי:

יו קוז מי גאלאנה מי קירו איר

רומאנסה דוס

ליטעה רומחנסח חליירם חיל פחסחזי דילום מחנקיבוס קי חיב־
טחן קירבייכלו חל קירביקיו מיליטחר

אה! חיכלומי פור חיקטחק מחריס, כחביגי קון לס פורטונס, קחמי חין פיירלחק חזיכחס, חכדי כון מי קונוקיחן, חכדי כון קחכטחבֿס גחייו, כי מיכוס פירו מחחוליחן, חכדי ברחמיחס חיל ליחון חי לס ליחונס ריקפונדיחס:

אנדי! קריסי לס נחרחבֿס, חי חיל ליחון חי לס קירלס, חכדי קרי־כי לס יירבֿס קילריס, חי קובֿחס חי גרחבֿיחיכחס, חכדי קריפי כולס מיכודס. גוחדריחס דילחס קריחטורחס:

אה! ייוליי פחלכו חי טרחחיזור, קחבֿזחכטיס די לוס מיס מחליס, חיכנרלחטיס חין מי בֿחליר, חון דיחס די חיכבֿירלחכו, חקוזיטיס לס פלור די מי, לס חקוזיטיס חס גרפחכו חס גרחכו, קון טוס חבֿלחס דיליקחדחס, חי מי חיכגחכייחספטיס;

אה! לחמחס קי דירלחן די מי, לחס קי חמי מי קונוקיחן, קי קון מי קי קונורטחבֿחן מוגחבֿיקחס, סייכלו חיזה די קיין סו, מי קחזח־טים קון חון פולחכו, חיזו חירה די חון גוחירטילחכו, חי די לס מי גוחירטס:

— 3 —

אה! ייוליין בֿאמוס די אקי, די איסטי ארבֿול סין פֿלוריס, לובֿייא
קאייגה דילוס סיילוס, אי מוס מאטי.

רומאנסה טרים

איסטה נוג'י מיס קאבֿאליירוס, דורמיר קירו קון אונאס סינייורס
אי דורמיר קירו קון אונה סינייורה, און דינייה די לוס מיס דיאס, כון
טופי אוטרס קומו איליאס.

אי כון טופי אוטרס קומו איליאס, בלאנקה איס אי קולוראדה, אירמו-
זה קומו לה איסטריליה.

אי אירמוזה קומו לה איסטריליה, לה אבאמאלה די און ריאו, אי
אלה סובֿידה די און בֿאליי.

אי אלה סובֿידה די און בֿאליי, אינקונטרי קון מי איזילה, לה איזה
דיל אימפירדור.

אי לה איזה דיל אימפירדור, קי בֿיניאן די לוס באנייוס, אי דילוס
באנייוס די לאבֿארסי.

אי דילוס באנייוס די לאבֿארסי, די לאבֿארסי אי איכטרינסארסי, אי
די מודארסי אונה דילגאדה.

אי די מודארסי אונה דילגאדה, דימו לה קונדיסה אל קונדי, אי קונ-
די פונקי כון קאזאטים.

אי קונדי פונקי כון קאזאטים, קאזארי סי איל דייו קיירי, אי קאזארי
סי לה איל לי פלאזי:

אי קאזארי סי לה איל דייו לי פלאזי, טומארי מוזיר ג'יקיטה אי ג'י-
קה די לה בוקה אידאדי.

אי ג'יקה דילה פוקה אידאדי, קי סיאה ג'יקה די אנייוס, אי די איל
אינטינדימיינטו גראנדי:

— 4 —

אי די איל אינטינדימיינטו גראנדי, קי סיאס אלטה סין גאפינים אי אירמוזאס קין אפֿייטארסי:

אי אירמוזאס קין אפֿייטארסי, נוס איז׳יקוס קי מי פאריירי, מי אסי-מיז׳ין אלאס מאדרי:

אי מי אסימיז׳ין אלאס מאדרי, פוקו מאס או פוקו מאנקו, קי מי אסי-מיז׳ין אה איל פאדרי.

רומאנסה קואטרו

איסטאב״ה לה ריינה אילינה, אי אין סו באסטידור לאבֿראנדו:

אי אין סו באסטידור לאבֿראנדו, אגוז׳יקאס די אורו אין מאנו, אי און פינדון די אמור לאבֿראנדו:

אי און פינדון די אמור לאבֿראנדו, קואנדו לי קאייי לאס אגוז׳אס, אי קואנדו לי קאייי איל דידאלי:

אי קואנדו לי קאייי איל דידאלי, אי קואנדו לי קאייי לאס טיז׳ירה נון טייני קין קי קורטארי:

אי נון טייני קין קי קורטארי, פור אאי פאסו פאריזי, איל סו לינ-דו נאמוראדו;

אי איל סו לינדו נאמוראדו, פאראס איסטי פואירטו פאריזי, קי אופֿי-סייו אבֿים טומאדו:

אי קי אופֿיסייו אבֿים טומאדו, מירקאדיר סו לה מי סינייורה, אי מירקאדיר אי איסקריבֿאנו:

אי מירקאדיר אי איסקריבֿאנו, טריס נאבֿים טינגו אין איל פורטו, קארגאדאס די אורו אי ברוקאדו:

אי קארגאדאס די אורו אי ברוקאדו, לה נאבֿי קי ייו בֿינגו, אבֿיאה און ריקו מאנסאנו;

— 5 —

·אי אב̈יאה און ריקו מאנסאבו, קי איג̈אב̈ה מאנסאנאס די אמוריס,
אין אינב̈יירנו אי אין אינב̈יראנו:

·אי אין אינב̈יירנו אי אין אינב̈יראנו, קי סי איכסו אים ב̈ירדאד
פאליזי, לורייס אים די לו קונטארי:

·אי לורייס אים דילו קונטארי, סי ב̈וס פלאזיאה פאליזי, די ב̈וס
איר אה ב̈יזיטארי:

·אי די ב̈וס איר אה ב̈יזיטארי, ב̈ינגאס אין בואינאס אורה ריינה
ב̈וס אי ב̈ואיסטרו ריינאדו:

·אי ב̈וס אי ב̈ואיסטרו ריינאדו, דיקי לה ב̈ידו ב̈ינירי, ארמו ב̈ילאס
אי אליב̈אנטו גאנג̈ו:

·אי ארמו ב̈ילאס אי אליב̈אנטו גאנג̈ו, די פארטי די פאראנסייאס קי
לה ייב̈ארון:

רומאנסה סינקו

און אמור טאן קירינסייוזו, קי אולב̈ידאר כון לאס פואידילאס.
·אי קי אולב̈ידאר כון לאס פואידילאס, לה מאנייאניקה אי לה טארדי,
אה ב̈יזיטאר ייה לה איזה:

·אי אה ב̈יזיטאר ייה לה איזה, קי לה טופאב̈ה דורמיינדו, לה קא־
קונ̈יזאב̈ה אי סי איבה:

·אי לה קונ̈יזאב̈ה אי סי איבה, סי לה טופאב̈ה דישפיירטה, אה
פלאטיקאר סי לי מיטיאה:

·אי אה פלאטיקאר סי לי מיטיאה, לה דיזאב̈ה אי לה אבראסאב̈ה, אי
אה ייוראר סי לי מיטיאה:

·אי אה ייוראר סי לי מיטיאה, די קי ייוראש קאב̈אליירו, אי די קי
ייוראש בנה גראנדה:

— 6 —

אי די קי ייורבאן בוזאס גריאס, טריס מאל די אמורים, אי איטשא-
באן דיזין פריסייאדאס:

אי איספאנבאן דיזין פריסייאדאס, כון טריס מאל לאמורים, כי איב-
טאבאס דיזין פריסייאדאס:

אי כי איסטאבאס דיזין פריסייאדאס, סי בולו קונטו איל בואין די-
אפיאדים אה. מיס פאלאבראס:

אי אפיאדים אה מיס פאלאבראס, ייו בולו קריאדה אין סופיאה.
איכטרי בואינה ביכטי אוכורדאס:

אי איכטרי בואינה ביכטי אוכורדאס, און קאבאלייכו איכלאדרליטו,
קי די מי סי כאיורדאבה:

אי קי די מי סי כאמורדאבה, איסקאליריקה לי איזו ליבאמו די סוס
ביכטאנאס:

אי ליבאמו די סוס ביכטאנאס פארה קי אבוזה אי קי לבאמי קומו
סי פואירה סו קאזה:

אי קומו סי פואירה סו קאזה, טריס כוביס דורמייו קון איליים, לי
פאריקייו טריס סימאנאס:

אי לי פאריקייו טריס סימאנאס, אה לה פין די לאס טריס כוביס
סי פואי אה בוסקאר מואיבה אמאדה:

אי כי פואי אה בוסקאר מואיבה אמאדה. איליים סי פואי ליטראס
די איל. פור ביר סי אירה מאס גאלאנה:

רומאנסה סייש

טריס לאמאס באן אלה מילכה, אה איר לה אורלאסיון, איכטרי
איכמידייו לה מי איספוזה, לה קי מאס קיריאה ייו:

אי איכטרי איכמידייו לה מי איספוזה, לה קי מאס קיריאה ייו

— ז —

קאמיזה די אולאנדה ייבֿה. סירמה אי פירלה אל קאבֿיסון:

אי סירמה אי פירלה אל קאבֿיסון, סאייו ייבֿה קוזֿרי סאלייו, אי און סיבויי די אלטורכאסייון:

אי און סיבויי די אלטורכאסייון, סו קאבֿיסה אונה טורנגֿה, סוס קאבֿילייוס ברילים סון:

אי סוס קאבֿילייוס ברילים סון. לה סו פֿיזֿיקה איכארקאדה, ארקול די טירהר ייה סון:

אי ארקול די טירהר ייה סון, לוס סוס אוזֿוס ג׳יקיטיקוס, איספי-זֿוס די איסטאמבול:

אי איספיזֿוס די איסטאמבול. לאס סוס קאראס קורולאדאס. מאנסא-נאס די איסקופייה סון:

אי מאנסאנאס די איסקופייה סון. סו נאריז אפירפֿילאדה, פינדולה די איסקריבֿיר ייה סון:

אי פינדולה די איסקריבֿיר ייה סון, לה סו בוקה ג׳יקיטיקה, נון לי קאבֿי און פינייון:

אי נון לי קאבֿי און פינייון, סוס דיינטיס טאן מינודיקוס, פירלה די אינפֿילאר ייה סון:

רומאנסה סייטי

סאליר קיירי אל מאר די מאיו, אי אינטראר קיירי אל מאר די אבֿ-ריל, קואנדו אל טריגו איסטה אין גראנו, אי לאס פֿלוריס קירין סאליר:

אי קואנדו אל טריגו איסטה אין גראנו, אי לאס פֿלוריס קירין סאליר, אי קואנדו אל קונדאלימארי, פארה פֿראנסייה קיזֿו איר:

אי קואנדו אל קונדאלימארי, פארה פֿראנסייה קיזֿו איר, קון סיגו אל סי ייבֿאבֿה. אונרה אי פֿאמה אי טאן ג׳ינטיל:

— 8 —

אי קון קירו ד כי ייבֿאבֿה, אונדה אי שאמה אי שאן בֿינבֿיל, אי און בֿואליטו די מארפיל, ייה קילו מיטי אין לה בוקה כון לה ספאבֿילה ליזיר;

אי ייה קילו מיטי אין לה בוקה, אי כון לה ספאבֿילה ליזיר, ייה מא-לאכייו שאל בֿואליטי, לאס דובלאס קי די פור טי;

אי ייה מאלאכייו באל בֿואליטו, לאס דובלאס קי די פור טי. אי אטו-כאס שאנטאס יו לי דירה. קי מי לו קיטין די אקי:

אי אוירדאס ניסטנאס יו לי דירה. קי מי לו קיטין די אקי, אי ייה לו קיטאן לה בֿינדירי. פור פלאסאס אי פור בֿארטים;

אי ייה לו קיטאן לה בֿינדירי, פור פלאסאס אי פור בֿארטים. ריבגוטס לי דאבֿאן פריקייו. כי און אספרו כי קוביר;

אי ריבגוטס לי דאבֿאן פריקייו כי און אספרו כי קוביר, שאלבֿו סולי די בוקה אין בוקס. סולי אין בוקס די אמאלי;

אי באלבו סולי די בוקה אין בוקס, סולי אין בוקס די אמאלי אי אוירדאס שאנטאס יו לי דירה, קי מי לו טראייגאן אקי

רומאנסה אוג׳י

פור לוס פאלאסייוס די קארלו, כון פאסאן סי כון בֿוגארי.

אי כון פאסאן כי כון בֿוגארי, כון בֿוגאן פלאטאס כי אורו כי כון דיאס אי קיבֿדאדיס.

אי כי כון דיאס אי קיבֿדאדיס, גאנו קאיירו אה גאייפירו, סוס די-אס אי סוס קיבֿדאדיס.

אי סוס דיאס אי סוס קיבֿדאדיס, גאנו גאייפירו אה קארלו, אי אה לה סו מוגיר ריאלי.

אי לה סו מוג׳יר ריאלי, מאס באליאה אה פידריראס, אה פידרירלה קי קן גאנארי.

— 9 —

אי אס פילדירלס קי כון גאנאלי, סוב'רינו איל מי סוב'רינו אי איל מי סוב'רינו קארדנאלי.

אי איל מי סוב'רינו קארדונאלי, ייו ב'וס קריאי ג'יקיטיקו איל דייו, ני איזו באראגאני

אי איל דייו ני איזו באראגאני, איל ני דייו באראב'יקס לוגס, אי אין נו פודירשו פ'ודירקס גראנדי.

אי אין נו פודירשו פ'ודירקס גראנדי, ייו ב'וס די אס באלאנקס קי־ייס, פור מוז'יר אי פור איגואלי.

אי פור מוז'יר אי פור איגואלי, פ'ודירים און אומברי קוב'אדו, ב'ולו דיסאמיס ייב'ארי.

אי ב'ולו דיסאמיס ייב'ארי, און דיאה אין לה מילסה, אין איל ב'יר־ג'יל די ב'ואיסטרו פאדרי.

אי אין איל ב'ירג'יל די ב'ואיסטרו פאדרי, קוז'ינדו ראמאס אי פ'לוריס, מאנייאנאס די סאנב'יגואלי.

אי מאנייאנאס די סאנב'יגואלי, מאלדיזיין ב'וס איז'ו איל מי סוב'רינו, סי כון לה ב'אמה אס בושקארי.

אי סי כון לה ב'אמה אס בושקארי, פור לוס קאמינוס קי ב'אמה, כון טודוס כי ב'ינו כי פארי.

אי כון טודוס ב'ינו כי פארי, כי מינוס ליב'ידו אין בולסאס, פארה איל קאמינו גאסטארי.

אי פארה איל קאמינו גאספארי, כון ליאס סיב'אדאס אס לה מדאס כי קארני קרודה אל גאב'ילאנו.

אי כי קארני קרודה לל גאב'ילאנו, לה מוז'יר קי ב'וס טוב'יירלאס כון ב'וס גואדרי קרואילדאד.

אי כון ב'וס גואדרי קרואילדאד, לוס אוז'וס קי ב'וס מיראירי, כון ב'וס קיטוקאן פור פאדרי.

— 10 —

רומאנסה מואיב״י

און דיל דיאה אי קאנדילארה, קי איל דיאה ... דאה איל קולי א
לה נוג׳י קלארו לונארי.

אי לה נוג׳י קלארה לונארי. לאס מאנייאניקאס לאה. איסטריאס, אי
קואנדו קירי אלבוריאר.

אי קואנדו קירי אלבוריאר, סי פאסיאה ניאו די סו פאדרי, ג׳ונטוס
באן אה און באראבאר.

אי ג׳ונטוס באן אה און באראבאר, קי קאבאליירוס ייבאן די און
פריסייו, אי סו ביר קואל קוריאה מאס

אי סו ביר קואל קוריאה מאס, קי קורי אונו אי קורי אוטרו אי
ג׳ונטוס באן אה און באראבאר.

אי ג׳ונטוס באן אה און באראבאר, אבלאנדו אי פלאטיקאנדו לוקי
לים אימפורטה מאס.

אי לוקי לים אימפורטה מאס, אונה מירקיד לי כוגו עיאו. קואל אה
לה אבים די אטורגאר.

אי קואל אי לה אבים די אטורגאר, קי מי ליב לה בלאנקה ניניה.
סור מוזיר אי סור איגואל.

אי סור מוזיר אי סור איגואל, איסטה מירקיד איל מי פאדריכו, כון
בוס לה פואידו אטורגאר.

אי נון בולה פואידו אטורגארי. קואנדו בולה אביאה דאדו, כון לה
קיזיטים טומאר.

אי כון לה קיזיטים טומאר, קי דאדה לה טינגו אין פראנסייס סור
ביין כונבלאס אי אלגו מאס.

אי סור ביין כונבלאס אי אלגו מאס, ליקסוזאלה לה טינגו אין פראנ-
סייה, אי קון איל קונדי אליגוראנאר.

— 11 —

אי קון איל קונדי אליגורנאל, גירירו סום איל מי סוב'רינו, אי לה פואידיס מויי ביין גאנאר.

אי לה פואידיס מויי ביין גאנאר, דיסטי קאמפוס דילגאדוס, סירמה אי פירלה אין סו קוייאר.

אי סירמה פירלה אין סו קוייאר, אי ייה סי איספארטי איל קאב'אליירו, אי ייה סי איספארטי אי ייה סי ב'ה.

אי ייה סי איספארטי אי ייה סי ב'ה. פור קאלייס קי אב'יאס ג'ינטיס קאמינאב'ה די אב'אגאר.

אי קאמינאב'ה די אב'אגאר, פור לאס קאלייס קי נון אב'יאס ג'ינטיב סינטיאס אזיאס סאלטאר.

אי סינטיאס אזיאס סאלטאר. קיין אים איסטי מונו קי לה סיב'דאד ב'ה דירוקאר.

רומאנסה דייז

סי פאסיאה פאסטור פ'יאיל, קון סו גאנאדו די אקיאס טאדרי.

אי קון סו גאנאדו די אקיאס טאדרי קון רימולינוס אי טרואינוס, אי לוס רילאמפאגוס מויי גראנדיס.

אי לוס רילאמפאגוס מויי גראנדיס, פינייור סינייור סי פיקי, איל מי גאנאדו נון לו פ'אאי.

אי איל מי גאנאדו נון לו פ'אאי; סי איל מי גאנאדו פיקו, לו קי נון אים מיאו איסקאפאמי.

אי לו קי נון אים מיאו איסקאפאמי. איסטו קי סינטיירון לאס נוב'יס סי ב'ולטארון פור אוטראס פארטיס.

אי סי ב'ולטארון פור אוטראס פארטיס. סי דאב'אן לי פינייס אין פינייס. אי פור אגואס קוריאס סאנגרי.

— 12 —

לג סור אגואס קוריאס פ'אגרי. ייראב'אן לוס קאפיטאנים, אי טודוס
לוס קי אין לה מאר,

לד טודוס לוס קי אין לה מאר, און גראנדי אי אינגרי אליירו,
קי אין איליאס כון אג'יטארי,

לה קי אין איליאס כון אג'יטארי, סינייורה לה מי סינייורה די איס-
טה פ'ירטונה איסקאפארי.

לו די איסטה פ'ירטונה איסקאפארי, סי די איסטה פ'ורטונה די איס-
קאפארה, קון אורו ג'ם איסקורונארי,

לז קון אורו ג'ם איסקורונארי, איסטו סינטייו איל פאטרון די אי
ירודה. לאס אגואס מאס קונפ'ירטייארי,

לח לאס אגואס מאס קונפ'ירטייארי, ג'אמי ג'אטי, טו מאריאס קי קון
כי כון לירוגארי:

לט קי קון כי כון אירוגארי, איריאס אין פארדי פילאהו קי מו-
ג'אס מארמאג'יאס איס אוי;

מ מוג'אס מארמאג'יאס מוס אוי, מי לאס אגס די קונטינו, די פרי-
סה קי כון די גואדרי.

מא די פריסה קי כון די גואדרי, איל קי קיירי לה כאזי דיל גולפו,
קומו לה פארידה קי פארי;

מב קומו לה פארידה קי פארי, אנסי אגס קון לוס פאזימוס די פרי-
סה קי כון די גואדרי.

מג די פריסה קי כון די גואדרי; קי מיגומוס קי כון סי דיזיספירין,
כי קי פיידראן לה איספיראנסה;

מד כי קי פיידראן לה איספיראנסה. קי ליספוגיס די לאס פ'ורטונאס
איל מאר מאנדי לה בונאנסה.

— 13 —

רומאנסה אונזי

בי פחביחס לחק לוצי פלוריס, חינטרי חינבחידייו חונה קונבה,
דיפו לה קונבה חלחק פלוריס חויי חיס דיחה די פחקיחרי.
בי פחסיחס לה לינדה דינה פור לוס קחמפוס דיל ריי חמור
חה קולומברה דיל מוחלו, קי כון לה חימפחכייחרה חיל קול:
קון פחבור די סוס לוצי חירמחנוס קחמינחבה קין טימור:
חירימוס, חה חונה טיינדה, פינקחנדו קי כון חיי בחרון:
ביקטו לה חוביירה ביקטו, שכס חיל חיזו דיל ריי חמור:
חייגוסי פחרה חילייה, טריס פחלחבריקחס לי חבלו:
לינדה סוס לה לינדה דינה, קין חפייטי חי סין קולור;
לינדוס סון לוס בוחיקטידוס חירמחנוס. מחס קי בוס ליינחס לה פליני
חה סין לינדוס חו כון סין לינדוס, חויי ויי לוס גוחדרו חיל דייו;
חייגוסי פחרה חילייה, חיזו לוקי כון חיס רחזון:
בי חיספחרטי לה לינדה דינה. קי בה חנדי חיל סו קירייר:
חיל פחדרי דיס קי לו סופו, חריביביר לה כחליי:
קיין בוס דימודו לה קחרה, חי קיין בוס דימודו לה קולור;
בו לה דימודו חיל חיירי חו בו לה דימודו חיל סול;
ני מי לה דימודו חיל חיירי, ני מי לה דימודו חיל סול,
מי לה דימודו חון מוחביקו שכם חיל חיזו דיל ריי חמור:
חיקטו קי סיקטייו חיל פחדרי קחחמיינטירוס לי מחבלו.

* * *

יבר ני יימחטיק מוס קונלינחקטיס חה חיל מונעל, קי נודו דיין מוכלו חיקבחיוס די על. קי נו קיק פור קיימפרי נכה קלה ועל:

עיל בינלחדים מוס חגחק הגורה חין חיקטח חיבה, קי חין חיספיי פוחיגו כון מוס קידו כי רויחדור כי פליבה. חי נחיגדיין לה קריבה חה כוס מוס חיקטריבה:

כרוב סי חיל קי ני יימחה די קורחקין. ני רוגחמיב בחקעחמי קי מוס קומסנחה מוחיקטרה רלון. כוחיקטרה פורטונה חבולניים די נריקטיזה חה בבין.

בלוך סוס ייחמחר חזוס כביס קומטרה נחעורה. ני רוגחיוב דייר קי לה קחריזה די חגורה חיי חכייוב קי עורה קי מוס חיקקחפיב די נחבטה ביקחעורה:

דין. נאביגחרי לי קומסנחב מונגחק בוס חרי, פור חורחק חה נילוב מיס קליחיגטיס חדיחו בוס ליכו.

— 14 —

אקי קונטייני לאס ברכות די ברת מילה אין ליטראס פראנסיזאס
אי לשון הקדש

Achré tivhar outkarev yichkon hasséréha

Barouh ata Adonaï éloénon meleh aolam acher Kidechanou bemisvotav vessivanou léahnisso bivrito chel Avraam avinou.

Barouh ata Adonaï éloénou meleh aolam chééhiyanou vekiyemanou veigianou la zeman aze.

איסטוס ה׳ בייכזוס דיכס איל פאכילו

אשרי תיבחר ותקרב ישכון חציריך

דיספואיס דיכס ליטאק לוס ברכות

ברוך אתה ה״ אלוהינו מלך העולם אשר קדשנו במצותיו וציונו להכניסו בבריתו של אברהם אבינו

ברוך אתה ה״ אילוהינו מלך העולם שהחיינו וקיימנו והגיענו לזמן הזה.

קאכודאכלו אל פאכילו קון בסימן טוב

— 15 —

אורדינאר קירו אין קאנטאר. קונטרי די איל דייו אינקומינסאר. קי
טומו אינקומינסאר לה סיב'ידאד די טבריה:

בינדיגו סיאה סו נומברי, אין בוקה די טודו אומברי, קי אינקומינסי אי
קי קונטרי לאס קיבלאל די טבריה: פאסאריס

גון עשטאבאן אליגריאס, אגאן פור טודאס לאס ביאס, קי סי פרגוניאבה
אין סוס דיאס, לה טיירה די טבריה: פאסאריס

דין לואוריס אה איל דייו, בוינו איל קי אים ביניו, פורקי סי אלרי-
ביביין, איל לוגאר די טבריה: פאסאריס

הילייס אים גראנדי די אמאס, טודו איל קי לה בי לה אמה, קי ני
אליגראס לס סו אלמאס, איל אייר די טבריה: פאסאריס

ויינדו מאן קלארו אביר, קי אים גראן קוזה די ביר, אי מוי מירב-
סו ביביר, איל אגואה די טבריה: פאסאריס

זכות גראנדי ייה טוביאמוס, קי אין איליאס קונביסיימוס, ביניינדו לי-
פרנטאמוס איל קבר די טבריה: פאסאריס

חזאכים קי סי גאסטאריאס, סיינטו קון אבאסטאריאס, אה קי ביניאן
גודיריאה אס מוראר אין טבריה: פאסאריס

טיימפו מונגו פואי פאסאדו, קי איסטאבה דיזיירטאדו, כי מניין איראס
אבוקאטאדו, (קומו אגורה) פור קדיש אין טבריה: פאסאריס

יס איספאנייה די איספינוס, אין לוגאר די אביר פינוס, אלאראמוס
סאביין איביסינוס, לאס בוטירטאס די טבריה: פאסאריס

כומו אבריס לאס אלאבאנסאס, אי סוס פרוטוס איספירנסאס, כי אין
ירושלים דאבה, לאס פרוטאס די טבריה: פאסאריס

לואוריס אה איל דייו לאריאמוס, סאבאבין לו ביכלידיאמוס, מוי פריס-
סו עוס אראטאריאמוס די ביינים די טבריה: פאסאריס

באסה איי קוזה די ולגאר, סאבריס לאס אומבריס אולגאר. כון איי אין
מיגאן לוגאר, לאס ליגאס די טבריה:

— 16 —

נון מי קידה כי ריפוזו, די אלאבאר אה מי גוזו, עאמביין די מיס איל פוזו, אין לה מאר די טבריה: פאסארים

סו סגואה טייני אוכה קוזה, קי איס מוכ׳ה ב׳ירטואוזה, קי לוגו קינקייה לי פוזה, קי לה ב׳ינ׳י אין טבריה: פאסארים

עיך כון טייני כי טאל, כי כי טופה ליקו מיטאל, אי איל **רב חיים ויטאל**, לאס ביב׳ייו אין טבריה: פאסארים

פרואבה פואי איסטאנטי, קי פואי קיזה די איכקאנטי, קינסיים לי ב׳ינו באסטאנטי. סופיטו אין טבריה: פאסארים

צאן איל קי איס גוזו, מירה מוכידה די אזיר, ב׳יניד אה טומאר פלאזיר, גאסטארלאס אין טבריה:

כון מוס פואי זוכה אה איסטו, מוס אמוספרי די ביין איל ריסטו, מויי פריסטו אי מויי קומפואיסטו, פארה פואר אין טבריה: פאסא
רים

ריאליס פירלאן ב׳ינידוס, לוס קי איסטאן איספארטידוס, אה קי פירלאן אקוז׳ידוס, אין פלאסאס די טבריה: פאסארים

שירפו אקי טורנארלאן, קי לוס **סנהדרין** בוזגארלאן, אי די אקי סי ריג׳ירלאן, פריימיר לין די טבריה: פאסארים

תסלות אה איל דייו לאבימוס, אי אה לה פאליסטינה מוס אירימוס, די אקי אה טבריה:

פאסארים אגורה אי ב׳יניס לאס קאליז׳אס דילה אימטירה. פאסארים אגורה אי ב׳יניס קומו איסטאן מוליסטרוס אירמאנוס אלה פירה:

פין

אימפרימיריאה · נוב״יל ·

קאליי באלאטין נומירו 2 אימיבליס דיל פורטו

LOCATIONS OF THE COPIES OF YONÁ'S CHAPBOOKS REPRODUCED IN THE PRESENT EDITION

I.	SGM:	Yivo Institute for Jewish Research (New York).
II.	GSA:	Instituto Arias Montano (Madrid).
III.	GRA:	Private library of R. Menéndez Pidal (Madrid).
IV.	LRI:	Private library of I. S. Révah (Paris).
V.	RSA:	Ben-Zvi Institute (Jerusalem).
VI.	BRI:	Ben-Zvi Institute (Jerusalem).
VII.	RHP:	Ben-Zvi Institute (Jerusalem).
VIII.	GRI:	JNUL 39A838 + JNUL 51A726 (Jerusalem).

BIBLIOGRAPHY

The following criteria have informed our search for Hispanic and extra-Hispanic analogs to Yoná's ballads. Our bibliography of Judeo-Spanish balladry is, to the best of our knowledge, exhaustive, although some publications may, of course, have escaped our attention. As to the modern Peninsular and Hispanic-American traditions, we have attempted to index all major collections and as many minor publications as time has permitted. This work is currently going forward and, hopefully, abundant additional references, especially to the complex and diffuse Spanish American and Catalan bibliographies, can be added to subsequent volumes of our collection. In the archaic *Romancero* we have usually limited our indexing to texts and references appearing in modern publications. For the various European linguistic traditions and their overseas extensions, we have sought to index either standard "canon" collections (Child, Bronson, DgF, DVM), text-type indexes (Coffin, Balys, Bērzkalne), comparative surveys (Seemann, Schirmunski), or exhaustive analyses (Leader; Vargyas, *Researches*; Baud-Bovy, *Textes*). Where such publications were not available, we selected one or more representative collections. Special attention has been accorded the Modern Greek tradition as a hitherto unknown source from which Eastern Judeo-Spanish ballad narratives derive. (See the commentary to no. 23 *supra,* and for further examples NSR, pp. 75-76, and our articles, "A Judeo-Spanish Derivative of the Ballad of *The Bridge of Arta,*" *JAF,* 76 [1963], 16-20; "Exclamaciones turcas y otros rasgos orientales en el Romancero judeo-español" [to appear in *Sef*]. We plan an extensive separate study on the problem of Greek ballad loans in the Judeo-Spanish *Romancero.*) More extensive indexing of

Pan-European balladry will be carried out in the preparation of subsequent volumes of our collection.

ABBREVIATIONS OF JOURNALS AND SERIAL PUBLICATIONS

AEA = *Anuario de Estudios Atlánticos,* Madrid - Las Palmas.
AEM = *Anuario de Estudios Medievales,* Barcelona.
AFA = *Archivo de Filología Aragonesa,* Zaragoza.
AFC = *Archivos del Folklore Cubano,* Havana.
ALAn = *Al-Andalus,* Madrid.
ALG = *Archiv für Litteraturgeschichte,* Leipzig.
ALM = *Anuario de Letras,* Mexico City.
ALV = *Archiv für Literatur und Volksdichtung,* Lahr, Baden.
AnFFE = *Anales de la Facultad de Filosofía y Educación, Universidad de Chile, Sección de Filología,* Santiago de Chile.
AnM = *Anuario Musical,* Barcelona.
AO = *Archivum,* Oviedo.
AUCh = *Anales de la Universidad de Chile,* Santiago de Chile.
AVF = *Archivos Venezolanos de Folklore,* Caracas.
BAAEE = *Biblioteca de Autores Españoles,* Madrid.
BAE = *Boletín de la Real Academia Española,* Madrid.
BAH = *Boletín de la Real Academia de la Historia,* Madrid.
BBMP = *Boletín de la Biblioteca Menéndez Pelayo,* Santander.
Ber = *Berceo,* Logroño.
BFL = *Boletim de Filologia,* Lisbon.
BHi = *Bulletin Hispanique,* Bordeaux.
BHS = *Bulletin of Hispanic Studies,* Liverpool.
BHTP = *Bulletin d'Histoire du Théâtre Portugais,* Lisbon.
BIEA = *Boletín del Instituto de Estudios Asturianos,* Oviedo.
BIF = *Boletín del Instituto de Folklore,* Caracas.
BN = *Blanco y Negro,* Madrid.
Brasilia = *Brasilia,* Coimbra.
Bs = *Biblos,* Coimbra.
BUG = *Boletín de la Universidad de Granada,* Spain.
CE = *Cultura Española,* Madrid.
Clav = *Clavileño,* Madrid.
CuA =*Cuadernos Americanos,* Mexico City.
CuC = *Cuba Contemporánea,* Havana.
Davar = *Davar,* Buenos Aires.
DCELC = J. Corominas, *Diccionario crítico etimológico de la lengua castellana.*
DL = *Douro Litoral,* Oporto.
EETS = *Early English Text Society,* London.
EMP = *Estudios dedicados a Menéndez Pidal,* Madrid, 1950-1957.

EMu = *Ethnomusicology,* Middletown, Connecticut.
ER = *Estudis Romànics,* Barcelona.
FA = *Folklore Americas,* Los Angeles.
FICU = *Folklore: Boletín del Departamento de Folklore del Instituto de Cooperación Universitaria de los Cursos de Cultura Católica,* Buenos Aires.
Fil = *Filología,* Buenos Aires.
H = *Hispania,* Baltimore.
HCA = *L'Hellénisme Contemporain,* Athens.
HMP = *Homenaje a Menéndez Pidal,* Madrid, 1925.
HR = *Hispanic Review,* Philadelphia.
Ilustração Trasmontana = *Ilustração Trasmontana,* Oporto.
Ilerda = *Ilerda,* Lérida.
JAF = *Journal of American Folklore,* Philadelphia.
JFI = *Journal of The Folklore Institute,* Bloomington.
JPh = *Journal of Philology,* Cambridge, England.
JREL = *Jahrbuch für Romanische und Englische Literatur,* Berlin.
JS = *Le Judaïsme Séphardi,* London.
JVF = *Jahrbuch für Volksliedforschung,* Berlin.
Laog = *Laografía,* Salonika.
LR = *Les Lettres Romanes,* Louvain.
MAe = *Medium Aevum,* Oxford.
MEAH = *Miscelánea de Estudios Árabes y Hebraicos,* Granada.
Mélusine = *Mélusine,* Paris.
MHRA = *Bulletin of the Modern Humanities Research Association,* London.
MLF = *The Modern Language Forum,* Los Angeles.
MLN = *Modern Language Notes,* Baltimore.
MLQ = *Modern Language Quarterly,* Seattle.
MPh = *Modern Philology,* Chicago.
NBAE = *Nueva Biblioteca de Autores Españoles.*
NRFH = *Nueva Revista de Filología Hispánica,* México City.
PMLA = *Publications of the Modern Language Association of America,* Baltimore.
QIA = *Quaderni Ibero-Americani,* Turin.
RABM = *Revista de Archivos, Bibliotecas y Museos,* Madrid.
RBC = *Revista Bimestre Cubana,* Havana.
RBFo = *Revista Brasileira de Folclore,* Rio de Janeiro.
RChHG = *Revista Chilena de Historia y Geografía,* Santiago de Chile.
RDM = *Revue des Deux Mondes,* Paris.
RDTP = *Revista de Dialectología y Tradiciones Populares,* Madrid.
REE = *Revista de Estudios Extremeños,* Badajoz.
REJ = *Revue des Études Juives,* Paris.
Rěšumôə = *Rěšumôə,* Tel-Aviv.
Revista Ibérica = *Revista Ibérica,* Madrid.
RF = *Romanische Forschungen,* Köln.
RFE = *Revista de Filología Española,* Madrid.

RFH = *Revista de Filología Hispánica,* Buenos Aires.
RFLC = *Revista de la Facultad de Letras y Ciencias, Universidad de la Habana.*
RHi = *Revue Hispanique,* Paris.
RHM = *Revista Hispánica Moderna,* New York.
RIHGB = *Revista do Instituto Histórico e Geográfico Brasileiro,* Rio de Janeiro.
RL = *Revista Lusitana,* Lisbon.
RLC = *Revue de Littérature Comparée,* Paris.
RNC = *Revista Nacional de Cultura,* Caracas.
Ro = *Romania,* Paris.
ROcc = *Revista de Occidente,* Madrid.
RPF = *Revista Portuguesa de Filologia,* Coimbra.
RPh = *Romance Philology,* Berkeley.
RR = *The Romanic Review,* New York.
S = *Symposium,* Syracuse, New York.
SATF = *Société des Anciens Textes Français,* Paris.
Sef = *Sefarad,* Madrid.
SFQ = *Southern Folklore Quarterly,* Gainesville, Florida.
Sp = *Speculum,* Cambridge, Massachusetts.
StM = *Studi Medievali,* Turin.
TI = *Tribuna Israelita,* Mexico City.
UCPMPh = *University of California Publications in Modern Philology,* Berkeley - Los Angeles.
VR = *Vox Romanica,* Bern.
WF = *Western Folklore,* Berkeley.
Yeda^{c}-^{c}*Ām* = *Yeda*^{c}-^{c}*Ām,* Tel-Aviv.
ZRPh = *Zeitschrift für Romanische Philologie,* Tübingen.
ZVLRL = *Zeitschrift für Vergleichende Literaturgeschichte und Renaissance-Literatur,* Berlin.
ZVVk = *Zeitschrift des Vereins für Volkskunde,* Berlin.

BALLAD COLLECTIONS

EASTERN JUDEO-SPANISH:

Adatto [Schlesinger], E., *A Study of the Linguistic Characteristics of the Seattle Sefardí Folklore,* Master's thesis, Univ. of Washington, Seattle, 1935.

Algazi, L., *Chants séphardis,* London, 1958.

Armistead, S. G., and J. H. Silverman, "Dos romances fronterizos en la tradición sefardí oriental," *NRFH,* XIII (1959), 88-98.

———, "El romance de *Celinos y la adúltera* entre los sefardíes de Oriente," *ALM,* II (1962), 5-14.

Armistead, S. G., and J. H. Silverman: See also DRH, "Hispanic Balladry," NSR, SICh.

Attias = Attias, M., *Romancero sefaradí: romanzas y cantes populares en judeo-español,* Jerusalem, 1956; 2d ed., Jerusalem, 1961.

Attias, M., "Minhagê niśû'în bĕ-Śaloniki (Marriage Customs in Salonika)," *Edoth* (Jerusalem), I (1945-46), 28-35, 61-62.

Babini, I., "Romansa," *Voz Sefaradí* (Mexico City), II:13 (June 1967), p. 25.

Baruch, Kalmi, "Španske romanse bosanskih Jevreja," *Godišnjak* (Sarajevo-Belgrade, 1933), pp. 272-288.

Bassan [Warner], S., *Judeo-Spanish Folk Poetry,* Master's thesis, Columbia University, New York, 1947.

BdR = B. Yosef, Binyamin, *'El bukyeto de romansas,* Istanbul, 5686 (= 1926).

B. Yosef, Binyamin: See BdR, SR.

Benardete = Benardete, M. J., *Los romances judeo-españoles en Nueva York,* Master's thesis, Columbia University, New York, 1923.

Besso, H. V., "Matrimonios sefardíes de ayer," *JS,* no. 4 (May, 1954), 177-183; no. 5 (Nov., 1954), 198-200; no. 6 (March, 1955), 273-277.

Bidjarano, H., "Los judíos españoles de Oriente: Lengua y literatura popular," *Boletín de la Institución Libre de Enseñanza* (Madrid), IX (1885), 23-27.

BRI = Yoná, Y. A., *Brošura de romansas 'importantes,* Salonika, 1913.

Cantera Burgos, F., *Los sefardíes,* Madrid, 1960.

Cantera Ortiz de Urbina, J., *Los sefardíes* (*Temas españoles,* no. 252), Madrid, 1958; 2d ed. (*Temas españoles,* no. 352), Madrid, 1965.

Catalán, D.: See Menéndez Pidal, R., *Romancero tradicional,* Vol. III.

CBU = Larrea Palacín, A. de, "El cancionero de Baruh Uziel," *VR,* 18 (1959), 324-365.

Coello = Menéndez Pelayo, M., "Romances castellanos tradicionales entre los judíos de Levante," *Antología de poetas líricos castellanos,* IX, "Ed. Nac.," XXV (Santander, 1945), 387-439. We reference separately nos. 1-4, 6, 8-12, collected by Carlos Coello y Pacheco.

Danon, A., "Recueil de romances judéo-espagnoles chantées en Turquie," *REJ,* XXXII (1896), 102-123, 263-275; XXXIII (1896), 122-139, 255-268.

Díaz-Plaja, G., "Aportación al cancionero judeo español del Mediterráneo oriental," *BBMP,* XVI (1934), 44-61.

DRH = Armistead, S. G., and J. H. Silverman, *Diez romances hispánicos en un manuscrito sefardí de la Isla de Rodas,* Pisa, 1962.

Elnecavé, D., "Folklore de los sefardíes de Turquía," reprinted from *Sef,* XXIII (1963). References allude to the ballad numbers in Section III.

Estrugo, J. M., "Reminiscencias de la judería sefardí del cercano Oriente," *RDTP,* XIV (1958), 70-77.

Estrugo, J. M., *Los sefardíes,* Havana, 1958.

Galante, A., "Quatorze romances judéo-espagnols," *RHi,* X (1903), 594-606.

Gil = Gil, R., *Romancero judeo-español,* Madrid, 1911.

Giménez Caballero, E., "Monograma sobre la judería de Escopia," *ROcc,* VIII, No. LXXXI (1930), 356-376.

González-Llubera, Ig., "Three Jewish Spanish Ballads in MS. *British Museum Add.* 26967," *MAe,* VII (1938), 15-28.

Granell, M., "Rodas, la isla encantada," in C. A. Del Real, J. Marías, and M. Granell, *Juventud en el mundo antiguo* (*Crucero universitario por el Mediterráneo*) (Madrid, 1934), pp. 288-292.

GRA = Yoná, Y. A., *Gu'erta de romansas antiguas de pasatyempo* (title page lacking; before 1908?).

GRI = Yoná, Y. A., *Gu'erta de romansos 'inportantes,* [Salonika], 1920.

GSA = Yoná, Y. A., *Gu'erta de romansos 'importantes,* Salonika, before 1905.

Hemsi = Hemsi, A., *Coplas sefardíes* (*Chansons judéo-espagnoles*), 5 fascicles, Alexandria, 1932-1937.

Hemsi, A., "Sur le folklore séfardi," *JS,* 18 (April, 1959), 794-795.

———, "Évocation de la France dans le folklore séphardi," *JS,* 24 (July, 1962), 1055-1057, 1059; 25 (Dec., 1962), 1091-1093.

"Hispanic Balladry" = Armistead, S. G., and J. H. Silverman, "Hispanic Balladry among the Sephardic Jews of the West Coast," *WF,* XIX (1960), 229-244.

Idelsohn, A. Z., *Hebräisch-Orientalischer Melodienschatz. Band IV: Gesänge der orientalischen Sefardim,* Jerusalem-Berlin-Vienna, 1923.

Katz, I. J., *Judeo-Spanish Traditional Ballads from Jerusalem,* 2 vols., Ph. D. dissertation, University of California, Los Angeles, 1967.

———, "A Judeo-Spanish Romancero," *EMu,* XII (1968), 72-85.

Kayserling: See **Archaic Judeo-Spanish Incipits.**

Larrea Palacín, A. de: See CBU.

Levy = Levy, I., *Chants judéo-espagnols,* London, [1959].

Levy, I. J.: See SBS.

LRI = Yoná, Y. A., *Livriko de romansas 'importantes,* Sofia, 1908.

LSO = Molho, M., *Literatura sefardita de Oriente,* Madrid-Barcelona, 1960.

MacCurdy, R. R., and D. D. Stanley, "Judaeo-Spanish Ballads from Atlanta, Georgia," *SFQ,* XV (1951), 221-238.

Manrique de Lara, M., "Romances españoles en los Balkanes," *BN,* Vol. 26 (Jan. 2, 1916), no. 1285, 3 pages (no pagination).

Menéndez Pelayo = Menéndez Pelayo, M., "Romances castellanos tradicionales entre los judíos de Levante," *Antología de poetas líricos castellanos,* IX, "Ed. Nac.," XXV (Santander, 1945), 387-439.

Menéndez Pelayo, M.: See Coello.

Menéndez Pidal, G., *Romancero* ("Biblioteca Literaria del Estudiante," no. 25), 2d ed., Madrid, 1936.

Menéndez Pidal, R., "Un viejo romance cantado por Sabbatai Ceví," *Mediaeval Studies in Honor of Jeremiah Denis Matthias Ford* (Cambridge, Mass., 1948), pp. 183-190.

———, "El Romancero y los sefardíes," *TI,* V, no. 51 (Feb., 1949), pp. xxi-xxii.

———, *Romancero tradicional,* Vol. III, ed. D. Catalán (in press).

Menéndez Pidal, R.: See also MP, RoH.

Milwitzky, Wm., "El viajero filólogo y la antigua España," *Cuba y América* (Havana), XIX, no. 17 (July 23, 1905), 307-309, 325-327.

———, "Judeo-Spanish [Literature]," *Encyclopedia of Literature,* ed. J. T. Shipley (New York, 1946), 650-653.

Molho, M., "Cinq élégies en judéo-espagnol," *BHi,* XLII (1940), 231-235.

———, *Usos y costumbres de los sefardíes de Salónica,* Madrid-Barcelona, 1950.

Molho, M., "Tres romances de tema bíblico y dos canciones de cuna," *Comentario* (Buenos Aires), IV, no. 15 (April-May-June, 1957), 64-70.

Molho, M.: See LSO.

Morley, "A New Jewish-Spanish Romancero": See **Critical Works.**

MP = Menéndez Pidal, R., "Catálogo del romancero judío-español," *CE,* I (1906), 1045-1077; V (1907), 161-199. Republished in slightly abbreviated form in *El Romancero: Teorías e investigaciones* (Madrid, [1928]), pp. 101-183, and under the title "Romancero judíoespañol" in *Los romances de América y otros estudios,* 6th ed. (Madrid, "Austral," 1958), pp. 114-179.

Moya, I., "Romances judeo-españoles en Buenos Aires," in *Romancero,* 2 vols. (Buenos Aires, 1941), II, 255-259.

NSR = See **Critical Works.**

Patai, R., "Sephardi Folklore," in *The World of the Sephardim* (New York, 1960), pp. 22-36 (Herzl Institute Pamphlet, no. 15).

PTJ = See **Moroccan Judeo-Spanish.**

Pulido = Pulido Fernández, A., *Intereses Nacionales: Españoles sin patria y la raza sefardí,* Madrid, 1905.

RHP = Yoná, Y. A., *'Un remorso por la Hagādāh de Ḥag ha-Pesaḥ,* Salonika, 1915.

RoH = See **Critical Works.**

Romey, D., *A Study of Spanish Tradition in Isolation as Found in the Romances, Refranes, and Storied Folklore of the Seattle Sephardic Community,* Master's thesis, University of Washington, Seattle, 1950.

RSA = Yoná, Y. A., *Romansos,* n.p., before 1909.

Rubiato, M. T., "El repertorio musical de un sefardí," *Sef,* XXV (1965), 453-463.

San Sebastián = S[an] S[ebastián], P. José Antonio de, *Canciones sefardíes para canto y piano,* Tolosa, Spain, [1945 (?)].

Sánchez Moguel, A., "Un romance español en el dialecto de los judíos de Oriente," *BAH,* XVI (1890), 497-509.

SBS = Levy, I. J., *Sephardic Ballads and Songs in the United States: New Variants and Additions,* Master's thesis, University of Iowa, Iowa City, 1959.

Sciaky, L., *Farewell to Salonica: Portrait of an Era,* New York, 1946.

Shipley, J. T.: See Milwitzky, Wm.

SICh = Armistead, S. G., and J. H. Silverman, "Judeo-Spanish Ballads in a MS by Salomon Israel Cherezli," *Studies in Honor of M. J. Benardete* (New York, 1965), pp. 367-387.

SGM = Yoná, Y. A., *Sēfer gĕdûlaɵ Mōšeh,* n.p., 1891.

SR = B. Yosef, Binyamin, *Sēfer rĕnānôɵ,* [Jerusalem], 5668 (= 1908).

Spomenica = *Spomenica: 400 godina od dolaska jevreja u Bosnu i Hercegovinu (1566-1966),* Sarajevo, 1966.

UR = Uziel, B., "Ha-folklor šel ha-yĕhûdîm ha-sĕfāradîm," *Rĕšumôɵ,* V (1927), 324-337; VI (1930), 359-397.

UYA = Uziel, B., "Šālōš romansôɵ: Mi-pî yĕhûdîm sĕfāradîm," pp. 75-76; "Šālôš romansôɵ: Mi-pî yĕhûdê Sĕfārad," pp. 172-177; "Šĕɵê romansôɵ: Min ha-folklor ha-yĕhûdî ha-sĕfāradî," pp. 261-265, *Yedaᶜ-ᶜĀm,* II (1953-1954).

Uziel, B.: See CBU, UR, UYA.

Wiener, L., "Songs of the Spanish Jews in the Balkan Peninsula," *MPh,* I (1903-1904), 205-216, 259-274.

Yoná, Y. A.: See BRI, GRA, GRI, GSA, LRI, RHP, RSA, SGM.

Zara, R., "Romances judéo-espagnoles," *JS,* no. 1 (May, 1953), 32.

ARCHAIC JUDEO-SPANISH INCIPITS:

Aguilar, E., and D. A. De Sola, *The Ancient Melodies of the Liturgy of the Spanish and Portuguese Jews,* London, 1857.

ASW = See **Castilian.**

Avenary, H., "Études sur le Cancionero judéo-espagnol (XVIe et XVIIe siècles)," *Sef,* XX (1960). 377-394.

Danon: See **Eastern Judeo-Spanish.**

Frenk Alatorre, M., "El antiguo cancionero sefardí," *NRFH,* XIV (1960), 312-318.

Kayserling, M., *Biblioteca española-portugueza-judaica: Dictionnaire bibliographique,* Nieuwkoop, 1961.

Menéndez Pelayo, M.: See ASW.

Menéndez Pidal, R.: See RoH.

RoH = See **Critical Works.**

MOROCCAN JUDEO-SPANISH:

Alvar, M., "Romances de Lope de Vega vivos en la tradición oral marroquí," *RF,* 63 (1951), 282-305.

———, "El romance de Gerineldo entre los sefarditas marroquíes," *BUG,* XXIII (1951), 127-144.

———, "Cinco romances de asunto novelesco recogidos en Tetuán," *ER,* III (1951-1952), 57-87.

———, *Endechas judeo-españolas,* Granada, 1953; 2d ed., Madrid, 1969.

———, "Los romances de *La bella* [*en*] *misa* y de *Virgilios* en Marruecos," *AO,* IV (1954), 264-276.

———, "Amnón y Tamar en el romancero marroquí," *VR,* XV (1956), 241-258.

———, *Textos hispánicos dialectales: Antología histórica,* 2 vols., Madrid, 1960.

Alvar, M.: See also PTJ.

Arce, A., "Cinco nuevos romances del Cid," *Sef,* XXI (1961), 69-75.

Benardete = See **Eastern Judeo-Spanish.**

Benarroch Pinto, I., *El indiano, el kadi y la luna,* Tetuán, 1951.

Bénichou = Bénichou, P., "Romances judeo-españoles de Marruecos," *RFH,* VI (1944), 36-76, 105-138, 255-279, 313-381.

Bénichou, P.: See also BNE.

Benoliel, J., "Dialecto judeo-hispano-marroquí o hakitía," *BAE,* XIV (1927), 357-373 (Chap. XIII).

BNE = See **Critical Works.**

Catalán, D.: See RCan.

FN = See **Archaic Texts.**

Gil = See **Eastern Judeo-Spanish.**

Larrea = Larrea Palacín, A. de, *Romances de Tetuán,* 2 vols., Madrid, 1952.

Larrea Palacín, A. de, *Canciones rituales hispano-judías,* Madrid, 1954.

Levy = See **Eastern Judeo-Spanish.**

Martínez Ruiz, J.: See MRuiz.

Menéndez Pidal, R.: See FN, MP.

Milá y Fontanals, M.: See PHP.

Moya: See **Eastern Judeo-Spanish.**

MP = See **Eastern Judeo-Spanish.**

MRuiz = Martínez Ruiz, J., "Poesía sefardí de carácter tradicional (Alcazarquivir)," offprint from *AO,* XIII (1963), 79-215.

Ortega, M. L., *Los hebreos en Marruecos,* [1st ed.], Madrid, 1919; 3d ed., Madrid, 1929; 4th ed., Madrid, 1934.

PHP = See **Critical Works.**

PTJ = Alvar, M., *Poesía tradicional de los judíos españoles,* Mexico City, 1966.

Pulido = See **Eastern Judeo-Spanish.**

RCan = See **Canarian.**

Torner, "La canción tradicional española": See **Castilian.**

Torner, *Lírica hispánica*: See **Castilian.**

CASTILIAN:

Acevedo y Huelves, B., *Los vaqueiros de alzada en Asturias,* 2d ed., Oviedo, 1915.

Alonso Cortés, N.: See ART, RPC.

Amador de los Ríos, J., "Romanzen Asturiens aus dem Volksmunde zum ersten Mal gesammelt und herausgegeben," *JREL,* III (1861), 268-296; also published under the title: "Poesía popular de España: Romances tradicionales de Asturias," *Revista Ibérica,* I (1861), 24-51.

ART = Alonso Cortés, N., "Romances tradicionales," *RHi,* L (1920), 198-268.

ASW = Menéndez Pelayo, M., "Apéndices y suplemento a la *Primavera y flor de romances* de Wolf y Hoffmann," *Antología de poetas líricos castellanos,* IX, "Ed. Nac.," XXV, Santander, 1945.

Berrueta, M. D., *Del cancionero leonés,* León, 1941.

BTPE = *Biblioteca de las tradiciones populares españolas,* ed. A. Machado y Álvarez, 11 vols., I (Seville, 1883), II-VI (Seville, 1884), VII (Madrid, 1885), VIII-XI (Madrid, 1886).

Cabal, C., *Las costumbres asturianas: Su significación y sus orígenes,* Madrid, 1925.

Chacón y Calvo, "Romance de la dama y el pastor": See **Spanish American.**

Córdova y Oña, S., *Cancionero popular de la Provincia de Santander,* 4 vols., Santander, I (n.d.), II (1949), III (1952), IV (1955).

Cossío, J. M. de, "Romances recogidos de la tradición oral en la Montaña," *BBMP,* I (1919), 117-127, 171-179, 307-313; II (1920), 27-31, 69-75, 265-271.

Cossío, J. M. (and T. Maza Solano): See also RPM, RTO.

CPE = Gil, B., *Cancionero popular de Extremadura,* 2 vols., I, [1st ed.] (Valls, 1931), I, 2d ed. (Badajoz, 1961), II (Badajoz, 1956).

CPM = García Matos, M., with M. Schneider (Vols. I-II), J. Tomás Parés (Vol. III), and J. Romeu Figueras, *Cancionero popular de la Provincia de Madrid,* 3 vols., Barcelona-Madrid, 1951, 1952, 1960.

CVR = Menéndez Pidal, J., *Poesía popular: Colección de los viejos romances que se cantan por los asturianos en la danza prima, esfoyazas y filandones,* Madrid, 1885.

Durán, A.: See **Archaic Texts.**

Echevarría Bravo, P., *Cancionero musical popular manchego,* Madrid, 1951.

Espinosa, A. M., "Traditional Ballads from Andalucía," *Flügel Memorial Volume* (Stanford University, California, 1916,) pp. 93-107.

Estébanez Calderón, S. ("El Solitario"), *Escenas andaluzas,* Madrid, 1883.

Feito, J. M., "Romances de la tierra somedana," *BIEA,* XII (1958), 288-304; XIII (1959), 121-132.

Fernán Caballero, ¡*Pobre Dolores*! (*Obras completas,* VII), Madrid, 1906.

Fernández Núñez, M. F., "Folklore bañezano," *RABM,* XXX (1914), 384-422.

———, *Folk-lore leonés,* Madrid, 1931.

FN = See **Archaic Texts.**

Folk-lore Andaluz, El (Seville, 1882-1883). There are two paginations: pp. 1-64 + 1-523. Unless otherwise specified, references allude to the second pagination.

García de Diego, P., "Siete canciones infantiles," *RDTP,* VI (1950), 104-132.

García Matos, M., *Lírica popular de la Alta Extremadura,* Madrid, n.d.

García Matos, M., *et al.*: See CPM.

García Sanz, S., "Las *Ramas,*" *RDTP,* I (1945), 579-597.

Gil, B., "Folklore musical extremeño," *REE,* X (1936), 51-62, 183-192, 291-303.

———, "Canciones del folklore riojano recogidas por Kurt Schindler," reprinted from *Ber,* XI, no. 41 (Logroño, 1956).

Gil, B.: See also CPE, RPE, RTR.

González Palencia, A., "Del folklore aragonés: El romance de Gerineldo en Albarracín," *Aragón* (Zaragoza), V (1929), 23-24.

Goyri de Menéndez Pidal, M.: See RQDB-I, RQDB-II.

Güéjar = Martínez Ruiz, J., "Romancero de Güéjar Sierra (Granada)," *RDTP,* XII (1956), 360-386, 495-543.

Gutiérrez Macías, V., "Fiestas cacereñas," *RDTP,* XVI (1960), 335-357.

Hernáez Tobías, L., "Romancero caballeresco en La Rioja," *Ber,* VI (1951), 235-242.

Kundert, H., "Romancerillo sanabrés," *RDTP,* XVIII (1962), 37-124.

Ledesma, D., *Folk-lore o Cancionero salmantino,* Madrid, 1907.

Llano Roza de Ampudia, A. de, *Del folklore asturiano: Mitos, supersticiones, costumbres,* Madrid, 1922.

———, *Esfoyaza de cantares asturianos,* Oviedo, 1924.

Machado y Álvarez, A.: See BTPE.

Magaña, J., "Notas para un romancero religioso de La Rioja," *Ber,* II (1947), 445-461.

———, "Nuevas notas para un romancero religioso de La Rioja," *Ber,* VI (1951), 91-106.

Marín, I = Marín, P., "Contribución al Romancero español (Cinco versiones aragonesas)," *AFA,* III (1950), 261-273.

Marín, II = Marín, P., "Contribución al Romancero español (2 versiones aragonesas)," *AFA,* V (1953), 125-141.

Martínez Hernández, A., *Antología musical de cantos populares españoles y un suplemento de cantos populares portugueses,* Barcelona, 1930.

Martínez Ruiz, J.: See Güéjar.

Menéndez Pelayo, M.: See ASW, TRV.

Menéndez Pidal, G., *Romancero*: See **Eastern Judeo-Spanish.**

Menéndez Pidal, J.: See CVR.

Menéndez Pidal, R., *et al., Cómo vive un romance*: See **Critical Works.**

Menéndez Pidal, R., *et al., Romancero tradicional*: See **Archaic Texts.**

Menéndez Pidal, R.: See also FN.

Micrófilo = [J. A. Torre], *Un capítulo del folk-lore guadalcanalense,* Seville, 1891.

Milá = See **Catalan.**

Montalbán, R., *El corro de las niñas,* [Madrid, 1894].

Morán Bardón, C., *Poesía popular salmantina* (*Folklore*), Salamanca, 1924.

Munthe, Å. W., "Folkpoesi från Asturien," *Språkvetenskapliga Sällskapets i Upsala Förhandlingar* (Sept. 1885-May 1888): *Upsala Universitets Årsskrift*: *Filosofi, Språkvetenskap och Historiska Vetenskaper,* V (1887), 105-124.

Nuevo Zarracina, D. G., "Cancionero popular asturiano," *RDTP,* II (1946), 98-133, 246-277.

Pedrell, F., *Cancionero musical popular español,* 4 vols., I-II (2d. ed., Barcelona, n.d.), III (Valls, n.d.), IV (Valls, 1922).

Pérez de Castro, J. L., "Nuevas variantes asturianas del Romancero hispánico," *RDTP,* XVI (1960), 477-481.

Pérez Clotet, P., and G. Álvarez Beigbeder: See RSC.

Petit Caro, C.: See QRA.

Poncet y de Cárdenas, C., "Romancerillo de Entrepeñas y Villar de los Pisones," *RHi,* LVII (1923), 286-314; reprinted, with an additional appendix, in *AFC,* III (1928), 121-154. We cite from the later printing.

Primavera = See **Archaic Texts.**

Puig Campillo, A., *Cancionero popular de Cartagena,* Cartagena, 1953.

QRA = Petit Caro, C., *Quince romances andaluces,* Seville, 1946.

Rodríguez Marín, F., *Cantos populares españoles,* 5 vols., Madrid, n.d.

RPC = Alonso Cortés, N., *Romances populares de Castilla,* Valladolid, 1906.

RPE = Gil, B., *Romances populares de Extremadura recogidos de la tradición oral,* Badajoz, 1944.

RPM = Cossío, J. M. de, and T. Maza Solano, *Romancero popular de La Montaña*: *Colección de romances tradicionales,* 2 vols., Santander, 1933-1934.

RQDB-I = Goyri de Menéndez Pidal, M., "Romances que deben buscarse en la tradición oral," *RABM,* X (1906), 374-386; XI (1907), 24-36. Offprint: Madrid, 1907.

RQDB-II = Goyri de Menéndez Pidal, M., *Romances que deben buscarse en la tradición oral,* Madrid, [1929] (published as a booklet together with E. M. Torner, *Indicaciones prácticas sobre la notación musical de los romances*).

RSC = Pérez Clotet, P., and G. Álvarez Beigbeder, *Romances de la Sierra de Cádiz,* Larache, 1940.

RTCN = *Romances tradicionales y canciones narrativas existentes en el Folklore español (incipit y temas),* Barcelona: Instituto Español de Musicología, 1945.

RTO = Cossío, J. M. de, *Romances de tradición oral,* Buenos Aires-Mexico City, 1947.

RTR = Gil, B., "Romances tradicionales de La Rioja," reprinted from *Ber,* XVII and XVIII, Logroño, 1962.

Sampedro: See **Galician.**

Sánchez Fraile, A., *Nuevo cancionero salmantino: Colección de canciones y temas folklóricos inéditos,* Salamanca, 1943.

Schindler, K., *Folk Music and Poetry of Spain and Portugal (Música y poesía popular de España y Portugal),* New York, 1941. References allude to the ballad numbers in the section "Romances y relaciones," pp. 46-116.

Sevilla, A., *Cancionero popular murciano,* Murcia, 1921.

Teresa León, T., "Romances," *RDTP,* II (1946), 489-492.

Torner, E. M., *Cancionero musical de la lírica popular asturiana,* Madrid, 1920.

———, *Cuarenta canciones españolas armonizadas,* Madrid, 1924.

———, "Del folklore español: Persistencia de antiguos temas poéticos y musicales," *BSS,* I (1924), 62-70, 97-102.

———, "La canción tradicional española musicalmente considerada," in *Folklore y costumbres de España,* ed. F. Carreras y Candi, II, 2d ed. (Barcelona, 1934), 2-166.

———, "Índice de analogías entre la lírica española antigua y la moderna," *S,* I:1 (1946), 12-33; I:2 (1947), 4-35; I:3

(1947), 84-107; II:1 (1948), 84-105; II:2 (1948), 221-241; III:2 (1949), 282-320; IV:1 (1950), 141-180.

Torner, E. M., *Lírica hispánica: Relaciones entre lo popular y lo culto,* Madrid, 1966.

———, *El folklore en la escuela,* 3d ed., Buenos Aires, n.d.

Torre, J. A.: See Micrófilo.

TRV = See **Critical Works.**

Vergara, G. M., *Cantares populares recogidos en diferentes regiones de Castilla La Vieja y particularmente en Segovia y su tierra,* Madrid, 1912.

———, "Algunos romances populares de carácter geográfico recogidos en diferentes comarcas de España," *Boletín de la Sociedad Geográfica Nacional,* LXXIV (1934), 87-93.

Wolf, F. J., and C. Hofmann: See *Primavera.*

CANARIAN:

Catalán, D.: See RCan.

Cuscoy, L. D., *Folklore infantil* (*Tradiciones Populares,* Vol. II), La Laguna de Tenerife, 1943.

Espinosa, A., *et al., Folklore isleño: Romancero canario* (*Antiguos romances tradicionales de las Islas*), Santa Cruz de Tenerife, n.d. (Introduction dated Jan. 1932).

Morales, M., and M. J. López de Vergara: See RCan.

Pérez Vidal, J., "Romancero tradicional canario (Isla de La Palma)," *RDTP,* V (1949), 435-470; VI (1950), 554-573; VII (1951), 266-291, 424-445.

RCan = Morales, M., and M. J. López de Vergara, *Romancerillo canario: Catálogo-manual de recolección,* La Laguna, n.d. Introduction ("La recolección romancística en Canarias") by Diego Catalán (pp. [3-35]) dated May 1955.

SPANISH AMERICAN:

ASW = See **Castilian.**

Aramburu, J., *El folklore de los niños: Juegos, corros, rondas, canciones, romances, cuentos y leyendas,* 2d ed., Buenos Aires, [1944].

Bayo, C., "La poesía popular en la América del Sur," *RABM*, VI (1902), 43-49.

———, "Cantos populares americanos: El romance en América," *RHi*, XV (1906), 796-809.

———, *Poesía popular hispano-americana: Romancerillo del Plata (Contribución al estudio del Romancero ríoplatense)*, Madrid, 1913.

Bertini, G. M., *Romanze novellesche spagnole in America*, Turin, 1957.

Cadilla de Martínez, M., *Juegos y canciones infantiles de Puerto Rico*, San Juan, Puerto Rico, 1940.

Campa, A. L., *The Spanish Folksong in the Southwest (The University of New Mexico Bulletin: Modern Language Series*, Vol. 4, no. 1), Albuquerque, 1933.

———, "Bernal Francés y la esposa infiel," *FICU*, II:4 (1941), 35-36.

———, *Spanish Folk-poetry in New Mexico*, Albuquerque, 1946.

Carrera, G. L., "Una nueva versión venezolana del romance de Blancaniña," *BIF*, III:7 (1960), 277-290.

Carrizo, J. A., *Cancionero popular de Salta*, Buenos Aires, 1933.

———, *Cancionero popular de Jujuy*, Tucumán, 1934.

———, *Cancionero popular de Tucumán*, 2 vols., Buenos Aires - Mexico City, 1937.

———, *Cancionero popular de La Rioja*, 3 vols., Buenos Aires - Mexico City, [1942].

Castro Leal, A., "Dos romances tradicionales," *CuC*, Year II, Vol. VI:3 (1914), 237-244.

Catalán-Galmés, "El tema": See **Critical Works.**

Chacón y Calvo, J. M., "Nuevos romances en Cuba: *Gerineldo-Conde Olinos*," *RBC*, IX (1914), 199-210.

———, "Romances tradicionales en Cuba: Contribución al estudio del *folk-lore* cubano," *RFLC*, XVIII (1914), 45-121.

———, "Romance de la dama y el pastor," *AFC*, I (1924-1925), 289-297.

Córdova de Fernández, S., "El folklore del niño cubano," *AFC,* III (1928), 55-78.

Cuadra, P. A., "Horizonte patriótico del Folklore," *FICU,* no. 2 (1940), p. 23.

Deliz, M., *Renadío del cantar folklórico de Puerto Rico,* 1st ed., Madrid, 1951; 2d ed., Madrid, 1952.

Di Lullo, O., with J. A. Carrizo, *Cancionero popular de Santiago del Estero,* Buenos Aires, 1940.

Draghi Lucero, J., *Cancionero popular cuyano,* Mendoza, 1938.

Espinosa, A. M., "Romancero nuevomejicano," reprinted from *RHi,* XXXIII, New York - Paris, 1915.

———, "Romances de Puerto Rico," reprinted from *RHi,* XLIII, New York - Paris, 1918.

———, "Los romances tradicionales en California," *HMP,* I (1925), 299-313.

———, "Traditional Spanish Ballads in New Mexico," *H,* XV (1932), 89-102.

———, *Romancero de Nuevo Méjico,* Madrid, 1953.

Garrido [de Boggs], E., *Versiones dominicanas de romances españoles,* Santo Domingo, 1946.

Fernández, M., "*Romances* from the Mexican Tradition in Southern California," *FA,* XXVI (1966), 35-45.

Goodwyn, F., "A North Mexican Ballad: *José Lizorio,*" *WF,* VI (1947), 240-248.

Henríquez Ureña, P., and B. D. Wolfe, "Romances tradicionales en Méjico," *HMP,* II (Madrid, 1925), 375-390.

Laval, R. A., *Contribución al folklore de Carahue* (*Chile*), Madrid, 1916.

———, "Nuevas variantes de romances populares," *AFC,* III (1928), 16-26.

———, "Sobre dos cantos chilenos derivados de un antiguo romance español," *RChHG,* LXIII (1929), 40-47.

Lida de Malkiel, "El romance de la misa de amor": See **Critical Works.**

Liscano, J., *Poesía popular venezolana,* Caracas, 1945.

Lucero-White Lea, A., *Literary Folklore of the Hispanic Southwest,* San Antonio (Texas), 1953.

Lummis, C. F., "New Mexican Folk-songs" in *The Land of Poco Tiempo* (New York, 1923), pp. 215-250; facsimile reprint, Albuquerque, 1966.

Mason, J. A., "Spanish *Romances* from Porto Rico," *JAF,* 33 (1920), 76-79.

Mejía Sánchez, E., *Romances y corridos nicaragüenses,* Mexico City, 1946.

Mendoza, V. T., *El romance español y el corrido mexicano: Estudio comparativo,* Mexico City, 1939.

Menéndez Pelayo, M.: See ASW.

Menéndez Pidal, R., *et al., Cómo vive un romance*: See **Critical Works.**

Menéndez Pidal, R., "Un recuerdo de juventud": See **Critical Works.**

Menéndez Pidal, R.: See RTA.

Monroy Pittaluga, F., "Cuentos y romances tradicionales en Cazorla (Llanos del Guárico)," *AVF,* I (1952), 360-380.

Montesinos, P., "Dos romances viejos," *RNC,* año II, no. 24 (1940), 45-53.

Moya, I., *Romancero,* 2 vols., Buenos Aires, 1941.

Muñoz, D., "La poesía popular chilena," *AUCh,* CXIII:93 (1954), 31-48.

Olivares Figueroa, R., *Folklore venezolano,* Caracas, 1948.

Pardo, I. J., "Viejos romances españoles en la tradición popular venezolana," *RNC,* año V, no. 36 (1943), 35-74.

Poncet y de Cárdenas, C., "El romance de Cuba," *RFLC,* XVIII (1914), 180-260, 278-321. Offprint: Havana, 1914.

Ramón y Rivera, L. F., and I. Aretz, *Folklore tachirense,* 2 "Tomos" in 3 vols., Caracas, 1961 (I:1-I:2), 1963 (II).

Restrepo, A. J., *El cancionero de Antioquia,* 3d ed., Barcelona, 1930; reprinted, together with B. A. Gutiérrez, *Contribución al estudio del folklore de Antioquia y Caldas,* Medellín, 1955.

Romero, E., *El romance tradicional en el Perú,* Mexico City, 1952.

RTA = Menéndez Pidal, R., "Los romances tradicionales en América," *CE,* I (1906), 72-111. Reprinted in *El Romancero: Teorías e investigaciones* (Madrid, [1928]), 184-229, and in *Los romances de América y otros estudios,* 6th ed. (Madrid: "Austral," 1958), pp. 13-46.

Simmons, M. E.: See **Critical Works.**

Terrera, G. A., *Primer cancionero popular de Córdoba,* Córdoba (Argentina), 1948.

Vicuña Cifuentes, J., *Romances populares y vulgares recogidos de la tradición oral chilena,* Santiago de Chile, 1912.

Villablanca, C., "Estudio del folklore de Chillán," *AnFFE,* III (1941-1943), 185-223.

PHILIPPINE:

Eugenio, D. L., *Awit and Korido: A Study of Fifty Philippine Metrical Romances in Relation to Their Sources and Analogues,* Ph. D. dissertation, University of California, Los Angeles, 1965.

Fansler, D. S., "Metrical Romances in the Philippines," *JAF,* XXIX (1916), 203-235.

GALICIAN:

BTPE = See **Castilian.**

Carré Alvarellos, L., *Romanceiro popular galego de tradizón oral,* Oporto, 1959.

La Iglesia, A. de, *El idioma gallego: Su antigüedad y vida,* 3 vols., La Coruña, 1886.

Machado y Álvarez, A.: See BTPE.

Milá y Fontanals, M., "De la poesía popular gallega," *Ro,* VI (1877), 47-75; reprinted in *Obras completas,* Vol. V (Barcelona, 1893), 363-399.

Sampedro y Folgar, C., and J. Filgueira Valverde, *Cancionero musical de Galicia,* 2 vols., Madrid, 1942.

PORTUGUESE:

Albuquerque e Castro, J. de, "Conde Nino," *DL*, IV:iii-iv (1951), 125-128.

Almeida Garrett, Visconde de, *Romanceiro*, 3d ed., 3 vols., Lisbon, 1900-1901.

Alves, F. M., "Cancioneiro popular bragançano," *Memórias Arqueológico-históricas do Distrito de Bragança* ..., X (Oporto, 1938), pp. 347-585.

Athaide Oliveira, F. X. d', *Romanceiro e cancioneiro do Algarve* (*Lição de Loulé*), Oporto, 1905.

Basto, C., "Falas e tradições do Distrito de Viana-do-Castelo," *RL*, XVII (1914), 55-85.

Bellermann, Ch. F., *Portugiesische Volkslieder und Romanzen*, Leipzig, 1864.

Braga, Th., *Cantos populares do Archipélago açoriano*, Oporto, 1869.

———, "Ampliações ao Romanceiro das Ilhas dos Açores," *RL*, I (1887-1889), 99-116.

Braga = Braga, Th., *Romanceiro geral português*, 2d ed., 3 vols., Lisbon, 1906, 1907, 1909.

Catalán-Galmés, "El tema": See **Critical Works.**

Chaves, L., "O 'ciclo dos descobrimentos' na poesia popular do Brasil," *Brasilia*, II (1943), 81-157.

———, "O Romanceiro e o teatro popular do Norte do Douro," *Bs*, XXIV (1948), 347-419.

Delgado, M. J., *Subsídio para o cancioneiro popular do Baixo Alentejo*, 2 vols., Lisbon, 1955.

Dias, M. da C., "Tradições populares do Baixo Alemtejo (Ourique)," *RL*, XIV (1911), 41-61.

Estácio da Veiga, S. P. M., *Romanceiro do Algarve*, Lisbon, 1870.

Fernandes, J. A., "Terras de Arouca: II. Ciclo do Natal," *DL*, IV:v-vi (1951), 120-141.

Fernandes Thomás, P., *Velhas canções e romances populares portuguêses*, Coimbra, 1913.

Fernandes Thomás, P., *Canções portuguesas* (*Do século XVIII à actualidade*), Coimbra, 1934.

Folk-lore Andaluz: See **Castilian.**

Furtado de Mendonça, M. A., "Romances populares da Beira-Baixa," *RL,* XIV (1911), 1-35.

Gomes Pereira, A., "Folk-lore trasmontano: *Dona Silvana,*" *Ilustração Trasmontana,* I (1908), 176.

———, "Novo supplemento as tradições populares e linguagem de Villa Real," *RL,* XIII (1910), 95-109.

———, "Tradições populares do Porto," *RL,* XIV (1911), 125-144.

Hardung, V. E., *Romanceiro português,* 2 vols., Leipzig, 1877.

Joaquim, M., *O cancioneiro musical e poético da Biblioteca Públia Hortênsia,* Coimbra, 1940.

Kundert: See **Castilian.**

L[eite] de V[asconcellos], J., "Romance popular de D. Carlos," *RL,* IV (1896), 189-191.

Leite de Vasconcellos, J.: See also Vasconcellos, "Bibl. do Povo"; VRP.

Lopes Graça, F., *A canção popular portuguesa,* Lisbon, n.d.

Martins, F. A., *Folklore do Concelho de Vinhais,* 2 vols., I (Coimbra, 1928), II (Lisbon, 1939).

Michaëlis, "Estudos": See **Critical Works.**

Michaëlis de Vasconcelos, C.: See also RVP.

Monteiro do Amaral, C. A., "Tradições populares e linguagem de Atalaia," *RL,* XI (1908), 96-163.

Morais Machado, C. de, "Subsídios para a história de Mogadouro: Os marranos de Vilarinho dos Galegos (Notícia prévia)," *DL,* V:i (1952), 17-49.

Neves, C. das, and G. de Campos, *Cancioneiro de músicas populares contendo letra e música ...,* Vol. II, Oporto, 1895.

Nunes, J. J., "Subsídios para o Romanceiro português (Tradição popular do Algarve)," *RL,* VI (1900-1901), 151-188.

Pereira, M. P. da Silva, "Fafe: Contribuição para o estudo da linguagem, etnografia e folclore do concelho," *RPF,* III

(1949-1950), 196-220; IV (1951), 20-169, 374-416; V (1952), 221-319.

Pereira Monteiro, A., "Tradições populares do Marco-de-Canavezes," *DL*, II: i (1944), 71-75.

Pires de Lima, A. C. "Tradições populares de Santo Tirso," *RL*, XVII (1914), 282-337; XX (1917), 1-39.

———, *Estudos etnográficos, filológicos e históricos*, III (*Tradições populares de Santo Tirso*), Oporto, 1948; IV, Oporto, 1949.

——— and A. Lima Carneiro, *Romanceiro para o povo e para as escolas*, Oporto, n.d.

Pires de Lima, J. A., and F. de Castro Pires de Lima, *Contribuïção para o estudo do Romanceiro minhoto*, Oporto, 1943.

Reis Dâmaso, A., "Tradições populares (Colecção do Algarve): Romances," *Enciclopédia Republicana* (Lisbon, 1882), pp. 154-156, 171-173, 184; continued with the variant title: "Tradições populares do Algarve: Romances," pp. 201-204, 215-216, 232-237.

Rodrigues, D., "Folk-lore trasmontano," *Ilustração Trasmontana*, I (1908), 40, 53, 187.

Rodrigues de Azevedo, A., *Romanceiro do Archipélago da Madeira*, Funchal, 1880.

RVP = See **Archaic Texts.**

Schwarz, S., *Os cristãos-novos em Portugal no século XX*, Lisbon, 1925.

———, "The Crypto-Jews of Portugal," *The Menorah Journal* (New York), XII (1926), 138-149, 283-297.

Schindler: See **Castilian.**

Serrano, F., *Romances e canções populares da minha terra*, Braga, 1921.

Tavares, J. A., "Romanceiro trasmontano," *RL*, VIII (1903-1905), 71-80; IX (1906), 277-323.

———, "Folk-lore trasmontano," *Ilustração Trasmontana*, I (1908), 24, 88, 103-104, 143; II (1909), 28, 124; III (1910), 40-41, 76, 93-94, 128, 135-136.

Thomás Pires, A., "Tradições poéticas de Entre-Douro-e-Minho," *RL,* VIII (1903-1905), 215-220.

———, *Lendas e romances* (*Recolhidos da tradição oral na província do Alentejo*), Elvas, 1920.

Vasconcellos, "Bibl. do Povo" = Leite de Vasconcellos, J., *Romanceiro português,* Lisbon: "Biblioteca do Povo e das Escolas," 1886.

VRP = Leite de Vasconcellos, J., *Romanceiro português,* 2 vols., Coimbra, 1958-1960.

BRAZILIAN:

Boiteux, L. A., "Poranduba catarinense," *RIHGB,* 184 (1944), 1-92.

Braga = See **Portuguese.**

Brandão, Th., *Folclore de Alagoas,* Maceió-Alagoas, 1949.

Câmara Cascudo, L. da, *Vaqueiros e cantadores: Folclore poético do sertão de Pernambuco, Paraíba, Rio Grande do Norte e Ceará,* Pôrto Alegre, [1939].

———, *História da literatura brasileira,* VI: *Literatura oral,* Rio de Janeiro, 1952.

Pereira da Costa, F. A., "Folk-lore pernambucano: Romanceiro," *RIHGB,* LXX (1907), 295-641.

Pereira de Mello, G. Th., *A música no Brasil desde os tempos coloniais até o primeiro decênio da República,* 2d ed., Rio de Janeiro, 1947.

Rodrigues de Carvalho, [no first name given], *Cancioneiro do Norte,* 2d ed., Paraíba do Norte, 1928.

Romero, S., *Cantos populares do Brasil,* 2 vols., Rio de Janeiro, 1954.

Santos Neves, G., "Presença do Romanceiro peninsular na tradição oral do Brasil," *RBFo,* I (1961), 44-62.

CATALAN:

AFC = Amades, J., *Folklore de Catalunya: Cançoner* (*Cançons - refranys - endevinalles*), Barcelona, 1951.

Aguiló y Fuster, M., *Romancer popular de la terra catalana: Cançons feudals cavalleresques,* Barcelona, 1893.

Ali-Ben-Noab-Tun: See Bulbena y Tosell, A.

Amades, I = Amades, J., *Cançons populars amoroses i cavalleresques,* Tárrega, 1935.

Amades, II = Amades, J., *Cançons populars históriques i de costums,* Tárrega, 1936.

Amades, J.: See also AFC.

ASW = See **Castilian.**

Avenç, I = *40 cançons populars catalanes: Primera serie,* 2d ed., Barcelona: Biblioteca Popular de "L'Avenç," 1909.

Avenç, II = *Segona serie de cançons populars catalanes,* Barcelona: Biblioteca Popular de "L'Avenç," 1909.

Avenç, III = *Tercera serie de cançons populars catalanes,* Barcelona: Biblioteca Popular de "L'Avenç," 1910.

Avenç, IV = *30 cançons populars catalanes aplegades per Adolf Carrera* (Quarta serie), Barcelona: Biblioteca Popular de L'Avenç, 1916.

Bertrán y Bros, P., *Cansons y follíes populars* (*inédites*) *recullides al peu de Montserrat,* Barcelona, 1885.

Briz, F. P., *Cansons de la terra: Cants populars catalans,* 5 vols., I (Barcelona, 1866), II (Barcelona, 1867), III (Barcelona, 1871), IV (Barcelona-Paris, 1874), V (Barcelona-Paris, 1877).

Bulbena y Tosell, A. (alias Ali-Ben-Noab-Tun), *Romancer popular català,* Barcelona, 1900.

Camps y Mercadal, F., *Folk-lore menorquín* (*De la pagesía*), Mahón, 1918.

Canteloube, J.: See **French.**

Capdevila, J., "Cancionero popular: 'Les cançons de collir olives' (Primera serie)," *Ilerda,* XIII (1955), 43-75.

Capmany, A., *Cançoner popular,* 3 series, Barcelona, 1901-1903, 1904-1907, [1907]-1913.

Macabich, I., *Romancer tradicional eivissenc,* Palma de Mallorca, 1954.

Massot Muntaner, J., "El Romancero tradicional español en Mallorca," *RDTP,* XVII (1961), 157-173.

Menéndez Pelayo, M.: See ASW.

Milá = Milá y Fontanals, M., *Romancerillo catalán: Canciones tradicionales,* 2d ed., Barcelona, 1882.

OCPC = *Obra del cançoner popular de Catalunya: Materials,* 3 vols., I, fasc. 1 (Barcelona, 1926), I, fasc. 2, and II (Barcelona, 1928), III (Barcelona, 1929). Unless otherwise specified references to Vol. I allude to fasc. 2.

Pedrell, *Cancionero*: See **Castilian.**

Pujol, F., *Cançons populars catalanes,* Madrid, 1921.

Sarri, J., "Cancionero de 'La Rosa de Bulner': Primera parte," *Ilerda,* XVI (1958), 91-126.

Segura, J., "Cansons catalanas aplegadas en la comarca d'Urgell," in *Miscelánea folk-lórica per los Srs. Almirall, Arabia, et al.* (Barcelona, 1887), pp. 105-125.

Serra i Pagès, R., *El cançoner musical popular catalá,* Manresa, 1918.

Serra i Vilaró, J., *El cançoner del Calic,* Barcelona, 1913.

Subirá, J., *Cançons populars catalanes: Lletra i música,* Barcelona, 1948.

Tomás i Parés, J., "L'Hereu Mill: Arxiu vivent de cançons populars catalanes," *Miscelánea en Homenaje a Monseñor Higinio Anglés,* II (Barcelona, 1958-1961), 923-940.

Torner, *Cuarenta canciones*: See **Castilian.**

Vidal, P., *Cansoner catalá de Rosselló y de Cerdanya,* 2 vols., Perpignan, 1885.

BASQUE:

Azkue, R. M. de, *Euskalerriaren yakintza* (*Literatura popular del país vasco*), 4 vols., I, 2d ed. (Madrid, 1959), II (1942), III (1945), IV (1947).

Lecuona, M. de, *Literatura oral vasca,* San Sebastián, 1964.

ARCHAIC CASTILIAN TEXTS:

Alonso, D., and J. M. Blecua, *Antología de la poesía española: Poesía de tipo tradicional,* Madrid, 1956.
Anglés, H.: See MME, V.

ASW = See **Castilian.**

Barbieri, F. Asenjo, *Cancionero musical español de los siglos XV y XVI,* Buenos Aires, 1945.

Blanchard-Demouge, P.: See Pérez de Hita, G.

Bonilla y San Martín, A., "Romances antiguos," in *Anales de la literatura española* (Madrid, 1904), pp. 29-46.

Cancionero general recopilado por Hernando del Castillo (Valencia, 1511), ed. A. Rodríguez-Moñino, Madrid, 1958.

Cancionero de obras de burlas provocantes a risa, London, 1841.

Castañeda-Huarte, I = Castañeda, V., and A. Huarte, *Colección de pliegos sueltos, agora de nuevo sacados,* [Madrid], 1929.

Castañeda-Huarte, II = Castañeda, V., and A. Huarte, *Nueva colección de pliegos sueltos,* Madrid, 1933.

Cejador y Frauca, J., *La verdadera poesía castellana: Floresta de la antigua lírica popular,* 9 vols. + Index, I-II (Madrid, 1921), III (1922), IV (1923), V (1924), VI-IX and Index (1930).

CSA = *Cancionero de romances impreso en Amberes sin año,* ed. R. Menéndez Pidal, Madrid, 1945.

Durán, A., *Romancero general o Colección de romances castellanos anteriores al siglo XVIII,* 2 vols. (*BAAEE* 10 and 16), Madrid, 1945.

FN = Menéndez Pidal, R., *Flor nueva de romances viejos,* Madrid, 1928; Madrid, 1943; 13th ed., Buenos Aires: "Austral," 1962.

Foulché-Delbosc, R., "Les romancerillos de la Bibliothèque Ambrosienne," *RHi,* XLV (1919), 510-624.

———, "Les cancionerillos de Prague," *RHi,* LXI (1924), 303-586.

Frenk Alatorre, M., "El Cancionero sevillano de la Hispanic Society (*ca.* 1568)," *NRFH*, XVI (1962), 355-394.

FRG = Rodríguez-Moñino, A., *Las fuentes del Romancero general (Madrid, 1600)*, 12 vols., Madrid, 1957.

Gallardo, B. J., *Ensayo de una biblioteca española de libros raros y curiosos*, 4 vols., I (Madrid, 1863), II (1866), III (1888), IV (1889); photographic reprint: Madrid, 1968.

González Palencia, A.: See *Romancero general de 1600.*

Horrent, *Roncesvalles*: See **Medieval Epic Poems.**

Joaquim: See **Portuguese.**

Levi, E., "El romance florentino de Jaume de Olesa," *RFE*, XIV (1927), 134-160; reprinted with an additional, final note in *Motivos hispánicos* (Florence, 1933), pp. 39-73. We cite the original article.

———, "Poesie catalane in un codice fiorentino," *Estudis Universitaris Catalans*, Vol. XV (Barcelona, 1930), 160-167.

López Estrada, F., *La conquista de Antequera en el Romancero y en la épica de los siglos de oro*, Seville, 1956.

Lucas Rodríguez = Rodríguez, Lucas, *Romancero hystoriado con mucha variedad de glosas y sonetos*, Madrid, 1875 ("Colección de Libros Españoles Raros o Curiosos," no. X).

Menéndez Pelayo, M.: See ASW, TRV.

Menéndez Pidal, R., *et al.*, *Romancero tradicional de las lenguas hispánicas* (*español-portugués-catalán-sefardí*), 2 vols., Madrid, 1957, 1963.

Menéndez Pidal, R.: See also CSA, FN, RoH.

Menéndez Pidal, R., "Poesía popular ... ," *Los romances de América* and *El Romancero Español*: See **Critical Works.**

Mey, Felipe, [*Tercera parte de Flor de varios romances*], Valencia, 1593 (= FRG, III).

Michaëlis de Vasconcelos, C.: See RVP.

MME, V = Anglés, H., *La música en la corte de los Reyes Católicos*: *Cancionero musical de palacio* (*siglos XV-XVI*), vol. I (II: *Polifonía profana*), *Monumentos de la Música Española*, V, Barcelona, 1947.

MME, VIII = Querol Gavaldá, M., *Cancionero musical de la Casa de Medinaceli (siglo XVI), I (Polifonía profana,* vol. I), *Monumentos de la Música Española,* VIII, Barcelona, 1949.

Moncayo, Pedro de, *Flor de varios romances nuevos y canciones,* Huesca, 1589 (= FRG, I).

———, *Tercera parte de Flor de varios romances,* Madrid, 1593 (= FRG, III).

Ontañón de Lope, P., "Veintisiete romances del siglo XVI," *NRFH,* XV (1961), 180-192.

Pedrell: See **Castilian.**

Pérez de Hita, G., *Guerras civiles de Granada,* ed. P. Blanchard-Demouge, 2 vols., Madrid, 1913, 1915.

Pliegos góticos = *Pliegos poéticos góticos de la Biblioteca Nacional,* 6 vols., I-II (Madrid, 1957), III (1958), IV (1960), V-VI (1961).

Pliegos de Praga = *Pliegos poéticos españoles en la Universidad de Praga,* 2 vols., Madrid, 1960.

Porębowicz, E., *Zbiór nieznanych hiszpańskich ulotnych Druków znajdujących się w Biblijotece Jagiellońskiej w Krakowie,* Krakow, 1891.

Primavera = Wolf, F. J., and C. Hofmann, *Primavera y flor de romances,* 2 vols., Berlin, 1856; 2d ed., M. Menéndez Pelayo, *Antología de poetas líricos castellanos,* VIII, "Ed. Nac.," XXIV, Santander, 1945.

Querol Gavaldá, M., "Importance historique et nationale du romance," *Colloques Internationaux du Centre National de la Recherche Scientifique: Sciences Humaines,* V: *Musique et Poésie au XVI*[e] *Siècle* (Paris, 1954), pp. 299-327.

Querol Gavaldá, M.: See also MME, VIII.

Rodríguez-Moñino, A., *Espejo de enamorados: Cancionero gótico,* Valencia, 1951.

———, *Cancionerillos góticos castellanos,* Valencia, 1954.

———, and D. Devoto, *Cancionero llamado Flor de enamorados* (Barcelona, 1562), Valencia, 1954.

———, *Flor de romances, glosas, canciones y villancicos* (Zaragoza, 1578), Valencia, 1954.

Rodríguez-Moñino, A., *Segunda parte del Cancionero general agora nueuamente copilado de lo más gracioso y discreto de muchos afamados trovadores* (Zaragoza, 1552), Valencia, 1956.

———, *El Cancionero general* (*Valencia, 1511-Anvers, 1573*): *Noticias bibliográficas sobre sus ediciones y sobre otros cancioneros que se derivan de él,* Madrid, 1958.

———, *Suplemento al Cancionero general de Hernando del Castillo* (Valencia, 1511), Valencia, 1959.

———, "La *Floresta de varios romances* de López de Tortajada (¿1711?-1764): Precisiones bibliográficas," reprinted from *BBMP,* 1960, pp. 225-248 (Santander, 1960).

———, *Los pliegos poéticos de la colección del Marqués de Morbecq* (*Siglo XVI*), Madrid, 1962.

———, "Los pliegos poéticos de la colección Campo de Alanje en la Biblioteca Nacional de Madrid (siglo XVI)," *RPh,* XVII (1963-1964), 373-380.

———, "Tres romances de la *Ensalada* de Praga (siglo XVI)," reprinted from *HR,* XXXI (1963).

Rodríguez-Moñino, A.: See also FRG, *Silva de 1561,* Timoneda.

RoH = See **Critical Works.**

Romancero general de 1600 = *Romancero general* (*1600, 1604, 1605*), ed. A. González Palencia, 2 vols., Madrid, 1947.

RVP = Michaëlis de Vasconcelos, C., *Estudos sôbre o Romanceiro peninsular: Romances velhos em Portugal,* 2d ed., Coimbra, 1934.

Schaeffer, A., "Ein unbekannter altspanischer Romancero," *RF,* VII (1893), 415-426.

Silva de 1561 = Rodríguez-Moñino, A., *Silva de varios romances* (Barcelona, 1561), Valencia, 1953.

Simón Díaz, J., *Bibliografía de la literatura hispánica,* "Tomo" III (in two vols.), Madrid, 1963-1965.

Thomas, H., *Romance del conde Dirlos printed by G. Coci, Saragossa, ca. 1510,* Cambridge, England, 1927.

———, *Romance de don Gayferos printed by J. Cromberger Seville ca. 1515 . . . ,* Cambridge, England, 1927.

Thomas, H., *Trece romances españoles impresos en Burgos, 1516-1517, existentes en el British Museum,* Barcelona, 1931.

Timoneda, J., *Rosas de romances* (Valencia, 1573), ed. A. Rodríguez-Moñino and D. Devoto, Valencia, 1963.

Torner: See **Castilian.**

TRV = See **Critical Works.**

Wilson, E. M., "Samuel Pepys's Spanish Chap-books, Part I," "Part II," and "Part III," reprinted from *Transactions of the Cambridge Bibliographical Society,* II:2 (1955), 127-154; II:3 (1956), 229-268; II:4 (1957), 305-322.

Wilson-Sage = Wilson, E. M., and J. Sage, *Poesías líricas en las obras dramáticas de Calderón: Citas y glosas,* London, 1964.

Wolf, F. J., *Ueber eine Sammlung spanischer Romanzen in fliegenden Blättern auf der Universitäts-Bibliothek zu Prag,* Vienna, 1850.

Wolf, F. J., and C. Hofmann: See also *Primavera.*

FRENCH and PROVENÇAL:

Arbaud, D., *Chants populaires de la Provence,* 2 vols., Aix, 1862-1864.

Canteloube, J., *Anthologie des chants populaires français groupés et présentés par pays ou provinces,* 4 vols., Paris, 1951.

Coirault, P.: See **Critical Works.**

Davenson, H., *Le livre des chansons,* 1st ed., Neuchâtel, 1944; 3d ed., Neuchâtel-Paris, 1955.

Decombe, L., *Chansons populaires recueillies dans le département d'Ille-et-Vilaine,* Rennes, 1884.

Doncieux, G., *Le Romancéro populaire de la France: Choix de chansons populaires françaises,* Paris, 1904.

Puymaigre, Le Comte de, *Chants populaires recueillis dans le Pays Messin,* 2 vols., 2d ed., Paris-Nancy-Metz, 1881.

Rolland, E., *Recueil de chansons populaires,* 6 vols., I (Paris, 1883), II (1886), III-V (1887), VI (1890); photographic reprint: 6 vols. in 3, Paris, 1967.

Tarbé, P., *Romancéro de Champagne,* 5 vols., Reims, 1863-1864.

Udry, A., *Les vieilles chansons patoises de tous les pays de France,* Paris, 1930.

CANADIAN FRENCH:

Barbeau, M., *Folk Songs of Old Quebec,* [Ottawa], n.d. (National Museum of Canada, *Anthropological Series,* no. 16: Bulletin 75).

Barbeau, M., and E. Sapir, *Folk Songs of French Canada,* New Haven, 1925.

Barbeau, M., *Romancéro du Canada,* Toronto, 1937.

———, *Jongleur Songs of Old Quebec,* New Brunswick-Toronto, 1962.

———, *Le rossignol y chante: Première partie du répertoire de la chanson folklorique française au Canada,* Ottawa, 1962.

Gagnon, E., *Chansons populaires du Canada,* 6th ed., Montreal, 1925.

LOUISIANA FRENCH:

Whitfield, I. Th., *Louisiana French Folk Songs,* University, Louisiana, 1939.

BRETON:

Canteloube, J.: See **French.**

Udry, A.: See **French.**

Villemarqué, Th. H. de la, *Barzaz-Breiz: Chants populaires de la Bretagne,* 4th ed., 2 vols., Paris-Leipzig, 1846.

ITALIAN:

Bronzini, G. B., *La canzone epico-lirica nell'Italia centro-meridionale,* 2 vols., Rome, 1956-1961.

Casetti, A., and V. Imbriani, *Canti popolari delle provincie meridionali,* 2 vols., Rome-Turin-Florence, 1871-72.

Liebrecht, *Zur Volkskunde*: See **Critical Works.**

Nigra, C., *Canti popolari del Piemonte,* Turin, 1888; reprinted: Turin, 1957.

Pitré, G., *Canti popolari siciliani,* 2 vols., Rome, 1940-1941.

Vidossi, G., "Canzoni popolari narrative dell'Istria," in *Saggi e scritti minori di folklore* (Turin, 1960), pp. 460-507.

ENGLISH:

Bronson, B. H., *The Traditional Tunes of the Child Ballads with Their Texts, According to the Extant Records of Great Britain and America,* 3 vols., Princeton, 1959, 1962, 1966.

Child = Child, F. J., *The English and Scottish Popular Ballads,* 5 vols., New York, 1965.

Sargent, H. Child, and G. L. Kittredge, *English and Scottish Popular Ballads,* Boston, 1932.

ANGLO-AMERICAN:

Bronson, B. H.: See **English.**

Coffin, T. P., *The British Traditional Ballad in North America,* Philadelphia, 1950; revised ed., Philadelphia, 1963.

Laws, G. M., *American Balladry from British Broadsides: A Guide for Students and Collectors of Traditional Song,* Philadelphia, 1957.

SCANDINAVIAN:

Andersson, O.: See FSF.

Arwidsson, A. I., *Svenska Fornsånger,* 3 vols., Stockholm, 1834, 1837, 1842.

Dal = Dal, E., *Danske Viser: Gamle folkeviser, Skæmte, Efterklang,* Copenhagen, 1962, and its identically numbered English version, *Danish Ballads and Folksongs,* trans. H. Meyer, Copenhagen-New York, 1967.

DgF = Grundtvig, S., with A. Olrik, H. Grüner Nielsen, and E. Abrahamsen, *Danmarks gamle Folkeviser,* 11 vols., I (Copenhagen, 1853), II (1856), III (1862), IV (1883), V:1 (1877-1878), V:2 (1890), VI (1895-1898), VII (1899-1904), VIII (1905-1919), IX (1920-1923), X:1 (1933), X:2 (1938), X:3 (1943), XI:1 (1935), XI:2 (1938); Vols. I-X reprinted: Copenhagen, 1966-67.

FSF = *Finlands svenska folkdiktning,* Vol. V: *Folkvisor*: 1. *Den äldre Folkvisan,* ed. O. Andersson, Helsinki, 1934.

Geijer-Afzelius = Geijer, E. G., and A. A. Afzelius, *Svenska Folkvisor,* ed. R. Bergström and L. Höijer, 3 vols., Stockholm, 1880.

Geijer-Afzelius-2 = Geijer, E. G., and A. A. Afzelius, *Svenska Folkvisor,* ed. J. Sahlgren, 4 vols., Uppsala, 1957, 1958 (II-III), 1960.

Greverus, I.-M., *Skandinavische Balladen des Mittelalters,* Reinbek bei Hamburg, 1963.

Grundtvig, S., and J. Sigurðsson, *Íslenzk fornkvæði,* 2 vols., Copenhagen, 1854-1858, 1859-1885.

Grundtvig, S., *et al.*: See also DgF.

Jonsson, B. R., *Svenska medeltidsballader,* 2d ed., Stockholm, 1966.

Olrik, I = Olrik, A., *Danske Folkeviser i Udvalg,* Copenhagen, 1899; 6th ed., Copenhagen, 1927.

Olrik, II = Olrik, A., *Danske Folkeviser i Udvalg*: *Anden Samling,* Copenhagen-Kristiania, 1909.

Olrik, A., *Nordens Trylleviser,* Copenhagen, 1934.

Olrik, A.: See also Smith-Dampier.

Pineau, L., *Le Romancéro scandinave,* Paris, 1906.

Prior, R. C. A., *Ancient Danish Ballads,* 3 vols., London-Edinburgh, 1860.

Smith-Dampier = Olrik, A., *A Book of Danish Ballads,* trans. E. M. Smith-Dampier, Princeton, 1939.

Warrens, R., *Schwedische Volkslieder der Vorzeit,* Leipzig, 1857.

GERMAN and DUTCH:

Butzmann, H., "Eine neue Handschrift des Liedes vom Edlen Moringer," *JVF,* VI (1938), 94-103.

DVM = Meier, J., with E. Seemann, W. Wiora, H. Siuts, *et al.*, *Deutsche Volkslieder mit ihren Melodien*: *Deutsche Volkslieder*: *Balladen*, 5 vols., I (Berlin-Leipzig, 1935), II (Berlin, 1939), III (1954), IV (1959), V (Freiburg-Breisgau, 1967).

Entwistle, "The Noble Moringer": See **Critical Works.**

Erk-Böhme = Erk, L., and F. M. Böhme, *Deutscher Liederhort*, 3 vols., Leipzig, 1893-94; reprinted: Hildesheim-Wiesbaden, 1963.

Meier, J., *Balladen*, 2 vols., Darmstadt, 1964.

Meier, J., *et al.*: See DVM.

Röhrich, L., and R. W. Brednich, *Deutsche Volkslieder*: *Texte und Melodien*, I: *Erzählende Lieder*: *Balladen-Schwänke-Legenden*, Düsseldorf, 1965.

YIDDISH:

Mlotek, E. G., "International Motifs in the Yiddish Ballad," in *Studies in Jewish Languages, Literature, and Society*: *For Max Weinreich on His Seventieth Birthday* (The Hague, 1964), pp. 209-228.

Rubin, R., "Some Aspects of Comparative Jewish Folksong," in *Studies in Biblical and Jewish Folklore*, ed. R. Patai *et al.* (Bloomington, 1960), pp. 233-252.

LITHUANIAN and LETTISH:

Balys, J., *Lithuanian Narrative Folksongs*: *A Description of Types and a Bibliography*, Washington, D.C., 1954.

Bērzkalne, A., *Typenverzeichnis lettischer Volksromanzen in der Sammlung Kr. Barons' Latvju Dainas*, Helsinki, 1938 (FF Communications, no. 123).

Seemann, E., "Deutsch-litauische Volksliedbeziehungen," *JVF*, VII (1941), 142-211.

HUNGARIAN:

Aigner, L., *Ungarische Volksdichtungen*, Budapest, [1872].

Járdányi, P., *et al.*, *Ungarische Volksliedtypen*, 2 vols., Mainz, 1964.

Leader, N. A. M., *Hungarian Classical Ballads and their Folklore,* Cambridge, England, 1967.

Vargyas, L., "Zur Verbreitung deutscher Balladen und Erzähllieder in Ungarn," *JVF,* IX (1964), 63-79.

———, "Rapports internationaux de la balade populaire hongroise," *Littérature hongroise-Littérature européenne* (Budapest, 1964), pp. 69-103.

———, *Researches into the Medieval History of Folk Ballad,* Budapest, 1967.

RUMANIAN

Alexandri, V., *Ballades et chants populaires de la Roumanie,* Paris, 1855.

Amzulescu, A. I., *Balade populare romîneşti,* 3 vols., Bucharest, 1964.

Beza, M., "Balkan Peasant Poetry," *The Balkan Review,* I (1919), 279-296.

Comişel, E., "The Rumanian Popular Ballad," *Studia Memoriae Belae Bartók Sacra,* 3d ed. (London, 1959), 31-54.

Cortés, L. L., *Antología de la poesía popular rumana,* Salamanca, 1955.

Fochi, A., "Die rumänische Volksballade *Uncheşeii* und ihre südosteuropäischen Paralelen (Das Thema der Rückkehr des Gatten zur Hochzeit seiner Frau)," *Revue des Études Sud-Est Européens* (Bucharest), IV (1966), pp. 535-574.

Franken, A., "Rumänische Volksdichtungen," *Realgymnasium zu St. Petri und Pauli,* Progr. no. 44 (1889) .

Leader, N.: See **Hungarian.**

Vrabie: See **Critical Works.**

MACEDO-RUMANIAN

Fochi, A.: See **Rumanian.**

Papahagi, T., *Antologie aromănească,* Bucharest, 1922.

Weigand, G., *Die Aromunen: Ethnographisch-philologisch-historische Untersuchungen über das Volk der sogenannten*

Makedo-Romanen oder Zinzaren: Zweiter Band: Volkslitteratur der Aromunen, Leipzig, 1895 and 1894.

SLAVIC:

Bartók, B., and A. B. Lord, *Serbo-Croatian Folk Songs,* New York, 1951.

Child = See **English.**

Dozon, A., *Chansons populaires bulgares inédites,* Paris, 1875.

EEB = See **Critical Works.**

Entwistle, W. J.: See EEB.

Fochi, A.: See **Rumanian.**

Gesemann, G., *Zweiundsiebzig Lieder des bulgarischen Volkes,* Berlin, [1944].

Lüdeke, "Griechische Volksdichtung": See **Greek.**

Schirmunski, V., *Vergleichende Epenforschung: I,* Berlin, 1961.

Stevenson Stanoyevich, B., *An Anthology of Jugoslav Poetry,* Boston, 1920.

Strausz, A., *Bulgarische Volksdichtungen,* Vienna-Leipzig, 1895.

Wlislocki: See **Greek.**

GREEK:

Abbott, G. F., *Songs of Modern Greece,* Cambridge, England, 1900.

———, *Macedonian Folklore,* Cambridge, England, 1903.

Akadēmía Aθēnōn, *Hellēnikà dēmotikà tragoúdia* (*Eklogḗ*), Vol. I, Athens, 1962.

Arabantinos, P., *Sullogê dēmōdōn asmátōn tēs Ēpeírou,* Athens, 1880.

Argenti, Ph. P., and H. J. Rose, *The Folk-lore of Chios,* 2 vols., Cambridge, England, 1949.

Baud-Bovy, *Textes* = Baud-Bovy, S., *La chanson populaire grecque du Dodécanèse, I: Les textes,* Paris, 1936.

Baud-Bovy, S., *Chansons du Dodécanèse,* 2 vols., I (Athens, 1935), II (Paris, 1938).

———, *Études sur la chanson cleftique,* Athens, 1958.

Bouvier, B., "Treize chansons populaires du XVIe siècle tirées d'un manuscrit du Mont Athos," *HCA,* IX (1955), 72-74.

———, *Dēmotikà tragoúdia apò cheirógrafo tēs Monēs tōn Ibērōn,* Athens, 1960.

Chianis, S., *Folk Songs of Mantineia, Greece,* Berkeley-Los Angeles, 1965.

Child = See **English.**

Dawkins, R. M., "Tragoúdia tōn Dōdekanēsōn," *Laog,* XIII (1950), 33-99.

Dieterich, K., *Sprache und Volksüberlieferungen der südlichen Sporaden,* Vienna, 1908.

D'Istria, D., "La nationalité hellénique d'après les chants populaires," *RDM,* LXX (1867), 587-627.

Edwards, W. M., "Greek Popular Poetry," *Proceedings of the Leeds Philosophical and Literary Society* (*Literary and Historical Section*), VI (i), Parts I-IV (1944-1947), pp. 1-18.

Fauriel, C., *Chants populaires de la Grèce moderne,* 2 vols., Paris, 1824-1825.

Firmenich, I = Firmenich-Richartz, J. M., *Tragoúdia rōmaïkà: Neugriechische Volksgesänge,* Berlin, 1840.

Firmenich, II = Firmenich-Richartz, J. M., *Tragoúdia rōmaïkà: Neugriechische Volksgesänge* (*Zweiter Teil*), Berlin, 1867.

Fotheringham, D. R., *War Songs of the Greeks and Other Poems,* Cambridge-London, 1907.

Garnett, L. M. J., *Greek Folk Poesy,* 2 vols., London, 1896.

Georgeakis, G., and L. Pineau, *Le folk-lore de Lesbos,* Paris, 1894 (*Les Littératures Populaires de Toutes les Nations,* Vol. XXXI).

Hadjilazaros, M., *Chants populaires des grecs,* Paris, 1951.

Haxthausen, W. von, *Neugriechische Volkslieder,* Münster, 1935.

Jeannaraki, A., *Ásmata krētikà metà distíchōn kaì paroimiōn: Kretas Volkslieder nebst Distichen und Sprichwörtern,* Leipzig, 1876; photographic reprint: Wiesbaden, 1967.

Kavadias, G. B., *Pasteurs-nomades méditerranéens: Les saracatsans de Grèce,* Paris, 1965.

Kerr, R., "Greek Folk-Songs," *The Balkan Review,* I (1919), 210-215; II (1919-1920), 238-242, 399-401.

Kind, Th., *Anthologie neugriechischer Volkslieder,* Leipzig, 1861.

Klaar, M., *Klephtenkrieg: Neugriechische Volkslieder,* Athens, 1938.

Lagarde, P. de, "Neugriechisches aus Kleinasien," reprinted from *Abhandlungen der Königlichen Gesellschaft der Wissenschaften zu Göttingen,* XXXIII, Göttingen, 1886.

Legrand, E., *Recueil de chansons populaires grecques,* Paris, 1874.

——— and H. Pernot, *Précis de prononciation grecque,* Paris, [1896].

Liebrecht, *Zur Volkskunde*: See **Critical Works.**

Lübke, H., *Neugriechische Volks- und Liebeslieder in deutscher Nachdichtung,* Berlin, 1895.

Lüdeke, H., *Im Paradies der Volksdichtung: Erinnerungen an meine volkskundlichen Sammel- und Forschungsreisen im griechischen Sprachgebiet,* Berlin, 1948.

———, "Griechische Volksdichtung," *ALV,* I (1949), 196-250, with a supplement by E. Seemann, pp. 251-254.

Lüdeke-Megas = Lüdeke, H., and G. A. Megas, *Neugriechische Volkslieder,* II: *Übertragungen,* Athens, 1964.

Marcellus, M. de, *Chants du peuple en Grèce,* 2 vols., Paris, 1851.

———, *Chants populaires de la Grèce moderne,* Paris, 1860.

Martinengo Cesaresco, E., *A Sheaf of Greek Folk Songs,* Oxford, 1922.

McPherson, F., *Poetry of Modern Greece: Specimens and Extracts,* London, 1884.

Meyer, G., *Griechische Volkslieder,* Stuttgart, 1890.

Michaelides Nouaros, M. G., *Dēmotikà ragoúdia Karpáθou,* Athens, 1928.

Montesanto, M., *La città sacra* (*Lindo*), Rome, [1930].

Pappadopoulos, G. G., "Ásmata dēmotikà tõn en Korsikē hellḗnōn," *Pandṓra* (Athens), XV (1864-1865), 413-420.

Passow, A., *Tragoúdia rōmaïkà: Popularia carmina Graeciae recentioris,* Athens-Leipzig, 1860; photographic reprint; Athens, 1958.

Pellegrini, A., *Canti popolari dei greci di Cargese* (*Corsica*), Bergamo, 1871.

Pernot, H., *Anthologie populaire de la Grèce moderne,* 2d ed., Paris, 1910.

———, *Études de linguistique néo-hellénique,* III: *Textes et lexicologie des parlers de Chio,* Paris, 1946.

Petropoulos, D., *Hellēnikà dēmotikà tragoúdia,* 2 vols., Athens, 1958-1959.

Petropoulos, *La comparaison*: See **Critical Works.**

Politis, N. G., *Eklogaì apò tà tragoúdia toũ hellēnikoũ laoũ,* Athens, 1958.

Proust, A., *Chants populaires de la Grèce moderne,* Niort, 1866.

Romaios, "*Le retour de l'expatrié*": See **Critical Works.**

Sakellarios, I = Sakellarios, A. A., *Tà Kupriaká,* Vol. III, Athens, 1868.

Sakellarios, II = Sakellarios, A. A., *Tà Kupriaká,* Vol. II, Athens, 1891.

Sanders, D. H., *Das Volksleben der Neugriechen dargestellt und erklärt aus Liedern, Sprichwörtern, Kunstgedichten . . .,* Mannheim, 1844.

Schmidt, B., *Griechische Märchen, Sagen und Volkslieder,* Leipzig, 1877.

Schmidt, *Das Volksleben*: See **Critical Works.**

Schrader, A., *Sammlung neugriechischer Volkslieder,* Berlin, 1910.

Sheridan, Ch. B., *The Songs of Greece,* London, 1825.

Theros, A., *Tà tragoúdia tõn hellēnōn,* 2 vols., Athens, 1951-1952.

Tommaseo, N., and P. E. Pavolini, *Canti popolari greci,* Milan - Palermo - Naples, [1905].

Tozer, H. F., "Modern Greek Ballads from Corsica," *JPh,* VI (1876), 196-205.

Wlislocki, H. von, "Zu neugriechischen Volksliedern," *ZVLRL,* I (1887-1888), 351-365.

ALBANIAN:

Camarda, D., *Appendice al saggio di grammatologia comparata sulla lingua albanese,* Prato, 1866.

Child = See **English.**

De Grazia, D., *Canti popolari albanesi tradizionali nel mezzogiorno d'Italia,* Noto, 1889.

Fochi, A.: See **Rumanian.**

Lambertz, M., *Die Volksepik der Albaner,* Halle (Saale), 1958.

Skendi, S., *Albanian and South Slavic Oral Epic Poetry,* Philadelphia, 1954.

TURKISH:

Reinhard, U., *Vor seinen Häusern eine Weide ...: Volksliedtexte aus der Süd-Türkei,* Berlin, 1965.

CRITICAL WORKS on BALLADRY:

Alonso, *Primavera temprana*: See **Medieval Epic Poems.**

Alvar, M., "Cantos de boda judeo-españoles de Marruecos," *Clav,* VI, no. 36 (1955), 12-23.

———, *Granada y el Romancero,* Granada, 1956.

Alvar, M., "Patología y terapéutica rapsódicas: Cómo una canción se convierte en romance," *RFE,* XLII (1958-1959), 19-35.

———, "Interpretaciones judeo-españolas del árabe *ġabba,*" *RPh,* XVII (1963-1964), 322-328.

———, "Paralelismo en los cantos de boda judeo-españoles," *ALM,* IV (1964), 109-159.

Armistead, S. G., and J. H. Silverman, "Sobre unos romances del Cid recogidos en Tetuán," *Sef,* XXII (1962), 385-396.

———, "Christian Elements and De-Christianization in the Sephardic *Romancero,*" in *Collected Studies in Honour of Américo Castro's Eightieth Year* (Oxford, England, 1965), pp. 21-38.

———, "A New Collection of Judeo-Spanish Ballads" (concerning LSO), *JFI,* III (1966), 133-153.

———, "Para un gran romancero sefardí," *Actas del Simposio Sefardí* (Madrid, in press).

Armistead, S. G., and J. H. Silverman: See also **NSR.**

Asensio, E., *Poética y realidad en el Cancionero peninsular de la Edad Media,* Madrid, 1957.

Beatie, B. A., "Oral-traditional Composition in the Spanish *Romancero* of the Sixteenth Century," *JFI,* I ([1964]), 92-113.

———, "Oral-traditional themes and story-pattern in the *romance* of Conde Dirlos," Program of the *Sixty-third Annual Meeting* of the *Philological Association of the Pacific Coast* (Los Angeles, Nov. 26-27, 1965), p. 12.

Bénichou, P., "La belle qui ne saurait chanter: Notes sur un motif de poésie populaire," *RLC,* XXVIII (1954), 257-281.

BNE = Bénichou, P., "Nouvelles explorations du romancero judéo-espagnol marocain," *BHi,* LXIII (1961), 217-248.

Braga = See **Portuguese.**

Brewster, P. G., and G. Tarsouli, "Two English Ballads and their Greek Counterparts," *JAF,* 69 (1956), 41-46.

Carrizo, J. A., *Antecedentes hispano-medioevales de la poesía tradicional argentina,* Buenos Aires, n.d.

Caso González, J., "Ensayo de reconstrucción del romance *¡Ay! un galán de esta villa,*" *AO,* IV (1954), iii-xl.

Castro, A., "*La Celestina*" *como contienda literaria* (*castas y casticismo*), Madrid, 1965.

Catalán, D., and A. Galmés, "El tema de la boda estorbada: Proceso de tradicionalización de un romance juglaresco," *VR*, XIII (1953), 66-98.

Catalán, D., "El 'motivo' y la 'variación' en la trasmisión tradicional del Romancero," *BHi*, LXI (1959), 149-182.

———, "A caza de romances raros en la tradición portuguesa," reprinted from *Actas do III Colóquio Internacional de Estudos Luso-Brasileiros*, I (Lisbon, 1959), 445-477.

Catalán, D.: See also RCan.

Cirot, G., "Deux notes sur les rapports entre romances et chroniques," *BHi*, XXX (1928), 250-255.

Coirault, P., *Recherches sur notre ancienne chanson populaire traditionelle*, 5 fascicles, I (Vannes, 1927), II (1928), III (n.p., 1929), IV (Vannes, 1929), V (Paris, 1933).

———, *Formation de nos chansons folkloriques*, 4 vols., [Paris], 1953, 1955, 1959, 1963.

CSA = See **Archaic Texts.**

Devoto, D., "El mal cazador," *Studia Philologica*: *Homenaje ofrecido a Dámaso Alonso* ..., 3 vols. (Madrid, 1960, 1961, 1963), I, 481-491.

Dieterich, K., "Die Volksdichtung der Balkanländer in ihren gemeinsamen Elementen: Ein Beitrag zur vergleichenden Volkskunde," *ZVVk*, XII (1902), 145-155, 272-291, 403-415.

———, "Die neugriechische Volkspoesie," in *Geschichte der byzantinischen und neugriechischen Litteratur* (Leipzig, 1902), pp. 121-152; notes and supplement: pp. 229-230, 237-238.

Doncieux, G., "*La Pernette*: Origine, histoire et restitution critique d'une chanson populaire romane," *Ro*, XX (1891), 86-135.

EEB = Entwistle, Wm. J., *European Balladry*, Oxford, 1939; revised reprint: Oxford, 1951.

Entwistle, Wm. J., "Concerning Certain Spanish Ballads in the French Epic Cycles of *Aymeri*, *Aïol* (Montesinos), and *Ogier de Dinamarche*," *A Miscellany of Studies in Romance*

Languages & Literatures Presented to Leon E. Kastner (Cambridge, England, 1932), pp. 207-216.

———, "*La Dama de Aragón*," *HR*, VI (1938), 185-192.

———, "Blancaniña," *RFH*, I (1939), 159-164.

———, "A Note on *La Dama de Aragón*," *HR*, VIII (1940), 156-159.

———, "La historia del cautivo," *RFH*, II (1940), 387-388.

———, "El Conde Dirlos," *MAe*, X (1941), 1-14.

———, "*The Noble Moringer*," MLF, XXXIV (1949), 3-10.

———, "New Light on the Epic-Ballad Problem," *JAF*, 62 (1949), 375-381.

———, "La chanson populaire française en Espagne," *BHi*, LI (1949), 253-268.

———, "El Conde Sol, o La Boda Estorbada," *RFE*, XXXIII (1949), 251-264.

———, "La *Odisea*, fuente del romance del Conde Dirlos," *EMP*, I (Madrid, 1950), 265-273.

———, "El Conde Olinos," *RFE*, XXXV (1951), 237-248.

———, "Second Thoughts Concerning *El Conde Olinos*," *RPh*, VII (1953), 10-18.

Entwistle, Wm. J.: See also EEB.

FN = See **Archaic Texts.**

Frenk Alatorre, M., *La lírica popular en los siglos de oro*, Mexico City, 1946.

———, "Lope, poeta popular," *ALM*, III (1963), 253-266.

García Blanco, M., "El Romancero," in *Historia general de las literaturas hispánicas*, ed. G. Díaz-Plaja, Vol. II (Barcelona, 1951), 1-51.

Gerould, G. H., *The Ballad of Tradition*, New York, 1957.

Goyri de Menéndez Pidal, M., *De Lope de Vega y del Romancero*, Zaragoza, 1953.

Gummere, F. B., *The Popular Ballad*, New York, 1959.

Hanssen, F., "Las coplas 1788-1792 del *Libro de Alexandre,*" *RFE,* II (1915), 21-30.

———, "Sobre la poesía épica de los visigodos," *AUCh,* CXV, nos. 107-108 (1957), 300-306.

Hodgart, M. J. C., *The Ballads,* London, 1964.

Horrent, J., "Sur les romances carolingiens de Roncevaux," *LR,* IX (1955), 161-176.

Kemppinen, I., *The Ballad of Lady Isabel and the False Knight,* Helsinki, 1954.

Krappe, A. H., *The Science of Folklore,* [London], 1962.

Laiglesia, E. de, *Tres hijuelos había el rey* ... (*Orígenes de un romance popular castellano*), Madrid, 1917.

Levi, E., "El romance florentino": See **Archaic Texts.**

Lida de Malkiel, M. R., "El romance de la misa de amor," *RFH,* III (1941), 24-42.

———, *El cuento popular hispano-americano y la literatura,* Buenos Aires, 1941.

———, "Una colección de romances judeo-españoles," *Davar,* X (1947), 5-26.

Liebrecht, F., *Zur Volkskunde: Alte und neue Aufsätze,* Heilbronn, 1879.

LSO = See **Eastern Judeo-Spanish.**

Massot, "El romancero tradicional español en Mallorca": See **Catalan.**

Menéndez Pelayo, M.: See TRV.

Menéndez Pidal, R., "Serranilla de la Zarzuela," *StM,* II (1906-1907), 263-270; reprinted in *Poesía árabe y poesía europea,* 3d ed. (Buenos Aires - Mexico City: "Austral," 1946), pp. 99-108.

———, *El Romancero Español,* [New York], 1910.

———, "Poesía popular y romancero," *RFE,* I (1914), 357-377; II (1915), 1-20, 105-136, 329-338; III (1916), 233-289.

———, "Sobre *Roncesvalles* y la crítica de los romances carolingios," *RFE,* V (1918), 396-398.

Menéndez Pidal, R., "Romances y baladas," *MHRA*, I (1927), 1-17.

———, "Los *Estudos sôbre o Romanceiro peninsular* de Doña Carolina," *Miscelânea de estudos em honra de D. Carolina Michaëlis de Vasconcellos = Revista da Universidade de Coimbra*, XI (1933), 493-500.

———, "Supervivencia del *Poema de Kudrun* (Orígenes de la balada)," *RFE*, XX (1933), 1-59; reprinted in *Los godos y la epopeya española*: *"Chansons de geste" y baladas nórdicas* (Madrid: "Austral," 1956), pp. 89-173.

———, "Poesía tradicional en el Romancero hispano-portugués," in *Castilla*: *La tradición—El idioma* (Buenos Aires - Mexico City: "Austral," 1945), pp. 41-74.

———, "La primitiva poesía lírica española," in *Estudios literarios*, 6th ed. (Buenos Aires - Mexico City: "Austral," 1946), 203-277.

———, *Poesía árabe y poesía europea*, 3d ed., Buenos Aires - Mexico City: "Austral," 1946.

———, "Poesía popular y poesía tradicional en la literatura española," in *Los romances de América y otros estudios*, 5th ed. (Buenos Aires - Mexico City: "Austral," 1948), pp. 52-91.

———, *Los romances de América y otros estudios*, 5th ed., Buenos Aires - Mexico City: "Austral," 1948; 6th ed., Madrid, 1958.

———, "Un recuerdo de juventud," *Estudios hispánicos*: *Homenaje a Archer M. Huntington*: *Anejo único*, Wellesley, Mass., 1952.

——— with D. Catalán and A. Galmés, *Cómo vive un romance*: *Dos ensayos sobre tradicionalidad*, Madrid, 1954.

———, "El romance tradicional en las Islas Canarias," reprinted from *AEA*, I (1955), 3-10.

———, "A propósito del *Romanceiro português* de J. Leite de Vasconcelos," reprinted from *Actas do III Colóquio Internacional de Estudos Luso-Brasileiros*, I (Lisbon, 1959), 493-499.

Menéndez Pidal, R.: See also CSA, FN, RoH.

Menéndez Pidal, R., *Los godos y la epopeya española*: See **Medieval Epic Poems.**

Michaëlis de Vasconcelos, C., "Estudos sôbre o Romanceiro peninsular," *RL,* II (1890-1892), 156-179, 193-240.

Michaëlis de Vasconcelos, C.: See also RVP.

Milá y Fontanals, M.: See PHP.

Molho, M.: See LSO.

Morales, M., and M. J. López de Vergara: See RCan.

Morley, S. G., "El romance del *Palmero,*" *RFE,* IX (1922), 298-310.

———, "Chronological List of Early Spanish Ballads," *HR,* XIII (1945), 273-287.

———, "A New Jewish-Spanish *Romancero,*" *RPh,* I (1947), 1-9.

NSR = Armistead, S. G., and J. H. Silverman, "A New Sephardic *Romancero* from Salonika" (concerning M. Attias, *Romancero sefaradí*), *RPh,* XVI (1962-1963), 59-82.

Nygard, H. O., *The Ballad of "Heer Halewijn": Its Forms and Variations in Western Europe: (A Study of the History and Nature of a Ballad Tradition),* Helsinki, 1958 (*FF Communications,* no. 169).

Onís, J. de, "El celo de los duendes: Una variante americana del romance del *Conde Olinos,*" *CuA,* XXIII (1964), 219-229.

Peirone, F. J., "Un caso di trasumanza del ciclo carolingio: *Gaiferos* dall'Iberia al Piemonte," *BFL,* XIX (1960), 45-62.

Pérez Vidal, J. "*Santa Irene* (Contribución al estudio de un romance tradicional)," *RDTP,* IV (1948), 518-569.

———, "*Floresvento* y *La esposa infiel,*" *DL,* IV: ix (1952), 37-40.

Petropoulos, D., *La comparaison dans la chanson populaire grecque,* Athens, 1954.

PHP = Milá y Fontanals, M., *De la poesía heroico-popular castellana,* ed. M. de Riquer y J. Molas, Barcelona, 1959.

Pons, J. S., "Poésie courtoise et poésie populaire: La Dame d'Aragon," *Mélanges offerts à ... Henri Gavel* (Toulouse, 1948), pp. 71-76.

Puymaigre, Le Comte de, *Les vieux auteurs castillans,* 2 vols., Metz-Paris, 1861-1862.

Puymaigre, Le Comte de, "Notes sur un recueil de romances judéo-espagnoles," *REJ*, XXXIII (1896), 269-276.

RCan = See **Canarian.**

Révah, I. S., "Edition critique du *romance* de don Duardos et Flérida," *BHTP*, III (1952), 107-139.

RoH = Menéndez Pidal, R., *Romancero hispánico* (*hispano-portugués, americano y sefardí*), 2 vols., Madrid, 1953.

Romaios, C., "La chanson populaire néogrecque *Le retour de l'expatrié*," *HCA*, VII (1953), 38-57.

RVP = See **Archaic Texts.**

Schmidt, B., *Das Volksleben der Neugriechen und das hellenische Alterthum*, Leipzig, 1871.

Schneider, M., "Los cantos de lluvia en España: Estudio etnológico comparativo sobre la ideología de los ritos de pluviomagia," *AnM*, IV (1949), 3-57.

Simmons, M. E., *A Bibliography of the 'Romance' and Related Forms in Spanish America*, Bloomington, 1963.

Spitzer, L., "Notas sobre romances españoles," *RFE*, XXII (1935), 153-174; "Adiciones ..." pp. 290-291.

———, "The Folkloristic Pre-Stage of the Spanish *Romance* 'Conde Arnaldos'," *HR*, XXIII (1955), 173-187; "Annex ...," XXIV (1956), 64-66.

Stern, S. M., "A *Romance* on Galiana," *BHS*, XXXVI (1959), 229-231.

Taylor, A., "The Themes Common to English and German Balladry," *MLQ*, I (1940), 23-35.

———, "The Parallels between Ballads and Tales," *JVF*, IX (1964), 104-115.

Toelken, J. B., "An Oral Canon for the Child Ballads: Construction and Application," *JFI*, IV (1967), 75-101.

TRV = Menéndez Pelayo, M., *Tratado de los romances viejos*, 2 vols., in *Antología de poetas líricos castellanos*, VI-VII, "Ed. Nac.," XXII-XXIII, Santander, 1944.

Vrabie, G., *Balada populară română*, Bucharest, 1966.

Webber, R. H., *Formulistic Diction in the Spanish Ballad*, *UCPMPh*, 34 (Berkeley - Los Angeles, 1951), 175-278.

Wimberly, L. C., *Folklore in the English and Scottish Ballads*, New York, 1959.

MEDIEVAL EPIC POEMS (TEXTS and CRITICISM)

Alonso, D., "La primitiva épica francesa a la luz de una nota emilianense," in *Primavera temprana de la literatura europea* (Madrid, 1961), pp. 81-200.

Armistead, S. G., " 'The Enamored Doña Urraca' in Chronicles and Balladry," *RPh*, XI (1957-1958), 26-29.

———, "An Unnoticed Epic Reference to Doña Elvira, Sister of Alfonso VI," *RPh*, XII (1958-1959), 143-147.

———, *A Lost Version of the 'Cantar de gesta de las Mocedades de Rodrigo' Reflected in the Second Redaction of Rodríguez de Almela's 'Compendio historial'*, *UCPMPh*, 38 (Berkeley - Los Angeles, 1963), 299-336.

———, "The Structure of the *Refundición de las Mocedades de Rodrigo*," *RPh*, XVII (1963-1964), 338-345.

———, "Para el texto de la *Refundición de las Mocedades de Rodrigo*," *AEM*, III (1966), 529-540.

Babbitt, Th., *'La Crónica de Veinte Reyes': A Comparison with the Text of the 'Primera Crónica General' and a Study of the Principal Latin Sources*, New Haven, 1936.

Bartsch, K.: See *Nibelungenlied*.

Bowra, C. M., *Heroic Poetry*, London, 1952.

Catalán, D., *Poema de Alfonso XI: Fuentes, dialecto, estilo*, Madrid, 1953.

———, "El taller historiográfico alfonsí: Métodos y problemas en el trabajo compilatorio," *Ro*, LXXXIV (1963), 354-375.

Cintra, L. F. Lindley, *Crónica Geral de Espanha de 1344*, 3 vols., Lisbon, 1951, 1954, 1961.

Crónica particular del Cid = *Chrónica del famoso cavallero Cid Ruydiez Campeador*, ed. V. A. Huber, Stuttgart, 1853.

de Vries, J., *Heroic Song and Heroic Legend,* London, 1963.

Erichsen, F.: See *Thidrekssaga.*

Fuks, L., *The Oldest Known Literary Documents of Yiddish Literature* (*ca. 1382*), 2 vols., Leiden, 1957.

Gayangos, P. de: See *Gran Conquista de Ultramar.*

Gómez Pérez, J., "Leyendas medievales españolas del ciclo carolingio," reprinted from *Anuario de Filología* (Facultad de Humanidades y Educación, Universidad de Zulia, Maracaibo, 1964), nos. 2-3 (1963-1964), pp. 7-136.

———, "Leyendas carolingias en España," reprinted from *Anuario de Filología* (Facultad de Humanidades y Educación, Universidad de Zulia, Maracaibo, 1966), no. 4 (1965), pp. 121-193.

Gran Conquista de Ultramar, La, ed. P. de Gayangos, *BAAEE,* Vol. 44, Madrid, 1951.

Hollander, L. M.: See *Poetic Edda.*

Horrent, J., *La Chanson de Roland dans les littératures française et espagnole au Moyen Âge,* Paris, 1951.

———, *'Roncesvalles': Étude sur le fragment de cantar de gesta conservé à l'Archivo de Navarra* (*Pampelune*), Paris, 1951.

Huber, V. A.: See *Crónica particular del Cid.*

Keller, J. P., "The Hunt and Prophecy Episode of the *Poema de Fernán González,*" *HR,* XXIII (1955), 251-258.

Kölbing, E., ed., *The Romance of Sir Beues of Hamtoun, EETS,* Extra Series, XLVI, XLVIII, LXV, London, 1885, 1886, 1894.

Kübel, M., *Das Fortleben des Kudrunepos,* Leipzig, 1929.

Kudrun, ed. B. Symons and B. Boesch, 4th ed., Tübingen, 1964.

Langosch, K.: See *Waltharius.*

Lévi-Provençal, E., and R. Menéndez Pidal, "Alfonso VI y su hermana la infanta Urraca," *ALAn,* XIII (1948), 157-166.

Menéndez Pelayo, M.: See TRV.

Menéndez Pidal, R., *La leyenda de los Infantes de Lara,* 1st ed., Madrid, 1896; 2d ed., Madrid, 1934.

Menéndez Pidal, R., "*Roncesvalles*: Un nuevo cantar de gesta español del siglo XIII," *RFE*, IV (1917), 105-204.

———, *Historia y epopeya*, Madrid, 1934.

———, *Cantar de Mio Cid*: *Texto, gramática y vocabulario*, 3 vols., Madrid, 1944, 1945, 1946.

———, *La epopeya castellana a través de la literatura española*, 1st ed., Buenos Aires-Mexico City, 1945; 2d ed., Madrid, 1959.

———, *La España del Cid.*, 2 vols., 4th ed., Madrid, 1947.

———, *Reliquias de la poesía épica española*, Madrid, 1951.

———, *Los godos y la epopeya española*: "*Chansons de geste*" *y baladas nórdicas*, Madrid: "Austral," 1956.

———, *La Chanson de Roland y el neotradicionalismo* (*orígenes de la épica románica*), Madrid, 1959.

———, *La Chanson de Roland et la tradition épique des Francs*, 2d ed., Paris, 1960.

Menéndez Pidal, R.: See also PCG, *Reliquias*.

Nibelungenlied, Das, ed. K. Bartsch, 11th ed., Leipzig, 1944.

PCG = Menéndez Pidal, R., *Primera Crónica General de España*, 1st ed., Madrid, 1906 (= *NBAE*, Vol. V); 2d ed., 2 vols., Madrid, 1955.

Poetic Edda, The, trans. L. M. Hollander, 2d ed., Austin, 1964.

Reig, C., *El cantar de Sancho II y Cerco de Zamora*, Madrid, 1947.

Reliquias: See Menéndez Pidal, *Reliquias de la poesía épica española*.

Riedel, F. C., *Crime and Punishment in the Old French Romances*, New York, 1938.

Riquer, M. de, *Los cantares de gesta franceses*, Madrid, 1952.

Schlauch, M.: See *Volsungasaga*.

Strecker, K., *Ekkehards Waltharius*, Berlin, 1907.

Strecker, K.: See also *Waldere*.

Symons, B., and B. Boesch: See *Kudrun.*

Thidrekssaga = *Die Geschichte Thidreks von Bern,* trans. F. Erichsen, Jena, 1942 (= *Thule,* Vol. XXII).

TRV = See **Critical Works.**

Volsungasaga = *The Saga of the Volsungs* . . . , trans. M. Schlauch, New York, 1964.

Wais, K., *Frühe Epik Westeuropas und die Vorgeschichte des Nibelungenliedes,* Vol. I, Tübingen, 1953.

Waldere = "Die Waldere-Bruchstücke" in Strecker, K., *Ekkehards Waltharius* (Berlin, 1907), pp. 94-99.

Waltharius = Langosch, K., *Waltharius-Ruodlieb-Märchenepen: Lateinische Epik des Mittelalters mit deutschen Versen,* Basel-Stuttgart, 1956.

BIBLIOGRAPHICAL WORKS CONCERNING Y. A. YONÁ

Armistead, S. G., and J. Silverman, "Algo más para la bibliografía de Yacob Abraham Yoná," *NRFH,* XVII (1963-64), 315-337.

———, "Un romancerillo de Yacob Abraham Yoná," *Homenaje a Rodríguez-Moñino,* 2 vols. (Madrid, 1966), I, 9-16.

Attias, M.: See **Eastern J.-Sp.**

Besso, H. V., "Bibliography of Judeo-Spanish Books in The Library of Congress (Washington) . . . ," *MEAH,* VIII (1959), 55-134.

———, *Ladino Books in the Library of Congress: A Bibliography,* Washington, 1963.

Catálogo de la Exposición Bibliográfica Sefardí Mundial, Madrid, 1959.

Gaon, M. D., *A Bibliography of the Judeo-Spanish (Ladino) Press* (in Hebrew), Tel Aviv, 1965.

LSO = See **Eastern Judeo-Spanish.**

Menéndez Pidal, R.: See RoH.

Menéndez Pidal, *El Romancero Español*: See **Critical Works.**

Milwitzky, "El viajero filólogo": See **Eastern Judeo-Spanish.**

Molho, M., *Sĕfārîm ᶜibrîm ᶜaθîkîm wĕ-sifrê ladino,* Buenos Aires, 1957.

Molho, M.: See also LSO.

Révah, I. S., "Para una bibliografía de las publicaciones folklóricas de Yacob Yoná," *NRFH*, XV (1961), 107-112.

RoH = See **Critical Works.**

Yaari, A., *Rĕšîmaθ sifrê ladino ha-nimçā'îm bĕ-bêθ ha-sĕfārîm ha-lĕ'ûmî wĕ-ha-'ûnîversîtā'î bĕ-Yĕrûšālayîm* [*Catalogue of Judaeo-Spanish Books in the Jewish National and University Library*], Jerusalem, 1934.

JUDEO-SPANISH LANGUAGE

Benoliel, J., "Dialecto judeo-hispano-marroquí o hakitía," *BAE,* XIII (1926), 209-233, 342-363, 507-538; XIV (1927), 137-168, 196-234, 357-373, 566-580; XV (1928), 47-61, 188-223; XXXII (1952), 255-289.

Cantera, F., "Hebraísmos en la poesía sefardí," *EMP,* V (1954), 67-97.

Cherezli, S. I., *Nouveau petit dictionnaire judéo-espagnol-français,* Jerusalem, 1898-1899.

Crews, C. M., *Recherches sur le judéo-espagnol dans les pays balkaniques,* Paris, 1935.

DRH = See **Eastern Judeo-Spanish.**

Kahane, H. and R., and A. Tietze, *The Lingua Franca in the Levant: Turkish Nautical Terms of Italian and Greek Origin,* Urbana, 1958.

LSO = See **Eastern Judeo-Spanish.**

Miklosich, F., "Die türkischen Elemente in den südost- und osteuropäischen Sprachen," *Denkschriften der Kaiserlichen Akademie der Wissenschaften: Philosophisch-Historische Classe* (Vienna), 34 (1884), 239-338; 35 (1885), 105-192.

Molho, *Usos*: See **Eastern Judeo-Spanish.**

NSR = See **Critical Works.**

Wagner, M. L., *Beiträge zur Kenntnis des Judenspanischen von Konstantinopel,* Vienna, 1914.

———, *Caracteres generales del judeo-español de Oriente,* Madrid, 1930.

———, "Espigueo judeo-español," reprinted from *RFE,* XXXIV (1950), 9-106.

BIBLIOGRAPHICAL EPILOG

Attention must be called to several important romancistic works that became available to us only after the present volume had reached final form. These include two fundamental publications by P. Bénichou: *Creación poética en el Romancero tradicional* (Madrid, 1968) and *Romancero judeo-español de Marruecos* (Madrid, 1968), the latter a thorough revision of the collection published in *RFH* (1944). Bénichou's sensitive and penetrating investigation of collective authorship in *Creación*—especially his first chapter on *El destierro del Cid* and his pp. 87-88 on *Abenámar*—supplements and confirms our observations concerning *Las almenas de Toro* and *El triste amador* (nos. 1 and 19 *supra*). Among a host of lesser topics, the revised commentaries to *El sueño de Doña Alda* (pp. 57 ff.), *Linda Melisenda* (69 ff.), *Robo de Elena* (91 ff.), *Conde Olinos* (123 ff.), *Mujer engañada* (129 ff.), *Bodas en París* (138 ff.), *Adúltera* (*ó*; 142 ff.), *Rico Franco* (160 ff.), *Vos labraré un pendón* (164 ff.), *Boda estorbada* (235 ff.), and *Soldados forzadores* (244 ff.) in *Romancero* should be taken into account vis-à-vis Yoná's ballads. A recent article by Henry V. Besso ("Los sefardíes y el idioma castellano," *RHM*, XXXIV [1968], 176-194) brings to light previously unedited texts of four Sephardic ballads, probably of Salonikan origin, which formed part of a New York music recital held on February 18, 1935: *Melisenda sale de los baños* (1), *El robo de Dina* (2), *La mujer de Juan Lorenzo* (3; the first two verses are from *El chuflete*), and *El sueño profético* (4). Joanne B. Purcell's fine edition and study of Portuguese *romances* painstakingly culled from the U. S. immigrant tradition was submitted as an M. A. thesis at UCLA in the spring of 1968 (*Portuguese Traditional Ballads from California*). The collection includes important versions of *El conde Alemán y la reina* (no. 1), *Conde Olinos* (2;5), *El navegante* (4), *Silvana* (9;18), *Frei João* (12), and *Rico Franco* (13-14), all of which parallel ballads published by Yoná. A selection of Mrs. Purcell's ballads, including texts of *Frei João* (3) and *El navegante* (6) appears in "Traditional Ballads Among the Portuguese in California," *WF*, XXVIII (1969), 1-19, 77-90. Antônio Lopes' *Presença do Romanceiro*: *Versões maranhenses* (Rio de Janeiro, 1967) offers Brazilian texts of *El navegante* (4), *Silvana* + *Delgadina* (7), *Conde Olinos* (9;32), *La mala suegra* (12), *El conde Alemán y la reina* (16), *Conde Claros fraile* (17), *Frei João* (28), and *Conde Claros y la princesa* (31). J. Massot i Muntaner's useful and well-documented "Aportació a l'estudi del Romancer balear," *ER*, VII (1959-1960), 63-155, —published in 1964— includes both a catalog and a selection of texts and documents not only such text types as *La dama de Aragón* (pp. 71, 73, 124-126, 151), *Conde Claros y la infanta* (73, 83), *Conde Claros fraile* (83-84), *Gaiferos y Melisenda* (84-85), *Escriveta* (88-89, 94-96), *La presó de Lleyda* and *La Pernette* (96-98), *El navegante* + *Conde Olinos* (100), *La mala suegra* (*N'Arbola*: 101-102), *Adúltera* (*ó*; 106-107), *Gerineldo* + *La boda estorbada* (114-115), and *The Transformations* (123-124, 150-151), but also numerous lesser *topoi*: the unlucky hunter (115-116, 149-150), mills grinding fine materials (117), and flowers from graves (121, 140-141, 155). A. Rodríguez-Moñino's magnificent editions (Madrid, 1967) of the *Cancionero de romances* (Anvers, 1550), *Romancero historiado* (Alcalá, 1582) of Lucas Rodríguez, and *Cancionero de romances* (Seville, 1584) of Lorenzo de Sepúlveda include numerous archaic *romances* pertinent to the study of Yoná's texts. F. J. Norton's and E. M. Wilson's beautiful *Two Spanish Verse Chap-books* (Cambridge, Eng., 1969) is fundamental to the exploration of the early stages of the *Romancero* and to the study of *La fuga del rey Marsín* in particular (pp. 35-40). The massive *Romancero canario* (now being edited by Diego Catalán), of which we have seen sample proofs pertaining to the ballad of *Silvana,* promises a wealth of new material from a tradition which rivals that of the Sephardim in its fidelity and archaism.

INDICES

Titles

Hispanic Ballads and Songs (including Castilian-, Catalan-, and Portuguese-speaking areas, as well as the J.-Sp. traditions. References are to page numbers. The letters B. E. refer to the "Bibliographical Epilog"):

Ballads and Songs from Other Traditions

Other Literary Works

First Verses

References are to page numbers. All first lines specifically cited in the text are included. In addition, the first hemistich of early (15th-17th c.) *romances* mentioned in the text —whether or not their *incipits* are specifically cited— are also included, followed whenever possible by their *Primavera* number in parentheses.

Proverbs

Hebrew and Aramaic Words, Phrases, and Versicles

(Arabic numbers refer to our list of Yoná's works in the Introduction; Roman numbers, to our descriptions of Yoná's ballad chapbooks.)

'ănî 'I' (1st pers. sing. pronoun): II.

'Ašrê ϴibḥar û-ϴĕkārēb yiškōn ḥăçērêkā (written *Achre tivhar outkarev yichkon hasséréha*) "Blessed is the man whom thou choosest, and causest to approach unto thee, that he may dwell in thy courts" (Psalms 65:4): VII, VIII.

bĕrākôϴ 'blessings': VI, VII, VIII. *See* Cantera, "Hebraísmos," no. 14.

bĕrîϴ mîlāh 'circumcision ceremony': II, VI, VII, VIII.

ceder. *See* sēder.

dôr 'generation': Ballad no. 16, n. 27.

'Êl 'God': I. Cantera, "Hebraísmos," no. 22. In certain cases Yoná uses *scriptio plena* to specify the vocalization of Hebrew words. The usual spelling is *'Ēl.*

'Ēl mālē' raḥămîm 'God, full of mercy': II.

gĕdûlaϴ Mōšeh 'the greatness of Moses': I.

gĕmārā' 'pamphlet' (cf. Révah, p. 109): I, V; gĕmārāh: II, IV.

gĕmārôϴ = pl. of *gĕmārā'* (q.v.): V.

gemrikas = J.-Sp. diminutive of *gĕmārā'* (q.v.): V; also n. 5 of the Introduction. The readings *gemrekas, gemarikas, gemarekas* are also possible.

Hagādāh: the order of the service of narrative and prayer on Passover night: 15, VII.

hăkānāh 'preparation': V.

Hā' laḥmā' ᶜanyā' (Aram.) "This is the bread of affliction" (Passover *Haggadah*): VII.

hy"w = Ha-Šēm yišměrēhû wě-yaçîlēhû 'May the Lord guard and preserve him': I, V.

ḥag ha-Pesaḥ 'the feast of Passover': 15, 19, IV, VII.

ḥ"r = Ḥāḥām Rabî 'learned rabbi': 10.

ḥăzîr 'pig': Ballad no. 17, n. 26.

Ḳě-ѳapûaḥ ba-ᶜăçê ha-yaᶜar ḳēn dôdî bên ha-bānîm "As the apple tree among the trees of the wood, so is my beloved among the sons" (Song of Songs 2:3): I.

kîdûšîn 'blessings': II. Cantera, "Hebraísmos," no. 45. The usual form is *kidûšîn*. Cf. *'Ēl*.

La-yě'ûdîm (read *yěhûdîm*) hāyěѳāh 'ôrāh wě-śimḥāh "For the Jews there was light and joy" (Esther 8:16; also the *Habdālāh*): VIII.

lěšôn ha-kôdeš 'the holy language', i.e., Hebrew: VIII. The spelling *kôdeš*—normally *kōdeš*—is another case of *scriptio plena*. See *'Ēl*.

mazāl 'luck': Ballad no. 14.22.

meᶜārāh 'cave': p. 126.

miçrî 'Egyptian': Ballad 9A-B.15.

môᶜădîm lě-śimḥāh 'joyful holidays': VII.

nêkāmāh 'vengeance': Ballad no. 16.7. The normal spelling is *někāmāh*.

nîsān: the first month of the Hebrew calendar: I; Ballad no. 9, n. 1.

nr"w = nātrêh raḥmānā' û-bārěḳêh (Aram.) 'May the Merciful One guard and bless him': 10.

'ôḥîlāh 'I hope': II; Ballad no. 11A and n. 7. This is the first word of a hymn for the New Year and the Day of Atonement: "'ôḥîlāh lā-'Ēl" 'I hope in God,' as cited in IV and the headnote to Ballad no. 11B.

Parᶜōh 'Pharoah': Ballad no. 9A-B.6.

rabênû 'our lord': 10, I, IV. Cantera, "Hebraísmos," no. 71. The usual form is *rabēnû*, as in IV. Cf. what we say under *'Ēl*.

raḥămān 'merciful': Ballad no. 10A.13. The reading *raḥmān* is also possible.

sēder (spelled *ceder*) 'order': III.

Sēfer gědûlaѳ Mōšeh 'Book of the Greatness of Moses': 1, I.

sĕneh 'bramble bush': Ballad no. 17, at n. 27.

sîmān 'sign': II. Cantera, "Hebraísmos," no. 84.

sîwān: the third month of the Hebrew calendar: 25.

s"t: II. The meaning of this abbreviation is problematic. *See* H. J. Zimmels, *Ashkenazim and Sephardim* (London, 1958), pp. 286-287; M. Halpern, *Ha-Nôtārîkôn, ha-Sîmānîm, wĕ-ha-Kinûyim* (Vilna, 1912), p. 188; S. Ashkenazi and D. Jarden, *Ozar Rashe Tevot: Thesaurus of Hebrew Abbreviations* (Jerusalem, 1965), col. 422.

Šābûcôɵ 'Pentecost': II, III, VI.

šālēm 'safe, in good health': Ballad no. 8, n. 3.

Šĕmôr libî macăneh (written, with metathesis, *Xeborlimi mané*) "May my heart preserve an answer" (from a *Šābûcôɵ* prayer included in the *Maḥăzôr Saloniki* [Salonika, 1876; reedited: Tel-Aviv, 1963], p. 532): III. This is the first verse of a hymn by Ibn Gabirol. The entire text may be seen in *Šîrê Šĕlōmōh ben Yĕhûdāh 'ibn Gabîrôl,* ed. H. N. Bialik and I. H. Ravnitzky, Vol. III (Tel-Aviv, 1927), pp. 135-154. Concerning our translation of the verse, see *op cit.,* Vol. IV, p. 73.

šĕnaɵ '[in] the year of': I, IV, VII.

ɵaḥaɵ memšeleɵ 'Ădônênû ha-Meleḳ 'under the rule of Our Lord the King': I. *'Ădônênû* is another case of *scriptio plena.* Cf. *'Êl.*

ɵĕfîlāh 'prayer': Ballad no. 9A.9.

ɵm' "h = ɵaḥaɵ memšeleɵ 'Ădônēnû ha-Meleḳ (q.v.): V.

Wa-niçcak 'el [Adonay] "And we cried unto the Lord" (Passover *Haggadah,* based on Deuteronomy 26:7): VII.

Wa-yābō' Yacăkōb šālēm cîr Šĕḳem: "Jacob arrived safe in the city of Shechem" (Genesis 33:18): Ballad no. 8, n. 3.

Wa-yikrĕbû yĕmê Yacăkōb Yônā lā-mûɵ wa-yikrā' "And the time drew nigh that [Yakob Yoná] must die and he called" (adapted from Genesis 47:29): IV.

Wĕ-'eɵ laḥăçênû. Zeh ha-dĕḥak "And our oppression: this refers to the vexation" (Passover *Haggadah,* "Wa-niçcak 'el [Adonay]"): VII. The form *laḥăçênû* —read *laḥăçēnû*—is in *scriptio plena.* Cf. *'Êl.*

Wĕ-Yacăkōb 'îš ɵām yôšēb 'ôhālîm "And Jacob was a plain man, dwelling in tents" (Genesis 25:27): I. *Scriptio plena* is used in *'ôhālîm.*

Xabuot. *See* Šābûcôɵ.

Xeborlimi mané. *See* Šĕmôr libî macăneh.

yāšār 'just, righteous': VIII.

Yiśrā'ēl 'Israel': Ballad no. 9A-B.2.

yr"h = yārûm hôdô 'may his majesty be exalted': I, V.

ᶜĒç ha-Ḥayîm 'tree of life' (usually *ᶜēç ḥayîm*): V.

ᶜ"h = ᶜālâw ha-šālôm 'peace be with him; may he rest in peace': I, IV.

Motifs

From S. Thompson, *Motif-Index of Folk-Literature*, 6 vols., 2d ed., I (Bloomington, 1955), II-III (1956), IV-V (1957), VI (1958), or, where specified, from G. Bordman, *Motif-Index of the English Metrical Romances*, Helsinki, 1963 (*FF Communications*, no. 190). References are to ballad numbers and verses (e.g., 1.1), to ballad numbers and notes to commentary (e.g., 1, n. 1), or to pages (e.g., p. 1).

A. MYTHOLOGICAL MOTIFS

A182.3. *God (angel) speaks to mortal*: 9.11.
A197. *Deity controls elements*: 10.3-5.
A2611.7. *Origin of rue*: *from drops of Christ's blood*: 19, n. 7.

B. ANIMALS

B50. *Bird-men*: 18, n. 7.
B82.1.2. *Harp music makes merman restore stolen bride*: 27, n. 19.
B147.2.2. *Bird of ill-omen*: 3, n. 3; 21, n. 25.
B151.2. *Bird determines road to be taken*: 18, n. 7.
B210.ff. *Speaking animals*: 13, n. 10.
B211.1.3. *Speaking horse*: 13.10, nn. 7, 9-10.
B214.1.5. *Singing lion*: 19.5; 21, n. 21.
B214.1.10. *Singing snake*: 21, nn. 22-23.
B401. *Helpful horse*: 13.10, nn. 7-13.
B455.2. *Helpful falcon*: 18, n. 7.
B535. *Animal nurse*: 21, n. 18.
B563.2. *Birds point out road to hero*: 18, n. 7.
B582.2.1. *Hero carried* [or led] *by bird to mistress' chamber*: 17, n. 31; 18.3*a*, nn. 3-4, 7.
B611.3. *Horse paramour*: 25.6.

B614.	*Bird paramour*: 18, n. 7.
B621.7.	*Horse as suitor*: 25.6.
B623.	*Bird as wooer*: 18, n. 7.
B641.6.	*Marriage to person in horse form*: 25.9.
B767.	*Animals attracted by music*: 27, nn. 10, 17, 19.
B767.1.	*Fish follow sound of music*: 27, nn. 10, 18-19.

C. TABU

C119.1.3.	*Tabu*: *intercourse at hunting season*: 18, n. 6.

D. MAGIC

D100.	*Transformation*: *man to animal*: 25, n. 7.
D131.	*Transformation*: *man to horse*: 25.7.
D150.	*Transformation*: *man to bird*: 12, nn. 9, 12-13, 23; 18, n. 7; 25, n. 7.
D170.	*Transformation*: *man to fish*: 12, nn. 10-12, 23; 25, n. 7.
D215.	*Transformation*: *man to tree*: 12, n. 9.
D261.	*Transformation*: *man to altar*: 12, n. 18.
D268.0.1.	*Transformation*: *man to church*: 12, nn. 17-18.
D332.	*Transformation*: *equine animal (domestic) to person*: 25.7.
D615.3.	*Transformation combat between lover and maid*: 12, n. 23.
D641.1.	*Lover as bird visits mistress*: 18, n. 7.
D642.3.	*Transformation to escape lover*: 12, n. 23.
D791.1.7.	*Disenchantment at cockcrow*: 21, n. 27.
D925.	*Magic fountain*: 1, n. 39; 12, nn. 16, 18.
D927.	*Magic spring*: 1, n. 39; 12, nn. 16, 18.
D965.16.	*Magic rue*: 19.4, n. 7; 20, n. 6; 21.7.
D1051.	*Magic cloth*: 22.13, nn. 2, 8, 13.
D1070.	*Magic ornaments*: 19, n. 7.
D1223.1.	*Magic flute*: 27.5, nn. 7-9, 18.
D1224.	*Magic pipe (musical)*: 27.5, n. 17.
D1224.1.	*Magic flageolet*: 27.5.
D1225.	*Magic whistle*: 27.5, nn. 7-8.
D1231.	*Magic harp*: 27, n. 17.
D1242.1.	*Magic water*: 12, nn. 16, 18.
D1263.	*Magic mill*: 1.26, nn. 31-39.
D1273.	*Magic formula (charm)*: 19, n. 7.
D1275.	*Magic song*: 8, n. 4; 12.4, nn. 2, 7, 20; 27, nn. 13-16, 18.
D1275.1.	*Magic music*: 27.14, nn. 15-19.
D1275.2.	*Magic melody*: 27.14, n. 19.
D1355.1.	*Love-producing music*: 12, n. 7; 27, nn. 10, 18.

E. THE DEAD

F. MARVELS

H. TESTS

J. THE WISE AND THE FOOLISH

K. DECEPTIONS

K1227.1. *Lover put off till girl bathes and dresses*: 20.9, n. 8.
K1310. *Seduction by disguise...*: 21, n. 6.
K1317. *Lover's place in bed usurped by another*: 20, n. 8.
K1317.5. *Woman substitutes for her daughter in the dark*: 20, nn. 9-10.
K1321. *Seduction by man disguising as woman*: 21, n. 6.
K1321.1. *Man disguised as woman admitted to women's quarters: seduction*: 21, n. 6.
K1323. *Man disguised as gardener enters convent and seduces nuns*: 21.9-16, n. 4.
K1332. *Seduction by taking aboard ship to inspect wares*: 11.5 ff., n. 5.
K1349.1. *Disguise to enter girl's room*: 21, n. 6.
K1500. *Deception connected with adultery*: 2.22, 16.13-16.
K1515. *The animal in the chest*: 16.13-16, nn. 25, 27, 31, 35.
K1528. *Wife confesses to disguised husband*: 4, n. 7.
K1555. *Husband carries off box containing hidden paramour*: 16.13-16.
K1816. *Disguise as menial*: 21.9-16, n. 4.
K1816.1. *Gardener disguise*: 21.9-16, n. 4.
K1836. *Disguise of man in woman's dress*: 21, n. 6.
K1840. *Deception by substitution*: 20, nn. 8-10.
K1843.ff. [...] *Substituted bedmate*: 20, nn. 8-10.
K1911.1.5. *Old woman substituted for bride in bridegroom's bed*: 20, n. 8.
K2112. *Woman slandered as adulteress (prostitute)*: 13.18.
K2213.3. *Faithless wife plots with paramour against husband's life*: 17.19 ff.
K2218.1. *Treacherous mother-in-law accuses innocent wife*: 13, nn. 2-4; 14.18.

L. REVERSAL OF FORTUNE

L101.1. *Unpromising hero*: *aged man*: 7.3, n. 8.
L113.1.0.1. *Heroine endures hardships with menial husband*: 22.3.
L161. *Lowly hero marries princess*: 21.14, n. 7.
L410.5. *King overthrown and made servant*: 18.15.

M. ORDAINING THE FUTURE

M113.1. *Oath taken on sword*: 14.20, n. 3.
M266. *Man promises to build church if he is saved at sea*: 10.10.
M400. *Curses*: 17.11, nn. 14-15.
M411.1. *Curse by parent*: 23, n. 3.

N. CHANCE AND FATE

Q. REWARDS AND PUNISHMENTS

R. CAPTIVES AND FUGITIVES

R10. *Abduction*: 13.6; pp. 255-266.
R10.1. *Princess (maiden) abducted*: 5.10; p. 120; 18.12; p. 266.
R10.1.1. *Maiden abducted by soldiers*: p. 266.
R12.4. *Girl enticed into boat and abducted*: 11.5 ff., n. 5.
R18. *Abduction by rejected suitor*: pp. 255-266.
R131.10. *Hermit rescues abandoned child*: 21, n. 18.
R131.15. *Children abandoned in a boat survive storm* . . . : 21.1.

S. UNNATURAL CRUELTY

S51. *Cruel mother-in-law*: 13, nn. 2-4; 14.18.
S112. *Burning to death*: 16, nn. 8-10.
S116.1. *Murder by grinding in mill*: 1, n. 39; 16, n. 11.
S139.2.2.1. *Heads of slain enemies impaled upon stakes*: 1, n. 27.

T. SEX

T55. *Girl as wooer*: *Forthputting woman*: 26.8 ff., n. 4.
T55.1. *Princess declares her love for lowly hero*: 26.8 ff., n. 4.
T61.2. *Parting lovers pledge not to marry for seven years*: 23.14.
T61.3. *At betrothal maid makes shirt for her lover*: 22, n. 13.
T80. *Tragic love*: 12.13.
T91. *Unequals in love*: 21.9-16, nn. 4-5; 26.8 ff., nn. 3-4.
T121. *Unequal marriage*: 2, n. 4; 17.3; 21.14, n. 7.
T121.3.1. *Princess marries lowly man*: 21.14, n. 7.
*T123. *Supposedly unequal marriage (princess and supposed commoner)* (Bordman): 21, n. 7.
T230. *Faithlessness in marriage*: 2.20; 5.14-18, n. 14; 16.11; 17.19 ff.
T232.4. *Woman enamored of repulsive and abusive lover*: 26.17 ff.
T237. *Old man married to young, unfaithful wife*: 2, n. 4; 17.17, nn. 3-7.
T323. *Escape from undesired lover by strategy*: 20, n. 8.
T410. *Incest*: 20.7, nn. 2-8.
T411. *Father-daughter incest*: 20.7, nn. 2-3.
T411.1. *Lecherous father. Unnatural father wants to marry his daughter*: 20.7, nn. 2-3.
T412. *Mother-son incest*: 20, nn. 5, 8.
T415. *Brother-sister incest*: 1.5, n. 4; 20, nn. 2, 4; 24, n. 23.

V. RELIGION

W. TRAITS OF CHARACTER

X. HUMOR

GLOSSARY

The Glossary includes words appearing in the 27 ballads edited here as well as words defined or commented upon in the text and footnotes. We list only "exotic" loanwords and Hispanic forms which diverge significantly from Standard Castilian. Obviously such a procedure offers a completely unbalanced picture of the lexicon of Eastern Judeo-Spanish balladry. We hope that a computerized concordance can be appended to the completed edition of our Eastern ballad collection.

The following norms are observed in the present glossary: Occurrences of *vos, non,* and diminutives in *-iko* are excluded. Alternation in the use of *d* vs. *đ* and *š* vs. *ś* is not recorded; forms are listed with whichever spelling they first occur. Obvious printing errors are barred. Nouns are normally listed in the singular; adjectives as masculine singular; verbs by their infinitive; finite uses of verb forms in *-are* are listed as if they were infinitives.

abašada 'descent, slope' 6.4*a* (var.).
abašar 'to descend, to go down' *abaše* 7A.16, 7B.15, 15.13.
abistar 'to be in sight' *abistare* 14.17.
aboltar 'to turn' *aboltaron* 9A-B.5; *avoltaron* p. 4, n. 5. See also **boltarse.**
adatéaš: See 16, n. 8.
adáteš: See 16, n. 8.
aderokar 'to destroy' 4A.19*b* (var.). Read *a derokar.*
admirar 'to concern, to refer to' Introduction, no. VIII.
adyentro 'in' 10B.8; 'into' 16.13.
afeytarse 'to adorn oneself' 6.12.
afiar 'to give credit to' *afiaréś* 15.9.
afri'isyyón 'affliction' Introduction, no. VII.
agiar 'to guide, to lead, to direct' *agiava* 2A.13.
ağar (read *a echar*) here 'to abort' 17.21.

ağetar 'to accept, to believe' 4A-B.10; *ağetare* 10A.8 (It. *accettare*).
A'ífto: See **Ayifto.**
a'índa 'even, only, just' 2A.30.
akožer 'to pluck' *akožites* 21A.10; *akozites* (read *akožites*) 21B.11.
alavasyón 'praise' Introduction, no. III.
alevantar 'to arise' *alevantéš* 12.6.
alevantarse 'to rise up, to arise' *se alevantó* 17.22.
alguža 'needle' 11B.3.
alḥad 'Sunday' Introduction, no. 25 (Ar. *al-ḥad*).
alḥavaka 'sweet basil' 16, n. 14, 19.2.
aligorné[s] 'from Leghorn (?)' 18.11.
almorzar: *almorzare* 14.8-9.
almušama '(the process of) salting' 1, n. 25.
altornasyyón: meaning? 24.4 (originally *tornasol*, a type of fine, dyed cloth). On the form's loss of meaning and subsequent developments in various J.-Sp. and Peninsular versions of the ballad, see DRH, pp. 27-28.
amador: *amadore* 19.6, 7, 11, 15.
amor (f.) 'love' 15.1.
amožar 'to drench' *amože* 21A.17, 21B.18.
andar: *andare* 3.14; *andaron* 25.9.
ande 'where' 9A-B.14-15, 14.6, 19.2-5, 21A-B.2-7; 'to (at) the house of' 3.14, 8.12, 14.7, 12, 18; 'where someone is' 13.9, 11.
ánde 'where' (interrog.) 9A-B.7, 12.15, 16.3, 17.22.
ansí 'thus' 7A.23, 7B.22, 8.10*b* (var.), 10A.16, 10B.15, 22.5.
antikozo 'ancient' Introduction, no. II.
apararse 'to look out of, to stand at (a window)' *se aparó* 20.17.
aparentar 'to adorn, to decorate' 13.3.
apareser 'to publish' Introduction, no. V.
apartar: *apartáme* 10B4.
aperfilada: See **aporfilado.**
aporfilado 'finely formed' or 'finely pointed (?)' 24.9; *aperfilada* 24.9*b* (var.).
apreto 'difficulty' 16.13.
april 'April' 27.1.
arefolgar 'to wake up' *arefolgare* 3.9.
aremirar 'to concern, to refer to' Introduction, no. VI.
arenovarse 'to be renewed' *se 'iva arenovando* 9A.15.
aresekar 'to dry up' *aresekando* 9B.14; *aresekado* 9A.14.
aresponder 'to answer' *arespondí'a* 21A-B.4.
aretorsidos 'twisted' 16.19.
areventarse literally 'to burst forth'; here, by extension, 'to fit very tightly' *se le areventa* 18.7.
arivar: *arivare* 7A.18, 14.16, 21.
árkol 'bow' 16.2, 24.6.
armar 'to raise (sails)' *armó* 11A.12, 11B.15.
arožar: *arožalde* 'shoot at her' 1.10.

asarrear 'to cling, to wrap around' 12, n. 14 (T. *sarmak*). The text should probably read *a sarrear.*
asemežar 'appearance' 17.8.
asender 'to light' *asyenda* 20.23.
asentarse 'to sit down' *me asento* 14.5; *se asentava* 26A-B.4; *se asentaron* 25.8; *asentađa* 14.1.
asobrevyyar 'to cause to be enraged' *asobrevyyó* 10B.11. See also **sobrevyyar.**
asoltar 'to interpret' *asoltareš* 3.12.
aspro 'small coin' 27.10 (Gk. *áspron*).
asuvir 'to go up' *asuva* 15.13*a* (var.).
atakanar 'to put on, to wear' 24, n. 7 (T. *takınmak*).
'atambyén 'also' 7A-B.11, 20.14.
'atan 'so' 7A-B.5, 23.1, 26A.21, 26B.11; *atan* 26A.14.
atorgar 'to grant' 4A-B.8; *atorgare* 'to give credence to' 10A.12 (var.).
atornar 'to stage (a counterattack)' *atorna* 2A.8; *atornan* 2B.30; 'to return' *atorna* 13.5.
avagar: *de avagar* 'in a leisurely manner, slowly' 4A.17; *de avagare* 13.14.
aver 'to have': pres. ind.: *'a* (1st pers. sing.) 7B.16; *ayy* (1st pers. sing.) 13.8; *ayy* (3d pers. sing.) 13.10.
avoltar: See **aboltar.**
avrir: *avrišme* 16.4*a-b* (var.).
ayegarse 'to approach' *ayegóse* 8.7, 11.
Ayifto 'Egypt' 9A.2; **A'ífto** 9B.2, Introduction, no. IV.
azer: *azévos* 17.19.

barabar: *'a 'un barabar* 'together' 4A-B.4, 6 (T. *beraber*; Dialectal T. *barabar*).
baragán: *baragane* 'a strong young man' 5.7.
bel 'waist' 18.7, 21-23 (T. *bel*).
bel 'beautiful' 4B.17, 12.1, 2*b* (var.), 15, 13.17, 22.
belo 'beautiful' 14.14. See also **bel.**
bendiğo 'blessed' 10B.13.
birería 'beer hall' Introduction, n. 27 (It. *birreria,* perhaps reinforced by Gk. *mbiraría*).
bolar 'to fly' 12.18; *bolando* 18.1.
boltarse 'to turn away' *se boltaron* 10A.5.
boz 'voice' 20.16.
brağo: *'a brağo* 'by the arm' 18.12 (It. *braccio*).
bramear 'to roar' *brame'a* 21A-B.4.
briles 'golden threads' 24.5 (*origin*?).
brośura 'pamphlet' Introduction, nos. 12, 13, 16, IV, VI, VII, VIII (Fr. *brochure*)
burako 'hole' 9A-B.10.
burlante 'a mocker, scoffer, blasphemer' 10A.8.
buškar: *buśkare* 5.13; *buški* 2A.33, 2B.22
byervo 'word'; also **verbo** Introduction, no. VII.

ğadir 'tent' 21A.9, 21B.9-10 (T. *çadır*).

chapura 'porgy, flatfish' 12, n. 11 (T. *çipura* 'a kind of sea fish'; perhaps influenced by T. *çapa* 'hoe' or Sp. *chapa* 'sheet, plate of metal'; T. *çipura* derives, in its turn, from Gk. *tsipoũra*).

ğarśí 'market place' 27.9 (T. *çarşı*).

chichek 'flower' 1, at n. 20 (T. *çiçek*).

ğiketo 'small, young' 5.7, 6.10, 23.8; *ğiketiko* 5.7*a* (var.), 24.7, 10; *ğiketikos* 'infantry, foot soldiers' 2A.9, 2B.31.

chikiles 'wagon (loads) of firewood' 16, n. 8 (T. *çeki* 'horse load [of firewood, etc.]').

ğok yyaśa 'long live!' Introduction, no. 22 (T. *çok yaşa*).

ğuflete 'flute, whistle' 27.5, 7; *ğuflet* 27.5*b* (var.), 7*a* (var.). See also 13, n. 7, 27, nn. 7-9.

dada 'a blow' 16.17.

dar: *dare* 13.8; *darle* (read *darle é*) 'I will give him' 1.12; *dalde* 4B.14; *daldeš* 4B.16, 17; *dešme* 4A.15, 18.21.

debaldes 'idle' 3.5.

dedal: *dedale* 11B.3.

dedyentro 'within, inside' 18.4.

delgada 'fine chemise' 6.7; *kamiza delgada* 4A.15.

derokar: See **aderokar.**

desfazer 'to tear apart' *desfizo* 12.18 (var.).

desfožar 'to strip off leaves, petals' *desfožólos* 12.18.

deske 'from the moment that, as soon as' 8.14, 11B.14.

desterar: *desteraldo* 7A.28, 7B.27.

dešar: *ša* (2d pers. sing. imperative) 7B.15.

detrás: *detraze* 14.11.

dezir: *dezire* 7A.17, 7B.16.

dita 'said, aforesaid' Introduction, nos. I-V, VIII.

doğe 'twelve' 8.1*a* (var.), 4*a* (var.).

dolor (f.) 'pain' 14.13.

dor 'generation' 16, n. 27 (H. *dôr*).

dormir: *dormir* (= *dormí*) 6.1.

dovlet 'success, prosperity, good luck' Introduction, n. 27 (T. *devlet*; Archaic T. *dovlet*).

dudún ḥanum 'beloved lady' Introduction, n. 27 (Archaic T. *dudu hanım*).

dyentro 'into' 2A.3, 2B.25, 25.4.

Dyez 'God' 5.7, 13.10, 14.5, 17.10.

Dyyo 'God' 5.7*b* (var.), 6.9, 20.14, 22.8.

'edad: *'edade* 6.10.

'embružar 'to envelope in' *'embružó* 2A.23; *'enbružóla* 2B.14.

'enbružar: See **'embružar.**

'éndavos: See **ir.**

'endelantre 'in the future' Introduction, no. V.
'enfinkar 'to thrust into' *'enfinkó* 18.23.
'enfitar 'to strike (with an arrow)' *'enfita* 1.11, 12.
'enforkarse 'to hang oneself' *'enfórkate* 26A.17 (var.), 26B.14.
'enganyyar: *'enganyyates* 21A.12*b*, 21B.9*b*, 12*b* (var.).
'enkolgarse 'to hang oneself' *'enkólgate* 26A.17.
'enkonyí'a: See **mala 'enkonyí'a.**
'enkoronar 'to crown' *'enkoronare* 10A.10.
'enkuvrir: *'enkuvrildo* 7A-B.9.
'enmentar 'to mention' Introduction, no. VIII.
'enpensar (?) 'to begin' *'enpensan* 27.13.
'enselar 'to conceal' *'enselava* 7A.8; *'enselaldo* 7A-B.9.
'entrar: *'entrates* 21A.9.
'envelyyutado 'woolly' 1.18.
'enverano 'summer' 11A.8, 11B.10, 21A.9, 21B.10.
'esfu'egra 'mother-in-law' 2A.21, 2B.13, 14.6.
'esfu'eler (?) 'to be wont to' *'esfu'ele* 2A.27, 2B.18.
'esfu'enyyo 'dream' 3.12.
esḥuela 'a tool used for pulling nails' 16, n. 27.
'eskapar 'to cause to escape' *'eskapas* 10A-B.10; *'eskápame* 10B.9; *eskapáme* 10A.4, 9; 'to deliver (someone from danger)' *'eskape* 14.5.
'eskontrar 'to meet' *'eskontrí* 6.5; *'eskontró* 2A.24.
'espartirse 'to depart' *se 'esparte* 4A.16, 4B.18, 8.12, 13.19; *se 'espartí'a* 1.28, 20.12.
espinato 'a type of fish' 12, n. 10.
'espozada 'betrothed, bride' 13.6.
'espuntar 'to glisten' *'espunta* 26A.16, 26B.13.
'estar: *'estare* 14.6; *'estó* 22.14; *'estareš* 3.11.
'estringar 'to tighten' *'estringéšme* 13.12.
'estru'ir 'to destroy' *'estru'í'a* here 'to wear out' 7A.12.

falkón 'falcon' 18.1.
favor 'fear' 8.4.
fayyar 'to find' *fa'e* 10A-B.3; *fayyó* 13.5, 6.
felek 'destiny, fortune' Introduction, nos. 7, III, VI, VII (T. *felek*). Among the Eastern Sephardim the word is synonymous with H. *dôr* 'generation'.
féridas 'fairs (?)' 27, n. 2.
filar 'to embroider, to spin' *filáš* 22.6; *filavan* 3.6; *filalda* 22.4, 5.
filo 'thread' 7A-B.10.
fin (f.) 'end' 3.10, 15.15*a* (var.), 25.10.
fin a 'down to, as far as' 18.6, 20, 23.14.
folgar 'rest, repose' 12.6.
folgar 'to rest' 17.13; *folgare* 'to amuse' 3.7.
fortuna 'storm' 10A.9, 10, 18, 10B.17 (Cast. *fortuna,* probably reinforced by the currency of related forms in Eastern Mediterranean languages: T. *fırtına,* Gk. *fourtoúna.* Cf. Kahane-Tietze 305).

fota 'boat' 10B.9, 10 (T. *fita, fota, futa*; see Kahane-Tietze, s.v. *boúta*).
franko 'foreign, European' 4A.19, 18.11, 21, 22 (cf. T. *frenk*).
fu'ir 'to flee' 2A.31, 32, 2B.20, 21; *fuyygáš* 2A.32, 2B.21.
fu'iteś: See **ser.**
fyero 'iron' 13.13.

galano 'graceful' 2A.18, 2B.9.
galea 'galley, ship' 2B.24.
ganađo 'livestock'; here 'possessions, goods, wealth' 10A.1, 10A-B.3, 4, 22.11. See also 10, n. 12.
ganğo 'anchor' 11A.12, 11B.15. Crews, *Recherches*, 423.
garbe 'bearing, stance' 2A.29.
gastar: *gastare* 5.15.
gavilán: *gavilane* 5.16, 14.10; *gavilano* 5.16*b* (var.).
gozar: *gozare* 7A.27, 7B.26.
grano: *'a grano 'a grano* 'gradually' 21A.10, 21B.11 (in addition to the literal meaning, as in our translation). Cf. the proverb *Grano a grano la gallina hintche el papo* (E. Saporta y Beja, *Refranero sefardí* [Madrid-Barcelona, 1957], p. 161).
grave'ína 'pink (flower)' 12.16, 19.2, 10, 21A-B.6. See DRH, s.v. *glavinas*; NSR, p. 80.
guadrar 'to guard, to protect, to keep' *guađra* 13.4; *guadre* 5.17, 8.10.
guadri'a 'guardian' 19.4, 21A.7.
gu'erta 'garden' 21A.15, 21B.16.
gu'ertelano 'gardener' 21A.15, 21B.16.
gu'eso 'bone' 14.11; *gu'esezikos* 'small bones' 12.22.
gu'estro 'your' 18.15-17.
gustar 'to taste' *gosto* 17.21.

ğ: See also **ch.**
ğaver 'witty' Introduction, no. V (T. *cevher, gevher* 'jewel; beautiful or witty saying').
ğidyyó 'Jew' 9A.9, 14; 9A-B.13.
ğudyyó 'Jew' 9A.9, 14.
ğugar 'to gamble' *ğugare* 5.1; *ğugan* 5.2, 18.10.
ğugo 'game' 18.10, 25.10.

ḥaberğí 'messenger' 14.21 (T. *haberci*).
ḥameado (Moroc. J.-Sp.) 'burnt' 16, n. 2 (Moroc. Ar. *ḥami* 'hot, burning').
ḥan 'lord, sovereign' Introduction, nos. I, V (T. *han*).
ḥarán: *ḥarán vos se aga* 'may it do you no good' 7A-B.13, 14 (T. *haram etmek* 'to forbid the use or enjoyment [of something]').
ḥazino 'sick' 10A.16, 10B.15.
ḥăzîr 'swine' 17.20, 21, 22; *ḥăzîre* 17.24 (H.). See also 17, n. 26.
ḥazmearse (Moroc. J.-Sp.) 'to bind tightly' 16, n. 2 (Moroc. Ar. *ḥezzem*).

'inda 'still, even' 2A.26.

'ir: *vo* 14.20, 17.21; *'ťa* 15.2, 3, 19.7, 15, 20.12; *'índome* 21A-B.1; *va* (2d pers. sing. imperative) 26A.17, 26B.14; *vate* 10A-B.12, 19.11, 26A-B.28; *'éndavos* 22.10.

jasmeado: See **ḥazmearse.**

kadrador 'carder (of wool)' 22.3.

kadrar 'to card (wool)' *kadrava* 22.4.

kaleža 'passageway' 9A-B.13. Usually 'street, road, alley'.

kanğikada 'blow with a whip' 13, n. 7 (T. *kamçı* 'whip', probably contaminated by *kancık* 'female animal; she-ass'). Cf. C. Crews, "Miscellanea Hispano-Judaica," *VR*, 16(1957), 224-245: p. 234.

kara sazán 'black carp' 12.23 (T. *kara sazan*). See 12, n. 10.

karas 'cheeks' 24.8, 26A.20, 26B.17.

kardale 'a type of cloth (?)' 3.6.

karonale 'related by blood' 5.6.

kativado 'captive; unfortunate' 15.6.

kavo 'side' 22.13.

kavzante 'person who causes (something)' 21A-B.8.

kazamyentero 'matchmaker' 8.19b (var.).

kazar 'to marry' *kazare* 3.13; *kazateś* 21A.14, 21B.15.

ken 'he who' 7A-B.11, 17.1, 2; 'who' 21A.14, 21B.15; *ken..., ken...* 'some..., others...' 9A-B.3.

kén 'who' (interrog.) 8.15*a* (var.), 16.8.

kerensyyozo 'affectionate' 15.1.

kerer: *kero* 26A-B (refrain); *kere* 4A-B.3, 17.1, 2, 13, 22.5, 27.1, 2; *keren* 27.2*b* (var.); *kižiteš* 4A.11; *kižo* 2A.2, 2B.24, 27.3; *kižeraš* 2A.32, 2B.21.

kiefal 'grey mullet' 12, n. 10 (T. *kefal*).

kitar 'to redeem' 4B.14.

klenğa: *'en klenğa* 'with the hair parted in two parts' 18.5.

kodas 'braids (of hair)' 18.6.

komande 'command' 3.11.

komer: *komere* 2A.7, 2B.29, 18.2.

konğá 'rose' 8.1, 2, 12.16, 19.10 (T. *konca* '[flower] bud').

konortarse 'to comfort oneself' *se konortavan* 21A.13, 21B.14.

kontar: *kontare* 7A.17, 7B.16, 11A.9, 11B.11.

kontino: *de kontino* 'continuously' 10A.14.

kontošiko 'a type of dress (?)' 18.7 (T. *kontoş*). See Miklosich, "Die türkischen Elemente," s.v. ('Art Kleid'). Molho (LSO, p. 379) records *contixico*, with the meaning 'cinturón' which seems to be incorrectly deduced from the context.

korale: *de gran korale* 'of great courage (?)' 3.4 (cf. the O. Sp. adj. *coral* 'pertaining to the heart'. Such a connection is dubious. *Korale* is probably a deformation of O. Sp. *coraje*).

korelado: See **korolado.**

korolado 'pink, rose colored; red; scarlet' 6.3, 9A.6, 24.8*a* (var.); *korelada* 6.3*a* (var.); *koreladas* 24.8*a* (var.), 26A.21 (var.).
kortar: *kortare* 11B.4.
kovado 'coward' 5.10.
kožer: *kožendo* 5.12.
kriar 'to create' 17.10; 'to educate, to bring up' *kre'i* 5.7.
kristal: *kristale* 12.2.
kristal (adj.) 'of glass' 17.7.
kru'eldad 'cruelty' 5.17*b* (var.); *kru'eldade* 5.17. The context requires the reading *fi'eldad* 'faith, fidelity'.
kuando: *de kuando* 'since, from the moment' 25.6.
kulpar: *kulpí* 2A.33*b* (var.).

lazare 'sorrel' 13.7, 18, 23 (= Cast. *alazán.* J.-Sp. *lazar(e)* is closer than is *alazán* to the hypothetical form **alazar* adduced by Corominas [*DCELC,* s.v. *alazán*] as the immediate derivative of Hispano-Ar. *'azᶜár* 'rubio, rojizo' [= Ar. *'ázᶜar*]). See our note in *RPh,* XXI (1967-1968), 510-512.
linguada 'flounder' 12, n. 10.
lonğe 'far away' 2A.20, 2B.11. See NSR, p. 80.
loryya 'glory' 11A.9, 11B.11, 12.4.
lunar 'moonlight' 4A-B.2, 4B.17; *lunare* 4A.2*b* (var.), 13.17.
luvyya 'rain' 21A.17, 21B.18.

mağyyo 'May' 27.1.
mala 'enkonyí'a 'melancholy' 20.19. The adj. *mala* and the verb *enconar* 'to infect' contaminate *melancolía* by popular etymology.
malanyya: See **malanyyo.**
malanyyo 'accursed be' 7B.11; 19.17; *malanyya* 7A.11, 27.7. See DRH, s.v. *malaña.*
mandar: *mandalde* 20.23.
manko 'less' 6.14.
mar: *mare* 10A.7.
matar: *matare* 7A-B.26, 7A.26, 14.20; *matí* 18.17.
ma'ulyyar 'to bark, to howl' *ma'úlyya* 21A-B.3.
mazal: *mazale* 'luck' 14.22 (H. *mazāl*).
meará 'cave' (H. *meᶜārāh*) p. 126.
meldar 'to read' 22.8.
merkar: *merkí* 2A.26, 30, 2B.17; 'to spend' *merkaldos* 22.12.
mezo: *por mezo de* 'through the mediation of' Introduction, nos. I, II; *mezo* alone is also used in the same sense: Introduction, no. VI (It. *mezzo*).
miçrî 'an Egyptian' 9A-B.15 (H.).
milsa 'mass, church, chapel' 5.11, 7B.15, 24.1*a* (var.).
mos 'us' 2B.28, 4A.2*a* (var.), 9A-B.7, 10A.18, 21A.17, 21B.18; *molas* 10A-B.14.
mu'erir 'to die' 2A.21*b* (var.), 9A.7, 8.
mu'evo 'new' 7A.15, 7B.12, 25.10.

muğağikitas 'small girls' 21B.14.
munğo 'many' 7B.23, 10A-B.13.
mušama 'oilcloth' 1.21; *mušamá* 1, n. 28 (T. *muşamba*; Archaic T. *muşamma*).

namorađa 'mistress, beloved' 1.14, 15, 16.3.
namorado 'lover' 11A.3, 11B.5, 16.11, 14.
namorarse 'to fall in love' 1.3; *namorava* 15.11.
naser: *nasites* 25.6.
navegar: *navegí* 21A-B.1.
negro 'bad, evil' 26A.28.
nêkāmāh literally 'vengeance' 16.7; humorously used here for *cama* 'bed.' See LSO, p. 381*b*. The normal Hebrew reading is *nĕkāmāh*.
nîsān 'first month of the Hebrew calendar' 9A-B.1.
nyyuđiko 'small knot' or 'bun (of hair)' 18.5.

'o'ir: *'o'ired̄eš* 12.7; *'oyygaméš* 20.14.
'okita 'small *oka* (a Turkish measure)' 22.4 (T. *okka*).

palomba 'dove' 12.19.
pan: *pane* 5.14.
pará 'money' Introduction, no. IV; *parikas* Introduction, no. V (T. *para*).
parir: *parire* 14.2, 5.
pasažiko: See **pažežiko.**
pasear: *paseare* 8.2*b* (var.).
pasežiko: See **pažežiko.**
pažežiko 'small page' 2B.17, 18; *pasažiko* 2A.26*a* (var.), 27*a* (var.); *pasežiko* 2A.26, 27.
pedrer 'to lose' 5.5; *pedrí* 1.23, 24, 25, 26; *pyedran* 10A.17.
peğo 'pocket' 23.10. See Crews, *Recherches*, 724.
pekar: *pekí* 10A-B.3.
pensativle 'pensive' 7A-B.1.
penseryyo 'thought' 7A-B.1.
perkyya 'perch' 12.23 (Cast. *perca* + Gk. *pérkē*?). See 12, n. 10.
personale 'a group of people (?)' 13.20.
peškar 'to fish' 12.24; *peškólos* 12.25.
peynar: *peynare* 26A.15, 26B.12.
piađađ 'pity' 13.13.
poder: *pu'edéš* 4A.14; *pu'edí'a* 2A.4*b* (var.), 2B.26.
pontés 'from Pontus (?)' 18.4. The toponym seems too erudite in character to fit this context.
porto 'port' 11A.6, 11B.8, 27.14 (It. *porto*, probably through Gk. *pórto*).
prenyyado 'unborn child' 17.21.
preto 'black' 13.23.
pu'erpo 'body' 2A.18, 5.8, 11A.4, 11B.6, 17.8.
punto: *de todo punto* 'completely' 2A.3, 2B.25.
pye 'foot' *pyezes* 16.5.

quierco 'pig' 17, n. 26.

raḥămān 'merciful' 10A.13 (H.).
ravyyarse 'to become enraged' *ravyyóse* 25.4.
real: *reale* 3.16, 5.4.
relámparo 'lightening' p. 4, n. 5.
remorso 'selection' (?) Introduction, no. VII.
rengrasyyar 'to thank' Introduction, no. IV.
rey: *re'e* 'king' 1.1, 3, 7.
rezín 'recently' 15.7, 8. See Crews, *Recherches,* 1081.
rogar: rogo 4A-B.8.
romanso 'ballad' 20.3.
roši'ó 'nightingale' 12.3.
royyal: *royyale* 'royal' 13.9, 11, 16, 21.
rozal: *rozale* 12.1.
rublas 'rubles' 4A.12*b* (var.).

saltar: *saltare* 13.15.
sanğir = *San Gil* 2A.3, 4, 2B.25, 26. See commentary to no. 2.
sarayy 'palace' 14.3 (T. *saray*).
sarnudar 'to sneeze' *sarnuda* 16.15; *sarnudava* 16.14.
sarrear: See **asarrear.**
sazán: See **kara sazán.**
selví: See 26, n. 15.
sená 'bramble bush' 17 (p. 237) (H. *sĕneh*).
sensyya 'knowledge' 13.10.
sentir 'to hear' *syento* 20.16; *sentí* 12.3.
ser: *so* 11A.5, 11B.7, 21A.14, 21B.15; *sé* (1st pers. sing. pres. indicative) 18.20; *sos* 10A-B.12; *soš* 8.8; *fu'ites* 25.6; *fu'iteś* 5.10.
sidrera 'citrus (?)' 21A-B.6.
simyente 'root' 12.2.
sinbultura 'sepulchre' 9A.8; *sumbultura* 9B.8.
sinon 'but' 2A.33, 2B.22.
sirma 'silver thread' 4A.15, 4B.16, 17, 22.12, 24.3 (T. *sırma*).
sivdađ 'city' 3.4, 15, 4A.19, 5.2, 3, 7A-B.2, 22.15, 23.12, 26A-B.1.
siyar 'to saddle' *siyando* 25.1; *si'ólo* 25.2.
sobrevyyar 'to cause to be enraged' *sobrevyyare* 10A.11. See also **asobrevyyar.**
sobrevyyarse 'to become violent' *se 'iva sobrevyyando* 9B.15; 'to become enraged' *se sobrevyyó* 25.3.
sol: *sole* 'sun, sunlight' 4A.2*a* (var.).
solombra 'shadow' 8.13.
somportar: *somportare* 'to bear, to put up with' 14.2.
sonyyar: *sonyí* 3.12.
sotađa 'blow (with a whip)' 13.13.
sóvere 'upon' 24.4*a* (var.).
spitales: *los spitales* 'hospitals' p. 5, n. 5.

subé 'doubt, suspicion, uncertainty' 16, n. 29 (T. *şübhe, şüphe*).
sumbultura: See **sinbultura.**
ša: See **dešar.**
śarkí 'song' Introduction, no. 24 (T. *şarkı*).
šeđré: *la šeđré* 'chess' 18.10.
śiboyy 'waistcoat' 24.4. See NSR, p. 80.
šulik 'hammer' 16, n. 27 (origin? ; possibly T. *çelık* 'A piece of wood or metal beveled or tapering at one or both ends').
šupé: See **subé.**

tadre 'afternoon' 10A.1, 15.2.
tadre 'late' 10A-B.14, 10A.16.
tađri'ozo 'dilatory' Introduction, no. V.
tambyén 'neither' 18.18.
tayyfa 'group' 2A.13, 16, 17, 2B.4, 7, 8 (T. *taife* has possibly reinforced Cast. *taifa*; both are from Ar. *ṭā'ifa*).
teretemblo 'earthquake' Introduction, no. 5.
tomar: *tomare* 14.13; *tomí* 16.2; *tomateš* 7A.15, 7B.12; *tomalda* 1.10; *tomaldo* 22.9.
topar 'to find' *topa* 7A.19; *topava* 15.3, 4; *topavan* 18.2; *topí* 6.2; *topó* 19.8, 10; *toparéš* 22.11.
toparse 'to find oneself' *se topó* 16.13.
topḥaná 'arsenal' 13, at n. 6 (T. *tophane*).
torna 'counterattack' 2A.8*a* (var.).
tornađa 'counterattack' 2A.8, 2B.30.
tornarse 'to be repeated' *se torna* 2A.2*b* (var.), 2B.3*b* (var.), 3.3*b* (var.).
traer: *trago* 19.12; *truśites* 9A-B.7.
trensados 'tresses' 7A.22.
trezoro 'treasury' Introduction, no. 12.
truelos 'thunder' p. 4, n. 5.
truvyyo 'turbid' 25.3.
turkeska: *ala turkeska* 'in Turkish fashion' 18.6.

θĕfîlāh 'prayer' 9A.9 (H.).

veluntad: *de veluntad* 'with all one's heart' 17.14, 16, 23.3, 4, 5.
vender: *vendere* 22.15, 27.9.
venir: *venire* 11B.14; *vení* 16.18, 17.24, 22.9.
vente 'twenty' 7A-B.3.
ver: *ví'a* 7A-B.8; *vide* 17.20; *vido* 8.14; *viteš* 7A-B.9, 13.21, 17.24.
verbo: See **byervo.**
vergu'ela 'shame' 2A.5.
vigu'ela 'guitar' 3.7, 20.2.
vilano 'peasant' 21A.14, 21B.15.
vi'ola: *nošadas de vi'ola* 'the night preceding the day of a circumcision' Introduction, No. II. See Molho, *Usos*, pp. 62-64.

visyyo 'pleasure, relaxation' 3.8.
vižitar 'to visit' 15.2; *vižitare* 11A.10, 11B.12.
vos: *vo* (+ obj. pronoun) 4A.10*b* (var.), 4B.10, 4A.11*a* (var.), 5.10, 8.16, 15.9.

xabaló (Moroc. J.-Sp.) meaning (?) 16, n. 3.

yelada 'frost' 16.5.
yemes 'reins' Introduction, n. 29 (T. *gem* 'bit [of a horse]').
yevar: *yevare* 5.10; *yevateš* 8.9.
yul 'rose' Introduction, n. 29 (T. *gül*).

zyafet 'party, banquet' Introduction, no. II (T. *ziyafet*).